SONCINO BOOKS OF THE BIBLE

EDITOR: REV. DR. A. COHEN M.A. Ph.D., D.H.L.

Isaiah

HEBREW TEXT & ENGLISH TRANSLATION WITH AN INTRODUCTION AND COMMENTARY

by

THE REV. DR. I. W. SLOTKI, M.A., Litt.D.

Revised by

RABBI A. J. ROSENBERG

And all thy children shall be taught of the Lord;
And great shall be the peace of thy children.

ISAIAH LIV. 13

THE SONCINO PRESS, LTD.
New York • 1987

REVISED EDITION
FIRST IMPRESSION 1983
SECOND IMPRESSION 1987

© THE SONCINO PRESS LTD. 1983

ISBN 0-900689-28-5

PUBLISHERS' NOTE

*Thanks are due to the
Jewish Publication Society of America
for permission to use their beautiful
English text of the Scriptures*

PRINTED IN THE UNITED STATES OF AMERICA

PUBLISHERS' INTRODUCTION
TO THE REVISED SECOND EDITION

JUST over thirty-five years ago THE PSALMS, the first in a series of the SONCINO BOOKS OF THE BIBLE, saw the light of day, to be followed in the next six years by the remaining thirteen books. Whereas the earlier edition drew from various non-Jewish, as well as Jewish, sources, the publishers now feel there is a need to acquaint the reader with the pure Jewish view of these holy books, and this revised edition therefore limits its scope to the traditional classic Jewish commentaries and source material.

We are indebted to The Judaica Press for allowing us to use material from the Judaica Books of the Prophets.

FOREWORD BY THE GENERAL EDITOR TO THE FIRST EDITION

BY general consent the Book of Isaiah is regarded as the supreme example of the prophetic literature of the Hebrew Bible. In loftiness of thought, beauty of diction and rhetorical force the Book occupies a place of its own. Avoiding critical problems which loom so large in the standard commentaries, the exposition of *Isaiah* presented in this series of THE SONCINO BOOKS OF THE BIBLE has the one aim of making the language of the prophet intelligible to the layman.

The series is distinctive in the following respects:

(*i*) Each volume contains the Hebrew text and English translation together with the commentary. (*ii*) The exposition is designed primarily for the ordinary reader of the Bible rather than for the student, and aims at providing this class of reader with requisite direction for the understanding and appreciation of the Biblical Book. (*iii*) The commentary is invariably based upon the received Hebrew text. When this presents difficulties, the most probable translation and interpretation are suggested, without resort to textual emendation. (*iv*) It offers a *Jewish* commentary. Without neglecting the valuable work of Christian expositors, it takes into account the exegesis of the Talmudical Rabbis as well as of the leading Jewish commentators.

All Biblical references are cited according to chapter and verse as in the Hebrew Bible. It is unfortunate that, unlike the American-Jewish translation, the English Authorized and Revised Versions, although made direct from the Hebrew text, did not conform to its chapter divisions. An undesirable complication was thereby introduced into Bible study. In the Hebrew the longer headings of the Psalms are counted as a separate verse; consequently Ps. xxxiv. 12, e.g., corresponds to verse 11 in A.V. and R.V. It is also necessary to take into account a marginal note like that found against 1 Kings iv. 21, 'ch. v. 1 in Heb.', so that the Hebrew 1 Kings v. 14 tallies with iv. 34 in the English.

It is hoped that this Commentary, though more particularly planned for the needs of Jews, will prove helpful to all who desire a fuller knowledge of the Bible, irrespective of their creed.

A. COHEN

CONTENTS

INTRODUCTION

NATURE OF THE COMMENTARY

Biblical critics and commentators on the Book of Isaiah have vied with each other not only in its interpretation, which presents many difficulties, but also in the attempted solution of questions of authorship and chronology of the oracles. The commentary presented in this volume, intended as it is for the layman, avoids all theoretical speculation, conjectural emendation and far-fetched hypotheses. Loyally true to Jewish tradition, the commentator has nevertheless kept a constant eye on the latest researches in the fields of Biblical scholarship, criticism and exegesis. Due note has been taken of these, though no direct reference was deemed necessary.

SOURCES AND AUTHORITIES

It is humanly impossible to quote on each page of a modern commentary the numerous authorities to whom a writer is indebted. In many cases it is even an impossibility to trace the information to the first source, since very often several commentators have independently arrived at the same interpretation. No references are, therefore, given in the notes, except on rare occasions, and the reader is directed to the list of 'Authorities Consulted or Quoted' which might also serve the needs of a student desirous to continue and widen his study of any particular question.

For all interpretations or explanations, however, that occur in no previous work, the present writer himself must take responsibility.

LIGHT FROM THE EXCAVATIONS

Discoveries of cuneiform inscriptions between 1840 and 1854 at Khorsabad, Kujundshik and Nimrud, now stored in the British Museum and the Louvre, have brought to light new facts bearing on the times of Isaiah. These illustrate and supplement the Biblical records, and help us also to understand more than ever before much of the background of Isaiah's prophecies and activities, as well as the general condition of the nations and countries with whom Judah at that period came in friendly or hostile contact.

ISAIAH AND HIS FAMILY

The name 'Isaiah' signifies in its original Hebrew (*Yeshayah*) 'help (or deliverance) of God,' a name in complete harmony with the great prophet's teaching and hopes.

From Isaiah's own mouth we learn that he was a married man, and that his wife, in her own right or by virtue of her husband's vocation, was called by the honourable title, 'the prophetess.' He had at least two sons, *Shear-jashub*, meaning 'a remnant shall return,' and *Maher - shalal - hash - baz*, 'the spoil speedeth, the prey hasteth.' The latter son was so named as a symbol and warning on the fate of Damascus and Samaria, representing Syria and the kingdom of Israel, whose wealth was to be carried away by Assyria. The name of the former son was a message of comfort to the future exiles of Judah.

There is a tradition that Isaiah was a member of the tribe of Judah, his father Amoz, who also was said to be a prophet, being the brother of Amaziah, one of the kings of Judah.

HIS LIFE AND DEATH

Isaiah's public career extended over a period of forty (according to others, 46 or 61) years, corresponding with the last forty years of the eighth century B.C.E. He apparently received the call to his prophetic mission in the closing year of the life of Uzziah or Azariah (740-739 B.C.E.), and his activities continued throughout the reigns of the succeeding kings of Judah, Jotham, Ahaz and Hezekiah.

There is no written record of the date or cause of the prophet's death, but a tradition is preserved in both the Babylonian and Palestinian Talmudim and elsewhere that he met a tragic and violent death at the hands of Manasseh whose long and wicked reign followed that of his pious father Hezekiah.

CHARACTER AND GENIUS

Prophet and statesman, he united deep religious feeling with a profound knowledge of the world and everyday life.

His intellectual gifts and fine qualities of heart were harmoniously blended, his vision was clear and his judgment unerring. Great in thought and action, he was inflexible in his religious demands and unhesitating in his political advice or direction to king and people. He was justly described as one standing 'with his head in the clouds and his feet on the solid earth, with his heart in the things of eternity and with his hands and mouth in the things of time, with his spirit in the eternal counsel of God and his body in a very definite moment of history.'

HIS MISSION

Isaiah was endowed with the richest qualities of highest genius and since his early manhood, when he was called to his prophetic office, he devoted all the powers of his mind, all his moral and spiritual strength, even the incidents of his private and social life, to the performance of his mission, endeavouring to lead his countrymen in the ways of God and to impose the Divine will upon the conduct of the State, its rulers and its citizens. He was rightly described as 'the prophet of faith.' In words of fire he sought to impress this faith upon his generation, and to convince them that the Divine government of the world was based on morality, justice and equity. Animated by the fervour of his religious enthusiasm, his entire being, in the course of a long and strenuous career, was wholeheartedly and unselfishly laid on the altar of his sacred vocation, to which he was Divinely called and which he had readily shouldered.

It fell to his lot to live in one of the most critical periods in the history of his people, when the greatest empire of the time was threatening its very existence. With singleness of aim and complete selflessness, he took the lead in advancing a policy which was not popular but the only one which he knew could avert complete disaster.

COMPOSITION OF THE BOOK

The Book of Isaiah consists of sixty-six chapters embodying, in the main, oracles and discourses on Judah, and also on other nations: such as Egypt, Babylon, Moab, Edom, Tyre, Syria and Arabia as well as Israel or Ephraim. The time which comes under review in the Book may be roughly divided into pre-exilic, exilic and post-exilic: the first being the period when Judah was still an unconquered State; the second, when the State was lost and Judah in captivity; and the third, when the exiles had returned from Babylon to rebuild their country.

AUTHORSHIP

The sections of the Book of Isaiah that bear respectively on these divisions of time show also different characteristics of style and tone, religious and political background and even changes of natural scenery. A consideration of these phenomena has led Bible critics to the conclusion that the Book of Isaiah did not emanate from a single mind, but is the result of composite efforts of prophets to whose collected productions has been appended the name of the great Isaiah who could be held responsible at most for the first thirty-nine chapters only. To a prophet of the Babylonian captivity, whom the critics name Deutero-(second) Isaiah, are attributed chapters xl to lv, while the closing chapters, lvi to lxvi, are ascribed to a Palestinian prophet who is named Trito-(third) Isaiah and assumed to have been active after the return.

TRADITIONAL VIEW

Most modern scholars regard the evidence for the tripartite division of the Book as conclusive. But there are others who deny the validity of the conclusions and maintain the traditional view of the unity of authorship. The variations in style and historical, political and religious situations or in the natural scenery are attributed by them to the character and substance of the prophecies which deal respectively with (a) conditions of the present, (b) the future in captivity, and (c) the subsequent years in Judea. The exilic and post-exilic oracles are viewed as Divine predictions of future conditions and events by the same great prophet, Isaiah of Jerusalem.

THE WRITER OR EDITOR

In the Book of Isaiah there is no mention at all that the prophet himself, or that any other writer, has put on record all the prophecies the Book contains. According to a Talmudic statement, however, king Hezekiah, or his College, was the writer of the oral prophecies, or the editor of the documents that had been prepared by Isaiah or his disciples.

PLACE IN THE CANON

The place of the Book of Isaiah in the Biblical canon is, according to the Talmud, after the Book of Ezekiel, the order of the books of the Later Prophets being: Jeremiah, Ezekiel, Isaiah, the Twelve Prophets. In the Septuagint the Twelve Prophets also precede Isaiah. In the printed editions of the Hebrew Bible and in the best MSS., however, as well as according to the Masorah and the English Versions of Scripture, Isaiah's place is first in the Later Prophets, immediately following the Books of Kings, the last Book in the Early Prophets.

STYLE AND DICTION

Scholars pay wholehearted tribute to Isaiah's brilliance of imagination and his picturesque and graphic descriptions, his command of powerful metaphor, alliteration, assonance, and the fine balance and rhythmic flow of his sentences (Whitehouse). His poetical diction is superb (Driver), and every word of his kindles, stirs and strikes its mark (Dillmann). His thought constantly and spontaneously blossoms into imagery, and the images are no mere rhetorical embellishments but are always impressive in themselves and always appropriate and natural expressions of his ideas (Skinner).

ORATORY

Isaiah, like the other prophets of his calibre, was essentially a public orator whose impassioned utterances were subsequently recorded. Literature was used as a means of preserving the substance of the spoken word; but when the prophet addressed his audiences he had to rely upon the immediate effect and appeal of his spoken message. Unlike the writer of a book, the orator cannot trust to the application of the listener's mind or to his concentrated attention. The audiences have to be caught and their attention held by the sheer force of the oratory.

The brilliance of Isaiah's diction and the excellence of his periods are largely due to this fact. His written, like his spoken, word grips and holds the attention. The reader has the same experience as the original listeners who were addressed by the living prophet in Jerusalem. The written prophecies are faithful and effective reproductions of the impressive verbal oratory.

FORMS AND FEATURES OF ANCIENT HEBREW POETRY

A distinction must be drawn between ancient Hebrew poetry, examples of which are preserved in Isaiah and other Books of the Bible, and Hebrew poetry of the Middle Ages or modern times. The forms of the latter are well known but those of the former are generally uncertain.

Some scholars deny altogether the existence of metre in the Bible, while others maintain that the laws of metre are definite and that, furthermore, any Biblical poetry that does not conform to these rules is corrupt.

Gustav Bickell, for example, in his *Carmina Veteris Testamenti Metrica* has added about 2,600 syllables and changed about 3,811 vowels in the Book of Psalms alone to justify his metrical system; and C. A. Briggs in the *International Critical Commentary* has cut down many psalms to a half or less of their original length to conform to his rules of metre.

Between the extreme views on the subject there are other opinions approximating in various degrees to the one or the other.

The present writer has tried to find a way through this confusion in the course of a series of articles in the *Journal of Theological Studies*, vol. XXIX, pp. 255-268; XXXI, pp. 387-395 and 186-189; vol. XXXII, pp. 367-370; vol. XXXIII, pp. 341-354; the *Journal of the Manchester Egyptian and Oriental Society*, No. XVI, pp. 31-49; *Zeitschrift für die Alttestamentliche Wissenschaft*, N.F. Band VIII, pp. 211-222; the *Jewish Quarterly Review*, N.S., vol. XXVI, pp. 199-219, the *Journal of Biblical Literature*, vol. LI, pp. 214-226 and the *Expository Times*, vol. XLVI, pp. 517-522.

From these the conclusion has been drawn that, while the last word on the forms of ancient Hebrew poetry has not yet been spoken, it is nevertheless safe to say that certain laws of form may be regarded as well established. The most important of these is parallelism (synonymous, antithetic, synthetic and climactic). The second is rhythm or metre, by which is meant the beat of the accent, each word usually containing one principal beat, the stichoi or lines being arranged in combinations of three beats and two beats (3+2) or double three beats (3+3), sometimes 4+2, 2+2+2 and, rarely, 4+3 and 3+4, and each stanza or strophe consisting of 2, 3, 4, or any greater number of lines.

Rhyme is found in a number of passages, but is rather rare and cannot be viewed as a feature of the poetry. Assonance is more extensive than is commonly supposed, but its use like that of the acrostic needs further investigation.

Another very important characteristic of ancient Hebrew and other eastern poetry is 'oral repetition' and 'short written arrangement,' by which is meant that poems may have been recited in a certain long form and recorded in a shorter one. Sometimes, though very seldom, ancient poems have actually been preserved in two forms, the long and the short one (or the oral and the written), sometimes in the longer form and sometimes in the shorter form only.

In recitation, chanting or singing the poet may have indulged in frequent repetition or reduplication of terms, phrases and even complete sentences. In the written form, however, economy was often practised and whenever space, time or other causes required it, words, phrases or sentences, which were to be repe d appeared in writing only once, som plan of arrangement being adopted whereby the necessity for repetition was indicated.

For details of this arrangement the reader is referred to the articles mentioned, where he will also find support for the thesis in the ancient inscriptions on the baked clay tablets unearthed in Babylon and on papyri discovered in Egypt.

Psalm cxxxv. 11-12 is an example of a short written form:

> Lesichón mélech ha-emorí
> Uleóg mélech habashán
> Ulechól mamlechóth Cenáan
> Venathán artsám nachaláh
> Nachaláh leyisraél amó

Psalm cxxxvi. 19-22 is an example of the longer form of recital of the same poem:

> Lesichón mélech ha-emorí
> ki leolám chasdó
> Uleóg mélech habashán
> ki leolám chasdó
> Venathán artsám lenachaláh
> ki leolám chasdó
> Nachaláh leyisraél abdó
> ki leolám chasdó

Psalm xcviii. 9 and Psalm xcvi. 13 are another example of a short and long form respectively of the same stichos; so are Psalm cviii. 2 and Psalm lvii. 8. Space does not allow the quotation here of further examples.

By applying the principles which underlie the characteristics or features just described, many a difficult and obscure passage which exegesis has failed to explain satisfactorily has emerged in a natural, simple and clear light, making unnecessary all forced interpretation or radical emendation to which Bible critics have had recourse. One example of the successful application of the principles will be found in this Commentary on Isaiah ii. 12-13.

It may well be hoped that a large body of conjectural emendations, which owe their origin to textual or metrical difficulties, will have to be reconsidered and re-examined in the light of the principles here enunciated.

THE POLITICAL SCENE

Syro-Ephraimitic Invasion. In the Syro-Ephraimitic war on Judah (c. 735 B.C.E.), Isaiah assured the panic-stricken Ahaz that both Syria and Ephraim would be destroyed in an Assyrian onslaught on their countries. At the same time the prophet warned the king against seeking Assyrian protection, and urged implicit trust in God Who alone could save. Isaiah's prophecy was fully realized when Damascus, the

capital of Syria, was captured in 732
B.C.E. and when Samaria, the capital of
Israel, experienced a similar fate in
722 B.C.E.

The ravaging of Judah by both Assyria
and Egypt, as well as the overwhelming
disaster that would crush the former,
was also predicted by the prophet.
These were fulfilled in the course of the
struggle between the two great Powers
for the possession of Western Asia and
in the annihilation of Sennacherib's army
before the walls of Judah's capital.

The Land of Israel's Strategic Position.
In the eighth century B.C.E., there was
a critical change in the internal and
external affairs of Israel and Judah, both
passing through the most serious crisis
since Israel first entered the Promised
Land.

The two greatest world Powers of the
time were struggling for supremacy,
Assyria from the north or north-east
and Egypt from the south or south-west.

The Land of Israel, situated between
these two countries, was for centuries a
natural caravan route between them and
formed, therefore, the foundation of a
highway for armies marching north or
south.

Assyria and Judah. In the earlier part
of the eighth century, when the Assyrian
power was temporarily on the decline, an
opportunity was offered to the kings of
Israel and Judah to attain some of their
ambitions. Jeroboam II extended the
boundaries of Israel northwards, while
Uzziah was able to strengthen the
defences of Judah and increase its
defensive and military power.

With the accession, however, of
Tiglath-pileser III in 745 B.C.E., Assyria
had again risen to a very powerful height
which was maintained and further
increased by a succession of energetic
rulers, until Esarhaddon, in 670 B.C.E.,
succeeded in conquering Egypt.

Egypt and Assyria. During the prophetic ministry of Isaiah, therefore, the
Assyrian empire represented the greatest
force that threatened Judah and all
Western Asia. Egypt, the only nation
that could possibly offer any form of
resistance to Assyrian aggression, was
ruled in the middle of the eighth century

by the twenty-fourth dynasty under
which the country was rent by internal
dissension. Despite its eminence among
the smaller nations, it was quite impotent
to oppose an effective barrier to the
spread of the Assyrian conquests. On
more than one occasion Egypt dis-
appointed the Israelite kings who sought
her help. Her weakness led to pro-
crastination and culminated in disillusionment and loss of faith.

New life, however, was infused into
Egypt's foreign activities about 708
B.C.E. under the twenty-fifth dynasty,
which consisted of powerful Ethiopian
rulers who brought new hope to Judah
as to the other peoples around, and
inspired the Southern Kingdom with
courage to resist the Assyrian demands
and make a bid for independence.

Hezekiah's Rebellion and Illness. Isaiah
remonstrated against this reckless ad-
venture. He was convinced that the
safety of Judah lay not in independence
but in submission to Assyria, and in
resignation to the fate ordained by God.
But Isaiah was overruled by the strong
Egyptian party in the court of king
Hezekiah and a treaty was concluded
with Egypt. Judah was thus irrevocably
committed to a break with the greatest
empire of that age.

Sometime before Sennacherib's invasion of Judah, Hezekiah fell ill, and the
prophet advised him to prepare his will
since he would not recover. In answer
to the king's fervent prayer, however,
the prophet brought the good tidings
that God had added fifteen years to his life.

Miraculous Deliverance. When Sennacherib, in 701, had overrun all the
northern cities of Israel and was besieging
Jerusalem, Isaiah assured Hezekiah that
the Holy City would not fall into the
hands of the enemy whose entire army
would be destroyed before the walls of
the city of God. The prophecy was
fulfilled and all the 185,000 men of the
Assyrian expedition perished miraculously in one night.

MORAL, THEOLOGICAL AND NATIONAL
CONCEPTS

Moral Conditions. Isaiah has painted
a sad picture of the internal conditions of

Judah. The sin of idolatry, superstition, drunkenness, selfish greed of the rich, bribery and corruption of the judges were some of the evils which the prophet denounced. Misled by intoxicated prophets, the people disregarded the appeals of the true messenger of God and relied for safety on warlike preparations and military measures. The sanctuaries were crowded with worshippers, and the altars piled with sacrifices, while injustice, oppression, adultery and even murder were rife and unchecked. Religion had no effect upon conduct, and the people failed to understand that public as well as private life must be based on religious belief if stability was to be secured. They refused to listen to the prophet's warning that their sins would inevitably lead to national disaster and that trust in God and obedience to His will were the only safe course to follow.

Holiness. One of the titles by which Isaiah describes the Deity is the 'Holy one of Israel.' The fundamental conception underlying the word *kadosh,* as Isaiah used it, is 'righteousness' whereby God exalts and sanctifies Himself. It denotes God's supremacy, omnipotence and majesty. It is the attribute of Him Whose Presence cannot be approached or fully realized by mortals, Who alone is entitled to the adoration of all created beings.

God and Israel. That there is a special and everlasting relationship between God and Israel is another of the fundamentals of Isaiah's prophecy. God has chosen Israel from all the idol-worshipping nations to be the bearer of His message. Israel is, therefore, God's people in a particular sense and He is Israel's God in a particular relationship. In this sense 'holiness' is transformed from an abstract thought to practical religion, and the prophet can thus describe the Supreme Being as the 'Holy One of Israel.'

Glory. The concept of *glory* is the external manifestation of God's omnipotence, greatness and overwhelming, awe-inspiring majesty. The glory of

God is the honour and praise that are due to Him and the 'dazzling brightness' in which He arrays Himself when He manifests His Presence on earth. The ministering angels are but a faint reflection of His sublime majesty, and even they in their adorations, being conscious of their inferiority, do not venture into His Presence without first covering their feet and faces. All that exists in the world, all that is awesome in creation and all that is powerful are but the external manifestation and symbol of the supreme majesty of the Lord of all things.

Messianic Ideal. Isaiah's Messianic predictions embody the ideal of the Kingdom of God on earth and the eternal greatness of Zion. The city of Zion, which is the present abode of God's glory, will also be His habitation in the end of days.

INTERNATIONAL CONCEPTS AND HOPES

Universal Sovereign. Although the Lord is the God of Israel in a special sense, as the Creator of the Universe He is also the universal Sovereign Whose glory fills the earth. The Kingship of God is not limited to one nation. All are His peoples and He is their God, and He will tolerate no rival. The deities of the other nations are nonentities and the creation of man. There will be a day of judgment, and the retribution that will follow will prove to all that He alone is the Lord of all.

World Peace. Isaiah prophesied the advent of a time when the nations 'shall beat their swords into plowshares and their spears into pruning-hooks,' when 'nation shall not lift up sword against nation, neither shall they learn war any more.' He looked forward to the era when 'the wolf shall dwell with the lamb, the leopard lie down with the kid,' the infant 'play on the hole of the asp,' and the calf and the young lion together be led by a child. And the world 'shall be full of the knowledge of the Lord as the waters cover the sea.'

I. W. SLOTKI

ISAIAH

Introduction and Commentary
by
DR. I. W. SLOTKI, M.A., LITT.D.

Revised by
RABBI A. J. ROSENBERG

ISAIAH

1   CHAPTER I   א

1. THE vision of Isaiah the son of Amoz, which he saw concerning Judah and Jerusalem, in the days of Uzziah, Jotham, Ahaz, and Hezekiah, kings of Judah.

2. Hear, O heavens, and give ear, O earth,
For the LORD hath spoken:
Children I have reared, and brought up,
And they have rebelled against Me.

חֲזוֹן יְשַׁעְיָהוּ בֶן־אָמוֹץ אֲשֶׁר חָזָה ¹
עַל־יְהוּדָה וִירוּשָׁלָ͏ִם בִּימֵי עֻזִיָּהוּ
יוֹתָם אָחָז יְחִזְקִיָּהוּ מַלְכֵי יְהוּדָה:
שִׁמְעוּ שָׁמַיִם וְהַאֲזִינִי אֶרֶץ ²
כִּי יְהוָה דִּבֵּר
בָּנִים גִּדַּלְתִּי וְרוֹמַמְתִּי
וְהֵם פָּשְׁעוּ בִי:

v. 1. הפטרת אלה הדברים

CHAPTER I

THIS chapter, though the first in the Book, is not the earliest of Isaiah's prophecies, which should be looked for in chapter vi, where a graphic description of the prophet's call to, and initiation into, his high office precedes what is obviously his prophetic message. The position of the chapter at the opening of the Book is to be explained on the ground that it sets forth the fundamental ideas and cardinal principles of the prophet's teaching as was necessary for his generation (Kimchi). It has been well described as 'The great Arraignment.' According to Rashi, the date of the first part of the chapter, verses 2-17, is after the exile of the Kingdom of Israel. See verses 7 and 8. The chapter is read as the *haphtarah* of the Sabbath before the fast of the Ninth of Ab which, from its opening word *chazon,* is named 'Sabbath *Chazon.*'

1. The verse should be understood as the superscription of chapter i only. Chapter ii has its own superscription. Moreover, the subsequent chapters, containing prophecies on foreign nations, cannot be covered by the heading *concerning Judah and Jerusalem* (Abarbanel, Rashi).

vision. From the root *chazah* 'to see.' The

prophet 'sees' (perceives the Divine message) with the eye of the spirit (Metsudath Zion).

Isaiah. Hebrew *Yeshayah,* meaning 'salvation of the Lord.' Cf. Joshua, in Hebrew *Yehoshua.*

Amoz. According to a tradition he was the brother of Amaziah, king of Judah (Megillah 10b).

Judah. The people and the country.

Jerusalem. [Being the capital, it is singled out.]

in the days of Uzziah. In the last year of his reign (cf. vi. 1f.).

2. God's lament over Israel.

2. *hear, O heavens . . . earth.* i.e. be witnesses to the great benefactions the Lord had bestowed upon His people and Israel's ingratitude and backsliding. Moses, when rebuking Israel, similarly began, *Give ear, ye heavens . . . and let the earth hear* (Deut. xxxii. 1).

brought up. lit. 'exalted' to *a kingdom of priests and a holy nation* (Exod. xix. 6) (See Kimchi).

and they. [Emphatic in the Hebrew: *they* to whom I have shown such favor.]

rebelled. Against the Divine Sovereignty by violation of His will (Kimchi).

1

3. The ox knoweth his owner,
   And the ass his master's crib;
   But Israel doth not know,
   My people doth not consider.

4. Ah sinful nation,
   A people laden with iniquity,
   A seed of evil-doers,
   Children that deal corruptly;
   They have forsaken the LORD,
   They have contemned the Holy
     One of Israel,
   They are turned away backward.

5. On what part will ye be yet
     stricken,
   Seeing ye stray away more and
     more ?
   The whole head is sick,
   And the whole heart faint;

3 יָדַע שׁוֹר קֹנֵהוּ
וַחֲמוֹר אֵבוּס בְּעָלָיו
יִשְׂרָאֵל לֹא יָדַע
עַמִּי לֹא הִתְבּוֹנָן:
4 הוֹי | גּוֹי חֹטֵא
עַם כֶּבֶד עָוֹן
זֶרַע מְרֵעִים
בָּנִים מַשְׁחִיתִים
עָזְבוּ אֶת־יְהֹוָה
נִאֲצוּ אֶת־קְדוֹשׁ יִשְׂרָאֵל
נָזֹרוּ אָחוֹר:
5 עַל־מֶה תֻכּוּ
עוֹד תּוֹסִיפוּ סָרָה
כָּל־רֹאשׁ לָחֳלִי
וְכָל־לֵבָב דַּוָּי:

---

3. *the ox . . . crib.* Even dumb animals show more recognition and gratitude than Israel to their benefactors (Kimchi). The ox and the ass are mentioned probably on account of their being among the domesticated animals in Palestine (Ibn Ezra).

but. This word is not represented in the Hebrew, but is implied from the context (Malbim).

doth not know. That God is his Creator and Provider (Kimchi).

4–9. Isaiah's denunciation of Israel.

4. *sinful nation.* Israel's guilt is the heavier because he was chosen to be the depository of God's Revelation (See Rashi).

seed. Generation (Kimchi)

contemned. Or, 'provoked, spurned' (Rashi, Ibn Ezra, Kimchi).

Holy One of Israel. [This description of

God occurs 39 times in Isaiah and only five times in all the other Books of Scripture. It sums up Isaiah's conception of the Divine nature in its relationship to Israel.]

turned away. from God (Malbim).

5. *on what part.* Of the body, the nation being represented as an individual stricken and wounded from head to foot without any healthy part on which a new wound could be inflicted (Ibn Ezra, Abarbanel).

yet. This may be the rendering of the Hebrew *od* which, according to the accentuation, is to be joined to the preceding clause. Surprisingly, none of the classical exegetes interprets it in this manner.

the whole head . . . heart. lit. 'every head . . . heart.' The Hebrew is rendered as though the definite article preceded the nouns (Ibn Ezra).

6. From the sole of the foot even
   unto the head
   There is no soundness in it;
   But wounds, and bruises, and
   festering sores:
   They have not been pressed,
   neither bound up,
   Neither mollified with oil.

7. Your country is desolate;
   Your cities are burned with fire;
   Your land, strangers devour it in
   your presence,
   And it is desolate, as overthrown
   by floods.

8. And the daughter of Zion is left
   As a booth in a vineyard,
   As a lodge in a garden of
   cucumbers,
   As a besieged city.

6 מִכַּף־רֶגֶל וְעַד־רֹאשׁ

אֵין־בּוֹ מְתֹם

פֶּצַע וְחַבּוּרָה וּמַכָּה טְרִיָּה

לֹא־זֹרוּ וְלֹא חֻבָּשׁוּ

וְלֹא רֻכְּכָה בַּשָּׁמֶן:

7 אַרְצְכֶם שְׁמָמָה

עָרֵיכֶם שְׂרֻפוֹת אֵשׁ

אַדְמַתְכֶם לְנֶגְדְּכֶם זָרִים

אֹכְלִים אֹתָהּ

וּשְׁמָמָה כְּמַהְפֵּכַת זָרִים:

8 וְנוֹתְרָה בַת־צִיּוֹן

כְּסֻכָּה בְכָרֶם

כִּמְלוּנָה בְמִקְשָׁה

כְּעִיר נְצוּרָה:

---

6. *wounds ... sores.* [The Hebrew nouns are in the singular, but to be understood in the collective sense.]

pressed ... mollified. In Isaiah's time a wound was first *pressed out* to rid it of any purulent matter, then it was *mollified with oil* and *bound up* (Ibn Ezra). The Hebrew verbs for *pressed* and *bound up* are in the plural, but that for *mollified* is in the singular, referring only to the festering sore (Rashi).

7f. The metaphors of verses 5f. now give way to a plain enumeration of the calamities which had befallen the nation.

7. *desolate.* lit. 'a desolation.'

strangers. A reference to the Assyrians and the peoples they repatriated in Samaria and its environs (Abarbanel).

in your presence. And you can but helplessly look on (Kimchi, Kara).

floods. Better 'flood.' Hebrew *zarim,* usually rendered 'stranger' (so Targum,

Rashi), is here regarded as a variation of *zerem* 'flood' (Ibn Ezra, Kimchi).

8. *daughter of Zion.* [*Bath Zion,* construction of apposition meaning 'the daughter Zion,'] a personification of Jerusalem (Kimchi).

is left. Isolated and forlorn in the midst of a conquered and devastated country (Kimchi, Rashi, Ibn Ezra).

booth in a vineyard. [Such a booth was a frail structure raised from the ground several feet above the level of the vines by means of four poles driven into the earth and joined at their upper ends with cross-pieces supporting the booth.] It served as a shelter for the watchman who guarded the fruit from intruding animals and thieves. Even during the season it was a solitary habitation; but after the vintage, when it was deserted even by the watchman, it presented a complete picture of dreariness and loneliness (Kimchi).

lodge ... cucumbers. Similar in condition to the booth (Rashi).

9. Except the LORD of hosts
   Had left unto us a very small
   remnant,
   We should have been as Sodom,
   We should have been like unto
   Gomorrah.

10. Hear the word of the LORD,
    Ye rulers of Sodom;
    Give ear unto the law of our God,
    Ye people of Gomorrah.

11. To what purpose is the multitude
    of your sacrifices unto Me?
    Saith the LORD;
    I am full of the burnt-offerings
    of rams,
    And the fat of fed beasts;
    And I delight not in the blood
    Of bullocks, or of lambs, or of
    he-goats.

9 לוּלֵי יְהֹוָה צְבָאוֹת
הוֹתִיר לָנוּ שָׂרִיד כִּמְעָט
כִּסְדֹם הָיִינוּ
לַעֲמֹרָה דָּמִינוּ׃

10 שִׁמְעוּ דְבַר־יְהֹוָה
קְצִינֵי סְדֹם
הַאֲזִינוּ תּוֹרַת אֱלֹהֵינוּ
עַם עֲמֹרָה׃

11 לָמָּה־לִּי רֹב־זִבְחֵיכֶם
יֹאמַר יְהֹוָה
שָׂבַעְתִּי עֹלוֹת אֵילִים
וְחֵלֶב מְרִיאִים
וְדַם פָּרִים וּכְבָשִׂים
וְעַתּוּדִים לֹא חָפָצְתִּי׃

as a besieged city. Which is cut off from the outside world (See Abarbanel). A possible rendering is, 'like a city under close watch (Rabbenu Isaiah of Trani).' The first rendering treats *netsura* as the participle Niphal of *tsur* 'to besiege,' while the second regards it as the present participle passive Kal of *natsar* 'to watch.'

9. LORD *of hosts.* A title denoting God's omnipotence and universal Sovereignty. *Hosts* signifies the heavenly hosts of the angels as well as the earthly hosts of Israel (Kimchi).

very small. An adverbial phrase, joined in harmony with the Hebrew accents to the preceding *sarid,* 'remnant' (Ibn Ezra). Others connect it with the following half of the verse and render, 'we had almost been as,' etc. (Rashi).

Sodom . . . Gomorrah. Cf. Gen xviii. 23ff., xix. 24f.

10–17. False and true worship of God. The one (verses 11–15) is objection-able, the other (verses 16f.) is acceptable to Him.

10. *rulers of Sodom.* i.e. as wicked as those of Sodom (Targum, Rashi).

law. Hebrew *Torah,* 'instruction, direction'; generally religious teaching, in this case, the following reprimand (Kimchi).

11. *to what purpose.* No attack by the prophet is intended upon the offerings in the Temple. A sacrifice is welcomed from the sincere penitent but not from the hypocrite who brings it while still clinging to his evil ways (Rashi, Kimchi).

sacrifices. The Hebrew is *zebach,* 'an animal sacrifice.'

I am full of. lit. 'I am sated with.'

burnt-offerings. Animal sacrifices that were entirely burnt on the altar. Other sacrifices, such as peace-offerings, were eaten by the owners, and only the fat and blood were offered upon the altar. See Lev. i. 3.

12. When ye come to appear before
Me,
Who hath required this at your
hand,
To trample My courts?

13. Bring no more vain oblations;
It is an offering of abomination
unto Me;
New moon and sabbath, the
holding of convocations—
I cannot endure iniquity along
with the solemn assembly.

14. Your new moons and your
appointed seasons
My soul hateth;
They are a burden unto Me;
I am weary to bear them.

15. And when ye spread forth your
hands,
I will hide Mine eyes from you;
Yea, when ye make many
prayers,
I will not hear;
Your hands are full of blood.

16. Wash you, make you clean,

כִּי תָבֹאוּ לֵרָאוֹת פָּנַי 12
מִי־בִקֵשׁ זֹאת מִיֶּדְכֶם
רְמֹס חֲצֵרָי:
לֹא תוֹסִיפוּ הָבִיא מִנְחַת־שָׁוְא 13
קְטֹרֶת תּוֹעֵבָה הִיא לִי
חֹדֶשׁ וְשַׁבָּת קְרֹא מִקְרָא
לֹא־אוּכַל אָוֶן וַעֲצָרָה:
חָדְשֵׁיכֶם וּמוֹעֲדֵיכֶם שָׂנְאָה נַפְשִׁי 14
הָיוּ עָלַי לָטֹרַח
נִלְאֵיתִי נְשֹׂא:
וּבְפָרִשְׂכֶם כַּפֵּיכֶם 15
אַעְלִים עֵינַי מִכֶּם
גַּם כִּי־תַרְבּוּ תְפִלָּה
אֵינֶנִּי שֹׁמֵעַ
יְדֵיכֶם דָּמִים מָלֵאוּ:
רַחֲצוּ הִזַּכּוּ 16

---

12. *appear before Me.* The phrase used
of pilgrimage to the Temple three times
a year (Deut. xvi. 16). Although it is
obligatory, if it is performed without
sincerity, it is unacceptable (Abarbanel).

who hath required. The purpose of the
question is indicated in the note on the
preceding verse (Abarbanel).

13. *oblations.* The Hebrew singular
with collective force. The usual meaning
of the noun is 'meal-offering,' [but it is
also used of any sacrificial gift.]

offering. The word is usually rendered
'incense,' from a root meaning 'to
smoke.'

holding of convocations. Festival religious
assemblies (Lev. xxiii. 4), lit. 'to call a
calling.' The messengers of the Sanhedrin would go out to announce the New

Moon and inform the people when the
festivals would occur (Kara).

endure. To be supplied; the Hebrew is 'I
cannot.'

iniquity . . . assembly. A combination of
such opposites is intolerable (Rashi).

14. *appointed seasons.* The pilgrimage
Festivals (Lev. xxiii. 4).

15. *spread . . . hands.* Towards heaven
in an attitude of prayer (Metsudath
David).

full of blood. Metaphor for murder or
cruel oppression (cf. verse 21).

16f. God demands moral reformation
and a return to the paths of justice
and charity as the true performance
of His will and a prerequisite to the
acceptance of the people's offerings.

Put away the evil of your doings
From before Mine eyes,
Cease to do evil;

17. Learn to do well;
Seek justice, relieve the oppressed,
Judge the fatherless, plead for
the widow.

18. Come now, and let us reason
together,
Saith the LORD;
Though your sins be as scarlet,
They shall be as white as snow;
Though they be red like crimson,
They shall be as wool.

19. If ye be willing and obedient,
Ye shall eat the good of the land;

20. But if ye refuse and rebel,

הָסִירוּ רֹעַ מַעַלְלֵיכֶם
מִנֶּגֶד עֵינָי
חִדְלוּ הָרֵעַ׃
17 לִמְדוּ הֵיטֵב
דִּרְשׁוּ מִשְׁפָּט אַשְּׁרוּ חָמוֹץ
שִׁפְטוּ יָתוֹם רִיבוּ אַלְמָנָה׃
18 לְכוּ־נָא וְנִוָּכְחָה
יֹאמַר יְהֹוָה
אִם־יִהְיוּ חֲטָאֵיכֶם כַּשָּׁנִים
כַּשֶּׁלֶג יַלְבִּינוּ
אִם־יַאְדִּימוּ כַתּוֹלָע
כַּצֶּמֶר יִהְיוּ׃
19 אִם־תֹּאבוּ וּשְׁמַעְתֶּם
טוּב הָאָרֶץ תֹּאכֵלוּ׃
20 וְאִם־תְּמָאֲנוּ וּמְרִיתֶם

17. *learn to do well.* To be contrasted with *cease to do evil* in the preceding verse. A negative attitude to evil is not enough; it must be accompanied by positive acts of righteousness (Abarbanel).

relieve the oppressed. Better, 'strengthen the robbed (Rashi), or 'set straight the robbed (Ibn Ezra, Kimchi).' Force the robber to make amends for his crime.

judge. Listen to his plea in court (Kimchi).

fatherless . . . widow. They are helpless and the likeliest victims of the unscrupulous. The prophet demands justice from both rulers and people (cf. verse 10), even for the weakest members of society (Kimchi).

plead. The Hebrew *ribu* bears also the meaning of 'strive.' One should not hesitate to fight for the right (Kara).

18-20. God reasons with His people,

offers pardon, and prosperity to the penitent, death and destruction to the rebellious.

18. *come.* lit. 'go.' [The Hebrew language views the action from the starting point, the English from that of destination.]

let us reason together. The root-meaning of the verb is 'to prove, decide, adjudge (Kimchi).'

though your sins. Since the particle *im* usually bears the meaning of 'if,' some translate, 'if your sins be as scarlet, they shall be like snow. If they be red like crimson dye, they shall be like wool (Rashi).' The implication being that if you have sinned by yourselves and you repent, your sins will be forgiven completely. If you have caused others to sin, your sins will not be forgiven completely, just as white wool is not pure white (Malbim).

19. *and obedient.* lit. 'and hear.'

Ye shall be devoured with the
  sword;
For the mouth of the LORD hath
  spoken.

21. How is the faithful city
  Become a harlot!
  She that was full of justice,
  Righteousness lodged in her,
  But now murderers.

22. Thy silver is become dross,
  Thy wine mixed with water.

23. Thy princes are rebellious,
  And companions of thieves;
  Every one loveth bribes,
  And followeth after rewards;
  They judge not the fatherless,
  Neither doth the cause of the
    widow come unto them.

חֶרֶב תְּאֻכְּלוּ
כִּי פִּי יְהוָה דִּבֵּר׃
21 אֵיכָה הָיְתָה לְזוֹנָה
קִרְיָה נֶאֱמָנָה
מְלֵאֲתִי מִשְׁפָּט
צֶדֶק יָלִין בָּהּ
וְעַתָּה מְרַצְּחִים׃
22 כַּסְפֵּךְ הָיָה לְסִיגִים
סָבְאֵךְ מָהוּל בַּמָּיִם׃
23 שָׂרַיִךְ סוֹרְרִים
וְחַבְרֵי גַּנָּבִים
כֻּלּוֹ אֹהֵב שֹׁחַד
וְרֹדֵף שַׁלְמֹנִים
יָתוֹם לֹא יִשְׁפֹּטוּ
וְרִיב אַלְמָנָה לֹא־יָבוֹא אֲלֵיהֶם׃

20. *with the sword.* The construction is called by the grammarians 'the accusative of instruments,' there being no preposition in the Hebrew.

21ff. A dirge on the moral decay of Jerusalem. Like similar elegies it begins with the exclamation *echah* (*how*). Cf. Lam. i. 1.

21. *faithful city.* Jerusalem, symbolizing its inhabitants who were once loyal and faithful to the teaching of the Torah (Rashi).

harlot. astray from her God (Rashi). Just as the harlot is unfaithful to her husband and has affairs with other men, so did Jerusalem, the faithful city, after clinging tenaciously to the Temple service and abolishing the sacrifices on the high places during the reigns of David, Solomon, Asa, and Jehoshaphat, revert to sacrificing on high places and to asherim (Kimchi).

justice . . . righteousness. The latter is the principle of rectitude and just dealing of men with each other, while the former, also rendered 'judgment,' is the practice of the principle in the courts of law and daily life and action (Kimchi).

lodged. Better, 'abode', 'continued', 'endured' (Kimchi).

22. *silver . . . dross . . . wine . . . water.* The words may metaphorically symbolize, apart from their literal sense, the rulers and judges, the cream of the people in their moral deterioration (Ibn Ezra).

wine. This follows Rashi. Other renderings are 'choice drink,' 'strong drink' (Metsudath Zion).

23. *rebellious.* Against the Divine law (Abarbanel).

the fatherless. Who has no protector and can offer no bribes (Alshich).

neither doth . . . widow come. The orphan having been before the judges and

24. Therefore saith the Lord, the
LORD of hosts,
The Mighty One of Israel:
Ah, I will ease Me of Mine
adversaries,
And avenge Me of Mine enemies;

25. And I will turn My hand upon
thee,
And purge away thy dross as
with lye,
And will take away all thine alloy;

26. And I will restore thy judges as
at the first,
And thy counsellors as at the
beginning;
Afterward thou shalt be called
The city of righteousness,
The faithful city.

27. Zion shall be redeemed with
justice,
And they that return of her with
righteousness.

28. But the destruction of the transgressors and the sinners shall
be together,
And they that forsake the LORD
shall be consumed.

לָכֵן נְאֻם הָאָדוֹן יְהֹוָה צְבָאוֹת 24
אֲבִיר יִשְׂרָאֵל
הוֹי אֶנָּחֵם מִצָּרַי
וְאִנָּקְמָה מֵאוֹיְבָי׃
וְאָשִׁיבָה יָדִי עָלַיִךְ 25
וְאֶצְרֹף כַּבֹּר סִגָיִךְ
וְאָסִירָה כָּל־בְּדִילָיִךְ׃
וְאָשִׁיבָה שֹׁפְטַיִךְ כְּבָרִאשֹׁנָה 26
וְיֹעֲצַיִךְ כְּבַתְּחִלָּה
אַחֲרֵי־כֵן יִקָּרֵא לָךְ עִיר הַצֶּדֶק
קִרְיָה נֶאֱמָנָה׃
צִיּוֹן בְּמִשְׁפָּט תִּפָּדֶה 27
וְשָׁבֶיהָ בִּצְדָקָה׃ *
וְשֶׁבֶר פֹּשְׁעִים וְחַטָּאִים יַחְדָּו 28
וְעֹזְבֵי יְהֹוָה יִכְלוּ׃

v. 27. עד כאן

failed to secure justice, the widow, frail
and helpless, is afraid even to approach
the court (Rashi).

24. [The moral conditions being so
hopeless, God Himself, so to speak,
takes matters in His own hand.]

24. *The* LORD. Hebrew *haAdon,* 'the
Master, Sovereign'; when so used by
Isaiah in the absolute form, it always
introduces a warning or threat (Metsudath David).

ease Me. By the execution of vengeance
referred to in the following clause (Ibn
Ezra).

Mine enemies. Those who sin against the
moral and Divine law are the enemies of
God (Kimchi).

25. *My hand upon thee.* Striking again
and again (Rashi).

lye. An alkaline solution used in the
smelting of metals (Kimchi).

alloy. What is base and corrupting
(Rashi).

26. *as at the first.* Before corruption
had set in (Malbim). Others see in the
phrase an allusion to the days of David
(Ibn Ezra).

those shalt be called. lit. 'it shall be called
to thee.'

27. *with justice.* That will be executed
by its people and rulers (Rashi).

and they . . . her. From their evil ways to
the right path (Rashi, Ibn Ezra). An
alternative explanation is: from captivity to Zion (Kimchi).

28. *shall be together.* Better, in harmony
with the Hebrew, 'but the destruction of
transgressors and sinners together.'
Another possible rendering is, 'but
there shall be a destruction of transgressors and sinners together (See Kimchi).' Transgressors are the rebellious

29. For they shall be ashamed of the terebinths which ye have desired,
And ye shall be confounded for the gardens that ye have chosen.
30. For ye shall be as a terebinth whose leaf fadeth,
And as a garden that hath no water.
31. And the strong shall be as tow,
And his work as a spark;
And they shall both burn together,
And none shall quench them.

כִּי יֵבֹשׁוּ מֵאֵילִים אֲשֶׁר חֲמַדְתֶּם ‏29
וְתַחְפְּרוּ מֵהַגַּנּוֹת אֲשֶׁר בְּחַרְתֶּם:
כִּי תִהְיוּ כְּאֵלָה נֹבֶלֶת עָלֶהָ ‏30
וּכְגַנָּה אֲשֶׁר־מַיִם אֵין לָהּ:
וְהָיָה הֶחָסֹן לִנְעֹרֶת ‏31
וּפֹעֲלוֹ לְנִיצוֹץ
וּבָעֲרוּ שְׁנֵיהֶם יַחְדָּו
וְאֵין מְכַבֶּה:

---

2   CHAPTER II   ב

1. The word that Isaiah the son of Amoz saw concerning Judah and Jerusalem.

הַדָּבָר אֲשֶׁר חָזָה יְשַׁעְיָהוּ בֶּן־אָמוֹץ ‏1
עַל־יְהוּדָה וִירוּשָׁלָ͏ִם:

---

ones: apostates and idolators; sinners are those guilty of other infractions of the law (Rashi).

consumed. Without a trace of them being left (Metsudath David).

29–31. The return to the ways of righteousness wil also lead to a purified worship of God, all kinds of idols and alien forms of ritual being ignominiously rejected.

29. *terebinths ... gardens.* Emblems of nature worship.

ye have desired ... chosen. As objects of reverence (Kimchi, Kara).

30. *fadeth ... hath no water.* Symbols of disintegration and decay (Kimchi).

31. *strong.* The powerful worshipper (Jonathan, Abarbanel); others explain it of the idol (Kimchi).

his work. The idol (Targum). An alternative translation, in accordance with the Hebrew, is 'his maker' (Kimchi).

CHAPTERS II–IV

THE artistic and literary unity of these three chapters is evident from (a) the

superscription of ii. 1; (b) the introduction (ii. 2–4) describing the glories of the Messianic age, the dissemination of true religion and the spontaneous submission of the nations to the authority of the God of Israel; (c) the series of exhortations to the people, judges and princes (ii. 5–iv. 1) condemning idolatry, pride, robbery, oppression, ostentation and luxury, and announcing the retribution that would follow; and (d) the conclusion (iv. 2–6) alluding again to the Messianic times and enumerating the blessings that would be enjoyed by the escaped remnant, *every one that is written unto life* that *shall be called holy*, who would be protected, as was Israel of old (Exod. xiii. 21f.), by *a cloud and smoke by day, and the shining of a flaming fire by night.*

CHAPTER II

1. *the word.* Hebrew *haddabar,* 'the message, vision.'

saw. See on i. 1.

concerning ... Jerusalem. The superscription may refer (cf. the introductory note above) to the three chapters that follow (See Ibn Ezra iii. 1, where he connects

2. And it shall come to pass in the
　　end of days,
　That the mountain of the Lord's
　　house shall be established as
　　the top of the mountains,
　And shall be exalted above the
　　hills;
　And all nations shall flow unto it.
3. And many peoples shall go and
　　say:
　'Come ye, and let us go up to the
　　mountain of the Lord,
　To the house of the God of
　　Jacob;
　And He will teach us of His ways,
　And we will walk in His paths.'
　For out of Zion shall go forth the
　　law,
　And the word of the Lord from
　　Jerusalem.
4. And He shall judge between the
　　nations,
　And shall decide for many
　　peoples;
　And they shall beat their swords
　　into plowshares,
　And their spears into pruning-
　　hooks;

² וְהָיָה ׀ בְּאַחֲרִית הַיָּמִים
נָכוֹן יִהְיֶה הַר בֵּית־יְהֹוָה
בְּרֹאשׁ הֶהָרִים
וְנִשָּׂא מִגְּבָעוֹת
וְנָהֲרוּ אֵלָיו כָּל־הַגּוֹיִם׃
³ וְהָלְכוּ עַמִּים רַבִּים וְאָמְרוּ
לְכוּ ׀ וְנַעֲלֶה אֶל־הַר־יְהֹוָה
אֶל־בֵּית אֱלֹהֵי יַעֲקֹב
וְיֹרֵנוּ מִדְּרָכָיו
וְנֵלְכָה בְּאֹרְחֹתָיו
כִּי מִצִּיּוֹן תֵּצֵא תוֹרָה
וּדְבַר־יְהֹוָה מִירוּשָׁלָ͏ִם׃
⁴ וְשָׁפַט בֵּין הַגּוֹיִם
וְהוֹכִיחַ לְעַמִּים רַבִּים
וְכִתְּתוּ חַרְבוֹתָם לְאִתִּים
וַחֲנִיתוֹתֵיהֶם לְמַזְמֵרוֹת

chapter iii to chapter ii; Abarbanel, who connects iv to iii.

2-4. Zion as the center of religious instruction and the place of the supreme court of the nations. The reign of world peace. The passage occurs with slight variations in Micah iv. 1-4.

2. *end of days.* In the remote future, when wickedness will disappear and the Kingdom of God be firmly established (Ibn Ezra).

mountain . . . house. The Temple mount (Rashi, Ibn Ezra, Kimchi).

as the top. In respect of religious, moral and political eminence (Ibn Ezra).

all nations. lit. 'all the nations.'

shall flow. The Hebrew signifies 'stream like a river.'

3. *come.* lit. 'go' (see on i. 18).

house . . . Jacob. It is named after Jacob because it was he who called the locality *the house of God* (Gen. xxviii. 19).

and He will teach . . . walk. Better, 'that He may teach . . . and that we may walk.' The words express the purpose of the nations' streaming to God's house (Abarbanel).

for out of Zion . . . Jerusalem. This may be either the prophetic comment on the action of the nations (Kimchi), or the conclusion of the nations' exhortation to one another beginning with *come ye.* If the latter, the verb should be rendered 'goeth forth' (Kara).

law. Torah, i.e. religious and moral instruction to the nations (Kimchi).

4. God's Sovereignty culminates in the abolition of all warfare.

decide. Better, 'arbitrate.'

Nation shall not lift up sword against nation,
Neither shall they learn war any more.

5. O house of Jacob, come ye, and let us walk
In the light of the LORD.

6. For Thou hast forsaken Thy people the house of Jacob;
For they are replenished from the east,
And with soothsayers like the Philistines,
And they please themselves in the brood of aliens.

7. Their land also is full of silver and gold,
Neither is there any end of their treasures;
Their land also is full of horses,
Neither is there any end of their chariots.

לֹא־יִשָּׂא גוֹי אֶל־גּוֹי חֶרֶב
וְלֹא־יִלְמְדוּ עוֹד מִלְחָמָה:
5 בֵּית יַעֲקֹב לְכוּ וְנֵלְכָה
בְּאוֹר יְהֹוָה:
6 כִּי נָטַשְׁתָּה עַמְּךָ בֵּית יַעֲקֹב
כִּי מָלְאוּ מִקֶּדֶם
וְעֹנְנִים כַּפְּלִשְׁתִּים
וּבְיַלְדֵי נָכְרִים יַשְׂפִּיקוּ:
7 וַתִּמָּלֵא אַרְצוֹ כֶּסֶף וְזָהָב
וְאֵין קֵצֶה לְאֹצְרֹתָיו
וַתִּמָּלֵא אַרְצוֹ סוּסִים
וְאֵין קֵצֶה לְמַרְכְּבֹתָיו:

5. The verse introduces a thought suggested by the glorious future just depicted and leads on to the drab reality, the actual state of the people, described in the following verses. The prophet says in effect, 'Seeing that we are to have such a bright future, universal peace and the recognition of the law of our God by all the nations of the earth, let us ourselves begin here and now to *walk in the light of the* LORD. But alas! Israel is still sunk in the vices of idolatry and superstition, and for that reason God has forsaken them' (Kimchi).

come ye. lit. 'go,' as in verse 3.

6–9. The prophet in despair and bitterness turns away from his people, and addresses himself to God (Rashi).

6. *for Thou.* Better, 'yea, Thou.'

forsaken Thy people. Because they deliberately abandoned the way of life prescribed for them in the Torah (Rashi).

replenished. With sorcery which was substituted for the God-given prophecy (Ibn Ezra).

east. Aram, the land of magic and witchcraft (Rashi, Ibn Ezra).

with soothsayers. Better, 'and are soothsayers' (Isaiah of Trani).

please themselves in. This follows Rashi. An alternative rendering is: 'have a sufficiency of,' i.e. 'abound in' (Ibn Ezra).

brood of aliens. With children they have begotten by alien women (Rashi). Others understand the phrase as 'ideas of aliens.' They satisfy themselves with studying the wisdom of the heathens and do not seek God's prophecy (Ibn Ezra).

7. *their land also is full.* lit. 'and his (the people's) land has become filled.' Throughout verses 7f. the Hebrew singular 'his,' referring to the people collectively, is rendered by the plural (Targum).

silver and gold ... treasures ... horses. This refers to Solomon's time when silver and gold were plentiful, and the king accumulated huge stables of horses from Egypt (Kimchi).

11

8. Their land also is full of idols;
Every one worshippeth the work
of his own hands,
That which his own fingers have
made.

9. And man boweth down,
And man lowereth himself;
And Thou canst not bear with
them.

10. Enter into the rock,
And hide thee in the dust,
From before the terror of the
LORD,
And from the glory of His
majesty.

11. The lofty looks of man shall be
brought low,
And the haughtiness of men
shall be bowed down,
And the LORD alone shall be
exalted in that day.

וַתִּמָּלֵא אַרְצוֹ אֱלִילִים 8
לְמַעֲשֵׂה יָדָיו יִשְׁתַּחֲווּ
לַאֲשֶׁר עָשׂוּ אֶצְבְּעֹתָיו:
וַיִּשַּׁח אָדָם 9
וַיִּשְׁפַּל־אִישׁ
וְאַל־תִּשָּׂא לָהֶם:
בּוֹא בַצּוּר 10
וְהִטָּמֵן בֶּעָפָר
מִפְּנֵי פַּחַד יְהֹוָה
וּמֵהֲדַר גְּאֹנוֹ:
עֵינֵי גַּבְהוּת אָדָם שָׁפֵל 11
וְשַׁח רוּם אֲנָשִׁים
וְנִשְׂגַּב יְהֹוָה לְבַדּוֹ בַּיּוֹם הַהוּא:

---

8. *their land also is full.* A parallel to the opening words of the previous verse describing cause and effect: prosperity, idolatry. This refers to the end of Solomon's reign and the reign of Jeroboam, whho erected the golden calves (Kimchi).

idols. Hebrew *elilim,* lit. 'nonentities,' from *al* 'not,' objects which lack reality (Ibn Ezra).

9. *boweth . . . lowereth.* Evil practices result in the degradation of human dignity (Ibn Ezra). Others explain, 'is bowed down . . . is brought low,' i.e., Divine retribution inevitably follows (Kimchi). In the translation the word *man* occurs twice, but in the Hebrew they are distinguished, the first being *adam* and the second *ish.* The variant may be nothing more than poetical parallelism, but some expositors explain their meaning as 'mean man' and 'great man' (Rashi, Kimchi).

and Thou canst not bear with them. And so Thou hast forsaken them (verse 6). If the

beginning of the sentence means that God will punish them, this clause must signify, 'for Thou will not forgive them' (Rashi, Kimchi).

10. *and hide thee.* lit. 'and be hidden.' Since it cannot be supposed that Isaiah thought that man is able to escape God's punishment by hiding himself, Jewish commentators understand the verse as the cry which arose in the midst of the panic-stricken Israelites (Ibn Ezra, Kimchi). This may also be interpreted as an infinitive (Rashi, Ibn Ezra).

11. *the lofty looks of.* lit. 'the eyes of the haughtiness of.' This denotes a haughty spirit. Cf. Ps. ci. 5 (Rashi).

shall be brought low. The Hebrew verb is in the perfect tense. The prophet is so sure of the result that he describes it as an event that had already taken place. The verb is also singular, emphasizing the effect on each individual (Kimchi).

that day. The day of judgment described in the following verses (Kimchi).

12. For the LORD of hosts hath a day
Upon all that is proud and lofty,
And upon all that is lifted up,
and it shall be brought low;

13. And upon all the cedars of
Lebanon
That are high and lifted up,
And upon all the oaks of Bashan;

14. And upon all the high mountains,
And upon all the hills that are
lifted up;

15. And upon every lofty tower,
And upon every fortified wall;

12 כִּי יוֹם לַיהוָה צְבָאוֹת
עַל כָּל־גֵּאֶה וָרָם
וְעַל כָּל־נִשָּׂא וְשָׁפֵל׃

13 וְעַל כָּל־אַרְזֵי הַלְּבָנוֹן
הָרָמִים וְהַנִּשָּׂאִים
וְעַל כָּל־אַלּוֹנֵי הַבָּשָׁן׃

14 וְעַל כָּל־הֶהָרִים הָרָמִים
וְעַל כָּל־הַגְּבָעוֹת הַנִּשָּׂאוֹת׃

15 וְעַל כָּל־מִגְדָּל גָּבֹהַּ
וְעַל כָּל־חוֹמָה בְצוּרָה׃

12. *a day.* Of judgment, corresponding to *that day* (verse 11 (Metsudath David).

lofty. Or 'haughty' (Targum).

and it shall . . . low. This follows Targum, Ibn Ezra, and Kimchi. Malbim explains this to mean: 'one who is haughty, but in reality, of low character.' All will be humbled. Alternatively, 'everyone lifted up and humble,' i.e. haughty in his heart, but appearing humble on the surface (Abarbanel).

13. *the cedars of Lebanon.* This symbolizes the kings (Rashi). Kimchi elaborates by explaining that it symbolizes the heathen kings.

the oaks of Bashan. This symbolizes the governors. Just as the oaks are smaller than the cedars, so are the governors of lower status than the kings (Rashi).

14. *the high mountains.* the inhabitants of the high mountains (Rashi).

The prophet enumerates everything with which a person prides himself over others. All pride will be humbled on that day, for the Lord will be exalted over everyone, who will admit His exaltation and will humble himself before Him. A person takes pride in his high mountains and his hills that are

lifted up, where he can fortify himself against his enemies, and wage battle against them without being vulnerable to them. Likewise, he takes pride in a lofty tower or a fortified wall, where he can fortify himself against his enemies. Similarly, he takes pride in his wealth and in his many possessions imported from over the seas by ship (Redak).

15. *lofty tower.* In the king's palace (Ibn Ezra). This symbolizes those who trust in their fortifications for protection (Metsudath David).

16. *ships of Tarshish.* Targum explains *Tarshish* as a generic term for 'sea,' rendering 'those who dwell in the islands of the sea.' Rashi explains that those people must travel by ship, hence 'ships of Tarshish.' This coincides with Targum Onkelos (Exod. xxviii. 20), who renders *tarshish,* a stone on the breastplate of the High Priest, as one of the color of the sea, probably aquamarine. Rashi explains that the sea was named Tarshish. This is believed to be the Mediterranean, as in Targum Jonathan ibid. Cf. Rashi on Jonah i. 2.

Malbim (I Kings x. 22) identifies it with Tartessus in Spain, the farthest point to which merchant ships sailed from Phoenicia and other Mediterranean ports. [Owing to the long voyage

16. And upon all the ships of
Tarshish,
And upon all delightful imagery.

17. And the loftiness of man shall be
bowed down,
And the haughtiness of men shall
be brought low;
And the LORD alone shall be
exalted in that day.

18. And the idols shall utterly pass
away.

19. And men shall go into the caves
of the rocks,
And into the holes of the earth,
From before the terror of the
LORD,
And from the glory of His
majesty,
When He ariseth to shake
mightily the earth.

20. In that day a man shall cast away
His idols of silver, and his idols
of gold,
Which they made for themselves
to worship,
To the moles and to the bats;

16 וְעַל כָּל־אֳנִיּוֹת תַּרְשִׁישׁ
וְעַל כָּל־שְׂכִיּוֹת הַחֶמְדָּה׃

17 וְשַׁח גַּבְהוּת הָאָדָם
וְשָׁפֵל רוּם אֲנָשִׁים
וְנִשְׂגַּב יְהוָה לְבַדּוֹ בַּיּוֹם הַהוּא׃

18 וְהָאֱלִילִים כָּלִיל יַחֲלֹף׃

19 וּבָאוּ בִּמְעָרוֹת צֻרִים
וּבִמְחִלּוֹת עָפָר
מִפְּנֵי פַּחַד יְהוָה
וּמֵהֲדַר גְּאוֹנוֹ
בְּקוּמוֹ לַעֲרֹץ הָאָרֶץ׃

20 בַּיּוֹם הַהוּא יַשְׁלִיךְ הָאָדָם
אֵת אֱלִילֵי כַסְפּוֹ וְאֵת אֱלִילֵי זְהָבוֹ
אֲשֶׁר עָשׂוּ־לוֹ לְהִשְׁתַּחֲוֹת
לַחְפֹּר פֵּרוֹת וְלָעֲטַלֵּפִים׃

the ships had to make, they were
strongly built and of big capacity, and
thus came to be known as the largest
and strongest vessels of the time. Hence
the description *ships of Tarshish* may
denote all large and strongly built
ships.]

imagery. The noun occurs only here and
is possibly derived from the root *sakah*
('to see'), because images are attractive
to the eye (Kimchi, Shorashim). The
Jewish commentators understood it as
mosaic work on ornamented pave-
ments. Rashi relates it to *sakak* ('to
cover'), since it covers the ground under
the floor.

18. *pass away*. The Hebrew is singular;
each one of the idols will vanish (Targum, Rashi). Others render 'He will cut
off' (Kimchi, Ibn Ezra).

19. *and men shall go*. lit. 'and they shall
come.'

to shake mightily. Better, 'to break.' I.e. to

break the wicked of the earth (Targum,
Rashi, Kimchi). Kimchi remarks that the
pagans, unaware of God's omnipresence, will expect to find shelter in the
caves when He executes judgment upon
the wicked of the earth. Others render,
'to terrify' (Ibn Ezra).

20. *a man*. lit. 'a man.'

his idols . . . gold. lit. 'the idols of his
silver and the idols of his gold,' or 'his
silver idols and his gold idols.' Kimchi
relates that to this day, in the Far East,
there are people who worship idols of
silver and gold.

they made for themselves. lit. 'for him.' I.e.
which the makers made for him. It is
the indefinite subject (Ibn Ezra).

moles. The Hebrew *lachpor peroth* should
be understood as one word, *lachphar-
peroth*. Kimchi, however, maintains that
it is two words, since the name is related
to digging and means, 'to diggers of
holes'.

21. To go into the clefts of the rocks,
And into the crevices of the crags,
From before the terror of the
   Lord,
And from the glory of His
   majesty,
When He ariseth to shake
   mightily the earth.

22. Cease ye from man, in whose
   nostrils is a breath;
For how little is he to be accounted!

21 לָבוֹא בְּנִקְרוֹת הַצֻּרִים
וּבִסְעִפֵי הַסְּלָעִים
מִפְּנֵי פַּחַד יְהֹוָה
וּמֵהֲדַר גְּאוֹנ֑וֹ
בְּקוּמוֹ לַעֲרֹץ הָאָרֶץ:
22 חִדְלוּ לָכֶם מִן־הָאָדָם
אֲשֶׁר נְשָׁמָה בְּאַפּוֹ
כִּי בַמֶּה נֶחְשָׁב הוּא:

3   CHAPTER III   ג

1. For, behold, the Lord, the Lord
   of hosts,
Doth take away from Jerusalem
   and from Judah
Stay and staff,
Every stay of bread, and every
   stay of water;

2. The mighty man, and the man
   of war;
The judge, and the prophet,
And the diviner, and the elder;

1 כִּי הִנֵּה הָאָדוֹן יְהֹוָה צְבָאוֹת
מֵסִיר מִירוּשָׁלַ͏ִם וּמִיהוּדָה
מַשְׁעֵן וּמַשְׁעֵנָה
כֹּל מִשְׁעַן־לֶחֶם וְכֹל מִשְׁעַן־מָיִם:
2 גִּבּוֹר וְאִישׁ מִלְחָמָה
שׁוֹפֵט וְנָבִיא
וְקֹסֵם וְזָקֵן:

---

22. *cease ... man.* Who leads you
astray after false gods. The *man* here
recalls *man* in *man shall cast away,* etc.
(verse 20) (Rashi).

breath. Which is unsubstantial and
evanescent (Rashi, Kimchi).

for how little. lit. 'in what,' i.e. in nothing.
There is nothing in man upon which
one can rely or need fear (Kimchi).

CHAPTER III

1-4. Removal of all competent leaders
of society and State, and the assumption
of government by incompetent weaklings.

1. *the* Lord, *the* Lord. Better, 'the

Sovereign (or, the Master, *haAdon*), the
Lord' (see on i. 24).

stay and staff. The Hebrew text has both
the masculine and feminine forms of the
same noun, implying 'all kinds of support.' The change of gender is for poetic
beauty (Kimchi).

2f. The definite article in the English
version should be omitted throughout
in harmony with the Hebrew which is
more forcible. The list of prominent
men includes only tried and recognized
leaders. The reference to *charmer* and
enchanter will be explained further on.

diviner. Or soothsayer. One who foretells the future by means of astrology
(Ibn Ezra).

elder. Councillor (Kimchi).

3. The captain of fifty, and the man of rank,
And the counsellor, and the cunning charmer, and the skilful enchanter.

4. And I will give children to be their princes,
And babes shall rule over them.

5. And the people shall oppress one another,
Every man his fellow, and every man his neighbour;
The child shall behave insolently against the aged,
And the base against the honourable.

6. For a man shall take hold of his brother of the house of his father:
'Thou hast a mantle,
Be thou our ruler,
And let this ruin be under thy hand.'

7. In that day shall he swear, saying-
'I will not be a healer;
For in my house is neither bread nor a mantle;

שַׂר־חֲמִשִּׁים וּנְשׂוּא פָנִים 3
וְיוֹעֵץ וַחֲכַם חֲרָשִׁים וּנְבוֹן לָחַשׁ׃
וְנָתַתִּי נְעָרִים שָׂרֵיהֶם 4
וְתַעֲלוּלִים יִמְשְׁלוּ־בָם׃
וְנִגַּשׂ הָעָם אִישׁ בְּאִישׁ 5
וְאִישׁ בְּרֵעֵהוּ
יִרְהֲבוּ הַנַּעַר בַּזָּקֵן
וְהַנִּקְלֶה בַּנִּכְבָּד׃
כִּי־יִתְפֹּשׂ אִישׁ בְּאָחִיו בֵּית אָבִיו 6
שִׂמְלָה לְכָה
קָצִין תִּהְיֶה־לָּנוּ
וְהַמַּכְשֵׁלָה הַזֹּאת תַּחַת יָדֶךָ׃
יִשָּׂא בַיּוֹם הַהוּא | לֵאמֹר 7
לֹא־אֶהְיֶה חֹבֵשׁ
וּבְבֵיתִי אֵין לֶחֶם וְאֵין שִׂמְלָה

---

3. *man of rank*. lit. 'raised of countenance,' i.e. men commanding respect (Metsudath David).

and the cunning charmer. Jewish commentators reject this interpretation. They prefer 'skilful craftsman' (Ibn Ezra), or 'teacher of the wise' (Kimchi).

skilful enchanter. lit. 'understanding of whispering.' Ibn Ezra explains it as 'a snake charmer.' Others explain it as 'one skilled in speech, able to argue a point, such as a lawyer (Kimchi).

4. *children*. Men young in years and lacking experience or sagacity (Kimchi, Metsudath David).

and babes. [The Hebrew word is an abstract noun, and should rather be translated 'wantonness' or 'capriciousness.']

5. *the child*. Better, 'youth.'

6f. Fruitless efforts in the search for someone to accept the minor office of local justice to maintain some form of peace and order.

6. *for*. Better, 'when.' The entire verse is the protasis to verse 7 which is the apodosis (Rashi, Kimchi).

house of his father. A relative of his father with whom he is intimate (Kimchi).

mantle. Outer appearance of respectability (Kimchi).

ruler. Hebrew *katzin*, like the Arabic *kadi*, means 'decider, a local justice.' Kimchi explains the word in this manner.

this ruin. Or 'this obstacle.' Please instruct us concerning matters upon which we stumble (Rashi, Kimchi).

under thy hand. i.e. under thy control.

7. *swear*. lit. 'he will lift up.' He will raise his voice in an oath (Ibn Kaspi). Most exegetes explain that 'he will take God's name in his mouth' and swear (Rashi, Kimchi).

Ye shall not make me ruler of a people.'

8. For Jerusalem is ruined,
And Judah is fallen;
Because their tongue and their doings are against the LORD,
To provoke the eyes of His glory.

9. The show of their countenance doth witness against them;
And they declare their sin as Sodom, they hide it not.
Woe unto their soul!
For they have wrought evil unto themselves.

10. Say ye of the righteous, that it shall be well with him;
For they shall eat the fruit of their doings.

11. Woe unto the wicked! it shall be ill with him;
For the work of his hands shall be done to him.

12. As for My people, a babe is their master,

לֹא תְשִׂימֵנִי קְצִין עָם׃

8 כִּי כָשְׁלָה יְרוּשָׁלַ͏ִם
וִיהוּדָה נָפָל
כִּי־לְשׁוֹנָם וּמַעַלְלֵיהֶם אֶל־יְהֹוָה
לַמְרוֹת עֵנֵי כְבוֹדוֹ׃

9 הַכָּרַת פְּנֵיהֶם עָנְתָה בָּם
וְחַטָּאתָם כִּסְדֹם הִגִּידוּ לֹא כִחֵדוּ
אוֹי לְנַפְשָׁם
כִּי־גָמְלוּ לָהֶם רָעָה׃

10 אִמְרוּ צַדִּיק כִּי־טוֹב
כִּי־פְרִי מַעַלְלֵיהֶם יֹאכֵלוּ׃

11 אוֹי לְרָשָׁע רָע
כִּי־גְמוּל יָדָיו יֵעָשֶׂה לּוֹ׃

12 עַמִּי נֹגְשָׂיו מְעוֹלֵל

v. 8. חסר י

---

healer. lit. 'binder up, of the wounds of the people (Ibn Ezra).

in my house . . . mantle. The sense is, 'I have my own worries,' being completely destitute (Ibn Ezra).

This prophecy tells of the dire poverty that will exist in the city, that even those who appear well dressed, will, in reality, be impoverished (Abarbanel, Kimchi).

8. The prophet resumes his exhortation, His use of the verbs in the perfect indicates certainty of fulfillment.

is ruined. Better, 'is stumbling staggering.'

tongue . . . doings. In word and deed (Ibn Ezra).

9. *the show of their countenance.* Other renderings are, 'a look at their faces,' 'the expression of their faces,' 'the impudence of their faces.' The literal sense is 'the look, recognition of' (Kimchi).

woe unto their soul . . . themselves. Better, 'woe to themselves for they have done themselves evil.' The evil they planned and executed recoiled on their own heads (see Kara).

10f. Divine reward and punishment.

10. *say ye of . . . him.* The Hebrew exegetes render: 'Say ye to . . .'' (Rashi, Malbim). The Hebrew root *amar* may signify 'saying' or 'praising.' Hence the text may be rendered, 'praise ye the righteous *for it,*' etc., or, freely, 'praise unto the righteous for it . . .' (Kara). This rendering supplies an exact parallel to *woe unto the wicked,* etc. (Verse 11).

11. *work.* lit. 'reward' he will incur the penalty of his evil deeds.

12. *as for My people.* [Better, 'my people,' since the prophet is speaking. He mentions God in third person in verses 13f.] A.J. *My (with capital) interprets as God's people.*

babe . . . master. Better, 'its rulers are

And women rule over them.
O My people, they that lead
thee cause thee to err,
And destroy the way of thy
paths.
13. The LORD standeth up to plead,
And standeth to judge the
peoples.
14. The LORD will enter into judgment
With the elders of His people,
and the princes thereof:
'It is ye that have eaten up the
vineyard;
The spoil of the poor is in your
houses;
15. What mean ye that ye crush My
people,
And grind the face of the poor?'
Saith the Lord, the GOD of hosts.
16. Moreover the LORD said:
Because the daughters of Zion
are haughty,
And walk with stretched-forth
necks
And wanton eyes,

וְנָשִׁים מָשְׁלוּ בוֹ
עַמִּי מְאַשְּׁרֶיךָ מַתְעִים
וְדֶרֶךְ אֹרְחֹתֶיךָ בִּלֵּעוּ:
13 נִצָּב לָרִיב יְהֹוָה
וְעֹמֵד לָדִין עַמִּים:
14 יְהֹוָה בְּמִשְׁפָּט יָבוֹא
עִם־זִקְנֵי עַמּוֹ וְשָׂרָיו
וְאַתֶּם בִּעַרְתֶּם הַכֶּרֶם
גְּזֵלַת הֶעָנִי בְּבָתֵּיכֶם:
15 מַּלָּכֶם תְּדַכְּאוּ עַמִּי
וּפְנֵי עֲנִיִּים תִּטְחָנוּ
נְאֻם־אֲדֹנָי יְהֹוָה צְבָאוֹת:
16 וַיֹּאמֶר יְהֹוָה
יַעַן כִּי גָבְהוּ בְּנוֹת צִיּוֹן
וַתֵּלַכְנָה נְטוּוֹת גָּרוֹן
וּמְשַׂקְּרוֹת עֵינָיִם

v. 15. מה לכם ק׳   v. 16. נטיות ק׳

babes.' Although the noun is actually singular, the implication is that each of its rulers is a babe (Ibn Ezra). Alternatively, 'its rulers are mockers' (Rashi), or 'its rulers are gleaners' (Targum). They rob the people of their property like one who gleans a vineyard.

their master. lit. 'his,' i.e. the people's collectively.

women . . . them. lit. 'him.' The corrupting influence of the women gave rise to the denunciation of verses 16ff. (Rashi).

they that lead . . . err. The so-called leaders are misleaders (Rashi).

paths. Of equity and righteousness (Mestudath David).

13–15. God, in judging the peoples, declares that the social and political leaders are responsible for the oppression and exploitation of the helpless poor. By closing their eyes to the evils which they could have prevented, they become accessories to the act.

13. *peoples.* The plural form applies to the nations generally (Rashi, Kimchi), or, to the tribes of Israel (Rashi).

14. *it is ye.* The leaders, who should have prevented others from trespassing, are charged with having themselves plundered the vineyard (Abarbanel).

15. *what mean ye.* The kere, ma lachem, is written as one word, mallachem, lit. 'what to you' (Rashi, Ibn Ezra, Kimchi).

16. The prophet condemns the ostentation of the fashionable women of Jerusalem. Such pretentious displays were intended to attract the attention of the men and lead them to sin (Rashi). Also, since he reprimanded the men for their haughtiness, he now reprimands the women for that same sin (Kara).

Walking and mincing as they go,
And making a tinkling with their
feet;

17. Therefore the Lord will smite
with a scab
The crown of the head of the
daughters of Zion,
And the Lord will lay bare their
secret parts.

18. In that day the Lord will take
away the bravery of their anklets,
and the fillets, and the crescents;
19. the pendants, and the bracelets,
and the veils; 20. the headtires, and
the armlets, and the sashes, and the
corselets, and the amulets; 21. the
rings, and the nose-jewels; 22. the
aprons, and the mantelets, and the
cloaks, and the girdles; 23. and the
gauze robes, and the fine linen, and
the turbans, and the mantles. 24.
And it shall come to pass, that
Instead of sweet spices there shall
be rottenness;
And instead of a girdle rags;
And instead of curled hair baldness;

הָלוֹךְ וְטָפוֹף תֵּלַכְנָה
וּבְרַגְלֵיהֶם תְּעַכַּסְנָה:

17 וְשִׂפַּח אֲדֹנָי

קָדְקֹד בְּנוֹת צִיּוֹן

וַיהֹוָה פָּתְהֵן יְעָרֶה:

18 בַּיּוֹם הַהוּא יָסִיר אֲדֹנָי אֵת תִּפְאֶרֶת

הָעֲכָסִים וְהַשְּׁבִיסִים וְהַשַּׂהֲרֹנִים:

19 הַנְּטִפוֹת וְהַשֵּׁרוֹת וְהָרְעָלוֹת:

20 הַפְּאֵרִים וְהַצְּעָדוֹת וְהַקִּשֻּׁרִים וּבָתֵּי

21 הַנֶּפֶשׁ וְהַלְּחָשִׁים: הַטַּבָּעוֹת וְנִזְמֵי

22 הָאָף: הַמַּחֲלָצוֹת וְהַמַּעֲטָפוֹת

23 וְהַמִּטְפָּחוֹת וְהָחֲרִיטִים: הַגִּלְיֹנִים

וְהַסְּדִינִים וְהַצְּנִיפוֹת וְהָרְדִידִים:

24 וְהָיָה

תַּחַת בֹּשֶׂם מַק יִהְיֶה

וְתַחַת חֲגוֹרָה נִקְפָּה

וְתַחַת מַעֲשֶׂה מִקְשֶׁה קָרְחָה

16. *with stretched-forth necks.* with their
head in the air. They would stretch forth
their necks to display their finery
(Midrash).

and wanton eyes. Better, 'and ogling with
(their) eyes' (Rashi, Ibn Ezra).

walking and mincing. Since they did not
look at the ground, they were forced to
walk slowly (Talmud).

18-23. It need not be assumed that all
the twenty-one ornaments were worn at
one and the same time. Some of these
adornments are still in use by women in
the East.

18. *the bravery.* Better 'the glory,' or
'the beauty.'

19. *veils.* Hebrew *realoth,* sing. *realah.* A
veil with which they envelop their entire
countenance except the eye, so that a
man will desire to gaze at their cheeks
(Rashi).

20. *corselets.* Another translation is,
'clasps worn over the heart' (Rashi), or,
'jewels hanging over the heart'
(Kimchi).

22. *cloaks.* Or, 'shawls' (Ibn Ezra).

23. *gauze robes.* Others render, 'mir-
rors,' made of polished metal (Rashi,
Kimchi).

24. *a stomacher.* Perhaps this rendering
follows Ibn Ezra, who explains *pethigil*
as 'a fine embroidered garment worn

And instead of a stomacher a
girding of sackcloth;
Branding instead of beauty.

25. Thy men shall fall by the sword,
And thy mighty in the war.

26. And her gates shall lament and
mourn;
And utterly bereft she shall sit
upon the ground.

וְתַחַת פְּתִיגִיל מַחֲגֹרֶת שָׂק
כִּי תַחַת יֹפִי׃
25 מְתַיִךְ בַּחֶרֶב יִפֹּלוּ
וּגְבוּרָתֵךְ בַּמִּלְחָמָה׃
26 וְאָנוּ וְאָבְלוּ פְּתָחֶיהָ
וְנִקָּתָה לָאָרֶץ תֵּשֵׁב׃

4　　　　CHAPTER IV　　　ד

1. And seven women shall take hold
of one man in that day, saying:
'We will eat our own bread, and
wear our own apparel; only let us be
called by thy name; take thou away
our reproach.'

2. In that day shall the growth of
the LORD be beautiful and
glorious,

1 וְהֶחֱזִיקוּ שֶׁבַע נָשִׁים בְּאִישׁ אֶחָד בַּיּוֹם
הַהוּא לֵאמֹר לַחְמֵנוּ נֹאכֵל וְשִׂמְלָתֵנוּ
נִלְבָּשׁ רַק יִקָּרֵא שִׁמְךָ עָלֵינוּ אֱסֹף
חֶרְפָּתֵנוּ׃
2 בַּיּוֹם הַהוּא יִהְיֶה צֶמַח יְהֹוָה
לִצְבִי וּלְכָבוֹד

over the other garments.' It is, however,
unlikely.

branding. Better, 'a burn.' The Hebrew *ki*
is employed for the more regular
kewiyyah (root *kawah*) (Exod. xxi. 25)
(Kimchi).

25. The prophet addresses Jerusalem.

thy men. The warriors (Rashi).

thy mighty. lit. 'thy might' (Ibn Ezra,
Kimchi).

26. *gates.* Of the towns and the houses
(Rashi).

bereft. Of inhabitants (Kimchi).

sit . . . ground. The outward expression
of mourning (Kimchi).

CHAPTER IV

1. This verse is parallel with iii. 6
where, in the disturbed and anarchic
state of the land, the men are content
with the appointment of any sort of
leader. Here too the women, in batches,

are equally content with one husband
for all of them.

seven women. The number *seven* is not to
be taken literally in the context. Its sig-
nification here is 'many, a batch.' There
was a scarcity of men through heavy
casualties in war (Kimchi).

that day. The day of the great judgment
(Kimchi).

let us . . . name. lit. "let thy name be
named (called) over us.' A woman on
marriage assumes her husband's name
(Metsudath David).

our reproach. Of being unmarried. It was
a disgrace in the East for a woman to
remain a spinster (Kimchi).

2-6. A further description of the
Messianic age (cf. 11. 2-4) and the happy
state of the survivors of the storm in
which all the wicked have been swept
away. The land will be purified and the
glory of the Lord manifest, while His
Divine protection will ensure safety and

And the fruit of the land excellent and comely
For them that are escaped of Israel.

3. And it shall come to pass, that he that is left in Zion, and he that remaineth in Jerusalem, shall be called holy, even every one that is written unto life in Jerusalem;
4. when the Lord shall have washed away the filth of the daughters of Zion, and shall have purged the blood of Jerusalem from the midst thereof, by the spirit of judgment, and by the spirit of destruction.
5. And the LORD will create over the whole habitation of mount Zion, and over her assemblies, a cloud and smoke by day, and the shining of a flaming fire by night; for over all the glory shall be a canopy.
6. And there shall be a pavilion for a shadow in the day-time from the heat, and for a refuge and for a covert from storm and from rain.

וּפְרִי הָאָרֶץ לְגָאוֹן וּלְתִפְאֶרֶת
לִפְלֵיטַת יִשְׂרָאֵל:

3 וְהָיָה | הַנִּשְׁאָר בְּצִיּוֹן וְהַנּוֹתָר
בִּירוּשָׁלַם קָדוֹשׁ יֵאָמֶר לוֹ כָּל־
4 הַכָּתוּב לַחַיִּים בִּירוּשָׁלָם: אִם |
רָחַץ אֲדֹנָי אֵת צֹאַת בְּנוֹת־צִיּוֹן
וְאֶת־דְּמֵי יְרוּשָׁלַם יָדִיחַ מִקִּרְבָּהּ
5 בְּרוּחַ מִשְׁפָּט וּבְרוּחַ בָּעֵר: וּבָרָא
יְהֹוָה עַל כָּל־מְכוֹן הַר־צִיּוֹן וְעַל־
מִקְרָאֶהָ עָנָן | יוֹמָם וְעָשָׁן וְנֹגַהּ אֵשׁ
לֶהָבָה לָיְלָה כִּי עַל־כָּל־כָּבוֹד
6 חֻפָּה: וְסֻכָּה תִּהְיֶה לְצֵל־יוֹמָם
מֵחֹרֶב וּלְמַחְסֶה וּלְמִסְתּוֹר מִזֶּרֶם
וּמִמָּטָר:

eternal peace. The argument for the assignment of this passage to a later writer on the grounds of style and its pronounced apocalyptic character has no basis. Isaiah's prophecies provide many parallels with the idea here expressed.

2. *that day.* When justice has been meted out (Metsudath David).

growth of the LORD. Some take this literally: the land will yield rich produce (Ibn Ezra). Others regard it as symbolic of the Messiah (Targum, Kimchi) or the righteous who survived the day of wrath (Kara).

fruit of the land. This too may be taken literally or regarded as symbolizing the children of the righteous who will be the glory of the escaped remnant of Israel.

3. *written unto life.* Specifically approved by Providence. There will be no casual survivors (Kimchi).

4. This is the protasis to verse 3 which is the apodosis (Ibn Ezra, Kimchi).

when. Hebrew *im* (lit. 'if') referring to time (Ibn Ezra, Kimchi, Rashi).

filth ... blood. Metaphorical of moral degradation and the shedding of innocent blood (Metsudath David).

5. *and the* LORD. As a consequence of the process of purification, the LORD will create, etc. (Metsudath David).

cloud ... flaming fire. Symbols of Divine protection (Rashi).

6. *pavilion.* Hebrew *sukkah,* a noun applied to the festive booth in which Israelites were commanded to dwell during the feast of Tabernacles.

heat. An allusion to the great day which *burneth as a furnace, and all the proud, and all that work wickedness, shall be stubble; and the day that cometh shall set them ablaze* (Mal. iii. 19) (Rashi).

5   CHAPTER V   ה

1. Let me sing of my well-beloved,
   A song of my beloved touching
   his vineyard.
   My well-beloved had a vineyard
   In a very fruitful hill;

2. And he digged it, and cleared it
   of stones,
   And planted it with the choicest
   vine,
   And built a tower in the midst of
   it,
   And also hewed out a vat therein;
   And he looked that it should
   bring forth grapes,
   And it brought forth wild grapes.

3. And now, O inhabitants of
   Jerusalem and men of Judah,
   Judge, I pray you, betwixt me
   and my vineyard.

4. What could have been done
   more to my vineyard,
   That I have not done in it?
   Wherefore, when I looked that it
   should bring forth grapes,
   Brought it forth wild grapes?

5. And now come, I will tell you

אָשִׁירָה נָּא לִידִידִי 1
שִׁרַת דּוֹדִי לְכַרְמוֹ
כֶּרֶם הָיָה לִידִידִי
בְּקֶרֶן בֶּן־שָׁמֶן:
וַיְעַזְּקֵהוּ וַיְסַקְּלֵהוּ 2
וַיִּטָּעֵהוּ שֹׂרֵק
וַיִּבֶן מִגְדָּל בְּתוֹכוֹ
וְגַם־יֶקֶב חָצֵב בּוֹ
וַיְקַו לַעֲשׂוֹת עֲנָבִים
וַיַּעַשׂ בְּאֻשִׁים:
וְעַתָּה יוֹשֵׁב יְרוּשָׁלַם וְאִישׁ יְהוּדָה 3
שִׁפְטוּ־נָא בֵּינִי וּבֵין כַּרְמִי:
מַה־לַּעֲשׂוֹת עוֹד לְכַרְמִי 4
וְלֹא עָשִׂיתִי בּוֹ
מַדּוּעַ קִוֵּיתִי לַעֲשׂוֹת עֲנָבִים
וַיַּעַשׂ בְּאֻשִׁים:
וְעַתָּה אוֹדִיעָה־נָּא אֶתְכֶם 5

CHAPTER V

1–6. The parable of the vineyard. By means of its imagery the prophet subtly and effectively brings home to the people God's mercy and kindness towards them, which they repaid by ingratitude and disobedience. Dire retribution is threatened.

1. well-beloved. i.e. God (Kimchi).

vineyard. i.e. Israel (cf. verse 7).

a very fruitful hill. lit. 'a horn the son of fatness,' an allusion to the fertility of the Land of Israel (Kimchi).

2. and he looked. lit. 'and he hoped,'

expected, as the effect of his diligent care and labor (Metsudath David).

3. inhabitants . . . men. The Hebrew uses the singular in both cases to denote the people collectively. Some explain that the prophet was addressing each individual (Ibn Ezra).

5f. The disappointing results cannot be ignored by the owner of the vineyard and He will abandon it to ruin.

5. and now . . . do. Or, 'and now, let me tell you, pray, what I am about to do.' [The use of the Hebrew present implies irrevocable decision and prompt action.]

What I will do to my vineyard:
I will take away the hedge thereof,
And it shall be eaten up;
I will break down the fence
thereof,
And it shall be trodden down;
6. And I will lay it waste:
It shall not be pruned nor hoed,
But there shall come up briers
and thorns;
I will also command the clouds
That they rain no rain upon it.
7. For the vineyard of the Lord of
hosts is the house of Israel,
And the men of Judah the plant
of His delight;
And He looked for justice, but
behold violence;
For righteousness, but behold a
cry.
8. Woe unto them that join house
to house,
That lay field to field,

אֵת אֲשֶׁר־אֲנִי עֹשֶׂה לְכַרְמִי
הָסֵר מְשׂוּכָּתוֹ
וְהָיָה לְבָעֵר
פָּרֹץ גְּדֵרוֹ
וְהָיָה לְמִרְמָס׃
6 וַאֲשִׁיתֵהוּ בָתָה
לֹא יִזָּמֵר וְלֹא יֵעָדֵר
וְעָלָה שָׁמִיר וָשָׁיִת
וְעַל הֶעָבִים אֲצַוֶּה
מֵהַמְטִיר עָלָיו מָטָר׃
7 כִּי כֶרֶם יְהֹוָה צְבָאוֹת בֵּית יִשְׂרָאֵל
וְאִישׁ יְהוּדָה נְטַע שַׁעֲשׁוּעָיו
וַיְקַו לְמִשְׁפָּט וְהִנֵּה מִשְׂפָּח
לִצְדָקָה וְהִנֵּה צְעָקָה׃
8 הוֹי מַגִּיעֵי בַיִת בְּבַיִת

הכ' בדגש v. 5.

I will take away . . . I will break down. The
verbs *haser . . . parots* are absolute infinitives (lit. 'to take away . . . to break
down') (Rashi); they might be rendered
'take away (or, remove) . . . break down'
as imperatives, or we can understand a
preliminary phrase like 'My intention
is.'

hedge. Of thorns (Rashi, Kimchi).

fence. Of stones. A valued vineyard is
protected against trespass by both a
thorn-hedge and a more substantially
constructed fence. The prophet hints at
a pending invasion of the country
(Kimchi).

6. *and I will lay it waste.* lit. 'and I will
put it a destruction.'

but there shall . . . thorns. Better, in harmony with the Hebrew, 'but it shall go
up (in) briers and thorns.'

7. Application of the parable in verses
1–6.

men. Hebrew *ish,* used as a collective
noun.

justice . . . cry. The assonance of the
Hebrew strikingly emphasizes the contrasts: instead of *mishpat* (justice) there is
mispach (violence), instead of *tsedakah*
(righteousness) there is *tse'akah* (a cry)
(Kimchi).

8-25. An indictment under six counts
each beginning with the exclamation
woe. Each of the first two is followed by
a description of the inevitable punishment, while the last four are grouped
together, the threatened retribution
following the last count.

8-10. First count. Absorption of the
small holdings of the poorer peasants
by their wealthy neighbors (verse 8) and
the Divine punishment (verses 9f.).

8. *lay.* lit. 'bring near,' by dispossess-
ing neighbours of their land (Rashi,
Kimchi).

Till there be no room, and ye be
made to dwell
Alone in the midst of the land!
9. In mine ears said the LORD of
hosts:
Of a truth many houses shall be
desolate,
Even great and fair, without inhabitant.
10. For ten acres of vineyard shall
yield one bath,
And the seed of a homer shall
yield an ephah.
11. Woe unto them that rise up early
in the morning,
That they may follow strong
drink;
That tarry late into the night,
Till wine inflame them!
12. And the harp and the psaltery,
the tabret and the pipe,
And wine, are in their feasts;

שָׂדֶה בְשָׂדֶה יַקְרִיבוּ
עַד אֶפֶס מָקוֹם וְהוּשַׁבְתֶּם
לְבַדְּכֶם בְּקֶרֶב הָאָרֶץ:
9 בְּאָזְנָי יְהֹוָה צְבָאוֹת
אִם־לֹא בָּתִּים רַבִּים לְשַׁמָּה יִהְיוּ
גְּדֹלִים וְטוֹבִים מֵאֵין יוֹשֵׁב:
10 כִּי עֲשֶׂרֶת צִמְדֵּי־כֶרֶם
יַעֲשׂוּ בַּת אֶחָת
וְזֶרַע חֹמֶר יַעֲשֶׂה אֵיפָה:
11 הוֹי מַשְׁכִּימֵי בַבֹּקֶר
שֵׁכָר יִרְדֹּפוּ
מְאַחֲרֵי בַנֶּשֶׁף
יַיִן יַדְלִיקֵם:
12 וְהָיָה כִנּוֹר וָנֶבֶל תֹּף וְחָלִיל
וָיַיִן מִשְׁתֵּיהֶם

v. 9. קמץ בטרחא

---

there be no room. For the poor peasant
between two wealthy landowners (Rashi).

and ye. The rich landlords (Kimchi).

9f. The punishment

8. *in mine ears said.* The last word *said*
or some similar expression (e.g.
'revealed'), absent from the Hebrew, is
implied (Metsudath David).

of a truth. lit. 'if not,' a form of emphatic
affirmation, usually an oath (Kimchi).

houses. The residences of the trespassers
who will not be allowed to enjoy their
ill-gotten gains (Kimchi).

be desolate. lit. 'for a desolation.'

10. *acres of.* lit. 'yokes of.' A 'yoke of
land' is a plot that can be ploughed in a
day by a pair of oxen (Rashi, Kimchi).

one bath. Of wine; about fourteen gallons, or, according to some, close to
nine gallons, which is a very poor yield

for the amount of labour and the extent
of the field (Kimchi).

homer . . . ephah. The *ephah* is a tenth part
of the *homer,* a dry of the same capacity as
the *bath* which is a liquid measure. The
land will produce only a small fraction in
bulk of what had actually been sown
(Kimchi).

11–17. Second count against drunkenness and self-indulgence. The tragic
consequences that will follow.

11. *strong drink.* The Hebrew denotes
an alcoholic beverage made of raisins,
dates, honey or barley and the like
(Kimchi, Shorashim).

tarry late into the night. Drinking wine
(Rashi).

till . . . them. This follows Metsudath
David. Rashi renders, 'wine inflaming
them.'

harp . . . pipe. Others render, 'guitar and
harp, tambourine and flute' (see Rashi).

But they regard not the work of the LORD,
Neither have they considered the operation of His hands.

13. Therefore My people are gone into captivity,
For want of knowledge;
And their honourable men are famished,
And their multitude are parched with thirst.

14. Therefore the nether-world hath enlarged her desire,
And opened her mouth without measure;
And down goeth their glory, and their tumult, and their uproar,
And he that rejoiceth among them.

15. And man is bowed down,
And man is humbled,
And the eyes of the lofty are humbled;

16. But the LORD of hosts is exalted through justice,
And God the Holy One is sanctified through righteousness.

וְאֵת פֹּעַל יְהוָֹה לֹא יַבִּיטוּ
וּמַעֲשֵׂה יָדָיו לֹא רָאוּ׃
13 לָכֵן גָּלָה עַמִּי
מִבְּלִי־דָעַת
וּכְבוֹדוֹ מְתֵי רָעָב
וַהֲמוֹנוֹ צִחֵה צָמָא׃
14 לָכֵן הִרְחִיבָה שְּׁאוֹל נַפְשָׁהּ
וּפָעֲרָה פִיהָ לִבְלִי־חֹק
וְיָרַד הֲדָרָהּ וַהֲמוֹנָהּ
וּשְׁאוֹנָהּ וְעָלֵז בָּהּ׃
15 וַיִּשַּׁח אָדָם
וַיִּשְׁפַּל־אִישׁ
וְעֵינֵי גְבֹהִים תִּשְׁפַּלְנָה׃
16 וַיִּגְבַּה יְהוָֹה צְבָאוֹת בַּמִּשְׁפָּט
וְהָאֵל הַקָּדוֹשׁ נִקְדָּשׁ בִּצְדָקָה׃

regard not . . . hands. Owing to their absorption in sensual pleasures (Kimchi).

13. *are gone.* The Hebrew has the prophetic perfect, i.e. the event though in the future is depicted as having happened (Kimchi).

captivity. [This is the only specific mention of the exile in Isaiah.] *North?*

knowledge. Of God's ways and deeds, referred to in the previous verse (Metsudath David).

their honourable men. lit. 'his (the people's glory' (Rashi).

famished. lit. 'men of hunger' (Kimchi).

14–17. For the sins of the people the capital will be destroyed.

14. *nether-world.* Hebrew *sheol,* the

abode of the dead (see Rashi, Gen. xxxvii. 35).

desire. Or, 'appetite,' to swallow those killed by the invader (Ibn Ezra as quoted by Kimchi, Shorashim).

without measure. Better, 'without limit.'

down goeth their . . . them. Better, 'down goeth her (Jerusalem's) glory and her tumult and her uproar and (any one that is) jubilant in her' (Ibn Ezra).

15. *man . . . man.* The Hebrew uses different words, *adam* and *ish*; see on ii. 9. This refers to the survivors, who will repent and humble themselves before the Creator (Kara).

16. *through justice.* Which He will execute among His people (Rashi).

righteousness. His righteous judgments (Kimchi).

17. Then shall the lambs feed as in
their pasture,
And the waste places of the fat
ones shall wanderers eat.

18. Woe unto them that draw
iniquity with cords of vanity,
And sin as it were with a cart
rope,

19. That say: 'Let Him make speed,
let Him hasten His work,
That we may see it;
And let the counsel of the Holy
One of Israel draw nigh and
come,
That we may know it!'

20. Woe unto them that call evil
good,
And good evil;
That change darkness into light,
And light into darkness;
That change bitter into sweet,
And sweet into bitter!

21. Woe unto them that are wise in
their own eyes,
And prudent in their own sight!

22. Woe unto them that are mighty
to drink wine,
And men of strength to mingle
strong drink;

וְרָעוּ כְבָשִׂים כְּדָבְרָם 17
וְחָרְבוֹת מֵחִים גָּרִים יֹאכֵלוּ:

הוֹי מֹשְׁכֵי הֶעָוֹן בְּחַבְלֵי הַשָּׁוְא 18
וְכַעֲבוֹת הָעֲגָלָה חַטָּאָה:

הָאֹמְרִים יְמַהֵר ׀ יָחִישָׁה מַעֲשֵׂהוּ 19
לְמַעַן נִרְאֶה
וְתִקְרַב וְתָבוֹאָה עֲצַת
קְדוֹשׁ יִשְׂרָאֵל וְנֵדָעָה:

הוֹי הָאֹמְרִים לָרַע טוֹב וְלַטּוֹב רָע 20
שָׂמִים חֹשֶׁךְ לְאוֹר
וְאוֹר לְחֹשֶׁךְ
שָׂמִים מַר לְמָתוֹק
וּמָתוֹק לְמָר:

הוֹי חֲכָמִים בְּעֵינֵיהֶם 21
וְנֶגֶד פְּנֵיהֶם נְבֹנִים:

הוֹי גִּבּוֹרִים לִשְׁתּוֹת יָיִן 22
וְאַנְשֵׁי־חַיִל לִמְסֹךְ שֵׁכָר:

---

17. *then shall . . . feed.* Better, 'and
lambs shall graze.'

wanderers. Or, 'nomadic shepherds.'
Better, 'sojourners' (Ibn Ezra).

18f. Third count against addiction to
sin, scepticism and the mocking of the
prophet's warnings.

18. The underlying idea is that the
commission of minor offences (*draw
iniquity with cords of vanity* or 'slender
cords') gradually leads to graver crime
(*sin as . . . cart rope*) (Rashi, Kimchi).

19. *that say.* In derision or defiance
(Metsudath David).

let . . . speed. To carry out His threats
(Rashi, Kimchi).

20. Fourth count against wilful confusion of the standards of right and
wrong.

change darkness . . . bitter. The phrases are
metaphorical (Kimchi).

21. Fifth count against arrogance and
conceit.

22f. Sixth count against indulgence
and bribery which lead to corruption
and injustice.

23. That justify the wicked for a reward,
    And take away the righteousness of the righteous from him!
24. Therefore as the tongue of fire devoureth the stubble,
    And as the chaff is consumed in the flame,
    So their root shall be as rottenness,
    And their blossom shall go up as dust;
    Because they have rejected the law of the LORD of hosts,
    And contemned the word of the Holy One of Israel.
25. Therefore is the anger of the LORD kindled against His people,
    And He hath stretched forth His hand against them, and hath smitten them,
    And the hills did tremble,
    And their carcasses were as refuse in the midst of the streets.
    For all this His anger is not turned away,
    But His hand is stretched out still.
26. And He will lift up an ensign to the nations from far,
    And will hiss unto them from the end of the earth;
    And, behold, they shall come with speed swiftly;

23 מַצְדִּיקֵי רָשָׁע עֵקֶב שֹׁחַד
וְצִדְקַת צַדִּיקִים יָסִירוּ מִמֶּנּוּ׃
24 לָכֵן כֶּאֱכֹל קַשׁ לְשׁוֹן אֵשׁ
וַחֲשַׁשׁ לֶהָבָה יִרְפֶּה
שָׁרְשָׁם כַּמָּק יִהְיֶה
וּפִרְחָם כָּאָבָק יַעֲלֶה
כִּי מָאֲסוּ אֵת תּוֹרַת יְהוָה צְבָאוֹת
וְאֵת אִמְרַת קְדוֹשׁ־יִשְׂרָאֵל נִאֵצוּ׃
25 עַל־כֵּן חָרָה אַף־יְהוָה בְּעַמּוֹ
וַיֵּט יָדוֹ עָלָיו וַיַּכֵּהוּ
וַיִּרְגְּזוּ הֶהָרִים
וַתְּהִי נִבְלָתָם כַּסּוּחָה בְּקֶרֶב חֻצוֹת
בְּכָל־זֹאת לֹא־שָׁב אַפּוֹ
וְעוֹד יָדוֹ נְטוּיָה׃
26 וְנָשָׂא־נֵס לַגּוֹיִם מֵרָחוֹק
וְשָׁרַק לוֹ מִקְצֵה הָאָרֶץ
וְהִנֵּה מְהֵרָה קַל יָבוֹא׃

23. *justify ... reward.* Having received a bribe, the venal judges pronounce a verdict in favour of the guilty party (Metsudath David).

from him. The righteous or innocent contestant (Ibn Ezra, Kimchi).

24. In vivid language the fearful penalty is described.

chaff is consumed. The Hebrew verb signifies 'weakening' (Kimchi).

25. The use of the perfect and consecutive imperfect tenses may be regarded as prophetic perfects (see on verse 13).

the hills did tremble. To be understood metaphorically (Kimchi). Metsudath David takes it as a prophecy concerning the kings of Judah and their princes,

whereas Abarbanel takes it as the account of the downfall of the kings of Israel.

refuse. Or 'spittle' (Rashi).

26-30. A martial nation (probably the Assyrians), equipped, disciplined, powerful and swift is called *from the end of the earth* to complete the punishment of Israel for the sins enumerated in the six counts above (Kimchi).

26. *lift up an ensign.* A signal for assembly and attack (Rashi).

hiss unto them. Better, in agreement with the Hebrew sing., 'unto him,' i.e. the one nation selected from the assembled nations (Laniado).

they shall. Better, 'he,' the selected nation; similarly every *they* and *their* to

27. None shall be weary nor stumble
    among them;
    None shall slumber nor sleep;
    Neither shall the girdle of their
      loins be loosed,
    Nor the latchet of their shoes be
      broken;

28. Whose arrows are sharp,
    And all their bows bent;
    Their horses' hoofs shall be
      counted like flint,
    And their wheels like a whirl-
      wind;

29. Their roaring shall be like a lion,
    They shall roar like young lions,
      yea, they shall roar,
    And lay hold of the prey, and
      carry it away safe,
    And there shall be none to
      deliver.

30. And they shall roar against them
    in that day
    Like the roaring of the sea;
    And if one look unto the land,
    Behold darkness and distress,
    And the light is darkened in the
      skies thereof.

27 אֵין־עָיֵף וְאֵין־כּוֹשֵׁל בּוֹ
לֹא יָנוּם וְלֹא יִישָׁן
וְלֹא נִפְתַּח אֵזוֹר חֲלָצָיו
וְלֹא נִתַּק שְׂרוֹךְ נְעָלָיו:

28 אֲשֶׁר חִצָּיו שְׁנוּנִים
וְכָל־קַשְּׁתֹתָיו דְּרֻכוֹת
פַּרְסוֹת סוּסָיו כַּצַּר נֶחְשָׁבוּ
וְגַלְגִּלָּיו כַּסּוּפָה:

29 שְׁאָגָה לוֹ כַּלָּבִיא
וְשָׁאַג כַּכְּפִירִים וְיִנְהֹם
וְיֹאחֵז טֶרֶף וְיַפְלִיט
וְאֵין מַצִּיל:

30 וְיִנְהֹם עָלָיו בַּיּוֹם הַהוּא
כְּנַהֲמַת־יָם
וְנִבַּט לָאָרֶץ
וְהִנֵּה־חֹשֶׁךְ
צַר וָאוֹר חָשַׁךְ בַּעֲרִיפֶיהָ:

---

6   **CHAPTER VI**   ו

1. In the year that king Uzziah died

1 בִּשְׁנַת־מוֹת הַמֶּלֶךְ עֻזִּיָּהוּ וָאֶרְאֶה

v. 28. כצ״ל   v. 28. קמץ בז״ק   v. 29. ישאג ק׳   v. 1. הפטרת וישמע יתרו

---

the end of verse 30 should be read as
'he' and 'his' respectively.

28. *bows bent.* Ready for action
(Kimchi).

30. *and they . . . them.* Better, 'and he
shall growl over him, 'the invader over
Israel (Rashi).

unto the land. Better, 'earth' in contrast
to *skies* in the following clause.

CHAPTER VI

ISAIAH'S INITIATION
AND FIRST COMMISSION

1–4. A vision of the splendor, awe and
majestic holiness that surround the
throne of the Lord of Hosts. The scene
is the Temple.

1. *in the year . . . Uzziah died.* Uzziah
reigned from 790 to 739 B.C.E. The

I saw the Lord sitting upon a throne high and lifted up, and His train filled the temple. 2. Above Him stood the seraphim; each one had six wings: with twain he covered his face, and with twain he covered his feet, and with twain he did fly.

3. And one called unto another, and said:

Holy, holy, holy, is the LORD of hosts;

The whole earth is full of His glory.

4. And the posts of the door were moved at the voice of them that called, and the house was filled with

אֶת־אֲדֹנָי יֹשֵׁב עַל־כִּסֵּא רָם וְנִשָּׂא
וְשׁוּלָיו מְלֵאִים אֶת־הַהֵיכָל: שְׂרָפִים 2
עֹמְדִים ׀ מִמַּעַל לוֹ שֵׁשׁ כְּנָפַיִם שֵׁשׁ
כְּנָפַיִם לְאֶחָד בִּשְׁתַּיִם ׀ יְכַסֶּה פָנָיו
וּבִשְׁתַּיִם יְכַסֶּה רַגְלָיו וּבִשְׁתַּיִם
יְעוֹפֵף:
וְקָרָא זֶה אֶל־זֶה וְאָמַר 3
קָדוֹשׁ ׀ קָדוֹשׁ קָדוֹשׁ יְהֹוָה צְבָאוֹת
מְלֹא כָל־הָאָרֶץ כְּבוֹדוֹ:
וַיָּנֻעוּ אַמּוֹת הַסִּפִּים מִקּוֹל הַקּוֹרֵא 4

---

vision must accordingly have taken place about 739, either before or after the king's death. Since Isaiah prophesied during the reign of Uzziah, as in i. 1, it must have taken place before his death. According to tradition, this verse is to be explained, 'in the year during which King Uzziah was smitten with leprosy,' based on the maxim that a leper is regarded as a dead person. In that case, the vision took place twenty-seven years before Uzziah's death. See 2 Chron. xvi. 21, 2 Kings xv. 5 (Rashi after Targum and various midrashim).

I saw. In a vision. The prophets, under the influence of Divine inspiration, behold mysterious and spiritual scenes which are invisible to ordinary men.

the Lord. The Hebrew means 'the Sovereign,' 'the Master.'

high and lifted up. This phrase qualifies *the throne*, not *the Lord* (Ibn Ezra).

2. *above Him stood the seraphim*. Better, 'seraphim were standing over Him,' i.e. in attendance upon Him (Rashi).

covered his face. As a mark of reverence. Even the ministering angels do not ven-

ture to gaze upon the Divine Presence (Rashi).

covered his feet. In his modesty he does not expose all his body (Rashi). A Midrashic interpretation refers to Ezek. i. 17, *and the sole of their feet was like the sole of a calf's foot*: a calf recalls the sin of the golden calf, and the seraphim cover their feet so as not to recall that sin before God (Rashi from Tanchuma).

3. *holy*. The threefold repetition indicates the superlative degree of holiness. 'Holy in the highest heaven, holy upon the earth, holy for ever and ever' (Targum Jonathan). 'The Holy One, blessed be He' is the usual designation of God in Rabbinic literature.

the whole . . . glory. Better, 'that which fills the whole earth is His glory.'

4. *posts . . . moved*. Better, 'shook.' An allusion to the earthquake mentioned in Zech. xiv. 5 (Rashi).

them . . . called. The Hebrew uses the singular in a collective sense (Ibn Ezra).

was filled. Rather, 'began to fill with' (Ibn Ezra).

smoke. 5. Then said I:

Woe is me! for I am undone;

Because I am a man of unclean
lips,

And I dwell in the midst of a
people of unclean lips;

For mine eyes have seen the
King,

The LORD of hosts.

6. Then flew unto me one of the
seraphim, with a glowing stone in
his hand, which he had taken with
the tongs from off the altar; 7. and
he touched my mouth with it, and
said:

Lo, this hath touched thy lips;

And thine iniquity is taken away,

And thy sin expiated.

8. And I heard the voice of the
Lord, saying:

Whom shall I send,

And who will go for us?

Then I said: 'Here am I; send me.'

וְהַבַּיִת יִמָּלֵא עָשָׁן׃

5 וָאֹמַר

אוֹי־לִי כִי־נִדְמֵיתִי

כִּי אִישׁ טְמֵא־שְׂפָתַיִם אָנֹכִי

וּבְתוֹךְ עַם־טְמֵא שְׂפָתַיִם אָנֹכִי יֹשֵׁב

כִּי אֶת־הַמֶּלֶךְ

יְהוָה צְבָאוֹת רָאוּ עֵינָי׃

6 וַיָּעָף אֵלַי אֶחָד מִן־הַשְּׂרָפִים וּבְיָדוֹ

רִצְפָּה בְּמֶלְקַחַיִם לָקַח מֵעַל

הַמִּזְבֵּחַ׃

7 וַיַּגַּע עַל־פִּי וַיֹּאמֶר

הִנֵּה נָגַע זֶה עַל־שְׂפָתֶיךָ

וְסָר עֲוֹנֶךָ

וְחַטָּאתְךָ תְּכֻפָּר׃

8 וָאֶשְׁמַע אֶת־קוֹל אֲדֹנָי אֹמֵר

אֶת־מִי אֶשְׁלַח

וּמִי יֵלֶךְ־לָנוּ

וָאֹמַר הִנְנִי שְׁלָחֵנִי׃

smoke. A similar manifestation of God
was also accompanied by smoke (cf.
Exod. xx. 18).

5. undone. Isaiah feels that his own
spiritual shortcomings, as well as those
of the people among whom he dwells,
create an insurmountable barrier
between him and the Divine call
(Kimchi).

for mine eyes. A second reason why he is
undone (cf. Exod. xxxiii. 20, for man shall
not see Me and live) (see Kimchi).

6. from . . . altar. The fire on the altar

was heavenly and holy, and as such
burned away, so to speak, the impurities
of sin (Ibn Ezra).

7. and he . . . it. lit. 'and he caused to
touch upon my mouth.'

8. for us. The plural includes the
angelic host (Ibn Ezra, Kimchi).

here am I; send me. [Note his ready and
spontaneous acceptance of the Divine
mission even before its nature was
revealed to him.] This verse denotes the
beginning of Isaiah's mission as a
prophet (Ibn Ezra).

9. And He said: 'Go, and tell this people:

> Hear ye indeed, but understand not;
>
> And see ye indeed, but perceive not.

10. Make the heart of this people fat,
> And make their ears heavy,
> And shut their eyes;
> Lest they, seeing with their eyes,
> And hearing with their ears,
> And understanding with their heart,
> Return, and be healed.'

11. Then said I: 'Lord, how long?' And He answered:

> 'Until cities be waste without inhabitant,
> And houses without man,
> And the land become utterly waste,

12. And the LORD have removed men far away,
> And the forsaken places be many in the midst of the land.

9 וַיֹּאמֶר לֵךְ וְאָמַרְתָּ לָעָם הַזֶּה
שִׁמְעוּ שָׁמוֹעַ וְאַל־תָּבִינוּ
וּרְאוּ רָאוֹ וְאַל־תֵּדָעוּ:

10 הַשְׁמֵן לֵב־הָעָם הַזֶּה
וְאָזְנָיו הַכְבֵּד
וְעֵינָיו הָשַׁע
פֶּן־יִרְאֶה בְעֵינָיו
וּבְאָזְנָיו יִשְׁמָע
וּלְבָבוֹ יָבִין
וָשָׁב וְרָפָא לוֹ:

11 וָאֹמַר עַד־מָתַי אֲדֹנָי
וַיֹּאמֶר
עַד אֲשֶׁר אִם־שָׁאוּ עָרִים מֵאֵין יוֹשֵׁב
וּבָתִּים מֵאֵין אָדָם
וְהָאֲדָמָה תִּשָּׁאֶה שְׁמָמָה:

12 וְרִחַק יְהוָה אֶת־הָאָדָם
וְרַבָּה הָעֲזוּבָה בְּקֶרֶב הָאָרֶץ:

v. 10. קמץ ברביע

9f. The message.

9. *hear ... perceive not.* The people's insensibility to all that is Divine and indifferent to the prophet's exhortation result in lack of understanding and absence of perception. This inevitable result is viewed by the prophet, perhaps ironically, as if that had been its purpose (Metsudath David).

10. *heart.* Synonymous with mind, understanding.

fat. Dull, insensitive (Metsudath David).

shut their eyes. lit. 'smear their eyes' (Rashi, Ibn Ezra, Kimchi).

11-13 Only desolation, destruction and exile of the sinful majority will bring to an end the deplorable conditions.

11. *Lord, how long?* A heartrending cry of the prophet. How long, he asks, will this insensibility and blind obduracy persist?

become utterly waste. lit. 'be ruined (into) a desolation.'

12. *and the forsaken places be many.* lit. 'and great be the forsakenness' (Targum).

31

13. And if there be yet a tenth in it, it shall again be eaten up; as a terebinth, and as an oak, whose stock remaineth, when they cast their leaves, so the holy seed shall be the stock thereof.'

וְעוֹד בָּהּ עֲשִׂרִיָּה וְשָׁבָה וְהָיְתָה 13

לְבָעֵר כָּאֵלָה וְכָאַלּוֹן אֲשֶׁר בְּשַׁלֶּכֶת

מַצֶּבֶת בָּם זֶרַע קֹדֶשׁ מַצַּבְתָּהּ׃

7   CHAPTER VII   ז

1. And it came to pass in the days of Ahaz the son of Jotham, the son of Uzziah, king of Judah, that Rezin the king of Aram, and Pekah the son of Remaliah, king of Israel, went up to Jerusalem to war against it; but could not prevail against it. 2. And it was told the house of David, saying: 'Aram is confederate

וַיְהִי בִּימֵי אָחָז בֶּן־יוֹתָם בֶּן־עֻזִּיָּהוּ 1

מֶלֶךְ יְהוּדָה עָלָה רְצִין מֶלֶךְ־אֲרָם

וּפֶקַח בֶּן־רְמַלְיָהוּ מֶלֶךְ־

יִשְׂרָאֵל יְרוּשָׁלַם לַמִּלְחָמָה עָלֶיהָ

וְלֹא יָכֹל לְהִלָּחֵם עָלֶיהָ׃ וַיֻּגַּד לְבֵית 2

דָּוִד לֵאמֹר נָחָה אֲרָם עַל־אֶפְרָיִם

v. 2. מלעיל   v. 18.

13. *tenth.* The Kingdom of Judah remained after the ten tribes that formed the Northern Kingdom had gone into captivity (Abarbanel).

again be eaten up. Judah too was repeatedly assailed and finally exiled (Abarbanel).

stock. The vital and indestructible element from which the tree springs into life again (Abarbanel).

when they .... leaves. or, 'when the branches are cast off' and pruned (Abarbanel).

so the holy seed. The escaped remnant (Rashi, Ibn Ezra).

CHAPTER VII

CRISIS OF THE SYRO-EPHRAIMITISH INVASION

ISAIAH brings to Ahaz a Divine message of assurance and a warning. The event

described took place in the year 734-4 B.C.E.

1-3.   Introduction to the message.

1.   The apparently unnecessary genealogy is in fact an explanation why God has shown consideration to a wicked king like Ahaz. It states in effect that, though he be unworthy of Divine help, the merit of his fathers secures that aid for him (Rashi from Midrash).

but could not prevail. lit. 'but he could not war.' The city was indeed blockaded (cf. 2 Kings xvi. 5) but could not be taken. This was due to Divine protection, not to the strength of the city's defences or the prowess of the people who, in fact (cf. next verse), shook with fear like trees in the wind (Rashi, Kimchi).

2.   *house of David.* The royal family or the court. The king's name is not mentioned. A wicked man, declares a Rabbinic tradition, does not deserve the honour of being named (Rashi).

confederate with. lit. 'rested upon.'

32

with Ephraim.' And his heart was moved, and the heart of his people, as the trees of the forest are moved with the wind.

3. Then said the LORD unto Isaiah: 'Go forth now to meet Ahaz, thou, and Shear-jashub thy son, at the end of the conduit of the upper pool, in the highway of the fullers' field; 4. and say unto him: Keep calm, and be quiet; fear not, neither let thy heart be faint, because of these two tails of smoking firebrands, for the fierce anger of Rezin and Aram, and of the son of Remaliah. 5. Because Aram hath counselled evil against thee, Ephraim also, and the son of Remaliah, saying: 6. Let us go up against Judah, and vex it, and let us make a breach therein for us, and set up a king in the midst of it, even the son of Tabeel; 7. thus saith the Lord GOD:

It shall not stand, neither shall it come to pass.

וַיָּ֤נַע לְבָבוֹ֙ וּלְבַ֣ב עַמּ֔וֹ כְּנ֥וֹעַ עֲצֵי־

3 יַ֖עַר מִפְּנֵי־רֽוּחַ׃ וַיֹּ֤אמֶר יְהוָה֙ אֶל־
יְשַׁעְיָ֔הוּ צֵא־נָא֙ לִקְרַ֣את אָחָ֔ז אַתָּ֕ה
וּשְׁאָ֖ר יָשׁ֣וּב בְּנֶ֑ךָ אֶל־קְצֵ֗ה תְּעָלַת֙
הַבְּרֵכָ֣ה הָעֶלְיוֹנָ֔ה אֶל־מְסִלַּ֖ת שְׂדֵ֥ה

4 כוֹבֵֽס׃ וְאָמַרְתָּ֣ אֵ֠לָיו הִשָּׁמֵ֨ר וְהַשְׁקֵ֜ט
אַל־תִּירָ֗א וּלְבָבְךָ֙ אַל־יֵרַ֔ךְ מִשְּׁנֵ֨י
זַנְב֧וֹת הָאוּדִ֛ים הָעֲשֵׁנִ֖ים הָאֵ֑לֶּה
בָּחֳרִי־אַ֛ף רְצִ֥ין וַאֲרָ֖ם וּבֶן־

5 רְמַלְיָֽהוּ׃ יַ֗עַן כִּֽי־יָעַ֥ץ עָלֶ֛יךָ אֲרָ֖ם
רָעָ֑ה אֶפְרַ֥יִם וּבֶן־רְמַלְיָ֖הוּ לֵאמֹֽר׃

6 נַעֲלֶ֤ה בִֽיהוּדָה֙ וּנְקִיצֶ֔נָּה וְנַבְקִעֶ֖נָּה
אֵלֵ֑ינוּ וְנַמְלִ֥יךְ מֶ֨לֶךְ֙ בְּתוֹכָ֔הּ אֵ֖ת בֶּן־
טָֽבְאַֽל׃

7 כֹּ֤ה אָמַר֙ אֲדֹנָ֣י יְהֹוִ֔ה
לֹ֥א תָק֖וּם וְלֹ֥א תִֽהְיֶֽה׃

Ephraim. The Kingdom of Israel consisting of the Ten Tribes was so named on account of its first king, Jeroboam, who was an Ephraimite (Ibn Ezra).

with the wind. lit. 'before the wind.'

3. Isaiah, accompanied by his son, is directed by God to meet Ahaz outside the city (Kimchi, Ibn Ezra).

Shear-jashub. Meaning 'a remnant shall return,' i.e. to the true worship of God (Abarbanel).

upper pool. Identified by many authorities with *Birket el-Mamilla,* about half a mile to the west of Jerusalem. Tukachinski, however, places it between the Tower of David and Yemin Moshe.

4-9. God's message to the king.

4. *keep calm.* This follows Rashi and Ibn Ezra. Targum Jonathan and Saadya render, 'take heed.'

son of Remaliah. viz. Pekah. Isaiah is too contemptuous of the usurper to utter his name (Abarbanel).

5-7. These verses form one sentence, verse 5f, being the protasis and verse 7 the apodosis.

6. *son of Tabeel.* Probably a famous prince in Syria or Israel (Ibn Ezra). Some authorities hold that Pekah is intended (Rashi).

7. *it.* i.e. the plan detailed in verse 6 (Rashi, Ibn Ezra).

8. For the head of Aram is Damascus,
And the head of Damascus is
Rezin;
And within threescore and five
years
Shall Ephraim be broken, that it
be not a people;
9. And the head of Ephraim is
Samaria,
And the head of Samaria is
Remaliah's son.
If ye will not have faith, surely ye
shall not be established.'
10. And the LORD spoke again
unto Ahaz, saying: 11. 'Ask thee a
sign of the LORD thy God: ask it
either in the depth, or in the height
above.' 12. But Ahaz said: 'I will
not ask, neither will I try the LORD.'
13. And he said: 'Hear ye now,
O house of David: Is it a small thing
for you to weary men, that ye will

8 כִּי לֹאשׁ אֲרָם דַּמֶּשֶׂק
וְרֹאשׁ דַּמֶּשֶׂק רְצִין
וּבְעוֹד שִׁשִּׁים וְחָמֵשׁ שָׁנָה
יֵחַת אֶפְרַיִם מֵעָם:
9 וְרֹאשׁ אֶפְרַיִם שֹׁמְרוֹן
וְרֹאשׁ שֹׁמְרוֹן בֶּן־רְמַלְיָהוּ
אִם לֹא תַאֲמִינוּ כִּי לֹא תֵאָמֵנוּ:
10 וַיּוֹסֶף יְהֹוָה דַּבֵּר אֶל־אָחָז לֵאמֹר:
11 שְׁאַל־לְךָ אוֹת מֵעִם יְהֹוָה אֱלֹהֶיךָ
הַעְמֵק שְׁאָלָה אוֹ הַגְבֵּהַּ לְמָעְלָה:
12 וַיֹּאמֶר אָחָז לֹא־אֶשְׁאַל וְלֹא־אֲנַסֶּה
13 אֶת־יְהֹוָה: וַיֹּאמֶר שִׁמְעוּ־נָא בֵּית
דָּוִד הַמְעַט מִכֶּם הַלְאוֹת אֲנָשִׁים כִּי

8f. The underlying thought seems to
be that Rezin and Pekah might well be
the sovereigns of their respective countries and capitals (which by the way, the
prophet asserts, will not endure very
long), but never will they achieve the
conquest of Judah or Jerusalem which
will ever enjoy the merciful protection
of God (Rashi, Ibn Ezra).

8. and within . . . people. A parentheti-
cal clause.

threescore and five years. Calculated from
the time of the earthquake in the reign
of Uzziah, when the prophet announced
that Israel shall surely be led away captive out of his land (cf. Amos i. 1, vii. 17)
(Rashi).

9. have faith . . . established. Or, 'for
you are not established.' I.e. you are not
established in the faith of God (Kimchi).

10. the LORD spoke. Through Isaiah
(Ibn Ezra, Kimchi).

again. [This prophetic message, apparently, though not necessarily, followed
close upon the preceding.]

11. sign. to verify the prophet's message. All this time Ahaz refused to
acknowledge the Divine origin of
Isaiah's utterance (Rashi).

12. Ahaz in his obduracy does not
want to be convinced.

13. he said. The subject is the prophet
(Ibn Ezra).

house of David. See on verse 2. Alternatively, Isaiah addresses the court and
the members of the royal family present
(Abarbanel).

is it a small thing. Better, 'is it too little for
you (Metsudath David).

weary my God also? 14. Therefore the Lord Himself shall give you a sign: behold, the young woman shall conceive, and bear a son, and shall call his name Immanuel. 15. Curd and honey shall he eat, when he knoweth to refuse the evil, and choose the good. 16. Yea, before the child shall know to refuse the evil, and choose the good, the land whose two kings thou hast a

יד תִּלְאוּ גַּם אֶת־אֱלֹהָי: לָכֵן יִתֵּן אֲדֹנָי הוּא לָכֶם אוֹת הִנֵּה הָעַלְמָה הָרָה וְיֹלֶדֶת בֵּן וְקָרָאת שְׁמוֹ עִמָּנוּ אֵל:
טו חֶמְאָה וּדְבַשׁ יֹאכֵל לְדַעְתּוֹ מָאֹס
טז בָּרָע וּבָחוֹר בַּטּוֹב: כִּי בְּטֶרֶם יֵדַע הַנַּעַר מָאֹס בָּרָע וּבָחוֹר בַּטּוֹב תֵּעָזֵב הָאֲדָמָה אֲשֶׁר־אַתָּה קָץ מִפְּנֵי שְׁנֵי

ע. 14. נ"א עמנואל.

my God. [The emphasis is on my. Ahaz had just declared his unbelief and thus shown his unworthiness to be included in the company of the faithful.]

14. therefore. Because of the king's scepticism (Kimchi).

the young woman. Hebrew ha'almah means an adolescent woman, one of marriage-able age. The contention that the word must necessarily connote 'virgin' is unwarranted. The Hebrew for 'virgin' is bethulah, though almah too sometimes bears this meaning. It is difficult to say with certainty who was the young woman referred to. Chronological considera-tions exclude the mother of Hezekiah (Rashi, Ibn Ezra, Kimchi); and the fact that the birth (or the name) of the child was to serve as a sign to convince Ahaz of the certain fulfillment of the prophecy rules out the Christological interpreta-tion that the young woman and son are identical with persons who lived 700 years later. The wife of Isaiah (Rashi, Ibn Ezra), a wife of King Ahaz (Kimchi), or a woman of the Royal Family (Abarbanel) may have been the young woman of the text.

and shall call. lit. 'and she shall call.' According to some authorities, the sign given by Isaiah was not the birth, but the striking and symbolic name, of the child which would spontaneously be given to him by his mother (Rashi).

Immanuel. Made up of immanu 'with us,'

el 'God.' 'God is with us' was the battle-cry adopted by Gustavus Adolphus in the Thirty Years War.

15. A parenthesis describing the prim-itive conditions of life in which Immanuel will spend his youth (cf. verse 22).

curd and honey shall he eat. The land will be replete with all good (Rashi). Others explain that as soon as the child is born, he will eat curds and honey, symbolic of all sweet foods. He will reject all bitter foods fed him and eat all sweet foods, knowing to reject bad and choose good (Kimchi).

when he knoweth . . . good. The prophet seems to indicate that the time of the invasion will precede Immanuel's attainment of the age of discretion when he has the ability to discriminate. For the Hebrew, cf. Gen. ii. 9, 17; Deut 1. 39.

16. yea. Or, 'for,' joining the verse to verse 14.

the land. Syria and Ephraim are treated as one country ruled by two kings (see Rashi, Abarbanel).

be forsaken. Cf. In the days of Pekah king of Israel came Tiglath-pileser king of Assyria, and took Ijon . . . captive to Assyria (2 Kings xv. 29); And the king of Assyria went up against Damascus, and took it, and carried the people of it captive to Kir, and slew Rezin (2 Kings xvi. 9).

horror of shall be forsaken. 17.
The LORD shall bring upon thee,
and upon thy people, and upon thy
father's house, days that have not
come, from the day that Ephraim
departed from Judah; even the king
of Assyria.'

18. And it shall come to pass in that
day,
That the LORD shall hiss for the
fly
That is in the uttermost part of
the rivers of Egypt,
And for the bee that is in the
land of Assyria.

19. And they shall come, and shall
rest all of them
In the rugged valleys, and in the
holes of the rocks,
And upon all thorns, and upon
all brambles.

20. In that day shall the Lord shave
with a razor that is hired in the parts
beyond the River, even with the king
of Assyria, the head and the hair of
the feet; and it shall also sweep
away the beard.

21. And it shall come to pass in

מַלְכֵיהֶ׃ יָבִיא יְהוָֹה עָלֶיךָ וְעַל־ 17
עַמְּךָ וְעַל־בֵּית אָבִיךָ יָמִים אֲשֶׁר
לֹא־בָאוּ לְמִיּוֹם סוּר־אֶפְרַיִם מֵעַל
יְהוּדָה אֵת מֶלֶךְ אַשּׁוּר׃
וְהָיָה ׀ בַּיּוֹם הַהוּא 18
יִשְׁרֹק יְהוָֹה לַזְּבוּב
אֲשֶׁר בִּקְצֵה יְאֹרֵי מִצְרָיִם
וְלַדְּבוֹרָה אֲשֶׁר בְּאֶרֶץ אַשּׁוּר׃
וּבָאוּ וְנָחוּ כֻלָּם 19
בְּנַחֲלֵי הַבַּתּוֹת וּבִנְקִיקֵי הַסְּלָעִים
וּבְכֹל הַנַּעֲצוּצִים וּבְכֹל הַנַּהֲלֹלִים׃
בַּיּוֹם הַהוּא יְגַלַּח אֲדֹנָי בְּתַעַר 20
הַשְּׂכִירָה בְּעֶבְרֵי נָהָר בְּמֶלֶךְ אַשּׁוּר
אֶת־הָרֹאשׁ וְשַׂעַר הָרַגְלָיִם וְגַם אֶת־
הַזָּקָן תִּסְפֶּה׃ וְהָיָה בַּיּוֹם הַהוּא 21

17. The theme of verse 15 and the
unwelcome sign are now dealt with. The
threat to Judah is not, as Ahaz feared,
that of the two neighbouring allies,
Pekah and Rezin, but the all-powerful
king of Assyria sent by the Lord of
Hosts to execute punishment for the
unbelief and godlessness of Ahaz
(Kimchi).

day . . . Judah. The rebellion of the Ten
Tribes under Jeroboam against the
house of David was the greatest disaster
in the history of Judah (Laniado).

18-20. The invasion.

18f. When the king of Assyria returned
from Egypt, he marched on Judah,
accompanied by an army of Egyptians
(Malbim).

18. the fly . . . the bee. Metaphors for
the swiftness of movement of the Egyptian and Assyrian hosts. The fly is asso-
ciated with Egypt on account of its
weakness in comparison to Assyria,

resembling the weakness of the fly in
comparison to the bee (Malbim).

rivers of Egypt. Or, 'canals of Egypt,' the
irrigation ditches, extending from the
Nile, to water the land, not favoured by
rainfall (Rashi).

19. The metaphor of flying insects is
sustained.

20. With a change of metaphor,
Assyria is being shaven with a razor.

shave . . . beard. Symbolizing the annihilation of the Assyrian hosts. The beard
in the Orient was a mark of dignity
(Kimchi).

hired. A hired razor is exceedingly sharp
(Ibn Ezra). This symbolizes the angel
who destroyed the camp (Ibn Ezra).

beyond the River. Upon those who dwell
beyond the River, viz. 'the king of
Assyria, etc.' (Rashi). The River is the
Euphrates.

that day, that a man shall rear a young cow, and two sheep; 22. and it shall come to pass, for the abundance of milk that they shall give, he shall eat curd; for curd and honey shall every one eat that is left in the midst of the land.

23. And it shall come to pass in that day, that every place, where there were a thousand vines at a thousand silverlings, shall even be for briers and thorns. 24. With arrows and with bow shall one come thither; because all the land shall become briers and thorns. 25. And all the hills that were digged with the mattock, thou shalt not come thither for fear of briers and thorns, but it shall be for the sending forth of oxen, and for the treading of sheep.

יַחְיֶה־אִישׁ עֶגְלַת בָּקָר וּשְׁתֵּי־צֹאן: 22 וְהָיָה מֵרֹב עֲשׂוֹת חָלָב יֹאכַל חֶמְאָה כִּי־חֶמְאָה וּדְבַשׁ יֹאכֵל כָּל־הַנּוֹתָר 23 בְּקֶרֶב הָאָרֶץ: וְהָיָה בַּיּוֹם הַהוּא יִהְיֶה כָל־מָקוֹם אֲשֶׁר יִהְיֶה־שָּׁם אֶלֶף גֶּפֶן בְּאֶלֶף כָּסֶף לַשָּׁמִיר וְלַשַּׁיִת 24 יִהְיֶה: בַּחִצִּים וּבַקֶּשֶׁת יָבוֹא שָׁמָּה כִּי־שָׁמִיר וָשַׁיִת תִּהְיֶה כָל־הָאָרֶץ: 25 וְכֹל הֶהָרִים אֲשֶׁר בַּמַּעְדֵּר יֵעָדֵרוּן לֹא־תָבוֹא שָׁמָּה יִרְאַת שָׁמִיר וָשָׁיִת וְהָיָה לְמִשְׁלַח שׁוֹר וּלְמִרְמַס שֶׂה:

21-25. The deplorable condition of the land after the invader had left his mark upon it and God's blessing.

21f. Agricultural activity ceased, primitive conditions have returned, and the survivors of the storm and strife live on the abundance of the produce of their flocks (Rashi, Kimchi).

21. *cow . . . sheep.* No more will remain since the armies have pillaged all the livestock, but God will bestow His blessing on the remnant (Rashi).

22. *they shall give.* The abundance of milk these two sheep shall produce (Rashi).

honey. This too will be plentiful in Hezekiah's time, when the land will, literally, flow with milk and honey (Kimchi).

every one. Of the righteous who survived the sword of Sennacherib (Rashi).

23-25. The forlorn state of the most precious vineyards.

23. *shall be for briers and thorns.* When

their owners flee the invaders, they will abandon their precious vineyards (Rashi).

24. *with arrows . . . come thither.* To protect oneself against highwaymen and wild beasts haunting such desolate and unfrequented places (Rashi, Ibn Ezra).

25. *hills.* These are ideal sites for vineyard plantations (Ibn Ezra).

that were digged. Before the invasion and consequent desolation (Ibn Ezra).

thou shalt not come thither for fear. Better, 'fear of briers and thorns shall not come thither.' The vineyards on the hills will not be overgrown with briers and thorns, but will be cultivated so successfully that, even though cattle and sheep will graze there undisturbed, there will still be plenty (Ibn Ezra). Others explain that the vineyards will be completely abandoned because the people will be preoccupied with Torah study and will not think of drinking wine. The hills will be 'digged with the mattock' for grain fields, necessary for sustenance (Rashi).

8

CHAPTER VIII   ח

1. And the Lord said unto me: 'Take thee a great tablet, and write upon it in common script: The spoil speedeth, the prey hasteth; 2. and I will take unto Me faithful witnesses to record, Uriah the priest, and Zechariah the son of Jeberechiah.' 3. And I went unto the prophetess; and she conceived, and bore a son. Then said the Lord unto me: 'Call his name ¹Mahershalal-hash-baz. 4. For before the child shall have knowledge to cry: My father, and: My mother, the riches of Damascus and the spoil of Samaria shall be carried away before the king of Assyria.'

1 וַיֹּאמֶר יְהוָֹה אֵלַי קַח־לְךָ גִּלָּיוֹן גָּדוֹל וּכְתֹב עָלָיו בְּחֶרֶט אֱנוֹשׁ לְמַהֵר שָׁלָל 2 חָשׁ בַּז: וְאָעִידָה לִּי עֵדִים נֶאֱמָנִים אֵת אוּרִיָּה הַכֹּהֵן וְאֶת־זְכַרְיָהוּ בֶּן 3 יְבֶרֶכְיָהוּ: וָאֶקְרַב אֶל־הַנְּבִיאָה וַתַּהַר וַתֵּלֶד בֵּן וַיֹּאמֶר יְהוָֹה אֵלַי 4 קְרָא שְׁמוֹ מַהֵר שָׁלָל חָשׁ בַּז: כִּי בְּטֶרֶם יֵדַע הַנַּעַר קְרֹא אָבִי וְאִמִּי יִשָּׂא ׀ אֶת־חֵיל דַּמֶּשֶׂק וְאֵת שְׁלַל שֹׁמְרוֹן לִפְנֵי מֶלֶךְ אַשּׁוּר:

---

¹ That is, *The spoil speedeth, the prey hasteth.*

CHAPTER VIII

1–3. The prophet attempts to impress the people by two concrete manifestations. He first displays on a tablet an ominous inscription attested by trustworthy witnesses, and then adopts the same inscription as the name of his newly-born son.

1. *tablet.* Of metal, wood or stone (Targum). Others translate 'a roll' (Rashi).

in common script. i.e easily legible by the ordinary man (Rashi). The Hebrew literally means 'stylus of a man.' This denotes that the words were actually to be written and that this was not merely a prophetic vision (Kimchi). Ibn Ezra explains that the letters were cast on the cylinder just as the form of a man is cast.

spoil . . . hasteth. Others prefer the translation: 'speeding (to the) spoil, hasting (to the) prey (Rashi).

2. *and I will take.* The continuation of God's speech beginning with *take thee* in the preceding verse (Malbim, see Rashi, Ibn Ezra).

faithful witnesses. i.e. witnesses trusted by the people (see Ibn Ezra).

Uriah the priest. Mentioned again in 2 Kings xvi. 11; the name of the other witness is otherwise unknown (Ibn Ezra, Metsudath David).

3. *prophetess.* The prophet's wife. A husband confers his title upon his wife irrespective of her own qualifications and attainments (Ibn Ezra).

4. Explanation of the name of Isaiah's son and therefore, also of the inscription as predicting the speedy fall of both Ephraim and Syria.

my father . . . my mother. i.e. the child has the ability to distinguish his parents from other persons. This he would be able to do at a very early age; so the threatened invasion would soon come to pass (Kimchi, Ibn Ezra).

Damascus. The capital of Syria.

Samaria. The capital of Ephraim, the Northern Kingdom of Israel.

shall be carried away. lit. 'one will carry away,' the subject being indefinite (Ibn Ezra).

the king of Assyria. viz. Tiglath-Pileser III (745–727 B.C.E.)

5. And the LORD spoke unto me
yet again, saying:
6. Forasmuch as this people hath
refused
  The waters of Shiloah that go
softly,
  And rejoiceth with Rezin and
Remaliah's son;
7. Now therefore, behold, the Lord
bringeth up upon them
  The waters of the River, mighty
and many,
  Even the king of Assyria and all
his glory;
  And he shall come up over all his
channels,
  And go over all his banks;
8. And he shall sweep through
Judah,
  Overflowing as he passeth
through;
  He shall reach even to the neck;
  And the stretching out of his
wings
  Shall fill the breadth of thy land,
O Immanuel.
9. Make an uproar, O ye peoples,
and ye shall be broken in
pieces;

5 וַיֹּסֶף יְהוָֹה דַּבֵּר אֵלַי עוֹד לֵאמֹר׃
6 יַעַן כִּי מָאַס הָעָם הַזֶּה
אֵת מֵי הַשִּׁלֹחַ הַהֹלְכִים לְאָט
וּמְשׂוֹשׂ אֶת־רְצִין וּבֶן־רְמַלְיָהוּ׃
7 וְלָכֵן הִנֵּה אֲדֹנָי מַעֲלֶה עֲלֵיהֶם
אֶת־מֵי הַנָּהָר הָעֲצוּמִים וְהָרַבִּים
אֶת־מֶלֶךְ אַשּׁוּר וְאֶת־כָּל־כְּבוֹדוֹ
וְעָלָה עַל־כָּל־אֲפִיקָיו
וְהָלַךְ עַל־כָּל־גְּדוֹתָיו׃
8 וְחָלַף בִּיהוּדָה
שָׁטַף וְעָבַר
עַד־צַוָּאר יַגִּיעַ
וְהָיָה מֻטּוֹת כְּנָפָיו
מְלֹא רֹחַב אַרְצְךָ עִמָּנוּ אֵל׃
9 רֹעוּ עַמִּים וָחֹתּוּ

v. 6. פתח באתנח

5–8. The Assyrian invasion of Judah is
threatened in symbolic language.

6. *this people.* The disaffected men of
Judah (see Rashi).

the waters, etc. A metaphor for the house
of David (Targum).

Shiloah. The modern Ain Silwan, south-
west of the Temple Mount.

and rejoiceth. The Hebrew has a noun
instead of a verb, 'and joy with.' I.e.
those who chose the joy that will accom-
pany the rule of Rezin and Pekah
(Metsudath David). Perhaps a party is
indicated which described to come to
terms with the enemy (Kimchi).

Remaliah's son. See on vii. 4.

7. *upon them.* The people of Judah (Ibn
Ezra).

the River. The Euphrates; a metaphor
for Assyria, as explained later in the
verse. The picture of the invading army

as a rising river is suggested by the
summer overflow of the banks of the
Euphrates.

and all his glory. i.e. that in which he
glorifies, his mighty army (Kimchi).

8. *stretching out of his wings.* He previously delineated the length of the
armies, that they would extend
throughout all the cities of Judah. Then
he delineated the height, that it would
reach up to Jerusalem, the highest point
in Judah, and now he delineates the
width, that the armies would fill the
breadth of the land (Kara).

Immanuel. A name for the land of Judah,
as in vii. 14 for the prophet's son, indicating the conviction that Divine protection will be extended to it (Rashi).

9f. The evil designs of the nations
against Israel will be frustrated.

9. *make an uproar.* Other possible ren-

39

And give ear, all ye of far
countries;
Gird yourselves, and ye shall be
broken in pieces;
Gird yourselves, and ye shall be
broken in pieces.

10. Take counsel together, and it
shall be brought to nought;
Speak the word, and it shall not
stand;
For God is with us.

11. For the LORD spoke thus to
me with a strong hand, admonishing
me that I should not walk in the way
of this people, saying: 12. 'Say ye
not: A conspiracy, concerning all
whereof this people do say: A conspiracy; neither fear ye their fear,
nor account it dreadful. 13. The
LORD of hosts, Him shall ye sanctify;
and let Him be your fear, and let
Him be your dread. 14. And He
shall be for a sanctuary; but for a

וְהַאֲזִינוּ כֹּל מֶרְחַקֵּי־אָרֶץ
הִתְאַזְּרוּ וָחֹתּוּ
הִתְאַזְּרוּ וָחֹתּוּ׃
10 עֻצוּ עֵצָה וְתֻפָר
דַּבְּרוּ דָבָר וְלֹא יָקוּם
כִּי עִמָּנוּ אֵל׃
11 כִּי כֹה אָמַר יְהֹוָה אֵלַי כְּחֶזְקַת הַיָּד
וְיִסְּרֵנִי מִלֶּכֶת בְּדֶרֶךְ הָעָם־הַזֶּה
12 לֵאמֹר׃ לֹא־תֹאמְרוּן קֶשֶׁר לְכֹל
אֲשֶׁר־יֹאמַר הָעָם הַזֶּה קֶשֶׁר וְאֶת־
מוֹרָאוֹ לֹא־תִירְאוּ וְלֹא תַעֲרִיצוּ׃
13 אֶת־יְהֹוָה צְבָאוֹת אֹתוֹ תַקְדִּישׁוּ וְהוּא
14 מוֹרַאֲכֶם וְהוּא מַעֲרִצְכֶם׃ וְהָיָה
לְמִקְדָּשׁ וּלְאֶבֶן נֶגֶף וּלְצוּר מִכְשׁוֹל

derings are: 'associate yourselves' (Targum), 'be broken' (Ibn Ezra, Kimchi).

and ye . . . pieces. This alludes to the
destruction of the Assyrian camp
(Rashi).

gird yourselves. For battle, against the
Lord and His people (Rashi).

10. *the word.* lit. 'a word,' the resolu-
tion they had formed (Malbim).

for . . . with us. Hebrew *Immanuel*; see on
verse 8.

11–15. The prophet had been commanded by God to hold firmly to his
principles, and this enabled him to
stand out alone, disregarding all dangerous though popular demands or
tendencies (See Rashi, Kimchi).

11. *with a strong hand.* Or, 'while the
hand (of the Lord) grasped (me).' The
prophet's mind was under the direct
and overwhelming influence of the
Holy Spirit; so he was in a position to

view the situation in true perspective
uninfluenced by any disturbing elements (Rashi, Kimchi).

admonishing . . . walk. Or, 'and warned
me against walking.'

the way of this people. The prophet was
not to be moved by the currents of passing popular views and emotions (See
Rashi).

12. *conspiracy.* Alluding to the coalition
between Syria and Ephraim against
Judah. This had filled the Israelite
people with dread; but it should not
produce the same effect upon the
prophet (Kara).

13. *let Him be your fear.* God alone, not
foreign kings, is to be feared (Kimchi).

14. *for a sanctuary.* To those who
believe in Him and obey His instruction. A *sanctuary* is also a place of refuge
(cf. I Kings i. 50; Ezek. xi. 16) (Ibn Ezra,
Kimchi).

stone of stumbling and for a rock of offence to both the houses of Israel, for a gin and for a snare to the inhabitants of Jerusalem. 15. And many among them shall stumble, and fall, and be broken, and be snared, and be taken.'

16. 'Bind up the testimony, seal the instruction among My disciples'. 17. And I will wait for the LORD, that hideth His face from the house of Jacob, and I will look for Him. 18. Behold, I and the children whom the LORD hath given me shall be for signs and for wonders in Israel from the LORD of hosts, who dwelleth in mount Zion. 19. And when they shall say unto you: 'Seek unto the

לְשֵׁנֵי בָתֵּי יִשְׂרָאֵל לְפַח וּלְמוֹקֵשׁ
15 לְיוֹשֵׁב יְרוּשָׁלָ͏ִם: וְכָשְׁלוּ בָם רַבִּים
16 וְנָפְלוּ וְנִשְׁבָּרוּ וְנוֹקְשׁוּ וְנִלְכָּדוּ: צוֹר
תְּעוּדָה חֲתוֹם תּוֹרָה בְּלִמֻּדָי:
17 וְחִכִּיתִי לַיהֹוָה הַמַּסְתִּיר פָּנָיו מִבֵּית
18 יַעֲקֹב וְקִוֵּיתִי־לוֹ: הִנֵּה אָנֹכִי
וְהַיְלָדִים אֲשֶׁר נָתַן־לִי יְהֹוָה לְאֹתוֹת
וּלְמוֹפְתִים בְּיִשְׂרָאֵל מֵעִם יְהֹוָה
19 צְבָאוֹת הַשֹּׁכֵן בְּהַר צִיּוֹן: וְכִי־
יֹאמְרוּ אֲלֵיכֶם דִּרְשׁוּ אֶל־הָאֹבוֹת

v. 15. קמץ בז״ק

for a stone of stumbling. To unbelievers and the disobedient (Kimchi).

15. *many among them.* But not all; for a remnant shall escape. Ibn Ezra has 'many shall stumble thereon,' viz. on the stone and snares, and this corresponds more closely with the order of the words in the Hebrew.

16-18. The prophet entrusts his disciples with a written and sealed record of his instruction rather than reveal it to the public at large, who were not willing to obey the prophetic teaching (Kimchi).

16. *bind ... seal.* God addresses Isaiah as in verse II (Targum).

testimony ... instruction. The evidential and practical elements respectively in the revelation concerning the coming troubles and dangers (Rashi, Ibn Ezra).

disciples. lit. 'taught,' the intimate associates whom the prophet taught God's Torah and to whom he imparted His message (Rashi, Kimchi).

17. *and I will,* etc. The prophet speaks (Rashi, Ibn Ezra).

hideth His face. A common metaphor of the Bible for God's displeasure.

look for Him. Better, 'hope in Him.' The prophet avows his reliance upon God in contrast to the disbelief of the king and mass of the people (Rashi).

18. *for signs and for wonders.* The second noun signifies 'portents.' Isaiah, by writing on a tablet and the children by their names, viz. *Shear-jashub* 'a remnant will return,' and *Maher-shalal-hash-baz* 'the spoil speedeth, the prey hasteth.' The mere mention of such names, or sight of the persons bearing them, brings to mind their significance and directs attention to the prophetic message (Kimchi).

mount Zion. The earthly habitation of God's glory. The Divine Presence in Zion is the assurance that He will save His Temple and His Holy Mount (Abarbanel).

19-22. The coming of despair and affliction, resort to necromancy, dreariness and hunger.

19. This verse and the following draw a contrast between the religion of God and common superstition.

they shall say. The subject is the godless, and *you* refers to the faithful (Metsudath David).

41

ghosts and the familiar spirits, that chirp and that mutter; should not a people seek unto their God? on behalf of the living unto the dead 20. for instruction and for testimony?'—Surely they will speak according to this word, wherein there is no light.—21. And they shall pass this way that are sore bestead and hungry; and it shall come to pass that, when they shall be hungry, they shall fret themselves, and curse by their king and by their God, and, whether they turn their faces upward, 22. or look unto the earth, behold distress and darkness, the gloom of anguish, and outspread thick darkness. 23. For is there no gloom to her that was stedfast? Now the former hath lightly afflicted

וְאֶל־הַיִּדְּעֹנִים הַמְצַפְצְפִים וְהַמַּהְגִּים הֲלוֹא־עַם אֶל־אֱלֹהָיו יִדְרֹשׁ בְּעַד הַחַיִּים אֶל־הַמֵּתִים׃

20 לְתוֹרָה וְלִתְעוּדָה אִם־לֹא יֹאמְרוּ כַּדָּבָר הַזֶּה אֲשֶׁר אֵין־לוֹ שָׁחַר׃

21 וְעָבַר בָּהּ נִקְשֶׁה וְרָעֵב וְהָיָה כִי־ יִרְעַב וְהִתְקַצַּף וְקִלֵּל בְּמַלְכּוֹ

22 וּבֵאלֹהָיו וּפָנָה לְמָעְלָה׃ וְאֶל־אֶרֶץ יַבִּיט וְהִנֵּה צָרָה וַחֲשֵׁכָה מְעוּף צוּקָה

23 וַאֲפֵלָה מְנֻדָּח׃ כִּי לֹא מוּעָף לַאֲשֶׁר מוּצָק לָהּ כָּעֵת הָרִאשׁוֹן הֵקַל אַרְצָה

---

ghosts and the familiar spirits. To attempt by these means to penetrate the future is forbidden by the Torah (Lev. xix. 31, xx. 6; Deut. xviii. 11).

chirp . . . mutter. The 'voices' which issue from ghosts and familiar spirits are indistinct. (Rashi).

should not . . . testimony? This is the reply the prophet's disciples are to give to those who suggest the use of occult media for ascertaining the future (Rashi).

20. *for instruction and for testimony?* According to R.V., 'to the law and to the testimony!'; the words are part of Isaiah's retort to the popular plea. Instead of turning to the dead for guidance, let them look to the revealed word of the living God! But A.J. is to be preferred and is supported by the Jewish commentators.

surely they, etc. The prophet's comment (Rashi).

21f. The scene of desolation and misery.

they. The Hebrew has the singular throughout the two verses, the subject being anyone who passes through the land during the Assyrian siege on Samaria (Rashi).

curse by their king, etc. According to Jewish commentaries, 'he will curse by his king and by his god,' alluding to the calves and the baalim of Samaria.

23. *for is there no gloom . . . stedfast?* A difficult clause which R. V. renders: 'but there shall be no gloom to her that was in anguish.' The Jewish commentators connect the noun *mu'aph* with the root *'iph,* 'to be faint' and interpret: 'For there is no faintness to him (the king of Assyria) who brings distress to her (the people of Israel)'; he carries on his campaign relentlessly.

the former . . . the latter. 'In the former troubled days, preceding the downfall of Samaria, Tiglath-pileser III had deprived the kingdom of Ephraim of its northern provinces, Zebulun and Naphtali. The ruin which Tiglath-pileser had begun Sargon completed in 722' (Marcus).

the land of Zebulun and the land of
Naphtali, but the latter hath dealt a
more grievous blow by the way of
the sea, beyond the Jordan, in the
district of the nations.

זְבֻלוּן וְאַרְצָה נַפְתָּלִי וְהָאַחֲרוֹן
הִכְבִּיד דֶּרֶךְ הַיָּם עֵבֶר הַיַּרְדֵּן גְּלִיל
הַגּוֹיִם׃

| 9 | CHAPTER IX | ט |

1. The people that walked in
darkness
Have seen a great light;
They that dwelt in the land of
the shadow of death,
Upon them hath the light shined.

2. Thou hast multiplied the nation,
Thou hast increased their joy;
They joy before Thee according
to the joy in harvest,
As men rejoice when they divide
the spoil.

¹ הָעָם הַהֹלְכִים בַּחֹשֶׁךְ
רָאוּ אוֹר גָּדוֹל
יֹשְׁבֵי בְּאֶרֶץ צַלְמָוֶת
אוֹר נָגַהּ עֲלֵיהֶם׃
² הִרְבִּיתָ הַגּוֹי
לֹא הִגְדַּלְתָּ הַשִּׂמְחָה
שָׂמְחוּ לְפָנֶיךָ כְּשִׂמְחַת בַּקָּצִיר
כַּאֲשֶׁר יָגִילוּ בְּחַלְּקָם שָׁלָל׃

v. 2. לו ק'

land of Zebulun . . . Naphtali. The northern extremity of the Land of Israel,
Galilee.

by the way of the sea. i.e. Lake Gen-
nesareth (Rashi). Or, 'in the direction of
the (Mediterranean) sea' (Kimchi). The
road from Acre to Damascus was
known as 'the way of the sea' (*Via Maris*)
in the time of the Crusaders.

beyond the Jordan. viz. Gilead.

the district (galil) of the nations. The entire
kingdom of Israel, composed of tribes,
often referred to as nations (Ibn Ezra).
When these regions were conquered,
Jerusalem, in the interior, was still free
(Kimchi). The Judeans are exhorted to
take heed of their sister nation and to
refrain from necromancy and the like
(Abarbanel).

CHAPTER IX

1-6. Deliverance and joy. The fall of
Assyria and the announcement of the
birth of Hezekiah.

1. *the people.* The inhabitants of Jerusalem who were besieged by the
Assyrian army (Rashi, Ibn Ezra).

have seen. This and the following perfects
are 'prophetic,' the prophet seeing the
future so vividly that to him it seems an
event of the past (According to
Malbim).

a great light. As the effect of the destruction of the Assyrian hosts (cf. xxxvii.
36f.) (Rashi).

2. *the joy in harvest.* The festival was the
time of national rejoicing (cf. Deut. xvi.
15; Ps. cxxxvi. 6) (Kimchi).

as men rejoice, etc. After a great victory
(cf. Ps. cxix. 162) (Kimchi).

43

3. For the yoke of his burden,
   And the staff of his shoulder,
   The rod of his oppressor,
   Thou hast broken as in the day
   of Midian.

4. For every boot stamped with
   fierceness,
   And every cloak rolled in blood,
   Shall even be for burning, for
   fuel of fire.

5. For a child is born unto us,
   A son is given unto us;
   And the government is upon his
   shoulder;
   And his name is called
   Pele-joez-el-gibbor-
   Abi-ad-sar-shalom;

³ כִּי | אֶת־עֹל סֻבֳּלוֹ
וְאֵת מַטֵּה שִׁכְמוֹ
שֵׁבֶט הַנֹּגֵשׂ בּוֹ
הַחִתֹּתָ כְּיוֹם מִדְיָן׃
⁴ כִּי כָל־סְאוֹן סֹאֵן בְּרַעַשׁ
וְשִׂמְלָה מְגוֹלָלָה בְדָמִים
וְהָיְתָה לִשְׂרֵפָה מַאֲכֹלֶת אֵשׁ׃
⁵ כִּי־יֶלֶד יֻלַּד־לָנוּ
בֵּן נִתַּן־לָנוּ
וַתְּהִי הַמִּשְׂרָה עַל־שִׁכְמוֹ
וַיִּקְרָא שְׁמוֹ
פֶּלֶא יוֹעֵץ אֵל גִּבּוֹר
אֲבִי־עַד שַׂר־שָׁלוֹם׃

3f. The destruction of the besieging army.

the yoke of his burden. i.e. the oppressive rule of the conqueror (Abarbanel).

the staff. It appears that Rashi construes *matteh* not as a noun but the Hiphil particle of *natah*: 'him who made his (Israel's shoulder to bow (and receive a burden).' For this idiom, cf. Gen. xlix. 15.

the day. Of battle (Kimchi).

Midian. On whom Gideon (Judg. vii) inflicted a crushing defeat with but three hundred men, comparative to the miraculous defeat of the Assyrians (Kimchi).

4. *boot.* A.J. renders the Hebrew word *seon* as corresponding to the Assyrian *senu,* 'shoe, sandal,' or the Aramaic *'sena,* meaning the same. Rashi, however, renders: For every victory shout sounds with clamor.

stamped with fierceness. Or, 'of him that goest booted in the din.'

be for burning. In the case of the defeat of Sennacherib, however, they will be burnt by the heavenly fire (Kimchi).

5. *a child.* The verse has been given a Christological interpretation by the Church, but modern non-Jewish exegetes agree that a contemporary person is intended. The Talmud and later Jewish commentators understood the allusion to be the son of Ahaz, viz. Hezekiah.

is born . . . is given. Better, in agreement with the Hebrew, 'has been born . . . has been given.'

the government is upon his shoulder. Unlike his father, who was a vassal to the king of Assyria (Kimchi).

pele-joez, etc. The meaning of the Hebrew words is 'Wonderful in counsel is God the Mighty, the Everlasting Father, The Ruler of Peace.' The child will bear these significant names in order to recall to the people the message which they embodied (Abarbanel).

6. That the government may be
increased,
And of peace there be no end,
Upon the throne of David, and
upon his kingdom,
To establish it, and to uphold it
Through justice and through
righteousness
From henceforth even for ever.
The zeal of the LORD of hosts
doth perform this.

7. The Lord sent a word into
Jacob,
And it hath lighted upon Israel.

8. And all the people shall know,
Even Ephraim and the inhabitant
of Samaria,
That say in pride and in arrogancy of heart:

⁶ לְםַרְבֵּ֞ה הַמִּשְׂרָ֜ה
וּלְשָׁל֣וֹם אֵֽין־קֵ֗ץ
עַל־כִּסֵּ֤א דָוִד֙ וְעַל־מַמְלַכְתּ֔וֹ
לְהָכִ֤ין אֹתָהּ֙ וּֽלְסַעֲדָ֔הּ
בְּמִשְׁפָּ֖ט וּבִצְדָקָ֑ה
מֵעַתָּה֙ וְעַד־עוֹלָ֔ם
קִנְאַ֛ת יְהוָ֥ה צְבָא֖וֹת תַּעֲשֶׂה־זֹּֽאת׃
⁷ דָּבָ֛ר שָׁלַ֥ח אֲדֹנָ֖י בְּיַעֲקֹ֑ב
וְנָפַ֖ל בְּיִשְׂרָאֵֽל׃
⁸ וְיָדְעוּ֙ הָעָ֣ם כֻּלּ֔וֹ
אֶפְרַ֖יִם וְיוֹשֵׁ֣ב שֹׁמְר֑וֹן
בְּגַאֲוָ֥ה וּבְגֹֽדֶל־לֵבָ֖ב לֵאמֹֽר׃

v. 6. מ׳ סתומה באמצע תיבה

6. *the government may be increased.* The Jewish commentators render: To the one who increases the government of the Lord upon himself (Rashi). Alternatively, 'To the one who increases the power of the government.

and of peace there be no end. The increased power of his government is not dependent on waging war, for there shall be peace in his days (Abarbanel).

for ever. During the lifetime of Hezekiah. The Hebrew word *olam* also signifies 'a considerable time' (Rashi).

the zeal of the LORD. Either God's zeal on behalf of His people (Rashi) or Hezekiah's zeal to perform the Divine Will by promoting the welfare of his subjects and his passion for justice.

doth perform this. i.e. assures the fulfillment of the promise.

7-20. An oracle on the Northern Kingdom arranged in three regular strophes, each ending with *For all this*

His anger is not turned away, but His hand is stretched out still. This section is regarded as the most artistically arranged of all the writings of Isaiah.

7-11. First strophe.

7-9. Introduction, stating that the arrogant inhabitants of Ephraim, and particularly those of Samaria, are the subject of the oracle.

7. *a word.* viz. the oracle that follows (Ibn Ezra).

Jacob . . . Israel. Synonymous with the Northern Kingdom as opposed to the Kingdom of Judah in the south (Rashi, Kara).

it hath lighted. i.e. it is soon to be realized (prophetic perfect) (Rashi).

8. *shall know.* By the immediate fulfillment of the prophet's prediction (Kimchi).

that say. lit. 'saying,' and 'as follows' is implied (Metsudath David, Rashi).

45

9. 'The bricks are fallen, but we will build with hewn stones; The sycomores are cut down, but cedars will we put in their place.'

10. Therefore the LORD doth set upon high the adversaries of Rezin against him, And spur his enemies;

11. The Arameans on the east, and the Philistines on the west; And they devour Israel with open mouth. For all this His anger is not turned away, But His hand is stretched out still.

12. Yet the people turneth not unto Him that smiteth them, Neither do they seek the LORD of hosts.

13. Therefore the LORD doth cut off from Israel head and tail, Palm-branch and rush, in one day.

14. The elder and the man of rank, he is the head; And the prophet that teacheth lies, he is the tail.

9 לְבֵנִים נָפָלוּ וְגָזִית נִבְנֶה
שִׁקְמִים גֻּדָּעוּ וַאֲרָזִים נַחֲלִיף:

10 וַיְשַׂגֵּב יְהוָה אֶת־צָרֵי רְצִין עָלָיו
וְאֶת־אֹיְבָיו יְסַכְסֵךְ:

11 אֲרָם מִקֶּדֶם וּפְלִשְׁתִּים מֵאָחוֹר
וַיֹּאכְלוּ אֶת־יִשְׂרָאֵל בְּכָל־פֶּה
בְּכָל־זֹאת לֹא־שָׁב אַפּוֹ
וְעוֹד יָדוֹ נְטוּיָה:

12 וְהָעָם לֹא־שָׁב עַד־הַמַּכֵּהוּ
וְאֶת־יְהוָה צְבָאוֹת לֹא דָרָשׁוּ:

13 וַיַּכְרֵת יְהוָה מִיִּשְׂרָאֵל רֹאשׁ וְזָנָב
כִּפָּה וְאַגְמוֹן יוֹם אֶחָד:

14 זָקֵן וּנְשׂוּא־פָנִים הוּא הָרֹאשׁ
וְנָבִיא מוֹרֶה־שֶּׁקֶר הוּא הַזָּנָב:

v. 9. קמץ בטרחא

9. The prophet makes his point the more forcefully by means of a metaphor. In their conceited self-confidence they claim to be able to make good any loss they might sustain, and even to improve upon their lost possessions. They would replace cheap *bricks* by costly *hewn stones* and the common *sycomores* by precious *cedars* (Rashi).

10f. The first calamity: invasion and plunder from the north, east and west. The attacks are not to be understood as taking place simultaneously, the prophet having in mind a long stretch of the history of the Northern Kingdom (Rashi).

10. *the adversaries of Rezin.* The Assyrians from the north who were also the adversaries of Ephraim, Rezin's ally (Rashi).

11. *with open mouth.* lit. 'with all mouth.'

is stretched out still. To mete out more drastic punishment (Targum).

12–16. Second strophe. The people still disregarding the prophet's warning and, despite the calamities enumerated, continuing in their wickedness and corruption are struck again. Their rulers and leaders are taken away, joy is withdrawn from their young men, and even their orphans and widows are deprived of the protection of God's mercy.

13. *head and tail.* Leader and follower (Kimchi).

palm-branch and rush. The tallest and shortest of plants, symbolizing the upper and lower classes (Metsudath David).

14. *he is the tail.* The false prophet is in reality no leader but a follower. In his prophecy he merely says what the ruling classes (*the elder and the man of rank*) wish him to say (Kimchi).

46

15. For they that lead this people
cause them to err;
And they that are led of them are
destroyed.

16. Therefore the Lord shall have
no joy in their young men,
Neither shall He have compassion on their fatherless and
widows;
For every one is ungodly and an
evil-doer,
And every mouth speaketh
wantonness.
For all this His anger is not
turned away,
But His hand is stretched out
still.

17. For wickedness burneth as the
fire;
It devoureth the briers and
thorns;
Yea, it kindleth in the thickets of
the forest,
And they roll upward in thick
clouds of smoke.

18. Through the wrath of the Lord
of hosts is the land burnt up;
The people also are as the fuel of
fire;
No man spareth his brother.

19. And one snatcheth on the right
hand, and is hungry;
And he eateth on the left hand,
and is not satisfied;
They eat every man the flesh of
his own arm:

15 וַיִּהְיוּ מְאַשְּׁרֵי הָעָם־הַזֶּה מַתְעִים
וּמְאֻשָּׁרָיו מְבֻלָּעִים׃

16 עַל־כֵּן עַל־בַּחוּרָיו
לֹא־יִשְׂמַח ׀ אֲדֹנָי
וְאֶת־יְתֹמָיו וְאֶת־אַלְמְנֹתָיו לֹא יְרַחֵם
כִּי כֻלּוֹ חָנֵף וּמֵרַע
וְכָל־פֶּה דֹּבֵר נְבָלָה
בְּכָל־זֹאת לֹא־שָׁב אַפּוֹ
וְעוֹד יָדוֹ נְטוּיָה׃

17 כִּי־בָעֲרָה כָאֵשׁ רִשְׁעָה
שָׁמִיר וָשַׁיִת תֹּאכֵל
וַתִּצַּת בְּסִבְכֵי הַיַּעַר
וַיִּתְאַבְּכוּ גֵּאוּת עָשָׁן׃

18 בְּעֶבְרַת יְהוָה צְבָאוֹת נֶעְתַּם אָרֶץ
וַיְהִי הָעָם כְּמַאֲכֹלֶת אֵשׁ
אִישׁ אֶל־אָחִיו לֹא יַחְמֹלוּ׃

19 וַיִּגְזֹר עַל־יָמִין וְרָעֵב
וַיֹּאכַל עַל־שְׂמֹאל וְלֹא שָׂבֵעוּ
אִישׁ בְּשַׂר־זְרֹעוֹ יֹאכֵלוּ׃

15. *they that lead . . . err.* The leaders
are misleaders (Rashi).

16. *neither shall He have compassion.*
Even widows and orphans must suffer in
the midst of such godlessness and corruption (Kimchi).

17-20. Third strophe. Utter confusion
and dejection, widespread anarchy and
fratricidal war.

17. *briers and thorns.* Representing the
common people who are the first to
suffer in the national demoralization
(Kimchi).

thickets of the forest. The elders and rulers
will not escape the effects of their corruption (Kimchi).

19. The verse describes a grim state of
famine culminating in insanity.

20. Manasseh, Ephraim; and
    Ephraim, Manasseh;
    And they together are against
    Judah.
    For all this His anger is not
    turned away,
    But His hand is stretched out
    still.

fratricide & betrayal

20 מְנַשֶּׁה אֶת־אֶפְרַיִם
וְאֶפְרַיִם אֶת־מְנַשֶּׁה
יַחְדָּו הֵמָּה עַל־יְהוּדָה
בְּכָל־זֹאת לֹא־שָׁב אַפּוֹ
וְעוֹד יָדוֹ נְטוּיָה׃

with strophe

10   CHAPTER X

1. Woe unto them that decree
   unrighteous decrees,
   And to the writers that write
   iniquity;
2. To turn aside the needy from
   judgment,
   And to take away the right of the
   poor of My people,
   That widows may be their spoil,
   And that they may make the
   fatherless their prey!
3. And what will ye do in the day
   of visitation,
   And in the ruin which shall
   come from far?
   To whom will ye flee for help?
   And where will ye leave your
   glory?

money

1 הוֹי הַחֹקְקִים חִקְקֵי־אָוֶן
וּמְכַתְּבִים עָמָל כִּתֵּבוּ׃
2 לְהַטּוֹת מִדִּין דַּלִּים
וְלִגְזֹל מִשְׁפַּט עֲנִיֵּי עַמִּי
לִהְיוֹת אַלְמָנוֹת שְׁלָלָם
וְאֶת־יְתוֹמִים יָבֹזּוּ׃
3 וּמַה־תַּעֲשׂוּ לְיוֹם פְּקֻדָּה
וּלְשׁוֹאָה מִמֶּרְחָק תָּבוֹא
עַל־מִי תָּנוּסוּ לְעֶזְרָה
וְאָנָה תַעַזְבוּ כְּבוֹדְכֶם׃

---

20. *Manasseh, Ephraim.* There will be
intertribal strife and fratricide (Ibn
Ezra, Kimchi).

CHAPTER X

1–4. A strophe ending with the same
refrain as the three strophes in the preceding chapter. It may be regarded as
the last of a poem of four strophes and
as referring still to the Northern Kingdom (Abarbanel); or it may be viewed
as being connected with the following
oracle and like it referring to the Kingdom of Judah (Kara).

1. *decree unrighteous decrees.* Or, 'draw
up mischievous ordinances' (Kimchi).

the writers that write iniquity. Both the
judges and the scribes are employed in
framing legislation which enables them
to exploit the poor and the helpless
under the mask of legality (Ibn Ezra,
Kimchi).

2. The verse describes the aim and the
result of the legislation spoken of in the
preceding verse (Malbim).

3. A day of reckoning will come.

glory. The Hebrew word *kabod* may also
be rendered 'wealth,' as in Gen. xxxi. 1
and elsewhere (Rashi, Metsudath Zion).

4. They can do nought except
   crouch under the captives,
   And fall under the slain.
   For all this His anger is not
   turned away,
   But His hand is stretched out
   still.

5. O Asshur, the rod of Mine anger,
   In whose hand as a staff is Mine
   indignation!

6. I do send him against an ungodly
   nation,
   And against the people of My
   wrath do I give him a charge,
   To take the spoil, and to take the
   prey,
   And to tread them down like the
   mire of the streets.

7. Howbeit he meaneth not so,
   Neither doth his heart think so;
   But it is in his heart to destroy,
   And to cut off nations not a few.

בִּלְתִּי כָרַע תַּחַת אַסִּיר 4
וְתַחַת הֲרוּגִים יִפֹּלוּ
בְּכָל־זֹאת לֹא־שָׁב אַפּוֹ
וְעוֹד יָדוֹ נְטוּיָה׃

הוֹי אַשּׁוּר שֵׁבֶט אַפִּי 5
וּמַטֶּה־הוּא בְיָדָם זַעְמִי׃

בְּגוֹי חָנֵף אֲשַׁלְּחֶנּוּ 6
וְעַל־עַם עֶבְרָתִי אֲצַוֶּנּוּ
לִשְׁלֹל שָׁלָל וְלָבֹז בַּז
וּלְשִׂימוֹ מִרְמָס כְּחֹמֶר חוּצוֹת׃

וְהוּא לֹא־כֵן יְדַמֶּה 7
וּלְבָבוֹ לֹא־כֵן יַחְשֹׁב
כִּי לְהַשְׁמִיד בִּלְבָבוֹ
וּלְהַכְרִית גּוֹיִם לֹא מְעָט׃

v. 6. וְלָשׂוּמוֹ ק׳

---

4. *they can do nought . . . slain.* Or, except one (that might here and there) crouch among captives and fall under the slain,' as though they themselves were slain. There will be no escape for them from the Divine wrath (Ibn Ezra).

5-34. The Assyrian onslaught on Judah. Sennacherib's arrogance and self-glorification and the consequent destruction of his power. The date of this oracle may be some time between 717 and 701 B.C.E.

5-15. Assyria is entrusted with a mission to execute the Divine judgment but abuses it.

5-7. A contrast is drawn between God's plan and the Assyrian ambition and brutality.

5. *the rod of Mine anger.* Wherewith to punish wicked nations (Ibn Ezra).

in whose hand . . . indignation. It is not the military power of the Assyrians that conquers a people, but God's indignation resulting in the chastisement of that people and in the use of the Assyrians as His instrument for that purpose (Rashi).

6. *an ungodly nation.* An allusion to Israel (Rashi).

the people of My wrath. The people against whom My wrath is directed (Ibn Ezra).

7. *he meaneth not so.* Assyria does not recognize the Divine commission with which she has been entrusted, and acts in sheer self-interest and lust for conquest (Kimchi).

8-11. The Assyrian boast of successes in the past and confident assurance of easy victories in the future.

49

8. For he saith:
'Are not my princes all of them
kings?
9. Is not Calno as Carchemish?
Is not Hamath as Arpad?
Is not Samaria as Damascus?
10. As my hand hath reached the
kingdoms of the idols,
Whose graven images did exceed
them of Jerusalem and of
Samaria;
11. Shall I not, as I have done unto
Samaria and her idols,
So do to Jerusalem and her
idols?'
12. Wherefore it shall come to pass,
that when the Lord hath performed
His whole work upon mount Zion

כִּי יֹאמַר 8
הֲלֹא שָׂרַי יַחְדָּו מְלָכִים:
הֲלֹא כְּכַרְכְּמִישׁ כַּלְנוֹ 9
אִם־לֹא כְאַרְפַּד חֲמָת
אִם־לֹא כְדַמֶּשֶׂק שֹׁמְרוֹן:
כַּאֲשֶׁר מָצְאָה יָדִי לְמַמְלְכֹת הָאֱלִיל 10
וּפְסִילֵיהֶם מִירוּשָׁלַם וּמִשֹּׁמְרוֹן:
הֲלֹא כַּאֲשֶׁר עָשִׂיתִי 11
לְשֹׁמְרוֹן וְלֶאֱלִילֶיהָ
כֵּן אֶעֱשֶׂה לִירוּשָׁלַם וְלַעֲצַבֶּיהָ:
וְהָיָה כִּי־יְבַצַּע אֲדֹנָי אֶת־כָּל־ 12
מַעֲשֵׂהוּ בְּהַר צִיּוֹן וּבִירוּשָׁלָ͏ם אֶפְקֹד

8. *he saith.* The speaker is the Assyrian king (Rashi, Kimchi).

princes . . . kings. Assyrian rulers had by that time already assumed the title of 'king of kings,' and many of their princes and officers were in fact kings whose territories they had conquered and whom they pressed into their service (Kimchi).

9. A number of cities north of Judah, conquered by Assyrian kings, are enumerated.

Calno. Presumed to be Kullani near Arpad, and captured about 738 by Tiglath-pileser III.

Carchemish. Identified with the ruins of Jerabis on the right bank of the Euphrates. Formerly the capital of the Hittites, in 717 it was incorporated by Sargon in the Assyrian empire.

Hamath. The modern Hamah, halfway between Carchemish and Damascus on the river Orontes; it was captured in 738 by Tiglath-pileser and again in 720 by Sargon.

Arpad. The modern Tell Erfad, some fifteen miles north of Aleppo, captured by Tiglath-pileser about 720 (See Carta's Atlas of the Bible).

Samaria. Taken by the Assyrians in 722.

Damascus. Conquered by them about 732.

10. *idols.* A term of contempt, from the Hebrew *elil*, 'nonentity' (Rashi Lev. xxix. 4). The proud king of Assyria, who so easily subdued their lands and peoples, naturally regarded himself as much superior to all of them (Kimchi).

exceed. In number and importance.

11. *idols . . . idols.* The Hebrew for the former means 'nonentities,' 'sadnesses,' because they cause sadness and disappointment to their worshippers (Chotam Tochnit, Malbim) and for the latter. The former have already been suppressed; the latter are now being put to the test.

12. The indignant answer of the prophet, interrupting the blasphemy of the Assyrian who ventures to compare the God of Israel with the useless heathen idols.

His whole work. The full punishment the people deserved (Rashi).

and on Jerusalem, I will punish the fruit of the arrogant heart of the king of Assyria, and the glory of his haughty looks. 13. For he hath said:

By the strength of my hand I
　have done it,
And by my wisdom, for I am
　prudent;
In that I have removed the
　bounds of the peoples,
And have robbed their treasures,
And have brought down as one
　mighty the inhabitants;

14. And my hand hath found as a
　nest the riches of the peoples;
And as one gathereth eggs that
　are forsaken,
Have I gathered all the earth;
And there was none that moved
　the wing,
Or that opened the mouth, or
　chirped.

15. Should the axe boast itself
　against him that heweth there-
　with?
Should the saw magnify itself
　against him that moveth it?

עַל־פְּרִי־גֹדֶל לְבַב מֶלֶךְ־אַשּׁוּר
וְעַל־תִּפְאֶרֶת רוּם עֵינָיו:

13 כִּי אָמַר
בְּכֹחַ יָדִי עָשִׂיתִי
וּבְחָכְמָתִי כִּי נְבֻנֹתִי
וְאָסִיר ׀ גְּבוּלֹת עַמִּים
וַעֲתוּדֹתֵיהֶם שׁוֹשֵׂתִי
וְאוֹרִיד כַּאבִּיר יוֹשְׁבִים:

14 וַתִּמְצָא כַקֵּן ׀ יָדִי לְחֵיל הָעַמִּים
וְכֶאֱסֹף בֵּיצִים עֲזֻבוֹת
כָּל־הָאָרֶץ אֲנִי אָסָפְתִּי
וְלֹא הָיָה נֹדֵד כָּנָף
וּפֹצֶה פֶה וּמְצַפְצֵף:

15 הֲיִתְפָּאֵר הַגַּרְזֶן עַל הַחֹצֵב בּוֹ
אִם־יִתְגַּדֵּל הַמַּשּׂוֹר עַל־מְנִיפוֹ

v. 13. בביר ק'　v. 13. ועתודתיהם ק'

---

fruit of the arrogant heart. The Assyrian king's boastful and blasphemous language (Kimchi).

13f. Resumption of the speech of the king of Assyria with self-glorification and the parading of his wisdom and brutal power.

13. *I am prudent.* Or, 'I have insight,' to plan successful campaigns (Metsudath David).

removed the bounds. To prevent possible rebellion, conquering despots deported entire populations from one country to another (Kara), or amalgamated several small countries under a single administration (Kimchi).

treasures. lit. 'things prepared' for future use; 'stores' is a better translation (Ibn Ezra, Kimchi).

as one mighty. This rendering follows the *kethib*; the *kerë* means 'many inhabitants' (Rashi).

14. *as one gathereth eggs.* Descriptive of the ease of the Assyrian conquests; while *there was none,* etc. pictures the helplessness of the stricken victims created by terror of their formidable enemy (All commentaries).

15. *the axe.* Assyria, a mere tool in the hand of the Almighty *that heweth therewith* (Rashi).

as if a rod, etc. Rashi and Ibn Ezra appear to have had a slightly different reading, viz. *we-eth* instead of *eth.* The former comments: 'As the rod lifted itself and the hand that raised it! Is it not that a rod does not lift itself but is lifted by a man?'

51

As if a rod should move them
  that lift it up,
Or as if a staff should lift up him
  that is not wood.

16. Therefore will the Lord, the
    Lord of hosts,
Send among his fat ones lean-
  ness;
And under His glory there shall
  be kindled
A burning like the burning of
  fire.

17. And the light of Israel shall be
  for a fire,
And his Holy One for a flame;
And it shall burn and devour
  his thorns
And his briers in one day.

18. And the glory of his forest and
  of his fruitful field,
He will consume both soul and
  body;
And it shall be as when a sick
  man wasteth away.

19. And the remnant of the trees of
  his forest shall be few,
That a child may write them
  down.

כְּהָנִיף שֵׁבֶט אֶת־מְרִימָיו
כְּהָרִים מַטֶּה לֹא־עֵץ׃
16 לָכֵן יְשַׁלַּח הָאָדוֹן
יְהוָה צְבָאוֹת בְּמִשְׁמַנָּיו רָזוֹן
וְתַחַת כְּבֹדוֹ
יֵקַד יְקֹד כִּיקוֹד אֵשׁ׃
17 וְהָיָה אוֹר־יִשְׂרָאֵל לְאֵשׁ
וּקְדוֹשׁוֹ לְלֶהָבָה
וּבָעֲרָה וְאָכְלָה
שִׁיתוֹ וּשְׁמִירוֹ בְּיוֹם אֶחָד׃
18 וּכְבוֹד יַעְרוֹ וְכַרְמִלּוֹ
מִנֶּפֶשׁ וְעַד־בָּשָׂר יְכַלֶּה
וְהָיָה כִּמְסֹס נֹסֵס׃
19 וּשְׁאָר עֵץ יַעְרוֹ מִסְפָּר יִהְיוּ
וְנַעַר יִכְתְּבֵם׃

not wood. A compound noun,
'notwood,' denoting a human being. It
is the man that lifts up the staff, but
the staff does not lift up the man. All the
metaphors in the verse symbolize
Assyria's impotence in the absence of
the directing hand of the Ruler of the
universe (Rashi).

16–23. The fall of Assyria and the
return of the survivors of Israel unto
God.

16–19. Assyria will be destroyed by
disease and fire.

16. the Lord, the Lord of hosts. See on
1. 24.

among his fat ones. Or, 'into his fat limbs.'
The reference is to the mighty Assyrian
warriors who were to be slain by the

angel on the night of the destruction of
the Assyrian camp (Ibn Ezra, Kimchi).

17. light of Israel. Some explain as God
(Ibn Ezra), others as the Torah (Rashi).

his Holy one. Israel's God. Others understand it as the righteous men of the time
(Laniado).

thorns . . . briers. The rank and file, as in
ix. 17 (Laniado).

18. the glory . . . field. Alluding to the
captains and officers (Laniado).

19. a child may write them down. So few
of them will remain that even a child
could write down all their names. Their
is a Rabbinical tradition that only ten
men survived and, as this number is
represented in Hebrew by the letter yod
which is a mere stroke, a little child
could do it (Sanh. 95b).

20. And it shall come to pass in that
    day,
    That the remnant of Israel,
    And they that are escaped of the
    house of Jacob,
    Shall no more again stay upon
    him that smote them;
    But shall stay upon the LORD,
    the Holy One of Israel, in
    truth.
21. A remnant shall return, even
    the remnant of Jacob,
    Unto God the Mighty.
22. For though thy people, O Israel,
    be as the sand of the sea,
    Only a remnant of them shall
    return;
    An extermination is determined,
    overflowing with righteous-
    ness.
23. For an extermination wholly
    determined
    Shall the Lord, the GOD of hosts,
    make in the midst of all the
    earth.

20 וְהָיָה ׀ בַּיּוֹם הַהוּא
לֹא־יוֹסִיף עוֹד
שְׁאָר יִשְׂרָאֵל
וּפְלֵיטַת בֵּית־יַעֲקֹב
לְהִשָּׁעֵן עַל־מַכֵּהוּ
וְנִשְׁעַן עַל־יְהֹוָה
קְדוֹשׁ יִשְׂרָאֵל בֶּאֱמֶת:
21 שְׁאָר יָשׁוּב שְׁאָר יַעֲקֹב
אֶל־אֵל גִּבּוֹר:
22 כִּי אִם־יִהְיֶה
עַמְּךָ יִשְׂרָאֵל כְּחוֹל הַיָּם
שְׁאָר יָשׁוּב בּוֹ
כִּלָּיוֹן חָרוּץ שׁוֹטֵף צְדָקָה:
23 כִּי כָלָה וְנֶחֱרָצָה
אֲדֹנָי יְהֹוִה צְבָאוֹת
עֹשֶׂה בְּקֶרֶב כָּל־הָאָרֶץ:

20–23. The survivors in Israel will return to God and henceforth place their trust in Him alone.

20. *no more again stay upon.* The reference is to Assyria with whom Ahaz had made an alliance (cf. 2 Kings xvi 7ff.) against the wish of Isaiah (Kimchi).

him that smote them. viz. Assyria. The folly of the alliance was fully realized in the reign of Hezekiah (Kimchi).

the Holy One of Israel, in truth. I.e. with sincerity (Kimchi, Abarbanel, Metsu-dath David).

21. *a remnant shall return.* Hebrew *shear jashub,* the name given to one of Isaiah's

sons (vii. 3) as a sign and prediction which is now being fulfilled (Ibn Ezra). *God the mighty* (*el gibbor*) is similarly a reference to the name assigned to the young Hezekiah in ix. 5.

22. *as the sand of the sea.* In fulfillment of the promise made to the patriarchs (cf. Gen. xxii. 17, xxxii. 13).

overflowing with righteousness. Since the punishment of the wicked and corrupt majority was well deserved (Metsudath David).

23. *in the midst of all the earth.* Involving the Assyrians in particular, but Israel will not be immune from God's process of extermination (Abarbanel).

24. Therefore thus saith the Lord, the GOD of hosts: O My people that dwellest in Zion, be not afraid of Asshur, though he smite thee with the rod, and lift up his staff against thee, after the manner of Egypt. 25. For yet a very little while, and the indignation shall be accomplished, and Mine anger shall be to their destruction. 26. And the LORD of hosts shall stir up against him a scourge, as in the slaughter of Midian at the Rock of Oreb; and as His rod was over the sea, so shall He lift it up after the manner of Egypt. 27. And it shall come to pass in that day, that

His burden shall depart from off thy shoulder,
And his yoke from off thy neck,
And the yoke shall be destroyed by reason of fatness.

28. He is come to Aiath, He is passed through Migron;

כ֣ד לָכֵ֗ן כֹּֽה־אָמַ֞ר אֲדֹנָ֧י יְהוִ֛ה צְבָא֖וֹת
אַל־תִּירָ֥א עַמִּ֛י יֹשֵׁ֥ב צִיּ֖וֹן מֵֽאַשּׁ֑וּר
בַּשֵּׁ֣בֶט יַכֶּ֔כָּה וּמַטֵּ֖הוּ יִשָּֽׂא־עָלֶ֑יךָ
כה בְּדֶ֣רֶךְ מִצְרָֽיִם: כִּי־ע֖וֹד מְעַ֣ט מִזְעָ֑ר
וְכָ֣לָה זַ֔עַם וְאַפִּ֖י עַל־תַּבְלִיתָֽם:
כו וְעוֹרֵ֨ר עָלָ֜יו יְהוָ֤ה צְבָאוֹת֙ שׁ֔וֹט
כְּמַכַּ֥ת מִדְיָ֖ן בְּצ֣וּר עוֹרֵ֑ב וּמַטֵּ֙הוּ֙
עַל־הַיָּ֔ם וּנְשָׂא֖וֹ בְּדֶ֥רֶךְ מִצְרָֽיִם:
כז וְהָיָ֣ה ׀ בַּיּ֣וֹם הַה֗וּא
יָס֤וּר סֻבֳּלוֹ֙ מֵעַ֣ל שִׁכְמֶ֔ךָ
וְעֻלּ֖וֹ מֵעַ֣ל צַוָּארֶ֑ךָ
וְחֻבַּ֥ל עֹ֖ל מִפְּנֵי־שָֽׁמֶן:
כח בָּ֥א עַל־עַיַּ֖ת
עָבַ֣ר בְּמִגְר֑וֹן

24–27. A message of comfort and hope, addressed to the faithful remnant.

24. *therefore.* Since the righteous will survive (Abarbanel).
after the manner of Egypt. The bondage endured by the early Israelites in Egypt (Rashi).

25. *their destruction.* The destruction of the Assyrians (Ibn Ezra, Kimchi).

26. *against him.* The Assyrian oppressor (all commentaries).

as . . . Oreb. Cf. Judg. vii. 25.

as His rod was over the sea. When Israel was delivered and the Egyptians were drowned (Exod. xiv. 21 ff.) (all commentaries). The ending of this verse is meant to be contrasted with the ending of verse 24.

27. *the yoke . . . fatness.* As the increasing fatness of an animal would burst the

yoke on its neck, so would Israel's renewed vigour and growing prosperity break down all foreign oppression (See Kimchi, Metsudath David).

28–32. A graphic description of the march of the Assyrian army through various towns on the northern approaches to Jerusalem.

28. *Aiath.* Assumed to be the ancient town of Ai (Josh. vii. 2), about two miles north-west from Michmash (Malbim). Some identify it with Khirbat E-tell, northwest of Deir-dibon, near Beitin (identified with Bethel). Some believe that it is one of the ruins near Beitin, whose identity is yet unknown (Daath Mikra).

Migron. [An unidentified place which was probably situated between Michmash and Ai. Some identify it with the modern Makrun, a ruined site north of Michmash.]

(handwritten marginalia: "2 mi ne of Geva", "3 mi ne of Jeru", "3 aw?")

At Michmas he layeth up his
    baggage;

29. They are gone over the pass;
    They have taken up their lodging
        at Geba;
    Ramah trembleth;
    Gibeath-shaul is fled.

30. Cry thou with a shrill voice, O
        daughter of Gallim!
    Hearken, O Laish! O thou poor
        Anathoth!

31. Madmenah is in mad flight;
    The inhabitants of Gebim flee
        to cover.

32. This very day shall he halt at
        Nob,
    Shaking his hand at the mount
        of the daughter of Zion,
    The hill of Jerusalem.

33. Behold, the Lord, the LORD of
        hosts,
    Shall lop the boughs with terror;
    And the high ones of stature shall
        be hewn down,
    And the lofty shall be laid low.

לְמִכְמָשׂ יַפְקִיד כֵּלָיו:

29 עָבְרוּ מַעְבָּרָה
    גֶּבַע מָלוֹן לָנוּ
    חָרְדָה הָרָמָה
    גִּבְעַת שָׁאוּל נָסָה:

30 צַהֲלִי קוֹלֵךְ בַּת־גַּלִּים
    הַקְשִׁיבִי לַיְשָׁה עֲנִיָּה עֲנָתוֹת:

31 נָדְדָה מַדְמֵנָה
    יֹשְׁבֵי הַגֵּבִים הֵעִיזוּ:

32 עוֹד הַיּוֹם בְּנֹב לַעֲמֹד
    יְנֹפֵף יָדוֹ הַר בֵּית־צִיּוֹן
    גִּבְעַת יְרוּשָׁלָ͏ִם:

33 הִנֵּה הָאָדוֹן יְהוָה צְבָאוֹת
    מְסָעֵף פֻּארָה בְּמַעֲרָצָה
    וְרָמֵי הַקּוֹמָה גְּדֻעִים
    וְהַגְּבֹהִים יִשְׁפָּלוּ:

v. 32. הפטרת יום שמיני של פסח בת ק'

Michmash. The city Michmash, now
called Muchmas, lies less than two miles
north-east of Geba (cf. I Sam. xiii. 2ff.)
(See Carta's Atlas of the Bible).

layeth up his baggage. To cross the wadi,
the banks of which are very steep (See
Malbim).

28. *the pass.* Near Michmash in the
hills of Judah about eight miles north-
east from Jerusalem (Malbim).

Geba. A city south of the pass of Michmash, five miles north of Jerusalem (See
Carta).

Gibeath-shaul. Probably Tell el-Ful,
about midway between Jerusalem and
Ramah (Carta).

30. *Gallim . . . Laish.* Both these villages are unknown.

Anathoth. Full three miles north-east
from the capital; the home of Jeremiah
(Jer. i. 1).

31. The places mentioned in this verse
cannot be traced on our maps.

32. *Nob.* Described as *the city of the
priests* in I Sam. xxii. 19. It cannot be
identified though it was obviously a
place near Jerusalem. It has been suggested that it may have been situated on
Mount Scopus to the north of the city
on which the Hebrew University now
stands.

33f. The Assyrian army's destruction
at the very moment when it believed
itself to be knocking at the gates of victory. The metaphor is that of a forest
being cut down by the axe of the wood-
man.

34. And He shall cut down the thickets of the forest with iron, And Lebanon shall fall by a mighty one.

וְנִקַּף סִבְכֵי הַיַּעַר בַּבַּרְזֶל
וְהַלְּבָנוֹן בְּאַדִּיר יִפּוֹל: 34

11   CHAPTER XI   יא

1. And there shall come forth a shoot out of the stock of Jesse, And a twig shall grow forth out of his roots.

וְיָצָא חֹטֶר מִגֵּזַע יִשָׁי
וְנֵצֶר מִשָּׁרָשָׁיו יִפְרֶה: 1

2. And the spirit of the LORD shall rest upon him, The spirit of wisdom and understanding, The spirit of counsel and might, The spirit of knowledge and of the fear of the LORD.

וְנָחָה עָלָיו רוּחַ יְהֹוָה
רוּחַ חָכְמָה וּבִינָה
רוּחַ עֵצָה וּגְבוּרָה
רוּחַ דַּעַת וְיִרְאַת יְהֹוָה: 2

---

33. *the Lord*, etc. See on i. 24.

with terror. This translation is not found in the Jewish commentaries. Rashi renders: 'with a saw'; Ibn Ezra and Kimchi, 'with might.'

34. *with iron*. In Deut. xix. 5 the word denotes the metal part of an axe.

Lebanon. The proud status of Assyria is likened to the majestic cedars on the Lebanon mount (Rashi).

a mighty one. God's angel (cf. xxxvii. 36) (Rashi, Kimchi).

CHAPTER XI

THE MESSIANIC AGE

THE prophet consoled the survivors in Jerusalem during the reign of Hezekiah. Now he consoles the exiles, who will be returned to the Holy Land by the Messiah son of David (Rashi).

1. *a shoot*. This contrasts with the last two verses of the previous chapter. The Assyrian forest will be cut down and end in everlasting desolation, but the stock of Judah will produce fresh shoots and new life (Malbim).

Jesse. The father of David symbolizes the Davidic dynasty (Metsudath David).

a twig . . . roots. Or, 'a branch out of his roots shall bear fruit' (Metsudath Zion).

2. The qualities which will distinguish the ideal ruler are enumerated under three headings, each of which consists of two terms relating to his intellectual, administrative and spiritual attributes respectively (Malbim).

wisdom and understanding. Similarly with Bezalel, *the spirit of God* manifested itself in *wisdom and understanding* (Exod. xxxv. 31).

3. And his delight shall be in the
  fear of the LORD;
And he shall not judge after the
  sight of his eyes,
Neither decide after the hearing
  of his ears;

4. But with righteousness shall he
  judge the poor,
And decide with equity for the
  meek of the land;
And he shall smite the land with
  the rod of his mouth,
And with the breath of his lips
  shall he slay the wicked.

5. And righteousness shall be the
  girdle of his loins,
And faithfulness the girdle of his
  reins.

6. And the wolf shall dwell with
  the lamb,
And the leopard shall lie down
  with the kid;
And the calf and the young lion
  and the fatling together;
And a little child shall lead them.

³ וַהֲרִיחוֹ בְּיִרְאַת יְהֹוָה
וְלֹא־לְמַרְאֵה עֵינָיו יִשְׁפּוֹט
וְלֹא־לְמִשְׁמַע אָזְנָיו יוֹכִיחַ׃

⁴ וְשָׁפַט בְּצֶדֶק דַּלִּים
וְהוֹכִיחַ בְּמִישׁוֹר לְעַנְוֵי־אָרֶץ
וְהִכָּה־אֶרֶץ בְּשֵׁבֶט פִּיו
וּבְרוּחַ שְׂפָתָיו יָמִית רָשָׁע׃

⁵ וְהָיָה צֶדֶק אֵזוֹר מָתְנָיו
וְהָאֱמוּנָה אֵזוֹר חֲלָצָיו׃

⁶ וְגָר זְאֵב עִם־כֶּבֶשׂ
וְנָמֵר עִם־גְּדִי יִרְבָּץ
וְעֵגֶל וּכְפִיר וּמְרִיא יַחְדָּו
וְנַעַר קָטֹן נֹהֵג בָּם׃

3-5. His government will be one of
impartial justice, marked by righteousness and fear of God.

3. *his delight.* lit. 'his smelling' (of satisfaction). Others render: 'And his smelling shall be through the fear of the
Lord.' His perception will be so keen, it
will be as though he smelled the facts
(Ibn Ezra, Metsudath David).

his eyes . . . his ears. He will not be guided
by the superficial impressions of the
senses (Ibn Ezra).

4. *the poor.* Usually deprived of their
rights by the wealthy (Kimchi).

the meek. Or, 'the oppressed' (Targum).

the land. i.e. the guilty men in the land
(Targum). Some render *the earth* (Abarbanel) interpreting the sphere of the
ideal ruler as universal.

5. *girdle.* A symbol of strength. He will

derive his power and influence from the
sources of righteousness and faith
(Kimchi).

6-8. Universal peace and harmony
among men will also be extended to the
animal world. The wild beasts will not
prey on the weak and domesticated
animals, nor will man and beast stand
in fear of each other. According to
some, this will be true only in the Holy
Land (Kimchi).

6. Harmonious association of the
beasts of prey, the domestic animals
and the human being. A similar idyllic
scene is drawn in lxv. 25.

a little child shall lead them. The superior-
ity of the human race, represented by a
young child, with its potentialities for
the universal good, will be acknowledged by the submission of the animal
kingdom (Hirsch).

7. And the cow and the bear shall
    feed;
   Their young ones shall lie down
    together;
   And the lion shall eat straw like
    the ox.
8. And the sucking child shall play
    on the hole of the asp,
   And the weaned child shall put
    his hand on the basilisk's den.
9. They shall not hurt nor destroy
   In all My holy mountain;
   For the earth shall be full of the
    knowledge of the LORD,
   As the waters cover the sea.
10. And it shall come to pass in that
    day,
    That the root of Jesse, that
    standeth for an ensign of the
    peoples,
    Unto him shall the nations seek;
    And his resting-place shall be
    glorious.
11. And it shall come to pass in that
    day,
    That the Lord will set His hand
    again the second time
    To recover the remnant of His
    people,

7 וּפָרָה וָדֹב תִּרְעֶינָה
יַחְדָּו יִרְבְּצוּ יַלְדֵיהֶן
וְאַרְיֵה כַּבָּקָר יֹאכַל־תֶּבֶן׃
8 וְשִׁעֲשַׁע יוֹנֵק עַל־חֻר פָּתֶן
וְעַל מְאוּרַת צִפְעוֹנִי גָּמוּל יָדוֹ הָדָה׃
9 לֹא־יָרֵעוּ וְלֹא־יַשְׁחִיתוּ
בְּכָל־הַר קָדְשִׁי
כִּי־מָלְאָה הָאָרֶץ דֵּעָה אֶת־יְהֹוָה
כַּמַּיִם לַיָּם מְכַסִּים׃
10 וְהָיָה בַּיּוֹם הַהוּא
שֹׁרֶשׁ יִשַׁי אֲשֶׁר עֹמֵד לְנֵס עַמִּים
אֵלָיו גּוֹיִם יִדְרֹשׁוּ
וְהָיְתָה מְנֻחָתוֹ כָּבוֹד׃
11 וְהָיָה ׀ בַּיּוֹם הַהוּא
יוֹסִיף אֲדֹנָי ׀ שֵׁנִית יָדוֹ
לִקְנוֹת אֶת־שְׁאָר עַמּוֹ

---

7. The animals will no longer prey on
each other. Even the wild beasts will
lose their blood-thirstiness and be satisfied with a meal of straw.

8. The poisonous serpent, too, will be
harmless.

den. (Targum). Others translate, 'glittering eye' (Targum).

9. The first part of the verse may have
as its antecedent the animals mentioned
in the preceding three verses, or the
subject may be indefinite (Ibn Ezra) and
the meaning be 'none shall hurt,' etc.
(Kara).

My holy mountain. Zion, or all the Land
of Israel (Kimchi).

10–16. The return of the exiles.

10. This verse seems to be detached
from the following, forming by itself a
complete thought.

root. A descendant (Kimchi).

an ensign. A signal for rallying the
people (Kimchi).

unto him shall the nations seek. To pledge
their allegiance to him and await his
commands (Kimchi).

resting-place. Residence (Targum).

11. set His hand. The verb set is
implied.

the second time. The first time was the
exodus from Egypt (All commentaries).

That shall remain from Assyria,
and from Egypt,
And from Pathros, and from
Cush, and from Elam,
And from Shinar, and from
Hamath, and from the islands
of the sea.

12. And He will set up an ensign for
the nations,
And will assemble the dispersed
of Israel,
And gather together the scattered
of Judah
From the four corners of the
earth.

13. The envy also of Ephraim shall
depart,
And they that harass Judah shall
be cut off;
Ephraim shall not envy Judah,
And Judah shall not vex
Ephraim.

14. And they shall fly down upon
the shoulder of the Philistines
on the west;
Together shall they spoil the
children of the east;
They shall put forth their hand
upon Edom and Moab;
And the children of Ammon shall
obey them.

אֲשֶׁר יִשָּׁאֵר מֵאַשּׁוּר וּמִמִּצְרַיִם
וּמִפַּתְרוֹס וּמִכּוּשׁ וּמֵעֵילָם
וּמִשִּׁנְעָר וּמֵחֲמָת וּמֵאִיֵּי הַיָּם:

12 וְנָשָׂא נֵס לַגּוֹיִם
וְאָסַף נִדְחֵי יִשְׂרָאֵל
וּנְפֻצוֹת יְהוּדָה יְקַבֵּץ
מֵאַרְבַּע כַּנְפוֹת הָאָרֶץ:

13 וְסָרָה קִנְאַת אֶפְרַיִם
וְצֹרְרֵי יְהוּדָה יִכָּרֵתוּ
אֶפְרַיִם לֹא יְקַנֵּא אֶת יְהוּדָה
וִיהוּדָה לֹא יָצֹר אֶת אֶפְרָיִם:

14 וְעָפוּ בְכָתֵף פְּלִשְׁתִּים יָמָּה
יַחְדָּו יָבֹזּוּ אֶת בְּנֵי קֶדֶם
אֱדוֹם וּמוֹאָב מִשְׁלוֹחַ יָדָם
וּבְנֵי עַמּוֹן מִשְׁמַעְתָּם:

Pathros. In Upper Egypt (Biberfeld).

Cush. i.e. Ethiopia. Pathros and Cush
were among the dependencies of Egypt
(Biberfeld).

Elam. Susiana, north-east of the Persian
Gulf (Biberfeld).

Shinar. Babylonia (cf. Gen. x. 10).

Hamath. See on x. 9. The last three
places were dependencies of Assyria.

islands of the sea. The Mediterranean
coast-lands (Rashi, Kimchi).

12.   *an ensign for the nations.* A signal for
the afore-mentioned nations to yield up
the Israelite exiles in their midst, or for
the exiles to see and gather round it (All
commentaries).

13.   *the envy also of Ephraim.* Toward
Judah (Ibn Ezra).

they that harass Judah. The parallelism
requires, and the second part of the
verse confirms, the translation: 'the
adversaries (of Ephraim) in Judah,' a
rendering which is rather forced, but
may be grammatically justified (Kimchi).

14.   *upon the shoulder.* The land of the
Philistines. Or, 'upon its side.' The land
of the Philistines on the west coast of the
Holy Land (Kimchi).

the children of the east. The Arabian tribes
who live in the eastern desert (Daath
Mikra, Judg. vi. 3).

put forth their hand upon. lit. 'the putting
forth of their hand.' Edom, Moab and
Ammon were inveterate enemies of
Israel, but they will submit to the ideal
ruler (Rashi).

15. And the LORD will utterly
destroy the tongue of the
Egyptian sea; _Suez_
And with His scorching wind
will He shake His hand over
the River,
And will smite it into seven
streams,
And cause men to march over
dryshod. _in sandals_

16. And there shall be a highway for
the remnant of His people,
That shall remain from Assyria;
Like as there was for Israel
In the day that he came up out
of the land of Egypt.

וְהֶחֱרִים יְהֹוָה אֵת לְשׁוֹן יָם־מִצְרַיִם 15

וְהֵנִיף יָדוֹ עַל־הַנָּהָר בַּעְיָם רוּחוֹ

וְהִכָּהוּ לְשִׁבְעָה נְחָלִים

וְהִדְרִיךְ בַּנְּעָלִים:

וְהָיְתָה מְסִלָּה לִשְׁאָר עַמּוֹ 16

אֲשֶׁר יִשָּׁאֵר מֵאַשּׁוּר

כַּאֲשֶׁר הָיְתָה לְיִשְׂרָאֵל

בְּיוֹם עֲלֹתוֹ מֵאֶרֶץ מִצְרָיִם:

12   CHAPTER XII   יב

1. And in that day thou shalt say:
'I will give thanks unto Thee, O
LORD;
For though Thou wast angry
with me,
Thine anger is turned away, and
Thou comfortest me.

וְאָמַרְתָּ בַּיּוֹם הַהוּא 1

אוֹדְךָ יְהֹוָה

כִּי אָנַפְתָּ בִּי

יָשֹׁב אַפְּךָ וּתְנַחֲמֵנִי:

---

shall obey them. lit. 'their obedience.'

15f. As at the exodus from Egypt, a
highway will be prepared for the returning exiles.

15. _the tongue of the Egyptian sea._ The
gulf of Suez, for the exiles to cross when
returning from the direction of Egypt.
Jewish commentators, however, identify
it with the Nile (Kimchi, Abarbanel).

the River. The Euphrates, for those
journeying from the direction of Assyria
(Rashi, Kimchi, Targum).

seven. The number is not to be taken
literally. It is here synonymous with
'many' (Kimchi).

dryshod. lit. 'in sandals.'

16. _highway._ Through gulf and river
(Rashi).

CHAPTER XII

THE chapter, consisting of two hymns, is
regarded by certain authorities as the
conclusion of the first division of
Isaiah's prophecies which began with
chapter i.

1f. The two verses are thought to com-
pose a hymn that was sung by the community here visualized as one individual.

1. _in that day._ Of deliverance and
return to Zion (Malbim).

thou shalt say. The prophet addresses the
community (Ibn Ezra).

though. Implied in the context (Ibn
Ezra).

2. Behold, God is my salvation;
I will trust, and will not be
afraid;
For GOD the LORD is my strength
and song;
And He is become my salvation.'

3. Therefore with joy shall ye draw
water
Out of the wells of salvation.

4. And in that day shall ye say:
'Give thanks unto the LORD,
proclaim His name,
Declare His doings among the
peoples,
Make mention that His name is
exalted.

5. Sing unto the LORD; for He hath
done gloriously;
This is made known in all the
earth.

6. Cry aloud and shout, thou
inhabitant of Zion;
For great is the Holy One of
Israel in the midst of thee.'

² הִנֵּה אֵל יְשׁוּעָתִי
אֶבְטַח וְלֹא אֶפְחָד
כִּי עָזִּי וְזִמְרָת יָהּ יְהֹוָה
וַיְהִי־לִי לִישׁוּעָה:

³ וּשְׁאַבְתֶּם־מַיִם בְּשָׂשׂוֹן
מִמַּעַיְנֵי הַיְשׁוּעָה:

⁴ וַאֲמַרְתֶּם בַּיּוֹם הַהוּא
הוֹדוּ לַיהֹוָה קִרְאוּ בִשְׁמוֹ
הוֹדִיעוּ בָעַמִּים עֲלִילֹתָיו
הַזְכִּירוּ כִּי נִשְׂגָּב שְׁמוֹ:

⁵ זַמְּרוּ יְהֹוָה כִּי גֵאוּת עָשָׂה
מְיֻדַּעַת זֹאת בְּכָל־הָאָרֶץ:

⁶ צַהֲלִי וָרֹנִּי יוֹשֶׁבֶת צִיּוֹן
כִּי־גָדוֹל בְּקִרְבֵּךְ קְדוֹשׁ יִשְׂרָאֵל:

13 CHAPTER XIII

1. The burden of Babylon, which
Isaiah the son of Amoz did see.

¹ מַשָּׂא בָּבֶל אֲשֶׁר חָזָה יְשַׁעְיָהוּ בֶּן־
אָמוֹץ:

v. 6. ק׳ מוֹדַעַת v. 5. ע״ב

---

2. The second section of the verse is
almost a repetition of Exod. xv. 2, and
both verses 2 and 3 form the beginning
of the *Habdalah* or the benediction and
Scriptural texts recited at the termina-
tion of the Sabbath.

3. *dr*... *wells of salvation*. A metaphor special appeal to an Eastern
people which depended for life upon
wells. A promise of God's bounty. Cf.
Jer. ii. 13 where God is described as *the
fountain of living waters* (See Kimchi).

4. *shall ye say*. The delivered people to
one another (Ibn Ezra, Kimchi).

6. *inhabitant of Zion*. lit. 'inhabitress,'

Zion, as elsewhere, being addressed as a
female.

CHAPTER XIII

THE DOOM OF BABYLON

A NEW section begins with this chapter
extending to the end of xxiii in which
the prophet surveys the neighbouring
peoples with whom Israel has had relations and pronounces their fate. He first
deals with Babylon in xiii. 1-xiv. 23.

1. Superscription.

burden. This is the literal meaning of the
Hebrew word *massa*. It signifies 'a lifting

2. Set ye up an ensign upon the
   high mountain,
   Lift up the voice unto them,
   Wave the hand, that they may go
   Into the gates of the nobles.

3. I have commanded My consecrated ones,
   Yea, I have called My mighty
   ones for Mine anger,
   Even My proudly exulting ones.

4. Hark, a tumult in the mountains,
   Like as of a great people!
   Hark, the uproar of the kingdoms
   Of the nations gathered together!
   The LORD of hosts mustereth
   The host of the battle.

² עַל הַר־נִשְׁפֶּה שְׂאוּ־נֵס
הָרִימוּ קוֹל לָהֶם
הָנִיפוּ יָד וְיָבֹאוּ
פִּתְחֵי נְדִיבִים׃
³ אֲנִי צִוֵּיתִי לִמְקֻדָּשָׁי
גַּם קָרָאתִי גִבּוֹרַי לְאַפִּי
עַלִּיזֵי גַאֲוָתִי׃
⁴ קוֹל הָמוֹן בֶּהָרִים
דְּמוּת עַם־רָב
קוֹל שָׁאוֹן
מַמְלְכוֹת גּוֹיִם נֶאֱסָפִים
יְהוָה צְבָאוֹת מְפַקֵּד
צְבָא מִלְחָמָה׃

Bab-ilu – gate of God.

up' or 'a gift,' given to the prophet by
the Almighty (Abarbanel).

2–4. The muster of the hosts.

2. *an ensign.* A signal for the armies to
assemble for the advance against Babylon (Rashi, Kimchi).

upon the high mountain. So that the signal
could be seen from afar (Ibn Ezra,
Kimchi). An alternative translation is
'tranquil mountain,' trusting, unaware
of its impending doom (Targum,
Rashi).

unto them. The invading hosts (Rashi,
Ibn Ezra, Kimchi).

gates of the nobles. Suggestive of the name
of Babylon which is derived from Babel
(*Bab-ilu*), 'gate of God.' The traditional
Hebrew etymology of the name is 'con-
fusion' (cf. Gen. xi. 9) (See Biberfeld,
Universal Jewish History, vol. 1, p. 96).

3. The voice of God.

My consecrated ones. Most Jewish commentators render: 'My designated
ones.' The Medes and the Persians who

were designated by God to carry out
His will against Babylon (Targum,
Rashi, Ibn Eza, Kimchi).

My proudly exulting ones. i.e. soldiers
exulting in the assurance of victory (Ibn
Ezra).

4. The prophet can already hear the
noise and tumult of the gathering
legions.

the mountains. The land of the Medes
north-east of Babylonia beyond the
Zagros range. 'This was the quarter
from which the forces of Cyrus, attacked
the empire of Nabonidus and brought
about its overthrow in 538–6' Forsee-
ing the end of the kingdom, Nabonidus
moved his capital to the Desert of Tema,
leaving Belshazzar in Babylon, to conduct government affairs. He was slain
on the night of the attack (Carta).

5–8. The avenging hosts are commanded by the Lord Himself. Babylon's
feeling of terror and helplessness is
described.

5. *the weapons of His indignation.* They

5. They come from a far country,
   From the end of heaven,
   Even the LORD, and the weapons
      of His indignation,
   To destroy the whole earth.

6. Howl ye; for the day of the LORD
      is at hand;
   As destruction from the Al-
      mighty shall it come.

7. Therefore shall all hands be
      slack,
   And every heart of man shall
      melt.

8. And they shall be affrighted;
   Pangs and throes shall take hold
      of them;
   They shall be in pain as a woman
      in travail;
   They shall look aghast one at
      another;
   Their faces shall be faces of
      flame.

9. Behold, the day of the LORD
      cometh,
   Cruel, and full of wrath and
      fierce anger;
   To make the earth a desolation,
   And to destroy the sinners
      thereof out of it.

10. For the stars of heaven and the
      constellations thereof

5 בָּאִים מֵאֶרֶץ מֶרְחָק
מִקְצֵה הַשָּׁמָיִם
יְהֹוָה וּכְלֵי זַעְמֹו
לְחַבֵּל כָּל־הָאָרֶץ:

6 הֵילִילוּ כִּי קָרֹוב יֹום יְהֹוָה
כְּשֹׁד מִשַּׁדַּי יָבֹוא:

7 עַל־כֵּן כָּל־יָדַיִם תִּרְפֶּינָה
וְכָל־לְבַב אֱנֹושׁ יִמָּס:

8 וְנִבְהָלוּ |
צִירִים וַחֲבָלִים יֹאחֵזוּן
כַּיֹּולֵדָה יְחִילוּן
אִישׁ אֶל־רֵעֵהוּ יִתְמָהוּ
פְּנֵי לְהָבִים פְּנֵיהֶם:

9 הִנֵּה יֹום־יְהֹוָה בָּא
אַכְזָרִי וְעֶבְרָה וַחֲרֹון אָף
לָשׂוּם הָאָרֶץ לְשַׁמָּה
וְחַטָּאֶיהָ יַשְׁמִיד מִמֶּנָּה:

10 כִּי־כֹוכְבֵי הַשָּׁמַיִם וּכְסִילֵיהֶם

Joel 1.15

Orion

v. 8. קמץ בז״ק

---

are the attacking forces about to execute
the Divine purpose determined by
God's anger against Babylon (Kimchi).

whole earth. Better, 'the whole land,'
meaning 'the whole land of Babylonia
(Rashi, Kimchi, Abarbanel).

6. *as destruction from the Almighty.* The
Hebrew, *keshod mi-shaddai,* is an alliteration that cannot be reproduced in translation. Apart from the introductory
word, the verse is identical with Joel i.
15.

7. *all hands be slack.* So terror-stricken

will the Babylonians be that they will
lose the power to resist attack (Kimchi).

8. *faces of flame.* Burning with shame or
with impotent rage (Kimchi).

9-16. A fuller description of Babylon's day of doom.

9-12. The terror and destruction, and
the extermination of wickedness and
arrogance.

9. *the earth.* Babylon is intended as in
verse 5.

10. *the constellations thereof.* lit. 'their
Orions' (cf. Amos v. 8).

Shall not give their light;
The sun shall be darkened in his
going forth,
And the moon shall not cause
her light to shine.

11. And I will visit upon the world
their evil,
And upon the wicked their
iniquity;
And I will cause the arrogancy
of the proud to cease,
And will lay low the haughtiness
of the tyrants.

12. I will make man more rare than
fine gold,
Even man than the pure gold of
Ophir.

13. Therefore I will make the
heavens to tremble,
And the earth shall be shaken
out of her place,
For the wrath of the LORD of
hosts,
And for the day of His fierce
anger.

14. And it shall come to pass, that as
the chased gazelle,
And as sheep that no man
gathereth,
They shall turn every man, to
his own people,
And shall flee every man to his
own land.

לֹא יָהֵלּוּ אוֹרָם

חָשַׁךְ הַשֶּׁמֶשׁ בְּצֵאתוֹ

וְיָרֵחַ לֹא־יַגִּיהַּ אוֹרוֹ:

11 וּפָקַדְתִּי עַל־תֵּבֵל רָעָה

וְעַל־רְשָׁעִים עֲוֺנָם

וְהִשְׁבַּתִּי גְּאוֹן זֵדִים

וְגַאֲוַת עָרִיצִים אַשְׁפִּיל:

12 אוֹקִיר אֱנוֹשׁ מִפָּז

וְאָדָם מִכֶּתֶם אוֹפִיר:

13 עַל־כֵּן שָׁמַיִם אַרְגִּיז

וְתִרְעַשׁ הָאָרֶץ מִמְּקוֹמָהּ

בְּעֶבְרַת יְהֹוָה צְבָאוֹת

וּבְיוֹם חֲרוֹן אַפּוֹ:

14 וְהָיָה כִּצְבִי מֻדָּח

וּכְצֹאן וְאֵין מְקַבֵּץ

אִישׁ אֶל־עַמּוֹ יִפְנוּ

וְאִישׁ אֶל־אַרְצוֹ יָנוּסוּ:

shall not give their light. Frequently in the prophets the day of doom is pictured as enshrouded in complete darkness (cf. v. 30, viii. 22; Joel ii. 10) (Kimchi).

11f. God speaks (cf. verse 3). The widespread wickedness will be the cause of a co-extensive extermination and therefore practically complete.

11. *the world.* Alluding to the many nations conquered by Cyrus, as in Ezra i. 2 (Ibn Ezra). Alternatively, 'the land,' referring to Babylonia (Rashi, Kimchi).

12. *more rare than fine gold.* The survivors will be so few that they will be rarer even than the rare precious metal (Malbim).

Ophir. Probably to be located in South Arabia; a place famed for its gold (cf. I Kings x. 11; Ps. xiv. 10).

13-16. In the panic all foreign residents will flee to their own countries; while the native population, even women and children, will be mercilessly exterminated.

make the heavens to tremble. By the downfall of the guardian angel of Babylon (Rashi).

the earth shall be shaken. By Babylon's overwhelming disaster (Metsudath David).

14. *they shall turn.* The foreign merchants and residents. As an important centre of trade, merchants in large numbers came to Babylon (Kimchi).

15. Every one that is found shall be
    thrust through;
    And every one that is caught
    shall fall by the sword.
16. Their babes also shall be dashed
    in pieces before their eyes;
    Their houses shall be spoiled,
    And their wives ravished.
17. Behold, I will stir up the Medes
    against them,
    Who shall not regard silver,
    And as for gold, they shall not
    delight in it.
18. And their bows shall dash the
    young men in pieces;
    And they shall have no pity on
    the fruit of the womb;
    Their eye shall not spare child-
    ren.
19. And Babylon, the glory of king-
    doms,
    The beauty of the Chaldeans'
    pride,
    Shall be as when God overthrew
    Sodom and Gomorrah.

כָּל־הַנִּמְצָא יִדָּקֵר 15

וְכָל־הַנִּסְפֶּה יִפּוֹל בֶּחָרֶב:

וְעֹלְלֵיהֶם יְרֻטְּשׁוּ לְעֵינֵיהֶם 16

יִשַּׁסּוּ בָּתֵּיהֶם

וּנְשֵׁיהֶם תִּשָּׁגַלְנָה:

הִנְנִי מֵעִיר עֲלֵיהֶם אֶת־מָדָי 17

אֲשֶׁר־כֶּסֶף לֹא יַחְשֹׁבוּ

וְזָהָב לֹא יַחְפְּצוּ־בוֹ:

וּקְשָׁתוֹת נְעָרִים תְּרַטַּשְׁנָה 18

וּפְרִי־בֶטֶן לֹא יְרַחֵמוּ

עַל־בָּנִים לֹא־תָחוּס עֵינָם:

וְהָיְתָה בָבֶל צְבִי מַמְלָכוֹת 19

תִּפְאֶרֶת גְּאוֹן כַּשְׂדִּים

כְּמַהְפֵּכַת אֱלֹהִים

אֶת־סְדֹם וְאֶת־עֲמֹרָה:

v. 16. תשכבנה ק'

---

15. *every one that is found . . . caught.*
The natives who failed to escape from
the doomed city (Abarbanel).

17-19. The invaders hitherto spoken
of in general terms are now specified as
the cruel Medes; and Babylon, the
object of their attack, is named. The
Medes are mentioned alone because
they were more cruel than their Persian
allies (Ibn Ezra). Moreover, Darius the
Mede reigned instead of Bel-Shazzar.
Cyrus the Persian assumed the throne
after his death (Kimchi).

17. *the Medes.* This people, which
occupied the district southwest of the
Caspian Sea, could not have become a
real menace to Babylon before the reign
of Cyrus, though it was one of the lead-

ing powers of Asia since 606 B.C.E.,
when, together with the Chaldeans, it
conquered and divided the spoils of the
Assyrian empire. The Medes and the
Persians formed a united kingdom of
Persia under Cyrus when, in 549, he
overthrew the Median dynasty. The date
of this prophecy cannot be determined.

who shall not regard, etc. Their motive
being not the desire for plunder, but
sheer lust of destruction (Ibn Ezra).

18. *their bows. Their* is implied in the
context (Targum).

19. *God overthrew Sodom and Gomorrah.*
Cf. Gen. xix. 24f.; a proverbial expression for utter ruin (cf. i. 9).

20. It shall never be inhabited,
    Neither shall it be dwelt in from
        generation to generation;
    Neither shall the Arabian pitch
        tent there;
    Neither shall the shepherds make
        their fold there.
21. But wild-cats shall lie there;
    And their houses shall be full of
        ferrets;
    And ostriches shall dwell there,
    And satyrs shall dance there.
22. And jackals shall howl in their
        castles,
    And wild-dogs in the pleasant
        palaces;
    And her time is near to come,
    And her days shall not be pro-
        longed.

20 לֹא־תֵשֵׁב לָנֶצַח
וְלֹא תִשְׁכֹּן עַד־דּוֹר וָדוֹר
וְלֹא־יַהֵל שָׁם עֲרָבִי
וְרֹעִים לֹא־יַרְבִּצוּ שָׁם׃
21 וְרָבְצוּ־שָׁם צִיִּים
וּמָלְאוּ בָתֵּיהֶם אֹחִים
וְשָׁכְנוּ שָׁם בְּנוֹת יַעֲנָה
וּשְׂעִירִים יְרַקְּדוּ־שָׁם׃
22 וְעָנָה אִיִּים בְּאַלְמְנוֹתָיו
וְתַנִּים בְּהֵיכְלֵי עֹנֶג
וְקָרוֹב לָבוֹא עִתָּהּ
וְיָמֶיהָ לֹא יִמָּשֵׁכוּ׃

14   CHAPTER XIV   יד

1. For the LORD will have compassion on Jacob, and will yet
choose Israel, and set them in their

1 כִּי יְרַחֵם יְהֹוָה אֶת־יַעֲקֹב וּבָחַר
עוֹד בְּיִשְׂרָאֵל וְהִנִּיחָם עַל־אַדְמָתָם

20–22. Babylon's complete and eternal
desolation. It shall be the haunt of wild
creatures and other denizens of the
desert. With this passage cf. Jer. l. 39f.

20. *the Arabian.* Even the wandering
tribes of the desert will avoid it (Rashi).

pitch tent. The Hebrew verb *yahel* is a
shortened form with the omission of the
aleph after the first letter (Rashi).

21. *ferrets.* Hebrew *ochim,* a word that
does not occur elsewhere, apparently
means 'animals with a howling cry'
(Kimchi).

ostriches. Several times mentioned as
dwelling in desolate places (cf. xxxiv.
13; Jer. l. 39).

satyrs. Goat-shaped demons. The
Hebrew also means 'goats' (Kimchi).

22. *castles.* The Hebrew word is spelt
almenothaw for the usual *armenothaw,*
with *lamed* instead of *resh* (Rashi, Ibn
Ezra, Kimchi).

her time . . . her days. Of the fulfillment of
the prophecy (Rashi, Kimchi).

CHAPTER XIV

1–23. In this section, the pronouncement over Babylon is continued, consisting of an introduction, ode and
epilogue. The ode has been described as
'one of the most spirited of all Hebrew
poems.'

own land: and the stranger shall join himself with them, and they shall cleave to the house of Jacob. 2. And the peoples shall take them, and bring them to their place; and the house of Israel shall possess them in the land of the LORD for servants and for handmaids; and they shall take them captive, whose captives they were; and they shall rule over their oppressors.

3. And it shall come to pass in the day that the LORD shall give thee rest from thy travail, and from thy trouble, and from the hard service wherein thou wast made to serve, 4. that thou shalt take up this parable against the king of Babylon, and say:

How hath the oppressor ceased!
The exactress of gold ceased!

וְנִלְוָה הַגֵּר עֲלֵיהֶם וְנִסְפְּחוּ עַל־בֵּית
יַעֲקֹב: וּלְקָחוּם עַמִּים וֶהֱבִיאוּם ²
אֶל־מְקוֹמָם וְהִתְנַחֲלוּם בֵּית־
יִשְׂרָאֵל עַל אַדְמַת יְהֹוָה לַעֲבָדִים
וְלִשְׁפָחוֹת וְהָיוּ שֹׁבִים לְשֹׁבֵיהֶם וְרָדוּ
בְּנֹגְשֵׂיהֶם: וְהָיָה בְּיוֹם הָנִיחַ יְהֹוָה ³
לְךָ מֵעָצְבְּךָ וּמֵרָגְזֶךָ וּמִן־הָעֲבֹדָה
הַקָּשָׁה אֲשֶׁר עֻבַּד־בָּךְ: וְנָשָׂאתָ ⁴
הַמָּשָׁל הַזֶּה עַל־מֶלֶךְ בָּבֶל וְאָמָרְתָּ
אֵיךְ שָׁבַת נֹגֵשׂ
שָׁבְתָה מַדְהֵבָה:

v. 3. הַמֵּ׳ בחירק

1-4a. Introduction serving as a link between the preceding oracle against Babylon and the following ode on Israel's triumph over the proud aggressor.

1. The fall of Babylon is followed by the deliverance of Israel. Babylon was destroyed because of its harsh treatment of Israel (Kimchi). The allusion is probably to the reign of Cyrus, though some commentators regard it as referring also to the Messianic age (Rashi, Kimchi).

yet choose. Better, 'again choose.' Israel will again be given the privilege of building the Temple in Jerusalem (Abarbanel).

stranger. The text uses the term *ger,* 'proselyte' which it acquired in later Hebrew. This alludes to the Idumeans converted by Hyrcanus, king of Judah, as narrated in Josippon (Abarbanel).

2. *the peoples shall take them,* etc. A prediction of the help given by Cyrus to the restoration of the Judean exiles (Ibn Ezra).

shall possess them ... handmaids. This alludes to the Babylonians, who were possessed by the Jews as slaves during the Second Commonwealth (Abarbanel). Others take it as an allusion to the Messianic Era, when the nations of the world will serve the Jews (Kimchi).

4a. *parable.* Hebrew *mashal,* originally 'similitude'; hence 'proverb, parable' and also 'satire, a satirical song.'

4b-21. The ode is generally regarded as one of the finest specimens of the Hebrew poetry of the Bible.

4b-8. General relief and joy over the defeat of the Babylonian king.

4b. *the exactress of gold.* The Hebrew *madhebah* is of uncertain meaning. Many commentators connected it with *dehab,* the Aramaic equivalent of *zahab,* 'gold.' Hence most Jewish commentators have explained it as 'the golden city' (Abarbanel), either on account of Babylon's wealth or in allusion to Nebuchadnezzar of whom it was said, *Thou art the head of gold* (Dan. ii. 38) (Kara). Ibn Ezra renders, 'exactress of gold,' as our translation. Kimchi combines both interpretations: Babylon was called 'the golden kingdom' because of the gold

5. The LORD hath broken the staff
   of the wicked,
   The sceptre of the rulers,

6. That smote the peoples in wrath
   With an incessant stroke,
   That ruled the nations in anger,
   With a persecution that none
   restrained.

7. The whole earth is at rest, and
   is quiet;
   They break forth into singing.

8. Yea, the cypresses rejoice at thee,
   And the cedars of Lebanon:
   'Since thou art laid down,
   No feller is come up against us.'

9. The nether-world from beneath
   is moved for thee
   To meet thee at thy coming;
   The shades are stirred up for
   thee,
   Even all the chief ones of the
   earth;
   All the kings of the nations
   Are raised up from their thrones.

שָׁבַר יְהֹוָה מַטֵּה רְשָׁעִים 5
שֵׁבֶט מֹשְׁלִים׃
מַכֶּה עַמִּים בְּעֶבְרָה 6
מַכַּת בִּלְתִּי סָרָה
רֹדֶה בָאַף גּוֹיִם
מֻרְדָּף בְּלִי חָשָׂךְ׃
נָחָה שָׁקְטָה כָּל־הָאָרֶץ 7
פָּצְחוּ רִנָּה׃
גַּם־בְּרוֹשִׁים שָׂמְחוּ לְךָ 8
אַרְזֵי לְבָנוֹן
מֵאָז שָׁכַבְתָּ
לֹא־יַעֲלֶה הַכֹּרֵת עָלֵינוּ׃
שְׁאוֹל מִתַּחַת רָגְזָה לְךָ 9
לִקְרַאת בּוֹאֶךָ
עוֹרֵר לְךָ רְפָאִים
כָּל־עַתּוּדֵי אָרֶץ
הֵקִים מִכִּסְאוֹתָם
כֹּל מַלְכֵי גוֹיִם׃

v. 9. קמץ בז״ק

she exacted from all the nations. It is noteworthy that Rashi also defines the meaning as 'pride,' but whether he had a different reading is doubtful.

8. *cypress.* Or, 'box trees' (Kimchi, Shorashim).

no feller. The cutting of the trees of Lebanon is known to have been among the exploits of the kings of Assyria (cf. Hab. ii. 17); and though there is no specific record that Nebuchadnezzar had acted similarly, his inscriptions found in Lebanon confirms the implication of the text. Ibn Ezra, too, interprets

this passage literally, that Nebuchadnezzar hewed the cedars of the Lebanon for military purposes.

9–11. The scene in the nether-world where Babylon's former victims greet its king with derision.

9. *the shades.* Hebrew *rephaim,* lit. 'the powerless ones' (Ibn Ezra, Kimchi, Metsudath Zion).

chief ones. lit. 'he-goats,' as leaders of the flock (cf. Jer. l. 8); used figuratively of chieftains (again in Ezek. xxxiv. 17) (Rashi, Ibn Ezra).

10. All they do answer
And say unto thee:
'Art thou also become weak as
we?
Art thou become like unto us?

11. Thy pomp is brought down to
the nether-world,
And the noise of thy psalteries;
The maggot is spread under thee,
And the worms cover thee.'

12. How art thou fallen from heaven,
O day-star, son of the morning!
How art thou cut down to the
ground,
That didst cast lots over the
nations!

13. And thou saidst in thy heart:
'I will ascend into heaven,
Above the stars of God
Will I exalt my throne;

כֻּלָּם יַעֲנוּ 10
וְיֹאמְרוּ אֵלֶיךָ
גַּם־אַתָּה חֻלֵּיתָ כָמוֹנוּ
אֵלֵינוּ נִמְשָׁלְתָּ׃

הוּרַד שְׁאוֹל גְּאוֹנֶךָ 11
הֶמְיַת נְבָלֶיךָ
תַּחְתֶּיךָ יֻצַּע רִמָּה
וּמְכַסֶּיךָ תּוֹלֵעָה׃

אֵיךְ נָפַלְתָּ מִשָּׁמַיִם 12
הֵילֵל בֶּן־שָׁחַר
נִגְדַּעְתָּ לָאָרֶץ
חוֹלֵשׁ עַל־גּוֹיִם׃

וְאַתָּה אָמַרְתָּ בִלְבָבְךָ 13
הַשָּׁמַיִם אֶעֱלֶה
מִמַּעַל לְכוֹכְבֵי־אֵל
אָרִים כִּסְאִי

11. *the noise of thy psalteries*. The songs, accompanied by music, which lauded his triumphs (Rashi).

maggot . . . worms. He who had thought himself an immortal god experiences the fate of an ordinary human (Abarbanel).

12-15. The prophet apostrophizes the king of Babylon, contrasting his former pride and splendor with his grievous degradation and fall.

12. *day-star*. [Or, 'Lucifer' (lightbearer). The morning-star (*son of the morning*) under the name of Istar was worshipped by the Babylonians, and Nebuchadnezzar's days of power and glory are well represented by their comparison with the shining star.] Abar-

banel points out that this star, namely Venus, is the heavenly prince of Babylon.

cast lots. To determine the days on which the respective nations shall render service (Rashi). Others render, 'thou didst slay the nation (Targum, Ibn Ezra, Kimchi).

13f. Worldly power was not enough for him. He aspired to be the equal of God (Kimchi).

13. *above the stars of God*. Which are fixed in the *firmament* (Gen. i. 17), dividing the celestial from the terrestrial region.

the mount of meeting. Or, 'the appointed mount.' The mount is assumed to be

And I will sit upon the mount of meeting,

In the uttermost parts of the north;

14. I will ascend above the heights of the clouds;

I will be like the Most High.'

15. Yet thou shalt be brought down to the nether-world,

To the uttermost parts of the pit.

16. They that saw thee do narrowly look upon thee,

They gaze earnestly at thee:

'Is this the man that made the earth to tremble,

That did shake kingdoms;

17. That made the world as a wilderness,

And destroyed the cities thereof;

That opened not the house of his prisoners?'

18. All the kings of the nations,

All of them, sleep in glory,

Every one in his own house.

וָאֵשֵׁב בְּהַר־מוֹעֵד
בְּיַרְכְּתֵי צָפוֹן׃
14 אֶעֱלֶה עַל־בָּמֳתֵי עָב
אֶדַּמֶּה לְעֶלְיוֹן׃
15 אַךְ אֶל־שְׁאוֹל
תּוּרָד אֶל־יַרְכְּתֵי־בוֹר׃
16 רֹאֶיךָ אֵלֶיךָ יַשְׁגִּיחוּ
אֵלֶיךָ יִתְבּוֹנָנוּ
הֲזֶה הָאִישׁ מַרְגִּיז הָאָרֶץ
מַרְעִישׁ מַמְלָכוֹת׃
17 שָׂם תֵּבֵל כַּמִּדְבָּר
וְעָרָיו הָרָס
אֲסִירָיו לֹא־פָתַח בָּיְתָה׃
18 כָּל־מַלְכֵי גוֹיִם כֻּלָּם
שָׁכְבוּ בְכָבוֹד
אִישׁ בְּבֵיתוֹ׃

that of Zion (cf. Ps. xlviii. 3) (Rashi, Ibn Ezra, Kimchi), while others identify it with Aralu the sacred mountain on which, in Babylonian mythology, the chief gods meet. Nebuchadnezzar's ambition was to join the assembly of his people's chief gods (See Malbim).

14. *I will be like.* Better, 'I will make myself like' (Ibn Ezra, Kimchi).

15. *the pit.* Often used as a synonym of Sheol (cf. xxxviii. 18; Ps. xxviii. I) (Kimchi).

16–19. The scene shifts from the nether-world to the battlefield, where the unburied corpse of the tyrant lies exposed to the elements and the beasts and birds of prey.

16. *saw.* Those who saw you in this world in your glory (Kara).

17. *opened not . . . prisoners.* This follows Ibn Ezra, Kimchi, and Kara. According to some editions of Rashi, we render, 'let not loose his prisoners to their home,' or 'each to his home.'

18f. The dignified burial of other kings is contrasted with the indignities to which the king of Babylon is exposed.

18. *house.* i.e. the family tomb (cf. I Kings ii. 34; Job xxx. 23) (Targum, Rashi, Ibn Ezra, Kimchi).

19. But thou art cast forth away from
    thy grave
    Like an abhorred offshoot,
    In the raiment of the slain, that
      are thrust through with the
      sword,
    That go down to the pavement
      of the pit,
    As a carcass trodden under foot.
20. Thou shalt not be joined with
    them in burial,
    Because thou hast destroyed thy
    land,
    Thou hast slain thy people;
    The seed of evil-doers shall not
    Be named for ever.
21. Prepare ye slaughter for his
    children
    For the iniquity of their fathers;
    That they rise not up, and
    possess the earth,
    And fill the face of the world with
    cities.
22. And I will rise up against them,
saith the LORD of hosts, and cut off
from Babylon name and remnant,

19 וְאַתָּה הָשְׁלַכְתָּ מִקִּבְרְךָ֙
כְּנֵ֣צֶר נִתְעָ֔ב
לְבֻ֥שׁ הֲרֻגִ֖ים מְטֹ֣עֲנֵי חָ֑רֶב
יוֹרְדֵ֥י אֶל־אַבְנֵי־ב֖וֹר
כְּפֶ֥גֶר מוּבָֽס׃

20 לֹא־תֵחַ֤ד אִתָּם֙ בִּקְבוּרָ֔ה
כִּֽי־אַרְצְךָ֥ שִׁחַ֖תָּ
עַמְּךָ֣ הָרָ֑גְתָּ
לֹֽא־יִקָּרֵ֥א לְעוֹלָ֖ם זֶ֥רַע מְרֵעִֽים׃

21 הָכִ֥ינוּ לְבָנָ֖יו מַטְבֵּ֑חַ
בַּעֲוֺ֖ן אֲבוֹתָ֑ם
בַּל־יָקֻ֙מוּ֙ וְיָ֣רְשׁוּ אָ֔רֶץ
וּמָלְא֥וּ פְנֵֽי־תֵבֵ֖ל עָרִֽים׃

22 וְקַמְתִּ֣י עֲלֵיהֶ֔ם נְאֻ֖ם יְהֹוָ֣ה צְבָא֑וֹת
וְהִכְרַתִּ֨י לְבָבֶ֜ל שֵׁ֤ם וּשְׁאָר֙ וְנִ֣ין וָנֶ֔כֶד

v. 21. קמץ בז״ק

---

19. *from thy grave.* i.e. the elaborate
sepulchre which is thy due as a king;
instead thy body lies ignominiously
unburied (Abarbanel).

like an abhorred offshoot. Which, when cut
off from the tree, is unceremoniously
cast away (Abarbanel).

in the raiment of the slain. lit. 'clothed with
the slain.' His corpse is surrounded by
the dead bodies of his soldiers (Abarbanel).

pavement of the pit. lit. 'stones of the pit,'
its very bottom (Rashi).

20f His destruction of his own land and
massacre of his own people are the
causes of the king's indignities and the
extermination of his children.

20. *joined with them.* With the kings
mentioned in verse 18 (Rashi).

destroyed thy land. By heavy taxation,
forced labour and other rigorous measures (Rashi).

slain thy people. Imposing the death
penalty for the most trivial offences
(Rashi).

the seed of evil-doers. Members of the
royal family (Rashi).

not be named. Even their names will be
forgotten (Rashi, Kimchi).

21. *fill . . . with cities.* Inhabited by
wicked men like themselves. Others
render *arim*, the Hebrew word for *cities,*
as 'enemies' (Rashi).

22f. Epilogue.

22. *offshoot and offspring.* In the two
other passages where the phrase occurs
(Gen. xxi. 23; Job xviii. 19), A. J. translates *son* and *son's son.*

71

and offshoot and offspring, saith the
LORD.   23. I will also make it a
possession for the bittern, and pools
of water; and I will sweep it with
the besom of destruction, saith the
LORD of hosts.

24. The LORD of hosts hath
sworn, saying:
Surely as I have thought, so
   shall it come to pass;
And as I have purposed, so shall
   it stand,
25. That I will break Asshur in My
   land,
And upon My mountains tread
   him under foot;
Then shall his yoke depart from
   off them,
And his burden depart from off
   their shoulder.
26. This is the purpose that is
   purposed upon the whole
   earth;
And this is the hand that is
   stretched out upon all the
   nations.
27. For the LORD of hosts hath
   purposed,
And who shall disannul it?
And His hand is stretched out,
And who shall turn it back?
28. In the year that king Ahaz
died was this burden.

כג נְאֻם־יְהֹוָה: וְשַׂמְתִּיהָ לְמוֹרַשׁ קִפֹּד
וְאַגְמֵי־מָיִם וְטֵאטֵאתִיהָ בְּמַטְאֲטֵא
הַשְׁמֵד נְאֻם יְהֹוָה צְבָאוֹת:

כד נִשְׁבַּע יְהֹוָה צְבָאוֹת לֵאמֹר
אִם־לֹא כַּאֲשֶׁר דִּמִּיתִי כֵּן הָיָתָה
וְכַאֲשֶׁר יָעַצְתִּי הִיא תָקוּם:

כה לִשְׁבֹּר אַשּׁוּר בְּאַרְצִי
וְעַל־הָרַי אֲבוּסֶנּוּ
וְסָר מֵעֲלֵיהֶם עֻלּוֹ
וְסֻבֳּלוֹ מֵעַל שִׁכְמוֹ יָסוּר:

כו זֹאת הָעֵצָה הַיְּעוּצָה
עַל־כָּל־הָאָרֶץ
וְזֹאת הַיָּד הַנְּטוּיָה עַל־כָּל־הַגּוֹיִם:

כז כִּי־יְהֹוָה צְבָאוֹת
יָעָץ וּמִי יָפֵר
וְיָדוֹ הַנְּטוּיָה
וּמִי יְשִׁיבֶנָּה:

כח בִּשְׁנַת־מוֹת הַמֶּלֶךְ אָחָז הָיָה הַמַּשָּׂא
הַזֶּה:

v. 24. קמץ בזק   v. 27. קמץ בטרחא

---

23. *bittern*, (Kimchi). Or, 'hedgehog'
(Rashi).

pools of water. Marshy land (Targum).

24-27. The destruction of the Assyrian
in all the land of Judah and the threat of
a similar fate to all other nations who
have evil designs against it.

25. *My land.* The Land of Israel
(Kimchi).

My mountains. The mountains of Judah
(Kimchi).

26. *upon the whole earth.* The collapse of
Assyria was an event which affected the
whole of the then known world (See Ibn
Kaspi).

28-32. The threatened danger to
Philistia, and the peace and security
promised to Judah.

28. Superscription.

king Ahaz died. Probably in the year 720
B.C.E.

burden. See on xiii 1.

29. Rejoice not, O Philistia, all of thee,
Because the rod that smote thee is broken:
For out of the serpent's root shall come forth a basilisk,
And his fruit shall be a flying serpent.

30. And the first-born of the poor shall feed,
And the needy shall lie down in safety;
And I will kill thy root with famine,
And thy remnant shall be slain.

31. Howl, O gate; cry, O city;
Melt away, O Philistia, all of thee;
For there cometh a smoke out of the north,
And there is no straggler in his ranks.

29 אַל־תִּשְׂמְחִי פְלֶשֶׁת כֻּלֵּךְ
כִּי נִשְׁבַּר שֵׁבֶט מַכֵּךְ
כִּי־מִשֹּׁרֶשׁ נָחָשׁ יֵצֵא צֶפַע
וּפִרְיוֹ שָׂרָף מְעוֹפֵף:
30 וְרָעוּ בְּכוֹרֵי דַלִּים
וְאֶבְיוֹנִים לָבֶטַח יִרְבָּצוּ
וְהֵמַתִּי בָרָעָב שָׁרְשֵׁךְ
וּשְׁאֵרִיתֵךְ יַהֲרֹג:
31 הֵילִילִי שַׁעַר זַעֲקִי־עִיר
נָמוֹג פְּלֶשֶׁת כֻּלֵּךְ
כִּי מִצָּפוֹן עָשָׁן בָּא
וְאֵין בּוֹדֵד בְּמוֹעָדָיו:

29. *all of thee*. No district or town is excluded from the warning (Metsudath David).

the rod that smote thee is broken. This may refer to the death of Tiglath-pileser III in 727, of Shalmaneser IV in 722 or of Sargon in 705 (Ibn Kaspi). Others take it as referring to Ahaz whose death, as mentioned above, is assumed to have taken place in 720 (Ibn Ezra).

serpent's root. On the allusion, see the previous note.

a basilisk. Hezekiah is meant (Rashi, Ibn Ezra, Kimchi).

his fruit, etc. The purport of the verse is that, though the foreign ruler under whom they had hitherto suffered is dead, a descendant of his would arise and be mightier and more dangerous than the deceased king (Rashi, Kimchi).

flying serpent. It is said to be the deadliest of its species (Ibn Ezra).

30. Philistia will be fatally hit and subdued, but Judah will prosper.

first-born of the poor. The poorest of the poor (Kimchi). According to others it means 'the first of the poor.' Israel, who was impoverished before any other nation, will have plenty, while the wealthy Philistines will be impoverished (Ibn Ezra).

31. *a smoke*. Metaphor for the devastating hosts, burning buildings and crops in their way (Rashi).

out of the north. See on verse 29. Assyria was to the north of Philistia; (Ibn Ezra) but Judah, whose capital Jerusalem lay to the north-east, may also be described as being in the north (Rashi).

straggler. lit. 'alone,' 'apart' from the main body of the troops (Rashi).

32. What then shall one answer the
messengers of the nation?

That the LORD hath founded
Zion,

And in her shall the afflicted of
His people take refuge.

32 וּמַה־יַּעֲנֶה מַלְאֲכֵי־גוֹי

כִּי יְהֹוָה יִסַּד צִיּוֹן

וּבָהּ יֶחֱסוּ עֲנִיֵּי עַמּוֹ׃

15   CHAPTER XV   טו

1. The burden of Moab.

For in the night that Ar of Moab
is laid waste,

He is brought to ruin;

For in the night that Kir of
Moab is laid waste,

He is brought to ruin.

2. He is gone up to Baith, and to
Dibon,

To the high places, to weep;

1 מַשָּׂא מוֹאָב

כִּי בְּלֵיל

שֻׁדַּד עָר מוֹאָב נִדְמָה

כִּי בְּלֵיל

שֻׁדַּד קִיר־מוֹאָב נִדְמָה׃

2 עָלָה הַבַּיִת וְדִיבֹן

הַבָּמוֹת לְבֶכִי

---

32. *messengers.* Probably envoys from
Philistia seeking an alliance with Judah.

the nation. Philistia.

the LORD *hath founded Zion.* No alliances
are necessary when God is Protector.
This interpretation, however, is not
found in the Jewish commentaries.
Rashi and Ibn Ezra render: 'and what
shall each of the messengers of the
nation answer?' The nation is then
Judah, and the messengers are those
sent by Hezekiah to carry the tidings of
his deliverance from Sennacherib.

CHAPTERS XV-XVI

THE INVASION AND FALL OF MOAB

THE invader, whose name is not mentioned, is presumed by Rashi, Abarbanel, and Ibn Kaspi, to be Sennacherib, king of Assyria and contemporary of Hezekiah. With this oracle

over Moab, Jer. xlviii should be
compared.

CHAPTER XV

THE PITTABLE CONDITION OF MOAB

1. Ar and Kir, Moab's most important
cities, are laid waste in one night (Abarbanel).

Ar. On the southern bank of the Arnon
and capital of Moab (See Kaftor
Vaferach).

Kir. The modern Kerak, about 17 miles
south of the Arnon (Map in Kafter
Vaferach).

2-4. Moab's cry of agony.

2. *Baith . . . Dibon.* Where presumably
sanctuaries (*the high places*) were situated.
Baith cannot be located. *Dibon is six
miles north of the Arnon* (See Kaftor
Vaferach).

Sof Nebo (handwritten note)

Upon Nebo, and upon Medeba,
  Moab howleth;
On all their heads is baldness,
Every beard is shaven.
3. In their streets they gird them-
  selves with sackcloth;
On their housetops, and in their
  broad places,
Every one howleth, weeping
  profusely. *4 mi NE of Nebo* (handwritten note)
4. And Heshbon crieth out, and
  Elealeh; *Close by* (handwritten note)
Their voice is heard even unto
  Jahaz;
Therefore the armed men of
  Moab cry aloud;
His soul is faint within him.
5. My heart crieth out for Moab;
Her fugitives reach unto Zoar, *Sodom* (handwritten note)
A heifer of three years old;

עַל־נְב֣וֹ וְעַ֤ל מֵידְבָא֙ מוֹאָ֣ב יְיֵלִ֔יל
בְּכָל־רֹאשָׁ֣יו קָרְחָ֔ה
כָּל־זָקָ֖ן גְּרוּעָֽה׃
3 בְּחוּצֹתָ֖יו חָ֣גְרוּ שָׂ֑ק
עַל־גַּגּוֹתֶ֤יהָ וּבִרְחֹֽבֹתֶ֙יהָ֙
כֻּלֹּ֣ה יְיֵלִ֔יל יֹרֵ֖ד בַּבֶּֽכִי׃
4 וַתִּזְעַ֤ק חֶשְׁבּוֹן֙ וְאֶלְעָלֵ֔ה
עַד־יַ֖הַץ נִשְׁמַ֣ע קוֹלָ֑ם
עַל־כֵּ֗ן חֲלֻצֵ֤י מוֹאָב֙ יָרִ֔יעוּ
נַפְשׁ֖וֹ יָ֥רְעָה לּֽוֹ׃
5 לִבִּי֙ לְמוֹאָ֣ב יִזְעָ֔ק
בְּרִיחֶ֖הָ עַד־צֹ֑עַר
עֶגְלַ֖ת שְׁלִשִׁיָּ֑ה

v. 2. v. 5. נ״א גדועה קמץ בז״ק

Nebo. A town near the mountain of the same name on which Moses passed away. It lay east of the northern coast of the Dead Sea (Carta).

Medeba. Not far from Nebo and to the south of it (Daath Mikra, Jos. xii. 9).

baldness . . . shaven. These are oriental manifestations of grief and mourning (Kimchi).

3. *weeping profusely.* lit. 'going down in weeping.' Elsewhere 'the eye' is said to 'go down in tears' (Jer. ix. 17; Lam. i. 16, iii. 48), but only here is the phrase used of the whole person (Kimchi).

4. *Heshbon.* Some four miles north-east of Nebo, the capital of the Amorites (Num. xxi. 26) (Kaftor Vaferach).

Elealeh. [About six miles north-east of Nebo.]

Jahaz. Probably not far from Heshbon

(cf. Num xxi. 23), but its position is not known.

is faint. Or, 'crieth out' (Rashi, Ibn Ezra, Kimchi).

5-7. The fugitives make their way through the ruins of their country to Edom, collecting their belongings which they were able to carry away at the brook of the willows.

5. *my heart crieth out.* The Hebrew prophet, viewing Moab's calamity, is moved to commiseration, and he cannot help expressing his sympathy with a suffering people even though they had ill-treated Israel (Rashi).

Zoar. South-east of the Dead Sea, near Sodom (cf. Gen. xix. 22).

heifer of three years old. A symbol of health and vigour. The phrase is in apposition to Zoar (Kimchi, Ibn Ezra). Abarbanel

For by the ascent of Luhith
With weeping they go up;
For in the way of Horonaim
They raise up a cry of destruction.

6. For the Waters of Nimrim shall be desolate;
For the grass is withered away, the herbage faileth,
There is no green thing.

7. Therefore the abundance they have gotten,
And that which they have laid up,
Shall they carry away to the brook of the willows.

8. For the cry is gone round about
The borders of Moab;
The howling thereof unto Eglaim,
And the howling thereof unto Beer-elim.

כִּי ׀ מַעֲלֵה הַלּוּחִית
בִּבְכִי יַעֲלֶה־בּוֹ
כִּי דֶּרֶךְ חוֹרֹנַיִם
זַעֲקַת־שֶׁבֶר יְעֹעֵרוּ׃

6 כִּי־מֵי נִמְרִים מְשַׁמּוֹת יִהְיוּ
כִּי־יָבֵשׁ חָצִיר כָּלָה דֶשֶׁא
יֶרֶק לֹא הָיָה׃

7 עַל־כֵּן יִתְרָה עָשָׂה
וּפְקֻדָּתָם
עַל נַחַל הָעֲרָבִים יִשָּׂאוּם׃

8 כִּי־הִקִּיפָה הַזְּעָקָה
אֶת־גְּבוּל מוֹאָב
עַד־אֶגְלַיִם יִלְלָתָהּ
וּבְאֵר אֵלִים יִלְלָתָהּ׃

---

explains that Moab is complaining that, in addition to being pillaged, her fugitives did not manage to flee to a large city in which to fortify themselves, but to a small town, as Zoar is described in Gen. xix. 20. This is the comparison to the three-year-old heifer.

Luhith. Between Zoar and Rabba.

Horonaim. Apparently in the vicinity of Zoar to the south (See Carta).

6. *the Waters of Nimrim.* Identified with Wadi Sahib, a tributary of the Jordan, about eight miles from its mouth or, more probably, with Wadi Numeirah which flows into the Dead Sea not far from Kerak (Carta).

shall be desolate. Instead of watering the land, as the waters of Nimrim were wont to do, this river will dry up, caus-

ing the grass to wither away and the herbage to fail (Abarbanel).

7. *brook of the willows.* This was evidently on the border between Moab and Edom and may, therefore, be identified with Wadi el-Ahsa (valley of water pits) which formed the boundary between those lands.

8. The territorial extent of the destruction.

the cry. Mentioned in the previous verses.

Eglaim . . . Beer-elim. Abarbanel theorizes that both these cities are on the border of Moab, one on one side and one on the other. Malbim theorizes that they are both outside the border of Moab, Eglaim being near the border and Beer-elim far from the border.

9. For the waters of Dimon are full
   of blood;
   For I will bring yet more upon
   Dimon,
   A lion upon him that escapeth of
   Moab,
   And upon the remnant of the
   land.

⁹ כִּי מֵי דִימוֹן מָלְאוּ דָם

כִּי־אָשִׁית עַל־דִּימוֹן נוֹסָפוֹת

לִפְלֵיטַת מוֹאָב אַרְיֵה

וְלִשְׁאֵרִית אֲדָמָה׃

16   CHAPTER XVI   טז

1. Send ye the lambs for the ruler
   of the land
   From the crags that are toward
   the wilderness,
   Unto the mount of the daughter
   of Zion.

2. For it shall be that, as wandering
   birds,
   As a scattered nest,
   So shall the daughters of Moab
   be
   At the fords of Arnon.

¹ שִׁלְחוּ־כַר מֹשֵׁל־אֶרֶץ

מִסֶּלַע מִדְבָּרָה

אֶל־הַר בַּת־צִיּוֹן׃

² וְהָיָה כְעוֹף־נוֹדֵד

קֵן מְשֻׁלָּח

תִּהְיֶינָה בְּנוֹת מוֹאָב

מַעְבָּרֹת לְאַרְנוֹן׃

Dimon . . . blood. A play on words, the Hebrew for blood being *dam* (Rashi).

bring yet more. Of the evil specified in the second part of the verse and in xvi. 2 (Ibn Ezra).

a lion. The allusion is to some powerful invader, and the king of Assyria has been suggested (Ibn Ezra).

CHAPTER XVI

IN this chapter the oracle on Moab is continued.

1-6. The prophet advises the Moabites that the only way they will be saved is by sending a messenger (or tribute) to Judah to beg for admittance into the country (Malbim).

1. *lambs.* The Hebrew singular is used as a collective noun. The lambs were to be sent as tribute. In 2 Kings iii. 4 it is

recorded that Moab used to send to the king of Israel a large quantity of wool annually. Now they should seek the favour of the ruler of the Southern Kingdom (Rashi, Kimchi).

ruler of the land. The king of Judah (Kara). Others take this as addressed to the ruler of the land of Moab (Rashi, Kimchi).

crags. Jewish commentators understand this as a proper noun, *Sela-Midbarah,* the capital of Moab. Send the tribute from Sela-Midbarah to the mount of the daughter of Zion (Rashi, Kimchi).

2. *daughters of Moab.* The inhabitants of the provincial towns, uprooted from their homes and in search of a resting place (Ibn Ezra).

fords of Arnon. This river formed the frontier of the country of Moab (Kimchi).

(handwritten margin note: Moab's plea)

3. 'Give counsel, execute justice;
   Make thy shadow as the night in
      the midst of the noonday;
   Hide the outcasts; betray not the
      fugitive.
4. Let mine outcasts dwell with
      thee;
   As for Moab, be thou a covert to
      him from the face of the
      spoiler.'
   For the extortion is at an end,
      spoiling ceaseth,
   They that trampled down are
      consumed out of the land;
5. And a throne is established
      through mercy,
   And there sitteth thereon in
      truth, in the tent of David,
   One that judgeth, and seeketh
      justice, and is ready in
      righteousness.
6. We have heard of the pride of
      Moab;
   He is very proud;
   Even of his haughtiness, and his
      pride, and his arrogancy,
   His ill-founded boastings.

(handwritten margin note: Judah's reply)

הָבִיאוּ עֵצָה עֲשׂוּ פְלִילָה ³
שִׁיתִי כַלַּיִל צִלֵּךְ בְּתוֹךְ צָהֳרָיִם
סַתְּרִי נִדָּחִים נֹדֵד אַל־תְּגַלִּי׃
יָגוּרוּ בָךְ נִדָּחַי ⁴
מוֹאָב הֱוִי־סֵתֶר לָמוֹ מִפְּנֵי שׁוֹדֵד
כִּי־אָפֵס הַמֵּץ כָּלָה שֹׁד
תַּמּוּ רֹמֵס מִן־הָאָרֶץ׃
וְהוּכַן בַּחֶסֶד כִּסֵּא ⁵
וְיָשַׁב עָלָיו בֶּאֱמֶת בְּאֹהֶל דָּוִד
שֹׁפֵט וְדֹרֵשׁ מִשְׁפָּט וּמְהִר צֶדֶק׃
שָׁמַעְנוּ גְאוֹן־מוֹאָב ⁶
גֵּא מְאֹד
גַּאֲוָתוֹ וּגְאוֹנוֹ וְעֶבְרָתוֹ
לֹא־כֵן בַּדָּיו׃

v. 3. הֲבִיאִי ק׳   v. 3. עֲשׂוּ ק׳

3–5. Moab's appeal to Judah.

3. *give counsel, execute justice.* Devise effective means to secure us against our enemy.

make thy shadow, etc. A figurative expression for protection.

the outcasts. Of Moab.

4. *mine outcasts.* The refugees forced to leave Moab.

thee. In Judah.

thou. The Judean king (Malbim).

for the extortion . . . land. This explanation is not found in any classic Jewish commentary. Ibn Ezra explains that the prophet castigates Moab for not affording asylum to the Israelites of Samaria, fleeing the Assyrian armies. Since now 'the extortion is at an end . . . They that trampled down are consumed out of the land,' had you afforded them asylum,

they would be able to return to their homes.

5. *is established.* Firmly without danger of being overthrown, as happened with Moab's royal house. Implied is a desire by the appellants to be allowed to live in the security of allegiance to the dynasty of David.

6. Judah's reply declining Moab's request, recalling her notorious pride and arrogance which would constitute a menace to any country that gave her shelter (Malbim).

the pride of Moab. This characteristic is referred to again in xxv. 11, also in Jer. xlviii. 29 and Zeph. ii. 10.

his arrogancy. Better 'his anger.' The hatred he bore against Israel (Rashi).

his ill-founded boastings. Or, 'false (lit. not right) are his pratings' (Metsudath David).

7. Therefore shall Moab wail for
   Moab,
   Every one shall wail;
   For the sweet cakes of Kir-
   hareseth shall ye mourn,
   Sorely stricken.
8. For the fields of Heshbon
   languish,
   And the vine of Sibmah,
   Whose choice plants did over-
   come
   The lords of nations;
   They reached even unto Jazer,
   They wandered into the wilder-
   ness;
   Her branches were spread
   abroad,
   They passed over the sea.
9. Therefore I will weep with the
   weeping of Jazer
   For the vine of Sibmah;
   I will water thee with my tears,

לָכֵן יְיֵלִיל מוֹאָב לְמוֹאָב 7
כֻּלֹּה יְיֵלִיל
לַאֲשִׁישֵׁי קִיר־חֲרֶשֶׂת תֶּהְגּוּ
אַךְ־נְכָאִים:
כִּי שַׁדְמוֹת חֶשְׁבּוֹן אֻמְלָל 8
גֶּפֶן שִׂבְמָה
בַּעֲלֵי גוֹיִם
הָלְמוּ שְׂרוּקֶּיהָ
עַד־יַעְזֵר נָגָעוּ
תָּעוּ מִדְבָּר
שְׁלֻחוֹתֶיהָ נִטְּשׁוּ
עָבְרוּ יָם:
עַל־כֵּן אֶבְכֶּה בִּבְכִי יַעְזֵר 9
גֶּפֶן שִׂבְמָה
אֲרַיָּוֶךְ דִּמְעָתִי

v. 8. דגש אחר ת״ג v. 8. קמץ בטרחא v. 8. מלעיל v. 9. מלעיל

7-10. Moab's position being now hopeless, the prophet resumes his pronouncement over her fall.

7. *shall Moab wail for Moab.* i.e. the remaining Moabites for their fallen brethren (Kimchi).

the sweet cakes. These were made from raisins and flour and were regarded as a dainty (cf. Cant. ii. 5); the Moabites will lament the loss of the rich food they formerly ate. This follows Rashi (Cant. ii. 5). Here, however, it is rendered variously as 'walls' (Rashi), 'foundations,' symbolizing the nobles (Kimchi), or 'flagons' (Ibn Ezra).

Kir-hareseth. According to Kimchi, this is a place-name, identified by some with Kir of Moab (xv. 1). It is the same as Kir-heres in verse 11 (Carta) (Kimchi).

8. *the fields of Heshbon.* As in Deut.

xxxii. 32, *shadmoth* here denotes more particularly 'vineyards' (Ibn Ezra). For Heshbon, see on xv. 4.

Sibmah. In the neighborhood of Heshbon and famous for its vineyards. Some identify it with Khirbeth-sumia situated north of Heshbon, and some claim that it was south of Heshbon (Daath Mikra, Jos. xiii. 19).

did overcome. Jewish exegetes render: 'Lords of nations broke its choice plants' (Kimchi, Abarbanel).

they. viz. the *choice plants,* symbolizing the once flourishing vine-culture of the country (Ibn Ezra).

reached . . . wandered . . . passed over. To Jazer in the north, the desert in the east and the Dead Sea in the west.

9-11. The prophet expresses his sympathy with the desolate city.

79

O Heshbon, and Elealeh;
For upon thy summer fruits and
  upon thy harvest
The battle shout is fallen.

10. And gladness and joy are taken
  away
Out of the fruitful field;
And in the vineyards there shall
  be no singing,
Neither shall there be shouting;
No treader shall tread out wine
  in the presses;
I have made the vintage shout to
  cease.

11. Wherefore my heart moaneth
  like a harp for Moab,
And mine inward parts for
  Kir-heres.

12. And it shall come to pass, when
it is seen that Moab hath wearied
himself upon the high place, that he
shall come to his sanctuary to pray;
but he shall not prevail.

  13. This is the word that the LORD

חֶשְׁבּוֹן וְאֶלְעָלֵה
כִּי עַל־קֵיצֵךְ וְעַל־קְצִירֵךְ
הֵידָד נָפָל׃
10 וְנֶאֱסַף שִׂמְחָה וָגִיל
מִן־הַכַּרְמֶל
וּבַכְּרָמִים לֹא־יְרֻנָּן
לֹא יְרֹעָע
יַיִן בַּיְקָבִים לֹא־יִדְרֹךְ הַדֹּרֵךְ
הֵידָד הִשְׁבַּתִּי׃
11 עַל־כֵּן מֵעַי לְמוֹאָב
כַּכִּנּוֹר יֶהֱמוּ
וְקִרְבִּי לְקִיר חָרֶשׂ׃
12 וְהָיָה כִי־נִרְאָה כִּי־נִלְאָה מוֹאָב
עַל־הַבָּמָה וּבָא אֶל־מִקְדָּשׁוֹ
13 לְהִתְפַּלֵּל וְלֹא יוּכָל׃ זֶה הַדָּבָר

v. 10. פתח בס"פ

---

9. *Elealeh.* See on xv. 4.

battle shout. The Hebrew *hedad* means 'shouting,' 'cheering.' It signifies both the cry of winepressers (Jer. xxv. 30) and of charging soldiers (Jer. li. 14). The prophet may be implying that it used to be the former, but now it is the latter (Rashi, Kimchi).

10. *there shall be no singing.* Better, 'there is no singing,' a rendering which harmonizes the verse with the expressions of sympathy to which he is giving utterance.

neither shall there be. Better, 'neither is there'; similarly substitute 'treads' for *shall tread.*

I have made . . . cease. It is not clear to whom the pronoun refers, and the per-

fect of the verb disturbs the preceding tenses of the verb. The context seems to require a rendering somewhat like 'the vintage shout is ceased.'

11. *heart.* lit. 'bowels,' in Hebrew the seat of the emotions.

12. *wearied himself.* In battle (Rashi) or, according to others, in invoking the help of his gods (cf. xv. 2) (Ibn Ezra).

shall not prevail. Neither physical defence (or worship) on the *high place* nor prayer to his idols in their sanctuary will save a people the Lord had condemned (Malbim).

13f. Epilogue, intimating that the destruction of Moab is to take place within three years (Rashi, Kimchi).

spoke concerning Moab in time past.
14. But now the LORD hath spoken,
saying: 'Within three years, as the
years of a hireling, and the glory of
Moab shall wax contemptible for all
his great multitude; and the remnant
shall be very small and without
strength.'

אֲשֶׁר דִּבֶּר יְהוָה אֶל־מוֹאָב מֵאָז׃
14 וְעַתָּה דִּבֶּר יְהוָה לֵאמֹר בְּשָׁלֹשׁ שָׁנִים
כִּשְׁנֵי שָׂכִיר וְנִקְלָה כְּבוֹד מוֹאָב בְּכֹל
הֶהָמוֹן הָרָב וּשְׁאָר מְעַט מִזְעָר לוֹא
כַּבִּיר׃

17 CHAPTER XVII יז

1. The burden of Damascus.

Behold, Damascus is taken away
from being a city,
And it shall be a ruinous heap.

2. The cities of Aroer are forsaken;
They shall be for flocks,

1 מַשָּׂא דַּמֶּשֶׂק
הִנֵּה דַמֶּשֶׂק מוּסָר מֵעִיר
וְהָיְתָה מְעִי מַפָּלָה׃
2 עֲזֻבוֹת עָרֵי עֲרֹעֵר
לַעֲדָרִים תִּהְיֶינָה

---

13. *in time past.* The phrase modifies
the verb *spoke.* The *time,* according to
tradition, is that when Balak hired
Balaam to curse Israel (cf. Num. xxiiff.)
(Rashi).

14. *as the years of a hireling.* Cf. xxi. 16.
As a hireling does not work a moment
longer than the stipulated time, so the
fall of Moab will not be deferred for a
moment longer than the three years'
period mentioned (Rashi, Kimchi).

without strength. lit. 'not strong.'

CHAPTER XVII

DOOM OF DAMASCUS AND THE
NORTHERN KINGDOM

1–11. Announcement of the
approaching ruin of Damascus and the
fall of the kingdom of Israel. The date
of the prophecy is held to be about 735
B.C.E.

1–3. The destruction of the kingdom
of Damascus on whose protection Israel
had relied (Kimchi).

1. *the burden.* See on xiii. 1.

Damascus. The title can obviously apply
to no more than the first three verses of
the chapter, the remainder of which is
concerned mainly with the fate of the
kingdom of Israel (Abarbanel).

is taken away. Such will be the complete-
ness of devastation, that Damascus will
not be acknowledged any longer as a
city (Malbim).

2. *cities of Aroer.* There may have been
an Aroer in the Syrian kingdom
(Kimchi, Abarbanel); but if the reference is to the well-known Aroer on the
Arnon in the south (Num. xxxii. 34;
Deut. ii. 36), the verse must be applied
to the kingdom of Israel to which the
city once belonged (Rashi). Others render *aroer* as 'ruined cities,' and in that
case the text refers to Syria (Targum).

Which shall lie down, and none
  shall make them afraid.
3. The fortress also shall cease from
  Ephraim,
  And the kingdom from Damascus,
  And the remnant of Aram shall
  be as the glory of the children
  of Israel,
  Saith the LORD of hosts.
4. And it shall come to pass in that
  day,
  That the glory of Jacob shall be
  made thin,
  And the fatness of his flesh shall
  wax lean.
5. And it shall be as when the
  harvestman gathereth the
  standing corn,
  And reapeth the ears with his
  arm;
  Yea, it shall be as when one
  gleaneth ears
  In the valley of Rephaim.
6. Yet there shall be left therein
  gleanings,
  As at the beating of an olive-tree,
  Two or three berries

וְרָבְצוּ וְאֵין מַחֲרִיד׃

3 וְנִשְׁבַּת מִבְצָר מֵאֶפְרַיִם
וּמַמְלָכָה מִדַּמֶּשֶׂק וּשְׁאָר אֲרָם
כִּכְבוֹד בְּנֵי־יִשְׂרָאֵל יִהְיוּ
נְאֻם יְהוָה צְבָאוֹת׃

4 וְהָיָה בַּיּוֹם הַהוּא
יִדַּל כְּבוֹד יַעֲקֹב
וּמִשְׁמַן בְּשָׂרוֹ יֵרָזֶה׃

5 וְהָיָה כֶּאֱסֹף קָצִיר קָמָה
וּזְרֹעוֹ שִׁבֳּלִים יִקְצוֹר
וְהָיָה כִּמְלַקֵּט שִׁבֳּלִים
בְּעֵמֶק רְפָאִים׃

6 וְנִשְׁאַר־בּוֹ עוֹלֵלֹת
כְּנֹקֶף זַיִת
שְׁנַיִם שְׁלֹשָׁה גַּרְגְּרִים

---

none shall make them afraid. The site will
be without any human inhabitants to
frighten the animals (Metsudath David).

3. *fortress.* The kingdom of Syria which
was to serve as a bulwark against Assyria
for the kingdom of Israel (Malbim,
Laniado). According to some commentators, the *fortress* is Samaria (Ibn Ezra,
Kimchi).

and the remnant of Aram shall be. This rendering, which the exegetes seem to
prefer, disregards the Hebrew accentuation, according to which a new clause
begins with *Aram*: 'and the kingdom
from Damascus, and the remnant of
Syria; they shall be' etc. (so A.V., R.V.).

4–6. A description, in figurative
speech, of Israel's calamities.

4. *in that day.* When the ten tribes are
exiled (Kimchi).

glory. Power, prosperity, wealth (Targum).

made thin. Or, 'impoverished' (Kimchi).

5. As the reaper leaves no more than
isolated ears here and there, so will the
conqueror leave but stragglers, the
entire population being led away into
captivity.

the valley of Rephaim. A plain south-west
of Jerusalem (Josh. xviii. 16; 2 Sam.
xxiii. 13), the harvest scenes of which
must have been familiar to Isaiah's
audience (Rashi).

6. *beating of an olive-tree.* By beating
with a stick (cf. Deut. xxiv. 20), the olives
of the upper branches were knocked
down and only very few remained on
the tree (Kimchi).

In the top of the uppermost
  bough,
Four or five in the branches of
  the fruitful tree,
Saith the LORD, the God of
  Israel.

7. In that day shall a man regard
  his Maker,
And his eyes shall look to the
  Holy One of Israel.

8. And he shall not regard the
  altars,
The work of his hands,
Neither shall he look to that
  which his fingers have made,
Either the Asherim, or the sun-
  images.

9. In that day shall his strong
cities be as the forsaken places,
which were forsaken from before the
children of Israel, after the manner
of woods and lofty forests; and it
shall be a desolation.

10. For thou hast forgotten the God
  of thy salvation,
And thou hast not been mindful
  of the Rock of thy stronghold;
Therefore thou didst plant plants
  of pleasantness,

בְּרֹאשׁ אָמִיר

אַרְבָּעָה חֲמִשָּׁה בִּסְעִפֶיהָ פֹּרִיָּה

נְאֻם־יְהֹוָה אֱלֹהֵי יִשְׂרָאֵל׃

7 בַּיּוֹם הַהוּא יִשְׁעֶה הָאָדָם עַל־עֹשֵׂהוּ

וְעֵינָיו אֶל־קְדוֹשׁ יִשְׂרָאֵל תִּרְאֶינָה׃

8 וְלֹא יִשְׁעֶה אֶל־הַמִּזְבְּחוֹת

מַעֲשֵׂה יָדָיו

וַאֲשֶׁר עָשׂוּ אֶצְבְּעֹתָיו לֹא יִרְאֶה

וְהָאֲשֵׁרִים וְהָחַמָּנִים׃

9 בַּיּוֹם הַהוּא יִהְיוּ עָרֵי מָעֻזּוֹ כַּעֲזוּבַת

הַחֹרֶשׁ וְהָאָמִיר אֲשֶׁר עָזְבוּ מִפְּנֵי בְּנֵי

יִשְׂרָאֵל וְהָיְתָה שְׁמָמָה׃

10 כִּי שָׁכַחַתְּ אֱלֹהֵי יִשְׁעֵךְ

וְצוּר מָעֻזֵּךְ לֹא זָכָרְתְּ

עַל־כֵּן תִּטְּעִי נִטְעֵי נַעֲמָנִים

7f. Men will turn away from idol-
worship to the God of Israel.

7. *his Maker ... the Holy One of Israel.*
These are common designations of God
in this Book. For the former, cf. li. 13,
liv. 5; for the latter, see on i. 4.

8. *Asherim.* Trees worshipped (Metsudath Zion). They will not even look at
them as intermediaries between them
and God (Malbim).

sun-images. Images made like chariots in
honor of the sun, as stated in the history
of King Manasseh in 2 Kings xxi. 3 (Ibn
Ezra).

9-11. Forgetfulness of God is the
cause of disillusionment and desolation.

9. *which were forsaken.* The literal
meaning of the Hebrew verb is active:
'they forsook,' but the previous clause

supplies no apparent subject. Hence the
passive sense (Targum). Ibn Ezra and
Kimchi see 'Canaanites' as the subject,
as mentioned below.

from before the children of Israel. An allusion to the time of the conquest of
Canaan by Joshua, when the cities were
forsaken by their inhabitants who fled
before the children of Israel (Ibn Ezra,
Kimchi).

after the manner of woods, etc. Which are
uninhabited (Rashi).

10. *plants of pleasantness.* Originally,
you planted plants of pleasantness, i.e.
you worshipped God, but now you
did set it with slips of a stranger, i.e.
now you have worshipped idols (Kimchi). Others explain this figuratively as
referring to the children they bore and
reared. Until now, you begot pleasant
children from Jewish wives, but now

And didst set it with slips of a
  stranger;

11. In the day of thy planting thou
    didst make it to grow,
  And in the morning thou didst
    make thy seed to blossom—
  A heap of boughs in the day of
    grief
  And of desperate pain.

12. Ah, the uproar of many peoples,
  That roar like the roaring of the
    seas;
  And the rushing of nations, that
    rush
  Like the rushing of mighty
    waters!

13. The nations shall rush like the
    rushing of many waters;
  But He shall rebuke them, and
    they shall flee far off,
  And shall be chased as the chaff
    of the mountains before the
    wind,
  And like the whirling dust before
    the storm.

14. At eventide behold terror;

וּזְמֹרַת זָר תִּזְרָעֶנּוּ׃

11 בְּיוֹם נִטְעֵךְ תְּשַׂגְשֵׂגִי
וּבַבֹּקֶר זַרְעֵךְ תַּפְרִיחִי
נֵד קָצִיר בְּיוֹם נַחֲלָה
וּכְאֵב אָנוּשׁ׃

12 הוֹי הֲמוֹן עַמִּים רַבִּים
כַּהֲמוֹת יַמִּים יֶהֱמָיוּן
וּשְׁאוֹן לְאֻמִּים כִּשְׁאוֹן
מַיִם כַּבִּירִים יִשָּׁאוּן׃

13 לְאֻמִּים כִּשְׁאוֹן מַיִם רַבִּים יִשָּׁאוּן
וְגָעַר בּוֹ וְנָס מִמֶּרְחָק
וְרֻדַּף כְּמֹץ הָרִים לִפְנֵי־רוּחַ
וּכְגַלְגַּל לִפְנֵי סוּפָה׃

14 לְעֵת עֶרֶב וְהִנֵּה בַלָּהָה

you set it with slips of a stranger; you
intermarried with gentiles (Abarbanel).

slips of a stranger. i.e. of a strange god.
Figurative for idol-worship of gentile
wives, as above.

11. *a heap of boughs.* All this care and
labour were spent in the expectation of
a fruitful result; but what they will
experience is only bitter disappointment (Metsudath David, Kimchi).

12-14. An oracle on Assyria. A graphic
picture of the onrush of its hosts against
Jerusalem and their sudden destruction
of her walls. The assonance and verbal
force of the Hebrew original cannot be
reproduced in translation.

12. *uproar.* Or 'multitude' (Abarbanel).

many peoples. The contingents of the subject nations composing the Assyrian
army of invasion (Rashi, Ibn Ezra).

13. *they shall flee.* The Hebrew has this
and the following verb in the singular.
Sennacherib alone *shall flee,* or the multitude of many peoples, i.e. the survivors, shall flee. Since this is a collective
noun, it appears in the singular (Abarbanel).

the chaff of the mountains. Wherever possible, threshing-floors were located on
tops of hills so that the wind might carry
off the chaff (Kimchi, Metsudath David).

14. *at eventide . . . before the morning.*
The destruction of Sennacherib's army
actually occurred between evening and
the following morning (cf. xxxvii. 36).

terror. The Assyrians were terrified by
the angel smiting them (Abarbanel).

And before the morning they
are not.
This is the portion of them that
spoil us,
And the lot of them that rob us.

בְּטֶרֶם בֹּקֶר אֵינֶנּוּ
זֶה חֵלֶק שׁוֹסֵינוּ
וְגוֹרָל לְבֹזְזֵינוּ:

18 ~~Shadow?~~ CHAPTER XVIII   יח

1. Ah, land of the buzzing of wings,
   Which is beyond the rivers of
   Ethiopia;
2. That sendeth ambassadors by
   the sea,
   Even in vessels of papyrus upon
   the waters!
   Go, ye swift messengers,

¹ הוֹי אֶרֶץ צִלְצַל כְּנָפָיִם
אֲשֶׁר מֵעֵבֶר לְנַהֲרֵי־כוּשׁ:
² הַשֹּׁלֵחַ בַּיָּם צִירִים
וּבִכְלֵי־גֹמֶא עַל־פְּנֵי־מַיִם
לְכוּ | מַלְאָכִים קַלִּים

Alternatively, the inhabitants of Jerusalem were terrified by the Assyrians
(Ibn Ezra).

they are not. The subject is the survivors;
the Hebrew has here also the singular,
the antecedent being 'the multitude'
(Abarbanel).

CHAPTER XVIII

RETURN OF ISRAEL TO ITS LAND

AFTER prophesying the downfall of
Assyria and the salvation that took place
during Hezekiah's reign, the prophet
proceeds to depict the great salvation to
take place in Messianic times (Kimchi).

1. *buzzing of wings.* Jewish exegetes render, 'shaded by wings.' This refers to the
allies of Gog and Magog, *Persia, Cush,*
and *Put* (Ezek. xxxviii. 5), whose countries are warm, and where birds assemble, thus shading the country with their
wings (Rashi). Others take this as an
allusion to the sails of the boats they will
send to Israel (Targum), or the mountains surrounding their country (Abarbanel).

beyond the rivers of Ethiopia. As mentioned
above, Ethiopia, or Cush, will be an ally
of Gog and Magog (Abarbanel). Ibn
Ezra takes this as the location of Assyria,
whence the ten tribes will return.

2. *that sendeth ambassadors by the sea.* The
king of the land on the other side of the
rivers of Ethiopia, will send ambassadors by way of the sea (Kimchi).

vessels of papyrus. The ambassadors from
Ethiopia to Jerusalem would come
down the Nile in light and swift skiffs
built of the leaves of the papyrus, ac-
comodating one or two passengers.
They were used on that part of the river
which ordinary boats could not navi-
gate (Kimchi, Abarbanel).

go. The king's charge to the ambassadors begins here. The king orders them
to ascertain whether it is true that Israel
has returned to its land (Rashi, Ibn
Ezra).

swift messengers. Who came by the swift
skiffs (Kimchi).

to a nation. Israel (Rashi, Ibn Ezra,
Kimchi).

tall and of glossy skin. Jewish exegetes render, 'pulled and torn.' Israel was pulled
from its place by the gentile nations,
like a lamb, pulled by its wool until the
wool is torn out and the flesh is torn.
This represents the destruction of their
bodies and their own land (Kimchi).

terrible . . . onward. From their very
inception, they were a terrible, or awe-

To a nation tall and of glossy
skin,
To a people terrible from their
beginning onward;
A nation that is sturdy and
treadeth down,
Whose land the rivers divide!

3. All ye inhabitants of the world,
and ye dwellers on the earth,
When an ensign is lifted up on
the mountains, see ye;
And when the horn is blown,
hear ye.

4. For thus hath the LORD said unto
me:
I will hold Me still, and I will
look on in My dwelling-place,
Like clear heat in sunshine,
Like a cloud of dew in the heat of
harvest.

5. For before the harvest, when the
blossom is over,
And the bud becometh a ripen-
ing grape,

אֶל־גּוֹי מְמֻשָּׁךְ וּמוֹרָט

אֶל־עַם נוֹרָא מִן־הוּא וָהָלְאָה

גּוֹי קַו־קָו וּמְבוּסָה

אֲשֶׁר־בָּזְאוּ נְהָרִים אַרְצוֹ:

3 כָּל־יֹשְׁבֵי תֵבֵל וְשֹׁכְנֵי אָרֶץ
כִּנְשֹׂא־נֵס הָרִים תִּרְאוּ
וְכִתְקֹעַ שׁוֹפָר תִּשְׁמָעוּ:

4 כִּי כֹה אָמַר יְהוָה אֵלַי
אֶשְׁקוֹטָה וְאַבִּיטָה בִמְכוֹנִי
כְּחֹם צַח עֲלֵי־אוֹר
כְּעָב טַל בְּחֹם קָצִיר:

5 כִּי־לִפְנֵי קָצִיר כְּתָם־פֶּרַח
וּבֹסֶר גֹּמֵל יִהְיֶה נִצָּה

4 יתיר ר׃ ד.

some nation. People saw in them wonders and marvels, for God was with
them in their success and in their distress. When they were good, they were
more prosperous than any other nation.
When they disobeyed God's word, He
would punish them, to chastise them,
not to destroy them, for, no matter how
much the nations pull and tear them,
they are unable to annihilate them
(Kimchi).

sturdy. Jewish exegetes render, 'punished in kind,' lit. 'a line for a line'
(Rashi).

treadeth down. According to Jewish commentaries, 'trodden.'

3. The prophet illustrates the need-
lessness of the voyage, since the whole
world will soon be aware of Israel's
return to its land (Rashi).

ensign ... horn. See below xxvii. 13.
According to Kimchi, all this is figurative, for when a person wishes to gather
a large throng, he raises an ensign on

the mountains so that they will see it
from afar and come. He also sounds a
horn, so that they will hear the sound
and come. So will the Israelites be gathered from all the countries of their
exile. The nations will bring them as
though an ensign was raised and a horn
sounded. Traditionally, the horn will
actually be sounded to herald the
ingathering of the exiles.

4. *I will hold ... look on.* Then, when
the redemption is realized, will I be
silent from moaning for My people
Israel (Kimchi).

My dwelling-place. viz. the Temple in
Jerusalem (Kimchi).

like clear heat ... harvest. As the heat and
the dew mysteriously and slowly but
steadily and surely ripen the crops, so
will God's purposes against the army of
Gog and Magog silently mature and
manifestly come to fruition (Kimchi).

5. *before the harvest.* The metaphor of
the preceding verse is continued; but

He will cut off the sprigs with
pruning-hooks,
And the shoots will He take
away and lop off.
6. They shall be left together unto
the ravenous birds of the
mountains,
And to the beasts of the earth;
And the ravenous birds shall
summer upon them,
And all the beasts of the earth
shall winter upon them.
7. In that time shall a present be
brought unto the LORD of hosts of a
people tall and of glossy skin, and
from a people terrible from their
beginning onward; a nation that is
sturdy and treadeth down, whose
land the rivers divide, to the place
of the name of the LORD of hosts,
the mount Zion.

וְכָרַת הַזַּלְזַלִּים בַּמַּזְמֵרוֹת
וְאֶת־הַנְּטִישׁוֹת הֵסִיר הֵתַז:
6 יֵעָזְבוּ יַחְדָּו לְעֵיט הָרִים
וּלְבֶהֱמַת הָאָרֶץ
וְקָץ עָלָיו הָעַיִט
וְכָל־בֶּהֱמַת הָאָרֶץ עָלָיו תֶּחֱרָף:
7 בָּעֵת הַהִיא יוּבַל־שַׁי לַיהוָה צְבָאוֹת
עַם מְמֻשָּׁךְ וּמוֹרָט וּמֵעַם נוֹרָא מִן־
הוּא וָהָלְאָה גּוֹי | קַו־קָו וּמְבוּסָה
אֲשֶׁר בָּזְאוּ נְהָרִים אַרְצוֹ אֶל־מְקוֹם
שֵׁם־יְהוָה צְבָאוֹת הַר־צִיּוֹן:

19   CHAPTER XIX   יט

1. The burden of Egypt.
Behold, the LORD rideth upon a
swift cloud,

1 מַשָּׂא מִצְרָיִם
הִנֵּה יְהוָה רֹכֵב עַל־עָב קַל

v. 5. ה׳ רפה   v. 5. פתח בס״פ

---

the *harvest* here symbolizes Gog's hope
of conquest which will be suddenly frustrated, for *He will cut off*, etc.

sprigs . . . shoots. The various ranks of the
army of Gog and Magog (Rashi,
Kimchi).

6. The metaphor is now dropped, and
the fate of the invading host is described
in all its stark horror.

they. The corpses of the warriors lying
before the walls of Jerusalem (Rashi,
Kimchi).

shall summer . . . winter. The bodies will
have no burial, and would remain
exposed to the beasts and birds both in
summer and winter, throughout the
years (Rashi, Kimchi).

7. *a present.* The Jews will be brought
to their land by the nations as a gift to

the Lord of Hosts Whose earthly dwelling-place is in Zion (Kimchi).

in that time. When the predicted events
will have come to pass.

a nation, etc. See on verse 2.

CHAPTER XIX

ORACLE ON EGYPT

IT is difficult to assign a definite date for
the historical allusions, and the following three possible dates have been suggested: 720, 711, and 702 B.C.E.

1–15. God's judgment on Egypt and
the consequences of her religious,
social, political and industrial conditions.

1. *the burden.* See on xiii. 1.

a swift cloud. Symbolizing speedy fulfil-

And cometh unto Egypt;
And the idols of Egypt shall be
   moved at His presence,
And the heart of Egypt shall
   melt within it.

2. And I will spur Egypt against
   Egypt;
And they shall fight every one
   against his brother,
And every one against his neigh-
   bour;
City against city, and kingdom
   against kingdom.

3. And the spirit of Egypt shall be
   made empty within it;
And I will make void the counsel
   thereof;
And they shall seek unto the
   idols, and to the whisperers,
And to the ghosts, and to the
   familiar spirits.

4. And I will give over the Egyptians
Into the hand of a cruel lord;
And a fierce king shall rule over
   them,
Saith the Lord, the LORD of
   hosts.

5. And the waters shall fail from
   the sea,
And the river shall be drained
   dry.

וּבָא מִצְרַיִם

וְנָעוּ אֱלִילֵי מִצְרַיִם מִפָּנָיו

וּלְבַב מִצְרַיִם יִמַּס בְּקִרְבּוֹ׃

2 וְסִכְסַכְתִּי מִצְרַיִם בְּמִצְרַיִם

וְנִלְחֲמוּ אִישׁ־בְּאָחִיו

וְאִישׁ בְּרֵעֵהוּ

עִיר בְּעִיר מַמְלָכָה בְּמַמְלָכָה׃

3 וְנָבְקָה רוּחַ־מִצְרַיִם בְּקִרְבּוֹ

וַעֲצָתוֹ אֲבַלֵּעַ

וְדָרְשׁוּ אֶל־הָאֱלִילִים וְאֶל־הָאִטִּים

וְאֶל־הָאֹבוֹת וְאֶל־הַיִּדְּעֹנִים׃

4 וְסִכַּרְתִּי אֶת־מִצְרַיִם

בְּיַד אֲדֹנִים קָשֶׁה

וּמֶלֶךְ עַז יִמְשָׁל־בָּם

נְאֻם הָאָדוֹן יְהוָה צְבָאוֹת׃

5 וְנִשְּׁתוּ־מַיִם מֵהַיָּם

וְנָהָר יֶחֱרַב וְיָבֵשׁ׃

ment of the judgment (Rashi, Ibn Ezra, Kimchi).

the idols . . . moved. Better, 'shall quake.' The Egyptians will be powerless to save their people (Rashi, Kimchi).

the heart . . . melt. Indicating loss of self-confidence.

2–4. God speaks.

2. *Egypt against Egypt.* Social discord and civil war will prevail (Kimchi).

city . . . kingdom. Political chaos will undermine the national stability (Kimchi).

3. *make void the counsel thereof.* Losing

the power of logical reasoning, the Egyptians have recourse to sorcery and witchcraft (Kimchi).

4. *cruel lord . . . fierce king.* Cambyses or Xerxes has been suggested by some authorities; others think of Esarhaddon or Asshurbanipal who ravaged Egypt in 672 and 662 respectively. Rashi, Ibn Ezra, and Kimchi identify this king merely as the king of Assyria.

5–10. Agricultural and industrial ruin.

5. *sea . . . river.* Since the sea will not return the waters of the Nile, but the Nile will empty into it and not refill, it will be as though the sea shall dry up (Rashi).

6. And the rivers shall become foul;
The streams of Egypt shall be
minished and dried up;
The reeds and flags shall wither.

7. The mosses by the Nile, by the
brink of the Nile,
And all that is sown by the Nile,
Shall become dry, be driven
away, and be no more.

8. The fishers also shall lament,
And all they that cast angle into
the Nile shall mourn,
And they that spread nets upon
the waters shall languish.

9. Moreover they that work in
combed flax,
And they that weave cotton,
shall be ashamed.

10. And her foundations shall be
crushed,
All they that make dams shall be
grieved in soul.

11. The princes of Zoan are utter
fools;

6 וְהֶאֶזְנִיחוּ נְהָרוֹת
דָּלְלוּ וְחָרְבוּ יְאֹרֵי מָצוֹר
קָנֶה וָסוּף קָמֵלוּ:
7 עָרוֹת עַל־יְאוֹר עַל־פִּי יְאוֹר
וְכֹל מִזְרַע יְאוֹר
יִבַשׁ נִדַּף וְאֵינֶנּוּ:
8 וְאָנוּ הַדַּיָּגִים
וְאָבְלוּ כָּל־מַשְׁלִיכֵי בַיְאוֹר חַכָּה
וּפֹרְשֵׂי מִכְמֹרֶת
עַל־פְּנֵי־מַיִם אֻמְלָלוּ:
9 וּבֹשׁוּ עֹבְדֵי פִשְׁתִּים שְׂרִיקוֹת
וְאֹרְגִים חוֹרָי:
10 וְהָיוּ שָׁתֹתֶיהָ מְדֻכָּאִים
כָּל־עֹשֵׂי שֶׂכֶר אַגְמֵי־נָפֶשׁ:
11 אַךְ־אֱוִלִים שָׂרֵי צֹעַן

---

6. *rivers ... streams.* The irrigation
canals and watercourses which inter-
sected the lands of the Nile (Kimchi).

7. Destruction of agriculture.

the mosses. The Hebrew word is of uncertain meaning. A proposed translation
is: 'bare places are on the Nile, on the
very brink of the Nile' (Ibn Ezra).

all that is sown by the Nile. Better, 'the
seed-land of the Nile,' i.e. the alluvial
deposit which is left after the inunda-
tion and makes the soil fertile (Targum).

cast angle ... spread nets. Both these
methods of fishing are depicted on
Egyptian monuments.

9. Cessation of the manufacture of
textiles.

cotton. lit. 'white stuffs' (Kimchi).

10. *foundations.* Of the fishing ponds
and sluices (Metsudath David).

that they make dams. To collect the water.
On this translation, the verse refers, like
verse 8, to the fishing industry; but this
is impossible in view of the intervention
of verse 8. This difficulty can be solved
by rendering in verse 9, 'they that weave
nets,' as Rashi indeed renders it.

11-15. The stupidity of Egypt's counsellors.

11. *Zoan.* Synonymous with Egypt as
often in the Scriptures. Zoan or Tanis
occupies an important place in Egyptian history and dates back, according
to some authorities, to the time of the

The wisest counsellors of
Pharaoh are a senseless
counsel;
How can ye say unto Pharaoh:
'I am the son of the wise,
The son of ancient kings'?
12. Where are they, then, thy wise
men?
And let them tell thee now;
And let them know what the
LORD of hosts
Hath purposed concerning
Egypt.
13. The princes of Zoan are become
fools,
The princes of Noph are de-
ceived;
They have caused Egypt to go
astray,
That are the corner-stone of her
tribes.
14. The LORD hath mingled within
her
A spirit of dizziness;
And they have caused Egypt to
stagger in every work thereof,
As a drunken man staggereth in
his vomit.

חַכְמֵי֙ יֹעֲצֵ֣י פַרְעֹ֔ה עֵצָ֖ה נִבְעָרָ֑ה
אֵ֚יךְ תֹּאמְר֣וּ אֶל־פַּרְעֹ֔ה
בֶּן־חֲכָמִ֥ים אֲנִ֖י בֶּן־מַלְכֵי־קֶֽדֶם׃

12 אַיָּם֙ אֵפ֔וֹא חֲכָמֶ֔יךָ
וְיַגִּ֥ידוּ נָ֖א לָ֑ךְ
וְיֵ֣דְע֔וּ מַה־יָּעַ֛ץ
יְהוָ֥ה צְבָא֖וֹת עַל־מִצְרָֽיִם׃

13 נֽוֹאֲלוּ֙ שָׂ֣רֵי צֹ֔עַן
נִשְּׁא֖וּ שָׂ֣רֵי נֹ֑ף
הִתְע֥וּ אֶת־מִצְרַ֖יִם
פִּנַּ֥ת שְׁבָטֶֽיהָ׃

14 יְהוָ֛ה מָסַ֥ךְ בְּקִרְבָּ֖הּ ר֣וּחַ עִוְעִ֑ים
וְהִתְע֤וּ אֶת־מִצְרַ֙יִם֙ בְּכָל־מַעֲשֵׂ֔הוּ
כְּהִתָּע֥וֹת שִׁכּ֖וֹר בְּקִיאֽוֹ׃

---

sixth dynasty. Situated on the right
bank of the Tanitic arm of the Nile, it
was the seat of the Hyksos kings (Biberfeld, Malbim).

I am the son, etc. The boast of each counsellor, claiming to be a direct descendant from the priestly caste which produced the early dynasties, and whose
possession of the wisdom of Egypt was
regarded as hereditary (Rashi, Kimchi).

12. The prophet turns from the counsellors to Pharaoh himself (Metsudath
David).

where are they. A rhetorical question, the
expected answer to which is 'nowhere;
they cannot tell, and even they themselves do not know' (Malbim).

13. *Noph.* Memphis, situated on the
left bank of the Nile, near Cairo. It was
the famous capital of Lower Egypt and
a centre of learning and religion. In
Hos. ix. 6 the name is spelt *Moph*; in
Egyptian it is Mnoph (Malbim).

the corner-stone. The heads, rulers
(Kimchi).

tribes. The castes or nomes in which the
Egyptian population was classified (See
Malbim).

14. *dizziness.* Metsudath Zion has 'perverseness.' The root-meaning is 'distor-
tion'; the mind cannot think clearly.

in every work thereof. Or, 'in all its doing.'

staggereth. Better, 'goeth astray.'

15. Neither shall there be for Egypt
   any work,
   Which head or tail, palm-branch
   or rush, may do.
16. In that day shall Egypt be like
unto women; and it shall tremble
and fear because of the shaking of
the hand of the LORD of hosts, which
He shaketh over it. 17. And the
land of Judah shall become a terror
unto Egypt, whensoever one maketh
mention thereof to it; it shall be
afraid, because of the purpose of the
LORD of hosts, which He purposeth
against it.
18. In that day there shall be five
cities in the land of Egypt that speak
the language of Canaan, and swear
to the LORD of hosts; one shall be
called The city of destruction.
19. In that day shall there be an

15 וְלֹא־יִהְיֶה לְמִצְרַיִם מַעֲשֶׂה
אֲשֶׁר יַעֲשֶׂה רֹאשׁ וְזָנָב כִּפָּה וְאַגְמוֹן:
16 בַּיּוֹם הַהוּא יִהְיֶה מִצְרַיִם כַּנָּשִׁים
וְחָרַד ׀ וּפָחַד מִפְּנֵי תְּנוּפַת יַד־יְהוָה
צְבָאוֹת אֲשֶׁר־הוּא מֵנִיף עָלָיו:
17 וְהָיְתָה אַדְמַת יְהוּדָה לְמִצְרַיִם לְחָגָּא
כֹּל אֲשֶׁר יַזְכִּיר אֹתָהּ אֵלָיו יִפְחָד
מִפְּנֵי עֲצַת יְהוָה צְבָאוֹת אֲשֶׁר־הוּא
18 יוֹעֵץ עָלָיו: בַּיּוֹם הַהוּא יִהְיוּ חָמֵשׁ
עָרִים בְּאֶרֶץ מִצְרַיִם מְדַבְּרוֹת שְׂפַת
כְּנַעַן וְנִשְׁבָּעוֹת לַיהוָה צְבָאוֹת עִיר
19 הַהֶרֶס יֵאָמֵר לְאֶחָת: בַּיּוֹם הַהוּא

15. The chaotic character of the
country will prevent concrete or fruitful
action on the part of any of its citizens.

head ... rush. Metaphors for members
of different ranks of society (see on ix.
13) (Rashi).

16f. Egypt will be in terror of the Lord
of Hosts and of His people in the land
of Judah.

16. *like unto women.* Weak and timid
(Kimchi).

shaking ... it. To strike it down i.e. the
city destined to be destroyed (Targum).
Kimchi states that the five cities entered
into a pact that, should any city revert to
idolatry, that city would be destroyed.
This is in agreement with the reading of
the consonantal text (*ha-heres*). Because
of the ability of gutteral letters to be
interchanged, the Targum and Talmud
explain this to mean 'city of the sun'
(*ha-cheres*).

17. The semicolon after *to it* should be
transported to appear after *unto Egypt,*
in agreement with the Hebrew accentuation.

land of Judah. i.e. the inhabitants of
Judea. Others take *land* literally. The

Egyptians being in terror of the Lord
(verse 16), the land of Judah, which is
His dwelling-place, also becomes a
terror to them.

whatsoever one maketh ... afraid. Or,
everyone to whom mention is made
thereof shall be afraid,' 'everyone'
meaning every Egyptian.

18. *five cities,* i.e. a union of five cities
(Abarbanel).

the language of Canaan. viz. Hebrew. The
reference is to Egyptians who were converted to the worship of God and
adopted Hebrew as their language, i.e.
the city destined to be destroyed (Targum). Kimchi states that the five cities
entered into a pact that, should any city
revert to idolatry, that city would be
destroyed. This is in agreement with the
reading of the consonantal text (*ha-
heres*). Because of the ability of guttural
letters to be interchanged, the Targum
and Talmud explain this to mean 'city of
the sun' (*ha-cheres*).

The city of destruction. i.e. Heliopolis, one
of the oldest, if not the oldest, of the
cities of Egypt, situated near the southern end of the Nile Delta. Targum
Jonathan, therefore, renders, 'the city of

altar to the Lord in the midst of the land of Egypt, and a pillar at the border thereof to the Lord. 20. And it shall be for a sign and for a witness unto the Lord of hosts in the land of Egypt; for they shall cry unto the Lord because of the oppressors, and He will send them a saviour, and a defender, who will deliver them. 21. And the Lord shall make Himself known to Egypt, and the Egyptians shall know the Lord in that day; yea, they shall worship with sacrifice and offering, and shall vow a vow unto the Lord, and shall perform it. 22. And the Lord will smite Egypt, smiting and healing; and they shall return unto the Lord, and He will be entreated of them, and will heal them.

23. In that day shall there be a highway out of Egypt to Assyria, and the Assyrian shall come into Egypt, and the Egyptian into Assyria; and the Egyptians shall worship with the Assyrians.

יִֽהְיֶ֤ה מִזְבֵּ֙חַ֙ לַֽיהוָ֔ה בְּת֖וֹךְ אֶ֣רֶץ
מִצְרָ֑יִם וּמַצֵּבָ֥ה אֵֽצֶל־גְּבוּלָ֖הּ
20 לַֽיהוָֽה׃ וְהָיָ֨ה לְא֥וֹת וּלְעֵ֛ד לַֽיהוָ֥ה
צְבָא֖וֹת בְּאֶ֣רֶץ מִצְרָ֑יִם כִּֽי־יִצְעֲק֤וּ
אֶל־יְהוָה֙ מִפְּנֵ֣י לֹֽחֲצִ֔ים וְיִשְׁלַ֥ח לָהֶ֛ם
21 מוֹשִׁ֥יעַ וָרָ֖ב וְהִצִּילָֽם׃ וְנוֹדַ֤ע יְהוָה֙
לְמִצְרַ֔יִם וְיָֽדְע֥וּ מִצְרַ֖יִם אֶת־יְהוָ֑ה
בַּיּ֣וֹם הַה֔וּא וְעָֽבְדוּ֙ זֶ֣בַח וּמִנְחָ֔ה
22 וְנָֽדְרוּ־נֵ֥דֶר לַֽיהוָ֖ה וְשִׁלֵּֽמוּ׃ וְנָגַ֧ף
יְהוָ֛ה אֶת־מִצְרַ֖יִם נָגֹ֣ף וְרָפ֑וֹא וְשָׁ֙בוּ֙
עַד־יְהוָ֔ה וְנֶעְתַּ֥ר לָהֶ֖ם וּרְפָאָֽם׃
23 בַּיּ֣וֹם הַה֗וּא תִּֽהְיֶ֨ה מְסִלָּ֤ה מִמִּצְרַ֙יִם֙
אַשּׁ֔וּרָה וּבָֽא־אַשּׁ֥וּר בְּמִצְרַ֖יִם וּמִצְרַ֣יִם
בְּאַשּׁ֑וּר וְעָֽבְד֥וּ מִצְרַ֖יִם אֶת־אַשּֽׁוּר׃

Beth-shemesh, which is destined to be destroyed, is said to be one of them.'

19. Josephus (*The Jewish War, vii. x. 3*) records that Onias IV, who built a Jewish temple at Leontopolis, *c.* 154 B.C.E., appealed to this text in support of the validity of his enterprise, which was bitterly opposed in Jerusalem as being contrary to the Mosaic legislation (See also Men. 109b).

an altar. For sacrifices (Malbim).

a pillar. A monumental symbol of the recognition of the Sovereignty of God (Malbim).

20. *it.* viz. the altar (Rashi).

the oppressors. The Hebrew omits the definite article.

21. *make Himself known.* The suffering inflicted upon the Egyptians and their salvation will be recognized by them as the act of God and induce in them a change of heart (Kimchi).

sacrifice. Of beasts.

offering. Of flour and oil.

22. *smiting and healing.* The chastisement will be disciplinary. It will last only while the people deviate from the right path. As soon as they return to the ways of morality they will be finally healed (Metsudath David).

23–25. Cordial relations will exist between Assyria and Egypt (*a highway*), who will be united with Israel in a triple alliance in the Kingdom of God culminating in universal blessing (Metsudath David).

23. *a highway.* Through the Land of Israel, connecting Assyria in the north with Egypt in the south. There will be unrestricted intercourse between the three nations, evidencing a state of peace (Metsudath David).

shall worship. The true God. The Hebrew could be translated, 'the Egyptian shall serve Assyria.' It was so understood by the Targum and other ancient versions and adopted by Ibn Ezra; but Kimchi construes as A.J. and is supported by

24. In that day shall Israel be the third with Egypt and with Assyria, a blessing in the midst of the earth; 25. for that the LORD of hosts hath blessed him, saying: 'Blessed be Egypt My people and Assyria the work of My hands, and Israel Mine inheritance.'

24 בַּיּוֹם הַהוּא יִהְיֶה יִשְׂרָאֵל שְׁלִישִׁיָּה
לְמִצְרַיִם וּלְאַשּׁוּר בְּרָכָה בְּקֶרֶב
25 הָאָרֶץ: אֲשֶׁר בֵּרֲכוֹ יְהוָה צְבָאוֹת
לֵאמֹר בָּרוּךְ עַמִּי מִצְרַיִם וּמַעֲשֵׂה
יָדַי אַשּׁוּר וְנַחֲלָתִי יִשְׂרָאֵל:

20 CHAPTER XX ב

1. In the year that (Tartan) came unto Ashdod, when Sargon the king of Assyria sent him, and he fought against Ashdod and took it; 2. at that time the LORD spoke by Isaiah the son of Amoz, saying: 'Go, and loose the sackcloth from off thy

1 בִּשְׁנַת בֹּא תַרְתָּן אַשְׁדּוֹדָה בִּשְׁלֹחַ
אֹתוֹ סַרְגוֹן מֶלֶךְ אַשּׁוּר וַיִּלָּחֶם
2 בְּאַשְׁדּוֹד וַיִּלְכְּדָהּ: בָּעֵת הַהִיא דִּבֶּר
יְהוָה בְּיַד־יְשַׁעְיָהוּ בֶן־אָמוֹץ לֵאמֹר
לֵךְ וּפִתַּחְתָּ הַשַּׂק מֵעַל מָתְנֶיךָ וְנַעַלְךָ

the next verse where the three peoples are described as equals.

24. The triple alliance will be a blessing to the world.

the third. Partner in this league of nations (Metsudath David).

25. *blessed him.* viz. Israel (Rashi, Ibn Ezra).

My people . . . work of My hands . . . Mine inheritance. The titles assigned to them are in ascending order of Divine affection (Ibn Ezra).

CHAPTER XX

SYMBOLIC acts by the prophet which announced an Assyrian conquest of Egypt and Ethiopia.

1. *in the year.* 711 B.C.E.

Tartan. Turtanu in Assyrian, the military title of the supreme commander or chief of staff (Marcus).

Ashdod. A centre of disaffection against Assyria, captured by Sargon in 711.

Sargon. He reigned 722–705 B.C.E. The father of Sennacherib, who reigned after Shalmaneser. He was virtually unknown until the ruins of his palace were discovered in Tel-Nebi-Yonus (Marcus).

2. *sackcloth.* A garment made of coarse linen or some hairy material, worn by ascetics or mourners as an upper garment. Isaiah was in mourning for the exile of the tribes of the Northern Kingdom (Kimchi, Abarbanel).

loins, and put thy shoe from off thy foot.' And he did so, walking naked and barefoot.

3. And the Lord said: 'Like as My servant Isaiah hath walked naked and barefoot to be for three years a sign and a wonder upon Egypt and upon Ethiopia, 4. so shall the king of Assyria lead away the captives of Egypt, and the exiles of Ethiopia, young and old, naked and barefoot, and with buttocks uncovered, to the shame of Egypt. 5. And they shall be dismayed and ashamed, because of Ethiopia their expectation, and of Egypt their glory. 6. And the inhabitant of this coast-land shall say in that day: Behold, such is our expectation, whither we fled for help to be delivered from the king of Assyria; and how shall we escape?'

תַּחֲלֹץ מֵעַל רַגְלֶךָ וַיַּעַשׂ כֵּן הָלֹךְ
3 עָרוֹם וְיָחֵף: וַיֹּאמֶר יְהֹוָה כַּאֲשֶׁר
הָלַךְ עַבְדִּי יְשַׁעְיָהוּ עָרוֹם וְיָחֵף שָׁלֹשׁ
שָׁנִים אוֹת וּמוֹפֵת עַל־מִצְרַיִם וְעַל־
4 כּוּשׁ: כֵּן יִנְהַג מֶלֶךְ־אַשּׁוּר אֶת־שְׁבִי
מִצְרַיִם וְאֶת־גָּלוּת כּוּשׁ נְעָרִים
וּזְקֵנִים עָרוֹם וְיָחֵף וַחֲשׂוּפַי שֵׁת עֶרְוַת
5 מִצְרָיִם: וְחַתּוּ וָבֹשׁוּ מִכּוּשׁ מַבָּטָם
6 וּמִן־מִצְרַיִם תִּפְאַרְתָּם: וְאָמַר יֹשֵׁב
הָאִי הַזֶּה בַּיּוֹם הַהוּא הִנֵּה־כֹה
מַבָּטֵנוּ אֲשֶׁר־נַסְנוּ שָׁם לְעֶזְרָה לְהִנָּצֵל
מִפְּנֵי מֶלֶךְ אַשּׁוּר וְאֵיךְ נִמָּלֵט אֲנָחְנוּ:

<hr>

21   CHAPTER XXI   כא

1. The burden of the wilderness of the sea.

1 מַשָּׂא מִדְבַּר־יָם

הפ׳ בפתח .4 v.

<hr>

naked. This means with torn clothing, not really naked (Rashi).

3. Resumes the narrative begun in verse 1 and explains the symbolism of the prophet's action. He shall go in this manner for three years. This proves that Tartan took Ashdod three years prior to the exile of Ethiopia and Egypt. They were exiled when Sennacherib marched on Jerusalem, bringing his captives from Ethiopia and Egypt (Rashi).

a wonder. i.e. a portent.

4. buttocks uncovered. For the practice of this indignity, cf. 2 Sam. x. 4.

to the shame of Egypt. lit. 'the nakedness of Egypt,' its exposure to humiliation (Ibn Ezra).

5. and they. The people of Judah on witnessing the tragic plight of their neighbours upon whom they had relied for protection against Assyria (Kimchi).

6. inhabitant. Collective noun for 'inhabitants.'

this coast-land. Judah and all other countries in that region, though in its stricter sense it describes the land of the Philistines which adjoined the Mediterranean (Kimchi).

such is our expectation. If the protecting nations could not withstand the onslaught of Assyria, what hope is there for the peoples who relied on their protection (Metsudath David).

how shall we escape? The pronoun we is emphatic in the text.

CHAPTER XXI

ORACLES in the wilderness of the sea (Babylon), Dumah (Edom) and Arabia. They are characterized by sympathy with these suffering nations.

As whirlwinds in the South
sweeping on,
It cometh from the wilderness,
from a dreadful land.
2. A grievous vision is declared
unto me:
'The treacherous dealer dealeth
treacherously, and the spoiler
spoileth.
Go up, O Elam! besiege, O
Media!
All the sighing thereof have I
made to cease.'
3. Therefore are my loins filled with
convulsion;

כְּסוּפוֹת בַּנֶּגֶב לַחֲלֹף

מִמִּדְבָּר בָּא מֵאֶרֶץ נוֹרָאָה:

² חָזוּת קָשָׁה הֻגַּד־לִי

הַבּוֹגֵד ׀ בּוֹגֵד וְהַשּׁוֹדֵד ׀ שׁוֹדֵד

עֲלִי עֵילָם צוּרִי מָדַי

כָּל־אַנְחָתָה הִשְׁבַּתִּי:

³ עַל־כֵּן מָלְאוּ מָתְנַי חַלְחָלָה

v. 2. הד׳ רפה v. 2. פתח בס״ם

1–10. Oracle on the capture of Babylon by the Persians under Cyrus in 538 B.C.E. (Rashi, Kimchi, Abarbanel).

1. *the burden.* See on xiii 1.

wilderness of the sea. Babylon is so described on account of its situation near the Persian Gulf (See Ibn Ezra). In the cuneiform inscriptions only South Babylonia is called 'land of the sea,' but the name may have been extended by the prophet to the entire country. Others render 'wilderness of the west,' Babylon being situated on the west of Persia and separated from it by a wilderness (Kimchi, Ibn Ezra).

the South. Hebrew *negeb,* the 'dry' (so lit.) pastoral country, now a desert area, south of Palestine whose storms and whirlwinds sweep on to the north (According to Targum). Others render, 'an arid land' (Kimchi, Rashi).

it. The menace to Babylon. Better, 'he,' referring to the enemy (Ibn Ezra).

from the wilderness. The flat region that intervenes between Babylon and Persia (Kimchi).

a dreadful land. Persia, which was the terror of Babylon's inhabitants (Kimchi).

2. *a grievous vision.* The prophet expresses his sympathies and commiseration even with the foreign and harsh

Babylonians in the calamity that hangs over their heads. See below verse 3.

the treacherous dealer . . . spoileth. Descriptive of Babylon's treatment of her captives. Most commentaries, however, render, 'the treacherous dealer—one will deal treacherously with him, and the spoiler—one will spoil him.' This refers to Cyrus, who will conquer Babylon (Kimchi).

Elam . . . Media. Both these countries were under the rule of the Persian king, Cyrus. Elam lay on the north of the Persian Gulf and east of the Tigris; Media extended to the north of it. Cyrus first ruled over Anshan in the north of the latter and conquered Media in 549 B.C.E, uniting both countries in one kingdom.

sighing. Of the victims of Babylon's oppression (Rashi, Ibn Ezra, Kimchi).

thereof. Some omit this word in accordance with the Masoretic form of the Hebrew and render 'all sighing (i.e. wherever in the world the effects of Babylon's ruthlessness were felt) have I made to cease' (Rashi).

3f. The prophet, in sympathy with the suffering Babylonians, expresses his terror and bewilderment at the approaching disaster. On another interpretation, the prophet gives expression to the feeling of each of the Babylonian victims (Rashi).

Pangs have taken hold upon me,
as the pangs of a woman in
travail;
I am bent so that I cannot hear;
I am affrighted so that I cannot
see.

4. My heart is bewildered, terror
hath overwhelmed me;
The twilight that I longed for
hath been turned for me into
trembling.

5. They prepare the table, they
light the lamps, they eat, they
drink—
'Rise up, ye princes, anoint the
shield.'

6. For thus hath the LORD said
unto me:
Go, set a watchman;
Let him declare what he seeth!

7. And when he seeth a troop,
horsemen by pairs,
A troop of asses, a troop of
camels,
He shall hearken diligently with
much heed.

צִירִים אֲחָזוּנִי כְּצִירֵי יוֹלֵדָה
נַעֲוֵיתִי מִשְּׁמֹעַ
נִבְהַלְתִּי מֵרְאוֹת׃

4 תָּעָה לְבָבִי פַּלָּצוּת בִּעֲתָתְנִי
אֵת נֶשֶׁף חִשְׁקִי שָׂם לִי לַחֲרָדָה׃

5 עָרֹךְ הַשֻּׁלְחָן
צָפֹה הַצָּפִית אָכוֹל שָׁתֹה
קוּמוּ הַשָּׂרִים מִשְׁחוּ מָגֵן׃

6 כִּי כֹה אָמַר אֵלַי אֲדֹנָי
לֵךְ הַעֲמֵד הַמְצַפֶּה
אֲשֶׁר יִרְאֶה יַגִּיד׃

7 וְרָאָה רֶכֶב צֶמֶד פָּרָשִׁים
רֶכֶב חֲמוֹר רֶכֶב גָּמָל
וְהִקְשִׁיב קֶשֶׁב רַב־קָשֶׁב׃

---

4. *heart.* In Hebrew usage, it is the seat of the intellect. *Bewildered* is lit. 'strayeth'; his mind reels.

twilight . . . longed for. i.e. the twilight when I longed for merriment and revelry to celebrate the Babylonian victory over the Persian army (Rashi). Others render: 'twilight of my pleasure,' i.e. the evening I spent in celebration of my ascent to the throne (Kimchi).

5. A vivid portrayal of the Babylonian night revelry suddenly brought to an abrupt end by a peremptory call to arms.

they prepare . . . light . . . eat . . . drink. The Hebrew use of infinitives adds vividness to the picture.

light the lamps. Other translations of the phrase are: 'play music' (Ibn Ezra) and 'set the watch' (Kimchi).

anoint the shield. A shield was oiled (cf. 2

Sam i. 21). to keep it smooth, to make the enemy's arrows glide off it (Rashi).

6–9. From the realistic but general description of the threatened doom of Babylon in the preceding verses, the prophet proceeds to delineate the graphic manner in which it was conveyed to him.

6. *for.* This seems to refer back to the beginning of verse 2, *a grievous vision is declared unto me* (Laniado).

set a watchman. It is as though the prophet is standing in Babylon and is speaking for the princes of Babylon, who exhort one another to set a watchman to keep them informed of the progress of the enemy (Kimchi).

7. *a troop.* Better, 'cavalcades' (lit. 'chariot' or the singular in a collective sense (symbolizing the Persian and Median hosts in their advance (Rashi).

asses . . . camels. These may have been used for transport behind the lines or,

8. And he cried as a lion: 'Upon the watch-tower, O Lord, I stand continually in the day-time, And I am set in my ward all the nights.'

9. And, behold, there came a troop of men, horsemen by pairs. And he spoke and said: 'Fallen, fallen is Babylon; And all the graven images of her gods are broken unto the ground.'

10. O thou my threshing, and the winnowing of my floor, That which I have heard from the LORD of hosts, The God of Israel, have I declared unto you.

11. The burden of Dumah. One calleth unto me out of Seir: 'Watchman, what of the night? Watchman, what of the night?'

8 וַיִּקְרָא אַרְיֵה עַל־מִצְפֶּה ׀ אֲדֹנָי
אָנֹכִי עֹמֵד תָּמִיד יוֹמָם
וְעַל־מִשְׁמַרְתִּי
אָנֹכִי נִצָּב כָּל־הַלֵּילוֹת:
9 וְהִנֵּה־זֶה בָא רֶכֶב אִישׁ
צֶמֶד פָּרָשִׁים
וַיַּעַן וַיֹּאמֶר
נָפְלָה נָפְלָה בָּבֶל
וְכָל־פְּסִילֵי אֱלֹהֶיהָ שִׁבַּר לָאָרֶץ:
10 מְדֻשָׁתִי וּבֶן־גָּרְנִי
אֲשֶׁר שָׁמַעְתִּי מֵאֵת יְהֹוָה צְבָאוֹת
אֱלֹהֵי יִשְׂרָאֵל הִגַּדְתִּי לָכֶם:
11 מַשָּׂא דּוּמָה
אֵלַי קֹרֵא מִשֵּׂעִיר
שֹׁמֵר מַה־מִּלַּיְלָה
שֹׁמֵר מַה־מִּלֵּיל:

as some maintain, in actual battle (Metsudath David).

8. *he cried.* The subject is the watchman (Ibn Ezra).

and I am set ... nights. Or, 'and on my sentry guard I take my stand through all the nights.'

9. The cavalcade anticipated in verse 7 is already approaching.

all the graven images. The destruction of a people's gods was an indication of its utter defeat by the enemy (Cp. Exodus xii. 12).

10. The prophet addresses Israel.

O thou my threshing ... floor. Better, 'O my trodden one and child of my threshing-floor.' Israel had been oppressed and trodden down by the Babylonian tyrant (See Rashi).

11f. An oracle on Dumah or Edom. Its date is uncertain, but may be identical with that of the preceding oracle.

11. *burden.* See on xiii. 1.

Dumah. Synonymous with Edom which was known in ancient Egyptian as *Aduma* and in Assyrian as *Udumu.* According to Rabbinic tradition, the allusion is to Rome, the chief city of Edom. The literal meaning is 'silence' which imparts an element of mystery to our exile, known as the exile of Edom (Abarbanel). Others identify the name with one of the sons of Ishmael mentioned in Gen. xxv. 14 (Ibn Ezra, Kimchi).

Seir. Sometimes called mount Seir and synonymous with Edom.

watchman. Not the same Hebrew noun as in verse 6 but one meaning 'guardian' (Rashi).

12. The watchman said:
'The morning cometh, and also
the night—
If ye will inquire, inquire ye;
return, come.'

13. The burden upon Arabia.
In the thickets in Arabia shall ye
lodge, O ye caravans of Dedanites.

14. Unto him that is thirsty bring ye
water!
The inhabitants of the land of
Tema did meet the fugitive
with his bread.

15. For they fled away from the
swords, from the drawn sword,
And from the bent bow, and
from the grievousness of war.

יב אָמַר שֹׁמֵר

אָתָא בֹקֶר וְגַם־לָיְלָה

אִם־תִּבְעָיוּן בְּעָיוּ שֻׁבוּ אֵתָיוּ׃

יג מַשָּׂא בַּעְרָב

בַּיַעַר בַּעְרַב תָּלִינוּ אֹרְחוֹת דְּדָנִים׃

יד לִקְרַאת צָמֵא הֵתָיוּ מָיִם

יֹשְׁבֵי אֶרֶץ תֵּימָא בְּלַחְמוֹ קִדְּמוּ נֹדֵד׃

טו כִּי־מִפְּנֵי חֲרָבוֹת נָדָדוּ

מִפְּנֵי | חֶרֶב נְטוּשָׁה

וּמִפְּנֵי קֶשֶׁת דְּרוּכָה

וּמִפְּנֵי כֹּבֶד מִלְחָמָה׃

what of the night? i.e. how far is the night spent? How long is the darkness with its frightening uncertainties to last? How near is the dawn of redemption? (Rashi).

12. *the morning cometh, and also the night.* An enigmatic answer which leads the enquirer to guess the meaning. *Morning* is symbolic of deliverance, *night* of darkness, uncertainty and oppression. The answer may mean morning comes for the righteous and night for the wicked, (as Rashi) or a period of prosperity will be followed by one of adversity (as Kimchi).

if ye will inquire. Though a clear answer cannot or would not be given now, a repeated enquiry on some future day may be more successful (Kimchi).

return, come. Or, 'come again.' Some explain: return first from your evil ways and then you may come to enquire about your destiny (Rashi).

13–17. An oracle on Arabia. The date is uncertain, but the reference may be to one of the military expeditions of Tiglath-pileser III or Sargon. We know from the cuneiform inscriptions that Arabian rulers paid tribute to Tiglath-pileser III in 738 and 734 and to Sargon

in 720 and 715. Ibn Ezra, too, mentions the King of Assyria.

13. *in the thickets.* Away from the regular caravan route which had been destroyed by the enemy.

shall ye lodge. More lit. 'shall ye pass the night' (R.V. margin).

Dedanites. These were an important trading tribe of Arabs living near Edom, somewhere to the north of the Gulf of Akaba (cf. Ezek. xxvii. 20).

14. Unable to procure their food supplies from the normal stations on the regular route, the Dedanite caravans, thirsty and hungry, are dependent on the mercy of the tribes that occupied the country bordering on the less-frequented paths.

Tema. Modern Teima in the north of Arabia on the edge of the Arabian desert, east of the pilgrim route from Damascus to Mecca. Its inhabitants were engaged in commerce and presumably stood in friendly intercourse with the Dedanites.

his bread. The bread he was in need of (Ibn Ezra).

15. *the swords.* Of the raiding bands

16. For thus hath the Lord said unto me: 'Within a year, according to the years of a hireling, and all the glory of Kedar shall fail; 17. and the residue of the number of the archers, the mighty men of the children of Kedar, shall be diminished; for the LORD, the God of Israel, hath spoken it.'

16 כִּי־כֹה אָמַר אֲדֹנָי אֵלַי בְּעוֹד שָׁנָה
כִּשְׁנֵי שָׂכִיר וְכָלָה כָּל־כְּבוֹד קֵדָר׃
17 וּשְׁאָר מִסְפַּר־קֶשֶׁת גִּבּוֹרֵי בְנֵי־קֵדָר
יִמְעָטוּ כִּי יְהֹוָה אֱלֹהֵי־יִשְׂרָאֵל
דִּבֵּר׃

CHAPTER XXII   כב

1. The burden concerning the Valley of Vision.

   What aileth thee now, that thou
   art wholly gone up to the
   housetops,

2. Thou that art full of uproar, a
   tumultuous city, a joyous
   town?

   Thy slain are not slain with the
   sword, nor dead in battle.

1 מַשָּׂא גֵּיא חִזָּיוֹן
מַה־לָּךְ אֵפוֹא
כִּי־עָלִית כֻּלָּךְ לַגַּגּוֹת׃
2 תְּשֻׁאוֹת ׀ מְלֵאָה עִיר הוֹמִיָּה
קִרְיָה עַלִּיזָה
חֲלָלַיִךְ לֹא חַלְלֵי־חֶרֶב
וְלֹא מֵתֵי מִלְחָמָה׃

which infested the caravan routes (Kimchi).

16f. A prosaic conclusion of the oracle on Arabia.

16. *according . . . hireling.* See on xvi. 14.

Kedar. A pastoral tribe in the Syrian desert (cf. lx. 7). In the context it is synonymous with Arabia (Targum).

17. *archers.* The Hebrew is literally 'bow.' Archery was practiced among the northern Arabs from remote antiquity. According to Gen. xii. 20 their ancestor Ishmael was an archer in the wilderness.

CHAPTER XXII

1-14. The calamities that are to befall Jerusalem. The prophecy evidently relates to the invasion of Judah in 586 B.C.E. by Nebuchadnezzar (Kara, Abarbanel, Malbim).

1-4. Jerusalem, which, at one time had abandoned itself to mirth and revelry, is now plunged into deep sorrow and gloom.

1. *Valley of Vision.* Jerusalem is described as a *valley* because it is surrounded by hills, and *of visions* because it was the scene for, or the object of, many of the prophetic visions (Rashi).

what aileth thee now. The literal meaning is, 'what, pray, (hath come) to thee?' or, 'what, pray, meanest thou?' The prophet, weighed down by forebodings, asks the question ironically of the city's population who have no cares on their mind. The prophet pictures a man watching all that transpires in Jerusalem from the beginning of the siege until the city is conquered. He witnesses strange occurrences, which demonstrate that the city was not conquered in the usual manner, but that the hand of God was against it to destroy it (Malbim).

the housetops. The flat roofs of the houses were vantage ground for watching the approaching armies coming to beiege the city (Rashi, Ibn Ezra).

2f. A vision of the impending calamities.

3. All thy rulers are fled together,
   Without the bow they are bound;
   All that are found of thee are
       bound together, they are fled
       afar off.

4. Therefore said I: 'Look away
       from me, I will weep bitterly;
   Strain not to comfort me, for the
       destruction of the daughter of
       my people.'

5. For it is a day of trouble, and of
       trampling, and of perplexity,
   From the Lord, the GOD of
       hosts, in the Valley of Vision;
   Kir shouting, and Shoa at the
       mount.

6. And Elam bore the quiver, with
       troops of men, even horsemen;

כָּל־קְצִינַיִךְ נָדְדוּ־יַחַד ³
מִקֶּשֶׁת אֻסָּרוּ
כָּל־נִמְצָאַיִךְ אֻסְּרוּ יַחְדָּו
מֵרָחוֹק בָּרָחוּ:
עַל־כֵּן אָמַרְתִּי ⁴
שְׁעוּ מִנִּי אֲמָרֵר בַּבֶּכִי
אַל־תָּאִיצוּ לְנַחֲמֵנִי
עַל־שֹׁד בַּת־עַמִּי:
כִּי יוֹם מְהוּמָה וּמְבוּסָה וּמְבוּכָה ⁵
לַאדֹנָי יֱהוִֹה צְבָאוֹת בְּגֵי חִזָּיוֹן
מְקַרְקַר קִר וְשׁוֹעַ אֶל־הָהָר:
וְעֵילָם נָשָׂא אַשְׁפָּה ⁶
בְּרֶכֶב אָדָם פָּרָשִׁים

2. *thy slain . . . battle.* They will not die like heroes on the battlefield, but perish from starvation (contrast Lam. iv. 9) or lose their lives by ignominious execution (Rashi, Kara, Targum).

3. *rulers.* Zedekiah and his officers, who went out to flee at night (Rashi).

without the bow . . . bound. Having thrown away their bows in their precipitous flight. Jewish exegetes, however, render: 'they are bound by the archers.' By *bound* is meant 'taken prisoners' (Kimchi).

they are fled afar off. i.e. as well as those who fled. Both they who were found in the city as well as they who fled shared the same fate (Kimchi).

4. The prophet, overcome by sorrow in view of the approachingd disaster, refuses to be comforted (Ibn Ezra, Kimchi, Abarbanel).

look away from me. Better 'leave me alone' (Targum).

the daughter of my people. This phrase, common in Jeremiah and Lamentations, occurs only here in this Book.

5-11. The prophet's vision of the future, begun in verses 2f., is resumed.

5. *trouble . . . trampling . . . perplexity.* The impressive assonance of the Hebrew, *mehumah umebusah umebuchah*, cannot be reproduced in translation.

Kir . . . Shoa. Probably tribes participating in the invasion (Kara). Others render the second part of the verse: 'battering down the wall and a cry (of distress ascends) to the mountain' (Ibn Ezra).

6. *Elam.* See on xxi. 2. Jer. xlix. 35 speaks of tne might of *the bow of Elam,* its men being expert archers.

with troops . . . horsemens. The phrase may mean 'men on horseback among the chariots.'

Aram

And Kir uncovered the shield.

7. And it came to pass, when thy choicest valleys were full of chariots,

And the horsemen set themselves in array at the gate,

8. And the covering of Judah was laid bare,

that thou didst look in that day to the armour in the house of the forest. 9. And ye saw the breaches of the city of David, that they were many; and ye gathered together the waters of the lower pool. 10. And ye numbered the houses of Jerusalem, and ye broke down the houses to fortify the wall; 11. ye made also a basin between the two walls for the water of the old pool—

But ye looked not unto Him that had done this,

Neither had ye respect unto Him that fashioned it long ago.

וְקִיר עֵרָה מָגֵן:

7 וַיְהִי מִבְחַר־עֲמָקַיִךְ מָלְאוּ רֶכֶב
וְהַפָּרָשִׁים שֹׁת שָׁתוּ הַשָּׁעְרָה:

8 וַיְגַל אֵת מָסַךְ יְהוּדָה
וַתַּבֵּט בַּיּוֹם הַהוּא אֶל־נֶשֶׁק בֵּית

9 הַיָּעַר: וְאֵת בְּקִיעֵי עִיר־דָּוִד
רְאִיתֶם כִּי־רָבּוּ וַתְּקַבְּצוּ אֶת־מֵי

10 הַבְּרֵכָה הַתַּחְתּוֹנָה: וְאֶת־בָּתֵּי
יְרוּשָׁלַםִ סְפַרְתֶּם וַתִּתְצוּ הַבָּתִּים

11 לְבַצֵּר הַחוֹמָה: וּמִקְוָה עֲשִׂיתֶם בֵּין
הַחֹמֹתַיִם לְמֵי הַבְּרֵכָה הַיְשָׁנָה
וְלֹא הִבַּטְתֶּם אֶל־עֹשֶׂיהָ
וְיֹצְרָהּ מֵרָחוֹק לֹא רְאִיתֶם:

v. 10. הת׳ רפה

Kir. The place of origin of the Arameans (cf. Amos ix. 7).

uncovered the shield. To enter into battle. Shields were kept in leather coverings when not in use (Rashi, Ibn Ezra).

7. *and it came to pass.* [With prophetic foresight Isaiah envisages the scene] (Kimchi).

set . . . gate. (Kimchi). Alternatively 'placed the implements of siege at the gate (Rashi, Ibn Ezra). Kimchi suggests 'attacked the gate.'

8. *covering . . . bare.* Its defencelessness was made evident by the ease with which it was overrun (Rashi, Ibn Ezra).

of the forest. Of Lebanon which, since the days of Solomon (cf. I Kings vii. 2ff., x. 17) seems to have been used as an arsenal (Rashi, Kimchi).

9. *ye saw.* i.e. you inspected in preparation for the attack by the enemy (Kimchi).

city of David. The citadel of mount Zion.

the lower pool. Some identify it with the *upper pool* (vii. 3). The water that flowed outside the wall was then gathered inside to be ready for making mortar to repair the wall (Kimchi), or so that the enemies would not find any water (Kara).

10. *numbered the houses.* To ascertain how many could be spared for use in the fortification of the wall (Rashi).

11. *basin.* Better, 'reservoir.'

the two walls. It is suggested that the spot was the entrance to the Tyropoean Valley, where the wall of Zion and that of the western hill met.

the old pool. Possibly the pool of Siloam whose surplus water was to be gathered in the reservoir.

this . . . it. viz. the evil decree (Ibn Ezra).

101

12. And in that day did the Lord,
    the God of hosts, call
    To weeping, and to lamentation,
    and to baldness, and to girding
    with sackcloth;

13. And behold joy and gladness,
    Slaying oxen and killing sheep,
    Eating flesh and drinking wine—
    'Let us eat and drink, for to-
    morrow we shall die!'

14. And the Lord of hosts revealed
    Himself in mine ears:
    Surely this iniquity shall not be
    expiated by you till ye die,
    Saith the Lord, the God of hosts.

15. Thus saith the Lord, the God of
    hosts:
    Go, get thee unto this steward,

וַיִּקְרָא אֲדֹנָי יְהוִה 12
צְבָאוֹת בַּיּוֹם הַהוּא
לִבְכִי וּלְמִסְפֵּד
וּלְקָרְחָה וְלַחֲגֹר שָׂק:

וְהִנֵּה ׀ שָׂשׂוֹן וְשִׂמְחָה 13
הָרֹג ׀ בָּקָר וְשָׁחֹט צֹאן
אָכֹל בָּשָׂר וְשָׁתוֹת יָיִן
אָכוֹל וְשָׁתוֹ כִּי מָחָר נָמוּת:

וְנִגְלָה בְאָזְנָי יְהוָה צְבָאוֹת 14
אִם־יְכֻפַּר הֶעָוֹן
הַזֶּה לָכֶם עַד־תְּמֻתוּן
אָמַר אֲדֹנָי יְהוִה צְבָאוֹת:

כֹּה אָמַר אֲדֹנָי יְהוִה צְבָאוֹת 15
לֶךְ־בֹּא אֶל־הַסֹּכֵן הַזֶּה

קמץ בטרחא **v.** 14.

12-14. Instead of lamentation and penitence the people indulged in merriment. Such complacency cannot be forgiven.

12. *call.* Warning the people by the threatening signs of the times and through His prophets to return unto Him in repentance and humility (Kimchi).

weeping . . . sackcloth. The outward signs of mourning or penitence (Kimchi).

13. *let us eat and drink.* The Hebrew use of infinitives, 'to eat and to drink,' implies continuous and excessive indulgence in revelries and orgies. The sentence may have been the slogan of the reckless revellers who would enjoy themselves while they could, for life was short and death might come at any moment (Ibn Ezra, Kimchi, Abarbanel).

14. *surely this iniquity . . . die.* God's message through the prophet (Targum).

till ye die. Only death will purge the sins from you (Kimchi). Others explain, 'the punishment will be nothing less than death' (Targum).

saith . . . hosts. Repetition of the first part of the verse for emphasis. This followed Targum. Others render: 'In My ears it was revealed, I, the Lord of Hosts. Surely . . .' sayeth the Lord . . . According to this, there is no repetition (Ibn Ezra, Kimchi).

15-25. Denunciation of Shebna, a powerful politician in the reign of Hezekiah, and his replacement by a worthier man.

15-19. Condemnation, deposition and exile of Shebna who held the influential office of vizier.

15. *over the house.* The royal palace (Ibn Ezra, Kimchi). Others believe him to have been the trustee over the Temple (Rashi from Midrash).

Even unto Shebna, who is over
the house:
16. What hast thou here, and whom
hast thou here,
That thou hast hewed thee out
here a sepulchre,
Thou that hewest thee out a
sepulchre on high,
And gravest a habitation for thyself in the rock?
17. Behold, the LORD will hurl thee
up and down with a man's
throw;
Yea, He will wind thee round
and round;
18. He will violently roll and toss
thee
Like a ball into a large country;
There shalt thou die, and there
shall be the chariots of thy
glory,
Thou shame of thy lord's house.
19. And I will thrust thee from thy
post,
And from thy station shalt thou
be pulled down.

עַל־שֶׁבְנָא אֲשֶׁר עַל־הַבָּיִת:
16 מַה־לְךָ פֹה וּמִי־לְךָ פֹה
כִּי־חָצַבְתָּ לְךָ פֹּה קָבֶר
חֹצְבִי מָרוֹם קִבְרוֹ
חֹקְקִי בַסֶּלַע מִשְׁכָּן לוֹ:
17 הִנֵּה יְהֹוָה מְטַלְטֶלְךָ טַלְטֵלָה גָּבֶר
וְעֹטְךָ עָטֹה:
18 צָנוֹף יִצְנָפְךָ צְנֵפָה
כַּדּוּר אֶל־אֶרֶץ רַחֲבַת יָדָיִם
שָׁמָּה תָמוּת וְשָׁמָּה מַרְכְּבוֹת כְּבוֹדֶךָ
קְלוֹן בֵּית אֲדֹנֶיךָ:
19 וַהֲדַפְתִּיךָ מִמַּצָּבֶךָ
וּמִמַּעֲמָדְךָ יֶהֶרְסֶךָ:

16. Scripture denigrates him because
he plotted to surrender Hezekiah to the
king of Assyria, as the Rabbis relate in
Sanh. 26a (Rashi).

what has thou here. What claims have you,
who are not even a native of Jerusalem,
to hew a sepulchre among the
sepulchres of the House of David?
(Kimchi).

whom hast thou here. You have not even
one relative among the nobility or the
higher classes of society (Rashi).

hewed thee out here. Among the
sepulchres of the aristocracy (Rashi).

on high. Perhaps literally, on a hill or
mountain (Malbim). The Hebrew may
also signify 'among the great.' What
Shebna was doing evidenced his presumption and arrogance (Rashi).

17. the LORD will hurl . . . throw. Or,
'will fling thee forth violently, O thou
man.' Shebna will be deprived both of
position and influence (Ibn Ezra,
Kimchi).

18. He will violently roll. The verb is
found elsewhere only in Lev. xvi. 4,
'wind a turban around the head.' The
literal rendering is: 'He will entirely
wind thee with a winding' (Rashi).

and toss thee like a ball. The first four
words are to be supplied in translation.
The Hebrew is simply 'ball,' but the
construction is pregnant (Kimchi).

a large country. The Rabbis identify this
place as Casiphia, a Babylonian city,
where many Jews settled in their exile.
See Ezra viii. 2 (Rashi from Midrash).

there shall be the chariots of thy glory. Either
an ironical eulogy, or a jibe at his ostentation (Malbim).

thy lord's. viz. Hezekiah's (Malbim).

19. I will thrust thee. The change of person is rather difficult; an instance of it
occurred in x. 12. The first half of the
verse seems to be spoken by God, and
shalt thou be pulled down is literally 'He
(meaning God) will pull thee down'
(Kimchi).

20. And it shall come to pass in that day,
    That I will call my servant Eliakim the son of Hilkiah;
21. And I will clothe him with thy robe,
    And bind him with thy girdle,
    And I will commit thy government into his hand;
    And he shall be a father to the inhabitants of Jerusalem, and to the house of Judah.
22. And the key of the house of David will I lay upon his shoulder;
    And he shall open, and none shall shut;
    And he shall shut, and none shall open.
23. And I will fasten him as a peg in a sure place;
    And he shall be for a throne of honour to his father's house.
24. And they shall hang upon him all the glory of his father's house,

20 וְהָיָה בַּיּוֹם הַהוּא
וְקָרָאתִי לְעַבְדִּי
לְאֶלְיָקִים בֶּן־חִלְקִיָּהוּ:
21 וְהִלְבַּשְׁתִּיו כֻּתָּנְתֶּךָ
וְאַבְנֵטְךָ אֲחַזְּקֶנּוּ
וּמֶמְשַׁלְתְּךָ אֶתֵּן בְּיָדוֹ
וְהָיָה לְאָב
לְיוֹשֵׁב יְרוּשָׁלַ͏ִם וּלְבֵית יְהוּדָה:
22 וְנָתַתִּי מַפְתֵּחַ בֵּית־דָּוִד עַל־שִׁכְמוֹ
וּפָתַח וְאֵין סֹגֵר
וְסָגַר וְאֵין פֹּתֵחַ:
23 וּתְקַעְתִּיו יָתֵד בְּמָקוֹם נֶאֱמָן
וְהָיָה לְכִסֵּא כָבוֹד לְבֵית אָבִיו:
24 וְתָלוּ עָלָיו כֹּל | כְּבוֹד בֵּית־אָבִיו

20–23. The promotion and installation of Eliakim, God's *servant,* as successor to Shebna.

20. *that day.* When the prophecy will be fulfilled (Kimchi).

my servant Eliakim. He was the servant of the Lord (*my* should be printed *My*); Shebna served his own interests. In xxxvi. 3 Eliakim is said to be *over the household* of Hezekiah (Ibn Ezra).

21. *robe . . . girdle.* The king's officers wore distinguishing liveries to mark their respective offices and ranks. The *robe* (*kuttoneth*) is said to have been a long garment made of linen cloth (Ibn Ezra).

a father. Counsellor, friend and bene-

volent administrator (cf. Gen. xlv. 8) (Kimchi).

22. *the key.* The recognized symbol of outstanding authority in the royal palace and in the country generally (Ibn Ezra).

upon his shoulder. The officials of the king's household would wear a key on their shoulder as an emblem of their position (Malbim).

he shall open, etc. He will have supreme power in all State affairs (Kimchi).

23. *fasten . . . place.* A simile denoting permanency of office (Rashi).

24. Eliakim's entire family, great and small, young and old, will find security and safety in his eminence.

the offspring and the issue, all vessels of small quantity, from the vessels of cups even to all the vessels of flagons. 25. In that day, saith the LORD of hosts, shall the peg that was fastened in a sure place give way; and it shall be hewn down, and fall, and the burden that was upon it shall be cut off; for the LORD hath spoken it.

הַצֶּאֱצָאִים֙ וְהַצְּפִעֹ֔ות כֹּ֖ל כְּלֵ֣י הַקָּטָ֑ן מִכְּלֵי֙ הָֽאַגָּנֹ֔ות וְעַ֖ד כָּל־כְּלֵ֥י הַנְּבָלִֽים׃ 25 בַּיֹּ֣ום הַה֗וּא נְאֻם֙ יְהוָ֣ה צְבָאֹ֔ות תָּמוּשׁ֙ הַיָּתֵ֔ד הַתְּקוּעָ֖ה בְּמָקֹ֣ום נֶאֱמָ֑ן וְנִגְדְּעָ֣ה וְנָפְלָ֗ה וְנִכְרַת֙ הַמַּשָּׂ֣א אֲשֶׁר־עָלֶ֔יהָ כִּ֥י יְהוָ֖ה דִּבֵּֽר׃

---

23 CHAPTER XXIII **כג**

1. The burden of Tyre.
   Howl, ye ships of Tarshish,
   For it is laid waste, so that there
      is no house, no entering in;
   From the land of Kittim it is
      revealed to them.

מַשָּׂ֖א צֹ֑ר 1
הֵילִ֣ילוּ ׀ אֳנִיֹּ֣ות תַּרְשִׁ֗ישׁ
כִּֽי־שֻׁדַּ֤ד מִבַּ֙יִת֙ מִבֹּ֔וא
מֵאֶ֥רֶץ כִּתִּ֖ים נִגְלָה־לָֽמֹו׃

the issue. The Hebrew word denotes something emanating from the body. Comp. iv. 15 (Rashi).

25. The phraseology (*the peg that was fastened in a sure place*) seems to connect this verse with the preceding one, the reference still being to Eliakim. But it is difficult to reconcile this unexpected fall with the greatness and permanency of position foretold in the previous verses. Many commentators refer the verse back to Shebna's dismissal: Eliakim will be a *peg in a sure place* and remain so and thus be a reliable support for all his relatives and dependants; but Shebna, *the peg that was fastened in a sure place,* will give way and the entire load of dependants will, like himself, come down with a crash (Rashi, Ibn Ezra, Kimchi, Abarbanel).

CHAPTER XXIII

ORACLE ON TYRE AND ZIDON

A PROPHETIC message on the destruction

of Phoenicia and particularly its principal cities and harbours, Tyre and Zidon.

1. Tidings of the destruction of the Phoenician ports are brought to the ships of Tarshish while calling at Cyprus on their homeward journey.

ships of Tarshish. Cf. ii. 16. The great merchant vessels of the time, or ships that traded with Tarshish (Tartessus) in Spain on the mouth of the river Guadalquivir (Malbim, I Kings x. 22).

for it. Tyre or all Phoenicia.

no entering in. Into port (Malbim).

land of Kittim. Cyprus, so named from Kition or Kitium in the south of the island (Alshich, Biberfeld).

it is revealed to them. By the fugitive of Tyre who fled to Cyprus, that disaster had overtaken their homeland (Rashi).

2. The prophet addresses the inhabitants of Phoenicia.

2. Be still, ye inhabitants of the coastland;
   Thou whom the merchants of Zidon, that pass over the sea, have replenished.
3. And on great waters the seed of Shihor, *east Nile*
   The harvest of the Nile, was her revenue;
   And she was the mart of nations.
4. Be thou ashamed, O Zidon; for the sea hath spoken,
   The stronghold of the sea, saying:
   'I have not travailed, nor brought forth,
   Neither have I reared young men, nor brought up virgins.'
5. When the report cometh to Egypt,
   They shall be sorely pained at the report of Tyre.
6. Pass ye over to Tarshish;
   Howl, ye inhabitants of the coastland.
7. Is this your joyous city,

² דֹּמּוּ יֹשְׁבֵי אִי
סֹחֵר צִידוֹן עֹבֵר יָם מִלְאוּךְ׃
³ וּבְמַיִם רַבִּים זֶרַע שִׁחֹר
קְצִיר יְאוֹר תְּבוּאָתָהּ
וַתְּהִי סְחַר גּוֹיִם׃
⁴ בּוֹשִׁי צִידוֹן כִּי אָמַר יָם
מָעוֹז הַיָּם לֵאמֹר
לֹא־חַלְתִּי וְלֹא־יָלַדְתִּי
וְלֹא גִדַּלְתִּי בַחוּרִים
רוֹמַמְתִּי בְתוּלוֹת׃
⁵ כַּאֲשֶׁר־שֵׁמַע לְמִצְרָיִם
יָחִילוּ כְּשֵׁמַע צֹר׃
⁶ עִבְרוּ תַּרְשִׁישָׁה
הֵילִילוּ יֹשְׁבֵי אִי׃
⁷ הֲזֹאת לָכֶם עַלִּיזָה

be still. Sit silently and mourn, you dwellers of the island of the sea, for the seafaring merchants of Zidon were wont to replenish you with all merchandise. Now, when Tyre falls, Zidon will fall, for they were within a day's journey from one another (Rashi).

coastland. Of Phoenicia.

merchants. The Hebrew singular is used in a collective sense.

Zidon. The second of the two biggest harbours of Phoenicia and, according to some authorities, the most ancient of the Phoenician settlements (Malbim, Jos. xix. 29).

have replenished. Enriched with the wealth of their commercial enterprise (Kimchi).

3. *the seed of Shihor.* The Nile or its Pelusiac branch is also named *Shihor* (cf. Jer. ii. 18); and *the seed* is the grain or

other produce which Egypt, as one of the most important granaries of the ancient world, supplied to the Mediterranean countries. The grain, as well as the other Nile products (*harvest of the Nile*), was shipped in Egyptian vessels to the ports of Zidon and Tyre (Rashi, Kimchi).

4. The sea bordering on the Phoenician coast is now deserted and lonely like a long bereaved mother who forgot that she ever had any children (Rashi, Kimchi).

5. Egypt, who was in fear of Nebuchadnezzar, trembles when she hears of the fall of Tyre (Kimchi).

6. The Phoenicians are urged to escape from their doomed country to seek refuge in their distant colony in Spain (Rashi).

7. The prophet recalls the former prosperity and ramifications of Tyre,

Whose feet in antiquity,
In ancient days,
Carried her afar off to sojourn?
8. Who hath devised this against
   Tyre, the crowning city,
   Whose merchants are princes,
   Whose traffickers are the honoured
   able of the earth?
9. The LORD of hosts hath devised
   it,
   To pollute the pride of all glory,
   To bring into contempt all the
   honourable of the earth.
10. Overflow thy land as the Nile,
    O daughter of Tarshish! there is
    no girdle any more.
11. He hath stretched out His hand
    over the sea,

מִימֵי־קֶדֶם קַדְמָתָהּ
יֹבִלוּהָ רַגְלֶיהָ
מֵרָחוֹק לָגוּר׃
8 מִי יָעַץ זֹאת עַל־צֹר הַמַּעֲטִירָה
אֲשֶׁר סֹחֲרֶיהָ שָׂרִים
כִּנְעָנֶיהָ נִכְבַּדֵּי־אָרֶץ׃
9 יְהוָה צְבָאוֹת יְעָצָהּ
לְחַלֵּל גְּאוֹן כָּל־צְבִי
לְהָקֵל כָּל־נִכְבַּדֵּי־אָרֶץ׃
10 עִבְרִי אַרְצֵךְ כַּיְאֹר
בַּת־תַּרְשִׁישׁ אֵין מֵזַח עוֹד׃
11 יָדוֹ נָטָה עַל־הַיָּם

---

either in sympathy or in irony (Abarbanel).

in antiquity . . . days. Tyre is said by Josephus to have been founded 240 years before Solomon built his Temple in Jerusalem (*Antiquities*, VIII. iii. 1). Its antiquity is also attested by the classical historians, Herodotus and Strabo (See Ibn Ezra, Kimchi).

carried . . . to sojourn. Jewish exegetes render: 'Is this your joyous city from antiquity whose feet carry her afar off to sojourn?' This refers to the Tyrians fleeing to Tarshish and other lands (Rashi, Kimchi).

8f. Tyre's reverse of fortune is not accidental. It has been ordained and devised by God (Kimchi).

8. *the crowning city.* Better, 'the bestower of crowns'; the city which produced kings. Tarshish, Carthage and Kition were settled by Phoenicians and ruled by kings who owed allegiance to the mother city (Targum).

traffickers. The Hebrew is literally 'her Canaanites.' They carried on an extensive trade throughout the Mediterra-

nean lands and consequently 'Canaanite' and 'trafficker' became synonymous terms (Ibn Kaspi).

9. *the earth.* i.e. her downfall will cause all the honorable of the earth to humble themselves lest they meet the same fate as the honored men of Tyre (Kimchi).

10–14. The fugitives of Phoenicia will find no safety or rest even in Cyprus or Tarshish, the colonies which they themselves had founded. The natives, hitherto oppressed by the settlers, would take advantage of the weakness of the ruling class to break away.

10. *Overflow thy land.* Cross thy land to go into exile (Rashi).

as the Nile. As swiftly as the Nile and go into exile (Kimchi).

O daughter of Tarshish. Tyre, which is situated on the Sea of Tarshish (Rashi).

no girdle. No strength (Rashi).

11. *He.* The subject is God (Ibn Ezra, Kimchi).

the sea. The Mediterranean which washes the shore of Phoenicia and its dependencies (Kimchi).

He hath shaken the kingdoms;
The Lord hath given commandment concerning Canaan,
To destroy the strongholds thereof;

12. And He said: 'Thou shalt no
more rejoice.'
O thou oppressed virgin daughter
of Zidon,
Arise, pass over to Kittim; *Cyprus*
Even there shalt thou have no
rest.

13. Behold, the land of the Chaldeans
—this is the people that was not,
when Asshur founded it for shipmen—they set up their towers, they
overthrew the palaces thereof; it is
made a ruin.

14. Howl, ye ships of Tarshish,
For your stronghold is laid waste.

15. And it shall come to pass in
that day, that Tyre shall be forgotten
seventy years, according to the days
of one king; after the end of seventy

הִרְגִּיז מַמְלָכוֹת
יְהוָה צִוָּה אֶל־כְּנַעַן
לַשְׁמִד מָעֻזְנֶיהָ:

12 וַיֹּאמֶר לֹא־תוֹסִיפִי עוֹד לַעְלוֹז
הַמְעֻשָּׁקָה בְּתוּלַת בַּת־צִידוֹן
כִּתִּים קוּמִי עֲבֹרִי
גַּם־שָׁם לֹא־יָנוּחַ לָךְ:

13 הֵן ׀ אֶרֶץ כַּשְׂדִּים זֶה הָעָם לֹא הָיָה
אַשּׁוּר יְסָדָהּ לְצִיִּים הֵקִימוּ בַחִינָיו
עוֹרְרוּ אַרְמְנוֹתֶיהָ שָׂמָהּ לְמַפֵּלָה:

14 הֵילִילוּ אֳנִיּוֹת תַּרְשִׁישׁ
כִּי שֻׁדַּד מָעֻזְּכֶן:

15 וְהָיָה בַּיּוֹם הַהוּא וְנִשְׁכַּחַת צֹר
שִׁבְעִים שָׁנָה כִּימֵי מֶלֶךְ אֶחָד מִקֵּץ

v. 12. בחוניו ק׳   v. 13. כתים ק׳

---

kingdoms. The nations that attacked
Phoenicia (Kimchi).

Canaan. Synonymous in the context with
Phoenicia whose inhabitants called
their land 'Canaan' (Rashi).

12. *oppressed.* Or, 'outraged, ravished.'
Zidon is described as a *virgin daughter*
because it had not been previously conquered (Kimchi).

Zidon. Unlike Tyre, Zidon is referred to
as 'ravished.' Tyre, immediately after its
conquest by Nebuchadnezzar, was inun-
dated by the sea, unlike Zidon, which
was plundered by the Chaldees (Malbim).

Kittim. i.e. Cyprus (Alshich).

13. The place of this verse in the context is very difficult to explain. An allusion has been read into it by some commentators to Babylon's conquest of
Assyria which the prophet cites as an
illustration of a conquering nation

being, in turn, conquered by another
nation (Kimchi).

that was not. Originally in the land
(Kimchi).

Asshur founded it for shipmen. A.J. identifies *tsiyyim* with *tsi* used in xxxiii. 21 for
ship, following Rashi. Others render,
'Assyria hath appointed it for nomads'
(Kimchi).

their towers. Structures erected for the
attack upon walled cities (Ibn Ezra).

14. *your stronghold.* viz. Tyre (Kimchi).

15-18. The restoration of the stricken
country after the lapse of seventy years,
when its regained wealth will be consecrated to God to be used by the righteous who dwell before Him.

15. Tyre or Phoenicia will be forgotten
for seventy years.

the days of one king. This means the usual
span of life for a man, even a king (cf.

years it shall fare with Tyre as in the song of the harlot:

16. Take a harp,
Go about the city,
Thou harlot long forgotten;
Make sweet melody,
Sing many songs,
That thou mayest be remembered.

17. And it shall come to pass after the end of seventy years, that the LORD will remember Tyre, and she shall return to her hire, and shall have commerce with all the kingdoms of the world upon the face of the earth. 18. And her gain and her hire shall be holiness to the LORD; it shall not be treasured nor laid up; for her gain shall be for them that dwell before the LORD, to eat their fill, and for stately clothing.

שִׁבְעִים שָׁנָה יִהְיֶה לְצֹר כְּשִׁירַת הַזּוֹנָה:

16 קְחִי כִנּוֹר
סֹבִּי עִיר
זוֹנָה נִשְׁכָּחָה
הֵיטִיבִי נַגֵּן
הַרְבִּי־שִׁיר
לְמַעַן תִּזָּכֵרִי:

17 וְהָיָה מִקֵּץ | שִׁבְעִים שָׁנָה יִפְקֹד יְהֹוָה אֶת־צֹר וְשָׁבָה לְאֶתְנַנָּה וְזָנְתָה אֶת־כָּל־מַמְלְכוֹת הָאָרֶץ עַל־

18 פְּנֵי הָאֲדָמָה: וְהָיָה סַחְרָהּ וְאֶתְנַנָּה קֹדֶשׁ לַיהֹוָה לֹא יֵאָצֵר וְלֹא יֵחָסֵן כִּי לַיֹּשְׁבִים לִפְנֵי יְהֹוָה יִהְיֶה סַחְרָהּ לֶאֱכֹל לְשָׂבְעָה וְלִמְכַסֶּה עָתִיק:

v. 17. לֹא מַפִּיק ה׳ v. 18. מַפִּיק ה׳

Ps. xc. 10); or, the Hebrew may signify 'a certain king,' i.e. David who lived seventy years (Rashi).

as in the song of the harlot. By which a neglected harlot seeks to attract attention (Rashi).

16. A popular dancing song which comes to the mind of the prophet as he envisages Phoenicia's vicissitudes (Malbim).

make sweet melody. Or, 'play skilfully'; a free rendering is: 'touch the strings deftly.'

17. Application of the song.

return to her hire. She will again engage in her profitable activities and commerce. The noun used for *hire* and the verb *shall have commerce* arc technical terms respectively used elsewhere for the fee and self-surrender of the harlot. The language is, of course, metaphorical (Rashi).

18. *holiness to the* LORD. The riches which accrue from the resumption of Phoenician trade will be disposed of by God in accordance with His wishes (Ibn Ezra).

not be treasured nor laid up. For the benefit of the Phoenicians themselves (Rashi).

dwell before the LORD. Or, 'sit,' enjoying His Presence; viz. the righteous (Alschich).

24 CHAPTER XXIV

1. Behold, the LORD maketh the
earth empty and maketh it
waste,
And turneth it upside down, and
scattereth abroad the inhabitants thereof.

2. And it shall be, as with the
people, so with the priest;
As with the servant, so with his
master;
As with the maid, so with her
mistress;
As with the buyer, so with the
seller;
As with the lender, so with the
borrower;
As with the creditor, so with the
debtor.

3. The earth shall be utterly
emptied, and clean despoiled;
For the LORD hath spoken this
word.

4. The earth fainteth and fadeth
away,
The world faileth and fadeth
away,
The lofty people of the earth do
fail.

כד

1 הִנֵּה יְהוָה בּוֹקֵק הָאָרֶץ וּבוֹלְקָהּ
וְעִוָּה פָנֶיהָ וְהֵפִיץ יֹשְׁבֶיהָ:
2 וְהָיָה כָעָם כַּכֹּהֵן
כַּעֶבֶד כַּאדֹנָיו
כַּשִּׁפְחָה כַּגְּבִרְתָּהּ
כַּקּוֹנֶה כַּמּוֹכֵר
כַּמַּלְוֶה כַּלֹּוֶה
כַּנֹּשֶׁה כַּאֲשֶׁר נֹשֶׁא בוֹ:
3 הִבּוֹק | תִּבּוֹק הָאָרֶץ וְהִבּוֹז | תִּבּוֹז
כִּי יְהוָה דִּבֶּר אֶת־הַדָּבָר הַזֶּה:
4 אָבְלָה נָבְלָה הָאָרֶץ
אֻמְלְלָה נָבְלָה תֵּבֵל
אֻמְלְלוּ מְרוֹם עַם־הָאָרֶץ:

v. 2. כתיב

CHAPTERS XXIV–XXVII

THESE four chapters form a distinct
group of oracles, strongly marked by
their general apocalyptic character.
They speak of God's desolating judgment of the world, the terrors of that
great day, the suppression of the power
of evil in heaven and on earth, the
consequent blessings upon Israel and
humanity, the abolition of death for
ever and the wiping away of tears from
all faces (Kimchi, Abarbanel).

CHAPTER XXIV

THE day of universal judgment. The
wickedness of the people and consequent misery and wretchedness.

1. The day of retribution.

empty ... waste. The force of the
assonance of the Hebrew original in this
and in many of the following verses cannot be reproduced in English.

2. All classes and ranks are equally
affected.

as with the people ... priest. The Hebrew
is identical with Hos. iv. 9. The other
parallels in the verse suggest that the
priests formed the ruling class (Kimchi).

4. fainteth. Or, 'mourneth.'

world. Hebrew, tebel, i.e. the inhabited
parts of the earth (Metsudath Zion, Malbim). Traditionally tebel means the Land
of Israel (Rashi).

the lofty people. lit. 'the height of the
people,' denoting the nobility (Rashi,
Kimchi).

5. The earth also is defiled under
   the inhabitants thereof;
   Because they have transgressed
   the laws, violated the statute,
   Broken the everlasting covenant.
6. Therefore hath a curse devoured
   the earth,
   And they that dwell therein are
   found guilty;
   Therefore the inhabitants of the
   earth waste away, *are parched*
   And men are left few.
7. The new wine faileth, the vine
   fadeth,
   All the merry-hearted do sigh.
8. The mirth of tabrets ceaseth, *tambourines*
   The noise of them that rejoice
   endeth,
   The joy of the harp ceaseth.
9. They drink not wine with a song;
   Strong drink is bitter to them
   that drink it.
10. Broken down is the city of
    wasteness; *Chaos*
    Every house is shut up, that none
    may come in.

5 וְהָאָרֶץ חָנְפָה תַּחַת יֹשְׁבֶיהָ
כִּי־עָבְרוּ תוֹרֹת חָלְפוּ חֹק
הֵפֵרוּ בְּרִית עוֹלָם:

6 עַל־כֵּן אָלָה אָכְלָה אֶרֶץ
וַיֶּאְשְׁמוּ יֹשְׁבֵי בָהּ
עַל־כֵּן חָרוּ יֹשְׁבֵי אֶרֶץ
וְנִשְׁאַר אֱנוֹשׁ מִזְעָר:

7 אָבַל תִּירוֹשׁ אֻמְלְלָה־גָפֶן
נֶאֶנְחוּ כָּל־שִׂמְחֵי־לֵב:

8 שָׁבַת מְשׂוֹשׂ תֻּפִּים
חָדַל שְׁאוֹן עַלִּיזִים
שָׁבַת מְשׂוֹשׂ כִּנּוֹר:

9 בַּשִּׁיר לֹא יִשְׁתּוּ־יָיִן
יֵמַר שֵׁכָר לְשֹׁתָיו:

10 נִשְׁבְּרָה קִרְיַת־תֹּהוּ
סֻגַּר כָּל־בַּיִת מִבּוֹא:

---

5. *the everlasting covenant.* The Torah of
Moses which was given at Sinai as a
covenant between God and Israel
(Rashi). Others refer the phrase to the
Noachide covenant made between God
and the human race after the flood
(Gen. ix. 16). Under this covenant every
member of the human race is subject to
certain moral laws, one of which is the
prohibition of murder (Gen. ix. 5f.)
(Abarbanel).

6. *and . . . found guilty.* Better perhaps,
'they that dwell therein having been
found guilty.' Others render: And they
that dwell therein are wasted (Targum,
Kimchi).

waste away. Or, 'are parched' by the

consuming heat of God's wrath (Rashi,
Ibn Ezra, Kimchi).

7-9.   All joy and festivity have ceased.

7.   With this verse cf. Joel i. 10, 12.

8.   *the mirth of tabrets.* The reference is to
the musical celebrations at the vintage
festivals (cf. Amos viii. 3, 10).

10-12.   Sadness and desolation prevail
everywhere.

10.   *wasteness.* When it is broken, it will
be called 'the city of wasteness' (Rashi,
Kimchi).

shut up. Most houses will be deserted,
and there will be no one to enter them
(Ibn Ezra). Alternatively, most of the
houses will be in ruins (Kimchi).

11. There is a crying in the streets
amidst the wine;
All joy is darkened,
The mirth of the land is gone.
12. In the city is left desolation,
And the gate is smitten unto ruin.
13. For thus shall it be in the midst
of the earth, among the
peoples,
As at the beating of an olive-tree,
As at the gleanings when the
vintage is done.
14. Those yonder lift up their voice,
they sing for joy;
For the majesty of the LORD they
shout from the sea:
15. 'Therefore glorify ye the LORD
in the regions of light,
Even the name of the LORD, the
God of Israel, in the isles of
the sea.'

11 צְוָחָה עַל־הַיַּיִן בַּחוּצוֹת
עָרְבָה כָּל־שִׂמְחָה
גָּלָה מְשׂוֹשׂ הָאָרֶץ׃
12 נִשְׁאַר בָּעִיר שַׁמָּה
וּשְׁאִיָּה יֻכַּת־שָׁעַר׃
13 כִּי־כֹה יִהְיֶה
בְּקֶרֶב הָאָרֶץ בְּתוֹךְ הָעַמִּים
כְּנֹקֶף זַיִת
כְּעוֹלֵלֹת אִם־כָּלָה בָצִיר׃
14 הֵמָּה יִשְׂאוּ קוֹלָם יָרֹנּוּ
בִּגְאוֹן יְהֹוָה צָהֲלוּ מִיָּם׃
15 עַל־כֵּן בָּאֻרִים כַּבְּדוּ יְהֹוָה
בְּאִיֵּי הַיָּם שֵׁם יְהֹוָה אֱלֹהֵי יִשְׂרָאֵל׃

11. *amidst the wine.* Their orgies of drinking are interrupted by the bitter cry of the sufferers (See Malbim). Other renderings are: 'for the want of wine.' (Kimchi) 'instead of wine,' (Ibn Ezra) 'because of wine' (R.V.), i.e. the vineyards which are destroyed (cf. xxxii. 12).

mirth of the land. Applied traditionally to Jerusalem (Rashi), but perhaps to be interpreted more widely (Kimchi).

12. *in the city.* Here, too, tradition thinks of Jerusalem; see, however, on verse 10.

is left desolation. In place of *mirth* which *is gone* (verse 11) (Kimchi).

13. Tradition applies the verse to the remnant of Israel among the Gentiles (Rashi). Others see in it a visitation upon all the human race of which a small remnant only will survive (Kimchi).

beating of an olive-tree . . . is done. When only a few olives remain on the branches of the olive-tree and a few grapes on the vine (cf. xvii. 6).

14f. Those who survive the catastrophe will from the distant parts of the earth offer hymns and praises to God.

14. *those yonder.* Some apply the pronoun (the Hebrew is lit. 'they') to the Israelites in the Diaspora (Targum, Rashi).

from the sea. From the direction of the Mediterranean. The Hebrew word *yam* also means 'the west' (Kimchi).

15. The verse gives the word which *those yonder* (in the previous verse) will sing (Malbim).

the regions of light. This is a peculiar rendering, not found in any classical Jewish commentary. It is variantly rendered as, 'in the valleys' (Kimchi) 'in the crevices' (Menahem), 'with fires' (Abarbanel).

16. From the uttermost part of the earth have we heard songs: 'Glory to the righteous.'
But I say: I waste away, I waste away, woe is me!
The treacherous deal treacherously;
Yea, the treacherous deal very treacherously.

17. Terror, and the pit, and the trap, are upon thee, O inhabitant of the earth.

18. And it shall come to pass, that he who fleeth from the noise of the terror shall fall into the pit;
And he that cometh up out of the midst of the pit shall be taken in the trap;
For the windows on high are opened,
And the foundations of the earth do shake;

19. The earth is broken, broken down,
The earth is crumbled in pieces,
The earth trembleth and tottereth;

20. The earth reeleth to and fro like a drunken man,
And swayeth to and fro as a lodge;

מִכְּנַף הָאָרֶץ 16
זְמִרֹת שָׁמַעְנוּ צְבִי לַצַּדִּיק
וָאֹמַר רָזִי־לִי רָזִי־לִי אוֹי לִי
בֹּגְדִים בָּגָדוּ
וּבֶגֶד בּוֹגְדִים בָּגָדוּ:
פַּחַד וָפַחַת וָפָח 17
עָלֶיךָ יוֹשֵׁב הָאָרֶץ:
וְהָיָה הַנָּס מִקּוֹל הַפַּחַד 18
יִפֹּל אֶל־הַפַּחַת
וְהָעוֹלֶה מִתּוֹךְ הַפַּחַת יִלָּכֵד בַּפָּח
כִּי־אֲרֻבּוֹת מִמָּרוֹם נִפְתָּחוּ
וַיִּרְעֲשׁוּ מוֹסְדֵי אָרֶץ:
רֹעָה הִתְרֹעֲעָה הָאָרֶץ 19
פּוֹר הִתְפּוֹרְרָה אָרֶץ
מוֹט הִתְמוֹטְטָה אָרֶץ:
נוֹעַ תָּנוּעַ אֶרֶץ כַּשִּׁכּוֹר 20
וְהִתְנוֹדְדָה כַּמְּלוּנָה

v. 18. קמץ בז"ק   v. 16. קמץ בז"ק

16–20. The prophet hears jubilant songs ascending from the uttermost parts of the earth, perhaps from Persia or Ethiopia. But he exclaims in despair, 'Woe is me, I waste away, I waste away,' because the rejoicing is premature; the world has yet to pass through tribulation and sorrow before traitors and treachery would be swept away and the earth could be cleansed (Kimchi).

16. *I waste away*. lit. 'wasting away to me.' The prophet's realization of the true state of affairs brings on a feeling of sickness in contrast to the rejoicing of the peoples (Kimchi).

17. The wording of this verse and the first half of the next appears almost verbatim in Jer. xlviii. 43f. applies to Moab.

18. *windows on high*. An allusion to the flood in the days of Noah (cf. Gen. vii. 11, viii. 2) (Kimchi).

19f. The catastrophic manifestations of the day of Divine judgment.

19. The verse graphically describes the convulsions of an earthquake (Malbim).

20. *a lodge*. The frail hut of the watchman in a vineyard which sways in the wind (see on i. 8) (Metsudath David).

113

And the transgression thereof is heavy upon it,
And it shall fall, and not rise again.

21. And it shall come to pass in that day,
That the LORD will punish the host of the high heaven on high,
And the kings of the earth upon the earth.

22. And they shall be gathered together, as prisoners are gathered in the dungeon,
And shall be shut up in the prison,
And after many days shall they be punished.

23. Then the moon shall be confounded, and the sun ashamed;
For the LORD of hosts will reign in mount Zion, and in Jerusalem,
And before His elders shall be Glory.

וְכָבֵד עָלֶיהָ פִּשְׁעָהּ
וְנָפְלָה וְלֹא־תֹסִיף קוּם:

21 וְהָיָה בַּיּוֹם הַהוּא

יִפְקֹד יְהוָה

עַל־צְבָא הַמָּרוֹם בַּמָּרוֹם

וְעַל־מַלְכֵי הָאֲדָמָה עַל־הָאֲדָמָה:

22 וְאֻסְּפוּ אֲסֵפָה אַסִּיר עַל־בּוֹר

וְסֻגְּרוּ עַל־מַסְגֵּר

וּמֵרֹב יָמִים יִפָּקֵדוּ:

23 וְחָפְרָה הַלְּבָנָה

וּבוֹשָׁה הַחַמָּה

כִּי־מָלַךְ יְהוָה צְבָאוֹת

בְּהַר צִיּוֹן וּבִירוּשָׁלַ͏ִם

וְנֶגֶד זְקֵנָיו כָּבוֹד:

---

it shall fall . . . rise again. Under the heavy weight of its transgressions. Moral bankruptcy will bring about physical collapse. The sentence occurs again in Amos v. 2 (Kimchi).

21–23. The evil powers in heaven and on earth will be vanquished, imprisoned and punished, and God will reign supreme on mount Zion.

21. *host of the high heaven.* Some interpret this as an allusion to an eclipse of the sun and the moon, destined to take place prior to the Messianic era. Others explain as 'the patron angels of the nations' (Ibn Ezra).

kings of the earth. Who oppressed God's people (Malbim).

22. *And they shall be gathered together . . .* Kara equates this with Zechariah's prophecy (xiv. 2: *And I will gather all the nations to Jerusalem for war . . .* When they will be gathered there, not knowing God's intention, that this gathering is for their detriment, they will be imprisoned like prisoners in a dungeon.

23. *the moon shall be confounded,* etc. God's glory will outshine the celestial lights, the moon and the sun being eclipsed into insignificance (cf. lx. 19) (Ibn Ezra).

25   CHAPTER XXV   כה

1. O Lord, Thou art my God,
   I will exalt Thee, I will praise
   Thy name,
   For Thou hast done wonderful
   things;
   Even counsels of old, in faithfulness and truth.
2. For Thou hast made of a city a
   heap,
   Of a fortified city a ruin;
   A castle of strangers to be no city,
   It shall never be built.
3. Therefore shall the strong people
   glorify Thee,
   The city of the terrible nations
   shall fear Thee.
4. For Thou hast been a stronghold
   to the poor,
   A stronghold to the needy in his
   distress,
   A refuge from the storm, a
   shadow from the heat;
   For the blast of the terrible ones
   was as a storm against the wall.
5. As the heat in a dry place, Thou
   didst subdue the noise of
   strangers;

1 יְהֹוָה אֱלֹהַי אַתָּה
אֲרוֹמִמְךָ אוֹדֶה שִׁמְךָ
כִּי עָשִׂיתָ פֶּלֶא
עֵצוֹת מֵרָחֹק אֱמוּנָה אֹמֶן׃
2 כִּי שַׂמְתָּ מֵעִיר לַגָּל
קִרְיָה בְּצוּרָה לְמַפֵּלָה
אַרְמוֹן זָרִים מֵעִיר
לְעוֹלָם לֹא יִבָּנֶה׃
3 עַל־כֵּן יְכַבְּדוּךָ עַם־עָז
קִרְיַת גּוֹיִם עָרִיצִים יִירָאוּךָ׃
4 כִּי־הָיִיתָ מָעוֹז לַדָּל
מָעוֹז לָאֶבְיוֹן בַּצַּר־לוֹ
מַחְסֶה מִזֶּרֶם צֵל מֵחֹרֶב
כִּי רוּחַ עָרִיצִים כְּזֶרֶם קִיר׃
5 כְּחֹרֶב בְּצָיוֹן שְׁאוֹן זָרִים תַּכְנִיעַ

CHAPTER XXV

1–5. A psalm of praise and thanksgiving for the providential deliverance
of Israel and the downfall of his enemies (Ibn Ezra).

1. *of old.* lit. 'from afar,' from the days
of the covenant with Abraham (Gen. xv)
(Rashi).

in faithfulness and truth. God faithfully
and truly fulfilled the promise made to
the patriarch. The phrase may be translated 'in perfect faithfulness' (Kimchi).

2. *a city.* Of the enemy. According to
some the noun has a collective meaning,
'many cities' (Kimchi).

3. *the strong people.* A collective noun
meaning 'many strong peoples.' The
verbs are in the plural. Not only the

weak but even the strong will glorify the
Lord (Kimchi).

the city. Here, too, the noun is collective.
God will be feared by all, even by the
cities of the powerful nations.

4. The Divine protection of Israel.

poor . . . needy. i.e. Israel oppressed by
mighty neighbours (Kimchi).

storm against the wall. Torrents of rain
which overthrow a wall (Metsudath
Zion).

5. Suppression of Israel's enemies. As
the heat of the day, however fierce, is
abated by the shadow of a cloud, so will
God subdue the arrogant clamour or
triumphant song of the most violent
oppressors. The second part of the
verse is an amplification and interpretation of the first part (Malbim).

As the heat by the shadow of a
cloud, the song of the terrible
ones was brought low.

6. And in this mountain will the
LORD of hosts make unto all
peoples
A feast of fat things, a feast of
wines on the lees,
Of fat things full of marrow, of
wines on the lees well refined.

7. And He will destroy in this
mountain
The face of the covering that is
cast over all peoples,
And the veil that is spread over
all nations.

8. He will swallow up death for
ever;
And the Lord GOD will wipe
away tears from off all faces;
And the reproach of His people
will He take away from off all
the earth;
For the LORD hath spoken it.

חָרֶב בְּצֵל עָב זְמִיר עָרִיצִים יַעֲנֶה:

6 וְעָשָׂה יְהֹוָה צְבָאוֹת
לְכָל־הָעַמִּים בָּהָר הַזֶּה
מִשְׁתֵּה שְׁמָנִים מִשְׁתֵּה שְׁמָרִים
שְׁמָנִים מְמֻחָיִם שְׁמָרִים מְזֻקָּקִים:

7 וּבִלַּע בָּהָר הַזֶּה
פְּנֵי־הַלּוֹט ׀ הַלּוֹט
עַל־כָּל־הָעַמִּים
וְהַמַּסֵּכָה הַנְּסוּכָה עַל־כָּל־הַגּוֹיִם:

8 בִּלַּע הַמָּוֶת לָנֶצַח
וּמָחָה אֲדֹנָי יְהֹוִה
דִּמְעָה מֵעַל כָּל־פָּנִים
וְחֶרְפַּת עַמּוֹ יָסִיר מֵעַל כָּל־הָאָרֶץ
כִּי יְהֹוָה דִּבֵּר:

Thou didst subdue. (Kimchi). Others render: 'Thou wilt subdue,' and similarly substitute at the end 'shall be brought low.'

6f. Figuratively speaking, a great banquet will be served to the nations. They will think that, with almost no effort, they will conquer Israel. Instead, things will be bitter for them. They will meet their downfall, and confusion will reign among them (Rashi, Ibn Ezra, Kimchi).

6. *this mountain.* i.e. mount Zion (Ibn Ezra).

a feast of fat things. For they will think that it will be easy for them to conquer Israel, much like fat, which is smooth and soft. Instead, it will be converted for them into a feast of bitter dregs (Rashi).

fat things full of marrow. Soft and fat like the marrow of bones (Rashi).

wines on the lees. Lees completely refined of any liquid of wine or oil, for there will be only the lees. All this will be in the war of Gog and Magog (Rashi). This alludes to the poisoned cup mentioned in Obadiah xii. 2. xvi (Kimchi).

7. *covering . . . veil.* A metaphor for the shelter and protection these nations enjoy. God will remove this, making them vulnerable to the punishment due them (Kimchi).

8. *swallow up . . . ever.* An alternative translation, adopted in recent editions of the *Authorized Daily Prayer* Book, p. 324, reads: 'He maketh death to vanish (in life) eternal.'

reproach of His people. Their apparent neglect by Providence (Kimchi).

read "Tiqvat Chut" line   Rahab—Joz: 18 "htashani"

also 49.18   Tikvah

9. And it shall be said in that day:
'Lo, this is our God,
  For whom we waited, that He
    might save us;
This is the LORD, for whom we
  waited,
We will be glad and rejoice in
  His salvation.'

10. For in this mountain will the
  hand of the LORD rest,
And Moab shall be trodden down
  in his place,
Even as straw is trodden down
  in the dunghill.

11. And when he shall spread forth
  his hands in the midst thereof,
As he that swimmeth spreadeth
  forth his hands to swim,
His pride shall be brought down
  together with the cunning of
  his hands.

12. And the high fortress of thy
  walls will He bring down, lay
  low,
And bring to the ground, even to
  the dust.

9 וְאָמַר בַּיּוֹם הַהוּא
הִנֵּה אֱלֹהֵינוּ זֶה
קִוִּינוּ לוֹ וְיוֹשִׁיעֵנוּ
זֶה יְהֹוָה קִוִּינוּ לוֹ
נָגִילָה וְנִשְׂמְחָה בִּישׁוּעָתוֹ:

10 כִּי־תָנוּחַ יַד־יְהֹוָה בָּהָר הַזֶּה
וְנָדוֹשׁ מוֹאָב תַּחְתָּיו
כְּהִדּוּשׁ מַתְבֵּן בְּמוֹ מַדְמֵנָה:

11 וּפֵרַשׂ יָדָיו בְּקִרְבּוֹ
כַּאֲשֶׁר יְפָרֵשׂ הַשֹּׂחֶה לִשְׂחוֹת
וְהִשְׁפִּיל גַּאֲוָתוֹ עִם אָרְבּוֹת יָדָיו:

12 וּמִבְצַר מִשְׂגַּב חוֹמֹתֶיךָ הֵשַׁח הִשְׁפִּיל
הִגִּיעַ לָאָרֶץ עַד־עָפָר:

Moab's

26   CHAPTER XXVI   כו

1. In that day shall this song be
   sung in the land of Judah:

1 בַּיּוֹם הַהוּא
יוּשַׁר הַשִּׁיר־הַזֶּה בְּאֶרֶץ יְהוּדָה

v. 10. במו ק׳

---

9. A song of praise.

and it shall be said. lit. 'and he shall say,'
the pronoun referring back to *His people*
in the preceding verse (Rashi, Ibn Ezra,
Kimchi).

10-12. The subjection of Moab.

Moab. A nation that will be allied with
those coming from the north with Gog
and Magog, to attack Israel (Kimchi).

in his place. Where he stands.

in the dunghill. So the *kerë*; the *kethib*
means 'in the water of the dung-pit.'
The Hebrew for *dunghill* is *madmenah,*
and there may perhaps be a contemp-

tuous allusion to a Moabite city named
Madmen (Jer. xlviii. 2) (See Kimchi).

11. *shall be brought down.* lit. 'He (God)
shall bring down' (Ibn Ezra).

with the cunning of his hands. Or, 'despite
the skilful strokes (lit. wiles) of his
hands' (See Rashi).

12. The prophet addresses Moab
(Rashi, Ibn Ezra).

CHAPTER XXVI

1-6. A song of rejoicing and thankful-
ness for the protection of Jerusalem and
the fall and humiliation of the enemy
cities. The prophet is thinking of the

We have a strong city;
Walls and bulwarks doth He
   appoint for salvation.

2. Open ye the gates,
That the righteous nation that
   keepeth faithfulness may enter
   in.

3. The mind stayed on Thee Thou
   keepest in perfect peace;
Because it trusteth in Thee.

4. Trust ye in the LORD for ever,
For the LORD is God, an everlasting Rock.

5. For He hath brought down them
   that dwell on high,
The lofty city,
Laying it low, laying it low even
   to the ground,
Bringing it even to the dust.

6. The foot shall tread it down,
Even the feet of the poor, and the
   steps of the needy.

עִיר עָז־לָנוּ
יְשׁוּעָה יָשִׁית חוֹמוֹת וָחֵל׃

2 פִּתְחוּ שְׁעָרִים
וְיָבֹא גוֹי־צַדִּיק שֹׁמֵר אֱמֻנִים׃

3 יֵצֶר סָמוּךְ תִּצֹּר שָׁלוֹם שָׁלוֹם
כִּי בְךָ בָּטוּחַ׃

4 בִּטְחוּ בַיהֹוָה עֲדֵי־עַד
כִּי בְּיָהּ יְהֹוָה צוּר עוֹלָמִים׃

5 כִּי הֵשַׁח יֹשְׁבֵי מָרוֹם
קִרְיָה נִשְׂגָּבָה
יַשְׁפִּילֶנָּה יַשְׁפִּילָהּ עַד־אֶרֶץ
יַגִּיעֶנָּה עַד־עָפָר׃

6 תִּרְמְסֶנָּה רָגֶל
רַגְלֵי עָנִי פַּעֲמֵי דַלִּים׃

future rather than of what has taken
place.

1. *that day.* Of victory. If this chapter is
connected with the preceding, the *day* is
the time of Moab's humiliation (Kara,
Abarbanel).

strong city. i.e. Jerusalem (Rashi).

walls . . . salvation. Others prefer, 'salvation will He appoint in place of walls
and moat.' Jerusalem needs no material
defences, for God is its Guardian and
Protector (Kimchi).

2. Only the righteous and faithful
deserve to live in the holy city.

the righteous nation. A beautiful homiletic
interpretation of the Rabbis gives to the
phrase the meaning 'a righteous Gentile,' on the principle 'the righteous of
all peoples will have a share in the
world to come' (Yalkut Shimoni).

3. *the mind.* Better, 'a disposition,' lit.
'a formulation' (Metsudath Zion).

on Thee. This is not in the text but is
implied. Some render: 'a steadfast (lit.
supported) disposition' (cf. Ps. cxii. 8)
(Kara).

4. *the LORD is God.* The Hebrew is
literally 'in Yah is the Lord'; the grammarians term this use of the preposition
beth, 'in,' 'the *beth* of essence.'

5f. God may be well trusted, for He
can bring down to the dust even the
high and mighty, and make the
oppressed to triumph over their
oppressors (Kimchi).

5. The language of the verse recalls
xxv. 12.

6. *poor . . . needy.* i.e. Israel, as in xxv. 4
(Kimchi). Traditionally the *poor* is an
allusion to the Messiah (Rashi).

7. The way of the just is straight;
Thou, Most Upright, makest
plain the path of the just.
8. Yea, in the way of Thy judgments,
O LORD, have we waited for
Thee;
To Thy name and to Thy
memorial is the desire of our
soul.
9. With my soul have I desired
Thee in the night;
Yea, with my spirit within me
have I sought Thee earnestly;
For when Thy judgments are in
the earth,
The inhabitants of the world
learn righteousness.
10. Let favour be shown to the
wicked, yet will he not learn
righteousness;
In the land of uprightness will he
deal wrongfully,
And will not behold the majesty
of the LORD.
11. LORD, Thy hand was lifted up,
yet they see not;
They shall see with shame Thy
zeal for the people;
Yea, fire shall devour Thine
adversaries.

אֹרַח לַצַּדִּיק מֵישָׁרִים ⁷
יָשָׁר מַעְגַּל צַדִּיק תְּפַלֵּס:
אַף אֹרַח מִשְׁפָּטֶיךָ ⁸
יְהוָה קִוִּינוּךָ
לְשִׁמְךָ וּלְזִכְרְךָ תַּאֲוַת־נָפֶשׁ:
נַפְשִׁי אִוִּיתִךָ בַּלַּיְלָה ⁹
אַף־רוּחִי בְקִרְבִּי אֲשַׁחֲרֶךָּ
כִּי כַּאֲשֶׁר מִשְׁפָּטֶיךָ לָאָרֶץ
צֶדֶק לָמְדוּ יֹשְׁבֵי תֵבֵל:
יֻחַן רָשָׁע בַּל־לָמַד צֶדֶק ¹⁰
בְּאֶרֶץ נְכֹחוֹת יְעַוֵּל
וּבַל־יִרְאֶה גֵּאוּת יְהוָה:
יְהוָה רָמָה יָדְךָ בַּל־יֶחֱזָיוּן ¹¹
יֶחֱזוּ וְיֵבֹשׁוּ קִנְאַת־עָם
אַף־אֵשׁ צָרֶיךָ תֹאכְלֵם:

7-10. Implicit trust in God, and prayer to Him Whose direction and judgments are a wholesome discipline for mankind.

7. *Thou . . . just.* Another possible rendering is: 'straight dost Thou direct the path of the righteous' (Kimchi).

8. *Thy judgments.* Of the wicked (Rashi).

name . . . memorial. The two nouns are synonymous when applied to God (cf. Exod. iii. 15; Ps. cxxxv. 13), and denote the manifestation of Him as it is experienced by man and remembered from generation to generation (Metsudath David).

9. Israel is speaking.

in the night. A metaphor for sorrow or exile. Even when in trouble and distress the pure soul longs for its Creator (Kara).

for when . . . righteousness. Seeing as they do that ultimately the wicked do not escape their due retribution (Kimchi).

10. *in the land of uprightness.* Much more so in a land where evil prevails (Ibn Ezra).

11-15. Prayer for the destruction of the adversaries of God and for the peace of Israel; thanks for His mercies and a brief reference to past history.

11. *Thy hand was lifted up.* To punish the wicked who wantonly oppress Israel (Kimchi).

they see not. The cause of the calamities that befall them (Kimchi).

Thine adversaries. The enemies of Israel are the adversaries of God (Metsudath David).

12. LORD, Thou wilt establish peace
    for us;
    For Thou hast indeed wrought
      all our works for us.
13. O LORD our God, other lords
    beside Thee have had domi-
    nion over us;
    But by Thee only do we make
      mention of Thy name.
14. The dead live not, the shades
    rise not;
    To that end hast Thou punished
    and destroyed them, and made
    all their memory to perish.
15. Thou hast gotten Thee honour
    with the nations, O LORD,
    Yea, exceeding great honour with
    the nations;
    Thou art honoured unto the
    farthest ends of the earth.
16. LORD, in trouble have they
    sought Thee,
    Silently they poured out a prayer
    when Thy chastening was
    upon them.
17. Like as a woman with child, that
    draweth near the time of her
    delivery,
    Is in pain and crieth out in her
    pangs;
    So have we been at Thy presence,
    O LORD.

12 יְהוָה תִּשְׁפֹּת שָׁלוֹם לָנוּ

כִּי גַּם־כָּל־מַעֲשֵׂינוּ פָּעַלְתָּ לָּנוּ׃

13 יְהוָה אֱלֹהֵינוּ בְּעָלוּנוּ אֲדֹנִים זוּלָתֶךָ

לְבַד־בְּךָ נַזְכִּיר שְׁמֶךָ׃

14 מֵתִים בַּל־יִחְיוּ רְפָאִים בַּל־יָקֻמוּ

לָכֵן פָּקַדְתָּ וַתַּשְׁמִידֵם

וַתְּאַבֵּד כָּל־זֵכֶר לָמוֹ׃

15 יָסַפְתָּ לַגּוֹי יְהוָה

יָסַפְתָּ לַגּוֹי נִכְבָּדְתָּ

רִחַקְתָּ כָּל־קַצְוֵי־אָרֶץ׃

16 יְהוָה בַּצַּר פְּקָדוּךָ

צָקוּן לַחַשׁ מוּסָרְךָ לָמוֹ׃

17 כְּמוֹ הָרָה תַּקְרִיב לָלֶדֶת

תָּחִיל תִּזְעַק בַּחֲבָלֶיהָ

כֵּן הָיִינוּ מִפָּנֶיךָ יְהוָה׃

12. *Thou hast . . . us.* Without God's
help all Israel's efforts to save himself
would be of no avail (Ibn Ezra).

13. *other lords.* Foreign despots (Kimchi).

by Thee only. Through Thy help alone
(Ibn Ezra).

make mention of Thy name. In gratitude
(Ibn Ezra).

14. *the dead.* The despots just mentioned (Rashi,l Ibn Ezra).

live not. Even during their lifetime theyy
were considered dead, even more so
after their death (Ibn Kaspi).

the shades rise not. This is a repetition of
the preceding (Isaiah of Trani).

to that end. You resurrect them just to
punish them and then destroy them so
that all their memories perish (Kara).

15. The rendering of A.J. is doubtful,
and a closer translation of the text is:
'Thou hast increased the nation, O
Lord, Thou has increased the nation,
(and thereby) glorified Thyself; Thou
hast rejected all the ends of the earth.
Thou hast added Torah, greatness, and
honor to Thy nation Israel. Thou hast
added to Israel, and Thou hast been
honored by them. Thou hast rejected all
distant nations (Rashi).

16–19. Israel's appeal to God. The
unbearable sufferings of the people as
well as their prayers seem to have no
purpose. The promise of resurrection.

16. *silently . . . them.* This is a free rendering of a difficult text which may be
translated: 'they poured forth a whisper
(of prayer)' (Kimchi).

17. The agony of the times is com-

18. We have been with child, we
   have been in pain,
   We have as it were brought forth
   wind;
   We have not wrought any
   deliverance in the land;
   Neither are the inhabitants of
   the world come to life.
19. Thy dead shall live, my dead
   bodies shall arise—
   Awake and sing, ye that dwell
   in the dust—
   For Thy dew is as the dew of
   light,
   And the earth shall bring to life
   the shades.
20. Come, my people, enter thou
   into thy chambers,
   And shut thy doors about thee;
   Hide thyself for a little moment,
   Until the indignation be overpast.

הָרִינוּ חַלְנוּ 18
כְּמוֹ יָלַדְנוּ רוּחַ
יְשׁוּעֹת בַּל־נַעֲשֶׂה אֶרֶץ
וּבַל־יִפְּלוּ יֹשְׁבֵי תֵבֵל׃
יִחְיוּ מֵתֶיךָ נְבֵלָתִי יְקוּמוּן 19
הָקִיצוּ וְרַנְּנוּ שֹׁכְנֵי עָפָר
כִּי טַל אוֹרֹת טַלֶּךָ
וָאֶרֶץ רְפָאִים תַּפִּיל׃
לֵךְ עַמִּי בֹּא בַחֲדָרֶיךָ 20
וּסְגֹר דְּלָתְךָ בַּעֲדֶךָ
חֲבִי כִמְעַט־רֶגַע
עַד־יַעֲבָר־זָעַם׃

v. 20. יתיר י׳   v. 20. יתיר ר׳

pared with the agonizing pains of a woman in travail. The comparison is used by other prophets (cf. Hos. xiii. 13; Mic. iv. 10).

18. The simile of the preceding verse is continued.

brought forth wind. Prayer and suffering seem to be abortive (Rashi).

come to life. lit. 'fall.' The gentile kingdoms have not yet fallen. This indicates that the redemption is not yet at hand (Kimchi). The rendering of A.J. is doubtful.

19. This verse is the source of the belief in the resurrection of the dead, a fundamental of Jewish dogma. This is repeated by Daniel (xii. 2): *'And many of those sleeping in the earth shall awaken.'* The song mentioned at the beginning of this chapter terminates here. The prophet tells us that at the time of the ultimate redemption, the dead will sing this song, and then they will be resurrected. Isaiah addresses the Almighty, *'Thy dead,'* meaning the righteous who served God, *'shall live; with my dead body shall they rise.'* He knew that he was righ-

teous and would merit resurrection (Kimchi).

my dead bodies shall rise. This is the prophet's prayer for the dead of the Jewish people (Rashi). This differs slightly from the rendering quoted above.

awake and sing. The resurrection will lead to a new spiritual life, the resurrected engaging in devotional exercises and in the singing of hymns and praises to God (See Metsudath David).

Thy dew. The vivifying principle which God sends to bring the dead to life as the dew revives vegetation. Tradition speaks of the 'dew of life,' a supernatural dew which will descend on the dead and bring them back to life (See Abarbanel).

bring to life. lit. 'cause to fail,' or 'abort.' For *shades,* see on xiv. 9.

20f. A call on Israel or to the people of Jerusalem to retire into seclusion *until the indignation be overpast.*

20. *thy chambers.* Homiletically explained by the Rabbis as the places of

121

27. 2

21. For, behold, the LORD cometh
forth out of His place
To visit upon the inhabitants of
the earth their iniquity;
The earth also shall disclose her
blood,
And shall no more cover her
slain.

כִּי־הִנֵּה יְהֹוָה יֹצֵא מִמְּקוֹמוֹ 21
לִפְקֹד עֲוֺן יֹשֵׁב־הָאָרֶץ עָלָיו
וְגִלְּתָה הָאָרֶץ אֶת־דָּמֶיהָ
וְלֹא־תְכַסֶּה עוֹד עַל־הֲרוּגֶיהָ׃

27   CHAPTER XXVII   כז

1. In that day the LORD with His
sore and great and strong sword
will punish leviathan the slant
serpent, and leviathan the tortuous
serpent; and He will slay the dragon
that is in the sea.

2. In that day sing ye of her:
'A vineyard of foaming wine!'

בַּיּוֹם הַהוּא יִפְקֹד יְהֹוָה בְּחַרְבּוֹ 1
הַקָּשָׁה וְהַגְּדוֹלָה וְהַחֲזָקָה עַל לִוְיָתָן
נָחָשׁ בָּרִחַ וְעַל לִוְיָתָן נָחָשׁ עֲקַלָּתוֹן
וְהָרַג אֶת־הַתַּנִּין אֲשֶׁר בַּיָּם׃
בַּיּוֹם הַהוּא 2
כֶּרֶם חֶמֶד עַנּוּ־לָהּ׃

worship and study (Rashi, Yalkut
Shimoni).

thy doors. Similarly interpreted as the
doors of one's mouth, the lips. One
must not question or doubt the justice
of the Divine decree (Rashi).

21. *out of His place.* From heaven.
Understood by the Rabbis as from His
attribute of mercy to that of judgment
(Rashi).

shall disclose . . . slain. Cf. Gen. iv. 10.
Murder will be duly exposed and the
criminal will not have immunity
(Kimchi).

CHAPTER XXVII

1. This chapter continues the prophecy of the last verse of the previous
chapter. The three monsters symbolize
the three greatest powers of the time:
probably Assyria, Edom, or Rome, and
Egypt.

sore. lit. 'hard,' with the possible mean-

ing here of 'relentless.' Malbim,
however, explains it literally.

leviathan. One of the biggest sea monsters. Others regard it as the imaginary
axis or line through the centre of the
earth, and the two points in which the
ecliptic and the equator, or the ecliptic
and the orbit of the moon meet (Fried-
lander on Ibn Ezra).

the slant serpent. Mentioned again in Job.
xxvi. 13.

the dragon that is in the sea. If the allusion
is to Egypt, *the sea* here means the Nile.
Some commentators apply it to Tyre on
the Mediterranean sea (Ibn Ezra).

2–6. Song of the vineyard.

2. *that day.* The day of Israel's deliverance (Rashi).

a vineyard. Symbolizing Israel (Rashi).

foaming wine. The Hebrew word, *chemer,*
is only found again in Deut. xxxii. 14.
Several Hebrew MSS. read *chemed,* 'a
delightful vineyard' as in Amos v. 11.

3. I the LORD do guard it,
   I water it every moment;
   Lest Mine anger visit it,
   I guard it night and day.
4. Fury is not in Me;
   Would that I were as the briers
      and thorns in flame!
   I would with one step burn it
      altogether.
5. Or else let him take hold of My
      strength,
   That he may make peace with
      Me;
   Yea, let him make peace with
      Me.
6. In days to come shall Jacob take
      root,
   Israel shall blossom and bud;
   And the face of the world shall
      be filled with fruitage.
7. Hath He smitten him as He
      smote those that smote him?
   Or is he slain according to the
      slaughter of them that were
      slain by Him?

אֲנִי יְהוָה נֹצְרָהּ 3
לִרְגָעִים אַשְׁקֶנָּה
פֶּן יִפְקֹד עָלֶיהָ
לַיְלָה וָיוֹם אֶצֳּרֶנָּה:
חֵמָה אֵין לִי 4
מִי־יִתְּנֵנִי שָׁמִיר שַׁיִת בַּמִּלְחָמָה
אֶפְשְׂעָה בָהּ אֲצִיתֶנָּה יָּחַד:
אוֹ יַחֲזֵק בְּמָעֻזִּי 5
יַעֲשֶׂה שָׁלוֹם לִי
שָׁלוֹם יַעֲשֶׂה־לִּי:
הַבָּאִים יַשְׁרֵשׁ יַעֲקֹב 6
יָצִיץ וּפָרַח יִשְׂרָאֵל
וּמָלְאוּ פְנֵי־תֵבֵל תְּנוּבָה:
הַכְּמַכַּת מַכֵּהוּ הִכָּהוּ 7
אִם־כְּהֶרֶג הֲרֻגָיו הֹרָג:

v. 8. הצ׳ בח״ק   v. 4. הש׳ בח״ק

3. *lest Mine anger visit it.* there is nothing in the text corresponding to *Mine
anger*. The Hebrew is literally 'lest he
(unspecified subject) visit against it.'
A.V. and R.V. have 'lest any hurt it.'
This resembles Kimchi, who renders:
'Lest the enemy visit it.' Rashi, apparently, read: 'Lest I visit it' (Minchath
Shai).

4. An obscure verse. The Talmud
explains it to mean that though the
vineyard is unsatisfactory, symbolizing
Israel's backsliding, God can show no
fury against it. Would, He exclaims, that
He could muster a momentary but
flaming rage and make an end of it in
one overwhelming blow (Rashi).

in flame. lit. 'in battle.' Departing from
the accentuation, one may render:
'Who will give Me briers and thorns? In
battle I would stride against it, set it
altogether on fire!' (Kimchi).

5. If Israel, represented by the vineyard, desires to survive and live in
safety, let him immediately surrender to
the Sovereignty of God. Only by wholehearted obedience will he secure safety
and peace.

My strength. God's supreme power and
authority (Rashi, Kimchi). Another possible translation is: 'or let him take hold
of My stronghold,' seek safety in turning
to God for protection (Ibn Kaspi).

6. Israel's prosperity in the future
when he will acknowledge the true God
and loyally follow the path of morality
and religion.

in days to come. The word *days* is implied
(Ibn Ezra, Kimchi).

filled with fruitage. The blessing con-
ferred upon Israel will be enjoyed by
the whole world (Kimchi).

7-11. Israel's punishment, unlike that

8. In full measure, when Thou
sendest her away, Thou dost
contend with her;
He hath removed her with His
rough blast in the day of the
east wind.
9. Therefore by this shall the
iniquity of Jacob be expiated,
And this is all the fruit of taking
away his sin:
When he maketh all the stones
of the altar as chalkstones that
are beaten in pieces,
So that the Asherim and the sun-
images shall rise no more.
10. For the fortified city is solitary,
A habitation abandoned and
forsaken, like the wilderness;
There shall the calf feed, and
there shall he lie down,
And consume the branches thereof.
11. When the boughs thereof are
withered, they shall be broken
off;

8 בְּסַאסְּאָה בְּשַׁלְחָהּ תְּרִיבֶנָּה
הָגָה בְּרוּחוֹ הַקָּשָׁה בְּיוֹם קָדִים:
9 לָכֵן בְּזֹאת יְכֻפַּר עֲוֺן־יַעֲקֹב
וְזֶה כָּל־פְּרִי הָסֵר חַטָּאתוֹ
בְּשׂוּמוֹ ׀ כָּל־אַבְנֵי מִזְבֵּחַ
כְּאַבְנֵי־גִר מְנֻפָּצוֹת
לֹא־יָקֻמוּ אֲשֵׁרִים וְחַמָּנִים:
10 כִּי עִיר בְּצוּרָה בָּדָד
נָוֶה מְשֻׁלָּח וְנֶעֱזָב כַּמִּדְבָּר
שָׁם יִרְעֶה עֵגֶל וְשָׁם יִרְבָּץ
וְכִלָּה סְעִפֶיהָ:
11 בִּיבֹשׁ קְצִירָהּ תִּשָּׁבַרְנָה

v. 10. קמץ בטרחא

to be suffered by his enemies, was meted
out in moderation; and that fact promises better days when Israel would relin-
quish idolatry and return to God in
humble repentance.

7. *hath He,* etc. The answer required is
in the negative (Ibn Ezra).

him. viz. Israel (Kimchi).

8. *in full measure.* Just as much as
Israel's sins deserved; but no more (Ibn
Ezra, Kimchi).

sendeth her away. An allusion to the
captivity of Northern Israel after the
conquest of Samaria by the Assyrians
(Ibn Ezra).

east wind. The day of the exile to Assyria
(Laniado).

9. *therefore.* This refers back to verse 7.
Since Israel is punished in moderation
and the full anger of God is withheld,
there is hope for him in repentance and
return to God (Metsudath David).

by this. Which follows in the second part
of the verse (Kimchi).

Jacob. Synonymous with Israel.

the fruit. The means; repentance without
removal of the cause of the sin is not
enough (Kimchi).

when he maketh. Or, 'that he should
make.'

of the altar. That had been built for
idolatry (Ibn Ezra, Metsudath David).

Asherim . . . sun-images. See on xvii. 8.

10f. Why Jerusalem is deserted and
forsaken.

10. *the fortified city.* i.e. Jerusalem
(Kimchi).

there shall the calf feed. In places which
had formerly been inhabited but were
now deserted (Kimchi).

11. *the boughs,* etc. The picture of a
deserted city is continued. In the street
grass and wild bushes grow, and the

The women shall come, and set
   them on fire;
For it is a people of no understanding;
Therefore He that made them
   will not have compassion upon
   them,
And He that formed them will
   not be gracious unto them.
12. And it shall come to pass in that
   day,
   That the LORD will beat off [His
   fruit]
   From the flood of the River unto
   the Brook of Egypt,
   And ye shall be gathered one by
   one, O ye children of Israel.
13. And it shall come to pass in that
   day,
   That a great horn shall be blown;
   And they shall come that were
   lost in the land of Assyria,
   And they that were dispersed in
   the land of Egypt;
   And they shall worship the LORD
   in the holy mountain at
   Jerusalem.

נָשִׁים בָּאוֹת מְאִירוֹת אוֹתָהּ
כִּי לֹא עַם־בִּינוֹת הוּא
עַל־כֵּן לֹא־יְרַחֲמֶנּוּ עֹשֵׂהוּ
וְיֹצְרוֹ לֹא יְחֻנֶּנּוּ׃
וְהָיָה בַּיּוֹם הַהוּא   12
יַחְבֹּט יְהֹוָה
מִשִּׁבֹּלֶת הַנָּהָר עַד־נַחַל מִצְרָיִם
וְאַתֶּם תְּלֻקְּטוּ
לְאַחַד אֶחָד בְּנֵי יִשְׂרָאֵל׃
וְהָיָה ׀ בַּיּוֹם הַהוּא   13
יִתָּקַע בְּשׁוֹפָר גָּדוֹל
וּבָאוּ הָאֹבְדִים בְּאֶרֶץ אַשּׁוּר
וְהַנִּדָּחִים בְּאֶרֶץ מִצְרָיִם
וְהִשְׁתַּחֲווּ לַיהֹוָה
בְּהַר הַקֹּדֶשׁ בִּירוּשָׁלָ͏ִם׃

poor women use them for fuel
(Malbim).

set them on fire. The women collect the
branches to use them as fuel (Rashi).

12f. There will be a day when the
exiles from the most distant lands will
return to Jerusalem, and they will pay
homage to God on His holy mountain.

12. *beat off.* The collection of the scattered exiles is compared with the careful
collection of scattered fruit, olives for
instance, after it had been beaten off the
tree (Rashi).

the River. The Euphrates on the north-
east of Palestine, referring to the exile in
Assyria (Rashi).

the Brook of Egypt. Wadi el-Arish on the
south-west, referring to the exiles in
Egypt. The *River* and the *Brook* form the
farthest limits of the boundaries of the
Land of Israel. Others regard *the Brook
of Egypt* as the Nile (See Kaftor
Vaferach).

one by one. Not a single exile will be forgotten (Abarbanel).

13. An interpretation and amplification of the preceding verse. Even those
that were exiled in the distant parts of
Assyria, or dispersed in the remotest
corners of Egypt, will be brought back
(Kimchi).

horn. Hebrew *shophar,* ram's horn. The
blowing of the *shophar* is a signal for
assembly and return to God (Kimchi).

that were lost. Better, 'that were wandering,' as in Deut. xxvi. 5.

28. 4
pre-722

Skikur

Assyria
Shalmaneser V

28   CHAPTER XXVIII   כח

1. Woe to the crown of pride of the
   drunkards of Ephraim,
   And to the fading flower of his
     glorious beauty,
   Which is on the head of the fat
     valley of them that are smitten
     down with wine!
2. Behold, the Lord hath a mighty
     and strong one,
   As a storm of hail, a tempest of
     destruction,
   As a storm of mighty waters
     overflowing,
   That casteth down to the earth
     with violence.
3. The crown of pride of the
     drunkards of Ephraim
   Shall be trodden under foot;
4. And the fading flower of his
     glorious beauty,

1 הוֹי עֲטֶרֶת גֵּאוּת שִׁכֹּרֵי אֶפְרַיִם
וְצִיץ נֹבֵל צְבִי תִפְאַרְתּוֹ
אֲשֶׁר עַל־רֹאשׁ גֵּיא־שְׁמָנִים
הֲלוּמֵי יָיִן:
2 הִנֵּה חָזָק וְאַמִּץ לַאדֹנָי
כְּזֶרֶם בָּרָד שַׂעַר קָטֶב
כְּזֶרֶם מַיִם כַּבִּירִים שֹׁטְפִים
הִנִּיחַ לָאָרֶץ בְּיָד:
3 בְּרַגְלַיִם תֵּרָמַסְנָה
עֲטֶרֶת גֵּאוּת שִׁכּוֹרֵי אֶפְרַיִם:
4 וְהָיְתָה צִיצַת נֹבֵל צְבִי תִפְאַרְתּוֹ

CHAPTERS XXVIII-XXXII

THIS group of oracles, with the exception of xxviii. 1-6 which obviously deals with the Northern Kingdom and must be dated before the fall of Samaria in 722 B.C.E., is assigned to the early years of the reign of Sennacherib (705-702) (Kimchi). Throughout the prophecies in this group, God's purpose is contrasted with the foolish plans of the Judean politicians. Isaiah in the name of God warns against the fatal consequences of an alliance with Egypt. Chapter xxviii. 1-6, as an introduction to the series, may have been added as a reminder and a warning that the earlier fate of Samaria might also befall Jerusalem (Malbim).

CHAPTER XXVIII

DENUNCIATION OF THE ARISTOCRACY
IN THE NORTHERN KINGDOM

1-4. The fatal consequences of the misguided policy of the drunken nobles of Ephraim.

1. *the crown of pride.* Some interpret this verse as referring to the people of Samaria, who, in their haughtiness, made crowns to wear on their heads (Kimchi). Others interpret it as an allusion to their king (Ibn Ezra).

Ephraim, i.e. the Northern Kingdom (Kara, Kimchi).

fading flower. Another metaphor for the pride of the Ephraimites (Metsudath David).

on the head . . . wine. The Ephraimites are referred to figuratively as 'the fat valley,' since they are anointed profusely with perfumed oils (Kimchi).

smitten down with wine. They lie in the street in their drunken stupor as though smitten by the wine they drink (Kimchi).

2. *a mighty and strong one.* viz. the king of Assyria, the appointed agent of God against Samaria (Abarbanel).

a tempest of destruction. Or, 'pestilential wind,' metaphorically describing the Assyrian invasion (Abarbanel).

with violence. lit. 'with a hand.'

4. Assyria will greedily and easily devour Samaria as one snatches and

Which is on the head of the fat
    valley,
Shall be as the first-ripe fig
    before the summer,
Which when one looketh upon it,
While it is yet in his hand he
    eateth it up.
5. In that day shall the LORD of
    hosts be
    For a crown of glory, and for a
      diadem of beauty,
    Unto the residue of His people;
6. And for a spirit of judgment to
    him that sitteth in judgment,
    And for strength to them that
      turn back the battle at the gate.
7. But these also reel through wine,
    And stagger through strong
      drink;
    The priest and the prophet reel
      through strong drink,
    They are confused because of
      wine,
    They stagger because of strong
      drink;
    They reel in vision, they totter
      in judgment.

אֲשֶׁר עַל־רֹאשׁ גֵּיא שְׁמָנִים
כְּבִכּוּרָהּ בְּטֶרֶם קַיִץ
אֲשֶׁר יִרְאֶה הָרֹאֶה אוֹתָהּ
בְּעוֹדָהּ בְּכַפּוֹ יִבְלָעֶנָּה׃
5 בַּיּוֹם הַהוּא יִהְיֶה יְהוָה צְבָאוֹת
לַעֲטֶרֶת צְבִי וְלִצְפִירַת תִּפְאָרָה
לִשְׁאָר עַמּוֹ׃
6 וּלְרוּחַ מִשְׁפָּט לַיּוֹשֵׁב עַל־הַמִּשְׁפָּט
וְלִגְבוּרָה מְשִׁיבֵי מִלְחָמָה שָׁעְרָה׃
7 וְגַם־אֵלֶּה בַּיַּיִן שָׁגוּ
וּבַשֵּׁכָר תָּעוּ
כֹּהֵן וְנָבִיא שָׁגוּ בַשֵּׁכָר
נִבְלְעוּ מִן־הַיַּיִן
תָּעוּ מִן־הַשֵּׁכָר
שָׁגוּ בָּרֹאֶה פָּקוּ פְּלִילִיָּה׃

swallows the *first-ripe fig* which is
esteemed a great delicacy.

5f.   A glorious future (some regard it as
the Messianic Age) under the Sovereignty of God Who will be Israel's
strength in war and a source of justice in
civic life (See Kimchi).

5.   *in that day.* After the fall of Samaria
and the survival of a faithful remnant.
According to others, *that day* is the dawn
of the Messianic Age (See Kimchi).

the residue. The faithful who will survive
the destruction (Rashi).

6.   *to him . . . judgment.* The judge (Ibn
Ezra) or the king (Kimchi).

at the gate. Of their own city, i.e. they
will drive the enemy from the interior of
the city into which he had penetrated
(Isaiah of Trani). Others render:
'against them who bring back the battle
to the gate.' This alludes to the Assyrian
army, which brought the battle close to
the gate of Jerusalem. The Judeans did

not find it necessary to go out to engage
in battle with them. God was miraculous in their strength (Kimchi).

7f.   Having held up the fate of Samaria
as a warning to the people of Judah and
Jerusalem in verses 1–4, Isaiah now
turns to the latter who, he exclaims, are
no better either morally or politically.

7.   *these* also. Pointing to the inhabitants and leaders of Judah (Kimchi).

the priest. Whose mission it was to
instruct the people (Ibn Ezra).

the prophet. The false prophets whom the
people appointed to admonish them
(Kimchi, Metsudath David).

reel in vision. The prophets cannot dis-
cern the significance of the Divine message they receive and are, therefore,
unable to impart it. Or 'stray.' They
erred against the vision of the true
prophets and did not heed it (Kimchi).

totter in judgment. Better 'stumble in

8. For all tables are full of filthy vomit,
And no place is clean.
9. Whom shall one teach knowledge?
And whom shall one make to understand the message?
Them that are weaned from the milk,
Them that are drawn from the breasts?
10. For it is precept by precept, precept by precept,
Line by line, line by line;
Here a little, there a little.
11. For with stammering lips and with a strange tongue
Shall it be spoken to this people;

8 כִּי כָּל־שֻׁלְחָנוֹת מָלְאוּ קִיא צֹאָה
בְּלִי מָקוֹם׃
9 אֶת־מִי יוֹרֶה דֵעָה
וְאֶת־מִי יָבִין שְׁמוּעָה
גְּמוּלֵי מֵחָלָב
עַתִּיקֵי מִשָּׁדָיִם׃
10 כִּי צַו לָצָו צַו לָצָו
קַו לָקָו קַו לָקָו
זְעֵיר שָׁם זְעֵיר שָׁם׃
11 כִּי בְּלַעֲגֵי שָׂפָה וּבְלָשׁוֹן אַחֶרֶת
יְדַבֵּר אֶל־הָעָם הַזֶּה׃

judgment.' The priests and prophets, whose function it was to judge the people and instruct them in the laws of the Torah, stumble in judgment (Kimchi). Alternatively, the judges 'stumble in judgment' (Ibn Ezra). This does not mean that the judges were actually intoxicated. Even a small amount of alcoholic beverages can impair one's acuity in delivering a verdict. A judge may, therefore, not imbibe before deciding matters of law (Alschich).

and no place is clean. lit. 'without (a clean) place (*makom*).' The Hebrew word is used in Rabbinic literature to designate God as omnipresent; hence the homiletic interpretation 'without God' (Aboth).

8. *for all tables.* The general public, however, are castigated for their over-indulgence (Alschich).

9. *whom shall one teach.* Better, 'whom will he (the prophet) teach . . . will he make to understand?' (Kimchi).

message. lit. 'that which is heard,' i.e. a communication from God.

10f. Since they are drunk and indulge only in eating and drinking, the teacher who comes to instruct them—whom will he teach knowledge? Similarly, a prophet who brings them the message of God—to whom can he explain it, since they are like young children who soil themselves and have no sense to use the proper facilities? (Kimchi).

10. *precept by precept.* Since the populace has become very much estranged from the Torah, the prophet must teach them precept by precept, precept by precept, as one teaches young children (Ibn Ezra, Kimchi).

line by line. He teaches them to write line by line (Ibn Ezra).

here a little. He teaches them a little of one topic and a little of another topic, yet they do not accept it (Kimchi).

11. *stammering . . . tongue.* Everyone who speaks to them words of prophecy or admonition is to them like one who speaks with stammering lips or a strange tongue (Rashi, Kimchi, Malbim).

12. To whom it was said: 'This is
the rest,
Give ye rest to the weary;
And this is the refreshing';
Yet they would not hear.
13. And so the word of the LORD is
unto them
Precept by precept, precept by
precept,
Line by line, line by line;
Here a little, there a little;
That they may go, and fall back-
ward, and be broken,
And snared, and taken.
14. Wherefore hear the word of the
LORD, ye scoffers,
The ballad - mongers of this
people which is in Jerusalem:

אֲשֶׁר ׀ אָמַר אֲלֵיהֶם זֹאת הַמְּנוּחָה 12
הָנִיחוּ לֶעָיֵף
וְזֹאת הַמַּרְגֵּעָה
וְלֹא אָבוּא שְׁמוֹעַ:
וְהָיָה לָהֶם דְּבַר־יְהֹוָה 13
צַו לָצָו צַו לָצָו
קַו לָקָו קַו לָקָו
זְעֵיר שָׁם זְעֵיר שָׁם
לְמַעַן יֵלְכוּ וְכָשְׁלוּ אָחוֹר וְנִשְׁבָּרוּ
וְנוֹקְשׁוּ וְנִלְכָּדוּ:
לָכֵן שִׁמְעוּ דְבַר־יְהֹוָה אַנְשֵׁי לָצוֹן 14
מֹשְׁלֵי הָעָם הַזֶּה אֲשֶׁר בִּירוּשָׁלָ͏ִם:

v. 12. קמץ בז״ק   v. 13. כצ״ל

12. *it was said.* lit. 'to whom he said,' meaning the prophet (Rashi, Ibn Ezra).

this. viz. observing the word of God (Kimchi). Another interpretation is: This (city, Jerusalem) will be a place of rest and refreshment to those who trust in God during the Assyrian campaign (Ibn Ezra).

is the rest . . . refreshing. The true way of peace and safety for the troubled people was to keep away from any alliance with Egypt (Ibn Ezra).

the weary. Do not trouble the weary people by making them flee to Egypt or to Assyria (Ibn Ezra). Others explain: You false prophets, give rest to the weary people of Israel and teach them the word of God, which will bring them rest; do not burden them with your falsehoods and your rashness (Kimchi).

13. *And so the word of the Lord . . . pre-cept by precept.* It was to them merely a school exercise, not obligatory (Ibn Ezra).

precept . . . line. The Rabbinic interpreta-tion is *line by line* of retribution for every *precept by precept* they have wantonly transgressed; *here a little,* retribution will come within a very short time; *here a little,* only a few of them will survive the rigours of captivity (Rashi).

14f. The prophet addresses the scoffers and ballad-mongers, the pro-Egyptian party, who ridiculed the prophet's words in order that they might go to Egypt (Ibn Ezra).

14. *scoffers.* lit. 'men of scoffing,' *latson,* derived from *lets,* 'scoffer.' The Hebrew also bears the connotation of 'ungodly,' 'men who scorn all religious teaching.' The politicians of the pro-Egyptian party scoffed as the Divine message delivered by the prophet (Ibn Ezra).

ballad-mongers. Rather, 'composers of parables, or taunt-songs' (*mashal,* see on xiv. 4) (Rashi, Ibn Ezra). Others render: 'those that rule' (Targum). Kimchi ex-plains that they were the princes of Judah in Ahaz' time, who permitted him to execute his abominations.

"deal with the devil" (handwritten)

15. Because ye have said: 'We have
    made a covenant with death,
    And with the nether-world are
    we at agreement;
    When the scouring scourge shall
    pass through,
    It shall not come unto us;
    For we have made lies our refuge,
    And in falsehood have we hid
    ourselves';

16. Therefore thus saith the Lord
    God:
    Behold, I lay in Zion for a
    foundation a stone,
    A tried stone, a costly corner-
    stone of sure foundation;
    He that believeth shall not make
    haste.

17. And I will make justice the line,
    And righteousness the plummet;
    And the hail shall sweep away
    the refuge of lies,

כִּי אֲמַרְתֶּם כָּרַתְנוּ בְרִית אֶת־מָוֶת 15
וְעִם־שְׁאוֹל עָשִׂינוּ חֹזֶה
שׁוֹט שׁוֹטֵף כִּי־יַעֲבֹר
לֹא יְבוֹאֵנוּ
כִּי שַׂמְנוּ כָזָב מַחְסֵנוּ
וּבַשֶּׁקֶר נִסְתָּרְנוּ ׃
לָכֵן כֹּה אָמַר אֲדֹנָי יֱהֹוִה 16
הִנְנִי יִסַּד בְּצִיּוֹן אָבֶן
אֶבֶן בֹּחַן פִּנַּת יִקְרַת מוּסָד מוּסָּד
הַמַּאֲמִין לֹא יָחִישׁ ׃
וְשַׂמְתִּי מִשְׁפָּט לְקָו 17
וּצְדָקָה לְמִשְׁקָלֶת
וְיָעָה בָרָד מַחְסֵה כָזָב

"Shekel out" "plumbline" (handwritten)

v. 15. שׁוֹט ק׳ v. 16. יַעֲבֹר ק׳ v. 15. דגש אחר שורק v. 16.

15.　The verse is a protasis to verse 16ff.
which are the apodosis (Metsudath
David).

covenant with death. Accordingly death
has no terrors for us (Metsudath David).

with the nether-world . . . agreement. We
have called upon the powers of Sheol to
help us and secured their consent that
the enemy come not upon us (Abarbanel).

when the scouring scourge, etc. An assertion
of complete self-confidence.

we have made lies, etc. The prophet's
ironical reproduction of their confident
assertions. They claim to have found a
refuge and a shelter in the power of
idols but, he warns them, there is there
neither shelter nor refuge but only lies
and falsehood (Rashi). Kimchi takes it
as a reference to the false prophets.
Isaiah calls them 'lies' and falsehood.

16-22.　Apodosis to verse 15. Justice

will be permanently established, all
falsehood swept away, the scoffers and
the ungodly crushed beyond hope, and
only those who trust in the Lord will
achieve salvation.

16.　*behold, I lay.* The unusual Hebrew
construction may be translated 'Behold,
I (am He that) laid.' The *stone* is either
intended for the Messiah (Rashi) or
Hezekiah (Kimchi).

he that believeth . . . haste. He will remain
steadfast in his faith however long realization may be delayed (Ibn Ezra).

17.　Justice and righteousness will be
the standards of political and social
activities, completely sweeping away
intrigues and secret machinations.

line . . . plummet. Metaphors borrowed
from the builder's art (Rashi).

hail . . . waters. God's destructive agen-
cies, represented perhaps by the invading army of Assyria (Kimchi).

covered

And the waters shall overflow
the hiding-place.

18. And your covenant with death
shall be disannulled,
And your agreement with the
nether-world shall not stand;
When the scouring scourge shall
pass through,
Then ye shall be trodden down
by it.

19. As often as it passeth through, it
shall take you;
For morning by morning shall it
pass through,
By day and by night;
And it shall be sheer terror to
understand the message.

20. For the bed is too short for a
man to stretch himself;
And the covering too narrow
when he gathereth himself up.

21. For the LORD will rise up as in
mount Perazim,
He will be wroth as in the valley
of Gibeon;
That He may do His work,
strange is His work,
And bring to pass His act,
strange is His act.

וְסֵ֖תֶר מַ֥יִם יִשְׁטֹֽפוּ׃

18 וְכֻפַּ֤ר בְּרִֽיתְכֶם֙ אֶת־מָ֔וֶת
וְחָזוּתְכֶ֥ם אֶת־שְׁא֖וֹל לֹ֣א תָק֑וּם
שׁ֤וֹט שׁוֹטֵף֙ כִּ֣י יַֽעֲבֹ֔ר
וִהְיִ֥יתֶם ל֖וֹ לְמִרְמָֽס׃

19 מִדֵּ֤י עָבְרוֹ֙ יִקַּ֣ח אֶתְכֶ֔ם
כִּֽי־בַבֹּ֧קֶר בַּבֹּ֛קֶר יַֽעֲבֹ֖ר
בַּיּ֣וֹם וּבַלָּ֑יְלָה
וְהָיָ֥ה רַק־זְוָעָ֖ה הָבִ֥ין שְׁמוּעָֽה׃

20 כִּֽי־קָצַ֥ר הַמַּצָּ֖ע מֵֽהִשְׂתָּרֵ֑עַ
וְהַמַּסֵּכָ֥ה צָ֖רָה כְּהִתְכַּנֵּֽס׃

21 כִּ֤י כְהַר־פְּרָצִים֙ יָק֣וּם יְהֹוָ֔ה
כְּעֵ֥מֶק בְּגִבְע֖וֹן יִרְגָּ֑ז
לַֽעֲשׂ֤וֹת מַֽעֲשֵׂ֨הוּ֙ זָ֣ר מַֽעֲשֵׂ֔הוּ
וְלַֽעֲבֹד֙ עֲבֹ֣דָת֔וֹ נָכְרִיָּ֖ה עֲבֹֽדָתֽוֹ׃

folk saying

255.20 David Joshua 10.12 ff

255.25

255:17-25

---

hiding place. Of lies, mentioned above
(Rashi).

18. A retort to the arrogant boasts in
verse 15 with the use of similar phrases
and metaphors.

disannulled. lit. 'smeared over.'

then . . . by it. lit. 'then ye shall be unto it
a thing trodden down.'

19. The visitation will be continued
until all the guilty men are carried
away; and the retribution will be so ter-
rifying that even the report of it will
strike terror in the hearts of those who
grasp its significance.

it passeth through. viz. *the scouring scourge*
(Kimchi).

20. The impossible and vexatious
situation of the people is graphically

depicted by the use of what is perhaps a
popular saying. It is compared with that
of a man sleeping on a short bed under
a narrow covering. He cannot stretch
himself because the bed is too short;
and if he gathered himself up, his limbs
are exposed to the cold because the
covering is too narrow (Kimchi).

21. *mount Perazim.* Where, with God's
help, David inflicted a great defeat on
the Philistines (cf. 2 Sam. v. 20) (Ibn
Ezra, Kimchi).

the valley of Gibeon. All classic exegetes
take this as an allusion to the miracle of
the sun standing still in Gibeon in
Joshua's time, when he waged war
against the Canaanites (Josh. x. 12ff.).

strange in His work. Since He has never
dealt so harshly with His people
(Kimchi).

22. Now therefore be ye not scoffers,
    Lest your bands be made strong;
    For an extermination wholly
    determined have I heard from
    the Lord, the GOD of hosts,
    Upon the whole land.
23. Give ye ear, and hear my voice;
    Attend, and hear my speech.
24. Is the plowman never done with
    plowing to sow,
    With the opening and harrowing
    of his ground?
25. When he hath made plain the
    face thereof,
    Doth he not cast abroad the black
    cummin, and scatter the cum-
    min,

וְעַתָּה אַל־תִּתְלוֹצָצוּ 22
פֶּן־יֶחְזְקוּ מוֹסְרֵיכֶם
כִּי־כָלָה וְנֶחֱרָצָה שָׁמַעְתִּי
מֵאֵת אֲדֹנָי יֱהוִֹה צְבָאוֹת
עַל־כָּל־הָאָרֶץ ׃
הַאֲזִינוּ וְשִׁמְעוּ קוֹלִי 23
הַקְשִׁיבוּ וְשִׁמְעוּ אִמְרָתִי ׃
הֲכֹל הַיּוֹם יַחֲרֹשׁ הַחֹרֵשׁ לִזְרֹעַ 24
יְפַתַּח וִישַׂדֵּד אַדְמָתוֹ ׃
הֲלוֹא אִם־שִׁוָּה פָנֶיהָ 25
וְהֵפִיץ קֶצַח וְכַמֹּן יִזְרֹק

קמץ בז״ק .v 22.

22. Final thrust at the scoffers. Cf. verse 14, *hear the word of the* LORD, *ye scoffers,* etc.

but not ye scoffers. lit. 'scoff not'; do not treat the matter in a mocking spirit, lightly.

your bands. Chains of captivity (Ibn Ezra). Others render: 'your afflictions' (Targum, Rashi, Kimchi).

23-29. Isaiah, having described the judgment and retribution which God would bring upon the rulers and people, invites them now to listen to a parable taken from country life from which the obvious lessons might be drawn by them. The farmer ploughs and breaks up his land, but these acts are not an end in themselves. His object is to achieve the subsequent sowing and reaping. So God may inflict heartbreaking woe and suffering on His people, but His aim is their ultimate reaping and enjoying of the blessings that are in store for the faithful. God's wisdom directs the varied activities of the hus-

bandman who adapts his processes to the seasons of the year and the nature of the seeds; similarly the wisdom of God directs the destinies of His people, adapting His dealings to their characters and moral conditions. Other and similar comparisons readily suggest themselves.

23. The prophet addresses the rulers and the people inviting their careful and serious attention and contemplation.

24. *to sow.* Equals 'since his intention is to sow,' the ploughing being only the necessary preparation.

with the opening and harrowing of. lit. 'he opens and harrows.'

25. *made plain.* Levelled the ground.

black cumin. Or black cummel, *Nigella sativa.* It is cultivated in Egypt and Syria for its seeds, which are black and are used as a condiment (Kimchi).

cumin, i.e. *Cuminum sativum.* 'Its seeds are often used as a spice in the East (Kimchi).

And put in the wheat in rows
and the barley in the appointed
place
And the spelt in the border thereof?

26. For He doth instruct him aright;
His God doth teach him.

27. For the black cummin is not
threshed with a threshing-
sledge,
Neither is a cart-wheel turned
about upon the cummin;
But the black cummin is beaten
out with a staff,
And the cummin with a rod.

28. Is bread corn crushed?
Nay, he will not ever be threshing it;
And though the roller of his
wagon and its sharp edges
move noisily,
He doth not crush it.

29. This also cometh forth from the
LORD of hosts:
Wonderful is His counsel, and
great His wisdom.

וְשָׂ֤ם חִטָּה֙ שׂוֹרָ֔ה וּשְׂעֹרָ֖ה נִסְמָ֑ן
וְכֻסֶּ֖מֶת גְּבֻלָתֽוֹ׃

26 וְיִסְּר֖וֹ לַמִּשְׁפָּ֑ט
אֱלֹהָ֖יו יוֹרֶֽנּוּ׃

27 כִּ֣י לֹ֤א בֶֽחָרוּץ֙ י֣וּדַשׁ קֶ֔צַח
וְאוֹפַ֥ן עֲגָלָ֖ה עַל־כַּמֹּ֣ן יוּסָּ֑ב
כִּ֧י בַמַּטֶּ֛ה יֵחָ֥בֶט קֶ֖צַח
וְכַמֹּ֥ן בַּשָּֽׁבֶט׃

28 לֶ֣חֶם יוּדָ֔ק
כִּ֛י לֹ֥א לָנֶ֖צַח אָד֣וֹשׁ יְדוּשֶׁ֑נּוּ
וְ֠הָמַם גִּלְגַּ֧ל עֶגְלָת֛וֹ וּפָרָשָׁ֖יו
לֹֽא־יְדֻקֶּֽנּוּ׃

29 גַּם־זֹ֕את מֵעִ֖ם יְהֹוָ֣ה צְבָא֣וֹת יָצָ֑אָה
הִפְלִ֣יא עֵצָ֔ה הִגְדִּ֖יל תּוּשִׁיָּֽה׃

v. 27. ק׳ דגש אחר שורק v. 28. קמץ בז״ק

---

26. aright. The Hebrew word mishpat is
elsewhere usually rendered 'judgment,'
but here it bears the meaning of right
order or method (Ibn Ezra, Kimchi).
With the thought of this verse, cf. 'Hus-
bandry, which the Most High hath
ordained' (Ecclus. vii. 15).

27f. The appropriate methods of
threshing apply to the several kinds; but
how ruinous would be the method suitable for one kind if applied to another!
Neither cumin nor black cumin can
bear the heavy thrashing-sledge or the
cart-wheel; but the cumin can easily be
separated from its case with a rod and
the black cumin with a staff (Rashi).

28. and though ... noisily. The rendering of A.J. is questionable. Others
render: 'Bread corn is crushed, but he
will not ever be threshing it; lest the
wheel of his wagon and its sharp edges
break it, he doth not crush it (Kimchi).'
Others render: 'and the wheel of his
wagon shall break, and his separators
shall not crush it' (Rashi).

28. this also. Even this, the husband-
man's craft; much more so the fate and
destinies of mankind (Rashi).

wonderful is ... wisdom. lit. 'He produced wonderful counsel, He magnified
wisdom.' The last word, tushiyyah, is
common in Proverbs and Job, and con-
notes 'practical method' to accomplish
what is planned.

29   CHAPTER XXIX   כט

1. Ah, Ariel, Ariel, the city where
   David encamped!
   Add ye year to year,
   Let the feasts come round!

2. Then will I distress Ariel,
   And there shall be mourning and
   moaning;
   And she shall be unto Me as a
   hearth of God.

3. And I will encamp against thee
   round about,
   And will lay siege against thee
   with a mound,
   And I will raise siege works
   against thee.

4. And brought down thou shalt
   speak out of the ground,
   And thy speech shall be low out
   of the dust;
   And thy voice shall be as of a
   ghost out of the ground,
   And thy speech shall chirp out of
   the dust.

5. But the multitude of thy foes
   shall be like small dust,

1 הוֹי אֲרִיאֵל אֲרִיאֵל קִרְיַת חָנָה דָוִד
    סְפוּ שָׁנָה עַל־שָׁנָה חַגִּים יִנְקֹפוּ:

2 וַהֲצִיקוֹתִי לַאֲרִיאֵל
    וְהָיְתָה תַאֲנִיָּה וַאֲנִיָּה
    וְהָיְתָה לִי כַּאֲרִיאֵל:

3 וְחָנִיתִי כַדּוּר עָלָיִךְ
    וְצַרְתִּי עָלַיִךְ מֻצָּב
    וַהֲקִימֹתִי עָלַיִךְ מְצֻרֹת:

4 וְשָׁפַלְתְּ מֵאֶרֶץ תְּדַבֵּרִי
    וּמֵעָפָר תִּשַּׁח אִמְרָתֵךְ
    וְהָיָה כְּאוֹב מֵאֶרֶץ קוֹלֵךְ
    וּמֵעָפָר אִמְרָתֵךְ תְּצַפְצֵף:

5 וְהָיָה כְּאָבָק דַּק הֲמוֹן זָרָיִךְ

CHAPTER XXIX

THE FATE OF ZION

1–4. Jerusalem, now gay and festive, will be surrounded by many enemies and humbled to the dust.

1. The prophet apostrophizes Jerusalem.

Ariel. A.J. sees the Hebrew as a compound of 'hearth of' (*ari*) and 'God' (*El*). It is used in the sense of 'altar hearth' (cf. Ezek. xliii. 15f.); and the word is applied to Jerusalem as the location of the Temple. Classical Jewish exegetes, however, explain it as 'lion of God,' alluding to the fire on the altar which descended from heaven and lay crouched on the altar in the shape of a lion (Rashi after Targum).

the city where David encamped. Jerusalem, or Zion which formed a part of it. The place which recalled David's initial sacrifice (2 Sam. xxiv. 18–24) was now the scene of insincere worship (Kimchi).

all ye . . . round. The language is ironical. Let them go on enjoying themselves for a few more years; the approaching disaster will bring it all to an abrupt end (Malbim).

2. *mourning and moaning.* Hebrew *taaniyyah waaniyyah* (again in Lam. ii. 5) may be reproduced as 'moaning and bemoaning.'

as a hearth of God. Or, 'as the altar hearth' where the victims bleed and burn; so will Jerusalem be surrounded with the slain (Rashi, Metsudath David).

9. *I will encamp against thee.* God Himself, so to speak, will join the besieging army (Kimchi).

4. A scene of humiliation and dejection. Instead of the normally loud clamor of a city at peace, sepulchral voices will be heard like the mutterings of the necromancer (cf. viii. 19).

5–8. In the hour of his victory, the enemy is overwhelmed and destroyed.

And the multitude of the terrible
   ones as chaff that passeth
   away;
Yea, it shall be at an instant
   suddenly—

6. There shall be a visitation from
   the LORD of hosts
With thunder, and with earthquake, and great noise,
With whirlwind and tempest,
   and the flame of a devouring
   fire.

7. And the multitude of all the
   nations that war against Ariel,
Even all that war against her, and
   the bulwarks about her, and
   they that distress her,
Shall be as a dream, a vision of
   the night.

8. And it shall be as when a hungry
   man dreameth, and, behold,
   he eateth,
But he awaketh, and his soul is
   empty;
Or as when a thirsty man
   dreameth, and, behold, he
   drinketh,
But he awaketh, and, behold, he
   is faint, and his soul hath
   appetite—
So shall the multitude of all the
   nations be,
That fight against mount Zion.

9. Stupefy yourselves, and be
   stupid!
Blind yourselves, and be blind!

וּכְמֹץ עֹבֵר הֲמוֹן עָרִיצִים
וְהָיָה לְפֶתַע פִּתְאֹם׃

6 מֵעִם יְהֹוָה צְבָאוֹת תִּפָּקֵד
בְּרַעַם וּבְרַעַשׁ וְקוֹל גָּדוֹל
סוּפָה וּסְעָרָה וְלַהַב אֵשׁ אוֹכֵלָה׃

7 וְהָיָה כַּחֲלוֹם חֲזוֹן לַיְלָה
הֲמוֹן כָּל־הַגּוֹיִם
הַצֹּבְאִים עַל־אֲרִיאֵל
וְכָל־צֹבֶיהָ וּמְצֹדָתָהּ
וְהַמְּצִיקִים לָהּ׃

8 וְהָיָה כַּאֲשֶׁר יַחֲלֹם הָרָעֵב
וְהִנֵּה אוֹכֵל
וְהֵקִיץ וְרֵקָה נַפְשׁוֹ
וְכַאֲשֶׁר יַחֲלֹם הַצָּמֵא וְהִנֵּה שֹׁתֶה
וְהֵקִיץ וְהִנֵּה עָיֵף וְנַפְשׁוֹ שׁוֹקֵקָה
כֵּן יִהְיֶה הֲמוֹן כָּל־הַגּוֹיִם
הַצֹּבְאִים עַל־הַר צִיּוֹן׃

9 הִתְמַהְמְהוּ וּתְמָהוּ
הִשְׁתַּעַשְׁעוּ וָשֹׁעוּ

---

5. *thy foes.* lit. 'thy stranger,' the foreign invaders.

the terrible ones. Or, 'the tyrants.'

it shall be. viz. the change from triumph
to disaster.

6. *a visitation.* God's intervention to
save Jerusalem, by directing thunder,
etc. against the enemy (Rashi).

7f. The enemy's swift dispersal and
disillusionment.

7. *shall be as a dream.* That suddenly
vanishes (Ibn Ezra).

8. A realistic metaphor to describe
disillusionment and disappointment.

soul. The Hebrew word *nephesh* is twice
employed in the verse for 'appetite.' The
first instance may be more forcibly,
translated 'and his appetite is unsated,'
and the second 'and he (lit. his appetite)
craves (for water)' (Kimchi, Gen. xxiii.
8; Ibn Ganah).

9-12. The prophet denounces the
obtuseness of the people of Jerusalem
who fail to appreciate his warning.

Ye that are drunken, but not with
 wine,
That stagger, but not with strong
 drink.

10. For the LORD hath poured out
 upon you the spirit of deep
 sleep,
And hath closed your eyes;
The prophets, and your heads,
 the seers, hath He covered.

11. And the vision of all this is
become unto you as the words of a
writing that is sealed, which men
deliver to one that is learned, saying:
'Read this, I pray thee'; and he
saith: 'I cannot, for it is sealed';
12. and the writing is delivered to
him that is not learned, saying:
'Read this, I pray thee'; and he
saith: 'I am not learned.'

13. And the Lord said: Forasmuch
 as this people draw near,
And with their mouth and with
 their lips do honour Me,
But have removed their heart far
 from Me,
And their fear of Me is a commandment of men learned by
 rote;

שִׁכְרוּ וְלֹא־יַיִן
נָעוּ וְלֹא שֵׁכָר׃
10 כִּי־נָסַךְ עֲלֵיכֶם יְהֹוָה רוּחַ תַּרְדֵּמָה
וַיְעַצֵּם אֶת־עֵינֵיכֶם
אֶת־הַנְּבִיאִים וְאֶת־רָאשֵׁיכֶם
הַחֹזִים כִּסָּה׃
11 וַתְּהִי לָכֶם חָזוּת הַכֹּל כְּדִבְרֵי
הַסֵּפֶר הֶחָתוּם אֲשֶׁר־יִתְּנוּ אֹתוֹ אֶל־
יוֹדֵעַ הַסֵּפֶר לֵאמֹר קְרָא־נָא זֶה
12 וְאָמַר לֹא אוּכַל כִּי חָתוּם הוּא׃ וְנִתַּן
הַסֵּפֶר עַל אֲשֶׁר לֹא־יָדַע סֵפֶר
לֵאמֹר קְרָא־נָא זֶה וְאָמַר לֹא יָדַעְתִּי
סֵפֶר׃
13 וַיֹּאמֶר אֲדֹנָי יַעַן כִּי נִגַּשׁ הָעָם הַזֶּה
בְּפִיו וּבִשְׂפָתָיו כִּבְּדוּנִי
וְלִבּוֹ רִחַק מִמֶּנִּי
וַתְּהִי יִרְאָתָם אֹתִי
מִצְוַת אֲנָשִׁים מְלֻמָּדָה׃

v. 11. סֵפֶר ק׳

---

that stagger. Mentally, unable to make up
their mind (Ibn Ezra).

10. *the* LORD *hath poured out.* This
followed Targum and Rashi. Ibn Ezra
and Kimchi, however, render: 'has
covered you with . . . sleep.' As with the
hardening of Pharaoh's heart which
began with his own obduracy, so here
the people's mental and moral blindness was the effect of their failure to
listen to the prophet's warning message
from God.

11f. The learned and the ignorant are
alike unable to understand the prophet's communication.

13f. Rebuke of the people's mechanical and formal worship with its resultant
punishment.

13. *draw near.* To the Temple or to
worship. Against the accentuation, a
better balance is obtained by translat-
ing: 'draw near with their mouth'
(Metsudath David).

fear of Me. i.e. method of expressing
reverence of Me (Metsudath David).

14. Therefore, behold, I will again
do a marvellous work among
this people,
Even a marvellous work and a
wonder;
And the wisdom of their wise
men shall perish,
And the prudence of their
prudent men shall be hid.

15. Woe unto them that seek deep to
hide their counsel from the
LORD,
And their works are in the dark,
And they say: 'Who seeth us?
and who knoweth us?'

16. O your perversity!
Shall the potter be esteemed as
clay;
That the thing made should say
of him that made it: 'He made
me not';
Or the thing framed say of him
that framed it: 'He hath no
understanding?'

17. Is it not yet a very little while,
And Lebanon shall be turned
into a fruitful field,
And the fruitful field shall be
esteemed as a forest?

לָכֵן הִנְנִי יוֹסִף 14
לְהַפְלִיא אֶת־הָעָם־הַזֶּה
הַפְלֵא וָפֶלֶא
וְאָבְדָה חָכְמַת חֲכָמָיו
וּבִינַת נְבֹנָיו תִּסְתַּתָּר׃

הוֹי הַמַּעֲמִיקִים מֵיהוָה לַסְתִּר עֵצָה 15
וְהָיָה בְמַחְשָׁךְ מַעֲשֵׂיהֶם
וַיֹּאמְרוּ מִי רֹאֵנוּ וּמִי יֹדְעֵנוּ׃

הַפְכְּכֶם 16
אִם־כְּחֹמֶר הַיֹּצֵר יֵחָשֵׁב
כִּי־יֹאמַר מַעֲשֶׂה לְעֹשֵׂהוּ לֹא עָשָׂנִי
וְיֵצֶר אָמַר לְיֹצְרוֹ לֹא הֵבִין׃

הֲלֹא־עוֹד מְעַט מִזְעָר 17
וְשָׁב לְבָנוֹן לַכַּרְמֶל
וְהַכַּרְמֶל לַיַּעַר יֵחָשֵׁב׃

15-21. The prophet ridicules the arrogance and short-sightedness of the politicians, and reminds them of God's omnipotence and of the wonderful physical, moral and spiritual transformation He would bring about.

15. *unto them.* The political conspirators of the pro-Egyptian party who negotiated in secret (cf. xxxi. 1ff., xxxvi. 9) (Ibn Kaspi).

from the LORD. Who through His prophet counselled peace with Assyria.

16. Human presumption to outwit God is as foolish as if the potter should be put on a par with the clay he uses in the making of his pots; or as if a manufactured object should presume to question the intelligence of the man who made it or altogether deny the fact that he had made it.

shall the potter, etc. The answer, of course, is in the negative. According to the accentuation, however, it should be rendered: 'Shall it be esteemed as the potter's clay?' According to this rendering, the reply is in the affirmative (Rashi). Alternatively, 'Indeed, it is to be esteemed as the potter's clay.' Just as the potter's clay can easily be changed from one shape into another, so can I easily change you (Kimchi).

17. God in His omnipotence transforms Nature at will.

is it . . . while. i.e. almost at any moment (Rashi, Ibn Ezra).

Lebanon. Because it is covered with trees, it is here employed as a synonym for *forest.* This clause is repeated in xxxii. 15 and may have been a proverbial saying (Rashi).

18. And in that day shall the deaf
hear the words of a book,
And the eyes of the blind shall
see out of obscurity and out of
darkness.

19. The humble also shall increase
their joy in the LORD,
And the neediest among men
shall exult in the Holy One of
Israel.

20. For the terrible one is brought
to nought,
And the scorner ceaseth,
And all they that watch for
iniquity are cut off;

21. That make a man an offender by
words,
And lay a snare for him that
reproveth in the gate,
And turn aside the just with a
thing of nought.

22. Therefore thus saith the LORD,
who redeemed Abraham, concerning
the house of Jacob:
Jacob shall not now be ashamed,

וְשָׁמְעוּ בַיּוֹם־הַהוּא 18
הַחֵרְשִׁים דִּבְרֵי־סֵפֶר
וּמֵאֹפֶל וּמֵחֹשֶׁךְ עֵינֵי עִוְרִים תִּרְאֶינָה:
וְיָסְפוּ עֲנָוִים בַּיהֹוָה שִׂמְחָה 19
וְאֶבְיוֹנֵי אָדָם בִּקְדוֹשׁ יִשְׂרָאֵל יָגִילוּ:
כִּי־אָפֵס עָרִיץ 20
וְכָלָה לֵץ
וְנִכְרְתוּ כָּל־שֹׁקְדֵי אָוֶן:
מַחֲטִיאֵי אָדָם בְּדָבָר 21
וְלַמּוֹכִיחַ בַּשַּׁעַר יְקֹשׁוּן
וַיַּטּוּ בַתֹּהוּ צַדִּיק:
לָכֵן כֹּה־אָמַר יְהֹוָה אֶל־בֵּית יַעֲקֹב 22
אֲשֶׁר פָּדָה אֶת־אַבְרָהָם
לֹא־עַתָּה יֵבוֹשׁ יַעֲקֹב

(handwritten margin notes: "hypocrites", "— public speakers", "Nimrod furnace?")

18. A reference back to verses 11f.
God will effect a cure for spiritual deaf-
ness and blindness.

19. *shall increase their joy.* Or, 'shall
obtain fresh joy.' By the *humble* and
neediest are meant the depressed classes
who have been downtrodden by the
unscrupulous nobles (Kimchi).

20. *terrible one.* i.e. the wicked among
the Jews, who prevented the righteous
from observing the precepts. Those
were the princes and the judges in the
time of Ahaz (Kimchi).

watch for iniquity. Men who are on the
look out to work mischief (Rashi).

21. *by words.* Better, 'cause people to
sin with words.' An allusion to the false
prophets, who would mislead the
people with their false prophecies
(Rashi).

him that reproveth. The preacher, judge
or any one who condemns wickedness
and injustice (Abarbanel).

in the gate. The place where public affairs
were transacted (Abarbanel).

turn aside the just. From his rightful
claims (Targum, Rashi).

thing of nought. Flimsy arguments
(Metsudath Zion).

22-24. Israel's shame will become a
thing of the past; the rising generation
as well as the old will acknowledge their
subjection to the Holy God, and the
misguided and discontented will gain
understanding and learn the lessons of
true religion.

22. *therefore.* For the reason that follows in verse 23 (Kimchi, Metsudath
David).

redeemed Abraham. From the fiery furnace into which, according to tradition,
he had been cast by Nimrod for refusing to worship his idols (Rashi).

now. In the distant future which, in the
prophet's vivid vision, appears as the
present.

Neither shall his face now wax
pale;
23. When he seeth his children, the
work of My hands, in the
midst of him,
That they sanctify My name;
Yea, they shall sanctify the Holy
One of Jacob,
And shall stand in awe of the
God of Israel.
24. They also that err in spirit shall
come to understanding,
And they that murmur shall
learn instruction.

וְלֹא עַתָּה פָּנָיו יֶחֱוָרוּ׃

23 כִּי בִרְאֹתוֹ יְלָדָיו מַעֲשֵׂה יָדַי בְּקִרְבּוֹ
יַקְדִּישׁוּ שְׁמִי
וְהִקְדִּישׁוּ אֶת־קְדוֹשׁ יַעֲקֹב
וְאֶת־אֱלֹהֵי יִשְׂרָאֵל יַעֲרִיצוּ׃

24 וְיָדְעוּ תֹעֵי־רוּחַ בִּינָה
וְרוֹגְנִים יִלְמְדוּ־לֶקַח׃

Dedicate to Kay Warren 7/9?

Ki lekah tov

30   CHAPTER XXX

ל

1. Woe to the rebellious children,
saith the LORD,
That take counsel, but not of
Me;
And that ~~form~~ _weave out_ projects, but not
of My spirit,
That they may add sin to sin;
2. That walk to go down into Egypt,

1 הוֹי בָּנִים סוֹרְרִים נְאֻם־יְהוָה
לַעֲשׂוֹת עֵצָה וְלֹא מִנִּי
וְלִנְסֹךְ מַסֵּכָה וְלֹא רוּחִי
לְמַעַן סְפוֹת חַטָּאת עַל־חַטָּאת׃

2 הַהֹלְכִים לָרֶדֶת מִצְרַיִם

---

23. _when he._ viz. Jacob, the old generation (Kimchi).

sanctify . . . stand in awe. The same verbs
as in viii. 13.

24. _learn instruction._ The true knowledge of Torah (Ibn Ezra, Kimchi).

CHAPTER XXX

A BOLD and explicit denunciation of the
political intrigues of the pro-Egyptian
party, an exposure of the futility of
Egyptian power and an announcement
of the supernatural destruction of the
Assyrian invader (Kimchi).

1f. The proposed Egyptian alliance is
contrary to the will of God.

1. _rebellious children._ The members of
the pro-Egyptian party (Kimchi).

take counsel. Better, 'carry out a plan.'

form projects. lit. 'weave a web.' I.e. form
a plan. This is perhaps Ibn Ezra's rendering. Alternatively, it is an expression
of 'a covering,' denoting a secret plan of
alliance with Egypt or protection from
Egypt (Kimchi).

add sin to sin. The sin of trusting in
Pharaoh instead of God in addition to
their sins (Kimchi). Or the sin of returning to Egypt, in addition to their mis-
trust in God (Abarbanel).

not of My spirit. Not in agreement with
the Divine spirit which, in the Torah,
directed the warnings against returning
to Egypt (Abarbanel).

2. _walk to go down._ As envoys of the
people or of King Ahaz (Kimchi).

And have not asked at My
  mouth;
To take refuge in the stronghold
  of Pharaoh,
And to take shelter in the
  shadow of Egypt!
3. Therefore shall the stronghold of
  Pharaoh turn to your shame,
  And the shelter in the shadow of
  Egypt to your confusion.
4. For his princes are at Zoan,
  And his ambassadors are come
  to Hanes,
5. They shall all be ashamed of a
  people that cannot profit them,
  That are not a help nor profit,
  But a shame, and also a reproach.
6. The burden of the beasts of the
  South.
  Through the land of trouble and
  anguish,
  From whence come the lioness
  and the lion,
  The viper and flying serpent,
  They carry their riches upon the
  shoulders of young asses,

(margin annotations: 23rd dynasty @700 capital — Tanis — Delta; Ahaz & N. Israel; Tanis; Hyksos; Isle in Nile S. of Memphis; Heracleopolis? Magna; 1 com. s. of Memphis; — or maybe corruption of Tahpanes)

וּפִי לֹא שָׁאָלוּ
לָעוֹז בְּמָעוֹז פַּרְעֹה
וְלַחְסוֹת בְּצֵל מִצְרָיִם:
3 וְהָיָה לָכֶם מָעוֹז פַּרְעֹה לְבֹשֶׁת
וְהֶחָסוּת בְּצֵל־מִצְרַיִם לִכְלִמָּה:
4 כִּי־הָיוּ בְצֹעַן שָׂרָיו
וּמַלְאָכָיו חָנֵס יַגִּיעוּ:
5 כֹּל הִבְאִישׁ עַל־עַם לֹא־יוֹעִילוּ לָמוֹ
לֹא לְעֵזֶר וְלֹא לְהוֹעִיל
כִּי לְבֹשֶׁת וְגַם־לְחֶרְפָּה:
6 מַשָּׂא בַּהֲמוֹת נֶגֶב
בְּאֶרֶץ צָרָה וְצוּקָה
לָבִיא וָלַיִשׁ מֵהֶם
אֶפְעֶה וְשָׂרָף מְעוֹפֵף
יִשְׂאוּ עַל־כֶּתֶף עֲיָרִים חֵילֵיהֶם

‏א׳ נבה v. 6.   עירים ק׳ v. 5.

at My mouth. Through the prophet
(Targum).

3. The consequences of disobedience
to the word of God.

4f. Pharaoh may welcome the Judean
princes and ambassadors in Zoan and in
Hanes, but his promised help will result
in utter disappointment and shame.

4. *his.* Judah's or Ahaz' (Kimchi).
Other commentators explain the entire
prophecy as referring to the ambassadors of Hoshea son of Elah, who
appealed to So, King of Egypt, to protect him from Shalmaneser, king of
Assyria. Consequently, 'his' refers to the
king of Israel (Rashi, Abarbanel).

Zoan. See on xix. 11.

Hanes. Heracleopolis Magna, to the

south of Memphis on one of the Nile
islands. The two cities were on the
southern frontier of Lower Egypt
(Carta).

5. *they.* The Judean envoys or the
people they represent.

a people. The Egyptians (Malbim).

6f. The Judean envoys to Egypt had to
traverse the Negeb desert to the south of
Judah, a *land of trouble and anguish.* They
carried with them rich gifts from the
king of Judah to the Egyptian whose
help the prophet declares to be in vain
and empty (Rashi, Kimchi).

6. *beasts of the South.* The young asses
and camels mentioned later which had
to pass through the Negeb on their way
to Egypt. For Negeb, see on xxi. 1
(Rashi, Metsudath David).

And their treasures upon the
humps of camels,
To a people that shall not profit
them.

7. For Egypt helpeth in vain, and to
no purpose;
Therefore have I called her
Arrogancy that sitteth still.

8. Now go, write it before them on
a tablet, *poster?*
And inscribe it in a book, *permanent*
That it may be for the time to
come
For ever and ever.

9. For it is a rebellious people,
Lying children,
Children that refuse to hear the
teaching of the LORD;

10. That say to the seers: 'See not,'
And to the prophets: 'Prophesy
not unto us right things,
Speak unto us smooth things,
prophesy delusions;

11. Get you out of the way,
Turn aside out of the path,
Cause the Holy One of Israel
To cease from before us.'

וְעַל־דַּבֶּשֶׁת גְּמַלִּים אוֹצְרוֹתָם
עַל־עַם לֹא יוֹעִילוּ׃
7 וּמִצְרַיִם הֶבֶל וָרִיק יַעְזֹרוּ
לָכֵן קָרָאתִי לָזֹאת
רַהַב הֵם שָׁבֶת׃
8 עַתָּה בּוֹא כָתְבָהּ עַל־לוּחַ
אִתָּם וְעַל־סֵפֶר חֻקָּהּ
וּתְהִי לְיוֹם אַחֲרוֹן
לָעַד עַד־עוֹלָם׃
9 כִּי עַם מְרִי הוּא
בָּנִים כֶּחָשִׁים
בָּנִים לֹא־אָבוּ שְׁמוֹעַ תּוֹרַת יְהוָה׃
10 אֲשֶׁר אָמְרוּ לָרֹאִים לֹא תִרְאוּ
וְלַחֹזִים לֹא־תֶחֱזוּ־לָנוּ נְכֹחוֹת
דַּבְּרוּ־לָנוּ חֲלָקוֹת חֲזוּ מַהֲתַלּוֹת׃
11 סוּרוּ מִנֵּי־דֶרֶךְ
הַטּוּ מִנֵּי־אֹרַח
הַשְׁבִּיתוּ מִפָּנֵינוּ
אֶת־קְדוֹשׁ יִשְׂרָאֵל׃

v. 11. ב׳ נוניץ בצרי

7. *arrogancy.* Alluding to Egypt's false
pretence to be able to render help
(Metsudath David).

that sitteth still. Doing nothing while its
dupes are destroyed one by one (Rashi,
Metsudath David).

8. The prophet is directed to avoid the
Divine message so that it may serve as a
testimony for the future. The record
probably contained the numerous
warnings against the Egyptian alliance
(Abarbanel).

tablet . . . book. The former may have
been a temporary reminder for that
generation, whereas the book is a per-

manent record for posterity (Laniado,
Malbim).

9–11. The reason why a written record
is necessary.

9. *lying children.* Or, 'denying children,' children of God, who denied
Him, that He is not their father, for
they did not obey Him (Kimchi).

10. *smooth things . . . delusions.* These
are Isaiah's description of the kind of
message which the people wanted from
him (Kimchi).

11. *get you,* etc. i.e. stop preaching to
us words which are unpalatable (Rashi).

141

12. Wherefore thus saith the Holy
One of Israel:
Because ye despise this word,
And trust in oppression and
perverseness,
And stay thereon;

13. Therefore this iniquity shall be
to you
As a breach ready to fall, swelling
out in a high wall,
Whose breaking cometh suddenly at an instant.

14. And He shall break it as a
potter's vessel is broken,
Breaking it in pieces without
sparing;
So that there shall not be found
among the pieces thereof a
sherd
To take fire from the hearth,
Or to take water out of the
cistern.

15. For thus said the Lord GOD, the
Holy One of Israel:
In sitting still and rest shall ye
be saved,
In quietness and in confidence
shall be your strength;
And ye would not.

לָכֵן כֹּה אָמַר קְדוֹשׁ יִשְׂרָאֵל 12
יַעַן מָאָסְכֶם בַּדָּבָר הַזֶּה
וַתִּבְטְחוּ בְּעֹשֶׁק וְנָלוֹז
וַתִּשָּׁעֲנוּ עָלָיו:
לָכֵן יִהְיֶה לָכֶם הֶעָוֹן הַזֶּה 13
כְּפֶרֶץ נֹפֵל נִבְעֶה בְּחוֹמָה נִשְׂגָּבָה
אֲשֶׁר־פִּתְאֹם לְפֶתַע יָבוֹא שִׁבְרָהּ:
וּשְׁבָרָהּ כְּשֵׁבֶר נֵבֶל יוֹצְרִים 14
כָּתוּת לֹא יַחְמֹל
וְלֹא־יִמָּצֵא בִמְכִתָּתוֹ חֶרֶשׂ
לַחְתּוֹת אֵשׁ מִיָּקוּד
וְלַחְשֹׂף מַיִם מִגֶּבֶא:
כִּי כֹה־אָמַר אֲדֹנָי יֱהֹוִה 15
קְדוֹשׁ יִשְׂרָאֵל
בְּשׁוּבָה וָנַחַת תִּוָּשֵׁעוּן
בְּהַשְׁקֵט וּבְבִטְחָה תִּהְיֶה גְּבוּרַתְכֶם
וְלֹא אֲבִיתֶם:

---

cause . . . to cease. We do not want to hear communications which you bring to us in the name of *the Holy One of Israel* (Kimchi).

12-14. God's retort in a series of metaphors picturing the complete ruin of the State.

12. *this word.* viz. the true prophecy (Rashi, Ibn Ezra).

oppression. lit. 'that which is turned aside,' craftiness (Ibn Ezra).

13. *as a breach . . . wall.* lit. 'as a rent on the point of falling bulges in a high wall'; as a crack widens until the wall collapses (Rashi).

14. *as a potter's . . . sparing.* Or, 'like the breaking of a potter's jar smashed without remorse.'

among the pieces thereof. Better, 'among its fragments,' not one of which is sufficiently large to be used for any purpose (Malbim).

15. *in sitting still.* Grammatically, this is very doubtful. Better, 'in tranquility.' i.e. by staying in Jerusalem and resting there, you will be saved, not by going to Egypt (Rashi, Kimchi).

in quietness and in confidence. i.e. in quiet confidence in God (Rashi).

16. But ye said: 'No, for we will flee
    upon horses';
    Therefore shall ye flee;
    And: 'We will ride upon the
    swift';
    Therefore shall they that pursue
    you be swift.
17. One thousand shall flee at the
    rebuke of one,
    At the rebuke of five shall ye
    flee;
    Till ye be left as a beacon upon
    the top of a mountain,
    And as an ensign on a hill.
18. And therefore will the LORD
    wait, that He may be gracious
    unto you,
    And therefore will He be exalted,
    that He may have compassion
    upon you;
    For the LORD is a God of justice,
    Happy are all they that wait for
    Him.
19. For, O people that dwellest in
    Zion at Jerusalem,

וַתֹּאמְרוּ לֹא־כִי עַל־סוּס נָנוּס 16
עַל־כֵּן תְּנוּסוּן
וְעַל־קַל נִרְכָּב
עַל־כֵּן יִקַּלּוּ רֹדְפֵיכֶם:
אֶלֶף אֶחָד מִפְּנֵי גַּעֲרַת אֶחָד 17
מִפְּנֵי גַּעֲרַת חֲמִשָּׁה תָּנֻסוּ
עַד אִם־נוֹתַרְתֶּם
כַּתֹּרֶן עַל־רֹאשׁ הָהָר
וְכַנֵּס עַל־הַגִּבְעָה:
וְלָכֵן יְחַכֶּה יְהֹוָה לַחֲנַנְכֶם 18
וְלָכֵן יָרוּם לְרַחֶמְכֶם
כִּי־אֱלֹהֵי מִשְׁפָּט יְהֹוָה
אַשְׁרֵי כָּל־חוֹכֵי לוֹ:
כִּי־עַם בְּצִיּוֹן יֵשֵׁב בִּירוּשָׁלָ͏ִם 19

v. 16. קמץ בז"ק

16. *we will flee upon horses.* Or, 'we will mount horses' against the invaders (Ibn Ganah). The Hebrew for *horses* (*sus*) presents an assonance with *flee* (*nus*).

therefore shall ye flee. Away from the enemy, run away from the field of battle in defeat (Metsudath David).

17. *one thousand shall flee.* The verb 'shall ye flee,' applies to the first part of the verse as well (Metsudath David).

shall ye flee. All of you (Ibn Ezra).

as a beacon . . . hill. A picture of isolation and loneliness. The word for *beacon, toren,* 'a flagstaff.' In xxxiii. 23 and Ezek. xxvii. 5 it denotes 'a mast' of a ship (Rashi).

18. The verse is interpreted by some, including (Rashi, Abarbanel), as a threat, concluding the section and referring back to verse 16: 'therefore will the Lord wait before He will be gracious,' i.e. He will postpone His graciousness until your sins have been duly expiated (and similarly the following clause). By others it is regarded as the beginning of a new section in which God's graciousness and mercy are promised, the translation being: 'and so will the Lord expectantly wait to show you His graciousness, and so will He arise to show you compassion' (Ibn Ezra).

19-26. Promise of a bright future, when even Nature will be transformed for the benefit of the faithful survivors who will renounce and reject all forms of idolatry, devoting themselves entirely to the study and practice of the word of the Lord.

19. *people that dwelleth in Zion.* Others prefer, 'O people in Zion, that dwellest in Jerusalem.' The surviving faithful are addressed.

Thou shalt weep no more;
He will surely be gracious unto
   thee at the voice of thy cry,
When He shall hear, He will
   answer thee.

20. And though the Lord give you
   sparing bread and scant water,
Yet shall not thy Teacher hide
   Himself any more,
But thine eyes shall see thy
   Teacher;

21. And thine ears shall hear a word
   behind thee, saying:
'This is the way, walk ye in it,
When ye turn to the right hand,
   and when ye turn to the left.'

22. And ye shall defile thy graven
   images overlaid with silver,
And thy molten images covered
   with gold;
Thou shalt put them far away as
   one unclean;
Thou shalt say unto it: 'Get thee
   hence.'

23. And He will give the rain for thy
   seed, wherewith thou sowest
   the ground,

בְּכוֹ לֹא־תִבְכֶּה
חָנוֹן יָחְנְךָ לְקוֹל זַעֲקֶךָ
כְּשָׁמְעָתוֹ עָנָךְ׃

20 וְנָתַן לָכֶם אֲדֹנָי לֶחֶם צָר וּמַיִם לָחַץ
וְלֹא־יִכָּנֵף עוֹד מוֹרֶיךָ
וְהָיוּ עֵינֶיךָ רֹאוֹת אֶת־מוֹרֶיךָ׃

21 וְאָזְנֶיךָ תִּשְׁמַעְנָה דָבָר
מֵאַחֲרֶיךָ לֵאמֹר
זֶה הַדֶּרֶךְ לְכוּ בוֹ
כִּי תַאֲמִינוּ וְכִי תַשְׂמְאִילוּ׃

22 וְטִמֵּאתֶם אֶת־צִפּוּי פְּסִילֵי כַסְפֶּךָ
וְאֶת־אֲפֻדַּת מַסֵּכַת זְהָבֶךָ
תִּזְרֵם כְּמוֹ דָוָה
צֵא תֹּאמַר לוֹ׃

23 וְנָתַן מְטַר זַרְעֲךָ
אֲשֶׁר־תִּזְרַע אֶת־הָאֲדָמָה

20. *sparing bread and scant water.* The same phrase occurs in 1 Kings xxii. 27 to describe a prison diet. Here it may represent the reduced standard of the people's living during the siege from which they will be delivered (Ibn Ezra, Malbim).

thy Teacher. God Who instructs Israel through His Torah and prophets (Rashi). Others render 'teachers,' referring to Hezekiah and his company, who will stay in the land, confident of God's protection, and always be within view of the people (Kimchi, Ibn Ezra).

see thy Teacher. Metaphorical for God's manifestation in His act of deliverance (Metsudath David).

21. *hear a word behind thee.* They will be so anxious to hear the word of God from whatever direction it may come, that they will listen attentively even to the voice that might come from behind them (Rashi). Another explanation is, God will be behind them as a father walks behind his children to watch over them (Malbim).

saying. By the mouth of the prophets (Rashi).

22. All traces of idolatry will be removed from their midst.

thou shalt put them far away. lit. 'thou shalt disperse them' (Metsudath David).

23–25. Agricultural and pastoral prosperity will ensue.

23. *the rain for thy seed.* i.e. the 'early' rain which falls in October at the time of sowing (Abarbanel).

And bread of the increase of the
    ground, and it shall be fat and
    plenteous;
In that day shall thy cattle feed
    in large pastures.
24. The oxen likewise and the young
    asses that till the ground
    Shall eat savoury provender,
    Which hath been winnowed with
    the shovel and with the fan.
25. And there shall be upon every
    lofty mountain, and upon
    every high hill,
    Streams and watercourses,
    In the day of the great slaughter,
    when the towers fall.
26. Moreover the light of the moon
    shall be as the light of the sun,
    And the light of the sun shall be
    sevenfold, as the light of the
    seven days,
    In the day that the LORD
    bindeth up the bruise of His
    people,
    And healeth the stroke of their
    wound.

וְלֶ֫חֶם תְּבוּאַת הָאֲדָמָ֔ה
וְהָיָ֥ה דָשֵׁ֖ן וְשָׁמֵ֑ן
יִרְעֶ֥ה מִקְנֶ֛יךָ בַּיּ֥וֹם הַה֖וּא כַּ֥ר נִרְחָֽב:
24 וְהָאֲלָפִ֣ים וְהָעֲיָרִ֗ים עֹֽבְדֵי֙ הָ֣אֲדָמָ֔ה
בְּלִ֥יל חָמִ֖יץ יֹאכֵ֑לוּ
אֲשֶׁר־זֹרֶ֥ה בָרַ֖חַת וּבַמִּזְרֶֽה:
25 וְהָיָ֣ה ׀ עַל־כָּל־הַ֣ר גָּבֹ֗הַ
וְעַ֛ל כָּל־גִּבְעָ֖ה נִשָּׂאָ֑ה
פְּלָגִ֖ים יִבְלֵי־מָ֑יִם
בְּיוֹם֙ הֶ֣רֶג רָ֔ב בִּנְפֹ֖ל מִגְדָּלִֽים:
26 וְהָיָ֤ה אֽוֹר־הַלְּבָנָה֙ כְּא֣וֹר הַֽחַמָּ֔ה
וְא֤וֹר הַֽחַמָּה֙ יִֽהְיֶ֣ה שִׁבְעָתַ֔יִם
כְּא֖וֹר שִׁבְעַ֣ת הַיָּמִ֑ים
בְּי֗וֹם חֲבֹ֤שׁ יְהֹוָה֙ אֶת־שֶׁ֣בֶר עַמּ֔וֹ
וּמַ֥חַץ מַכָּת֖וֹ יִרְפָּֽא:

(handwritten margin note: Chametz (fermented) pointing to חָמִיץ)

24. *savoury provender*. The literal meaning of the Hebrew word for *provender* is
'mixture' (*belil*), having consisted of a
mixture of beans, barley, oats and
vetches. The Hebrew for *savoury* (*chamits*)
usually means 'acid' and is rendered by
some commentators as 'fermented.'
Such a slightly fermented fodder is
regarded as a dainty in food for cattle
(Abarbanel).

winnowed . . . fan. Clean and free from
all particles of straw and chaff (Rashi).

26. Even on the Judean mountains
and hills, which might be expected to be
dry and barren, there will flow streams
and watercourses that will fructify them
as well as the plains and valleys.

day of the great slaughter. Of the
enemies of God.

towers. Metaphor for the great and
mighty. viz. the generals and officers of
the Assyrian hosts (Rashi, Kimchi).

26. A representation in metaphorical
language of the abundant happiness
and prosperity in store for the people
after the downfall of Sennacherib or
during the Messianic era (Kimchi).
Others understand the text literally as a
miraculous increase in the radiance of
the heavenly luminaries (Rashi).

the seven days. Of the week, all their light
being concentrated in that of one day
(Rashi).

27-33. The sudden appearance of

27. Behold, the name of the LORD
cometh from far,
With His anger burning, and in
thick uplifting of smoke;
His lips are full of indignation,
And His tongue is as a devouring
fire;

28. And His breath is as an overflowing stream,
That divideth even unto the
neck,
To sift the nations with the sieve
of destruction;
And a bridle that causeth to err
shall be in the jaws of the
peoples.

29. Ye shall have a song
As in the night when a feast is
hallowed;
And gladness of heart, as when
one goeth with the pipe
To come into the mountain of
the LORD, to the Rock of
Israel.

30. And the LORD will cause His
glorious voice to be heard,

27 הִנֵּה שֵׁם־יְהוָה בָּא מִמֶּרְחָק
בֹּעֵר אַפּוֹ וְכֹבֶד מַשָּׂאָה
שְׂפָתָיו מָלְאוּ זַעַם
וּלְשׁוֹנוֹ כְּאֵשׁ אֹכָלֶת׃

28 וְרוּחוֹ כְּנַחַל שׁוֹטֵף
עַד־צַוָּאר יֶחֱצֶה
לַהֲנָפָה גוֹיִם בְּנָפַת שָׁוְא
וְרֶסֶן מַתְעֶה עַל לְחָיֵי עַמִּים׃

29 הַשִּׁיר יִהְיֶה לָכֶם
כְּלֵיל הִתְקַדֶּשׁ־חָג
וְשִׂמְחַת לֵבָב כַּהוֹלֵךְ בֶּחָלִיל
לָבוֹא בְהַר־יְהוָה אֶל־צוּר יִשְׂרָאֵל׃

30 וְהִשְׁמִיעַ יְהוָה אֶת־הוֹד קוֹלוֹ

God in His might and glory; the dramatic annihilation of the Assyrian host and Judah's festal rejoicing and songs of thanksgiving.

27. *name of the* LORD. Here it is synonymous with God's power and glory (Rashi).

from far. From His heavenly habitation, from His mysterious abode (Ibn Ezra). Traditionally *from far* means from times of old, in accordance with the promise He made long ago (Rashi).

28. Three metaphors of stream, sieve and bridle symbolizing the overwhelming catastrophe.

divideth even unto the neck, i.e. reaches up to, the water forming a division between the head and the neck (Rashi).

to sift the nations. Until none is left (Kimchi, Metsudath David).

a bridle that causeth to err. Diverting the enemy from his purpose and so frustrating his designs (Kimchi).

29. Israel's joy at the fall of the Assyrian invader.

ye shall have a song. On the deliverance from Assyria (Kimchi).

a feast is hallowed. The feast of Passover when hymns and psalms are sung in commemoration of the deliverance from Egypt (Rashi, Kimchi).

goeth with the pipe. In a pilgrim procession to the Temple accompanied with music (Rashi).

30. *His glorious voice.* Perhaps thunder is intended (Ibn Ezra).

And will show the lighting down *descent* ?
  of His arm,
With furious anger, and the
  flame of a devouring fire,
With a bursting of clouds, and a
  storm of rain, and hailstones.
31. For through the voice of the
  LORD shall Asshur be dismayed,
  The rod with which He smote.
32. And in every place where the
  appointed staff shall pass,
  Which the LORD shall lay upon
  him,
  It shall be with tabrets and
  harps;
  And in battles of *waving* wielding will
  He fight with them.
33. For a hearth is ordered of old;
  Yea, for the king it is prepared,
  Deep and large;
  The pile thereof is fire and much
  wood;
  The breath of the LORD, like a
  stream of brimstone, doth
  kindle it.

וְהִשְׁמִיעַ יְהֹוָה אֶת־הוֹד קוֹלוֹ וְנַחַת זְרוֹעוֹ יַרְאֶה
בְּזַעַף אַף וְלַהַב אֵשׁ אוֹכֵלָה
נֶפֶץ וָזֶרֶם וְאֶבֶן בָּרָד׃
31 כִּי־מִקּוֹל יְהֹוָה יֵחַת אַשּׁוּר
בַּשֵּׁבֶט יַכֶּה׃
32 וְהָיָה כֹּל מַעֲבַר מַטֵּה מוּסָדָה
אֲשֶׁר יָנִיחַ יְהֹוָה עָלָיו
בְּתֻפִּים וּבְכִנֹּרוֹת
וּבְמִלְחֲמוֹת תְּנוּפָה נִלְחַם־בָּהּ׃
33 כִּי־עָרוּךְ מֵאֶתְמוּל תָּפְתֶּה
גַּם־הוֹא לַמֶּלֶךְ הוּכָן
הֶעְמִיק הִרְחִב
מְדֻרָתָהּ אֵשׁ וְעֵצִים הַרְבֵּה
נִשְׁמַת יְהֹוָה כְּנַחַל גָּפְרִית בֹּעֲרָה בָּהּ׃

v. 33. היא ק׳   v. 32. בם ק׳

the lighting down. i.e. the descent. As often in the Bible, God manifests Himself in a storm (Rashi).

31. Assyria is now named as the enemy upon whom will fall the judgment hitherto described.

Asshur. i.e. Assyria.

the rod with which He smote. Other renderings are: 'who smote with the rod' (cf. x. 5), (Rashi, Kimchi). '(as though) He smites with the rod' (Ibn Ezra, Kimchi).

32. *the appointed staff.* Of Divine chastisement (Abarbanel).

upon him. Upon the Assyrian foe (Ibn Ezra, Kimchi).

with tabrets of harps. i.e. amidst popular rejoicing (Rashi).

battles of wielding. Or 'waving.' God waved them from their place to come in vain to attack Judah (Rashi). Others render: 'sifting' (Metsudath Zion). Still others explain that the battles were not waged with weapons, but it was as though the angel waved his baton to the musicians, and the camp was completely annihilated (Kimchi).

33. *a hearth.* A place for burning. The Hebrew *Topheth* has evidently to be connected with the Topheth, the place where human sacrifices were burnt to Moloch (2 Kings xxiii. 10; Jer. vii. 31). This place was later used to burn refuse, and smoke was continuously rising from it (Ibn Ezra).

yea. lit. 'it also.'

for the king. Of Assyria (Rashi, Ibn Ezra).

deep and large. lit. 'He made it deep, He made it broad.'

147

81　　　**CHAPTER XXXI**　　　　**לא**

1. Woe to them that go down to
   Egypt for help,
   And rely on horses,
   And trust in chariots, because
   they are many,
   And in horsemen, because they
   are exceeding mighty;
   But they look not unto the Holy
   One of Israel,
   Neither seek the LORD!

2. Yet He also is wise,
   And bringeth evil,
   And doth not call back His
   words;
   But will arise against the house
   of the evil-doers,
   And against the help of them that
   work iniquity.

3. Now the Egyptians are men, and
   not God,
   And their horses flesh, and not
   spirit;
   So when the LORD shall stretch
   out His hand,

1 הֹוי הַיֹּרְדִים מִצְרַיִם לְעֶזְרָה
וְעַל־סוּסִים יִשָּׁעֵנוּ
וַיִּבְטְחוּ עַל־רֶכֶב כִּי רָב
וְעַל פָּרָשִׁים כִּי־עָצְמוּ מְאֹד
וְלֹא שָׁעוּ עַל־קְדוֹשׁ יִשְׂרָאֵל
וְאֶת־יְהֹוָה לֹא דָרָשׁוּ׃
2 וְגַם־הוּא חָכָם
וַיָּבֵא רָע
וְאֶת־דְּבָרָיו לֹא הֵסִיר
וְקָם עַל־בֵּית מְרֵעִים
וְעַל־עֶזְרַת פֹּעֲלֵי אָוֶן׃
3 וּמִצְרַיִם אָדָם וְלֹא־אֵל
וְסוּסֵיהֶם בָּשָׂר וְלֹא־רוּחַ
וַיהֹוָה יַטֶּה יָדוֹ

CHAPTER XXXI

FURTHER denunciation of the pro-
Egyptian policy, and the contrast
between the futility of human power
and the effectiveness of Divine protection. To secure God's help repentance
and return to His ways are essential;
and the Assyrian army will be destroyed
through supernatural intervention of
the Holy One of Israel.

1–3. An oracle against the Northern
Kingdom which also foolishly trusted in
Egyptian power (Rashi).

1. *rely on horses.* Perhaps it was their
lack of war-horses, of which Assyria
had an abundance (cf. xxxvi. 8f.), that
made them turn to Egypt for help, since
that country was famed for its horses

(Rashi, Kimchi, Abarbanel). With the
thought of the verse, cf. Ps. xx. 8.

2. *yet He also is wise.* The prophet
speaks ironically. Wisdom is not a
monopoly of the politicians of the pro-
Egyptian party; God also possesses it!
(Kimchi, Metsudath David).

bringeth evil. i.e. calamity, to those who
deserve it (Kimchi).

His words. A reference to the oracles
against those who put their trust in man
in defiance of the counsel of God
through His prophet (Kimchi).

3. *flesh . . . spirit.* Mortal and frail, as
contrasted with what is enduring (Abarbanel).

he that helpeth. i.e. Egypt (Kimchi).

Egypt

Both he that helpeth shall stumble, and he that is helped shall fall,
And they all shall perish together.
4. For thus saith the LORD unto me:
Like as the lion, or the young lion, growling over his prey,
Though a multitude of shepherds be called forth against him,
Will not be dismayed at their voice,
Nor abase himself for the noise of them;
So will the LORD of hosts come down
To fight upon mount Zion, and upon the hill thereof.
5. As birds hovering,
So will the LORD of hosts protect Jerusalem;
He will deliver it as He protecteth it,
He will rescue it as He passeth over.
6. Turn ye unto Him
Against whom ye have deeply rebelled, O children of Israel.
7. For in that day they shall cast away
Every man his idols of silver, and his idols of gold,
Which your own hands have made unto you for a sin.
8. Then shall Asshur fall with the sword, not of man,

וְכָשַׁל עוֹזֵר וְנָפַל עָזֻר
וְיַחְדָּו כֻּלָּם יִכְלָיוּן׃
4 כִּי כֹה אָמַר־יְהוָה ׀ אֵלַי
כַּאֲשֶׁר יֶהְגֶּה הָאַרְיֵה וְהַכְּפִיר
עַל־טַרְפּוֹ
אֲשֶׁר יִקָּרֵא עָלָיו מְלֹא רֹעִים
מִקּוֹלָם לֹא יֵחָת
וּמֵהֲמוֹנָם לֹא יַעֲנֶה
כֵּן יֵרֵד יְהוָה צְבָאוֹת
לִצְבֹּא עַל־הַר־צִיּוֹן וְעַל־גִּבְעָתָהּ׃
5 כְּצִפֳּרִים עָפוֹת
כֵּן יָגֵן יְהוָה צְבָאוֹת עַל־יְרוּשָׁלָ͏ִם
גָּנוֹן וְהִצִּיל
פָּסֹחַ וְהִמְלִיט׃
6 שׁוּבוּ
לַאֲשֶׁר הֶעְמִיקוּ סָרָה בְּנֵי יִשְׂרָאֵל׃
7 כִּי בַּיּוֹם הַהוּא יִמְאָסוּן
אִישׁ אֱלִילֵי כַסְפּוֹ וֶאֱלִילֵי זְהָבוֹ
אֲשֶׁר עָשׂוּ לָכֶם יְדֵיכֶם חֵטְא׃
8 וְנָפַל אַשּׁוּר בְּחֶרֶב לֹא־אִישׁ

v. 4. קמץ בז״ק

---

that is helped. i.e. Israel (Kimchi).

4. Jerusalem is entirely under the protection of God, and He will come down with His heavenly hosts upon mount Zion to fight like a lion against the Assyrian hordes.

5. _hovering._ Over their helpless young to protect them against ravenous birds (Kara).

6. Israel is summoned to repentance.

ye have deeply. The text has the third person of the verb.

7. _cast away._ Better, 'reject,' 'despise.' For the thought of the verse, cf. ii. 20, xxx. 22.

8f. The supernatural fall of the Assyrians.

8. _not of man._ But of One Who is superhuman (Ibn Ezra, Kimchi).

And the sword, not of men, shall
　devour him;
And he shall flee from the sword,
And his young men shall become
　tributary.
9. And his rock shall pass away by
　reason of terror,
And his princes shall be dis-
　mayed at the ensign,
Saith the LORD, whose fire is in
　Zion,
And His furnace in Jerusalem.

וְחֶ֣רֶב לֹא־אִ֔ישׁ תֹּאכְלֶ֑נּוּ
וְנָ֥ס ל֖וֹ מִפְּנֵי־חֶ֑רֶב
וּבַחוּרָ֖יו לָמַ֥ס יִהְיֽוּ׃
9 וְסַלְעוֹ֙ מִמָּג֣וֹר יַעֲב֔וֹר
וְחַתּ֥וּ מִנֵּ֖ס שָׂרָ֑יו
נְאֻם־יְהֹוָ֗ה אֲשֶׁר־א֥וּר לוֹ֙ בְּצִיּ֔וֹן
וְתַנּ֥וּר ל֖וֹ בִּירוּשָׁלָֽ͏ִם׃

	32	CHAPTER XXXII	לב

1. Behold, a king shall reign in
　righteousness,
And as for princes, they shall rule
　in justice.
2. And a man shall be as in a
　hiding-place from the wind,
And a covert from the tempest;
As by the watercourses in a dry
　place,
As in the shadow of a great rock
　in a weary land.

1 הֵ֥ן לְצֶ֖דֶק יִמְלָךְ־מֶ֑לֶךְ
וּלְשָׂרִ֖ים לְמִשְׁפָּ֥ט יָשֹֽׂרוּ׃
2 וְהָיָה־אִ֥ישׁ כְּמַחֲבֵא־ר֖וּחַ
וְסֵ֣תֶר זָ֑רֶם
כְּפַלְגֵי־מַ֣יִם בְּצָי֔וֹן
כְּצֵ֥ל סֶֽלַע־כָּבֵ֖ד בְּאֶ֥רֶץ עֲיֵפָֽה׃

becomes tributary. The Hebrew word *mas*
means 'task-work, bond-service' (Malbim).

9. *his rock.* The king of Assyria (Abarbanel).

at the ensign. Which God will, so to
speak, set up (Kimchi). Another
interpretation of the first half of the
verse is: 'and he (Asshur) will pass by his
rock (i.e. his place of safe retreat) from
terror, and his officers flee from the
standard in panic' (Kimchi).

fire . . . furnace. Which will consume His
enemies and radiate light and warmth
to His beloved (Malbim).

CHAPTER XXXII

1–8. The moral restoration of the
commonwealth is foretold.

1f. A righteous and beneficent government will secure peace and safety for the
people.

1. *king.* Hezekiah (Ibn Ezra, Kara,
Kimchi, Abarbanel) or the Messiah
(commentators quoted by Abarbanel)
may be intended.

princes. The judges and officers of State
(Kimchi).

2. *and a man,* etc. Render: 'and he (the
king and each of the princes) shall be
like a hiding-place . . . and like the
watercourses . . . like the shadow' (Ibn
Ezra).

as a hiding-place, etc. An image of security (Rashi, Kimchi).

tempest. Better, 'rain-storm.'

as by the watercourses . . . weary land. An
image of prosperity (Kimchi).

ISAIAH

3. And the eyes of them that see
   shall not be closed,
   And the ears of them that hear
   shall attend.
4. The heart also of the rash shall
   understand knowledge,
   And the tongue of the stammerers shall be ready to speak
   plainly.
5. The vile person shall be no
   more called liberal,
   Nor the churl said to be noble.
6. For the vile person will speak
   villany,
   And his heart will work iniquity,
   To practise ungodliness, and to
   utter wickedness against the
   LORD,
   To make empty the soul of the
   hungry,
   And to cause the drink of the
   thirsty to fail.
7. The instruments also of the
   churl are evil;
   He deviseth wicked devices
   To destroy the poor with lying
   words,
   And the needy when he speaketh
   right.

³ וְלֹא תִשְׁעֶינָה עֵינֵי רֹאִים
וְאָזְנֵי שֹׁמְעִים תִּקְשַׁבְנָה:
⁴ וּלְבַב נִמְהָרִים יָבִין לָדָעַת
וּלְשׁוֹן עִלְּגִים תְּמַהֵר לְדַבֵּר צָחוֹת:
⁵ לֹא־יִקָּרֵא עוֹד לְנָבָל נָדִיב
וּלְכִילַי לֹא יֵאָמֵר שׁוֹעַ:
⁶ כִּי נָבָל נְבָלָה יְדַבֵּר
וְלִבּוֹ יַעֲשֶׂה־אָוֶן לַעֲשׂוֹת חֹנֶף
וּלְדַבֵּר אֶל־יְהֹוָה תּוֹעָה
לְהָרִיק נֶפֶשׁ רָעֵב
וּמַשְׁקֶה צָמֵא יַחְסִיר:
⁷ וְכֵלַי כֵּלָיו רָעִים
הוּא זִמּוֹת יָעָץ
לְחַבֵּל עֲנָוִים בְּאִמְרֵי שֶׁקֶר
וּבְדַבֵּר אֶבְיוֹן מִשְׁפָּט:

3f. A higher standard of morality and knowledge will be reached.

3. *shall not be closed.* To the word of God (Kimchi).

shall attend. To moral and religious instruction (Kimchi).

4. *the rash.* The hasty who act on their undisciplined impulses (Metsudath David).

the stammerers. Evil-minded persons who pretended to be unable to speak clearly and understand the language of the prophet, will speak clearly and study his words (Kimchi).

ready to speak plainly. Being morally regenerated (Kimchi).

5-8. Sham will be a thing of the past, men will be esteemed at their true moral value, and character will count for more than material wealth.

5. *the vile person.* For another description of this type of person, cf. Ps. xiv. 1ff.

liberal. Or, 'noble.'

churl. Or, 'knave.'

6f. The characteristics of the vile person and the churl.

6. *will work.* Targum Jonathan gives the verb *asah* here the meaning 'will think,' connecting it with a cognate Aramaic root (Aruch Completum, Lexicon Chaldaicum author Elija Levita).

to make empty. To defraud the poor of their means of subsistence (Kimchi).

7. The Hebrew for *churl* and *instrument* is *kelai* and *kelaw*, yielding an assonance.

instruments. i.e. methods (Kimchi).

when he speaketh right. When he pleads his cause before a tribunal with right on his side (Rashi).

8. But the liberal deviseth liberal
    things;
   And by liberal things shall he
    stand.
9. Rise up, ye women that are at
    ease, and hear my voice;
   Ye confident daughters, give ear
    unto my speech.
10. After a year and days shall ye be
    troubled, ye confident women;
   For the vintage shall fail, the
    ingathering shall not come.
11. Tremble, ye women that are at
    ease;
   Be troubled, ye confident ones;
   Strip you, and make you bare,
   And gird sackcloth upon your
    loins,
12. Smiting upon the breasts
   For the pleasant fields, for the
    fruitful vine;
13. For the land of my people
   Whereon thorns and briers come
    up;
   Yea, for all the houses of joy
   And the joyous city.

8 וְנָדִיב נְדִיבוֹת יָעָץ
וְהוּא עַל־נְדִיבוֹת יָקוּם:
9 נָשִׁים שַׁאֲנַנּוֹת קֹמְנָה שְׁמַעְנָה קוֹלִי
בָּנוֹת בֹּטְחוֹת הַאְזֵנָּה אִמְרָתִי:
10 יָמִים עַל־שָׁנָה תִּרְגַּזְנָה בֹּטְחוֹת
כִּי כָּלָה בָצִיר אֹסֶף בְּלִי יָבוֹא:
11 חִרְדוּ שַׁאֲנַנּוֹת
רְגָזָה בֹּטְחוֹת
פְּשֹׁטָה וְעֹרָה
וַחֲגוֹרָה עַל־חֲלָצָיִם:
12 עַל־שָׁדַיִם סֹפְדִים
עַל־שְׂדֵי־חֶמֶד
עַל־גֶּפֶן פֹּרִיָּה:
13 עַל אַדְמַת עַמִּי
קוֹץ שָׁמִיר תַּעֲלֶה
כִּי עַל־כָּל־בָּתֵּי מָשׂוֹשׂ
קִרְיָה עַלִּיזָה:

‎.9 ‏.v ‏א׳ ‏גחה

8. *by liberal things shall he stand.* Not
only does he devise them but he also
carries them out (Metsudath David).

9-20. A threatening address to the
frivolous women of Jerusalem (cf. the
attack on them in iii. 16ff.), followed by
a description of the new and prosperous
era which will ultimately emerge from
the ruin and desolation.

9. *are at ease ... confident.* Similar
phraseology is employed in Amos vi. 1.
The women are exhorted to *rise up* and
cast aside their complacency (Metsudath
David).

10. *after a year and days.* i.e. at the time
of the next year's harvest; lit. 'days over
a year' (Metsudath David).

the ingathering shall not come. The harvest
will not be reaped and gathered in
(Rashi).

11. The prophet sees the approaching
calamities so vividly that he calls upon
the women to go at once into mourning.

strip you. Of your garments (Metsudath
David).

gird sackcloth. The word *sackcloth* is absent
from the text. It is doubtful that it is
implied. The intention is: 'Place a girdle
upon your loins to cover your nakedness (Malbim, Ibn Kaspi, Metsudath
David).

12. *smiting upon the breasts.* A mourning
custom (Metsudath David).

for the pleasant fields. Which are lying in
ruins (Metsudath David).

14. For the palace shall be forsaken;
The city with its stir shall be
deserted;
The mound and the tower shall
be for dens for ever,
A joy of wild 'asses, a pasture of
flocks;

15. Until the spirit be poured upon
us from on high,
And the wilderness become a
fruitful field,
And the fruitful field be counted
for a forest.

16. Then justice shall dwell in the
wilderness,
And righteousness shall abide in
the fruitful field.

17. And the work of righteousness
shall be peace;
And the effect of righteousness
quietness and confidence for
ever.

18. And my people shall abide in a
peaceable habitation,
And in secure dwellings, and in
quiet resting-places.

19. And it shall hail, in the downfall
of the forest;
But the city shall descend into
the valley.

14 כִּי־אַרְמוֹן נֻטָּשׁ
הֲמוֹן עִיר עֻזָּב
עֹפֶל וָבַחַן
הָיָה בְעַד מְעָרוֹת עַד־עוֹלָם
מְשׂוֹשׂ פְּרָאִים מִרְעֵה עֲדָרִים׃

15 עַד־יֵעָרֶה עָלֵינוּ רוּחַ מִמָּרוֹם
וְהָיָה מִדְבָּר לַכַּרְמֶל
וְכַרְמֶל לַיַּעַר יֵחָשֵׁב׃

16 וְשָׁכַן בַּמִּדְבָּר מִשְׁפָּט
וּצְדָקָה בַּכַּרְמֶל תֵּשֵׁב׃

17 וְהָיָה מַעֲשֵׂה הַצְּדָקָה שָׁלוֹם
וַעֲבֹדַת הַצְּדָקָה
הַשְׁקֵט וָבֶטַח עַד־עוֹלָם׃

18 וְיָשַׁב עַמִּי בִּנְוֵה שָׁלוֹם
וּבְמִשְׁכְּנוֹת מִבְטַחִים
וּבִמְנוּחֹת שַׁאֲנַנּוֹת׃

19 וּבָרַד בְּרֶדֶת הַיָּעַר
וּבַשִּׁפְלָה תִּשְׁפַּל הָעִיר׃

v. 14. קמץ בז״ק v. 15. והכרמל ק׳

13. *the house of joy.* i.e. the houses
which were once joyful (Kimchi, Abarbanel).

14. *the mound.* Hebrew *ophel,* lit. 'swelling,' was the name given to the walled
citadel in Jerusalem (cf. Neh. iii. 27; 2
Chron. xxvii. 3). It and its watch-tower
will be deserted and become the lair of
beasts (Ibn Ezra).

for ever. For a long time, its end being
predicted in the next verse (Abarbanel).

15. *on high.* The heavens. For the
second half of the verse, cf. xxix. 17.

16. *dwell in the wilderness.* i.e. even in
the wilderness, much more so in the
inhabited places (Malbim).

17. *the work.* i.e. the result (Metsudath
David).

19. *it shall hail . . . forest.* Even when it
hails, it will not hail on plants that can
be destroyed, but in the forest (Ibn Ezra,
Kimchi, Metsudath David).

the city. Cities will be built in the valleys,
since they will not require fortification
to protect them from enemies (Metsudath David).

20. Happy are ye that sow beside all
waters,
That send forth freely the feet of
the ox and the ass.

²⁰ אַשְׁרֵיכֶ֕ם זֹרְעֵ֖י עַל־כָּל־מָ֑יִם
מְשַׁלְּחֵ֥י רֶֽגֶל־הַשּׁ֖וֹר וְהַחֲמֽוֹר׃

---

33   CHAPTER XXXIII   לג

1. Woe to thee that spoilest, and
thou wast not spoiled;
And dealest treacherously, and
they dealt not treacherously
with thee!
When thou hast ceased to spoil,
thou shalt be spoiled;
And when thou art weary with
dealing treacherously, they
shall deal treacherously with
thee.

2. O Lord, be gracious unto us;
We have waited for Thee;
Be Thou their arm every morning,
Our salvation also in the time of
trouble.

3. At the noise of the tumult the
peoples are fled;
At the lifting up of Thyself the
nations are scattered.

¹ ה֣וֹי שׁוֹדֵ֗ד וְאַתָּה֙ לֹ֣א שָׁד֔וּד
וּבוֹגֵ֖ד וְלֹא־בָ֣גְדוּ ב֑וֹ
כַּהֲתִֽמְךָ֤ שׁוֹדֵד֙ תּוּשַּׁ֔ד
כַּנְּלֹתְךָ֥ לִבְגֹּ֖ד יִבְגְּדוּ־בָֽךְ׃
² יְהֹוָ֥ה חָנֵּ֖נוּ
לְךָ֣ קִוִּ֑ינוּ
הֱיֵ֤ה זְרֹעָם֙ לַבְּקָרִ֔ים
אַף־יְשׁוּעָתֵ֖נוּ בְּעֵ֥ת צָרָֽה׃
³ מִקּוֹל֙ הָמ֔וֹן נָדְד֖וּ עַמִּ֑ים
מֵרֽוֹמְמֻתֶ֔ךָ נָפְצ֖וּ גּוֹיִֽם׃

v. 1. דגש אחר שורק

---

20. The prophet addresses the husbandmen of the rejuvenated and prosperous country in the new age which he foretells.

beside all waters. An assurance of an abundant water-supply for the field and cattle (Kimchi).

send . . . the ass. To feed in the rich pastures even though they trample the plants, since there will be plenty (Metsudath David).

CHAPTER XXXIII

THE DELIVERANCE OF ZION

1. *woe to thee.* The prophet apostrophizes Sennacherib who invaded the country in 701 B.C.E. (Kimchi, Metsudath David).

when thou art weary. This follows Targum. Others render: 'when thou hast ceased (Rashi, Kimchi).

2f. Turning away from the invader towards heaven, the prophet offers a prayer and expresses his confidence in God's power (Malbim).

2. *their arms.* Israel's help and defence. The abrupt change of person from the first to the third is not unusual in Hebrew style (Kimchi). Another explanation is 'an arm against them' (Isaiah of Trani).

every morning. Always, continually (Metsudath (David).

3. *tumult.* God's thunder and storm, the tumult of the angel destroying the Assyrian camp (Kimchi).

the peoples. The Assyrian hosts composed of many nationalities (Kimchi). Since the text has no definite article, it may be a general description of God's invincible might and the translation should be 'peoples . . . nations' (Kara).

4. And your spoil is gathered as the
   caterpillar gathereth;
   As locusts leap do they leap upon
   it.
5. The LORD is exalted, for He
   dwelleth on high;
   He hath filled Zion with justice
   and righteousness.
6. And the stability of thy times
   shall be
   A hoard of salvation—wisdom
   and knowledge,
   And the fear of the LORD which
   is His treasure.
7. Behold, their (valiant) ones cry
   without;
   The ambassadors of peace weep
   bitterly.
8. The highways lie waste,
   The wayfaring man ceaseth;
   He hath broken the covenant,
   He hath despised the cities,
   He regardeth not man.
9. The land mourneth and lan-
   guisheth;

וְאֻסַּף שְׁלַלְכֶם אֹסֶף הֶחָסִיל 4
בְּמַשַּׁק גֵּבִים שֹׁקֵק בּוֹ:
נִשְׂגָּב יְהֹוָה כִּי שֹׁכֵן מָרוֹם 5
מִלֵּא צִיּוֹן מִשְׁפָּט וּצְדָקָה:
וְהָיָה אֱמוּנַת עִתֶּיךָ 6
חֹסֶן יְשׁוּעֹת חָכְמַת וָדָעַת
יִרְאַת יְהֹוָה הִיא אוֹצָרוֹ:
הֵן אֶרְאֶלָּם צָעֲקוּ חֻצָה 7
מַלְאֲכֵי שָׁלוֹם מַר יִבְכָּיוּן:
נָשַׁמּוּ מְסִלּוֹת 8
שָׁבַת עֹבֵר אֹרַח
הֵפֵר בְּרִית
מָאַס עָרִים
לֹא חָשַׁב אֱנוֹשׁ:
אָבַל אֻמְלְלָה אָרֶץ 9

v. 9. קמץ בז״ק

---

4. The prophet addresses the
Assyrians (Kara).

as the caterpillar gathereth. Leaving nothing behind. The word for *caterpillar* signifies "the consumer," and denotes a
most destructive species of locusts
(Kimchi, Shorashim).

do they leap. Who gather the Assyrian
spoil. Others render: 'go' or 'gather'
(Ibn Ezra).

5f. Gratitude and adoration at the
prospect of the blessings to come; the
security and high social and religious
state which will prevail in Israel.

7–9. The present desolation, with its
bitter disappointment and ruin, is
described.

7. *their valiant ones.* The Hebrew *erallam*

is obscure. Some translate 'God's lions'
(i.e. angels) (Kimchi) or 'for their Ariel,'
meaning the altar (Rashi).

the ambassadors of peace. The envoys sent
to negotiate peace with the invaders are
overcome with emotion because the
enemy had violated the treaty (Malbim,
Isaiah of Trani).

8. *the highways,* etc. For a similar picture of desolation, cf. Judg. v. 6.

he. Sennacherib (Ibn Ezra).

the cities. Perhaps an allusion to *all the
fortified cities of Judah* which Sennacherib
had captured (xxxvi. 1) (See Metsudath).

9. *mourneth.* An expression of destruction (Kimchi). Lebanon, Sharon,
Bashan and Carmel are named as the
most fertile places (cf. xxxv. 2).

Lebanon is ashamed, is withereth;
Sharon is like a wilderness;
And Bashan and Carmel are clean bare.

10. Now will I arise, saith the LORD;
Now will I be exalted;
Now will I lift Myself up.

11. Ye conceive chaff, ye shall bring forth stubble;
Your breath is a fire that shall devour you.

12. And the peoples shall be as the burnings of lime;
As thorns cut down, that are burned in the fire.

13. Hear, ye that are far off, what I have done;
And, ye that are near, acknowledge My might.

14. The sinners in Zion are afraid;
Trembling hath seized the ungodly:
'Who among us shall dwell with the devouring fire?
Who among us shall dwell with everlasting burnings?'

15. He that walketh righteously, and speaketh uprightly;

הֶחְפִּיר לְבָנוֹן קָמַל
הָיָה הַשָּׁרוֹן כָּעֲרָבָה
וְנֹעֵר בָּשָׁן וְכַרְמֶל׃

10 עַתָּה אָקוּם יֹאמַר יְהוָה
עַתָּה אֵרוֹמָם
עַתָּה אֶנָּשֵׂא׃

11 תַּהֲרוּ חֲשַׁשׁ תֵּלְדוּ קַשׁ
רוּחֲכֶם אֵשׁ תֹּאכַלְכֶם׃

12 וְהָיוּ עַמִּים מִשְׂרְפוֹת שִׂיד
קוֹצִים כְּסוּחִים בָּאֵשׁ יִצַּתּוּ׃

13 שִׁמְעוּ רְחוֹקִים אֲשֶׁר עָשִׂיתִי
וּדְעוּ קְרוֹבִים גְּבֻרָתִי׃

14 פָּחֲדוּ בְצִיּוֹן חַטָּאִים
אָחֲזָה רְעָדָה חֲנֵפִים
מִי יָגוּר לָנוּ אֵשׁ אוֹכֵלָה
מִי־יָגוּר לָנוּ מוֹקְדֵי עוֹלָם׃

15 הֹלֵךְ צְדָקוֹת וְדֹבֵר מֵישָׁרִים

v. 9. פתח באתנח   v. 10. קמץ בז"ק   v. 11. פתח באתנח   v. 12. פתח בס"פ

10-12. God's answer to the prayer in verses 2f.

11. *ye.* The enemy; they provide the means for their own destruction (Ibn Ezra).

your breath. i.e. your speech, your blasphemy against God (Malbim).

12. *the peoples.* The Assyrians may be meant, as in verse 3 (Kimchi, Metsudath David).

13. The verse is taken either as the conclusion of the preceding sections or as an introduction to the one following.

14-16. The purged moral condition of Israel resulting from God's marvellous deeds which they were privileged to witness.

14. *shall dwell.* For the use of the verb in this connection, cf. Ps. xv. 1.

the devouring fire. i.e. God Whose flaming wrath destroys the wicked and purifies the penitent (Rashi).

everlasting burnings. Divine judgment is eternal like God Himself (Targum, Rashi, Abarbanel).

15f. The answer to the question in verse 14, *who among us,* etc. The faithful and the righteous will dwell in peace and tranquility even amidst the raging and consuming fire (Targum).

He that despiseth the gain of
    oppressions,
That shaketh his hands from
    holding of bribes,
That stoppeth his ears from
    hearing of blood,
And shutteth his eyes from look-
    ing upon evil;
16. He shall dwell on high;
His place of defence shall be the
    munitions of rocks;
His bread shall be given, his
    waters shall be sure.
17. Thine eyes shall see the king in
    his beauty;
They shall behold a land stretch-
    ing afar.
18. Thy heart shall muse on the
    terror:
'Where is he that counted, where
    is he that weighed?
Where is he that counted the
    towers?'
19. Thou shalt not see the fierce
    people:

מֹאֵס בְּבֶצַע מַעֲשַׁקּוֹת
נֹעֵר כַּפָּיו מִתְּמֹךְ בַּשֹּׁחַד
אֹטֵם אָזְנוֹ מִשְּׁמֹעַ דָּמִים
וְעֹצֵם עֵינָיו מֵרְאוֹת בְּרָע׃

16 הוּא מְרוֹמִים יִשְׁכֹּן
מְצָדוֹת סְלָעִים מִשְׂגַּבּוֹ
לַחְמוֹ נִתָּן מֵימָיו נֶאֱמָנִים׃

17 מֶלֶךְ בְּיָפְיוֹ תֶּחֱזֶינָה עֵינֶיךָ
תִּרְאֶינָה אֶרֶץ מַרְחַקִּים׃

18 לִבְּךָ יֶהְגֶּה אֵימָה
אַיֵּה סֹפֵר אַיֵּה שֹׁקֵל
אַיֵּה סֹפֵר אֶת־הַמִּגְדָּלִים׃

19 אֶת־עַם נוֹעָז לֹא תִרְאֶה

---

15. A similar description of the characteristics of the righteous is found in
Ps. xv. 2–5, xxiv. 4f.

oppressions. i.e. extortions from the
rightful owner (Kimchi).

from hearing of blood. Refusing to listen to
and take part in plots to murder
(Kimchi).

16. *he shall dwell on high.* The righteous
man is depicted as an impregnable fortress which will withstand any siege (Ibn
Ezra).

17–24. The righteous are now
addressed collectively as an individual.

17. *the king in his beauty.* Hezekiah in
his royal robes, in contrast to his torn
garments and sackcloth (cf. xxxvii. 1)
(Kimchi). Others see in the verse an
allusion to the Messiah (Abarbanel) or
an eschatological reference to the

Divine Presence which will be enjoyed
by the righteous in the hereafter (Rashi).

18f. In the coming times of peace, the
days of oppression will be recalled but
only as a memory.

18. *the terror.* Of the past time
(Kimchi).

where is he, etc. The Assyrian official who
oppressed the people (Kimchi).

that counted. The number of persons to
be subjected to forced labour or mone-
tary payment (Kimchi).

weighed. The tribute for the Assyrian
king (Kimchi).

counted the towers. To levy taxes according to the number of towers (Kimchi).

19. *the fierce people,* etc. The verse
describes a warlike, foreign invader
(Kimchi).

A people of a deep speech that
thou canst not perceive,
Of a stammering tongue that
thou canst not understand.

20. Look upon Zion, the city of our
solemn gatherings;
Thine eyes shall see Jerusalem a
peaceful habitation,
A tent that shall not be removed,
The stakes whereof shall never
be plucked up,
Neither shall any of the cords
thereof be broken.

21. But there the LORD will be with
us in majesty,
In a place of broad rivers and
streams;
Wherein shall go no galley with
oars,
Neither shall gallant ship pass
thereby.

22. For the LORD is our Judge,
The LORD is our Lawgiver,
The LORD is our King;
He will save us.

23. Thy tacklings are loosed;
They do not hold the stand of
their mast,
They do not spread the sail;

עַם עִמְקֵי שָׂפָה מִשְּׁמוֹעַ
נִלְעַג לָשׁוֹן אֵין בִּינָה׃
20 חֲזֵה צִיּוֹן קִרְיַת מוֹעֲדֵנוּ
עֵינֶיךָ תִרְאֶינָה יְרוּשָׁלַ͏ִם נָוֶה שַׁאֲנָן
אֹהֶל בַּל־יִצְעָן
בַּל־יִסַּע יְתֵדֹתָיו לָנֶצַח
וְכָל־חֲבָלָיו בַּל־יִנָּתֵקוּ׃
21 כִּי אִם־שָׁם אַדִּיר יְהוָה לָנוּ
מְקוֹם־נְהָרִים יְאֹרִים רַחֲבֵי יָדָיִם
בַּל־תֵּלֶךְ בּוֹ אֳנִי־שַׁיִט
וְצִי אַדִּיר לֹא יַעַבְרֶנּוּ׃
22 כִּי יְהוָה שֹׁפְטֵנוּ
יְהוָה מְחֹקְקֵנוּ
יְהוָה מַלְכֵּנוּ
הוּא יוֹשִׁיעֵנוּ׃
23 נִטְּשׁוּ חֲבָלָיִךְ
בַּל־יְחַזְּקוּ כֵן־תָּרְנָם
בַּל־פָּרְשׂוּ נֵס

v. 20. הע׳ בקמץ   v. 20. חצי הספר בפסוקים

---

that . . . understand. lit. 'without understanding,' incomprehensible to the
inhabitants of Judea (Kimchi).

20-24. The moral and material bliss
of Jerusalem.

20. A picture of permanent stability,
the city being represented as a tent
which is securely fixed to the ground.

21. Though fertile and prosperous,
the city will be in no fear of attack from
a hostile fleet. Jerusalem is compared

with a city surrounded by water as a
protection (cf. Nahum iii. 8) (Kimchi).

galley with oars. Or small boats.

22. The reason for the prophet's confidence.

23. The verse seems to connect with
verse 21 and is apparently addressed to
any enemy that might dare to take his
vessels of war through the *broad rivers
and streams* mentioned.

thy tacklings are loosed. Or, 'thy ropes
were abandoned' (Metsudath David).

Then is the prey of a great spoil
divided;
The lame take the prey.

אָז חֻלַּק עַד־שָׁלָל מַרְבֶּה

פִּסְחִים בָּזְזוּ בַז:

24. And the inhabitant shall not say:
'I am sick';
The people that dwell therein
shall be forgiven their iniquity.

24 וּבַל־יֹאמַר שָׁכֵן חָלִיתִי

הָעָם הַיֹּשֵׁב בָּהּ נְשֻׂא עָוֹן:

34 *Edom* CHAPTER XXXIV

לד

1. Come near, ye nations, to hear,
And attend, ye peoples;
Let the earth hear, and the ful-
ness thereof,
The world, and all things that
come forth of it.

1 קִרְבוּ גוֹיִם לִשְׁמֹעַ

וּלְאֻמִּים הַקְשִׁיבוּ

תִּשְׁמַע הָאָרֶץ וּמְלֹאָהּ

תֵּבֵל וְכָל־צֶאֱצָאֶיהָ:

2. For the LORD hath indignation
against all the nations,
And fury against all their host;
He hath utterly destroyed them,
He hath delivered them to the
slaughter.

2 כִּי קֶצֶף לַיהֹוָה עַל־כָּל־הַגּוֹיִם

וְחֵמָה עַל־כָּל־צְבָאָם

הֶחֱרִימָם

נְתָנָם לַטָּבַח:

3. Their slain also shall be cast out,
And the stench of their carcasses
shall come up,
And the mountains shall be
melted with their blood.

3 וְחַלְלֵיהֶם יֻשְׁלָכוּ

וּפִגְרֵיהֶם יַעֲלֶה בָאְשָׁם

וְנָמַסּוּ הָרִים מִדָּמָם:

v. 23. הב׳ בסגול   v. 3. קמץ בז״ק

divided. By the Judeans who will defeat
the attack (Kimchi).

the lame. i.e. even when cripples will be
able to take a share in the spoils, the
camp being near the city (Kimchi).

24. The verse resumes the description
of the happy state of Jerusalem. The
inhabitants will be free from pain, distress, and disease since all their sins will
be forgiven. All troubles are the consequences of the demoralization of the
soul (cf. Ps. ciii. 3).

CHAPTERS XXXIV, XXXV

THE doom and destruction of Edom are

contrasted with the promised redemption.

CHAPTER XXXIV

1–4. Before describing the vengeance
that is to come upon Edom, the prophet
begins with a summons to all the
nations of the world to hear an oracle
on the terrors of the Divine wrath when
God will sit in judgment on all peoples.

2. *utterly destroyed them.* Better, 'placed
them under a ban,' to be destroyed
(Targum).

3. *shall be cast out.* They will lie on the
ground unburied (Kimchi).

4. And all the host of heaven shall moulder away,
And the heavens shall be rolled together as a scroll;
And all their host shall fall down,
As the leaf falleth off from the vine,
And as a falling fig from the fig-tree.

5. For My sword hath drunk its fill in heaven;
Behold, it shall come down upon Edom,
And upon the people of My ban, to judgment.

6. The sword of the Lord is filled with blood,
It is made fat with fatness,
With the blood of lambs and goats,
With the fat of the kidneys of rams;
For the Lord hath a sacrifice in Bozrah,
And a great slaughter in the land of, Edom.

7. And the wild-oxen shall come down with them,
And the bullocks with the bulls;

וְנָמַקּוּ כָּל־צְבָא הַשָּׁמַיִם 4
וְנָגֹלּוּ כַסֵּפֶר הַשָּׁמָיִם
וְכָל־צְבָאָם יִבּוֹל
כִּנְבֹל עָלֶה מִגֶּפֶן
וּכְנֹבֶלֶת מִתְּאֵנָה:
כִּי־רִוְּתָה בַשָּׁמַיִם חַרְבִּי 5
הִנֵּה עַל־אֱדוֹם תֵּרֵד
וְעַל־עַם חֶרְמִי לְמִשְׁפָּט:
חֶרֶב לַיהֹוָה 6
מָלְאָה דָם הֻדַּשְׁנָה מֵחֵלֶב
מִדַּם כָּרִים וְעַתּוּדִים
מֵחֵלֶב כִּלְיוֹת אֵילִים
כִּי זֶבַח לַיהֹוָה בְּבָצְרָה
וְטֶבַח גָּדוֹל בְּאֶרֶץ אֱדוֹם:
וְיָרְדוּ רְאֵמִים עִמָּם 7
וּפָרִים עִם־אַבִּירִים

4. *the host of heaven.* Some explain as the heavenly luminaries, others as the celestial powers of the nations (cf. xxiv. 21) (Rashi).

fall down. More accurately, 'shall fade,' and similarly with *falleth off* and *falling fig* substitute 'fadeth' and 'fading' (Rashi).

5–17. The terrible doom of, and vengeance upon, Edom.

5–8. The land of Edom will be turned into a blood-bath from which none of the inhabitants will escape.

5. *drunk its fill.* Of slaying the heavenly princes of the nations (Rashi).

people of My ban. i.e. Edom upon whom the ban was laid by God (Targum).

6. *the sword of the Lord is filled.* More lit. 'the Lord hath a sword which is filled.'

made fat. Better, 'greased'; the Edomites are likened to slaughtered animals (Metsudath David).

lambs … goats … rams. Figurative for various types among the upper classes of Edom's inhabitants (Targum, Rashi, Ibn Ezra).

Bozrah. The capital of Edom, the modern Busaire, south of the Dead Sea (See Ibn Ezra). Others identify this with the Bozrah of Moab. It will be destroyed with Edom because it once supplied a king for Edom (Rashi from Pesikta).

7. *wild oxen … bullocks … bulls.* Also figurative for various ranks of heroes and governors (Targum). Kings and governors (Rashi).

come down. In the great slaughter (Kimchi).

And their land shall be drunken with blood,
And their dust made fat with fatness.

8. For the LORD hath a day of vengeance,
A year of recompense for the controversy of Zion.

9. And the streams thereof shall be turned into pitch,
And the dust thereof into brimstone,
And the land thereof shall become burning pitch.

10. It shall not be quenched night nor day,
The smoke thereof shall go up for ever;
From generation to generation it shall lie waste:
None shall pass through it for ever and ever.

11. But the pelican and the bittern shall possess it,
And the owl and the raven shall dwell therein;
And He shall stretch over it
The line of confusion, and the plummet of emptiness.

12. As for her nobles, none shall be there to be called to the kingdom;

וְרֻוְּתָה אַרְצָם מִדָּם
וַעֲפָרָם מֵחֵלֶב יְדֻשָּׁן׃

8 כִּי יוֹם נָקָם לַיהֹוָה
שְׁנַת שִׁלּוּמִים לְרִיב צִיּוֹן׃

9 וְנֶהֶפְכוּ נְחָלֶיהָ לְזֶפֶת
וַעֲפָרָהּ לְגָפְרִית
וְהָיְתָה אַרְצָהּ לְזֶפֶת בֹּעֵרָה׃

10 לַיְלָה וְיוֹמָם לֹא תִכְבֶּה
לְעוֹלָם יַעֲלֶה עֲשָׁנָהּ
מִדּוֹר לָדוֹר תֶּחֱרָב
לְנֵצַח נְצָחִים אֵין עֹבֵר בָּהּ׃

11 וִירֵשׁוּהָ קָאַת וְקִפּוֹד
וְיַנְשׁוֹף וְעֹרֵב יִשְׁכְּנוּ־בָהּ
וְנָטָה עָלֶיהָ
קַו־תֹהוּ וְאַבְנֵי־בֹהוּ׃

12 חֹרֶיהָ וְאֵין־שָׁם מְלוּכָה יִקְרָאוּ

v. 10. קמץ בז״ק v. 11. ת׳ רפה

---

with fatness. Of the slain (Abarbanel).

8. *day of vengeance.* Against Edom (Malbim).

a year . . . Zion. Better, 'a year of retribution in Zion's quarrel' with Edom (Targum, Rashi).

9f. Edom's complete destruction is represented as a conflagration of burning pitch which leaves nothing but desolation behind it.

9. [The prophet may have had in mind the account of the destruction of Sodom and Gomorrah (Gen. xix. 24) which were close to the land of Edom.]

10. *from generation . . . ever.* This and the destruction in the following verse depict the consequences of the meta-phorical conflagration or the Divine judgment.

11-15. A picturer of utter solitude and devastation.

11. The birds enumerated inhabit waste and solitary places (cf. xiv. 23).

line . . . plummet. Metaphors borrowed from builders' tools.

confusion. Or, 'desolation.' The Hebrew for *confusion* and *emptiness* is *tohu* and *bohu* as in Gen. i. 2.

12. *to the kingdom.* The preposition has to be supplied and does not occur in the Hebrew (Ibn Ezra). Another translation reads: 'as for her nobles, there are none there that proclaim the kingdom.' The nobility is wiped out (Rashi, Kimchi).

And all her princes shall be nothing.

13. And thorns shall come up in her palaces,
Nettles and thistles in the fortresses thereof;
And it shall be a habitation of wild-dogs,
An enclosure for ostriches.

14. And the wild-cats shall meet with the jackals,
And the satyr shall cry to his fellow;
Yea, the night-monster shall repose there,
And shall find her a place of rest.

15. There shall the arrowsnake make her nest, and lay,
And hatch, and brood under her shadow;
Yea, there shall the kites be gathered,
Every one with her mate.

16. Seek ye out of the book of the LORD, and read;
No one of these shall be missing,
None shall want her mate;

וְכָל־שָׂרֶיהָ יִהְיוּ אָפֶס׃

13 וְעָלְתָה אַרְמְנֹתֶיהָ סִירִים
קִמּוֹשׂ וָחוֹחַ בְּמִבְצָרֶיהָ
וְהָיְתָה נְוֵה תַנִּים
חָצִיר לִבְנוֹת יַעֲנָה׃

14 וּפָגְשׁוּ צִיִּים אֶת־אִיִּים
וְשָׂעִיר עַל־רֵעֵהוּ יִקְרָא
אַךְ־שָׁם הִרְגִּיעָה לִילִית
וּמָצְאָה לָהּ מָנוֹחַ׃

15 שָׁמָּה קִנְּנָה קִפּוֹז וַתְּמַלֵּט
וּבָקְעָה וְדָגְרָה בְצִלָּהּ
אַךְ־שָׁם נִקְבְּצוּ דַיּוֹת
אִשָּׁה רְעוּתָהּ׃

16 דִּרְשׁוּ מֵעַל־סֵפֶר יְהֹוָה וּקְרָאוּ
אַחַת מֵהֵנָּה לֹא נֶעְדָּרָה
אִשָּׁה רְעוּתָהּ לֹא פָקָדוּ

---

13. *enclosure*. The Hebrew word *chatsir*, here and in xxxv. 7; is only apparently identical with the normal word for 'grass'; it is cognate with the Arabic *chatir*, 'an enclosure' for cattle and with the Aramaic *chutra*, 'an enclosure' for flocks. With the verse, cf. xiii. 21f. Jewish exegetes identify it with *chatser*, a yard (Ibn Ezra, Kimchi).

14. The beasts mentioned in the verse are denizens of wild and lonely places.

night-monster. Or, 'night-hag.' The Hebrew *lilith*, in the Bible found only here, occurs frequently in Talmudic and particularly in Cabbalistic literature where it is the name of a female demon, Adam's first wife before Eve, roaming with her retinue in the darkest hours of

the night (Alfa-betha d'Ben Sira, Otzar Midrashim, p. 47).

15. *with her mate*. The preposition is implied (Kimchi).

16. The prophet addresses those who are to witness the fulfillment of his prediction.

the book of the LORD. The book in which are recorded the prophecies spoken in the name of God including the one on Edom (Kimchi).

no one of these. Not one of the desert birds or beasts enumerated above (Kimchi).

shall be missing. From the deserted and devastated land of Edom (Kimchi).

For My mouth it hath com-
manded,
And the breath thereof it hath
gathered them.

17. And He hath cast the lot for
them,
And His hand hath divided it
unto them by line; — *measuring*
They shall possess it for ever,
From generation to generation
shall they dwell therein.

כִּי־פִי הוּא צִוָּה
וְרוּחוֹ הוּא קִבְּצָן:
וְהוּא־הִפִּיל לָהֶן גּוֹרָל 17
וְיָדוֹ חִלְּקַתָּה לָהֶם בַּקָּו
עַד־עוֹלָם יִירָשׁוּהָ
לְדוֹר וָדוֹר יִשְׁכְּנוּ־בָהּ:

35   CHAPTER XXXV   לה

1. The wilderness and the parched
land shall be glad;
And the desert shall rejoice, and
blossom as the rose.

2. It shall blossom abundantly, and
rejoice,
Even with joy and singing;

יְשֻׂשׂוּם מִדְבָּר וְצִיָּה 1
וְתָגֵל עֲרָבָה וְתִפְרַח כַּחֲבַצָּלֶת:
פָּרֹחַ תִּפְרַח וְתָגֵל 2
אַף גִּילַת וְרַנֵּן

---

for My mouth. The prophet is speaking in
the name of God (Ibn Ezra).

the breath thereof. Of the mouth. A traditional interpretation takes *the book of the*
LORD to refer to the Book of Genesis,
written like the whole of the Torah at
the command of the Lord. *No one of these*
was (not *shall be*) *missing* is an allusion to
the animals which Noah, as instructed
by God, had taken with him into the ark
(Gen. vii. 8f.). The comparison between
the two groups of animals is in the
nature of an *a minori ad majus* deduction:
If the command of God caused none of
the animals to abstain from coming to
Noah's ark despite the obvious shortage
of foodstuffs, how much more would
His judgment and decree cause none of
the animals to abstain from coming to
Edom where there would be an abundant supply of flesh and fat! (Rashi).

17. *and He.* The subject is emphasized
in the text. What happened to Edom
was deliberately decreed by God
(Rashi).

cast the lot for them. Apportioning to each
animal its particular locality (Kimchi).

by line. By use of the measuring-line
(Kimchi).

CHAPTER XXXV

AN oracle on the salvation and future
happiness of Israel. Its position here
presents a remarkable contrast with the
desolation of Edom pictured in the preceding chapter.

1f. Judea, devastated by the Assyrian
hordes and deserted like a wilderness,
will be transformed into a land of smil-
ing fields and gardens.

1. *the wilderness . . . parched land . . .
desert.* The ravaged and desolate land of
Judah (Abarbanel, Metsudath David).

rose. This follows Kimchi and Targum.
Others define the Hebrew word as 'nar-
cissus' (Ibn Ganah, Aruch).

2. *with joy.* The preposition is implied.

The glory of Lebanon shall be
given unto it,
The excellency of Carmel and
Sharon;
They shall see the glory of the
LORD,
The excellency of our God.

3. Strengthen ye the weak hands,
And make firm the tottering
knees.

4. Say to them that are of a fearful
heart: 'Be strong, fear not';
Behold, your God will come
with vengeance,
With the recompense of God He
will come and save you.

5. Then the eyes of the blind shall
be opened,
And the ears of the deaf shall be
unstopped.

6. Then shall the lame man leap as
a hart,
And the tongue of the dumb
shall sing;
For in the wilderness shall
waters break out,
And streams in the desert.

כְּבוֹד הַלְּבָנוֹן נִתַּן־לָהּ
הֲדַר הַכַּרְמֶל וְהַשָּׁרוֹן
הֵמָּה יִרְאוּ כְבוֹד־יְהֹוָה
הֲדַר אֱלֹהֵינוּ׃
3 חַזְּקוּ יָדַיִם רָפוֹת
וּבִרְכַּיִם כֹּשְׁלוֹת אַמֵּצוּ׃
4 אִמְרוּ לְנִמְהֲרֵי־לֵב
חִזְקוּ אַל־תִּירָאוּ
הִנֵּה אֱלֹהֵיכֶם נָקָם יָבוֹא
גְּמוּל אֱלֹהִים הוּא יָבוֹא וְיֹשַׁעֲכֶם׃
5 אָז תִּפָּקַחְנָה עֵינֵי עִוְרִים
וְאָזְנֵי חֵרְשִׁים תִּפָּתַחְנָה׃
6 אָז יְדַלֵּג כָּאַיָּל פִּסֵּחַ
וְתָרֹן לְשׁוֹן אִלֵּם
כִּי־נִבְקְעוּ בַמִּדְבָּר מַיִם
וּנְחָלִים בָּעֲרָבָה׃

Lebanon . . . Carmel . . . Sharon. Cf. xxix.
17, xxxii. 15, xxxiii. 9.

3f. The prophet addresses his disciples
or the elders and leaders of the people,
exhorting them to pass on his message
of assurance to the doubters, the impa-
tient and the despondent.

3. With the language of the verse, cf.
Job iv. 3f.

4. *of a fearful heart.* Or, 'panic-stricken
in mind' (Kimchi).

behold . . . save you. The preposition *with*
has to be added before *vengeance* and *the
recompense* to make sense (Abarbanel).

Another rendering is: 'behold your
God will come to wreak vengeance and
to pay the recompense of God; He
Himself will come and save you'
(Metsudath David).

5-7. Defects will be removed from
both the land and its inhabitants, and
the people now physically fit and
healthy will enjoy the prosperity of their
land.

5. This and the next verse may be
interpreted literally (Ibn Ezra) or figuratively (Rashi, Kimchi). For the latter, cf.
xxix. 18, xxxii. 3f.

7. And the parched land shall
   become a pool,
   And the thirsty ground springs
   of water;
   In the habitation of jackals herds
   shall lie down,
   It shall be an enclosure for reeds
   and rushes.

8. And a highway shall be there,
   and a way,
   And it shall be called The way of
   holiness;
   The unclean shall not pass over
   it; but it shall be for those;
   The wayfaring men, yea fools,
   shall not err therein.

9. No lion shall be there,
   Nor shall any ravenous beast go
   up thereon,
   They shall not be found there;
   But the redeemed shall walk
   there;

10. And the ransomed of the LORD
    shall return,
    And come with singing unto
    Zion,
    And everlasting joy shall be upon
    their heads;
    They shall obtain gladness and
    joy,
    And sorrow and sighing shall
    flee away.

7 וְהָיָה הַשָּׁרָב לַאֲגַם
וְצִמָּאוֹן לְמַבּוּעֵי מָיִם
בִּנְוֵה תַנִּים רִבְצָהּ
חָצִיר לְקָנֶה וָגֹמֶא׃

8 וְהָיָה־שָׁם מַסְלוּל וָדֶרֶךְ
וְדֶרֶךְ הַקֹּדֶשׁ יִקָּרֵא לָהּ
לֹא־יַעַבְרֶנּוּ טָמֵא וְהוּא־לָמוֹ
הֹלֵךְ דֶּרֶךְ וֶאֱוִילִים לֹא יִתְעוּ׃

9 לֹא־יִהְיֶה שָׁם אַרְיֵה
וּפְרִיץ חַיּוֹת בַּל־יַעֲלֶנָּה
לֹא תִמָּצֵא שָׁם
וְהָלְכוּ גְּאוּלִים׃

10 וּפְדוּיֵי יְהֹוָה יְשֻׁבוּן
וּבָאוּ צִיּוֹן בְּרִנָּה
וְשִׂמְחַת עוֹלָם עַל־רֹאשָׁם
שָׂשׂוֹן וְשִׂמְחָה יַשִּׂיגוּ
וְנָסוּ יָגוֹן וַאֲנָחָה׃

7. *the parched land.* Rashi explains this
figuratively, he who longed for salvation, will find it.

herds shall lie down. lit. 'her lying down.'

enclosure. See on xxxiv. 13.

8–10. A highway, safe from all dangers and holy, will lead to Zion for the
joyful return of the redeemed of the
Lord.

8. *it shall be for those.* The redeemed
exiles returning to Zion. Abarbanel
connects the phrase with what follows
and translates: 'and He shall be to them
a Guide' (lit. walker in the way). The
former rendering, however, is accepted
by the vast majority of commentaries
since it follows the punctuation (See
Isaiah of Trani).

10. Repeated in li. 11

36   CHAPTER XXXVI   לו

1. Now it came to pass in the fourteenth year of king Hezekiah, that Sennacherib king of Assyria came up against all the fortified cities of Judah, and took them. 2. And the king of Assyria sent Rab-shakeh from Lachish to Jerusalem unto king Hezekiah with a great army. And he stood by the conduit of the upper pool in the highway of the fullers' field. 3. Then came forth unto him Eliakim the son of Hilkiah, that was over the household, and Shebna the scribe, and Joah the son of Asaph the recorder. 4. And Rab-shakeh said unto them:

1 וַיְהִי בְּאַרְבַּע עֶשְׂרֵה שָׁנָה לַמֶּלֶךְ
חִזְקִיָּהוּ עָלָה סַנְחֵרִיב מֶלֶךְ־אַשּׁוּר
עַל־כָּל־עָרֵי יְהוּדָה הַבְּצֻרוֹת
2 וַיִּתְפְּשֵׂם: וַיִּשְׁלַח מֶלֶךְ־אַשּׁוּר | אֶת־
רַבְשָׁקֵה מִלָּכִישׁ יְרוּשָׁלְַמָה אֶל־
הַמֶּלֶךְ חִזְקִיָּהוּ בְּחֵיל כָּבֵד וַיַּעֲמֹד
בִּתְעָלַת הַבְּרֵכָה הָעֶלְיוֹנָה בִּמְסִלַּת
3 שְׂדֵה כוֹבֵס: וַיֵּצֵא אֵלָיו אֶלְיָקִים
בֶּן־חִלְקִיָּהוּ אֲשֶׁר עַל־הַבָּיִת וְשֶׁבְנָא
הַסֹּפֵר וְיוֹאָח בֶּן־אָסָף הַמַּזְכִּיר:
4 וַיֹּאמֶר אֲלֵיהֶם רַבְשָׁקֵה אִמְרוּ־נָא

CHAPTERS XXXVI, XXXVII

A HISTORICAL record of the campaigns of Sennacherib in Judah, his threat to Hezekiah, the siege of Jerusalem, Hezekiah's prayer, the Divine message of assurance, the miraculous destruction of the Assyrian host and the deliverance of Jerusalem. 2 Kings xviii. 13-xix. 37 contains a parallel record with slight variations, omitting the Psalm of Hezekiah in xxxviii. 9-20. These events appear in both these books for different reasons. They appear in Kings as part of the history of Hezekiah, since that Book is dedicated to the historical records of the kings. They appear in Isaiah as the background of the prophecies mentioned therein (Abarbanel).

CHAPTER XXXVI

THE Assyrian invasion, Rab-shakeh's scoffing and threats and his demand for unconditional surrender.

1. *fourteenth year.* The invasion, it is generally agreed, took place in the year 701 B.C.E.

2. *Rab-shakeh.* The Assyrian is Rab-saqu, said to mean 'chief of the officers,' or 'general' (Marcus).

Lachish. A city in the Shephelah, identified with Tell-el-Hesy which is within a few miles of Umm Lakis. Standing in a commanding position on the road to Egypt, it is one of the most important fortresses of the Judean country (See Marcus).

upper pool. See on vii. 3.

3. *Eliakim.* Cf. xxii. 20ff., and for Shebna xxii. 15ff.

the recorder. lit. 'the remembrancer.' The same Hebrew noun is used for 'secretary' in modern Hebrew.

4-10. Rab-shakeh's first speech, arguing, insulting, threatening.

'Say ye now to Hezekiah: Thus saith the great king, the king of Assyria: What confidence is this wherein thou trustest? 5. I said: It is but vain words; for counsel and strength are for the war. Now on whom dost thou trust, that thou hast rebelled against me? 6. Behold, thou trustest upon the staff of this bruised reed, even upon Egypt; whereon if a man lean, it will go into his hand, and pierce it; so is Pharaoh king of Egypt to all that trust on him. 7. But if thou say unto me: We trust in the LORD our God; is not that He, whose high places and whose altars Hezekiah hath taken away, and hath said to Judah and to Jerusalem: Ye shall worship before this altar? 8. Now therefore, I pray thee, make a wager with my master, the king of Assyria, and I will give thee two thousand horses, if thou be able on thy part to set riders upon them. 9. How then canst thou turn away the face of one captain, even of the least of my master's servants? yet thou puttest thy trust on Egypt for chariots and

אֶל־חִזְקִיָּהוּ כֹּה־אָמַר הַמֶּלֶךְ
הַגָּדוֹל מֶלֶךְ אַשּׁוּר מָה הַבִּטָּחוֹן הַזֶּה
5 אֲשֶׁר בָּטָחְתָּ: אָמַרְתִּי אַךְ־דְּבַר־
שְׂפָתַיִם עֵצָה וּגְבוּרָה לַמִּלְחָמָה עַתָּה
6 עַל־מִי בָטַחְתָּ כִּי מָרַדְתָּ בִּי: הִנֵּה
בָטַחְתָּ עַל־מִשְׁעֶנֶת הַקָּנֶה הָרָצוּץ
הַזֶּה עַל־מִצְרַיִם אֲשֶׁר יִסָּמֵךְ אִישׁ
עָלָיו וּבָא בְכַפּוֹ וּנְקָבָהּ כֵּן פַּרְעֹה
מֶלֶךְ־מִצְרַיִם לְכָל־הַבֹּטְחִים
7 עָלָיו: וְכִי־תֹאמַר אֵלַי אֶל־יְהֹוָה
אֱלֹהֵינוּ בָּטָחְנוּ הֲלוֹא הוּא אֲשֶׁר
הֵסִיר חִזְקִיָּהוּ אֶת־בָּמֹתָיו וְאֶת־
מִזְבְּחֹתָיו וַיֹּאמֶר לִיהוּדָה וְלִירוּשָׁלַ͏ִם
8 לִפְנֵי הַמִּזְבֵּחַ הַזֶּה תִּשְׁתַּחֲווּ: וְעַתָּה
הִתְעָרֶב נָא אֶת־אֲדֹנִי הַמֶּלֶךְ אַשּׁוּר
וְאֶתְּנָה לְךָ אַלְפַּיִם סוּסִים אִם־תּוּכַל
9 לָתֶת לְךָ רֹכְבִים עֲלֵיהֶם: וְאֵיךְ
תָּשִׁיב אֵת פְּנֵי פַחַת אַחַד עַבְדֵי אֲדֹנִי
הַקְּטַנִּים וַתִּבְטַח לְךָ עַל־מִצְרַיִם

4. **confidence**. viz. expectation of help from Egypt.

5. **it is but vain words**. Hezekiah's assurance to his people that he can defy Assyria with impunity (Ibn Ezra).

for counsel ... war. Of which, Rabshakeh implies, Hezekiah has none (Metsudath David).

7. **is not that He,** etc. The abolition of local places of worship in favour of the one altar in Jerusalem (cf. 2 Kings xviii.

4) must have offended, in the view of the Assyrian heathen, Hezekiah's God Whose protection and help he could, therefore, no longer expect (Metsudath David).

8. A scornful thrust at the scanty manpower and poor equipment of the Judean army.

9. **captain**. The Hebrew word *pachath* signifies the governor of a province. (Rashi, Kara).

for horsemen! 10. And am I now come up without the LORD against this land to destroy it? The LORD said unto me: Go up against this land, and destroy it.'

11. Then said Eliakim and Shebna and Joah unto Rab-shakeh: 'Speak, I pray thee, unto thy servants in the Aramean language, for we understand it; and speak not to us in the Jews' language, in the ears of the people that are on the wall.' 12. But Rab-shakeh said: 'Hath my master sent me to thy master, and to thee, to speak these words? hath he not sent me to the men that sit upon the wall, to eat their own dung, and to drink their own water with you?' 13. Then Rab-shakeh stood, and cried with a loud voice in the Jews' language, and said: 'Hear ye the words of the great king, the king of Assyria. 14. Thus saith the king:

10 לָרֶכֶב וּלְפָרָשִׁים: וְעַתָּה הֲמִבַּלְעֲדֵי
יְהֹוָה עָלִיתִי עַל־הָאָרֶץ הַזֹּאת
לְהַשְׁחִיתָהּ יְהֹוָה אָמַר אֵלַי עֲלֵה
אֶל־הָאָרֶץ הַזֹּאת וְהַשְׁחִיתָהּ:

11 וַיֹּאמֶר אֶלְיָקִים וְשֶׁבְנָא וְיוֹאָח אֶל־
רַבְשָׁקֵה דַּבֶּר־נָא אֶל־עֲבָדֶיךָ
אֲרָמִית כִּי שֹׁמְעִים אֲנָחְנוּ וְאַל־
תְּדַבֵּר אֵלֵינוּ יְהוּדִית בְּאָזְנֵי הָעָם

12 אֲשֶׁר עַל־הַחוֹמָה: וַיֹּאמֶר רַבְשָׁקֵה
הַאֶל אֲדֹנֶיךָ וְאֵלֶיךָ שְׁלָחַנִי אֲדֹנִי
לְדַבֵּר אֶת־הַדְּבָרִים הָאֵלֶּה הֲלֹא
עַל־הָאֲנָשִׁים הַיֹּשְׁבִים עַל־הַחוֹמָה
לֶאֱכֹל אֶת־חָרְאֵיהֶם וְלִשְׁתּוֹת אֶת־

13 שֵׁינֵיהֶם עִמָּכֶם: וַיַּעֲמֹד רַבְשָׁקֵה
וַיִּקְרָא בְקוֹל־גָּדוֹל יְהוּדִית וַיֹּאמֶר
שִׁמְעוּ אֶת־דִּבְרֵי הַמֶּלֶךְ הַגָּדוֹל מֶלֶךְ

14 אַשּׁוּר: כֹּה אָמַר הַמֶּלֶךְ אַל־יַשִּׁא

v. 12. מֵימֵי רַגְלֵיהֶם ק'   v. 12. צוֹאָתָם ק'

10. The heathen's claim to be carrying out a Divine mission may have been mere pretence, its purpose being to impress his audience; or it may possibly have been the result of a genuine belief that since the God of Israel had allowed the Assyrian king to make so many conquests, He also expected and wished him to take Judah and Jerusalem (Kimchi, 2 Kings xviii. 25).

11f. A request by Hezekiah's representatives that Rab-shakeh should speak to them in a language that the people around did not understand is scornfully rejected. He, Rab-shakeh exclaims, came to speak to the common people, the real sufferers from their king's policy, and not to Hezekiah or to his representatives.

11. *Aramean*. This was the international medium of commercial and other intercourse throughout western Asia. Though unfamiliar to the populace, it was understood by Hezekiah's court (Rashi, 2 Kings xviii. 26).

the Jews' language. Hebrew, as in Neh. xiii. 24.

12. *to eat . . . water*. The direful effects of the siege (Rashi).

13-20. Rab-shakeh's harangue, persuasive at first and threatening in the end.

Let not Hezekiah beguile you, for he will not be able to deliver you; 15. neither let Hezekiah make you trust in the LORD, saying: The LORD will surely deliver us; this city shall not be given into the hand of the king of Assyria. 16. Hearken not to Hezekiah; for thus saith the king of Assyria: Make your peace with me, and come out to me; and eat ye every one of his vine, and every one of his fig-tree, and drink ye every one the waters of his own cistern; 17. until I come and take you away to a land like your own land, a land of corn and wine, a land of bread and vineyards. 18. Beware lest Hezekiah persuade you, saying: The LORD will deliver us. Hath any of the gods of the nations delivered his land out of the hand of the king of Assyria? 19. Where are the gods of Hamath and Arpad? where are the gods of Sepharvaim? and have they delivered Samaria out of my hand? 20. Who are they among all the gods of these countries, that have delivered their country out of my hand, that the LORD should deliver Jerusalem out of my hand?'

לָכֶם חִזְקִיָּהוּ כִּי לֹא־יוּכַל לְהַצִּיל
אֶתְכֶם: וְאַל־יַבְטַח אֶתְכֶם חִזְקִיָּהוּ 15
אֶל־יְהוָה לֵאמֹר הַצֵּל יַצִּילֵנוּ יְהוָה
לֹא תִנָּתֵן הָעִיר הַזֹּאת בְּיַד מֶלֶךְ
אַשּׁוּר: אַל־תִּשְׁמְעוּ אֶל־חִזְקִיָּהוּ 16
כִּי כֹה אָמַר הַמֶּלֶךְ אַשּׁוּר עֲשׂוּ־אִתִּי
בְרָכָה וּצְאוּ אֵלַי וְאִכְלוּ אִישׁ־גַּפְנוֹ
וְאִישׁ תְּאֵנָתוֹ וּשְׁתוּ אִישׁ מֵי־בוֹרוֹ:
עַד־בֹּאִי וְלָקַחְתִּי אֶתְכֶם אֶל־אֶרֶץ 17
כְּאַרְצְכֶם אֶרֶץ דָּגָן וְתִירוֹשׁ אֶרֶץ
לֶחֶם וּכְרָמִים: פֶּן־יַסִּית אֶתְכֶם 18
חִזְקִיָּהוּ לֵאמֹר יְהוָה יַצִּילֵנוּ הַהִצִּילוּ
אֱלֹהֵי הַגּוֹיִם אִישׁ אֶת־אַרְצוֹ מִיַּד
מֶלֶךְ אַשּׁוּר: אַיֵּה אֱלֹהֵי חֲמָת וְאַרְפָּד 19
אַיֵּה אֱלֹהֵי סְפַרְוָיִם וְכִי־הִצִּילוּ אֶת־
שֹׁמְרוֹן מִיָּדִי: מִי בְּכָל־אֱלֹהֵי 20
הָאֲרָצוֹת הָאֵלֶּה אֲשֶׁר־הִצִּילוּ אֶת־
אַרְצָם מִיָּדִי כִּי־יַצִּיל יְהוָה אֶת־

14. *beguile you.* By his assurance of ability to stand up against Assyria (Abarbanel).

16. *your peace.* lit. 'a blessing' (Targum).

and come out to me. i.e. surrender (Rashi).

eat ye ... cistern. Immediate submission would enable them to resume forthwith, though only temporarily, their usual economic pursuits and normal life (Rashi).

17. Though surrender meant deportation, the new land, Rab-shakeh assures them, was as fertile and productive as their own.

18-20. Rab-shakeh, comparing the Lord of hosts with the false gods of the nations Assyria had vanquished, argues that as the latter were powerless against Assyria so would be the God of Israel.

19. *Hamath and Arpad.* See on x. 9.

Sepharvaim. Rebelled against Sargon and were therefore repatriated to Samaria (Marcus).

have they delivered Samaria. Though the Samaritans had also worshipped the same gods (Rashi).

21. But they held their peace, and answered him not a word; for the king's commandment was, saying: 'Answer him not.' 22. Then came Eliakim the son of Hilkiah, that was over the household, and Shebna the scribe, and Joah the son of Asaph the recorder, to Hezekiah with their clothes rent, and told him the words of Rab-shakeh.

21 יְרוּשָׁלַ͏ִם מִיָּדִי: וַיַּחֲרִישׁוּ וְלֹא־עָנוּ
אֹתוֹ דָּבָר כִּי־מִצְוַת הַמֶּלֶךְ הִיא
22 לֵאמֹר לֹא תַעֲנֻהוּ: וַיָּבֹא אֶלְיָקִים
בֶּן־חִלְקִיָּהוּ אֲשֶׁר־עַל־הַבַּיִת
וְשֶׁבְנָא הַסֹּפֵר וְיוֹאָח בֶּן־אָסָף
הַמַּזְכִּיר אֶל־חִזְקִיָּהוּ קְרוּעֵי בְגָדִים
וַיַּגִּידוּ לוֹ אֵת דִּבְרֵי רַבְשָׁקֵה:

<hr/>

37   CHAPTER XXXVII   לז

1. And it came to pass, when king Hezekiah heard it, that he rent his clothes, and covered himself with sackcloth, and went into the house of the Lord. 2. And he sent Eliakim, who was over the household, and Shebna the scribe, and the elders of the priests, covered with sackcloth, unto Isaiah the prophet the son of Amoz. 3. And they said unto him: 'Thus saith Hezekiah: This day is a day of trouble, and of rebuke, and of contumely; for the children are come to the birth, and there is not strength to bring forth.

1 וַיְהִי כִּשְׁמֹעַ הַמֶּלֶךְ חִזְקִיָּהוּ וַיִּקְרַע
אֶת־בְּגָדָיו וַיִּתְכַּס בַּשָּׂק וַיָּבֹא בֵּית
2 יְהֹוָה: וַיִּשְׁלַח אֶת־אֶלְיָקִים אֲשֶׁר־
עַל־הַבַּיִת וְאֵת | שֶׁבְנָא הַסּוֹפֵר וְאֵת
זִקְנֵי הַכֹּהֲנִים מִתְכַּסִּים בַּשַּׂקִּים אֶל־
3 יְשַׁעְיָהוּ בֶן־אָמוֹץ הַנָּבִיא: וַיֹּאמְרוּ
אֵלָיו כֹּה אָמַר חִזְקִיָּהוּ יוֹם־צָרָה
וְתוֹכֵחָה וּנְאָצָה הַיּוֹם הַזֶּה כִּי בָאוּ
בָנִים עַד־מַשְׁבֵּר וְכֹחַ אַיִן לְלֵדָה:

v. 1. קמץ בז״ק

<hr/>

22. *clothes rent*. An expression of deep anguish and sorrow at the heathen's blasphemy and threats (Rashi, Metsudath David).

CHAPTER XXXVII

1-7. Hezekiah's distress and pathetic appeal to God through Isaiah, and the prophet's reassuring reply.

heard it. The report of Rab-shakeh's demand and threats recorded in the previous chapter as well as his blasphemy (Malbim).

went . . . Lord. To pray (Malbim).

2. *unto Isaiah*. In ch. x, Isaiah, had already prophesied that Sennacherib would fall on Mount Zion after blaspheming the name of God and when Jerusalem had come to such a state that it would no longer be able to survive. Hezekiah sent this delegation to appeal to Isaiah to pray to God to fulfill His promise although the people did not merit it (Malbim).

3. *for the children . . . bring forth*. Metaphor for a critical moment which finds one utterly helpless or unprepared (for the language, cf. lxvi. 9) (See Malbim).

4. It may be the LORD thy God will hear the words of Rab-shakeh, whom the king of Assyria his master hath sent to taunt the living God, and will rebuke the words which the LORD thy God hath heard; wherefore make prayer for the remnant that is left.'
5. So the servants of king Hezekiah came to Isaiah. 6. And Isaiah said unto them: 'Thus shall ye say to your master: Thus saith the LORD: Be not afraid of the words that thou hast heard, wherewith the servants of the king of Assyria have blasphemed Me. 7. Behold, I will put a spirit in him, and he shall hear a rumour, and shall return unto his own land; and I will cause him to fall by the sword in his own land.'
8. So Rab-shakeh returned, and found the king of Assyria warring against Libnah; for he had heard that he was departed from Lachish.
9. And he heard say concerning Tirhakah king of Ethiopia: 'He is come out to fight against thee.'

4 אוּלַי יִשְׁמַע יְהֹוָה אֱלֹהֶיךָ אֵת | דִּבְרֵי
רַבְשָׁקֵה אֲשֶׁר שְׁלָחוֹ מֶלֶךְ־אַשּׁוּר |
אֲדֹנָיו לְחָרֵף אֱלֹהִים חַי וְהוֹכִיחַ
בַּדְּבָרִים אֲשֶׁר שָׁמַע יְהֹוָה אֱלֹהֶיךָ
וְנָשָׂאתָ תְפִלָּה בְּעַד הַשְּׁאֵרִית
5 הַנִּמְצָאָה: וַיָּבֹאוּ עַבְדֵי הַמֶּלֶךְ
6 חִזְקִיָּהוּ אֶל־יְשַׁעְיָהוּ: וַיֹּאמֶר
אֲלֵיהֶם יְשַׁעְיָהוּ כֹּה תֹאמְרוּן אֶל־
אֲדֹנֵיכֶם כֹּה | אָמַר יְהֹוָה אַל־תִּירָא
מִפְּנֵי הַדְּבָרִים אֲשֶׁר שָׁמַעְתָּ אֲשֶׁר
7 גִּדְּפוּ נַעֲרֵי מֶלֶךְ־אַשּׁוּר אֹתִי: הִנְנִי
נֹתֵן בּוֹ רוּחַ וְשָׁמַע שְׁמוּעָה וְשָׁב אֶל־
אַרְצוֹ וְהִפַּלְתִּיו בַּחֶרֶב בְּאַרְצוֹ:
8 וַיָּשָׁב רַבְשָׁקֵה וַיִּמְצָא אֶת־מֶלֶךְ
אַשּׁוּר נִלְחָם עַל־לִבְנָה כִּי שָׁמַע כִּי
9 נָסַע מִלָּכִישׁ: וַיִּשְׁמַע עַל־תִּרְהָקָה
מֶלֶךְ־כּוּשׁ לֵאמֹר יָצָא לְהִלָּחֵם אִתָּךְ

v. 9. למדנחאי אל

4. *the living God.* [Contrasted with the inanimate gods with which Rab-shakeh had blasphemously compared Him.]

that is left. lit. 'that is found.'

6. *servants.* lit. 'boys lads'; i.e. Hezekiah need not be upset by the empty boasting of irresponsible youth (Rabinowitz, 2 Kings xix. 6).

7. *a spirit.* Better, 'a desire' (Metsudath Zion).

in him. In the king of Assyria.

hear a rumor. About Tirhakah's intentions (verse 9).

8. *Libnah.* Its position is not definitely known. Many identify it with Tel-e-tsafi, about fifteen kilometers north of Lachish (Daath Mikra, Josh. x. 29).

he had heard, etc. Rab-shakeh had heard that the king of Assyria had departed (Metsudath David).

departed from Lachish. Cf. xxxvi. 2.

9. *Tirhakah king of Ethiopia.* His accession is said to have taken place in the year 704 B.C.E., one year after that of Sennacherib to the throne of Assyria. His rule extended later over all the Nile countries, and he was continually occupied in endeavors to undermine the power of Assyria by inciting its vassals to rebellion.

And when he heard it, he sent messengers to Hezekiah, saying: 10. 'Thus shall ye speak to Hezekiah king of Judah, saying: Let not thy God in whom thou trustest beguile thee, saying: Jerusalem shall not be given into the hand of the king of Assyria. 11. Behold, thou hast heard what the kings of Assyria have done to all lands, by destroying them utterly; and shalt thou be delivered? 12. Have the gods of the nations delivered them, which my fathers have destroyed, Gozan, and Haran, and Rezeph, and the children of Eden that were in Telassar? 13. Where is the king of Hamath, and the king of Arpad, and the king of the city of Sepharvaim, of Hena, and Ivvah?'

14. And Hezekiah received the letter from the hand of the mes-

וַיִּשְׁמַע וַיִּשְׁלַח מַלְאָכִים אֶל־חִזְקִיָּהוּ

10 לֵאמֹר: כֹּה תֹאמְרוּן אֶל־חִזְקִיָּהוּ
מֶלֶךְ־יְהוּדָה לֵאמֹר אַל־יַשִּׁאֲךָ
אֱלֹהֶיךָ אֲשֶׁר אַתָּה בּוֹטֵחַ בּוֹ לֵאמֹר
לֹא תִנָּתֵן יְרוּשָׁלִַם בְּיַד מֶלֶךְ אַשּׁוּר:

11 הִנֵּה ׀ אַתָּה שָׁמַעְתָּ אֲשֶׁר עָשׂוּ מַלְכֵי
אַשּׁוּר לְכָל־הָאֲרָצוֹת לְהַחֲרִימָם

12 וְאַתָּה תִּנָּצֵל: הַהִצִּילוּ אוֹתָם אֱלֹהֵי
הַגּוֹיִם אֲשֶׁר־הִשְׁחִיתוּ אֲבוֹתַי אֶת־
גּוֹזָן וְאֶת־חָרָן וְרֶצֶף וּבְנֵי־עֶדֶן אֲשֶׁר

13 בִּתְלַשָּׂר: אַיֵּה מֶלֶךְ־חֲמָת וּמֶלֶךְ
אַרְפָּד וּמֶלֶךְ לָעִיר סְפַרְוַיִם הֵנַע

14 וְעִוָּה: וַיִּקַּח חִזְקִיָּהוּ אֶת־הַסְּפָרִים

10–13. A threatening message to Hezekiah from the king of Assyria, which is almost a repetition of Rabshakeh's harangue in verses 13–20 of the previous chapters.

12. *my fathers*. The Assyrian kings who reigned before him. Sennacherib was only the second king in the dynasty founded by his father Sargon. He was, however, descended from an earlier dynasty, that had since been deposed (Marcus).

Gozan. On the river Chaboras, a northern tributary of the Euphrates (Carta).

Haran. In northern Mesopotamia on the river Belikh which is also a tributary of the Euphrates to the west of Chaboras (Carta).

Rezeph. In the desert, about twenty miles south of the Euphrates and about sixteen miles south of Sura on the road from that town to Palmyra (Carta).

the children of Eden. The Hebrew *Benë Eden* corresponds to Bit Adini, situated on both banks of the middle Euphrates (Carta).

Telassar. Meaning 'the mound of Assur' was, as some suggest, the region called by its Hittite inhabitants Mitani (See Carta).

13. *Hamath . . . Arpad . . . Sepharvaim.* See on xxxvi. 19.

Hena, and Ivvah. Their exact location is unknown. They were apparently Syrian towns or regions. According to Targum, these are not placenames. He renders: 'he exiled them and twisted them.' Rabbenu Yeshayah considers both possibilities.

14. *the letter.* The Hebrew has the noun in the plural form, indicating that Sennacherib sent Hezekiah several letters. See 2 Kings xix. 14.

sengers, and read it; and Hezekiah went up unto the house of the LORD, and spread it before the LORD. 15. And Hezekiah prayed unto the LORD, saying: 'O LORD of hosts, the God of Israel, that sittest upon the cherubim, Thou art the God, even Thou alone, of all the kingdoms of the earth; Thou hast made heaven and earth. 17. Incline Thine ear, O LORD, and hear; open Thine eyes, O LORD, and see; and hear all the words of Sennacherib, who hath sent to taunt the living God. 18. Of a truth, LORD, the kings of Assyria have laid waste all the countries, and their land, 19. and have cast their gods into the fire; for they were no gods, but the work of men's hands, wood and stone; therefore they have destroyed them. 20. Now therefore, O LORD our God, save us from his hand, that all the kingdoms of the earth may know that Thou art the LORD, even Thou only.'

21. Then Isaiah the son of Amoz

מִיַּד הַמַּלְאָכִים וַיִּקְרָאֵהוּ וַיַּעַל בֵּית יְהֹוָה וַיִּפְרְשֵׂהוּ חִזְקִיָּהוּ לִפְנֵי יְהֹוָה:

15 וַיִּתְפַּלֵּל חִזְקִיָּהוּ אֶל־יְהֹוָה לֵאמֹר:

16 יְהֹוָה צְבָאוֹת אֱלֹהֵי יִשְׂרָאֵל יֹשֵׁב הַכְּרֻבִים אַתָּה־הוּא הָאֱלֹהִים לְבַדְּךָ לְכֹל מַמְלְכוֹת הָאָרֶץ אַתָּה עָשִׂיתָ אֶת־הַשָּׁמַיִם וְאֶת־הָאָרֶץ:

17 הַטֵּה יְהֹוָה אָזְנְךָ וּשֲׁמָע פְּקַח יְהֹוָה עֵינֶךָ וּרְאֵה וּשְׁמַע אֵת כָּל־דִּבְרֵי סַנְחֵרִיב אֲשֶׁר שָׁלַח לְחָרֵף אֱלֹהִים חָי:

18 אָמְנָם יְהֹוָה הֶחֱרִיבוּ מַלְכֵי אַשּׁוּר אֶת־כָּל־הָאֲרָצוֹת וְאֶת־

19 אַרְצָם: וְנָתֹן אֶת־אֱלֹהֵיהֶם בָּאֵשׁ כִּי לֹא אֱלֹהִים הֵמָּה כִּי אִם־מַעֲשֵׂה

20 יְדֵי־אָדָם עֵץ וָאֶבֶן וַיְאַבְּדוּם: וְעַתָּה יְהֹוָה אֱלֹהֵינוּ הוֹשִׁיעֵנוּ מִיָּדוֹ וְיֵדְעוּ כָּל־מַמְלְכוֹת הָאָרֶץ כִּי־אַתָּה יְהֹוָה

21 לְבַדֶּךָ: וַיִּשְׁלַח יְשַׁעְיָהוּ בֶן־אָמוֹץ

v. 17. קמץ בז"ק

---

spread it. viz. each letter, or the letter containing the blasphemies (Kimchi), a symbolic act, displaying the Assyrian's blasphemies in the presence of God.

16–20. Hezekiah's prayer.

16. *upon the cherubim.* Cf. Exod. xxv. 18–22.

17. *Thine eyes.* The Hebrew is written without the letter *yad,* the vowel indicating that the plural is meant. In Kings, the *yad* is present.

18. *all the countries, and their land.* Not only have they devastated the territories of other nations but even their own

land. Assyria, too, has been ruined as a result of their warlike aims and military preparations (cf. xiv. 20) (Abarbanel). Others regard *countries* in this context as synonymous with 'nations,' the noun used in the parallel passage, 2 Kings xix. 17, denoting the main cities and the village around them (Rashi, Kimchi).

20. *even Thou only.* lit. 'Thou alone.'

21–35. God's answer to Hezekiah's prayer is conveyed in a message through Isaiah.

21–29. A taunt-song on Sennacherib, introduced by *this is the word . . .him.*

sent unto Hezekiah, saying: 'Thus
saith the LORD, the God of Israel:
Whereas thou hast prayed to Me
against Sennacherib king of Assyria,
22. this is the word which the LORD
hath spoken concerning him:

> The virgin daughter of Zion
> Hath despised thee and laughed
> thee to scorn;
> The daughter of Jerusalem
> Hath shaken her head at thee.

23. Whom hast thou taunted and
blasphemed?
> And against whom hast thou
> exalted thy voice?
> Yea, thou hast lifted up thine
> eyes on high.
> Even against the Holy One of
> Israel!

24. By thy servants hast thou taunted
the Lord,
> And hast said: With the multi-
> tude of my chariots
> Am I come up to the height of
> the mountains,
> To the innermost parts of
> Lebanon;
> And I have cut down the tall
> cedars thereof,
> And the choice cypress-trees
> thereof;
> And I have entered into his
> farthest height,
> The forest of his fruitful field.

אֶל־חִזְקִיָּהוּ לֵאמֹר כֹּה־אָמַר יְהֹוָה
אֱלֹהֵי יִשְׂרָאֵל אֲשֶׁר הִתְפַּלַּלְתָּ אֵלַי
אֶל־סַנְחֵרִיב מֶלֶךְ אַשּׁוּר׃

22 זֶה הַדָּבָר אֲשֶׁר־דִּבֶּר יְהֹוָה עָלָיו
בָּזָה לְךָ לָעֲגָה לְךָ
בְּתוּלַת בַּת־צִיּוֹן
אַחֲרֶיךָ רֹאשׁ הֵנִיעָה
בַּת יְרוּשָׁלָ͏ִם׃

23 אֶת־מִי חֵרַפְתָּ וְגִדַּפְתָּ
וְעַל־מִי הֲרִימוֹתָה קּוֹל
וַתִּשָּׂא מָרוֹם עֵינֶיךָ
אֶל־קְדוֹשׁ יִשְׂרָאֵל׃

24 בְּיַד עֲבָדֶיךָ חֵרַפְתָּ ׀ אֲדֹנָי
וַתֹּאמֶר בְּרֹב רִכְבִּי
אֲנִי עָלִיתִי מְרוֹם הָרִים
יַרְכְּתֵי לְבָנוֹן
וְאֶכְרֹת קוֹמַת אֲרָזָיו
מִבְחַר בְּרֹשָׁיו
וְאָבוֹא מְרוֹם קִצּוֹ
יַעַר כַּרְמִלּוֹ׃

---

22. *virgin daughter.* See on xxiii. 12.

shaken her head. A gesture on contempt
(Metsudath David).

at thee. lit. 'behind thee,' an anticipation
of his coming flight. Or 'after you,'
alluding to his downfall (Metsudath
David).

23. *whom hast thou ... voice?* Two
rhetorical questions the answers to
which are obvious.

24f. The prophet quotes Sennacherib's boast of his easy victories and of
his power to overcome all obstacles in
his way of conquest. Some of the
expressions are obviously metaphorical.

24. *the tall cedars thereof.* lit. 'the height
of its cedars.'

farthest height. lit 'height of its end.'

the forest ... field. Cf. x. 18, xxix. 17,
xxxii. 15.

25. I have digged and drunk water,
And with the sole of my feet
have I dried up
All the rivers of Egypt.
26. Hast thou not heard?
Long ago I made it,
In ancient times I fashioned it;
Now have I brought it to pass,
Yea, it is done; that fortified
cities
Should be laid waste into ruinous
heaps.
27. Therefore their inhabitants were
of small power,
They were dismayed and confounded;
They were as the grass of the
field,
And as the green herb,
As the grass on the housetops,
And as a field of corn before it is
grown up.
28. But I know thy sitting down,
and thy going out, and thy
coming in,

25 אֲנִי קַרְתִּי וְשָׁתִיתִי מָיִם
וְאַחְרִב בְּכַף־פְּעָמַי
כֹּל יְאֹרֵי מָצוֹר:
26 הֲלוֹא־שָׁמַעְתָּ
לְמֵרָחוֹק אוֹתָהּ עָשִׂיתִי
מִימֵי קֶדֶם וִיצַרְתִּיהָ
עַתָּה הֲבֵאתִיהָ
וּתְהִי לְהַשְׁאוֹת
גַּלִּים נִצִּים עָרִים בְּצֻרוֹת:
27 וְיֹשְׁבֵיהֶן קִצְרֵי־יָד
חַתּוּ וָבֹשׁוּ
הָיוּ עֵשֶׂב שָׂדֶה
וִירַק דֶּשֶׁא
חֲצִיר גַּגּוֹת
וּשְׁדֵמָה לִפְנֵי קָמָה:
28 וְשִׁבְתְּךָ וְצֵאתְךָ וּבֹאֲךָ יָדַעְתִּי

25. *drunk water*. Of foreign conquered lands. The word 'foreign' occurs in the parallel phrase in 2 Kings xix. 24 (See Kimchi ad loc.).

with the sole . . . dried up. A reference to the multitudes of his armies (Rashi).

rivers of Egypt. The Nile streams. The last claim must be regarded as an empty boast since Sennacherib never invaded Egypt (Kimchi, 2 Kings xix. 24).

26f. The prophet in the name of God apostrophizes Sennacherib. All his power and achievements are due entirely to the will of God Who had decreed of old the fate of the nations he had conquered.

26. *made it*. The destiny of the nations defeated by Assyria (Rashi).

that fortified cities, etc. lit. 'that thou shouldest be (able) to lay fortified cities waste.'

27. *of small power*. lit. 'short of hands.'

as the grass, etc. Cf. Ps. cxxix. 6, symbolic of what is dried up and highly inflammable (Ralbag, 2 Kings xix. 26).

28f. None of Sennacherib's movements is hidden from the Lord and, as punishment for his arrogance in attributing his successes to his own power and his blasphemous raging against God, he will be taken under control like a wild beast and dragged back to his own lair.

28. *thy sitting down*. Cf. Ps. cxxix. 2.

30–35. The prophet now addresses Hezekiah.

And thy raging against Me.

29. Because of thy raging against
Me,
And for that thine uproar is
come up into Mine ears,
Therefore will I put My hook in
thy nose,
And My bridle in thy lips,
And I will turn thee back by the
way
By which thou camest.

30. And this shall be the sign unto
thee: ye shall eat this year that which
groweth of itself, and in the second
year that which springeth of the
same; and in the third year sow ye,
and reap, and plant vineyards, and
eat the fruit thereof. 31. And the
remnant that is escaped of the house
of Judah shall again take root
downward, and bear fruit upward.
32. For out of Jerusalem shall go
forth a remnant, and out of mount
Zion they that shall escape; the zeal
of the Lord of hosts shall perform
this. 33. Therefore thus saith the
Lord concerning the king of Assyria:
He shall not come unto this city,
nor shoot an arrow there, neither
shall he come before it with shield,

וְאֵת הִתְרַגֶּזְךָ אֵלָי:

29 יַעַן הִתְרַגֶּזְךָ אֵלַי
וְשַׁאֲנַנְךָ עָלָה בְאָזְנָי
וְשַׂמְתִּי חַחִי בְּאַפֶּךָ
וּמִתְגִּי בִּשְׂפָתֶיךָ
וַהֲשִׁיבֹתִיךָ בַּדֶּרֶךְ
אֲשֶׁר־בָּאתָ בָּהּ:

30 וְזֶה־לְּךָ הָאוֹת אָכוֹל הַשָּׁנָה סָפִיחַ
וּבַשָּׁנָה הַשֵּׁנִית שָׁחִיס וּבַשָּׁנָה
הַשְּׁלִישִׁית זִרְעוּ וְקִצְרוּ וְנִטְעוּ כְרָמִים
31 וְאִכְלוּ פִרְיָם: וְיָסְפָה פְּלֵיטַת בֵּית־
יְהוּדָה הַנִּשְׁאָרָה שֹׁרֶשׁ לְמָטָּה וְעָשָׂה
32 פְרִי לְמָעְלָה: כִּי מִירוּשָׁלַ͏ִם תֵּצֵא
שְׁאֵרִית וּפְלֵיטָה מֵהַר צִיּוֹן קִנְאַת
33 יְהֹוָה צְבָאוֹת תַּעֲשֶׂה־זֹּאת: לָכֵן
כֹּה־אָמַר יְהֹוָה אֶל־מֶלֶךְ אַשּׁוּר
לֹא יָבוֹא אֶל־הָעִיר הַזֹּאת וְלֹא־
יוֹרֶה שָׁם חֵץ וְלֹא־יְקַדְּמֶנָּה מָגֵן

v. 30. נ״א בת׳ v. 31. ואכלו ק׳

---

30. *the sign.* That the prophecy in the
following passage will be fulfilled
(Rashi).

groweth of itself. Hebrew *saphiach* (cf. Lev.
xxv. 5, 11), no sowing having taken
place because of the disturbed state of
the country (Rashi).

springeth of the same. Of the *saphiach* just
mentioned (Rashi after Targum).

sow ye . . . thereof. Normal conditions will
return to the land and it will again yield
its abundant produce (Abarbanel).

31. *remnant that is escaped.* lit. 'the
escaped of . . . that remained.'

32. *the zeal . . . shall perform this.* It is the
zeal of God for the vindication of His
profaned honour and not Israel's merit
that will be the cause of Assyria's downfall and Israel's deliverance. The phrase
occurred in ix. 6 (Rashi).

33. *therefore.* [Refers back to the beginning of verse 29. It is another result of
the Assyrian's raging and blasphemy.]

nor cast a mound against it. 34. By the way that he came, by the same shall he return, and he shall not come unto this city, saith the LORD. 35. For I will defend this city to save it, for Mine own sake, and for My servant David's sake.' 36. And the angel of the LORD went forth, and smote in the camp of the Assyrians a hundred and fourscore and five thousand; and when men arose early in the morning, behold, they were all dead corpses. 37. So Sennacherib king of Assyria departed, and went, and returned, and dwelt at Nineveh. 38. And it came to pass, as he was worshipping in the house of Nisroch his god, that Adrammelech and Sarezer his sons smote him with the sword; and they escaped into the land of Ararat. And Esarhaddon his son reigned in his stead.

וְלֹא־יִשְׁפֹּךְ עָלֶיהָ סֹלְלָה: בַּדֶּרֶךְ 34
אֲשֶׁר־בָּא בָּהּ יָשׁוּב וְאֶל־הָעִיר
הַזֹּאת לֹא יָבוֹא נְאֻם־יְהֹוָה: וְגַנּוֹתִי 35
עַל־הָעִיר הַזֹּאת לְהוֹשִׁיעָהּ לְמַעֲנִי
וּלְמַעַן דָּוִד עַבְדִּי: וַיֵּצֵא | מַלְאַךְ 36
יְהֹוָה וַיַּכֶּה בְּמַחֲנֵה אַשּׁוּר מֵאָה
וּשְׁמֹנִים וַחֲמִשָּׁה אָלֶף וַיַּשְׁכִּימוּ
בַבֹּקֶר וְהִנֵּה כֻלָּם פְּגָרִים מֵתִים:
וַיִּסַּע וַיֵּלֶךְ וַיָּשָׁב סַנְחֵרִיב מֶלֶךְ־ 37
אַשּׁוּר וַיֵּשֶׁב בְּנִינְוֵה: וַיְהִי הוּא 38
מִשְׁתַּחֲוֶה בֵּית | נִסְרֹךְ אֱלֹהָיו
וְאַדְרַמֶּלֶךְ וְשַׂרְאֶצֶר בָּנָיו הִכֻּהוּ
בַחֶרֶב וְהֵמָּה נִמְלְטוּ אֶרֶץ אֲרָרָט
וַיִּמְלֹךְ אֵסַר־חַדֹּן בְּנוֹ תַּחְתָּיו:

---

36. The sudden destruction of the Assyrian hosts by Divine intervention. This, according to tradition, occurred before the walls of Jerusalem to which Sennacherib had returned after defeating the king of Ethiopia. Another serious calamity befell the hosts of Sennacherib, according to an Egyptian tradition recorded by Herodotus. A plague of field-mice broke out in his camp at Pelusium in Egypt. In one night the mice gnawed the thongs of his armies' shields as well as their bows and, by depriving them of their main weapons, exposed them helpless to the mercy of their enemies.

37. *and dwelt at Nineveh*. This may signify that he remained in his capital and undertook no more campaigns (Kimchi, 2 Kings xxxvii. 37).

38. Sennacherib's assassination.

his sons smote him. The Babylon Chronicle

records that Sennacherib was killed 'on the 20th day of Tebeth, by his son, in an insurrection.' Some historians give Adrammelech as the name of his son. Sarezer, accordingly, may not have been guilty of actual murder which, however, may well be attributed to him as an accomplice who aided and abetted his brother. In a more recently discovered fragment of the prism of Esarhaddon, it states explicitly that the two brothers revolted and slew Sennacherib, their father (Biberfeld).

Ararat. i.e. Armenia, called by the Assyrians Urartu (Biberfeld).

Esarhaddon. According to an inscription, Esarhaddon, who was engaged in a military campaign elsewhere, on hearing of the murder of his father, collected his men and immediately marching on Nineveh defeated his brothers' armies (Cf. Marcus p. 169, Biberfeld, p. 27).

38 CHAPTER XXXVIII לח

1. In those days was Hezekiah sick unto death. And Isaiah the prophet the son of Amoz came to him, and said unto him: 'Thus saith the LORD: Set thy house in order; for thou shalt die, and not live.' 2. Then Hezekiah turned his face to the wall, and prayed unto the LORD, 3. and said: 'Remember now, O LORD, I beseech Thee, how I have walked before Thee in truth and with a whole heart, and have done that which is good in Thy sight.' And Hezekiah wept sore. 4. Then came the word of the LORD to Isaiah, saying: 5. 'Go, and say to Hezekiah: Thus saith the LORD, the God of David thy father: I have heard thy prayer, I have seen thy

א בַּיָּמִים הָהֵם חָלָה חִזְקִיָּהוּ לָמוּת
וַיָּבוֹא אֵלָיו יְשַׁעְיָהוּ בֶן־אָמוֹץ הַנָּבִיא
וַיֹּאמֶר אֵלָיו כֹּה־אָמַר יְהֹוָה צַו
לְבֵיתֶךָ כִּי מֵת אַתָּה וְלֹא תִחְיֶה:
ב וַיַּסֵּב חִזְקִיָּהוּ פָּנָיו אֶל־הַקִּיר
ג וַיִּתְפַּלֵּל אֶל־יְהֹוָה: וַיֹּאמַר אָנָּה
יְהֹוָה זְכָר־נָא אֵת אֲשֶׁר הִתְהַלַּכְתִּי
לְפָנֶיךָ בֶּאֱמֶת וּבְלֵב שָׁלֵם וְהַטּוֹב
בְּעֵינֶיךָ עָשִׂיתִי וַיֵּבְךְּ חִזְקִיָּהוּ בְּכִי
ד גָדוֹל: וַיְהִי דְּבַר־יְהֹוָה אֶל־יְשַׁעְיָהוּ
ה לֵאמֹר: הָלוֹךְ וְאָמַרְתָּ אֶל־חִזְקִיָּהוּ
כֹּה־אָמַר יְהֹוָה אֱלֹהֵי דָּוִד אָבִיךָ
שָׁמַעְתִּי אֶת־תְּפִלָּתֶךָ רָאִיתִי אֶת־

CHAPTER XXXVIII

HEZEKIAH's serious illness, his prayer to God, the Divine promise of a prolongation of his life and Hezekiah's thanksgiving. A parallel version with slight variations and the omission of Hezekiah's psalm of thanksgiving (verses 9–20) is in 2 Kings xx. 1-11.

1. *in those days.* Before the catastrophe that had befallen the Assyrian hosts (cf. verse 6). Traditionally Hezekiah's illness occurred three days before Sennacherib's fall. On the third day Hezekiah went up to the Temple to offer his prayer; and on the same day, which was the first day of Passover, Sennacherib's armies were miraculously destroyed while he himself fled to Nineveh (Rashi).

set thy house in order. lit. 'give instruction to thy house.' The phrase denotes the last instructions given by a dying man (Metsudath David).

and not live. i.e. thou shalt not live in the World to Come, since you have not married (Rashi).

2. *turned his face.* Since Hezekiah had no wife or children to instruct, he understood that he had sinned by not marrying and assuring the dynasty of permanence. He, therefore, turned his face to the wall to pray to God for forgiveness (Abarbanel).

to the wall. To concentrate his thoughts and commune alone with his Creator.

3. *with a whole heart.* This denotes his serving God in his heart, i.e. with fervent prayer (Kimchi, 2 Kings xx. 3).

and I did, etc. This denotes his serving God with his deeds (Kimchi, 2 Kings xx. 3).

5. *David thy father.* The Hebrew *ab,* 'father,' also signifies 'grandfather, ancestor.' The mention of David implies that Hezekiah's prayer was answered not for his own sake but for the merit of

tears; behold, I will add unto thy days fifteen years. 6. And I will deliver thee and this city out of the hand of the king of Assyria; and I will defend this city. 7. And this shall be the sign unto thee from the LORD, that the LORD will do this thing that He hath spoken: 8. behold, I will cause the shadow of the dial, which is gone down on the sun-dial of Ahaz, to return backward ten degrees.' So the sun returned ten degrees, by which degrees it was gone down.

9. The writing of Hezekiah king of Judah, when he had been sick, and was recovered of his sickness.

10. I said: In the noontide of my
  days I shall go,
  Even to the gates of the nether-
  world;
  I am deprived of the residue of
  my years.

11. I said: I shall not see the LORD,
  Even the LORD in the land of the
  living;

דִּמְעָתֶךָ הִנְנִי יוֹסִף עַל־יָמֶיךָ חֲמֵשׁ
6 עֶשְׂרֵה שָׁנָה: וּמִכַּף מֶלֶךְ־אַשּׁוּר
אַצִּילְךָ וְאֵת הָעִיר הַזֹּאת וְגַנּוֹתִי עַל־
7 הָעִיר הַזֹּאת: וְזֶה־לְּךָ הָאוֹת מֵאֵת
יְהֹוָה אֲשֶׁר יַעֲשֶׂה יְהֹוָה אֶת־הַדָּבָר
8 הַזֶּה אֲשֶׁר דִּבֵּר: הִנְנִי מֵשִׁיב אֶת־צֵל
הַמַּעֲלוֹת אֲשֶׁר יָרְדָה בְמַעֲלוֹת אָחָז
בַּשֶּׁמֶשׁ אֲחֹרַנִּית עֶשֶׂר מַעֲלוֹת וַתָּשָׁב
הַשֶּׁמֶשׁ עֶשֶׂר מַעֲלוֹת בַּמַּעֲלוֹת אֲשֶׁר
יָרָדָה:
9 מִכְתָּב לְחִזְקִיָּהוּ מֶלֶךְ־יְהוּדָה
10 בַּחֲלֹתוֹ וַיְחִי מֵחָלְיוֹ:
אֲנִי אָמַרְתִּי בִּדְמִי יָמַי אֵלֵכָה
בְּשַׁעֲרֵי שְׁאוֹל
פֻּקַּדְתִּי יֶתֶר שְׁנוֹתָי:
11 אָמַרְתִּי לֹא־אֶרְאֶה יָהּ
יָהּ בְּאֶרֶץ הַחַיִּים

his great ancestor (Rashi infra. xxxviii. 17).

fifteen years. His illness occurred in the fourteenth year of his reign (xxxvi. I) which lasted twenty-nine years (2 Kings xviii. 2).

6. *this city.* Jerusalem.

8. *dial.* lit. 'steps' or 'degrees.'

on the sun-dial of Ahaz. lit. 'on the steps of Ahaz in the sun' (Metsudath David).

9–20. A psalm by Hezekiah describing his suffering, fear and despair when he

was almost face to face with death, and his relief, joy and thanksgiving when his prayer for recovery was answered.

9. *the writing.* i.e. composition of thanksgiving (Targum, Rashi, Kimchi).

10. *I said.* I thought, I said to myself.

noontide. Most exegetes render: 'with the cutting off of my days'; i.e. with the shortening of my life, that I would not enjoy longevity, but die at a young age (Ibn Ezra, Kimchi, Abarbanel).

to the gates. lit. 'in the gates.' In Job xvii. 16 Sheol is described as having *bars.*

I shall behold man no more with
the inhabitants of the world.

12. My habitation is plucked up and
carried away from me
As a shepherd's tent;
I have rolled up like a weaver
my life;
He will cut me off from the
thrum;
From day even to night wilt
Thou make an end of me.

13. The more I make myself like
unto a lion until morning,
The more it breaketh all my
bones;
From day even to night wilt
Thou make an end of me.

14. Like a swallow or a crane, so do
I chatter,
I do moan as a dove;
Mine eyes fail with looking
upward.
O LORD, I am oppressed, be
Thou my surety.

15. What shall I say? He hath both
spoken unto me,

לֹא־אַבִּיט אָדָם
עוֹד עִם־יוֹשְׁבֵי חָדֶל׃
12 דּוֹרִי נִסַּע וְנִגְלָה מִנִּי
כְּאֹהֶל רֹעִי
קִפַּדְתִּי כָאֹרֵג חַיַּי
מִדַּלָּה יְבַצְּעֵנִי
מִיּוֹם עַד־לַיְלָה תַּשְׁלִימֵנִי׃
13 שִׁוִּיתִי עַד־בֹּקֶר כָּאֲרִי
כֵּן יְשַׁבֵּר כָּל־עַצְמוֹתָי
מִיּוֹם עַד־לַיְלָה תַּשְׁלִימֵנִי׃
14 כְּסוּס עָגוּר כֵּן אֲצַפְצֵף
אֶהְגֶּה כַּיּוֹנָה
דַּלּוּ עֵינַי לַמָּרוֹם
יְהוָה עָשְׁקָה־לִּי עָרְבֵנִי׃
15 מָה־אֲדַבֵּר וְאָמַר־לִי

v. 18. הכ׳ בקמץ

---

11. *world.* The word *chadel,* meaning
'cessation,' is taken as synonymous with
chaled, 'world' (Kimchi).

12. *my habitation.* The Hebrew *dor*
usually means 'generation,' but both
significations are derived from the same
root (Ibn Ezra, Kimchi).

carried away. lit. 'carried into exile' (Ibn
Ezra).

from the thrum. Jewish exegetes render:
'from illness.' Through his illness, God
would cut him off from the world (Ibn
Ezra, Kimchi, Abarbanel).

from day . . . end of me. Hezekiah, turning
in gratitude to God for his merciful
deliverance, recalls that his end seemed
so near, as if life were to be extinguished
from day even to night, i.e. in the briefest
span of time (Kimchi).

13. *like unto a lion.* Strong to endure
the agony of his pains (Rashi).

it breaketh. The subject is his illness
(Rashi).

14. *like a swallow,* etc. A description of
the invalid's moaning and sighing
(Kimchi).

or a crane. The word *or* is implied (Rashi,
Kimchi).

chatter. lit. 'twitter.'

with looking upward. lit. 'to the height,'
the abode of God (Metsudath David).

be Thou my surety. Death or the illness is
personified as a creditor demanding
retribution for the invalid's sins, and
God in His mercy and power to forgive
is asked, so to speak, to act as surety
(Ibn Ezra, Ibn Kaspi).

15. *what shall I say?* Hezekiah is unable
to express his feelings of gratitude
adequately (Rashi, Kimchi).

spoken. God promised recovery in the

And Himself hath done it;
I shall go softly all my years for
the bitterness of my soul.

16. O Lord, by these things men
live,
And altogether therein is the life
of my spirit;
Wherefore recover Thou me,
and make me to live.

17. Behold, for my peace I had
great bitterness;
But Thou hast in love to my soul
delivered it
From the pit of corruption;
For Thou hast cast all my sins
behind Thy back.

18. For the nether-world cannot
praise Thee,
Death cannot celebrate Thee;
They that go down into the pit
cannot hope for Thy truth.

19. The living, the living, he shall
praise Thee,
As I do this day;
The father to the children shall
make known Thy truth.

20. The LORD is ready to save me;

וְהוּא עָשָׂה
אֶדַּדֶּה כָל־שְׁנוֹתַי עַל־מַר נַפְשִׁי:
16 אֲדֹנָי עֲלֵיהֶם יִחְיוּ
וּלְכָל־בָּהֶן חַיֵּי רוּחִי
וְתַחֲלִימֵנִי וְהַחֲיֵנִי:
17 הִנֵּה לְשָׁלוֹם מַר־לִי מָר
וְאַתָּה חָשַׁקְתָּ נַפְשִׁי
מִשַּׁחַת בְּלִי
כִּי־הִשְׁלַכְתָּ אַחֲרֵי גֵוְךָ כָּל־חֲטָאָי:
18 כִּי־לֹא שְׁאוֹל תּוֹדֶךָּ
מָוֶת יְהַלְלֶךָּ
לֹא־יְשַׂבְּרוּ יוֹרְדֵי־בוֹר
אֶל־אֲמִתֶּךָ:
19 חַי חַי הוּא יוֹדֶךָ
כָּמוֹנִי הַיּוֹם
אָב לְבָנִים יוֹדִיעַ אֶל־אֲמִתֶּךָ:
20 יְהוָה לְהוֹשִׁיעֵנִי

message sent by Isaiah (Ibn Ezra,
Kimchi).

hath done it. He fulfilled His promise
(Rashi).

go softly. In meekness and humility
before God (Ibn Ezra).

for the bitterness. Which he had experienced during his illness (Kimchi).

16. *by these things.* Spoken of in the
preceding verse: the Divine promise
and fulfilment (Ibn Ezra).

17. *for my peace ... bitterness.* lit. 'for
peace bitter to me,' i.e. he had bitterness
instead of the peace he had expected
(Metsudath David).

but Thou ... it. lit. 'but Thou hast
desired my soul.'

corruption. Or, 'annihilation' (Ibn Ezra,
Kimchi).

cast ... back. Expressing complete
forgiveness (Kimchi).

18f. For the thought of these verses, cf.
Ps. cxv. 17f.

18. *death cannot.* The negative is
implied from the context (Ibn Ezra,
Kimchi).

Thy truth. God's fidelity in the fulfilment
of His promise (Rashi).

19. *as I do.* The verb is to be understood.

20. *is ready.* Not in the text and to be
implied. Better, 'God promised to save
me (Targum, Ibn Ezra, Kimchi).

Therefore we will sing songs to
the stringed instruments
All the days of our life in the
house of the LORD.
21. And Isaiah said: 'Let them take
a cake of figs, and lay it for a plaster
upon the boil, and he shall recover.'
22. And Hezekiah said: 'What is the
sign that I shall go up to the house
of the LORD?'

actually, before 163 [handwritten]

וּבִנְגִינוֹתַי נְנַגֵּן
כָּל־יְמֵי חַיֵּינוּ עַל־בֵּית יְהוָה:
21 וַיֹּאמֶר יְשַׁעְיָהוּ יִשְׂאוּ דְּבֶלֶת תְּאֵנִים
22 וְיִמְרְחוּ עַל־הַשְּׁחִין וְיֶחִי: וַיֹּאמֶר
חִזְקִיָּהוּ מָה אוֹת כִּי אֶעֱלֶה בֵּית
יְהוָה:

[handwritten marginal notes]

39   CHAPTER XXXIX   לט

1. At that time Merodach-baladan
the son of Baladan, king of Babylon,
sent a letter and a present to
Hezekiah; for he heard that he had

1 בָּעֵת הַהִיא שָׁלַח מְרֹאדַךְ בַּלְאֲדָן
בֶּן־בַּלְאֲדָן מֶלֶךְ־בָּבֶל סְפָרִים
וּמִנְחָה אֶל־חִזְקִיָּהוּ וַיִּשְׁמַע כִּי

we will sing . . . instruments. Or, 'we will
play with stringed music.' Better, 'we
will sing my songs.' My colleagues and I
will sing my compositions in the Temple
(Kimchi). Or, the Temple singers and I
will sing them (Ibn Ezra).

21f. Both verses describe events that
occurred before Hezekiah wrote the
psalm just concluded. Verse which had
no answer here is also found in 2 Kings
xx. 8 and is followed in verses 9–11 by
Isaiah's reply which corresponds, with a
number of variations, to verse 7f, of this
chapter.

21. *lay it for a plaster.* lit. 'rub, smear.'

22. *what is the sign . . .* LORD? This
question, as mentioned above, has no
answer here (Kimchi). Others render:
'what a good sign is this (the rapid cure)
that I will (also) go up to the house of
the Lord! (Rashi).

CHAPTER XXXIX

A BABYLONIAN embassy with gifts is
received by Hezekiah. Isaiah announces
to him the sack by Babylon of all that
he and his royal ancestors had accumulated and the subjection of his children

to the kings of that country. The corresponding passage, with variations, is 2
Kings xx. 12–19.

1. *at that time.* About 705-4 B.C.E. or,
according to others, about 714. According to Abarbanel, this took place after
Esarhaddon ascended the throne of
Assyria.

Merodach-baladan. Identified with the
Babylonian king Marduk-habal-iddina
who reigned from 721 to 709 B.C.E.
during the monarchy of the Assyrian
king Sargon who deposed him, and
again, for six months only, about 704 in
the reign of Sennacherib. As mentioned
above, Abarbanel maintains that he was
subordinate to Esarhaddon, who succeeded Sennacherib.

a letter. The Hebrew has the plural form
as in xxxvii. 14. Perhaps the plural is
indeed meant here, as appears from
Targum.

for he heard, etc. Some commentators
suggest that the real motive was to
secure Hezekiah's help in the protracted
struggle Merodach had carried on
against Sennacherib for the Babylonian
throne (Abarbanel).

been sick, and was recovered.
2. And Hezekiah was glad of them,
and showed them his treasure-
house, the silver, and the gold, and
the spices, and the precious oil, and
all the house of his armour, and all
that was found in his treasures;
there was nothing in his house, nor
in all his dominion, that Hezekiah
showed them not. 3. Then came
Isaiah the prophet unto king
Hezekiah, and said unto him: 'What
said these men? and from whence
came they unto thee?' And
Hezekiah said: 'They are come from
a far country unto me, even from
Babylon.' 4. Then said he: 'What
have they seen in thy house?'
And Hezekiah answered: 'All that
is in my house have they seen;
there is nothing among my treasures
that I have not shown them.'
5. Then said Isaiah to Hezekiah:
'Hear the word of the LORD of
hosts: 6. Behold, the days come,

חָלָה וַיֶּחֱזָק ׃ וַיִּשְׂמַח עֲלֵיהֶם חִזְקִיָּהוּ 2
וַיַּרְאֵם אֶת־בֵּית נְכֹתֹה אֶת־הַכֶּסֶף
וְאֶת־הַזָּהָב וְאֶת־הַבְּשָׂמִים וְאֵת |
הַשֶּׁמֶן הַטּוֹב וְאֵת כָּל־בֵּית כֵּלָיו
וְאֵת כָּל־אֲשֶׁר נִמְצָא בְּאוֹצְרֹתָיו
לֹא־הָיָה דָבָר אֲשֶׁר לֹא־הֶרְאָם
חִזְקִיָּהוּ בְּבֵיתוֹ וּבְכָל־מֶמְשַׁלְתּוֹ ׃
וַיָּבֹא יְשַׁעְיָהוּ הַנָּבִיא אֶל־הַמֶּלֶךְ 3
חִזְקִיָּהוּ וַיֹּאמֶר אֵלָיו מָה־אָמְרוּ |
הָאֲנָשִׁים הָאֵלֶּה וּמֵאַיִן יָבֹאוּ אֵלֶיךָ
וַיֹּאמֶר חִזְקִיָּהוּ מֵאֶרֶץ רְחוֹקָה בָּאוּ
אֵלַי מִבָּבֶל ׃ וַיֹּאמֶר מָה רָאוּ בְּבֵיתֶךָ 4
וַיֹּאמֶר חִזְקִיָּהוּ אֵת כָּל־אֲשֶׁר בְּבֵיתִי
רָאוּ לֹא־הָיָה דָבָר אֲשֶׁר לֹא־
הִרְאִיתִים בְּאוֹצְרֹתָי ׃ וַיֹּאמֶר 5
יְשַׁעְיָהוּ אֶל־חִזְקִיָּהוּ שְׁמַע דְּבַר־
יְהוָה צְבָאוֹת ׃ הִנֵּה יָמִים בָּאִים 6

2. *was glad.* On account both of the compliment paid to him by Merodach (Abarbanel) and the opportunity it afforded him of displaying his wealth to the Babylonian delegation (Malbim).

3. *from a far country.* Hezekiah answered the second of Isaiah's questions but evaded the first, apparently conscious of the prophet's objection to any coquetting with the Babylonian king. A Rabbinic tradition classes Hezekiah among three persons, the others being Cain and Balaam, whom God tested and found wanting. When the prophet came and asked him, *What said these*

men? and from whence came them unto thee? he should have replied, 'Thou art a prophet of the Lord to Whom all secrets are known, why then dost thou ask of me?' Instead he made a show of his greatness: *They are come from a far country unto me,* he boasted; 'they have travelled all that distance to pay honour to me and court my friendship.' On account of his arrogance and lack of faith in Providence, he was punished and the prophet forthwith delivered to him the ominous message (Rashi from Tanhuma).

5-7. Isaiah's announcement of Hezekiah's punishment.

183

that all that is in thy house, and that which thy fathers have laid up in store until this day, shall be carried to Babylon; nothing shall be left, saith the LORD. 7. And of thy sons that shall issue from thee, whom thou shalt beget, shall they take away; and they shall be officers in the palace of the king of Babylon.' 8. Then said Hezekiah unto Isaiah: 'Good is the word of the LORD which thou hast spoken.' He said moreover: 'If but there shall be peace and truth in my days.'

וְנִשָּׂא | כָּל־אֲשֶׁר בְּבֵיתֶךָ וַאֲשֶׁר
אָצְרוּ אֲבֹתֶיךָ עַד־הַיּוֹם הַזֶּה בָּבֶל
7 לֹא־יִוָּתֵר דָּבָר אָמַר יְהֹוָה: וּמִבָּנֶיךָ
אֲשֶׁר יֵצְאוּ מִמְּךָ אֲשֶׁר תּוֹלִיד יִקָּחוּ
וְהָיוּ סָרִיסִים בְּהֵיכַל מֶלֶךְ בָּבֶל:
8 וַיֹּאמֶר חִזְקִיָּהוּ אֶל־יְשַׁעְיָהוּ טוֹב
דְּבַר־יְהֹוָה אֲשֶׁר דִּבַּרְתָּ וַיֹּאמֶר כִּי
יִהְיֶה שָׁלוֹם וֶאֱמֶת בְּיָמָי:

40   CHAPTER XL

1. Comfort ye, comfort ye My
   people,
    Saith your God.
2. Bid Jerusalem take heart,
   And proclaim unto her,
   That her time of service is
    accomplished,

1 נַחֲמוּ נַחֲמוּ עַמִּי
   יֹאמַר אֱלֹהֵיכֶם:
2 דַּבְּרוּ עַל־לֵב יְרוּשָׁלַ͏ִם
   וְקִרְאוּ אֵלֶיהָ
   כִּי מָלְאָה צְבָאָהּ

v. 8. פתח באתנח   v. 1. הפטרת ואתחנן

---

8. *good is . . . spoke.* God is merciful in that He is postponing the calamity until after my death. Hezekiah acknowledges his error and submits to God's will, but sees in the deferment of the punishment evidence of His mercy to him (Rashi).

and truth. Or, 'steadfastness'; perhaps 'security.' Alternatively, 'the prophecy of peace will surely come true in my days' (Malbim, 2 Kings xx. 19).

CHAPTER XL

THE OMNIPOTENT GOD'S
DELIVERANCE OF ZION

A NEW section of the Book begins with this chapter; see the Introduction.

1f. A Divine instruction to the proph-
ets to comfort Israel and to announce the end of the Babylonian captivity (Rabbi Moshe Hakohen, quoted by Ibn Ezra, Ibn Kaspi).

1. *comfort ye.* The repetition indicates emphasis and occurs frequently in the latter section of the Book. According to the Targum the command is addressed to the prophets, and this view is adopted by most commentators (Rashi, Ibn Ezra, Kimchi, Metsudath David, Malbim).

2. *bid . . . heart.* lit. 'speak upon (or to) the heart of Jerusalem,' i.e. soothingly (Ibn Ezra). The city of Jerusalem is emblematic of the people of Israel (Ibn Ezra).

time of service. The sufferings in exile (Rashi, Ibn Ezra, Kimchi).

That her guilt is paid off;
That she hath received of the
  LORD's hand
Double for all her sins.
3. Hark! one calleth:
'Clear ye in the wilderness the
  way of the LORD,
Make plain in the desert
A highway for our God.
4. Every valley shall be lifted up,
And every mountain and hill
  shall be made low;
And the rugged shall be made
  level,
And the rough places a plain;
5. And the glory of the LORD shall
  be revealed,
And all flesh shall see it together;
For the mouth of the LORD hath
  spoken it.'
6. Hark! one saith: 'Proclaim!'

כִּי נִרְצָה עֲוֺנָהּ
כִּי לָקְחָה מִיַּד יְהֹוָה
כִּפְלַיִם בְּכָל־חַטֹּאתֶיהָ:
3 קוֹל קוֹרֵא
בַּמִּדְבָּר פַּנּוּ דֶּרֶךְ יְהֹוָה
יַשְּׁרוּ בָּעֲרָבָה
מְסִלָּה לֵאלֹהֵינוּ:
4 כָּל־גֶּיא יִנָּשֵׂא
וְכָל־הַר וְגִבְעָה יִשְׁפָּלוּ
וְהָיָה הֶעָקֹב לְמִישׁוֹר
וְהָרְכָסִים לְבִקְעָה:
5 וְנִגְלָה כְּבוֹד יְהֹוָה
וְרָאוּ כָל־בָּשָׂר יַחְדָּו
כִּי פִּי יְהֹוָה דִּבֵּר:
6 קוֹל אֹמֵר קְרָא

---

paid off. By her tribulation (Kimchi).

double. Of the penalties (Rashi).

3-5. A heavenly voice is heard calling for a highway to be prepared for the Lord Who is leading the exiles back to Zion. The language is figurative for the removal of all obstacles in the way of the deliverance (Kimchi).

3. *hark!* lit. 'a voice.'

in the wilderness. Between Babylon and Judea reminiscent of the wilderness the children of Israel traversed on their way from Egypt to the Promised Land (Malbim, with the exception that Malbim explains the chapter as referring to the final redemption, whereas we are following the commentators who explain it as referring to the return from Babylon).

4. *the rugged.* More probably the Hebrew *akob* is to be translated 'crooked road' (Kimchi). Its equivalent in Arabic denotes 'a steep mountain path.'

the rough places. The root from which the noun *rechasim* is derived occurs as a verb in Exod. xxviii. 28, xxxix. 21 with the meaning 'to bind' and signifies steep mountains, close together, very difficult to climb (Rashi).

5. *be revealed.* Or, 'shall reveal itself' by the fulfilment of His promise to Israel (Kimchi).

all flesh ... together. All mankind will recognize the working of Providence in the affairs of the world (Abarbanel).

6-8. The transience of human existence and enterprise is contrasted with the eternity of the word of God. Israel, therefore, fortified by Divine assurance need no longer be in fear of oppressors.

6. A heavenly voice is heard again (cf. verse 3).

And he saith: 'What shall I
proclaim?'
'All flesh is grass,
And all the goodliness thereof is
as the flower of the field;
7. The grass withereth, the flower
fadeth;
Because the breath of the LORD
bloweth upon it—
Surely the people is grass.
8. The grass withereth, the flower
fadeth;
But the word of our God shall
stand for ever.'
9. O thou that tellest good tidings
to Zion,
Get thee up into the high moun-
tain;
O thou that tellest good tidings to
Jerusalem,
Lift up thy voice with strength;
Lift it up, be not afraid;
Say unto the cities of Judah:
'Behold your God!'

וְאָמַר מָה אֶקְרָא
כָּל־הַבָּשָׂר חָצִיר
וְכָל־חַסְדּוֹ כְּצִיץ הַשָּׂדֶה:
7 יָבֵשׁ חָצִיר נָבֵל צִיץ
כִּי רוּחַ יְהֹוָה נָשְׁבָה בּוֹ
אָכֵן חָצִיר הָעָם:
8 יָבֵשׁ חָצִיר נָבֵל צִיץ
וּדְבַר אֱלֹהֵינוּ יָקוּם לְעוֹלָם:
9 עַל הַר־גָּבֹהַּ עֲלִי־לָךְ
מְבַשֶּׂרֶת צִיּוֹן
הָרִימִי בַכֹּחַ קוֹלֵךְ
מְבַשֶּׂרֶת יְרוּשָׁלָ͏ִם
הָרִימִי אַל־תִּירָאִי
אִמְרִי לְעָרֵי יְהוּדָה
הִנֵּה אֱלֹהֵיכֶם:

and he saith. Another supernatural voice
answers the call (Malbim).

all flesh, etc. The first voice responds
(Malbim).

goodliness. lit. 'loving-kindness.'

7. *the breath of the* LORD. A reference
probably to the sirocco or the hot east
wind which, when it blows in the spring,
blights the vegetation of Palestine (cf.
Ps. ciii. 16). Ibn Ezra renders: 'a wind of
the Lord,' i.e. a wind sent by the Lord.

the people. Mankind in general (Ibn
Ezra).

is grass. This is again a reference to the
frailty of Israel's captors when con-
fronted with the will of God (Metsudath
David, except that he explains it as an
allusion to the peoples accompanying
Gog and Magog).

8. *word of our God.* Spoken by His
prophets (Kimchi, Metsudath David).

stand for ever. Immutable; it is, as a commentator points out, the one permanent
factor in human history (Hirsch, Haf-
toroth).

9–11. A Divine voice requests the
prophets to announce from the mountain tops the advent of the Lord of hosts
leading the returning exiles like a
powerful and victorious warrior, but
also like a kind and gentle shepherd.

9. *thou that tellest . . . Jerusalem.* The
body of prophets is addressed collectively (Ibn Ezra).

Zion . . . Jerusalem. Both nouns are here
synonymous with the country or the
people or both since the tidings will
emanate from the main city of Judah
(Kimchi).

be not afraid. Of being contradicted or of
being hindered by an enemy (Metsudath
David).

10. Behold, the Lord GOD will come
as a Mighty One,
And His arm will rule for Him;
Behold, His reward is with
Him,
And His recompense before Him.
11. Even as a shepherd that feedeth
his flock,
That gathereth the lambs in his
arm,
And carrieth them in his bosom,
And gently leadeth those that
give suck.
12. Who hath measured the waters
in the hollow of his hand,
And meted out heaven with the
span,
And comprehended the dust of
the earth in a measure,
And weighed the mountains in
scales,
And the hills in a balance?

10 הִנֵּה אֲדֹנָי יֱהֹוִה בְּחָזָק יָבוֹא
וּזְרֹעוֹ מֹשְׁלָה לּוֹ
הִנֵּה שְׂכָרוֹ אִתּוֹ
וּפְעֻלָּתוֹ לְפָנָיו׃
11 כְּרֹעֶה עֶדְרוֹ יִרְעֶה
בִּזְרֹעוֹ יְקַבֵּץ טְלָאִים
וּבְחֵיקוֹ יִשָּׂא
עָלוֹת יְנַהֵל׃
12 מִי־מָדַד בְּשָׁעֳלוֹ מַיִם
וְשָׁמַיִם בַּזֶּרֶת תִּכֵּן
וְכָל בַּשָּׁלִשׁ עֲפַר הָאָרֶץ
וְשָׁקַל בַּפֶּלֶס הָרִים
וּגְבָעוֹת בְּמֹאזְנָיִם׃

10f. This may be a continuation of the Divine instruction to the prophets begun in the previous verse or Isaiah's own message.

10. *as a Mighty One.* Hebrew *bechazak,* lit. 'in (the character of) a strong one,' the *beth* of essence as in xxvi. 4 (Abarbanel).

arm. [Symbol of power.]

reward. For the righteous for their good deeds (Ibn Ezra, Kimchi, Kara).

recompense. Poetical parallel to *reward* (Metsudath David).

11. Though God, as has just been described, is a mighty warrior striking down Israel's oppressors, He is also like a good shepherd, gentle and considerate to His redeemed people.

carrieth them. The object is implied.

gently leadeth. The same expressive verb as in Ps. xxiii. 2.

12-20. The magnitude of God's

power and wisdom and His transcendent greatness are compared with the insignificance of the nations and the utter worthlessness of their manufactured gods.

12. The answer expected to the questions is that only God the Omnipotent is capable of measuring, meting and weighing such huge masses of the material world and of giving them their suitable shapes, forms and proportions.

comprehended. i.e. 'held.' Others translate 'measured,' the Hebrew *shalish* being the name of a dry measure. Cf. the following note (Ibn Ezra, Kimchi).

in a measure. Heb. *bashalish,* perhaps derived from *shalosh,* 'three,' but we are not familiar with the ancient measures. Cf. Ps. lxxx. 6, where it is used for 'a great measure' (Ibn Ezra). According to a traditional interpretation, the world was divided into three parts, one third wilderness, one third habitable land and one third seas and rivers (Rashi).

directed

13. Who hath meted out the spirit of
the LORD?
Or who was His counsellor that
he might instruct Him?

14. With whom took He counsel,
and who instructed Him,
And taught Him in the path of
right,
And taught Him knowledge,
And made Him to know the way
of discernment?

15. Behold, the nations are as a drop
of a bucket,
And are counted as the small
dust of the balance;
Behold, the isles are as a mote in
weight.

16. And Lebanon is not sufficient
fuel,
Nor the beasts thereof sufficient
for burnt-offerings.

17. All the nations are as nothing
before Him;
They are accounted by Him as
things of nought, and vanity.

18. To whom then will ye liken God?
Or what likeness will ye compare
unto Him?

13 מִֽי־תִכֵּ֞ן אֶת־ר֣וּחַ יְהֹוָ֗ה
וְאִ֥ישׁ עֲצָת֖וֹ יֽוֹדִיעֶֽנּוּ׃

14 אֶת־מִ֤י נוֹעַץ֙ וַיְבִינֵ֔הוּ
וַֽיְלַמְּדֵ֖הוּ בְּאֹ֣רַח מִשְׁפָּ֑ט
וַיְלַמְּדֵ֣הוּ דַ֔עַת
וְדֶ֥רֶךְ תְּבוּנ֖וֹת יוֹדִיעֶֽנּוּ׃

15 הֵ֤ן גּוֹיִם֙ כְּמַ֣ר מִדְּלִ֔י
וּכְשַׁ֥חַק מֹאזְנַ֖יִם נֶחְשָׁ֑בוּ
הֵ֥ן אִיִּ֖ים כַּדַּ֥ק יִטּֽוֹל׃

16 וּלְבָנ֕וֹן אֵ֥ין דֵּ֖י בָּעֵ֑ר
וְחַ֨יָּת֔וֹ אֵ֥ין דֵּ֖י עוֹלָֽה׃

17 כׇּל־הַגּוֹיִ֖ם כְּאַ֣יִן נֶגְדּ֑וֹ
מֵאֶ֥פֶס וָתֹ֖הוּ נֶחְשְׁבוּ־לֽוֹ׃

18 וְאֶל־מִ֖י תְּדַמְּי֣וּן אֵ֑ל
וּמַה־דְּמ֖וּת תַּעַ֥רְכוּ־לֽוֹ׃

tohu

primal chaos

13f. God's infinite wisdom. The questions are rhetorical and the obvious
answer is in the negative.

13. _meted out._ This follows Kara.
Others render: 'directed' (Ibn Ezra,
Kimchi).

spirit of the LORD. The Divine Will
(Kimchi, Metsudath David).

14. _path of right._ The order of Nature
(Kimchi).

discernment. Or, 'insight.'

15–17. The comparative nothingness
of the material world in the presence of
the Creator and His rule over its destinies.

15. _in weight._ Jewish exegetes suggest
'He takes up,' or 'casts away' (Ibn Ezra,
Kimchi). Others render: 'which is taken

up' (Rashi), or 'which flies away' (Targum).

16. Humanity cannot adequately pay
homage to the Ruler of the world. All
the forests of Lebanon, with their abundance of wood and beasts, will not
provide a sacrifice commensurate with
His greatness (Metsudath David).

fuel. lit. 'burning.'

17. _vanity._ Or, 'nonentity.' The
Hebrew _tohu_ signifies 'a waste,' 'chaos,'
'nothingness.'

18–20. The absurdity of representing
Deity by a metal or wooden man-made
image.

18. _to whom then will ye liken God?_
Because the nations compare God with
their own helpless deities, they deny
Him the power to deliver Israel
(Kimchi).

19. The image perchance, which the
    craftsman hath melted,
    And the goldsmith spread over
    with gold,
    The silversmith casting silver
    chains?
20. A holm-oak is set apart,
    He chooseth a tree that will not
    rot;
    He seeketh unto him a cunning
    craftsman
    To set up an image, that shall
    not be moved.
21. Know ye not? hear ye not?
    Hath it not been told you from
    the beginning?
    Have ye not understood the
    foundations of the earth?
22. It is He that sitteth above the
    circle of the earth,
    And the inhabitants thereof are
    as grasshoppers;

הַפֶּסֶל נָסַךְ חָרָשׁ 19
וְצֹרֵף בַּזָּהָב יְרַקְּעֶנּוּ
וּרְתֻקוֹת כֶּסֶף צוֹרֵף:
הַמְסֻכָּן תְּרוּמָה 20
עֵץ לֹא־יִרְקַב יִבְחָר
חָרָשׁ חָכָם יְבַקֶּשׁ־לוֹ
לְהָכִין פֶּסֶל לֹא יִמּוֹט:
הֲלוֹא תֵדְעוּ הֲלוֹא תִשְׁמָעוּ 21
הֲלוֹא הֻגַּד מֵרֹאשׁ לָכֶם
הֲלוֹא הֲבִינֹתֶם מוֹסְדוֹת הָאָרֶץ:
הַיֹּשֵׁב עַל־חוּג הָאָרֶץ 22
וְיֹשְׁבֶיהָ כַּחֲגָבִים

v. 21 קמץ בז"ק

19. A difficult verse the rendering of
which here is quite free. Its literal translation is: 'As for the image a workman
casts (it) and a refiner plates it with gold,
and the refiner casts for it chains of
silver (Kimchi, Metsudath David).

the image. Usually rendered elsewhere
'graven image.'

perchance, which. This is implied (Metsudath David).

goldsmith. The Hebrew for this word is
the same as that used later for silversmith.

casting. Implied from the cause which
otherwise has no predicate.

20. a holm-oak is set apart. This rendering is based on Targum, which has
been variously interpreted as 'laurel-
tree' (Kohut), or 'sapling' (Levita).
Other commentators render: 'he who is
too poor to set apart (gold or silver)'
(Kimchi): 'he who is expert in choosing
(wood)' (Rashi); 'the treasure of the
offering (Ibn Ezra).

he. The poorer worshipper who orders
an image of plain wood (Kimchi).

be moved. Or, 'slip, totter.'

21-26. The theme of verses 12-20 is
taken up again, and illustrations from
Nature and history re-emphasize the
omnipotence and magnificence of the
Creator and Ruler of heaven and earth.

21. Rhetorical questions demanding
an answer in the affirmative.

from the beginning. By age-old tradition
(Metsudath David).

understood . . . earth. That all creation
derives its existence from God alone
and that glory and worship are due to
Him only (Metsudath David).

22. circle of the earth. i.e. the heavens
which surround the earth like a circle
(Kimchi).

as grasshoppers. To those who are on
high, everything below appears very
small. This is an anthropomorphism
(Kimchi).

That stretcheth out the heavens
    as a curtain,
And spreadeth them out as a
    tent to dwell in;

23. That bringeth princes to no-
    thing;
He maketh the judges of the
    earth as a thing of nought.

24. Scarce are they planted,
Scarce are they sown,
Scarce hath their stock taken
    root in the earth;
When He bloweth upon them,
    they wither,
And the whirlwind taketh them
    away as stubble.

25. To whom then will ye liken Me,
    that I should be equal?
Saith the Holy One.

26. Lift up your eyes on high,
And see: who hath created these?
He that bringeth out their host
    by number,
He calleth them all by name;
By the greatness of His might,
    and for that He is strong in
    power,
Not one faileth.

הַנּוֹטֶה כַדֹּק שָׁמַיִם
וַיִּמְתָּחֵם כָּאֹהֶל לָשָׁבֶת׃
23 הַנּוֹתֵן רוֹזְנִים לְאָיִן
שֹׁפְטֵי אֶרֶץ כַּתֹּהוּ עָשָׂה׃
24 אַף בַּל־נִטָּעוּ
אַף בַּל־זֹרָעוּ
אַף בַּל־שֹׁרֵשׁ בָּאָרֶץ גִּזְעָם
וְגַם נָשַׁף בָּהֶם וַיִּבָשׁוּ
וּסְעָרָה כַּקַּשׁ תִּשָּׂאֵם׃
25 וְאֶל־מִי תְדַמְּיוּנִי וְאֶשְׁוֶה
יֹאמַר קָדוֹשׁ׃
26 שְׂאוּ־מָרוֹם עֵינֵיכֶם
וּרְאוּ מִי־בָרָא אֵלֶּה
הַמּוֹצִיא בְמִסְפָּר צְבָאָם
לְכֻלָּם בְּשֵׁם יִקְרָא
מֵרֹב אוֹנִים וְאַמִּיץ כֹּחַ
אִישׁ לֹא נֶעְדָּר׃

v. 26. עד כאן

a curtain. The Hebrew *dok* is derived from a root signifying 'thin, fine,' i.e. a curtain of fine material (Kimchi, Shorashim).

a tent. A poetic designation of the arch of heaven.

23f. Even the destinies of the greatest are in the hands of God, and their very existence, without His protection, is like stubble in a whirlwind.

23. *princes ... judges.* Both Hebrew terms embrace kings and governors as well as military and civil leaders (Kimchi, Shorashim; see also Introduction to Judges, Soncino ed.).

24. *scarce ... earth.* The Hebrew is

idiomatic, the literal meaning being 'also they were not planted,' etc.

when. lit. 'and also.' For the thought of this clause, cf. verse 7.

25. Cf. the similarity of idea and language in verse 18.

the Holy One. lit. 'holy,' the word being used as a proper noun (Metsudath David); again in Hab. iii. 3; Job vi. 10.

26. *these.* The stars (Kimchi).

calleth them all by name. Each star has been given a specific function (Kimchi).

not one faileth. To be called by name (Rashi).

judgment

27. Why sayest thou, O Jacob,
    And speakest, O Israel:
    'My way is hid from the LORD,
    And my right is passed over
    from my God'?
28. Hast thou not known? hast thou
    not heard
    That the everlasting God, the
    LORD,
    The Creator of the ends of the
    earth,
    Fainteth not, neither is weary?
    His discernment is past searching
    out.
29. He giveth power to the faint;
    And to him that hath no might
    He increaseth strength.
30. Even the youths shall faint and
    be weary,
    And the young men shall utterly
    fall;
31. But they that wait for the LORD
    shall renew their strength;

hope

27 לָמָּה תֹאמַר יַעֲקֹב
וּתְדַבֵּר יִשְׂרָאֵל
נִסְתְּרָה דַרְכִּי מֵיְהֹוָה
וּמֵאֱלֹהַי מִשְׁפָּטִי יַעֲבוֹר׃
28 הֲלוֹא יָדַעְתָּ אִם־לֹא שָׁמַעְתָּ
אֱלֹהֵי עוֹלָם ׀ יְהֹוָה
בּוֹרֵא קְצוֹת הָאָרֶץ
לֹא יִיעַף וְלֹא יִיגָע
אֵין חֵקֶר לִתְבוּנָתוֹ׃
29 נֹתֵן לַיָּעֵף כֹּחַ
וּלְאֵין אוֹנִים עָצְמָה יַרְבֶּה׃
30 וְיִעֲפוּ נְעָרִים וְיִגָעוּ
וּבַחוּרִים כָּשׁוֹל יִכָּשֵׁלוּ׃
31 וְקֹוֵי יְהֹוָה יַחֲלִיפוּ כֹחַ

v. 27. הפטרת לך לך

tikvet

27–31. The prophet, whose previous address may have been directed to mankind in general, now turns to Israel in particular and, pointing to God's omnipotence, assures them of His beneficence to those who trust in Him.

27. _Jacob ... Israel._ Synonymous for the entire people.

my way. i.e. my condition (Kimchi); according to others, my deeds in the service of God (Rashi).

is hid. Overlooked, unnoticed (Rashi).

my right. My rightful claim for consideration by God (Kimchi).

passed over. Ignored as though it did not exist (Kimchi).

28. _fainteth not,_ etc. If He does not respond to your plea and fails to intervene on your behalf, it is not due to His lack of power (Kimchi).

past searching out. Hence it is not for man to question His ways (Kimchi).

29. Far from being faint and weary, God grants power and strength to the _faint_ and _to him that hath no might_ if they are worthy of them (cf. verse 31) (Isaiah of Trani).

30f. Some construe the first of these verses as protasis and the second as apodosis rendering: 'and though youths faint and are weary and young men utterly fall (verse 30), yet they that wait,' etc. (verse 31) (Rashi, Kimchi).

30. _the young man._ Better, 'choice young men' (Kimchi, Shorashim).

31. _they that wait._ The subject is Israel (Rashi, Kimchi).

wait. Or, 'hope.'

shall renew their strength. Before their first strength is spent, God endows them with new strength (Ibn Ezra).

They shall mount up with wings
as eagles;
They shall run, and not be
weary;
They shall walk, and not faint.

יַעֲלוּ אֵבֶר כַּנְּשָׁרִים
יָרוּצוּ וְלֹא יִיגָעוּ
יֵלְכוּ וְלֹא יִיעָפוּ:

11/19

41   CHAPTER XLI

מא

1. Keep silence before Me, O
islands, *(to the nations)*
And let the peoples renew their
strength;
Let them draw near, then let
them speak;
Let us come near together to
judgment.

1 הַחֲרִישׁוּ אֵלַי אִיִּים
וּלְאֻמִּים יַחֲלִיפוּ כֹחַ
יִגְּשׁוּ אָז יְדַבֵּרוּ
יַחְדָּו לַמִּשְׁפָּט נִקְרָבָה:

mount up with wings. The verb can be parsed as kal or hiphil. If the latter, the sense would be 'cause feathers to grow' (Kimchi) or 'lift up wings'; since there is no preposition in the Hebrew, the phrase is best understood as the hiphil, as, indeed, all classical exegetes render it. Rabbi Saadiah writes that once in ten years the eagle flies up very high, until heated by the sun it throws itself into the sea for relief. Its feathers fall out then; new ones are grown, and its youth is renewed. But in the hundredth year it falls into the sea after its upward flight and dies (Kimchi).

they shall run. When they return to their land (Kimchi).

they shall walk. On the road (Kimchi). The sense of the entire verse appears to be that God will strengthen the Israelites, who hoped in Him, and bring them back to Jerusalem, but the mighty Babylonians will be weakened (Ibn Ezra).

CHAPTER XLI

GOD'S omniscience and omnipotence, the vanity of other gods, the Lord's loving care of Israel and the summons to Cyprus, the instrument for the liberation of His exalted people (Ibn Ezra).

1–4. The nations are invited to a judicial discussion in the presence of God Who is to prove His omnipotence and their utter impotence (Ibn Ezra).

1. *keep silence before Me.* lit. 'be silent (and listen) to Me.'

islands. The heathen inhabitants of the islands (Rashi, Kimchi).

renew their strength. To marshal their arguments in the discussion (Kimchi).

let them draw near. To hear My arguments (Kimchi).

judgment. A process at law (Kimchi).

2. Who hath raised up one from
the east, —
At whose steps victory attendeth?
He giveth nations before him,
And maketh him rule over kings;
His sword maketh them as the
dust,
His bow as the driven stubble.

3. He pursueth them, and passeth
on safely;
The way with his feet he treadeth
not.

4. Who hath wrought and done it?
He that called the generations
from the beginning.
I, the LORD, who am the first,
And with the last am the same.

5. The isles saw, and feared;
The ends of the earth trembled;
They drew near, and came.

6. They helped every one his
neighbour;
And every one said to his
brother:
'Be of good courage.'

² מִי הֵעִיר מִמִּזְרָח
צֶדֶק יִקְרָאֵהוּ לְרַגְלוֹ
יִתֵּן לְפָנָיו גּוֹיִם
וּמְלָכִים יַרְדְּ
יִתֵּן כֶּעָפָר חַרְבּוֹ
כְּקַשׁ נִדָּף קַשְׁתּוֹ:
³ יִרְדְּפֵם יַעֲבוֹר שָׁלוֹם
אֹרַח בְּרַגְלָיו לֹא יָבוֹא:
⁴ מִי־פָעַל וְעָשָׂה
קֹרֵא הַדֹּרוֹת מֵרֹאשׁ
אֲנִי יְהֹוָה רִאשׁוֹן
וְאֶת־אַחֲרֹנִים אֲנִי־הוּא:
⁵ רָאוּ אִיִּים וְיִירָאוּ
קְצוֹת הָאָרֶץ יֶחֱרָדוּ
קָרְבוּ וַיֶּאֱתָיוּן:
⁶ אִישׁ אֶת־רֵעֵהוּ יַעֲזֹרוּ
וּלְאָחִיו יֹאמַר חֲזָק:

2. *raised up one.* viz. Cyrus. The Targum and Jewish commentators understand it of the patriarch Abraham, but this is less appropriate to the context (Ibn Ezra).

from the east. Elam was northeast of Babylon (Ibn Ezra).

victory. lit. 'righteousness,' here with the sense of 'vindication of the right.'

attendeth. Shall meet him, or, 'shall call him wherever he goes' (Ibn Ezra).

3. *he pursues them.* He pursues the kings (Ibn Ezra).

the way . . . treadeth not. His victorious march is so rapid that his feet do not seem to touch the ground (Ibn Ezra).

4. *who hath wrought,* etc. [Who is responsible for Cyrus' spectacular victories?]

called . . . beginning. Determined their destinies and summoned each at the predestined historical time (Ibn Ezra).

5-7. The nations tremble and run for protection to their newly manufactured gods.

5. *the isles.* See on *islands* in verse 1.

and came. To take council how to stop Cyrus' triumphant advance (Kara).

6. The idol-worshippers try in vain to seek mutual help by intensifying their worship of their idols (Ibn Ezra).

7. So the carpenter encouraged the goldsmith,
And he that smootheth with the hammer him that smiteth the anvil,
Saying of the soldering: 'It is good';
And he fastened it with nails, that it should not be moved.

8. But thou, Israel, My servant,
Jacob whom I have chosen,
The seed of Abraham My friend;

9. Thou whom I have taken hold of from the ends of the earth,
And called thee from the uttermost parts thereof,
And said unto thee: 'Thou art My servant,
I have chosen thee and not cast thee away';

10. Fear thou not, for I am with thee,
Be not dismayed, for I am thy God;
I strengthen thee, yea, I help thee;
Yea, I uphold thee with My victorious right hand.

11. Behold, all they that were incensed against thee
Shall be ashamed and confounded;

וַיְחַזֵּק חָרָשׁ אֶת־צֹרֵף 7
מַחֲלִיק פַּטִּישׁ אֶת־הוֹלֶם פָּעַם
אֹמֵר לַדֶּבֶק טוֹב הוּא
וַיְחַזְּקֵהוּ בְמַסְמְרִים לֹא יִמּוֹט׃
וְאַתָּה יִשְׂרָאֵל עַבְדִּי 8
יַעֲקֹב אֲשֶׁר בְּחַרְתִּיךָ
זֶרַע אַבְרָהָם אֹהֲבִי׃
אֲשֶׁר הֶחֱזַקְתִּיךָ מִקְצוֹת הָאָרֶץ 9
וּמֵאֲצִילֶיהָ קְרָאתִיךָ
וָאֹמַר לְךָ עַבְדִּי־אַתָּה
בְּחַרְתִּיךָ וְלֹא מְאַסְתִּיךָ׃
אַל־תִּירָא כִּי עִמְּךָ־אָנִי 10
אַל־תִּשְׁתָּע כִּי־אֲנִי אֱלֹהֶיךָ
אִמַּצְתִּיךָ אַף־עֲזַרְתִּיךָ
אַף־תְּמַכְתִּיךָ בִּימִין צִדְקִי׃
הֵן יֵבֹשׁוּ וְיִכָּלְמוּ 11
כֹּל הַנֶּחֱרִים בָּךְ

v. 7. כ״ז ל״ל

7. The craftsmen engaged in the production of the images encourage one another.

that smiteth the anvil. The Targum has 'that striketh with the mallet.'

8–16. Having described the consternation and impotence of the idol-worshippers, the prophet, speaking in the name of God, addresses Israel, God's servant, assuring him of Divine care and protection and announcing the crushing defeat of his enemies.

8. God is speaking through his prophet.

Israel . . . Jacob. Both names are synonymous for the entire nation.

Abraham My friend. Better, 'who loved Me.' He loved Me and clung to Me, and abandoned the idolators (Kimchi). So again in 2 Chron. xx. 7.

9. *ends of the earth.* The reference is either to the scattered exiles (Kimchi) or to the patriarch Abraham, who came from the distant Ur of the Chaldees, as symbolizing the nation (Rashi).

10. *be not dismayed.* lit. 'do not turn around' in fear (Metsudath Zion).

victorious. lit. 'the right hand of My righteousness'; see on verse 2.

11–13. Confusion and annihilation of Israel's enemies. God stands behind His people to sustain them.

11. *incensed against.* lit. 'burned by,' roused to anger by (Metsudath Zion).

They that strove with thee
Shall be as nothing, and shall perish.

12. Thou shalt seek them, and shalt not find them,
Even them that contended with thee;
They that warred against thee
Shall be as nothing, and as a thing of nought.

13. For I the LORD thy God
Hold thy right hand,
Who say unto thee: 'Fear not, I help thee.'

14. Fear not, thou worm Jacob,
And ye men of Israel;
I help thee, saith the LORD,
And Thy Redeemer, the Holy One of Israel.

15. Behold, I make thee a new threshing-sledge
Having sharp teeth;
Thou shalt thresh the mountains, and beat them small,

יִהְיוּ כְאַיִן וְיֹאבְדוּ
אַנְשֵׁי רִיבֶךָ ׃
12 תְּבַקְשֵׁם וְלֹא תִמְצָאֵם
אַנְשֵׁי מַצֻּתֶךָ
יִהְיוּ כְאַיִן וּכְאֶפֶס
אַנְשֵׁי מִלְחַמְתֶּךָ ׃
13 כִּי אֲנִי יְהֹוָה אֱלֹהֶיךָ
מַחֲזִיק יְמִינֶךָ
הָאֹמֵר לְךָ אַל־תִּירָא
אֲנִי עֲזַרְתִּיךָ ׃
14 אַל־תִּירְאִי תּוֹלַעַת יַעֲקֹב
מְתֵי יִשְׂרָאֵל
אֲנִי עֲזַרְתִּיךְ נְאֻם־יְהֹוָה
וְגֹאֲלֵךְ קְדוֹשׁ יִשְׂרָאֵל ׃
15 הִנֵּה שַׂמְתִּיךְ לְמוֹרַג חָרוּץ חָדָשׁ
בַּעַל פִּיפִיּוֹת
תָּדוּשׁ הָרִים וְתָדֹק

13. *hold thy right hand.* To support and sustain (Metsudath David).

14–16. Israel is again bidden, as in verse 10, not to fear and a new reason is added. Not only is God his support, but Israel has an inherent spiritual strength and power of resistance to his enemies as the threshing-sledge to the corn.

14. *worm.* A symbol of weakness, meekness and humility. The worm crawling upon the ground is at the mercy of every passer-by (cf. Ps. xxii. 7) (Abarbanel).

Redeemer. The Hebrew *goël* is a technical term applied to the nearest relative whose duties included the redemption or buying back of the kinsman who sold himself, or his sold property or, if killed, the avenging of his blood by slaying the murderer. It is possibly in this sense applied to God, the Redeemer and Avenger of His people Israel (Abraham Azulai).

15. *having sharp teeth.* lit. 'possessor of mouths.' The literal rendering is: 'a new grooved threshing instrument having teeth' (Rashi, Metsudath Zion).

mountains . . . hills. These represent Israel's formidable enemies (Rashi, Kimchi). According to others, they symbolize the mighty worldly forces that obstruct the development and spread of the moral and spiritual ideas which Israel upholds (Hirsch).

And shalt make the hills as chaff.

16. Thou shalt fan them, and the
wind shall carry them away,
And the whirlwind shall scatter
them;
And thou shalt rejoice in the
LORD,
Thou shalt glory in the Holy
One of Israel.

17. The poor and needy seek water
and there is none,
And their tongue faileth for
thirst;
I the LORD will answer them,
I the God of Israel will not
forsake them.

18. I will open rivers on the high
hills,
And fountains in the midst of
the valleys;
I will make the wilderness a pool
of water,
And the dry land springs of
water.

19. I will plant in the wilderness the
cedar, the acacia-tree,
And the myrtle, and the oil-tree;

וּגְבָעוֹת כַּמֹּץ תָּשִׂים׃

16 תִּזְרֵם וְרוּחַ תִּשָּׂאֵם
וּסְעָרָה תָּפִיץ אֹתָם
וְאַתָּה תָּגִיל בַּיהוָה
בִּקְדוֹשׁ יִשְׂרָאֵל תִּתְהַלָּל׃

17 הָעֲנִיִּים וְהָאֶבְיוֹנִים
מְבַקְשִׁים מַיִם וָאַיִן
לְשׁוֹנָם בַּצָּמָא נָשָׁתָּה
אֲנִי יְהוָה אֶעֱנֵם
אֱלֹהֵי יִשְׂרָאֵל לֹא אֶעֶזְבֵם׃

18 אֶפְתַּח עַל־שְׁפָיִים נְהָרוֹת
וּבְתוֹךְ בְּקָעוֹת מַעְיָנוֹת
אָשִׂים מִדְבָּר לַאֲגַם־מַיִם
וְאֶרֶץ צִיָּה לְמוֹצָאֵי מָיִם׃

19 אֶתֵּן בַּמִּדְבָּר אֶרֶז שִׁטָּה
וַהֲדַס וְעֵץ שָׁמֶן

v. 16. עד כאן

---

16. The verse continues the agricultural figure of the preceding. Crushed to powder and reduced to chaff, the enemies will be carried off and scattered by the winds.

17-20. The present distressing condition of Israel in exile and the promise of a bright future. The text may be understood literally or figuratively.

17. *the poor.* Or, 'the afflicted.'

faileth for thirst. Or, 'is parched with thirst' (Rashi).

I the God. The pronoun is implied.

18. *springs of water.* Or, 'watercourses.' The root meaning of the Hebrew is 'going out,' 'issuing.' For the language of the second half of the verse, cf. Ps. cvii. 33.

19. *I will plant.* lit. 'I will give' or 'place.'

the oil-tree. This is not the olive but the pine (Kimchi).

I will set in the desert the cypress, the plane-tree, and the larch together;

20. That they may see, and know,
And consider, and understand together,
That the hand of the LORD hath done this,
And the Holy One of Israel hath created it.

21. Produce your cause, saith the LORD;
Bring forth your reasons, saith the King of Jacob.

22. Let them bring them forth, and declare unto us
The things that shall happen;
The former things, what are they?
Declare ye, that we may consider,
And know the end of them;
Or announce to us things to come.

23. Declare the things that are to come hereafter,
That we may know that ye are gods;
Yea, do good, or do evil,

אָשִׂים בָּעֲרָבָה
בְּרוֹשׁ תִּדְהָר וּתְאַשּׁוּר יַחְדָּו׃
20 לְמַעַן יִרְאוּ וְיֵדְעוּ
וְיָשִׂימוּ וְיַשְׂכִּילוּ יַחְדָּו
כִּי יַד־יְהוָה עָשְׂתָה זֹּאת
וּקְדוֹשׁ יִשְׂרָאֵל בְּרָאָהּ׃
21 קָרְבוּ רִיבְכֶם יֹאמַר יְהוָה
הַגִּישׁוּ עֲצֻמוֹתֵיכֶם
יֹאמַר מֶלֶךְ יַעֲקֹב׃
22 יַגִּישׁוּ וְיַגִּידוּ לָנוּ
אֵת אֲשֶׁר תִּקְרֶינָה
הָרִאשֹׁנוֹת ׀ מָה הֵנָּה
הַגִּידוּ וְנָשִׂימָה לִבֵּנוּ
וְנֵדְעָה אַחֲרִיתָן
אוֹ הַבָּאוֹת הַשְׁמִיעֻנוּ׃
23 הַגִּידוּ הָאֹתִיּוֹת לְאָחוֹר
וְנֵדְעָה כִּי אֱלֹהִים אַתֶּם
אַף־תֵּיטִיבוּ וְתָרֵעוּ

---

the plane-tree. Or, 'elm,' 'fir.'

the larch. Others define as the box-tree (Kimchi).

20. The reason for the wonderful transformation depicted in the last two verses.

they. Israel and the other nations (Abarbanel).

21-24. The discussion of verses 1-4 between God and the heathen nations is not resumed, but the address is directed both to the worshippers (verses 21, 22a) and to their idols or false gods (verses 22b, 23).

21. *produce*. lit. 'bring near.'

your reasons. lit. 'your strong (points)' (Rashi).

King of Jacob. The name refers back to verse 8.

22. Ability to explain the events of the past and a foreknowledge of the future are characteristics of a Divine Being. Can the false gods substantiate a claim to such power?

bring them. The reasons spoken of in the preceding verse (Kimchi).

what are they? Their meaning and purpose (Malbim).

the end of them. Their issue (Malbim).

That we may be dismayed, and
  behold it together.

24. Behold, ye are nothing,
  And your work a thing of nought;
  An abomination is he that
  chooseth you.

25. I have roused up one from the
  north, and he is come,
  From the rising of the sun one
  that calleth upon My name;
  And he shall come upon rulers as
  upon mortar,
  And as the potter treadeth clay.

26. Who hath declared from the
  beginning, that we may know?
  And beforetime, that we may say
  that he is right?
  Yea, there is none that declareth,
  Yea, there is none that announceth,
  Yea, there is none that heareth
  your utterances.

27. A harbinger unto Zion will I
  give: 'Behold, behold them,'
  And to Jerusalem a messenger of
  good tidings.

28. And I look, but there is no man;
  Even among them, but there is
  no counsellor,
  That, when I ask of them, can
  give an answer.

וְנִשְׁתָּעֶה וְנִרְאֶ֣ה יַחְדָּֽו׃

24 הֵן־אַתֶּ֣ם מֵאַ֔יִן
וּפָעָלְכֶ֖ם מֵאָ֑פַע
תּוֹעֵבָ֖ה יִבְחַ֥ר בָּכֶֽם׃

25 הַעִיר֤וֹתִי מִצָּפוֹן֙ וַיַּ֔את
מִמִּזְרַח־שֶׁ֖מֶשׁ יִקְרָ֣א בִשְׁמִ֑י
וְיָבֹ֤א סְגָנִים֙ כְּמוֹ־חֹ֔מֶר
וּכְמ֥וֹ יוֹצֵ֖ר יִרְמָס־טִֽיט׃

26 מִֽי־הִגִּ֤יד מֵרֹאשׁ֙ וְנֵדָ֔עָה
וּמִלְּפָנִ֖ים וְנֹאמַ֣ר צַדִּ֑יק
אַ֣ף אֵין־מַגִּ֗יד
אַ֚ף אֵ֣ין מַשְׁמִ֔יעַ
אַ֥ף אֵין־שֹׁמֵ֖עַ אִמְרֵיכֶֽם׃

27 רִאשׁ֥וֹן לְצִיּ֖וֹן הִנֵּ֣ה הִנָּ֑ם
וְלִירוּשָׁלַ֖͏ִם מְבַשֵּׂ֥ר אֶתֵּֽן׃

28 וְאֵ֙רֶא֙ וְאֵ֣ין אִ֔ישׁ
וּמֵאֵ֖לֶּה וְאֵ֣ין יוֹעֵ֑ץ
וְאֶשְׁאָלֵ֖ם וְיָשִׁ֥יבוּ דָבָֽר׃

v. 23. v. 26. קמץ בז״ק וְנִרְאֶה ק׳

---

23. *be dismayed*. lit. 'gaze at one another' (in rivalry) (Targum).

24. *nothing*. lit. '(made) of nothing.'

chooseth you. For his worshipper (Rashi).

25–29. Cyrus' rise and call to his high office, which was foretold by God through His prophet, are adduced as examples of events which the false gods did not foresee.

25. *one*. King Cyrus (Rashi, Ibn Ezra).

the north. Persia which lay to the north-east of Palestine and Babylonia (Rashi, Ibn Ezra).

calleth ... name. Acknowledges the

Sovereignty of God (cf. Ezra i. 2) (Metsudath David).

come upon. The preposition is implied (Rashi, Kimchi).

rulers. Or, 'princes,' e.g. the king of Babylon and his court (Rashi).

26. *who*. Among the false gods (Kimchi).

there is none. Other than God.

27. *a harbinger*. lit. 'first' to bring the news (Kimchi).

28. *no man*. i.e. not one of the worshippers of the false gods (Rashi, Ibn Ezra, Kimchi).

29. Behold, all of them,
    Their works are vanity and
        nought;
    Their molten images are wind
        and confusion.

הֵן כֻּלָּם 29
אָוֶן אֶפֶס מַעֲשֵׂיהֶם
רוּחַ וָתֹהוּ נִסְכֵּיהֶם:

chaos

Cyrus or Israel?

42   CHAPTER XLII   מב

1. Behold My servant, whom I
       uphold;
   Mine elect, in whom My soul
       delighteth;
   I have put My spirit upon him,
   He shall make the right to go
       forth to the nations.

2. He shall not cry, nor lift up,
   Nor cause his voice to be heard
       in the street.

3. A bruised reed shall he not break,
   And the dimly burning wick
       shall he not quench;
   He shall make the right to go
       forth according to the truth.

4. He shall not fail nor be crushed,

הֵן עַבְדִּי אֶתְמָךְ־בּוֹ 1
בְּחִירִי רָצְתָה נַפְשִׁי
נָתַתִּי רוּחִי עָלָיו
מִשְׁפָּט לַגּוֹיִם יוֹצִיא:
לֹא יִצְעַק וְלֹא יִשָּׂא 2
וְלֹא־יַשְׁמִיעַ בַּחוּץ קוֹלוֹ:
קָנֶה רָצוּץ לֹא יִשְׁבּוֹר 3
וּפִשְׁתָּה כֵהָה לֹא יְכַבֶּנָּה
לֶאֱמֶת יוֹצִיא מִשְׁפָּט:
לֹא יִכְהֶה וְלֹא יָרוּץ 4

---

among them. The false gods (Metsudath David).

29. *their works.* Of the man-made idols (Ibn Ezra).

confusion. Hebrew *tohu*; see on xl. 17.

CHAPTER XLII

1–4. The prophet in the name of God describes some of the characteristics of His ideal servant. Quiet and unobtrusive, his spiritual influence would spread throughout the world.

1. *My servant.* Israel (the LXX has the reading: 'Jacob is My servant, I will help him; Israel is My chosen, My soul has accepted him'); but according to others the allusion is to Cyrus (so Saadya quoted by Ibn Ezra). The Jewish

commentators are divided between Israel (Rashi), the king Messiah (Kimchi) and the prophet himself (Ibn Ezra).

the right. Justice and peace (Kimchi).

2. *lift up.* His voice. He will be obeyed although he is gentle and undemonstrative in manner (Kimchi).

3. He will not hurt even the weakest, yet he will firmly insist on right and truth.

dimly burning. lit. 'dim' (Metsudath David).

4. His perseverance and persistency in the fulfilment of his mission.

fail. The Hebrew verb comes from the same root as that for *dimly* in the previous verse.

Till he have set the right in the
earth;
And the isles shall wait for his
teaching.

5. Thus saith God the LORD,
He that created the heavens, and
stretched them forth,
He that spread forth the earth
and that which cometh out of
it,
He that giveth breath unto the
people upon it,
And spirit to them that walk
therein:

6. I the LORD have called thee in
righteousness,
And have taken hold of thy hand,
And kept thee, and set thee for
a covenant of the people,
For a light of the nations;

7. To open the blind eyes,
To bring out the prisoners from
the dungeon,

עַד־יָשִׂים בָּאָרֶץ מִשְׁפָּט
וּלְתוֹרָתוֹ אִיִּים יְיַחֵלוּ:
5 כֹּה־אָמַר הָאֵל | יְהֹוָה
בּוֹרֵא הַשָּׁמַיִם וְנוֹטֵיהֶם
רֹקַע הָאָרֶץ וְצֶאֱצָאֶיהָ
נֹתֵן נְשָׁמָה לָעָם עָלֶיהָ
וְרוּחַ לַהֹלְכִים בָּהּ:
6 אֲנִי יְהֹוָה קְרָאתִיךָ בְצֶדֶק
וְאַחְזֵק בְּיָדֶךָ
וְאֶצָּרְךָ וְאֶתֶּנְךָ לִבְרִית עָם
לְאוֹר גּוֹיִם:
7 לִפְקֹחַ עֵינַיִם עִוְרוֹת
לְהוֹצִיא מִמַּסְגֵּר אַסִּיר

v. 5. הפטרת בראשית

5–9. The Divine promise to His servant of full and constant support in the
accomplishment of the mission entrusted to him.

spread forth. lit. 'beats out,' implying
extension as well as firmness.

breath. Of physical life (Rashi).

spirit. The Divine element in man
(Rashi).

6. *in righteousness.* According to God's
set purpose; alternatively in God's righteous purpose (Hirsch).

and have taken. lit. 'and will take.' This
and the following two verbs which are
imperfect are rendered freely as perfects. Jewish exegetes, however, render
it literally.

taken . . . hand. To give you power over
all your adversaries (Abarbanel, Metsudath David).

kept thee. This rendering assumes the
root to be *natsar* (Ibn Ezra, Kimchi);
others consider the root to be *yatsar* and
translate 'form thee' (Targum, Rashi).

covenant of the people. The communication of the ideals entrusted to Israel will
lead to a bond of unity or a covenant of
peace among the peoples of the earth
(Abarbanel).

light of the nations. Their moral and religious counsellor and guide (Kimchi).

7. The subject of the two verbs
appears to be the servant (Rashi, Ibn
Ezra, Kimchi, Abarbanel).

to open the blind eyes. Bringing them spiritual enlightenment (Rashi, Abarbanel).

bring . . . dungeon. Either from actual
captivity (Rashi, Ibn Ezra, Kimchi,
Abarbanel) or from moral enslavement
(Hirsch).

200

And them that sit in darkness
out of the prison-house.

8. I am the LORD, that is My name;
And My glory will I not give to
another,
Neither My praise to graven
images.

9. Behold, the former things are
come to pass,
And new things do I declare;
Before they spring forth I tell
you of them.

10. Sing unto the LORD a new song,
And His praise from the end of
the earth;
Ye that go down to the sea, and
all that is therein,
The isles, and the inhabitants
thereof.

11. Let the wilderness and the cities
thereof lift up their voice,

מִבֵּית כֶּלֶא יֹשְׁבֵי חֹשֶׁךְ׃

8 אֲנִי יְהוָה הוּא שְׁמִי
וּכְבוֹדִי לְאַחֵר לֹא־אֶתֵּן
וּתְהִלָּתִי לַפְּסִילִים׃

9 הָרִאשֹׁנוֹת הִנֵּה־בָאוּ
וַחֲדָשׁוֹת אֲנִי מַגִּיד
בְּטֶרֶם תִּצְמַחְנָה אַשְׁמִיעַ אֶתְכֶם׃

10 שִׁירוּ לַיהוָה שִׁיר חָדָשׁ
תְּהִלָּתוֹ מִקְצֵה הָאָרֶץ
יוֹרְדֵי הַיָּם וּמְלֹאוֹ
אִיִּים וְיֹשְׁבֵיהֶם׃

11 יִשְׂאוּ מִדְבָּר וְעָרָיו

8. *the* LORD ... *My name. Name* signifies lordship and might. I must prove
that I am the Lord, and therefore My
glory will I not give to another (Rashi).

My glory ... to another. I will not allow
the heathens to rule over My children,
lest they claim that their god is powerful
(Rashi).

9. As God fulfilled His former predictions, so will He bring His new ones to
realization.

the former things. My prediction to
Abraham of his children's servitude in
Egypt and ultimate redemption (Rashi).
My predictions about Sennacherib (cf.
xxvii. 6f.) (Kimchi).

new things. Liberations from the Babylonian exile (Rashi, Kimchi).

before ... of them. And their fulfilment is
as assured as that of *the former things*
(Kimchi).

10–12. The marvels of the *new things* of
which he spoke in the preceding verse
suggest to the prophet the *new song* in
which he invites all Nature to join. It is
'new' in the sense that the idol-
worshippers who are to participate in it
have never before paid such homage to
God (Abarbanel).

and His praise. The conjunction *and* is
not in the text.

from ... earth. Throughout all the earth
(Rashi, Ibn Ezra, Kimchi).

that go down to the sea. Seafarers (cf. Ps.
cvii. 23).

and all that is therein. lit. 'and its fullness.'

11. *cities thereof.* Those situated in the
oases (Kimchi).

their voice. Implied from the context
(Rashi, Kimchi).

The villages that Kedar doth
    inhabit;
Let the inhabitants of Sela exult,
Let them shout from the top of
    the mountains.

12. Let them give glory unto the
    LORD,
And declare His praise in the
    islands.

13. The LORD will go forth as a
    mighty man,
He will stir up jealousy like a
    man of war;
He will cry, yea, He will shout
    aloud,
He will prove Himself mighty
    against His enemies.

14. I have long time held My peace,
I have been still, and refrained
    Myself;
Now will I cry like a travailing
    woman,
Gasping and panting at once.

15. I will make waste mountains and
    hills,
And dry up all their herbs;
And I will make the rivers
    islands,
And will dry up the pools.

16. And I will bring the blind by a
    way that they knew not,

חֲצֵרִים תֵּשֵׁב קֵדָר
יָרֹנּוּ יֹשְׁבֵי סֶלַע
מֵרֹאשׁ הָרִים יִצְוָחוּ׃
12 יָשִׂימוּ לַיהוָה כָּבוֹד
וּתְהִלָּתוֹ בָּאִיִּים יַגִּידוּ׃
13 יְהוָה כַּגִּבּוֹר יֵצֵא
כְּאִישׁ מִלְחָמוֹת יָעִיר קִנְאָה
יָרִיעַ אַף־יַצְרִיחַ
עַל־אֹיְבָיו יִתְגַּבָּר׃
14 הֶחֱשֵׁיתִי מֵעוֹלָם
אַחֲרִישׁ אֶתְאַפָּק
כַּיּוֹלֵדָה אֶפְעֶה
אֶשֹּׁם וְאֶשְׁאַף יָחַד׃
15 אַחֲרִיב הָרִים וּגְבָעוֹת
וְכָל־עֶשְׂבָּם אוֹבִישׁ
וְשַׂמְתִּי נְהָרוֹת לָאִיִּים
וַאֲגַמִּים אוֹבִישׁ׃
16 וְהוֹלַכְתִּי עִוְרִים בְּדֶרֶךְ לֹא יָדָעוּ

v. 16. קמץ בד"ק

Kedar. A pastoral tribe of the desert
(Kimchi).

Sela. Possibly Petra in Edom. Jewish
exegetes, however, render it as a generic
term, 'the rock dwellers,' those who
dwell in towers built on rocks and
mountains (Kimchi); The resurrected
dead, who were lying under the rocks
(Targum, Rashi).

13. Gives the reason why even the
idolworshippers, the enemies of God,
must now recognize His greatness and
join His people in the *new song*.

as a mighty man. Better, 'as a warrior.'

jealousy. Better, 'zeal,' ardour in battle
(Kimchi).

cry ... shout. Give forth battle-cries
(Kimchi).

14-17. The speaker is God and the
expressions are obviously anthropo-
morphisms (Ibn Ezra, Kimchi).

14. *will I cry.* Against the injustice
done to Israel. God will no longer
tolerate the sufferings of His people and
the continued ruin of their country
(Kimchi).

at once. Refer to the two preceding
verbs; at one and the same time
(Kimchi).

16. The return of the exiles.

blind. Those who do not know the way
(Metsudath David).

In paths that they knew not will
  I lead them;
I will make darkness light before
  them,
And rugged places plain.
These things will I do,
And I will not leave them
  undone.
17. They shall be turned back,
  greatly ashamed,
That trust in graven images,
That say unto molten images:
'Ye are our gods.'
18. Hear, ye deaf,
And look, ye blind, that ye may
  see.
19. Who is blind, but My servant?
Or deaf, as My messenger that
  I send?
Who is blind as he that is whole-
  hearted,
And blind as the LORD's servant?
20. Seeing many things, thou ob-
  servest not;

בִּנְתִיבוֹת לֹא־יָדְעוּ אַדְרִיכֵם
אָשִׂים מַחְשָׁךְ לִפְנֵיהֶם לָאוֹר
וּמַעֲקַשִּׁים לְמִישׁוֹר
אֵלֶּה הַדְּבָרִים עֲשִׂיתִם
וְלֹא עֲזַבְתִּים:
17 נָסֹגוּ אָחוֹר יֵבֹשׁוּ בֹשֶׁת
הַבֹּטְחִים בַּפָּסֶל
הָאֹמְרִים לְמַסֵּכָה
אַתֶּם אֱלֹהֵינוּ:
18 הַחֵרְשִׁים שְׁמָעוּ
וְהַעִוְרִים הַבִּיטוּ לִרְאוֹת:
19 מִי עִוֵּר כִּי אִם־עַבְדִּי
וְחֵרֵשׁ כְּמַלְאָכִי אֶשְׁלָח
מִי עִוֵּר כִּמְשֻׁלָּם
וְעִוֵּר כְּעֶבֶד יְהֹוָה:
20 רָאֹית רַבּוֹת וְלֹא תִשְׁמֹר

v. 20. ראות ק'

---

darkness. The desert, the trackless stretch
through which lies the way to the homeland (Kimchi, Metsudath David).

these things will I do. Better, 'these are the
things I have determined to do' (Rashi,
Kimchi, Targum).

17. graven images ... molten images.
[The Hebrew singulars are to be understood as collective nouns.] God's vindication of Israel will confound idolaters
by the revelation of His power
(Malbim).

18–25. The present pitiable plight of
Israel, the servant of God, is due to his
shortsightedness and disobedience of
the Divine will. His sufferings are a discipline imposed by God to fit him for
his great moral work for the benefit of
mankind (Hirsch).

18. deaf ... blind. Figurative terms for
mental and spiritual obtuseness (Ibn
Ezra, Kimchi).

19f. God's servant and messenger, who
might well be expected to have open
eyes to see the wonders of God as
revealed in Nature and history and
open ears to hear His message, is just
the reverse. He is both blind and deaf
(Rashi).

Opening the ears, he heareth not.

21. The LORD was pleased, for His righteousness' sake,
    To make the teaching great and glorious.

22. But this is a people robbed and spoiled,
    They are all of them snared in holes,
    And they are hid in prison-houses;
    They are for a prey, and none delivereth,
    For a spoil, and none saith: 'Restore.'

23. Who among you will give ear to this?
    Who will hearken and hear for the time to come?

24. Who gave Jacob for a spoil, and Israel to the robbers?
    Did not the LORD?
    He against whom we have sinned,
    And in whose ways they would not walk,
    Neither were they obedient unto His law.

פְּקוֹחַ אָזְנַיִם וְלֹא יִשְׁמָע׃
21 יְהוָה חָפֵץ לְמַעַן צִדְקוֹ
יַגְדִּיל תּוֹרָה וְיַאְדִּיר׃
22 וְהוּא עַם־בָּזוּז וְשָׁסוּי
הָפֵחַ בַּחוּרִים כֻּלָּם
וּבְבָתֵּי כְלָאִים הָחְבָּאוּ
הָיוּ לָבַז וְאֵין מַצִּיל
מְשִׁסָּה וְאֵין־אֹמֵר הָשַׁב׃
23 מִי בָכֶם יַאֲזִין זֹאת
יַקְשִׁב וְיִשְׁמַע לְאָחוֹר׃
24 מִי־נָתַן לִמְשִׁסָּה יַעֲקֹב
וְיִשְׂרָאֵל לְבֹזְזִים
הֲלוֹא יְהוָה
זוּ חָטָאנוּ לוֹ
וְלֹא־אָבוּ בִדְרָכָיו הָלוֹךְ
וְלֹא שָׁמְעוּ בְּתוֹרָתוֹ׃

v. 21. למשיסה ק' v. 24. עד כאן

19. *wholehearted*. The meaning of the Hebrew is uncertain. Some of the renderings suggested are: 'rewarded' (Ibn Ezra), 'paid' (Rashi), 'perfect one' (Kimchi).

20. *righteousness' sake*. The meaning here is 'steadfastness,' 'purpose.' God acts in accordance with His predetermined plan (Hirsch).

to make . . . great. lit. 'He will make great.'

the teaching. The Torah, embracing Divine revelation and moral and religious instruction to Israel, who is to be the appointed messenger for propagating its truth to all mankind and thus render the Torah *great and glorious* (Hirsch).

22–25. The present tragic condition of Israel and an exhortation to contemplate its cause.

22. *but this*. viz. Israel (Rashi, Kimchi).

23. *to this*. To the questions and answers in the following two verses (Rashi).

who will . . . come. So that in the future Israel may abandon his disobedience and rebellion and live up to the Divine ideal set before him (Targum, Rashi, Kimchi).

24f. The cause of Israel's bitter plight.

24. *Jacob . . . Israel*. Both names are synonymous with that of the entire people.

we have sinned . . . they would not walk. The first person refers to the present

25. Therefore He poured upon him
    the fury of His anger,
    And the strength of battle;   *Israel*
    And it set him on fire round
    about, yet he knew not,
    And it burned him, yet he laid it
    not to heart.

כה וַיִּשְׁפֹּ֤ךְ עָלָיו֙ חֵמָ֣ה אַפּ֔וֹ
וֶעֱז֖וּז מִלְחָמָ֑ה
וַתְּלַהֲטֵ֤הוּ מִסָּבִיב֙ וְלֹ֣א יָדָ֔ע
וַתִּבְעַר־בּ֖וֹ וְלֹא־יָשִׂ֥ים עַל־לֵֽב׃

43   CHAPTER XLIII   מג

1. But now thus saith the LORD
   that created thee, O Jacob,
   And He that formed thee, O
   Israel:
   Fear not, for I have redeemed
   thee,
   I have called thee by thy name,
   thou art Mine.
2. When thou passest through the
   waters, I will be with thee,
   And through the rivers, they
   shall not overflow thee;
   When thou walkest through the
   fire, thou shalt not be burned,
   Neither shall the flame kindle
   upon thee.

א וְעַתָּ֞ה כֹּֽה־אָמַ֤ר יְהֹוָה֙ בֹּרַאֲךָ֣ יַעֲקֹ֔ב
וְיֹצֶרְךָ֖ יִשְׂרָאֵ֑ל
אַל־תִּירָא֙ כִּ֣י גְאַלְתִּ֔יךָ
קָרָ֥אתִי בְשִׁמְךָ֖ לִי־אָֽתָּה׃
ב כִּֽי־תַעֲבֹ֤ר בַּמַּ֙יִם֙ אִתְּךָ֣ אָ֔נִי
וּבַנְּהָר֖וֹת לֹ֣א יִשְׁטְפ֑וּךָ
כִּֽי־תֵלֵ֤ךְ בְּמוֹ־אֵשׁ֙ לֹ֣א תִכָּוֶ֔ה
וְלֶהָבָ֖ה לֹ֥א תִבְעַר־בָּֽךְ׃

קמץ בז״ק v. 25.

generation; the third person to its
ancestors (Rashi).

25. *strength.* i.e. violence.

yet he knew not. Did not realize the significance of what had happened to him.

laid it not to heart. To associate cause and
effect (Kimchi).

CHAPTER XLIII

1–8. The section is contrasted with
verses 18–25 of the previous chapter.
God, it is there declared, has subjected
Israel to humiliation and exile as a punishment for his sins. Here Israel is
assured that, despite all this, he is still
the beloved people of God, and that a
bright future is in store for him. Israel
will pass unscathed through fire and
water, mighty nations will take his place
in bondage and Israel's scattered chil-

dren will be gathered from the farthest
corners of the earth and brought back
to their homeland (Rashi, Metsudath
David).

1. *but now.* The phrase introduces the
contrast (see the previous note) (Rashi,
Metsudath David).

have redeemed . . . have called. These are
the prophetic perfects, expressing a
future action with absolute certainty as
if it had already taken place. The latter
verb indicates the creation of a special
relationship between God and Israel
and the latter's appointment to His service (Kimchi, Hirsch).

2. *waters . . . rivers . . . fire . . . flame.*
Metaphors for perilous situations and
conditions. Israel's history proves this
to be only too true (Kimchi).

burned. Or, 'scorched' (Kimchi).

3. For I am the LORD thy God,
   The Holy One of Israel, thy
   Saviour;
   I have given Egypt as thy
   ransom,
   Ethiopia and Seba for thee.
4. Since thou art precious in My
   sight, and honourable,
   And I have loved thee;
   Therefore will I give men for
   thee,
   And peoples for thy life.
5. Fear not, for I am with thee;
   I will bring thy seed from the
   east,
   And gather thee from the west;
6. I will say to the north: 'Give up,'
   And to the south: 'Keep not
   back,
   Bring My sons from far,
   And My daughters from the end
   of the earth;
7. Every one that is called by My
   name,
   And whom I have created for My
   glory,

3 כִּי אֲנִי יְהֹוָה אֱלֹהֶיךָ
קְדוֹשׁ יִשְׂרָאֵל מוֹשִׁיעֶךָ
נָתַתִּי כָפְרְךָ מִצְרַיִם
כּוּשׁ וּסְבָא תַּחְתֶּיךָ׃
4 מֵאֲשֶׁר יָקַרְתָּ בְעֵינַי נִכְבַּדְתָּ
וַאֲנִי אֲהַבְתִּיךָ
וְאֶתֵּן אָדָם תַּחְתֶּיךָ
וּלְאֻמִּים תַּחַת נַפְשֶׁךָ׃
5 אַל־תִּירָא כִּי־אִתְּךָ אָנִי
מִמִּזְרָח אָבִיא זַרְעֶךָ
וּמִמַּעֲרָב אֲקַבְּצֶךָּ׃
6 אֹמַר לַצָּפוֹן תֵּנִי
וּלְתֵימָן אַל־תִּכְלָאִי
הָבִיאִי בָנַי מֵרָחוֹק
וּבְנוֹתַי מִקְצֵה הָאָרֶץ׃
7 כֹּל הַנִּקְרָא בִשְׁמִי
וְלִכְבוֹדִי בְּרָאתִיו

---

3. *Egypt . . . for these.* The liberation of Israel from Babylon by Cyrus when he captured it, and the conquest of Egypt and Seba by his son Cambyses, are described by the prophet as interdependent and predestined events. Persia is compensated for the loss of the Israelite captives by its conquest of the three African peoples (Ibn Ezra).

Seba. In the north of Ethiopia between the White and Blue Nile.

4. *and honourable.* This follows Kimchi, Metsudath David, and Malbim. Targum, however, renders, in agreement with the Hebrew, 'art honourable.' There appears to be no need to insert a copula.

men . . . peoples. Corresponding to the African peoples named in the previous verse (Kimchi).

5-7. The regathering of the scattered exiles.

6. *My sons . . . daughters.* Israel as a people is God's child and the individual members of the nation are His sons and daughters (Kimchi, Ibn Ezra).

7. *called by My name.* All the righteous, who are called by My name (Rashi, Kimchi).

for My glory. Those who believe that God created them and created the world, were created for God's glory, since they believe in Him and teach others that He created, formed and made them (Kimchi).

I have formed him, yea, I have
made him.'

8. The blind people that have eyes
   shall be brought forth,
   And the deaf that have ears.
9. All the nations are gathered
   together,
   And the peoples are assembled;
   Who among them can declare
   this,
   And announce to us former
   things?
   Let them bring their witnesses,
   that they may be justified;
   And let them hear, and say: 'It
   is truth.'
10. Ye are My witnesses, saith the
    LORD,
    And My servant whom I have
    chosen;
    That ye may know and believe
    Me, and understand

יְצַרְתִּיו אַף־עֲשִׂיתִיו:

8 הוֹצִיא עַם־עִוֵּר וְעֵינַיִם יֵשׁ
וְחֵרְשִׁים וְאָזְנַיִם לָמוֹ:

9 כָּל־הַגּוֹיִם נִקְבְּצוּ יַחְדָּו
וְיֵאָסְפוּ לְאֻמִּים
מִי בָהֶם יַגִּיד זֹאת
וְרִאשֹׁנוֹת יַשְׁמִיעֻנוּ
יִתְּנוּ עֵדֵיהֶם וְיִצְדָּקוּ
וְיִשְׁמְעוּ וְיֹאמְרוּ אֱמֶת:

10 אַתֶּם עֵדַי נְאֻם־יְהֹוָה
וְעַבְדִּי אֲשֶׁר בָּחָרְתִּי
לְמַעַן תֵּדְעוּ וְתַאֲמִינוּ לִי וְתָבִינוּ

v. 9. קמץ בז"ק

I have . . . yes, I have. Created him from
dust, formed his body, and given him
his daily sustenance (Kimchi).

8-13. Israel and the other nations are
summoned to a judicial process before
God. The nations are challenged to
produce evidence of the power and
foreknowledge they claim for their
gods, and this they are unable to do.
God, thereupon, calls upon His servant
Israel, far though he is from perfection,
to testify his personal experience of
God's omnipotence and omniscience.

8. *blind . . . eyes.* Israel, who despite his
imperfections (*blind*), has seen (*eyes*) the
wonders of God.

he brought forth. From exile (Rashi,
Kimchi).

9. *among them.* The gods of the nations
represented at the tribunal by their followers (Rashi, Metsudath David).

can declare this. What the prophet of God
had predicted (Kimchi).

former things. The prediction relating to
past events. Let them prove, if they can,
that they too have predicted the events
as did His prophets (Rashi).

bring their witnesses. To testify in support
of their claim (Rashi).

may be justified. Vindicated, their claims
proved (Rashi, Ibn Ezra, Kimchi).

let them hear. Let their witnesses hear the
plea of the nations (Ibn Ezra).

10. The nations and their gods being
unable to prove their contention, God
calls upon Israel, who is described as *My
witnesses* and *My servant*, to bear testimony to the uniqueness of His Divinity,
that there neither was nor ever would be
a God like unto Him.

That I am He;
Before Me there was no God
formed,
Neither shall any be after Me.
11. I, even I, am the LORD;
And beside Me there is no
saviour. ~told~
12. I have declared, and I have
saved,
And I have announced,
And there was no strange god
among you;
Therefore ye are My witnesses,
saith the LORD, and I am God.
13. Yea, since the day was I am He,
And there is none that can
deliver out of My hand;
I will work, and who can reverse
it?
14. Thus saith the LORD, your
Redeemer,
The Holy One of Israel:
For your sake I have sent to
Babylon,
And I will bring down all of
~them as~ fugitives,

כִּי־אֲנִי הוּא
לְפָנַי לֹא־נוֹצַר אֵל
וְאַחֲרַי לֹא־יִהְיֶה:
11 אָנֹכִי אָנֹכִי יְהֹוָה
וְאֵין מִבַּלְעָדַי מוֹשִׁיעַ:
12 אָנֹכִי הִגַּדְתִּי וְהוֹשַׁעְתִּי
וְהִשְׁמַעְתִּי
וְאֵין בָּכֶם זָר
וְאַתֶּם עֵדַי נְאֻם־יְהֹוָה וַאֲנִי־אֵל:
13 גַּם־מִיּוֹם אֲנִי הוּא
וְאֵין מִיָּדִי מַצִּיל
אֶפְעַל וּמִי יְשִׁיבֶנָּה:
14 כֹּה־אָמַר יְהֹוָה
גֹּאַלְכֶם קְדוֹשׁ יִשְׂרָאֵל
לְמַעַנְכֶם שִׁלַּחְתִּי בָבֶלָה
וְהוֹרַדְתִּי בְרִיחִים כֻּלָּם

I am He. Always the same, ever was, is,
and will be (Isaiah of Trani).

12. *there was no strange god.* When God
had *declared . . . saved . . . and announced,*
since no other god was capable of doing
these things. The word *god* is not in the
text, but is to be understood (Rashi).

13. *since the day.* The first day of creation (Rashi, Isaiah of Trani). Others
translate: 'before the day' (Kimchi).

14-21. The overthrow of Babylon and
the restoration of Israel. These events
and the miraculous highway for the
returning exiles across the desert, with
its supplies of water, will far surpass the
marvels of the exodus from Egypt and

the former journey of the Israelites
through the wilderness (Ibn Ezra).

14. *Redeemer.* See on xii. 14.

I have sent. The Persian hosts, the conquerors of Babylon under Cyrus
(Kimchi).

bring . . . them. The defeated Babylonians
(Kimchi).

as fugitives. There is no *as* in the text.
Some explain the first consonant of
barichim as the preposotion 'in' and
assumes a noun *riach,* connected with
ruach (wind), with the meaning 'wind-
driven boats,' 'sailing vessels' (Kimchi,
Targum).

Even the Chaldeans, in the ships
of their shouting.

15. I am the LORD, your Holy One,
The Creator of Israel, your King.

16. Thus saith the LORD, who
maketh a way in the sea,
And a path in the mighty waters;

17. Who bringeth forth the chariot
and horse,
The army and the power—
They lie down together, they
shall not rise,
They are extinct, they are
quenched as a wick:

18. Remember ye not the former
things,
Neither consider the things of
old.

19. Behold, I will do a new thing;
Now shall it spring forth; shall
ye not know it?
I will even make a way in the
wilderness,
And rivers in the desert.

20. The beasts of the field shall
honour Me,
The jackals and the ostriches;

וְכַשְׂדִּים בָּאֳנִיּוֹת רִנָּתָם׃

15 אֲנִי יְהֹוָה קְדוֹשְׁכֶם
בּוֹרֵא יִשְׂרָאֵל מַלְכְּכֶם׃

16 כֹּה אָמַר יְהֹוָה הַנּוֹתֵן בַּיָּם דָּרֶךְ
וּבְמַיִם עַזִּים נְתִיבָה׃

17 הַמּוֹצִיא רֶכֶב־וָסוּס
חַיִל וְעִזּוּז
יַחְדָּו יִשְׁכְּבוּ בַּל־יָקוּמוּ
דָּעֲכוּ כַּפִּשְׁתָּה כָבוּ׃

18 אַל־תִּזְכְּרוּ רִאשֹׁנוֹת
וְקַדְמֹנִיּוֹת אַל־תִּתְבֹּנָנוּ׃

19 הִנְנִי עֹשֶׂה חֲדָשָׁה
עַתָּה תִצְמָח הֲלוֹא תֵדָעוּהָ
אַף אָשִׂים בַּמִּדְבָּר דֶּרֶךְ
בִּישִׁמוֹן נְהָרוֹת׃

20 תְּכַבְּדֵנִי חַיַּת הַשָּׂדֶה
תַּנִּים וּבְנוֹת יַעֲנָה

v. 19. קמץ בז״ק

ships of their shouting. The shouting may
describe the lamentations of the Babylonian captives while the ships were sailing down the Euphrates (Kimchi).
Others render 'ships of their rejoicing,'
i.e. ships that were formerly used as
pleasure boats (Abarbanel).

15. The verb am is not in the Hebrew
and may be omitted in translation, the
verse defining the subject of I have sent
in verse 14 (Metsudath David).

16f. An allusion to the Israelites'
crossing of the Red Sea and the destruction of Pharaoh's hosts (Rashi).

17. bringeth forth. To their undoing
(Rashi).

wick. lit. 'flax,' of which a wick is made.

18. former things . . . of old. The signs
and wonders of the exodus from Egypt,
marvellous as they were, will be eclipsed
by the new marvels that God will show
to His people (Kimchi).

19. shall ye not know it? The answer is,
'Of course ye shall.'

rivers in the desert. A greater miracle than
turning the Red Sea to dry land
(Kimchi).

20. the beasts . . . jackals . . . ostriches.
Which will also be able to enjoy the
benefits of the water-supplies (Ibn Ezra,
Kimchi).

Because I give waters in the
wilderness,
And rivers in the desert,
To give drink to My people,
Mine elect;

21. The people which I formed for
Myself,
That they might tell of My
praise.

22. Yet thou hast not called upon
Me, O Jacob,
Neither hast thou wearied thyself
about Me, O Israel.

23. Thou hast not brought Me the
small cattle of thy burnt-
offerings;
Neither hast thou honoured Me
with thy sacrifices.
I have not burdened thee with a
meal-offering,
Nor wearied thee with frankincense.

כִּי־נָתַ֤תִּי בַמִּדְבָּר֙ מַ֔יִם
נְהָר֖וֹת בִּישִׁימֹ֑ן
לְהַשְׁק֖וֹת עַמִּ֥י בְחִירִֽי׃

21 עַם־זוּ֙ יָצַ֣רְתִּי לִ֔י
תְּהִלָּתִ֖י יְסַפֵּֽרוּ׃

22 וְלֹא־אֹתִ֥י קָרָ֖אתָ יַעֲקֹ֑ב
כִּֽי־יָגַ֥עְתָּ בִּ֖י יִשְׂרָאֵֽל׃

23 לֹֽא־הֵבֵ֤יאתָ לִּי֙ שֵׂ֣ה עֹלֹתֶ֔יךָ
וּזְבָחֶ֖יךָ לֹ֣א כִבַּדְתָּ֑נִי
לֹ֤א הֶעֱבַדְתִּ֙יךָ֙ בְּמִנְחָ֔ה
וְלֹ֥א הוֹגַעְתִּ֖יךָ בִּלְבוֹנָֽה׃

v. 21. הפטרת ויקרא

21. *the people.* lit. 'this people,' *My
people, Mine elect* of the previous verse
(Ibn Ezra).

tell of My praise. For the miracles I will
perform them when I redeem them
from exile (Kimchi).

22–28. Israel is unworthy of God's
bounties. He did nothing to please Him
but, on the contrary, always burdened
Him with his sins. For His own sake,
however, He will forgive his sins and
overlook his iniquities (Abarbanel).

22. *yet thou.* The address is directed
towards the people as a whole. It does
not, of course, exclude the existence of a
faithful minority. The appellation,
Israel, however, denotes the elite. Even
they were not beyond reproach (Malbim).

neither. The force of the Hebrew *ki* is
here the same as *aph ki,* 'much less.'

wearied thyself. Troubled thyself; Israel
did not care for God's service and neglected the high duties He imposed upon
him (Kimchi, Isaiah of Trani).

23f. Being captive in Babylon, Israel
could not bring sacrifices to the Temple

in Jerusalem. The purport of the exhortation, therefore, cannot be blamed for
not doing the impossible, but rather to
contrast God's treatment of His people
with their behaviour towards Him.
Israel, being in a foreign land, is indeed
no longer expected to bring animals or
other material sacrifices to God's Temple. He is no longer, so to speak, *burdened* or *wearied* by God (verses 23, 24a).
Yet Israel has *burdened* God with his sins
and *wearied* Him with his iniquities
attuned his mind and heart to the true
service of God and acted in the spirit, if
not in the letter, of the prescribed sacrificial ritual (Ibn Ezra).

23. *small cattle.* lit. 'lamb,' though the
noun is something applied also to goats
(Cf. Gen. xxx. 32).

thy burnt-offering. Two such offerings,
one in the morning and the other in the
evening, had to be offered daily in the
Temple in addition to any offerings
which individuals might bring during
the day (See Lev. i, Num. xxviii. 1–8).

sacrifices. Peace-offerings (Ibn Ezra).

frankincense. One of the ingredients of a
meal-offering (cf. Lev. ii. 1).

24. Thou hast bought Me no sweet
cane with money,
Neither hast thou satisfied Me
with the fat of thy sacrifices;
But thou hast burdened Me with
thy sins,
Thou hast wearied Me with thine
iniquities.
25. I, even I, am He that blotteth
out thy transgressions for
Mine own sake;
And thy sins I will not remember.
26. Put Me in remembrance, let us
plead together;
Declare thou, that thou mayest
be justified.
27. Thy first father sinned,
And thine intercessors have
transgressed against Me.
28. Therefore I have profaned the
princes of the sanctuary,

כד לֹא־קָנִיתָ לִּי בַכֶּסֶף קָנֶה
וְחֵלֶב זְבָחֶיךָ לֹא הִרְוִיתָנִי
אַךְ הֶעֱבַדְתַּנִי בְּחַטֹּאותֶיךָ
הֹוגַעְתַּנִי בַּעֲוֹנֹתֶיךָ׃
כה אָנֹכִי אָנֹכִי הוּא מֹחֶה פְשָׁעֶיךָ לְמַעֲנִי
וְחַטֹּאתֶיךָ לֹא אֶזְכֹּר׃
כו הַזְכִּירֵנִי נִשָּׁפְטָה יָחַד
סַפֵּר אַתָּה לְמַעַן תִּצְדָּק׃
כז אָבִיךָ הָרִאשֹׁון חָטָא
וּמְלִיצֶיךָ פָּשְׁעוּ בִי׃
כח וַאֲחַלֵּל שָׂרֵי קֹדֶשׁ

מלא ר v. 24.

24. *sweet cane.* It was one of the spices
used in the preparation of the holy
anointing oil (cf. Exod. xxx. 23). In the
Hebrew, *kanitha* (thou has bought) and
kaneh (sweet cane) are a play on words.

the fat of thy sacrifices. The fat of a peace-
offering had to be burned on the altar,
though the rest of the animal's flesh
could be consumed by the owner and
his friends (cf. Lev. iii. 3, 9f., 14ff.).

25. *I, even I.* I am He Who blotted out
your transgressions in the past and I
will do so again now (Rashi, Kimchi).

for Mine own sake. For the glory of God's
name which would have been profaned
if His people's sins were not forgiven
(Ibn Ezra, Kimchi, Abarbanel).

not remember. I will forget and forgive
(Metsudath David).

26. *put Me in remembrance.* If thou
knowest anything in thy favour that I
have overlooked (Kimchi).

plead together. I am not accusing thee
without giving thee first an opportunity

freely to state thy case (Metsudath
David).

declare thou. State thy case first if that will
add force to it (Kimchi).

justified. In thy right.

27. *thy first father.* According to
Kimchi, this refers to Adam (Gen. iii. 6,
17ff.); according to Rashi, it refers to
Abraham (by doubting God's words,
Gen. xv. 8).

intercessors. lit. 'interpreters,' the teachers
and prophets, the spokesmen of the
people. Even these have transgressed
the word of the Lord, and much more
so the people they led (Kimchi, Abarbanel).

28. *I have profaned . . . have given.* lit. 'I
will profane . . . will give.' Indeed,
many exegetes interpret it as future
(Kimchi, Abarbanel).

princes of the sanctuary. The priests (cf. 1
Chron. xxiv. 5) (Ibn Ezra). This may
also refer to the Levites, who were in
charge of the sanctuary (Kimchi, Isaiah
of Trani).

And I have given Jacob to
condemnation,
And Israel to reviling.

וְאֶתְּנָה לַחֵרֶם יַעֲקֹב
וְיִשְׂרָאֵל לְגִדּוּפִים:

44   CHAPTER XLIV   מד

1. Yet now hear, O Jacob My
servant,
And Israel, whom I have chosen;
2. Thus saith the LORD that made
thee,
And formed thee from the womb,
who will help thee:
Fear not, O Jacob My servant,
And thou, Jeshurun, whom I
have chosen.
3. For I will pour water upon the
thirsty land,
And streams upon the dry
ground;
I will pour My spirit upon thy
seed,
And My blessing upon thine
offspring;

1 וְעַתָּה שְׁמַע יַעֲקֹב עַבְדִּי
וְיִשְׂרָאֵל בָּחַרְתִּי בוֹ:
2 כֹּה־אָמַר יְהוָה עֹשֶׂךָ
וְיֹצֶרְךָ מִבֶּטֶן יַעְזְרֶךָּ
אַל־תִּירָא עַבְדִּי יַעֲקֹב
וִישֻׁרוּן בָּחַרְתִּי בוֹ:
3 כִּי אֶצָּק־מַיִם עַל־צָמֵא
וְנֹזְלִים עַל־יַבָּשָׁה
אֶצֹּק רוּחִי עַל־זַרְעֶךָ
וּבִרְכָתִי עַל־צֶאֱצָאֶיךָ:

have given Jacob. Or, 'had to deliver
Jacob.'

to condemnation. Better, 'to destruction'
(Metsudath Zion), or 'to slaying' (Targum, Kimchi).

to reviling. Among the gentiles. This
verse refers to all generations of Jewish
exile, when the leaders, or 'intercessors'
are slain because of the sins of the
populace, but the Jewish people will
never be annihilated (Kimchi).

CHAPTER XLIV

1–5. The severity and gloom of the
preceding section are now mitigated by
a promise of future happiness and
rejuvenation. The Divine spirit will
descend like refreshing rain, and the
rising generations will awaken to an
understanding of the honour and dignity of belonging to God's people.

1. *yet now.* The phrase introduces a
contrast as in xliii. 1 (Ibn Ezra).

2. *that made thee.* Cf. Deut. xxxii. 6.

the womb. Metaphor for the time of the
nation's birth (Ibn Ezra).

Jeshurun. lit. 'the upright one.' It is a
poetic term of honour applied to Israel;
again in Deut. xxxii. 15, xxxiii. 5, 26
(Kimchi, Metsudath David).

3. The two halves of the verse present
a comparison: *As I will pour . . . dry
ground, so I will pour . . . offspring* (Rashi,
Ibn Ezra, Kimchi).

My spirit. The spirit of prophecy. The
prophet predicts the restoration of
prophecy after the return of the exiles.
This coincides with Joel's prophecy (iii.
1f.) (Kimchi, Abarbanel).

seed . . . offspring. Children . . . grandchildren (Targum).

<table>
<tr><td>

4. And they shall spring up among
the grass,
As willows by the watercourses.

5. One shall say: 'I am the LORD's';
And another shall call himself by
the name of Jacob;
And another shall subscribe with
his hand unto the LORD,
And surname himself by the
name of Israel.

6. Thus saith the LORD, the King
of Israel,
And his Redeemer the LORD of
hosts:
I am the first, and I am the last,
And beside Me there is no God.

7. And who, as I, can proclaim—
Let him declare it, and set it in
order for Me—
Since I appointed the ancient
people?
And the things that are coming,
and that shall come to pass,
let them declare.

</td><td dir="rtl">

4 וְצָמְחוּ בְּבֵין חָצִיר
כַּעֲרָבִים עַל־יִבְלֵי־מָיִם:
5 זֶה יֹאמַר לַיהוָה אָנִי
וְזֶה יִקְרָא בְשֵׁם־יַעֲקֹב
וְזֶה יִכְתֹּב יָדוֹ לַיהוָה
וּבְשֵׁם יִשְׂרָאֵל יְכַנֶּה:
6 כֹּה־אָמַר יְהוָה מֶלֶךְ־יִשְׂרָאֵל
וְגֹאֲלוֹ יְהוָה צְבָאוֹת
אֲנִי רִאשׁוֹן וַאֲנִי אַחֲרוֹן
וּמִבַּלְעָדַי אֵין אֱלֹהִים:
7 וּמִי־כָמוֹנִי יִקְרָא
וְיַגִּידֶהָ וְיַעְרְכֶהָ לִי
מִשּׂוּמִי עַם־עוֹלָם
וְאֹתִיּוֹת וַאֲשֶׁר תָּבֹאנָה יַגִּידוּ לָמוֹ:

</td></tr>
</table>

4. The regeneration, fertility and freshness, physical and moral, of the nation is described in metaphorical language.

5. The rising generations will publicly and proudly proclaim their association with Israel and their attachment to his God.

I am the LORD's. A declaration of faith and implicit obedience (Metsudath David).

call himself . . . Jacob. He will be proud of his people and of their sacred mission (Ibn Ezra).

subscribe with his hand. Make public acknowledgment of his belief (Abarbanel).

surname . . . Israel. The name 'Israelite' will be all-sufficient. It will represent to him the most honoured and dignified name, far surpassing all other titles (Kimchi).

6–23. God's incomparable power and greatness contrasted with the vanities and absurdities of idolatry.

6–8. God is eternal and Israel is His witness.

6. *first . . . last.* I was the first King and I will be the last King (Ibn Ezra).

beside . . . no God. It is a cardinal belief of Judaism that 'He is One, and there is no second to compare to Him' (cf. *Hebrew Prayer Book,* ed. Singer, p. 3).

7. Provides proof for the preceding verse.

proclaim. Predict the future (Kimchi).

let him . . . Me. This is a parenthesis.

the ancient people. I.e. the entire creation. Let him tell Me all that has transpired from the Creation until now (Kimchi).

let them declare. Just as I am predicting the return from exile, although the Temple has not yet been destroyed, you have not yet been exiled, nor has Cyrus even been born (Rashi).

8. Fear ye not, neither be afraid;
   Have I not announced unto thee
   of old, and declared it?
   And ye are My witnesses.
   Is there a God beside Me?
   Yea, there is no Rock; I know
   not any.
9. They that fashion a graven
   image are all of them vanity,
   And their delectable things shall
   not profit;
   And their own witnesses see not,
   nor know;
   That they may be ashamed.
10. Who hath fashioned a god, or
    molten an image
    That is profitable for nothing?
11. Behold, all the fellows thereof
    shall be ashamed;
    And the craftsmen skilled above
    men;
    Let them all be gathered to-
    gether, let them stand up;
    They shall fear, they shall be
    ashamed together.

אַל־תִּפְחֲדוּ וְאַל־תִּרְהוּ 8
הֲלֹא מֵאָז הִשְׁמַעְתִּיךָ וְהִגַּדְתִּי
וְאַתֶּם עֵדָי
הֲיֵשׁ אֱלוֹהַּ מִבַּלְעָדַי
וְאֵין צוּר בַּל־יָדָעְתִּי׃
יֹצְרֵי־פֶסֶל כֻּלָּם תֹּהוּ 9
וַחֲמוּדֵיהֶם בַּל־יוֹעִילוּ
וְעֵדֵיהֶם הֵמָּה בַּל־יִרְאוּ וּבַל־יֵדְעוּ
לְמַעַן יֵבֹשׁוּ׃
מִי־יָצַר אֵל וּפֶסֶל נָסָךְ 10
לְבִלְתִּי הוֹעִיל׃
הֵן כָּל־חֲבֵרָיו יֵבֹשׁוּ 11
וְחָרָשִׁים הֵמָּה מֵאָדָם
יִתְקַבְּצוּ כֻלָּם יַעֲמֹדוּ
יִפְחֲדוּ יֵבֹשׁוּ יָחַד׃

v. 9. נָקוּד עַל הַמֵּ׳

8. Israel need have no fear of the coming troubles if he but trusted in God
Who as he knows, had foretold these
events which He Himself is bringing
about and are entirely under His control (Ibn Ezra).

announced ... declared. The future
(Kimchi).

Rock. Fortress and shelter (Hirsch).

9–20. Mordant exposure of the futility
of idol-worship.

9–11. The usefulness of the idols and
the frailty of their makers.

9. *vanity.* Hebrew *tohu* (see on xl. 17).

delectable things. Their idols; lit. 'their
beloved ones' (Ibn Ezra, Kimchi).

shall not profit. Are useless (Metsudath
David).

their own witnesses. They who profess a
belief in them, their worshippers (Ibn

Ezra). [The noun may have been chosen
in contrast to verse 8 where Israel is
called the 'witness' to God.]

that they. The witnesses (Ibn Ezra).

may be ashamed. This testimony will cause
the worshippers (Targum, Rashi);
according to others, the association of
the idol-makers (Ibn Ezra, Kimchi).

skilled above men. This follows Ibn Kaspi,
the Hebrew being literally 'from man.'
Kimchi renders: 'they are but craftsmen
of men.' These manufacturers of a 'god'
are neither angels nor seraphim, but
plain mortal man. Kara renders: 'they
are but the work of craftsmen, the work
of men.' Alternatively, 'they are but
craftsmen, and they are but of men.'
Surely, their product is worthless
(Rashi).

let them all. Both worshippers and craftsmen (Metsudath David).

12. The smith maketh an axe, *[iron]*
And worketh in the coals, and
fashioneth it with hammers,
And worketh it with his strong
arm;
Yea, he is hungry, and his
strength faileth;
He drinketh no water, and is
faint.

13. The carpenter stretcheth out a
line;
He marketh it out with a pencil;
He fitteth it with planes,
And he marketh it out with the
compasses,
And maketh it after the figure of
a man,
According to the beauty of a *[glory]*
man, to dwell in the house.

14. He heweth him down cedars,
And taketh the ilex and the oak,

חָרַשׁ בַּרְזֶל מַעֲצָד 12
וּפָעַל בַּפֶּחָם וּבַמַּקָּבוֹת יִצְּרֵהוּ
וַיִּפְעָלֵהוּ בִּזְרוֹעַ כֹּחוֹ
גַּם־רָעֵב וְאֵין כֹּחַ
לֹא־שָׁתָה מַיִם וַיִּיעָף׃
חָרַשׁ עֵצִים נָטָה קָו 13
יְתָאֲרֵהוּ בַשֶּׂרֶד
יַעֲשֵׂהוּ בַּמַּקְצֻעוֹת
וּבַמְּחוּגָה יְתָאֲרֵהוּ
וַיַּעֲשֵׂהוּ כְּתַבְנִית אִישׁ
כְּתִפְאֶרֶת אָדָם לָשֶׁבֶת בָּיִת׃
לִכְרָת־לוֹ אֲרָזִים 14
וַיִּקַּח תִּרְזָה וְאַלּוֹן

12f. A detailed description of the
laborious process in the manufacture of
an idol.

12. *smith.* lit. 'craftsman (in) iron.' The
verb *maketh* is implied (Kimchi).

fashioneth it. The material of which the
idol is made (Rashi).

is hungry . . . is faint. If the manufacturer
of the idol is so frail and dependent,
what can be expected from the idol he
makes! (Rashi).

13. *carpenter.* lit. 'workman (in) wood.'

stretcheth out a line. To trace out on the
block the dimensions of the idol he is
making (Kimchi).

the beauty of a man. A traditional explanation is 'female form' (Targum, Rashi).
Perhaps the phrase is ironical: the
choice is made of the human figure as
the most beautiful of all creatures
(Malbim).

to dwell in the house. In a temple or
shrine, unable to move (Kimchi).

14-17. The materials for the manufacture of the idol and for the cooking
of its worshippers' meals come from the
same tree. What an origin for a god!

14. *he heweth.* lit. 'to hew.' Something
like 'he goeth' is to be understood
before 'to hew' (See Kimchi).

And strengtheneth for himself
   one among the trees of the
   forest;
He planteth a bay-tree, and the
   rain doth nourish it.
15. Then a man useth it for fuel;
   And he taketh thereof, and
   warmeth himself;
   Yea, he kindleth it, and baketh
   bread;
   Yea, he maketh a god, and
   worshippeth it;
He maketh it a graven image,
   and falleth down thereto.
16. He burneth the half thereof in
   the fire;
   With the half thereof he eateth
   flesh;
He roasteth roast, and is satisfied;
   Yea, he warmeth himself, and
   saith: 'Aha,
I am warm, I have seen the fire';
17. And the residue thereof he
   maketh a god, even his graven
   image;
He falleth down unto it and
   worshippeth, and prayeth unto
   it,
And saith: 'Deliver me, for thou
   art my god.'
18. They know not, neither do they
   understand;
For their eyes are bedaubed, that
   they cannot see,
And their hearts, that they
   cannot understand.

וַיֹּאמֶץ־לוֹ בַּעֲצֵי־יָ֫עַר
נָטַע אֹ֫רֶן וְגֶ֫שֶׁם יְגַדֵּל׃
15 וְהָיָה לְאָדָם לְבָעֵר
וַיִּקַּח מֵהֶם וַיָּ֫חָם
אַף־יַשִּׂיק וְאָ֫פָה לָ֫חֶם
אַף־יִפְעַל־אֵל וַיִּשְׁתָּ֫חוּ
עָשָׂ֫הוּ פֶ֫סֶל וַיִּסְגָּד־לָ֫מוֹ׃
16 חֶצְיוֹ שָׂרַף בְּמוֹ־אֵשׁ
עַל־חֶצְיוֹ בָּשָׂר יֹאכֵל
יִצְלֶה צָלִי וְיִשְׂבָּע
אַף־יָחֹם וְיֹאמַר הֶאָח
חַמּ֫וֹתִי רָאִ֫יתִי אוּר׃
17 וּשְׁאֵרִיתוֹ לְאֵל עָשָׂה לְפִסְלוֹ
יִסְגָּד־לוֹ וְיִשְׁתַּ֫חוּ וְיִתְפַּלֵּל אֵלָיו
וְיֹאמַר הַצִּילֵ֫נִי כִּי אֵלִי אָ֫תָּה׃
18 לֹא יָדְעוּ וְלֹא יָבִ֫ינוּ
כִּי טַח מֵרְאוֹת עֵינֵיהֶם
מֵהַשְׂכִּיל לִבֹּתָם׃

v. 14. גוֹן זְעִירָא   v. 15. קמץ בז"ק   v. 17. יתיר ר

---

strengtheneth . . . one. Other translations
are: 'chooseth for himself the best one,'
(Kimchi, Kara) 'caused it to grow strong
for himself among the trees of the
forest,' i.e. he carefully tended the
growth of the selected tree (Abarbanel).

15. useth it. Any of the trees (Metsudath David).

taketh thereof. lit. 'of them,' the trees
mentioned (Rashi).

and worshippeth it. He prostrated himself
before it (Kimchi).

falleth down thereto. The Aramaic equivalent to the first part of the verse (Ibn
Ezra).

18–20. The intellectual level of the
idolater is so low that he is quite incapable of applying the most rudimentary
principles of logic to his absurd conduct.

18. their eyes . . . understand. Figurative
for intellectual blindness, lack of
reasoning power (Hirsch).

19. And none considereth in his
   heart,
   Neither is there knowledge nor
   understanding to say:
   'I have burned the half of it in
   the fire;
   Yea, also I have baked bread
   upon the coals thereof;
   I have roasted flesh and eaten it;
   And shall I make the residue
   thereof an abomination?
   Shall I fall down to the stock of
   a tree?'
20. He striveth after ashes,
   A deceived heart hath turned
   him aside,
   That he cannot deliver his soul,
   nor say:
   'Is there not a lie in my right
   hand?'
21. Remember these things, O Jacob,
   And Israel, for thou art My
   servant;
   I have formed thee, thou art
   Mine own servant;
   O Israel, thou shouldest not
   forget Me.
22. I have blotted out, as a thick
   cloud, thy transgressions,

וְלֹא־יָשִׁיב אֶל־לִבּוֹ 19
וְלֹא דַעַת וְלֹא־תְבוּנָה לֵאמֹר
חֶצְיוֹ שָׂרַפְתִּי בְמוֹ־אֵשׁ
וְאַף אָפִיתִי עַל־גֶּחָלָיו לֶחֶם
אֶצְלֶה בָשָׂר וְאֹכֵל
וְיִתְרוֹ לְתוֹעֵבָה אֶעֱשֶׂה
לְבוּל עֵץ אֶסְגּוֹד׃
רֹעֶה אֵפֶר 20
לֵב הוּתַל הִטָּהוּ
וְלֹא־יַצִּיל אֶת־נַפְשׁוֹ וְלֹא יֹאמַר
הֲלוֹא־שֶׁקֶר בִּימִינִי׃
זְכָר־אֵלֶּה יַעֲקֹב 21
וְיִשְׂרָאֵל כִּי עַבְדִּי־אָתָּה
יְצַרְתִּיךָ עֶבֶד־לִי אַתָּה
יִשְׂרָאֵל לֹא תִנָּשֵׁנִי׃
מָחִיתִי כָעָב פְּשָׁעֶיךָ 22

19. *considereth it.* lit. 'bringeth back to';
he does not reflect.

an abomination. Shall I make it into
something God regards as an abomination? (Kimchi).

20. *striveth after.* Better, 'feedeth on.'
'To strive after, or feed on, ashes' means
to rely on anything that is in vain, useless or worthless (Kimchi).

turned him aside. Away from the path of
right and reason (Ibn Ezra, Kimchi).

say. To himself, think.

a lie. Hebrew *sheker,* 'false belief or trust'
(Metsudath David).

21f. Israel is reminded of his special
relationship to God Who alone can blot
out his sins and deliver him from his
sufferings.

thou shouldest not forget Me. Although
this translation agrees with some Jewish
commentators (e.g. Metsudath David),
the verb is passive in form; hence Ibn
Ezra and Kimchi, 'thou shalt not be forgotten of Me.' You remember Me and I
will remember you.

22. *as a thick cloud.* Which rapidly scat-
ters and vanishes before the sun or the
winds. Israel's sins, too, will vanish likewise as soon as he will return wholeheartedly to his God (Ibn Ezra,
Malbim).

And, as a cloud, thy sins;
Return unto Me, for I have
redeemed thee.

23. Sing, O ye heavens, for the LORD
hath done it;
Shout, ye lowest parts of the
earth;
Break forth into singing, ye
mountains,
O forest, and every tree therein;
For the LORD hath redeemed
Jacob,
And doth glorify Himself in
Israel.

24. Thus saith the LORD, thy Re-
deemer,
And He that formed thee from
the womb:
I am the LORD, that maketh all
things;
That stretched forth the heavens
alone;
That spread abroad the earth by
Myself;

25. That frustrateth the tokens of
the impostors,
And maketh diviners mad;
That turneth wise men backward,
And maketh their knowledge
foolish;

וְכֶעָנָ֖ן חַטֹּאותֶ֑יךָ
שׁוּבָ֥ה אֵלַ֖י כִּ֥י גְאַלְתִּֽיךָ׃

23 רָנּ֨וּ שָׁמַ֜יִם כִּֽי־עָשָׂ֣ה יְהֹוָ֗ה
הָרִ֙יעוּ֙ תַּחְתִּיּ֣וֹת אָ֔רֶץ
פִּצְח֤וּ הָרִים֙ רִנָּ֔ה
יַ֖עַר וְכׇל־עֵ֣ץ בּ֑וֹ
כִּֽי־גָאַ֤ל יְהֹוָה֙ יַֽעֲקֹ֔ב
וּבְיִשְׂרָאֵ֖ל יִתְפָּאָֽר׃

24 כֹּֽה־אָמַ֤ר יְהֹוָה֙ גֹּֽאֲלֶ֔ךָ
וְיֹצֶרְךָ֖ מִבָּ֑טֶן
אָנֹכִ֤י יְהֹוָה֙ עֹ֣שֶׂה כֹּ֔ל
נֹטֶ֤ה שָׁמַ֙יִם֙ לְבַדִּ֔י
רֹקַ֥ע הָאָ֖רֶץ מֵאִתִּֽי׃

25 מֵפֵר֙ אֹת֣וֹת בַּדִּ֔ים
וְקֹסְמִ֖ים יְהוֹלֵ֑ל
מֵשִׁ֧יב חֲכָמִ֛ים אָח֖וֹר
וְדַעְתָּ֥ם יְסַכֵּֽל׃

I have redeemed thee. A prophetic perfect
(see on xliii. 1). The redemption is certain to follow Israel's spiritual revival
(Kimchi).

23. The prophet's call for all Nature
to join in song in celebration of the
marvellous redemption of God's
people, a redemption which is fraught
with the greatest consequences in the
religious history of the world.

hath done it. Prophetic perfect (Kimchi,
Abarbanel).

lower parts. Meaning 'the centre of the
earth' (Kimchi).

in Israel. Who is to disseminate God's
law of truth and justice among the
nations (Hirsch).

24–28. God, the Redeemer of Israel
and the Creator of the universe, has
appointed Cyrus to accomplish His
plans for His people.

24. *from the womb.* Cf. verse 2.

25. *the tokens.* The omens on which
forecasts are based (Metsudath David).

impostors. Or, 'praters.'

maketh . . . mad. Better, 'maketh fools of
diviners,' when their predictions are not
fulfilled (Abarbanel).

218

26. That confirmeth the word of
His servant,
And performeth the counsel of
His messengers;
That saith of Jerusalem: 'She
shall be inhabited';
And of the cities of Judah:
'They shall be built,
And I will raise up the waste
places thereof';
27. That saith to the deep: 'Be dry,
And I will dry up thy rivers';
28. That saith of Cyrus: 'He is My
shepherd,
And shall perform all My
pleasure';
Even saying of Jerusalem: 'She
shall be built';
And to the temple: 'Thy founda-
tion shall be laid.'

מֵקִים֙ דְּבַ֣ר עַבְדּ֔וֹ 26
וַעֲצַ֥ת מַלְאָכָ֖יו יַשְׁלִ֑ים
הָאֹמֵ֨ר לִירוּשָׁלִַ֜ם תּוּשָׁ֗ב
וּלְעָרֵ֤י יְהוּדָה֙ תִּבָּנֶ֔ינָה
וְחָרְבוֹתֶ֖יהָ אֲקוֹמֵֽם׃
הָאֹמֵ֥ר לַצּוּלָ֖ה חֳרָ֑בִי 27
וְנַהֲרֹתַ֖יִךְ אוֹבִֽישׁ׃
הָאֹמֵ֤ר לְכ֙וֹרֶשׁ֙ רֹעִ֔י 28
וְכָל־חֶפְצִ֖י יַשְׁלִ֑ם
וְלֵאמֹ֤ר לִירוּשָׁלִַ֙ם֙ תִּבָּנֶ֔ה
וְהֵיכָ֖ל תִּוָּסֵֽד׃

45   CHAPTER XLV   מה

1. Thus saith the LORD to His
anointed,
To Cyrus, whose right hand
I have holden,

כֹּה־אָמַ֤ר יְהֹוָה֙ לִמְשִׁיח֔וֹ 1
לְכ֙וֹרֶשׁ׀ אֲשֶׁר־הֶחֱזַ֣קְתִּי בִֽימִינ֔וֹ

קמץ ברביע v. 26.

26. *servant . . . messengers.* The prophets of God (Kimchi).

performeth. lit. 'completeth.'

27. The allusion is to the diversion of
the river Euphrates before the walls of
Babylon, as recorded by Herodotus,
whereby Cyrus was enabled to secure
an entrance into the fortified city.
Others regard the *deep* and *rivers* as a
figure of speech for the obstacles Cyrus
had to encounter. Jewish exegetes interpret it as figurative for the destruction
of Babylon's population and wealth
(Rashi, Kara, Kimchi).

28. *Cyrus.* Hebrew *Koresh*; the Persian
form is Kurush, the Greek Kuros, and
the Babylonian Kurash.

My shepherd. Cyrus will look after the
interests of Israel as a shepherd looks
after his flock's (Kimchi).

perform all My pleasure. Or, 'complete all
My purpose.'

to the temple. The preposition is implied
(Kimchi).

CHAPTER XLV

1-7. God's address to Cyrus, who is
promised easy victories and given the
reason and purpose of his mission.

1. Introduction

anointed. The Hebrew root of the verb
does not necessarily imply actual
anointment with oil. It may only mean
'consecration' or 'appointment to a
high office' (Rashi, Kimchi, Ibn Ezra).

right hand I have holden. An expression
denoting giving power (Metsudath
David).

To subdue nations before him,
And to loose the loins of kings;
To open the doors before him,
And that the gates may not be
   shut:

2. I will go before thee,
   And make the crooked places
      straight;
   I will break in pieces the doors
      of brass,
   And cut in sunder the bars of
      iron;

3. And I will give thee the treasures
      of darkness,
   And hidden riches of secret
      places,
   That thou mayest know that
      I am the LORD,
   Who call thee by thy name, even
      the God of Israel.

4. For the sake of Jacob My servant,
   And Israel Mine elect,
   I have called thee by thy name,
   I have surnamed thee, though
      thou hast not known Me.

[handwritten margin notes: "deprive of strength", "100 brass gates of Babylon — Herodotus", "No evidence of this", "Cyrus"]

לְבַד־לְפָנָיו גּוֹיִם
וּמָתְנֵי מְלָכִים אֲפַתֵּחַ
לִפְתֹּחַ לְפָנָיו דְּלָתַיִם
וּשְׁעָרִים לֹא יִסָּגֵרוּ׃

2 אֲנִי לְפָנֶיךָ אֵלֵךְ
וַהֲדוּרִים אֲיַשֵּׁר
דַּלְתוֹת נְחוּשָׁה אֲשַׁבֵּר
וּבְרִיחֵי בַרְזֶל אֲגַדֵּעַ׃

3 וְנָתַתִּי לְךָ אוֹצְרוֹת חֹשֶׁךְ
וּמַטְמֻנֵי מִסְתָּרִים
לְמַעַן תֵּדַע כִּי־אֲנִי יְהוָה
הַקּוֹרֵא בְשִׁמְךָ אֱלֹהֵי יִשְׂרָאֵל׃

4 לְמַעַן עַבְדִּי יַעֲקֹב
וְיִשְׂרָאֵל בְּחִירִי
וָאֶקְרָא לְךָ בִּשְׁמֶךָ
אֲכַנְּךָ וְלֹא יְדַעְתָּנִי׃

v. 2. אישר ק

---

to loose. lit. 'I will loose.' *To loose the loins* signifies to deprive of strength, to weaken. Its opposite, 'to gird up the loins,' implies the undertaking of an active task (cf. 1 Kings xviii. 46) (Rashi, Kimchi).

2f. Direct address to Cyrus.

2. *make ... straight.* Remove difficulties from his path (Kimchi).

doors of brass. Babylon, according to Herodotus, had a hundred gates of brass. But the phrase may be figurative, as in Ps. cvii. Rashi, Ibn Ezra, and Kimchi, however, explain it literally.

3. *treasures of darkness.* Treasures which are hidden in dark vaults for safety (Kimchi).

call thee by thy name. i.e. commission thee (cf. Exod. xxxi. 2) (Kimchi).

4. One of the purposes (the other is stated in verse 6) of the Divine elevation of Cyrus to his power and greatness.

surnamed thee. With dignified titles such as 'My anointed,' 'My shepherd' (Malbim).

hast not known Me. When he entered upon his career, Cyrus had not yet acknowledged the Sovereignty of God. His selection was not due to his merits, but to the Divine mission with which he had been entrusted (Malbim on verse 5).

5. I am the Lord, and there is none
  else,
  Beside Me there is no God;
  I have girded thee, though thou
  hast not known Me;
6. That they may know from the
  rising of the sun, and from
  the west,
  That there is none beside Me;
  I am the Lord, and there is none
  else;
7. I form the light, and create darkness;
  I make peace, and create evil;
  I am the Lord, that doeth all
  these things.
8. Drop down, ye heavens, from
  above,
  And let the skies pour down
  righteousness;
  Let the earth open, that they
  may bring forth salvation,

אֲנִי יְהֹוָה וְאֵין עוֹד ⁵
זוּלָתִי אֵין אֱלֹהִים
אֲאַזֶּרְךָ וְלֹא יְדַעְתָּנִי׃
לְמַעַן יֵדְעוּ ⁶
מִמִּזְרַח־שֶׁמֶשׁ וּמִמַּעֲרָבָה
כִּי־אֶפֶס בִּלְעָדָי
אֲנִי יְהֹוָה וְאֵין עוֹד׃
יוֹצֵר אוֹר וּבוֹרֵא חֹשֶׁךְ ⁷
עֹשֶׂה שָׁלוֹם וּבוֹרֵא רָע
אֲנִי יְהֹוָה עֹשֶׂה כָל־אֵלֶּה׃
הַרְעִיפוּ שָׁמַיִם מִמַּעַל ⁸
וּשְׁחָקִים יִזְּלוּ־צֶדֶק
תִּפְתַּח־אֶרֶץ וְיִפְרוּ־יֶשַׁע

5. *girded thee.* Given thee strength (cf.
the contrast, *loose the loins,* in verse 1)
(Metsudath David).

6. The second of the purposes.

that they may know. The subject is indefinite, 'all men,' and the phrase is the
equivalent of 'that it may be known'
(Metsudath David).

from the west. lit. 'from the going down
thereof' (Kimchi).

7. The pronouns are implied.

create evil. The term *evil* here denotes
calamity and suffering. These serve as
means of punishment for the sins of
man. Moral evil, on the other hand,
does not proceed from God, but is the
result of man's actions. In the *Hebrew
Prayer Book* (ed. Singer, p. 37), the
phrase is changed to 'create all things.'
Some commentators have detected in
this verse, in which God is declared to

be the universal Creator of both light
and darkness, peace and evil, a direct
allusion to, and intentional contradiction of, the Persian belief in dualism
according to which the world is ruled by
two antagonistic gods, Ahura Mazda,
the god of light and goodness, and
Ahriman, the god of darkness and evil
(Kimchi quoting Saadyah Gaon).

8. A short lyrical poem on the happy
state that will follow the liberation of
Israel by Cyrus and the establishment of
a reign of righteousness and salvation.

drop down. Like *pour down* in the following clause it is a transitive verb, the
object of both being *righteousness* in the
sense of 'victory' (see on xli. 2) (Rashi).

that they. The pronoun seems to refer to
heavens and *earth.* Some see the subject
as 'trees,' although not mentioned
(Isaiah of Trani).

And let her cause righteousness
    to spring up together;
I the Lord have created it.

9. Woe unto him that striveth with
    his Maker,
As a potsherd with the potsherds
    of the earth!
Shall the clay say to him that
    fashioneth it: 'What makest
    thou?'
Or: 'Thy work, it hath no hands'?

10. Woe unto him that saith unto
    his father: 'Wherefore be-
    gettest thou?'
Or to a woman: 'Wherefore
    travailest thou?'

11. Thus saith the Lord,
The Holy One of Israel, and his
    Maker:
Ask Me of the things that are to
    come;
Concerning My sons, and con-
    cerning the work of My hands,
    command ye Me.

12. I, even I, have made the earth,
And created man upon it;
I, even My hands, have stretched
    out the heavens,
And all their host have I com-
    manded.

13. I have roused him up in victory,
And I make level all his ways;

וּצְדָקָה תַצְמִיחַ יַחַד
אֲנִי יְהוָה בְּרָאתִיו׃
9 הוֹי רָב אֶת־יֹצְרוֹ
חֶרֶשׂ אֶת־חַרְשֵׂי אֲדָמָה
הֲיֹאמַר חֹמֶר לְיֹצְרוֹ מַה־תַּעֲשֶׂה
וּפָעָלְךָ אֵין־יָדַיִם לוֹ׃
10 הוֹי אֹמֵר לְאָב מַה־תּוֹלִיד
וּלְאִשָּׁה מַה־תְּחִילִין׃
11 כֹּה־אָמַר יְהוָה
קְדוֹשׁ יִשְׂרָאֵל וְיֹצְרוֹ
הָאֹתִיּוֹת שְׁאָלוּנִי
עַל־בָּנַי וְעַל־פֹּעַל יָדַי תְּצַוֻּנִי׃
12 אָנֹכִי עָשִׂיתִי אֶרֶץ
וְאָדָם עָלֶיהָ בָרָאתִי
אֲנִי יָדַי נָטוּ שָׁמַיִם
וְכָל־צְבָאָם צִוֵּיתִי׃
13 אָנֹכִי הַעִירֹתִהוּ בְצֶדֶק
וְכָל־דְּרָכָיו אֲיַשֵּׁר

9–13. An address apparently directed to Habakkuk, who was destined to question the length of Nebuchadnezzar's prosperity and Israel's exile in Babylon (Rashi).

9f. The objectors to God's apparent neglect of His people is compared with a potsherd questioning the wisdom of the potter, or a son daring to criticize his parent.

9. *striveth*. Contends, argues against, questions.

with the potsherds. Better, 'among the potsherds.'

no hands. It is as though thy work was made without hands. Thou hast no

power over it to do as thou desirest (Ibn Ezra).

10. *a woman*. i.e. his mother (Ibn Ezra).

11. *ask Me*. Emphasis is on *Me*; God alone can supply the answer (Rashi, Ibn Ezra, Kimchi).

Concerning My sons . . . Me. This is a question. Do you command Me concerning My sons and the work of My hands? I have already arranged the salvation for them, for I have created everything (Rashi, Kimchi).

12. *commanded*. Ordained.

13. *I have roused*. With emphasis on *I*.

him. Cyrus (Ibn Ezra, Kimchi).

He shall build My city,
And he shall let Mine exiles go
free,
Not for price nor reward,
Saith the LORD of hosts.

14. Thus saith the LORD:
The labour of Egypt, and the
merchandise of Ethiopia,
And of the Sabeans, men of
stature,
Shall come over unto thee, and
they shall be thine;
They shall go after thee, in
chains they shall come over;
And they shall fall down unto
thee,
They shall make supplication
unto thee:
Surely God is in thee, and there
is none else,
There is no other God.

15. Verily Thou art a God that
hidest Thyself,
O God of Israel, the Saviour.

"The best of Cyrus"

43.3

הוּא־יִבְנֶה עִירִי
וְגָלוּתִי יְשַׁלֵּחַ
לֹא בִמְחִיר וְלֹא בְשֹׁחַד
אָמַר יְהֹוָה צְבָאוֹת׃

14 כֹּה ׀ אָמַר יְהֹוָה
יְגִיעַ מִצְרַיִם וּסְחַר־כּוּשׁ
וּסְבָאִים אַנְשֵׁי מִדָּה
עָלַיִךְ יַעֲבֹרוּ וְלָךְ יִהְיוּ
אַחֲרַיִךְ יֵלֵכוּ בַּזִּקִּים יַעֲבֹרוּ
וְאֵלַיִךְ יִשְׁתַּחֲווּ
אֵלַיִךְ יִתְפַּלָּלוּ
אַךְ בָּךְ אֵל וְאֵין עוֹד
אֶפֶס אֱלֹהִים׃

15 אָכֵן אַתָּה אֵל מִסְתַּתֵּר
אֱלֹהֵי יִשְׂרָאֵל מוֹשִׁיעַ׃

---

reward. The Hebrew *shochad* is usually rendered 'bribe.'

14–17. The nations conquered by Cyrus will pay homage to Israel and acknowledge the omnipresence and omnipotence of God.

14. The prophet addresses Israel.

Egypt . . . Ethiopia . . . Sabeans. These are the nations mentioned in xliii. 3 as the ransom which God is giving to Persia for the release of Israel. Here they are described as becoming ultimately the possession of Israel. The possession need not necessarily imply physical domination. It may simply be an expression of acknowledgement by these nations of the power and Divinity of the God of Israel (This follows Ibn Ezra).

Sabeans. While Egypt and Ethiopia offer labour and merchandise respectively, the Sabeans present themselves as slaves (Isaiah of Trani).

in chains. [Symbol of complete moral or physical submission.]

surely God, etc. This is an admission which the Sabeans will make to Israel when offering themselves for service (Metsudath David).

15. *The nations acknowledge God.*

hidest Thyself. God had hitherto hidden His glory and never manifested His power in His dealings with Israel during the captivity (Rashi).

the Saviour. Now He has shown Himself to be the *God of Israel* and *the Saviour* of His suffering people (Rashi).

16. They shall be ashamed, yea,
confounded, all of them;
They shall go in confusion
together that are makers of
idols.

17. O Israel, that art saved by the
LORD with an everlasting salvation;
Ye shall not be ashamed nor
confounded ⹁world without
end.

18. For thus saith the LORD that
created the heavens,
He is God;
That formed the earth and made
it,
He established it,
He created it not a waste, He
formed it to be inhabited:
I am the LORD, and there is none
else.

19. I have not spoken in secret,
In a place of the land of darkness;
I said not unto the seed of Jacob:
'Seek ye Me in vain';
I the LORD speak righteousness,
I declare things that are right.

20. Assemble yourselves and come,
draw near together,

16 בֹּ֣ושׁוּ וְגַם־נִכְלְמ֔וּ כֻּלָּ֑ם
יַחְדָּ֣ו הָלְכ֣וּ בַכְּלִמָּ֔ה חָרָשֵׁ֖י צִירִֽים׃
17 יִשְׂרָאֵל֙ נֹושַׁ֣ע בַּֽיהֹוָ֔ה תְּשׁוּעַ֖ת עֹולָמִ֑ים
לֹא־תֵבֹ֥שׁוּ וְלֹא־תִכָּלְמ֖וּ
עַד־עֹ֥ולְמֵי עַֽד׃
18 כִּ֣י כֹ֣ה אָֽמַר־יְ֠הֹוָה בֹּורֵ֨א הַשָּׁמַ֜יִם
ה֣וּא הָאֱלֹהִ֗ים
יֹצֵ֨ר הָאָ֤רֶץ וְעֹשָׂהּ֙
ה֣וּא כֹֽונְנָ֔הּ
לֹא־תֹ֥הוּ בְרָאָ֖הּ לָשֶׁ֣בֶת יְצָרָ֑הּ
אֲנִ֥י יְהֹוָ֖ה וְאֵ֥ין עֹֽוד׃
19 לֹ֣א בַסֵּ֣תֶר דִּבַּ֗רְתִּי
בִּמְקֹום֙ אֶ֣רֶץ חֹ֔שֶׁךְ
לֹ֥א אָמַ֛רְתִּי לְזֶ֥רַע יַעֲקֹ֖ב
תֹּ֣הוּ בַקְּשׁ֑וּנִי
אֲנִ֤י יְהֹוָה֙ דֹּבֵ֣ר צֶ֔דֶק
מַגִּ֖יד מֵישָׁרִֽים׃
20 הִקָּבְצ֥וּ וָבֹ֖אוּ הִֽתְנַגְּשׁ֣וּ יַחְדָּו֙

16f. The prophet contrasts the confusion and shame of the idolmakers with
the eternal salvation of God's people.

17. *world without end.* lit. 'to the worlds
of everlasting,' to all eternity (Kimchi).

18–25. God is the sole Power of the
world which He created for man to
dwell in and not for confusion. He does
not hide in darkness but reveals Himself
in justice and righteousness. Idolatry is
sheer folly, and real help can come from
Him only. All who acknowledge His
Sovereignty shall find salvation.

18. *a waste.* Hebrew *tohu* (see on xl.
17).

19. God did not speak in darkness like
the dubious oracles obtained by magical arts which can be twisted or denied.
He spoke in the full light of day, and
when He invited Israel to seek Him, He
meant to respond to his prayer.

place of the land of darkness. Where no one
was witness to the revelation, but on
Mount Sinai, amidst thunder, lightning,
heavy clouds, and the sound of a shofar,
publicizing it to all neighboring peoples
(Kimchi).

in vain. Hebrew *tohu.*

20f. The remnants of the nations, the
Babylonians, were summoned together

Ye that are escaped of the
nations;
They have no knowledge that
carry the wood of their graven
image,
And pray unto a god that cannot
save.

21. Declare ye, and bring them near,
Yea, let them take counsel
together:
Who hath announced this from
ancient time,
And declared it of old? *among the idols*
Have not I the LORD?
And there is no God else beside
Me;
A just God and a Saviour;
There is none beside Me.

22. Look unto Me, and be ye saved,
All the ends of the earth;
For I am God, and there is none
else.

23. By Myself have I sworn,

פְּלִיטֵי הַגּוֹיִם
לֹא יָדְעוּ הַנֹּשְׂאִים אֶת־עֵץ פִּסְלָם
וּמִתְפַּלְלִים אֶל־אֵל לֹא יוֹשִׁיעַ:
21 הַגִּידוּ וְהַגִּישׁוּ
אַף יִוָּעֲצוּ יַחְדָּו
מִי הִשְׁמִיעַ זֹאת מִקֶּדֶם
מֵאָז הִגִּידָהּ
הֲלוֹא אֲנִי יְהוָה
וְאֵין־עוֹד אֱלֹהִים מִבַּלְעָדַי
אֵל־צַדִּיק וּמוֹשִׁיעַ
אַיִן זוּלָתִי:
22 פְּנוּ־אֵלַי וְהִוָּשְׁעוּ
כָּל־אַפְסֵי־אָרֶץ
כִּי אֲנִי־אֵל וְאֵין עוֹד:
23 כִּי נִשְׁבַּעְתִּי

to consider God's predictions and fulfilment concerning Cyrus, and to compare His power with the futility and
total incapacity of their false gods (Ibn
Ezra).

20. *escaped.* [The catastrophe that
befell the nations.]

that carry . . . image. The idols are so
helpless that they cannot even carry
themselves. They must be carried by
their worshippers to their temples, in
their processions or into battle (cf. 2
Sam. v. 21) (Kimchi).

21. *bring them.* Your servants (Ibn
Ezra); one another before your leaders
(Kimchi).

who has announced. Which of these idols
(Rashi, Kimchi).

this. The rise of Cyrus and the consequences for Israel (Ibn Kaspi).

22-25. All mankind will ultimately
find salvation in God unto Whom *every
knee shall bow.* He is the only Source of
strength and victory, and even His
enemies will come back to Him. Then
will Israel be vindicated and exult in the
glory of the Lord.

22. *look.* lit. 'turn' for help. The inten-
tion of the clause is: if you rely upon
Me, you will be saved (Rashi, Ibn Ezra,
Kimchi).

all the ends of the earth. All mankind
(Kimchi).

23. *by Myself have I sworn.* Cf. Gen. xxii.
16; Jer. xxii. 5.

The word is gone forth from My
mouth in righteousness,
And shall not come back,
That unto Me every knee shall
bow,
Every tongue shall swear.

24. Only in the LORD, shall one say
of Me, is victory and strength;
Even to Him shall men come in
confusion,
All they that were incensed
against Him.

25. In the LORD shall all the seed of
Israel
Be justified, and shall glory.

יָצָא מִפִּי צְדָקָה דָּבָר
וְלֹא יָשׁוּב
כִּי־לִי תִּכְרַע כָּל־בֶּרֶךְ
תִּשָּׁבַע כָּל־לָשׁוֹן׃
24 אַךְ בַּיהוָה לִי אָמַר צְדָקוֹת וָעֹז
עָדָיו יָבוֹא וְיֵבֹשׁוּ
כֹּל הַנֶּחֱרִים בּוֹ׃
25 בַּיהוָה יִצְדְּקוּ וְיִתְהַלְלוּ
כָּל־זֶרַע יִשְׂרָאֵל׃

CHAPTER XLVI

1. Bel boweth down, Nebo
stoopeth;
Their idols are upon the beasts,
and upon the cattle;
The things that ye carried about
are made a load,
A burden to the weary beast.

מו
1 כָּרַע בֵּל קֹרֵס נְבוֹ
הָיוּ עֲצַבֵּיהֶם לַחַיָּה וְלַבְּהֵמָה
נְשֻׂאֹתֵיכֶם עֲמוּסוֹת
מַשָּׂא לַעֲיֵפָה׃

the word . . . come back. Better, 'righteousness is gone from My mouth, a word
which shall not return.'

shall bow. In submission (Kimchi).

shall swear. Allegiance (Metsudath
David).

24. shall men come in confusion. lit. 'he
shall come and they shall be confused.'

incensed. The same verb as in xli. 11.

25. be justified, and shall glory. In contrast to the gentiles, who will be confused and ashamed of their previous
idolatry (Kimchi).

CHAPTER XLVI

FALL OF BABYLON'S DEITIES

1-4. The importance of the gods of
Babylon is contrasted with the supreme
power of the God of Israel. The former
are carried away from their country into
exile, while the God of Israel carries His
people from captivity into freedom.

1. Bel. A Babylonian deity, made in
the form of Nimrod, the first king of
Babylon (Abarbanel).

Nebo. A Babylonian deity, believed to
bestow prophecy on his prophets
(Abarbanel).

are upon the beasts. Being carried off for
safety on the approach of the invaders
(Kimchi).

the things that ye carried about. i.e. your
burdens, the fragments of the broken
idols, made of silver and gold, which
were very heavy for the weary beasts
(Kimchi).

2. They stoop, they bow down
   together,
   They could not deliver the
   burden;
   And themselves are gone into
   captivity.
3. Hearken unto Me, O house of
   Jacob,
   And all the remnant of the house
   of Israel,
   That are borne [by Me] from the
   birth,
   That are carried from the womb:
4. Even to old age I am the same,
   And even to hoar hairs will I
   carry you;
   I have made, and I will bear;
   Yea, I will carry, and will deliver.
5. To whom will ye liken Me, and
   make Me equal,
   And compare Me, that we may
   be like?
6. Ye that lavish gold out of the bag,
   And weigh silver in the balance;
   Ye that hire a goldsmith, that he
   make it a god,
   To fall down thereto, yea, to
   worship.
7. He is borne upon the shoulder,
   he is carried,

2 קָרְס֤וּ כָֽרְעוּ֙ יַחְדָּ֔ו
לֹ֥א יָכְל֖וּ מַלֵּ֣ט מַשָּׂ֑א
וְנַפְשָׁ֖ם בַּשְּׁבִ֥י הָלָֽכָה׃
3 שִׁמְע֤וּ אֵלַי֙ בֵּ֣ית יַעֲקֹ֔ב
וְכָל־שְׁאֵרִ֖ית בֵּ֣ית יִשְׂרָאֵ֑ל
הַֽעֲמֻסִים֙ מִנִּי־בֶ֔טֶן
הַנְּשֻׂאִ֖ים מִנִּי־רָֽחַם׃
4 וְעַד־זִקְנָה֙ אֲנִ֣י ה֔וּא
וְעַד־שֵׂיבָ֖ה אֲנִ֣י אֶסְבֹּ֑ל
אֲנִ֤י עָשִׂ֙יתִי֙ וַאֲנִ֣י אֶשָּׂ֔א
וַאֲנִ֥י אֶסְבֹּ֖ל וַאֲמַלֵּֽט׃
5 לְמִ֥י תְדַמְי֖וּנִי וְתַשְׁו֑וּ
וְתַמְשִׁל֖וּנִי וְנִדְמֶֽה׃
6 הַזָּלִ֤ים זָהָב֙ מִכִּ֔יס
וְכֶ֖סֶף בַּקָּנֶ֣ה יִשְׁקֹ֑לוּ
יִשְׂכְּר֤וּ צוֹרֵף֙ וְיַעֲשֵׂ֣הוּ אֵ֔ל
יִסְגְּד֖וּ אַף־יִֽשְׁתַּחֲוֽוּ׃
7 יִ֠שָּׂאֻהוּ עַל־כָּתֵ֤ף יִסְבְּלֻ֙הוּ֙

2. *they could not ... captivity.* Idol-worshippers believed that the images they worshipped were animate gods; but the prophet sarcastically remarks that not only were the gods powerless to enable the *burden* (the images) to escape, but they themselves *are gone into captivity* (Kimchi).

3. *all the remnant.* Referring to the two tribes of Judah and Benjamin, who remained in their land after the exile of the Northern Kingdom (Kimchi).

borne ... carried. Contrasted with the idols which cannot carry themselves (Malbim).

4. *to old age ... hoar hairs.* As God carried the Israelite nation in its infancy (*from the womb*), so will He continue to carry it in the future (Metsudath David).

5-7. The absurdity of idolatry (cf. xl. 18).

6f. Cf. the similar description of idolatry in xliv. 9-20.

the balance. lit. 'the beam' of the scales, used for the scales themselves (Rashi).

7. *is borne ... is carried.* lit. 'they bear it ... they carry it.'

8-11. The prophet appeals to the

And set in his place, and he
standeth,
From his place he doth not
remove;
Yea, though one cry unto him,
he cannot answer,
Nor save him out of his trouble.

8. Remember this, and stand fast;
Bring it to mind, O ye transgressors.

9. Remember the former things of
old:
That I am God, and there is
none else;
I am God, and there is none like
Me;

10. Declaring the end from the
beginning,
And from ancient times things
that are not yet done;
Saying: 'My counsel shall stand,
And all My pleasure will I do';

11. Calling a bird of prey from the
east,
The man of My counsel from a
far country;
Yea, I have spoken, I will also
bring it to pass,

וַיַּנִּיחֵהוּ תַחְתָּיו וְיַעֲמֹד
מִמְּקוֹמוֹ לֹא יָמִישׁ
אַף־יִצְעַק אֵלָיו וְלֹא יַעֲנֶה
מִצָּרָתוֹ לֹא יוֹשִׁיעֶנּוּ:

8 זִכְרוּ־זֹאת וְהִתְאֹשָׁשׁוּ
הָשִׁיבוּ פוֹשְׁעִים עַל־לֵב:

9 זִכְרוּ רִאשֹׁנוֹת מֵעוֹלָם
כִּי אָנֹכִי אֵל וְאֵין עוֹד
אֱלֹהִים וְאֶפֶס כָּמוֹנִי:

10 מַגִּיד מֵרֵאשִׁית אַחֲרִית
וּמִקֶּדֶם אֲשֶׁר לֹא־נַעֲשׂוּ
אֹמֵר עֲצָתִי תָקוּם
וְכָל־חֶפְצִי אֶעֱשֶׂה:

11 קֹרֵא מִמִּזְרָח עַיִט
מֵאֶרֶץ מֶרְחָק אִישׁ עֲצָתוֹ
אַף־דִּבַּרְתִּי אַף־אֲבִיאֶנָּה

עצתי ק v. 11.

---

transgressors to recall past events which
demonstrate that only God is omnipotent and omniscient, and that He
alone is able to carry His promises and
plans to full realization.

8. *mind.* lit. 'heart.'

9. *remember . . . of old.* Which you have
witnessed (Rashi).

that I am God. i.e. *the former things of old*
(the miraculous redemption of Israel
from Egypt and the destruction of the
Egyptian gods) demonstrate this fact
(Kimchi).

I am God. The first two words are
implied.

10. *declaring . . . beginning.* When a
period in history is just beginning God
declares how it will end (Metsudath
David).

from ancient . . . not yet done. [Thus prov-
ing His foreknowledge.]

pleasure. i.e. desire or purpose.

11. *a bird of prey.* viz. Cyrus, so
described from the rapidity of his
movements (Ibn Ezra, Kimchi).

from the east. Cf. xli. 2, 25.

the man of My counsel. Whom I have
chosen to execute My plan (Kimchi).

I have purposed, I will also do it.

formed

12. Hearken unto Me, ye stout-
hearted,
That are far from righteousness:

13. I bring near My righteousness, *justice*
it shall not be far off,
And My salvation shall not tarry;
And I will place salvation in Zion
For Israel My glory.

יְצָרְתִּי אַף־אֶעֱשֶׂנָּה:

12 שִׁמְעוּ אֵלַי אַבִּירֵי לֵב
הָרְחוֹקִים מִצְּדָקָה:

13 קֵרַבְתִּי צִדְקָתִי לֹא תִרְחָק
וּתְשׁוּעָתִי לֹא תְאַחֵר
וְנָתַתִּי בְצִיּוֹן תְּשׁוּעָה
לְיִשְׂרָאֵל תִּפְאַרְתִּי:

47   CHAPTER XLVII   מז

1. Come down, and sit in the dust,
O virgin daughter of Babylon, *usually Jeru (vulnerable)*
Sit on the ground without a
throne,
O daughter of the Chaldeans;
For thou shalt no more be called
Tender and delicate.

1 רְדִי ׀ וּשְׁבִי עַל־עָפָר
בְּתוּלַת בַּת־בָּבֶל
שְׁבִי־לָאָרֶץ אֵין־כִּסֵּא
בַּת־כַּשְׂדִּים
כִּי לֹא תוֹסִיפִי יִקְרְאוּ־לָךְ
רַכָּה וַעֲנֻגָּה:

v. 13. קמץ בז״ק   v. 1. מלרע

I have purposed. lit. 'I have formed,' the object to be understood being 'My design' (Kimchi).

12f. Announcement of the speedy salvation of Israel.

12. *stout-hearted.* Here the meaning 'perversely obstinate' (Ibn Ezra).

that are far from righteousness. Some explain this as referring to the Babylonians, who were far from performing deeds of righteousness and kindness to the Jews exiled to their land (Kimchi). Others render: 'far from receiving righteousness.' This refers to the Jews, who, in spite of their exile among the nations, were obstinate in adhering to God's worship, yet did not receive His righteousness, His kind deeds (Rashi).

CHAPTER XLVII

THE HUMILIATION OF BABYLON

1. *come down.* Descend from the heights of imperial power (Kimchi).

in the dust. lit. 'upon the dust,' the equivalent of *sit upon the ground* (iii. 26). There it denoted mourning, here humiliation (Abarbanel).

virgin daughter of Babylon. i.e. virgin daughter that is Babylon. For the meaning of the phrase, see on xxiii. 12.

thou shalt no more be called. lit. 'thou shalt no more (be in such a position that) they shall call thee' (Kimchi).

tender and delicate. One used to comfort and being pampered. The phrase occurs again in Deut. xxviii. 56 (Kimchi).

2. Take the millstones, and grind
   meal;
   Remove thy veil,
   Strip off the ~~train,~~ uncover the
   leg,
   Pass through the rivers.

3. Thy nakedness shall be un-
   covered,
   Yea, thy shame shall be seen;
   I will take vengeance,
   And will let no man intercede.

4. Our Redeemer, the LORD of
   hosts is His name,
   The Holy One of Israel.

5. Sit thou silent, and get thee into
   darkness,
   O daughter of the Chaldeans;
   For thou shalt no more be called
   The mistress of kingdoms.

6. I was wroth with My people,
   I profaned Mine inheritance,

קְחִי רֵחַיִם וְטַחֲנִי קָמַח 2
גַּלִּי צַמָּתֵךְ
חֶשְׂפִּי־שֹׁבֶל גַּלִּי־שׁוֹק
עִבְרִי נְהָרוֹת:
תִּגָּל עֶרְוָתֵךְ 3
גַּם תֵּרָאֶה חֶרְפָּתֵךְ
נָקָם אֶקָּח
וְלֹא אֶפְגַּע אָדָם:
גֹּאֲלֵנוּ יְהוָה צְבָאוֹת שְׁמוֹ 4
קְדוֹשׁ יִשְׂרָאֵל:
שְׁבִי דוּמָם וּבֹאִי בַחֹשֶׁךְ 5
בַּת־כַּשְׂדִּים
כִּי לֹא תוֹסִיפִי יִקְרְאוּ־לָךְ
גְּבֶרֶת מַמְלָכוֹת:
קָצַפְתִּי עַל־עַמִּי 6
חִלַּלְתִּי נַחֲלָתִי

v. 5. קמץ בז״ק   v. 3. מלרע

2.   The noble lady must descend to the
level of the female slave and dress and
work like her.

take the millstones, etc. This was the occu-
pation of captives (cf. Jud. xvi. 21)
(Kimchi).

veil . . . train. Most commentators render: 'remove thy veil, bare thy foot.'
The noble Babylonian ladies will have
to discard their finery and even bare
their feet and legs on their journey in
Persian captivity (Kimchi).

uncover . . . rivers. To be encountered on
the way to captivity (Kimchi).

3.   *thy nakedness,* etc. Thy garments will
be torn until thy nakedness shall be
uncovered (Malbim). Since Babylon is
likened to a tender and delicate woman,
the prophet continues to describe her

trials and tribulations in a manner a
propos of such a woman (Kimchi).

and will . . . intercede. lit. 'and I will meet
(or, entreat) no man' (Ibn Ezra)

4.   An exclamation by the prophet
(Rashi) or by the redeemed Israelites
(Ibn Ezra) at the sight of Babylon's fall.

5-7.   Babylon is again addressed. Her
ill-treatment of God's people is the
cause of her humiliation.

5.   *sit thou silent.* The attitude of a
mourner (Metsudath David).

darkness. Hidden from sight (Metsudath
David).

6.   God addresses Babylon.

Mine inheritance. This signifies Israel (cf.
xix. 25), as is apparent from the context
(Kimchi).

And gave them into thy hand;
Thou didst show them no mercy;
Upon the aged hast thou very
   heavily
Laid thy yoke.

7. And thou saidst:
  'For ever shall I be mistress';
So that thou didst not lay these
   things to thy heart,
Neither didst remember the end
   thereof.

8. Now therefore hear this, thou
   that art given to pleasures,
That sittest securely,
That sayest in thy heart:
'I am, and there is none else
   beside me;
I shall not sit as a widow,
Neither shall I know the loss of
   children';

9. But these two things shall come
   to thee in a moment
In one day,
The loss of children, and widowhood;

וָאֶתְּנֵם בְּיָדֵךְ
לֹא־שַׂמְתְּ לָהֶם רַחֲמִים
עַל־זָקֵן
הִכְבַּדְתְּ עֻלֵּךְ מְאֹד׃

7 וַתֹּאמְרִי
לְעוֹלָם אֶהְיֶה גְּבָרֶת
עַד לֹא־שַׂמְתְּ אֵלֶּה עַל־לִבֵּךְ
לֹא זָכַרְתְּ אַחֲרִיתָהּ׃

8 וְעַתָּה שִׁמְעִי־זֹאת עֲדִינָה
הַיּוֹשֶׁבֶת לָבֶטַח
הָאֹמְרָה בִּלְבָבָהּ
אֲנִי וְאַפְסִי עוֹד
לֹא אֵשֵׁב אַלְמָנָה
וְלֹא אֵדַע שְׁכוֹל׃

9 וְתָבֹאנָה לָּךְ שְׁתֵּי־אֵלֶּה רֶגַע
בְּיוֹם אֶחָד
שְׁכוֹל וְאַלְמֹן

---

upon the aged. And much more so upon the younger people (Metsudath David).

7. *didst not lay these things.* That God had delivered Israel into the hands of Babylon only for disciplinary punishment, that it was not Babylon's own power that prevailed (Malbim), and that the same could happen to them (Kimchi).

the end thereof. That when the period of chastisement will have terminated,

Israel will be restored to his former glory (Ibn Kaspi).

8f. Babylon's over-confidence in her power and vitality will be suddenly shattered by a twofold calamity.

8. *in thy heart.* lit. 'in her heart.' The clause *that sayest . . . beside me* occurs in Zeph. ii. 15.

a widow. When the figure is applied to a nation, it denotes the lack of a king, as *loss of children* means depopulation by a conqueror (Rashi).

In their full measure shall they
  come upon thee,
For the multitude of thy sorceries,
And the great abundance of
  thine enchantments.
10. And thou hast been secure in
  thy wickedness,
Thou hast said: 'None seeth me';
Thy wisdom and thy knowledge,
  It hath perverted thee;
And thou hast said in thy heart:
'I am, and there is none else
  beside me.'
11. Yet shall evil come upon thee;
Thou shalt not know how to
  charm it away;
And calamity shall fall upon
  thee;
Thou shalt not be able to put it
  away;
And ruin shall come upon thee
  suddenly,
Before thou knowest.
12. Stand now with thine enchantments,
And with the multitude of thy
  sorceries,

כְּתֻמָּם בָּאוּ עָלָיִךְ
בְּרֹב כְּשָׁפַיִךְ
בְּעָצְמַת חֲבָרַיִךְ מְאֹד׃
10 וַתִּבְטְחִי בְרָעָתֵךְ
אָמַרְתְּ אֵין רֹאָנִי
חָכְמָתֵךְ וְדַעְתֵּךְ
הִיא שׁוֹבְבָתֶךְ
וַתֹּאמְרִי בְלִבֵּךְ
אֲנִי וְאַפְסִי עוֹד׃
11 וּבָא עָלַיִךְ רָעָה
לֹא תֵדְעִי שַׁחְרָהּ
וְתִפֹּל עָלַיִךְ הֹוָה
לֹא תוּכְלִי כַּפְּרָהּ
וְתָבֹא עָלַיִךְ פִּתְאֹם
שֹׁאָה לֹא תֵדָעִי׃
12 עִמְדִי־נָא בַחֲבָרַיִךְ
וּבְרֹב כְּשָׁפַיִךְ

9. *thy sorceries.* The magical arts were
highly cultivated in Babylon, but they
were incapable of averting disaster
(Metsudath David).

10f. The ideas embodied in verses 8f.
are repeated with the addition of
further illustrations.

10. *hast been secure.* Or, 'hast been
confident.'

wickedness. The tyrannical use made by
Babylon of her power (cf. Nahum iii.
19).

none seeth me. There is no higher Power
to exact a reckoning of me (cf. Ps. x. 11)
(Kimchi).

wisdom . . . knowledge. Of the wrong
type, such as sorcery and witchcraft
(Kimchi).

11. *put it away.* The verb has the usual
meaning 'to atone, expiate' (Ibn Ezra).

12–15. Ironical encouragement of
Babylon passing into pathetic commiseration over her pitiable disappointment.

12. *stand now with.* Persist in (Rashi).

Wherein thou hast laboured from
  thy youth;
If so be thou shalt be able to
  profit,
If so be thou mayest prevail.

13. Thou art wearied in the multi-
  tude of thy counsels;
Let now the astrologers, the
  star-gazers,
The monthly prognosticators,
Stand up, and save thee
From the things that shall come
  upon thee.

14. Behold, they shall be as stubble;
The fire shall burn them;
They shall not deliver themselves
From the power of the flame;
It shall not be a coal to warm at,
Nor a fire to sit before.

15. Thus shall they be unto thee
With whom thou hast laboured;
They that have trafficked with
  thee from thy youth
Shall wander every one to his
  quarter;
There shall be none to save thee.

בַּאֲשֶׁר יָגַעַתְּ מִנְּעוּרָיִךְ
אוּלַי תּוּכְלִי הוֹעִיל
אוּלַי תַּעֲרוֹצִי׃
13 נִלְאֵית בְּרֹב עֲצָתָיִךְ
יַעַמְדוּ־נָא וְיוֹשִׁיעֻךְ
הֹבְרֵי שָׁמַיִם הַחֹזִים בַּכּוֹכָבִים
מוֹדִיעִים לֶחֳדָשִׁים
מֵאֲשֶׁר יָבֹאוּ עָלָיִךְ׃
14 הִנֵּה הָיוּ כְקַשׁ
אֵשׁ שְׂרָפָתַם
לֹא־יַצִּילוּ אֶת־נַפְשָׁם
מִיַּד לֶהָבָה
אֵין־גַּחֶלֶת לַחְמָם
אוּר לָשֶׁבֶת נֶגְדּוֹ׃
15 כֵּן הָיוּ־לָךְ אֲשֶׁר יָגַעַתְּ
סֹחֲרַיִךְ מִנְּעוּרַיִךְ
אִישׁ לְעֶבְרוֹ תָּעוּ
אֵין מוֹשִׁיעֵךְ׃

if so be thou shalt be able. More lit. 'perhaps thou art able.'

13. *the astrologers.* According to its
Arabic cognate, 'cutters of the heavens';
i.e. those who make definite decisions
according to the constellations of the
heavens. They would judge from the
location of the stars which was supposed to give information about inauspicious days or months, or the opposite, to undertake an enterprise (Kimchi,
Shorashim).

from the things. This may be qualified not
by *and save thee* but by *the monthly prognosticators*: 'who make known month by
month something of the things that will
come upon thee' (Rashi, Ibn Ezra,
Kimchi).

14. *behold, they.* The astrologers, star-
gazers, etc. (Rashi).

they shall not deliver themselves. Much less
others who depend upon their guidance
(Kimchi).

it shall not . . . sit before. The fire will not
be comfortable and beneficial, but fierce
and destructive (Kimchi).

15. *with whom thou hast laboured.* The
astrologers upon whom the Babylonians relied for advice (Kimchi).

trafficked with thee. Your friends, who
trafficked your land (Ibn Ezra, Kimchi).

to his quarter. lit. 'to (the path which is) in
front of him.'

48   CHAPTER XLVIII   מח

1. Hear ye this, O house of Jacob,
   Who are called by the name of Israel,
   And are come forth out of the *waters* fountain of Judah;
   Who swear by the name of the LORD,
   And make mention of the God of Israel,
   But not in truth, nor in righteousness.
2. For they call themselves of the holy city, *arrow*
   And stay themselves upon the God of Israel,
   The LORD of hosts is His name.
3. I have declared the former things from of old;
   Yea, they went forth out of My mouth, and I announced them;
   Suddenly I did them, and they came to pass.
4. Because I knew that thou art obstinate,
   And thy neck is an iron sinew,

1 שִׁמְעוּ־זֹאת בֵּית־יַעֲקֹב
הַנִּקְרָאִים בְּשֵׁם יִשְׂרָאֵל
וּמִמֵּי יְהוּדָה יָצָאוּ
הַנִּשְׁבָּעִים ׀ בְּשֵׁם יְהֹוָה
וּבֵאלֹהֵי יִשְׂרָאֵל יַזְכִּירוּ
לֹא בֶאֱמֶת וְלֹא בִצְדָקָה׃
2 כִּי־מֵעִיר הַקֹּדֶשׁ נִקְרָאוּ
וְעַל־אֱלֹהֵי יִשְׂרָאֵל נִסְמָכוּ
יְהֹוָה צְבָאוֹת שְׁמוֹ׃
3 הָרִאשֹׁנוֹת מֵאָז הִגַּדְתִּי
וּמִפִּי יָצְאוּ וְאַשְׁמִיעֵם
פִּתְאֹם עָשִׂיתִי וַתָּבֹאנָה׃
4 מִדַּעְתִּי כִּי קָשֶׁה אָתָּה
וְגִיד בַּרְזֶל עָרְפֶּךָ

v. 2. קמץ בז"ק

CHAPTER XLVIII

EXHORTATIONS to the Israelite exiles in Babylon (Rashi).

1f. They swear by the Name of the Lord and claim to trust in Him, but in reality their profession is hypocritical.

1. *hear ye this.* The exhortation beginning with verse 3.

fountain. lit. 'waters'; i.e. source, cf. *the fountain* (lit. well) *of Jacob* (Deut xxxiii. 28) and *the fountain of Israel* (the patriarch Jacob, Ps. lxviii. 27) (Metsudath David).

swear . . . LORD. As if they truly believed in Him (Ibn Ezra).

but not . . . righteousness. Their oaths in His name are not always true (Kimchi).

2. *the holy city.* Jerusalem in the state of holiness which should distinguish it (Kimchi).

stay themselves. They pretend to put their reliance in God (Ibn Ezra, Kimchi).

3–11. The ways of God's revelation to His people.

3. All that God predicted had been duly fulfilled, which is clear evidence of His omnipotence and power.

the former things. The events of the past such as the exodus from Egypt and the fall of Sennacherib (Rashi).

from of old. i.e. beforehand (Rashi).

they went forth. The predictions (Metsudath David).

4. *thy neck,* etc. Symbols of obstinacy (Ibn Ezra).

And thy brow brass;

5. Therefore I have declared it to thee from of old;

Before it came to pass I announced it to thee;

Lest thou shouldest say: 'Mine idol hath done them,

And my graven image, and my molten image, hath commanded them.'

6. Thou hast heard, see, all this;

And ye, will ye not declare it?

I have announced unto thee new things from this time,

Even hidden things, which thou hast not known.

7. They are created now, and not from of old,

And before this day thou heardest them not;

Lest thou shouldest say: 'Behold, I knew them.'

8. Yea, thou heardest not;

Yea, thou knewest not;

Yea, from of old thine ear was not opened;

For I knew that thou wouldest deal very treacherously,

וּמִצְחֲךָ נְחוּשָׁה׃

5 וָאַגִּיד לְךָ מֵאָז

בְּטֶרֶם תָּבוֹא הִשְׁמַעְתִּיךָ

פֶּן־תֹּאמַר עָצְבִּי עָשָׂם

וּפִסְלִי וְנִסְכִּי צִוָּם׃

6 שָׁמַעְתָּ חֲזֵה כֻּלָּהּ

וְאַתֶּם הֲלוֹא תַגִּידוּ

הִשְׁמַעְתִּיךָ חֲדָשׁוֹת מֵעַתָּה

וּנְצֻרוֹת וְלֹא יְדַעְתָּם׃

7 עַתָּה נִבְרְאוּ וְלֹא מֵאָז

וְלִפְנֵי־יוֹם וְלֹא שְׁמַעְתָּם

פֶּן־תֹּאמַר הִנֵּה יְדַעְתִּין׃

8 גַּם לֹא־שָׁמַעְתָּ

גַּם לֹא יָדַעְתָּ

גַּם מֵאָז לֹא־פִתְּחָה אָזְנֶךָ

כִּי יָדַעְתִּי בָּגוֹד תִּבְגּוֹד

---

5. *mine idol.* [This is perhaps an indication that some Jews had lapsed into idolatry while they were in Babylon, and explains the detailed raillery against the manufacture of images in which the prophet indulges.]

done them. The events mentioned (Metsudath David).

6-8. Having heard the predictions and witnessed their fulfillment, the people can no longer doubt that God alone plans and rules the destinies of nations. They must, therefore, also believe in the new predictions now made by His prophet.

6. *see.* The realization of what had been foretold to you (Rashi).

will ye not declare it? Will you not admit that it is indeed so? (Rashi).

new things. Such as the fall of Babylon, the redemption of Israel and the recognition of Divine Sovereignty (verse 20).

7. The events having been announced just before they had come to pass, no one can claim to have predicted or expected them (Metsudath David).

8. *yea, thou ... opened.* Others translate: 'thou hast neither heard nor known, nor was thine ear opened beforehand.'

And wast called a transgressor
from the womb.

9. For My name's sake will I defer
Mine anger,
And for My praise will I refrain
for thee,
That I cut thee not off.

10. Behold, I have refined thee, but
not as silver;
I have tried thee in the furnace
of affliction.

11. For Mine own sake, for Mine
own sake, will I do it;
For how should it be profaned?
And My glory will I not give to
another.

12. Hearken unto Me, O Jacob,
And Israel My called:
I am He; I am the first,
I also am the last.

13. Yea, My hand hath laid the
foundation of the earth,

וּפֹשֵׁעַ מִבֶּטֶן קֹרָא לָךְ ׃

9 לְמַעַן שְׁמִי אַאֲרִיךְ אַפִּי
וּתְהִלָּתִי אֶחֱטָם־לָךְ
לְבִלְתִּי הַכְרִיתֶךָ ׃

10 הִנֵּה צְרַפְתִּיךָ וְלֹא בְכָסֶף
בְּחַרְתִּיךָ בְּכוּר עֹנִי ׃

11 לְמַעֲנִי לְמַעֲנִי אֶעֱשֶׂה
כִּי אֵיךְ יֵחָל
וּכְבוֹדִי לְאַחֵר לֹא־אֶתֵּן ׃

12 שְׁמַע אֵלַי יַעֲקֹב
וְיִשְׂרָאֵל מְקֹרָאִי
אֲנִי־הוּא אֲנִי רִאשׁוֹן
אַף אֲנִי אַחֲרוֹן ׃

13 אַף־יָדִי יָסְדָה אֶרֶץ

---

from the womb. From national infancy Israel showed a tendency to be rebellious against God's commandments (Rashi, Kimchi).

9-11. Israel, despite his transgressions, has been preserved for the sake of God's name. By chastisement and suffering he was spiritually purified but, that the name of God be not profaned and His glory ascribed to another, he was not utterly destroyed.

9. *will I defer.* lit. 'make long.'

for My praise. The preposition is implied (Kimchi).

refrain. Mine anger. i.e. refrain from Mine anger. It is synonymous with the expression in the first part of the verse (Kimchi).

10. *not as silver.* lit. 'not in (a crucible for) silver,' i.e. the process of refining was not so severe, which would have

amounted to complete destruction (Ibn Ezra).

I have tried thee. This is the meaning of *becharticha* in Aramaic, the Hebrew equivalent being *bechanticha,* with *nun* instead of *resh.* The meaning of *becharticha* in Hebrew is 'I have chosen thee' (See Ibn Ezra, Levita).

the furnace of affliction. Which is not so destructive as the crucible for silver (Metsudath David).

11. *for how . . . profaned?* By allowing the extermination of His people, which would be interpreted by the other nations as due to God's powerlessness to save His people (Metsudath David).

My glory . . . another. By enabling the enemy to claim that his god, which helped him to prevail over Israel, has superseded Israel's God (Rashi).

12. *My called.* Called children of God (Ibn Ezra).

And My right hand hath spread
  out the heavens;
When I call unto them,
  They stand up together.
14. Assemble yourselves, all ye, and
  hear;
  Which among them hath de-
    clared these things?
  He whom the LORD loveth shall   *Cyrus*
    perform His pleasure on
    Babylon,
  And show His arm on the
    Chaldeans.
15. I, even I, have spoken, yea,
    I have called him;
  I have brought him, and he shall
    make his way prosperous.
16. Come ye near unto Me, hear ye
    this: *Isaiah speaking*
  From the beginning I have not
    spoken in secret;
  From the time that it was, there
    am I;
  And now the Lord GOD hath
    sent me, and His spirit.
17. Thus saith the LORD, the Re-
    deemer,
  The Holy One of Israel:

רְמִינִי טִפְּחָה שָׁמָיִם
קֹרֵא אֲנִי אֲלֵיהֶם
יַעַמְדוּ יַחְדָּו׃
14 הִקָּבְצוּ כֻלְּכֶם וּשְׁמָעוּ
מִי בָהֶם הִגִּיד אֶת־אֵלֶּה
יְהוָה אֲהֵבוֹ יַעֲשֶׂה חֶפְצוֹ בְּבָבֶל
וּזְרֹעוֹ כַּשְׂדִּים׃
15 אֲנִי אֲנִי דִּבַּרְתִּי אַף־קְרָאתִיו
הֲבִאֹתִיו וְהִצְלִיחַ דַּרְכּוֹ׃
16 קִרְבוּ אֵלַי שִׁמְעוּ־זֹאת
לֹא מֵרֹאשׁ בַּסֵּתֶר דִּבַּרְתִּי
מֵעֵת הֱיוֹתָהּ שָׁם אָנִי
וְעַתָּה אֲדֹנָי יְהוָה שְׁלָחַנִי וְרוּחוֹ׃
17 כֹּה־אָמַר יְהוָה גֹּאֲלֶךָ
קְדוֹשׁ יִשְׂרָאֵל

---

13. *they stand up together.* They implicitly obey the command of their Creator
(Ibn Ezra). Another explanation is, they
stand in the perfection of their forms
and functions through My power
(Kimchi).

14. *all ye* [All Israel].

among them. The worshippers of the false
gods of the nations (Metsudath David).

these things. The rise of Cyrus and his
conquests (Kimchi).

he whom the LORD *loveth.* An allusion to
Cyrus (Rashi, Ibn Ezra, Kimchi).

show His arm. Reveal God's powers. The
verb is implied (Kara).

16.   The prophet is speaking.

from the beginning. When God appointed

Cyrus as His agent against Israel's
oppressor (Kara).

in secret. Cf. xlv. 19.

it was. The decree against Babylon
(Kara).

there am I. The prophet was present to
receive the Divine message (Kara).

me, and His spirit. Both are the object of
sent, i.e. God has sent the prophet with
His *spirit* within him (Kimchi, Malbim).

17–19.   How bright and prosperous
would his condition have been if Israel
had followed the guidance of the Lord,
his beneficent Teacher and trustworthy
Guide!

17.   *thus saith . . . Israel.* A recurrent
phrase in this section of the Book (cf.
xli. 14, xliii. 14, xlix. 7).

I am the LORD thy God,
Who teacheth thee for thy
profit,
Who leadeth thee by the way
that thou shouldest go.

18. Oh that thou wouldest hearken
to My commandments!
Then would thy peace be as a
river,
And thy righteousness as the
waves of the sea;

19. Thy seed also would be as the
sand,
And the offspring of thy body
like the grains thereof;
His name would not be cut off
Nor destroyed from before Me.

20. Go ye forth from Babylon,
Flee ye from the Chaldeans;
With a voice of singing
Declare ye, tell this,
Utter it even to the end of the
earth;
Say ye: 'The LORD hath re-
deemed
His servant Jacob.

אֲנִי יְהֹוָה אֱלֹהֶיךָ
מְלַמֶּדְךָ לְהוֹעִיל
מַדְרִיכְךָ בְּדֶרֶךְ תֵּלֵךְ׃
18 לוּא הִקְשַׁבְתָּ לְמִצְוֺתָי
וַיְהִי כַנָּהָר שְׁלוֹמֶךָ
וְצִדְקָתְךָ כְּגַלֵּי הַיָּם׃
19 וַיְהִי כַחוֹל זַרְעֶךָ
וְצֶאֱצָאֵי מֵעֶיךָ כִּמְעֹתָיו
לֹא־יִכָּרֵת וְלֹא־יִשָּׁמֵד
שְׁמוֹ מִלְּפָנָי׃
20 צְאוּ מִבָּבֶל
בִּרְחוּ מִכַּשְׂדִּים
בְּקוֹל רִנָּה
הַגִּידוּ הַשְׁמִיעוּ זֹאת
הוֹצִיאוּהָ עַד־קְצֵה הָאָרֶץ
אִמְרוּ גָּאַל יְהֹוָה
עַבְדּוֹ יַעֲקֹב׃

18. *peace.* i.e. welfare, prosperity.

as a river. With its abundant water flowing on for ever; a symbol of endless
blessedness (Metsudath David).

righteousness. See on xlv. 8.

19. *as the sand.* For similar expressions,
cf. x. 22; Gen. xxii. 17.

body. lit. 'bowels.' [The Hebrew word
meëcha is used because of its resemb-
lance to *meothaw, the grains thereof.*]
(According to Targum, Kimchi).

his name. (Targum, Ibn Ezra). Or, 'its
name,' that of the *offspring* (Kimchi).

20–22. The exiles are bidden to hasten
their departure from Babylon with jubilant songs of praise, recounting far and
wide the wonders of their redemption
and the marvels of their journey
through the desert where waters flowed
for them from the barren rocks.

20. *from the Chaldees.* Or, 'from
Chaldea' (Targum).

utter it. The wonderful news of deliverance (Kimchi, Metsudath David).

21. And they thirsted not
    When He led them through the
        deserts;
    He caused the waters to flow
    Out of the rock for them;
    He cleaved the rock also,
    And the waters gushed out.'
22. There is no peace,
    Saith the LORD concerning the
        wicked.

21 וְלֹא צָמְאוּ בָּחֳרָבוֹת הוֹלִיכָם
מַיִם מִצּוּר הִזִּיל לָמוֹ
וַיִּבְקַע־צוּר וַיָּזֻבוּ מָיִם׃
22 אֵין שָׁלוֹם
אָמַר יְהֹוָה לָרְשָׁעִים׃

49   CHAPTER XLIX   מט

1. Listen, O isles, unto me,
    And hearken, ye peoples, from
        far:
    The LORD hath called me from
        the womb,
    From the bowels of my mother
        hath He made mention of my
        name;
2. And He hath made my mouth
        like a sharp sword,
    In the shadow of His hand hath
        He hid me;
    And He hath made me a polished
        shaft,
    In His quiver hath He concealed
        me;
3. And He said unto me: 'Thou art
    My servant,

1 שִׁמְעוּ אִיִּים אֵלַי
וְהַקְשִׁיבוּ לְאֻמִּים מֵרָחוֹק
יְהֹוָה מִבֶּטֶן קְרָאָנִי
מִמְּעֵי אִמִּי הִזְכִּיר שְׁמִי׃
2 וַיָּשֶׂם פִּי כְּחֶרֶב חַדָּה
בְּצֵל יָדוֹ הֶחְבִּיאָנִי
וַיְשִׂימֵנִי לְחֵץ בָּרוּר
בְּאַשְׁפָּתוֹ הִסְתִּירָנִי׃
3 וַיֹּאמֶר לִי עַבְדִּי־אָתָּה

21. The description is reminiscent of the journey of the Israelites through the wilderness of Sinai (cf. Exod. xvii. 6; Num xx. 11).

22. *the wicked.* Of Israel who paid no heed to Cyrus' proclamation to return to Judea. Others explain it of the Babylonians (Rashi) or Nebuchadnezzar and the offspring (Rashi, Kimchi). The verse recurs in lvii. 21 with *my God* substituted for *the* LORD.

CHAPTER XLIX

1–6. Isaiah (representing the ideal Israel), the servant of God, addresses the nations far and near on his Divine mission; his apparent failure and disappointment in the past and his final realization that he is not to be only the instrument of Israel's salvation, but also a spiritual light to all the world.

1. The call.

from the womb. Cf. xliv. 2, 24, xlvi. 3. The servant of God was predestined to undertake his mission (Rashi, Kimchi).

2. The servant's Divine equipment.

in the shadow . . . hid me. As a protection against adversaries (Rashi, Kimchi).

Israel, in whom I will be
glorified.'

4. But I said: 'I have laboured in
vain,
I have spent my strength for
nought and vanity;
Yet surely my right is with the
LORD,
And my recompense with my
God.'

5. And now saith the LORD
That formed me from the womb
to be His servant,
To bring Jacob back to Him,
And that Israel be gathered unto
Him—
For I am honourable in the eyes
of the LORD,
And my God is become my
strength—

6. Yea, He saith: 'It is too light a
thing that thou shouldest be
My servant
To raise up the tribes of Jacob,
And to restore the offspring of
Israel;
I will also give thee for a light of
the nations,
That My salvation may be unto
the end of the earth.'

7. Thus saith the LORD,
The Redeemer of Israel, his
Holy One,

יִשְׂרָאֵל אֲשֶׁר־בְּךָ אֶתְפָּאָר:

4 וַאֲנִי אָמַרְתִּי לְרִיק יָגַעְתִּי
לְתֹהוּ וְהֶבֶל כֹּחִי כִלֵּיתִי
אָכֵן מִשְׁפָּטִי אֶת־יְהֹוָה
וּפְעֻלָּתִי אֶת־אֱלֹהָי:

5 וְעַתָּה | אָמַר יְהֹוָה
יֹצְרִי מִבֶּטֶן לְעֶבֶד לוֹ
לְשׁוֹבֵב יַעֲקֹב אֵלָיו
וְיִשְׂרָאֵל לֹא יֵאָסֵף
וְאֶכָּבֵד בְּעֵינֵי יְהֹוָה
וֵאלֹהַי הָיָה עֻזִּי:

6 וַיֹּאמֶר נָקֵל מִהְיוֹתְךָ לִי עֶבֶד
לְהָקִים אֶת־שִׁבְטֵי יַעֲקֹב
וּנְצִירֵי יִשְׂרָאֵל לְהָשִׁיב
וּנְתַתִּיךָ לְאוֹר גּוֹיִם
לִהְיוֹת יְשׁוּעָתִי עַד־קְצֵה הָאָרֶץ:

7 כֹּה אָמַר־יְהֹוָה
גֹּאֵל יִשְׂרָאֵל קְדוֹשׁוֹ

v. 5. ק׳ לוֹ .6 v. וּנצורי ק

3. *Israel.* The nation (Kara, Ibn Kaspi);
or Isaiah, as the personification of the
people (Ibn Ezra).

4. Though for a time he was despondent, he soon realized that his cause was
safe under the protection of God.

I said. To myself; I thought (Ibn Ezra).

5f. The revelation to the servant of the
great mission to Israel and the nations
which had been entrusted to him.

gathered unto Him. The *Kethib* reads 'not'

for *unto Him,* and the meaning of the
phrase is then 'that Israel not die'
(Saadia Gaon).

6. *it is too light a thing.* The task of the
servant is greater than the restoration of
Israel to his land; it has a world-wide
significance (Kimchi).

the offspring. Better, 'the ruins of' (Ibn
Ezra, Kimchi).

7. From the lowest depths of degradation Israel will rise to the loftiest heights
of respect and honour.

To him who is despised of men,
To him who is abhorred of
  nations,
To a servant of rulers:
Kings shall see and arise,
Princes, and they shall prostrate
  themselves;
Because of the LORD that is
  faithful,
Even the Holy One of Israel,
  who hath chosen thee.
8. Thus saith the LORD:
In an acceptable time have
  I answered thee,
And in a day of salvation have
  I helped thee;
And I will preserve thee, and
  give thee
For a covenant of the people,
To raise up the land,
To cause to inherit the desolate
  heritages;
9. Saying to the prisoners: 'Go
  forth';
To them that are in darkness:
  'Show yourselves';
They shall feed in the ways,

לִבְזֹה־נֶ֫פֶשׁ
לִמְתָעֵב גּוֹי
לְעֶ֫בֶד מֹשְׁלִ֔ים
מְלָכִים יִרְא֣וּ וָקָ֔מוּ
שָׂרִים וְיִֽשְׁתַּחֲו֑וּ
לְמַ֤עַן יְהוָה֙ אֲשֶׁ֣ר נֶאֱמָ֔ן
קְדֹ֥שׁ יִשְׂרָאֵ֖ל וַיִּבְחָרֶֽךָ׃
8 כֹּ֣ה ׀ אָמַ֣ר יְהוָ֗ה
בְּעֵ֤ת רָצוֹן֙ עֲנִיתִ֔יךָ
וּבְי֥וֹם יְשׁוּעָ֖ה עֲזַרְתִּ֑יךָ
וְאֶצָּרְךָ֗ וְאֶתֶּנְךָ֙
לִבְרִ֣ית עָ֔ם
לְהָקִ֣ים אֶ֔רֶץ
לְהַנְחִ֖יל נְחָל֥וֹת שֹׁמֵמֽוֹת׃
9 לֵאמֹ֤ר לָֽאֲסוּרִים֙ צֵ֔אוּ
לַאֲשֶׁ֥ר בַּחֹ֖שֶׁךְ הִגָּל֑וּ
עַל־דְּרָכִ֣ים יִרְע֔וּ

v. 7. כצ"ל

---

to him who is despised of men. lit. 'to the
despised of (every) soul' (Isaiah of
Trani).

kings shall see. Israel's ascent to greatness
(Metsudath David).

and arise. As a mark of respect (Abarbanel).

shall prostrate themselves. Pay homage
(Kimchi).

the LORD *that is faithful.* To fulfil His
promises (Rashi, Ibn Ezra, Kimchi).

8-12. God's acceptance of the prayers
of the exiles, their redemption from
captivity, and their safe and pleasant
return to the homeland.

8. *an acceptable time.* Or, 'a season of
favour.'

a covenant of the people. Or, 'a covenant-
people,' as in xlii. 6.

to raise up. Or, 'to restore' to Israel
(Kimchi).

to cause to inherit. Others render: 'to
allot.'

9. *prisoners.* i.e. the captives in the
Diaspora (Kimchi, Rashi).

darkness. See on xlii. 16.

in the ways. Provision will be made for
them in the journey homewards (Metsudath David).

And in all high hills shall be their
  pasture;

10. They shall not hunger nor thirst,
  Neither shall the heat nor sun
  smite them;
  For He that hath compassion on
  them will lead them,
  Even by the springs of water will
  He guide them.

11. And I will make all My mountains a way,
  And My highways shall be
  raised on high.

12. Behold, these shall come from
  far;
  And, lo, these from the north and
  from the west,
  And these from the land of
  Sinim.

13. Sing, O heavens, and be joyful,
  O earth,
  And break forth into singing,
  O mountains;
  For the LORD hath comforted
  His people,
  And hath compassion upon His
  afflicted.

14. But Zion said: 'The LORD hath
  forsaken me,
  And the Lord hath forgotten
  me.'

וּבְכָל־שְׁפָיִים מַרְעִיתָם׃

10 לֹא יִרְעָבוּ וְלֹא יִצְמָאוּ
וְלֹא־יַכֵּם שָׁרָב וָשָׁמֶשׁ
כִּי־מְרַחֲמָם יְנַהֲגֵם
וְעַל־מַבּוּעֵי מַיִם יְנַהֲלֵם׃

11 וְשַׂמְתִּי כָל־הָרַי לַדָּרֶךְ
וּמְסִלֹּתַי יְרֻמוּן׃

12 הִנֵּה־אֵלֶּה מֵרָחוֹק יָבֹאוּ
וְהִנֵּה־אֵלֶּה מִצָּפוֹן וּמִיָּם
וְאֵלֶּה מֵאֶרֶץ סִינִים׃

13 רָנּוּ שָׁמַיִם וְגִילִי אָרֶץ
וּפִצְחוּ הָרִים רִנָּה
כִּי־נִחַם יְהֹוָה עַמּוֹ
וַעֲנִיָּו יְרַחֵם׃

14 וַתֹּאמֶר צִיּוֹן עֲזָבַנִי יְהֹוָה
וַאדֹנָי שְׁכֵחָנִי׃

v. 10. קמץ בז"ק   v. 13. קמץ בז"ק   v. 13. ופצחו ק'   v. 14. הפטרת עקב

10. *heat*. The Hebrew word *sharab* was
translated *parched land* in xxxv. 7. The
returning captives will be spared the
trials of desert travel (Ibn Ezra).

11. *highways ... on high*. All uneven-
ness and ruggedness in the highways
will be levelled. The thought is the same
as in xl. 4 (Rashi).

12. *land of Sinim*. Some render; 'the
land of the Chinese' (Biberfeld); alter-
natives proposed are 'a southern land'
(so the Targum), 'the land of Sin,' i.e.
Pelusium on the Egyptian border (Ibn
Ezra).

13. A short lyrical hymn concluding
the passage (cf. xliv. 23).

14-21. A poem of singular charm and
beauty, breathing the spirit of tender-
ness and sympathy, in which the
prophet announces the speedy return of
the exiled community to Zion, the
rebuilding of the city's ruins and the
increase of its inhabitants.

14. *Zion*. Represented as a deserted
and forgotten wife bemoaning her lot
(Abarbanel).

15. Can a woman forget her sucking
    child,
    That she should not have com-
    passion on the son of her
    womb?
    Yea, these may forget,
    Yet will not I forget thee.
16. Behold, I have graven thee upon
    the palms of My hands;
    Thy walls are continually before
    Me.
17. Thy children make haste;
    Thy destroyers and they that
    made thee waste shall go forth
    from thee.
18. Lift up thine eyes round about,
    and behold:
    All these gather themselves to-
    gether, and come to thee.
    As I live, saith the LORD,
    Thou shalt surely clothe thee
    with them all as with an
    ornament,
    And gird thyself with them, like
    a bride.

הֲתִשְׁכַּח אִשָּׁה עוּלָהּ 15

מֵרַחֵם בֶּן־בִּטְנָהּ

גַּם־אֵלֶּה תִשְׁכַּחְנָה

וְאָנֹכִי לֹא אֶשְׁכָּחֵךְ:

הֵן עַל־כַּפַּיִם חַקֹּתִיךְ 16

חוֹמֹתַיִךְ נֶגְדִּי תָּמִיד:

מִהֲרוּ בָּנָיִךְ 17

מְהָרְסַיִךְ וּמַחֲרִבַיִךְ מִמֵּךְ יֵצֵאוּ:

שְׂאִי־סָבִיב עֵינַיִךְ וּרְאִי 18

כֻּלָּם נִקְבְּצוּ בָאוּ־לָךְ

חַי־אָנִי נְאֻם־יְהֹוָה

כִּי כֻלָּם כָּעֲדִי תִלְבָּשִׁי

וּתְקַשְּׁרִים כַּכַּלָּה:

v. 18. קמץ בז״ק

15-21. God's answer, comforting and reassuring.

15. Is it likely that a mother's compassion for her child should fail? Of course not! But, even if such an unnatural possibility could be imagined, God's mindfulness of Zion is much more steadfast and enduring than the strongest of human ties of kinship.

these. Mothers (Ibn Ezra, Kimchi).

may forget. Their offspring (Kimchi).

16. A bold metaphor. God, having as it were engraved Zion on both His hands, can never forget her sad plight.

walls. Which are now in ruins (Kimchi). Others consider the imagery to refer to the plan of the rebuilt city which is engraved upon the Divine hands and so cannot be forgotten by Him (Alschich).

17-21. The prophet in his vision already sees Zion's children returning to their mother, the rebuilding of her ruins and the multitudes crowding within her walls.

17. *thy children.* The exiles. The Targum and other ancient versions explain the word as *bonayich,* 'thy builders,' but this is not supported by verses 20f.

make haste. To return to Zion (Rashi).

thy destroyers . . . waste. The Babylonian garrisons billeted upon the country (Ibn Kaspi). Others take the clause in a spiritual sense: the wicked men who were the cause of their people's fall (Ibn Ezra, Kimchi).

18. *all these.* Zion's children (Abarbanel).

clothe . . . bride. A vivid metaphor; the returning children will be like bridal ornaments.

19. For thy waste and thy desolate
places
And thy land that hath been
destroyed—
Surely now shalt thou be too
strait for the inhabitants,
And they that swallowed thee up
shall be far away.

20. The children of thy bereavement
Shall yet say in thine ears:
'The place is too strait for me;
Give place to me that I may
dwell.'

21. Then shalt thou say in thy heart:
'Who hath begotten me these,
Seeing I have been bereaved of
my children, and am solitary,
An exile, and wandering to and
fro?
And who hath brought up these?
Behold, I was left alone;
These, where were they?'

22. Thus saith the Lord GOD:

כִּי חָרְבֹתַיִךְ וְשֹׁמְמֹתַיִךְ 19
וְאֶרֶץ הֲרִסֻתֵךְ
כִּי עַתָּה תֵּצְרִי מִיּוֹשֵׁב
וְרָחֲקוּ מְבַלְּעָיִךְ:
עוֹד יֹאמְרוּ בְאָזְנַיִךְ 20
בְּנֵי שִׁכֻּלָיִךְ
צַר־לִי הַמָּקוֹם
גְּשָׁה־לִּי וְאֵשֵׁבָה:
וְאָמַרְתְּ בִּלְבָבֵךְ 21
מִי יָלַד־לִי אֶת־אֵלֶּה
וַאֲנִי שְׁכוּלָה וְגַלְמוּדָה
גֹּלָה וְסוּרָה
וְאֵלֶּה מִי גִדֵּל
הֵן אֲנִי נִשְׁאַרְתִּי לְבַדִּי
אֵלֶּה אֵיפֹה הֵם:
כֹּה־אָמַר אֲדֹנָי יְהוִה 22

19f. Zion's present solitude will give way to a teeming population that will overcrowd the city.

19. *for thy waste.* Perhaps 'as for thy waste.'

too strait. Owing to the returning multitudes (Rashi, Ibn Ezra).

that swallowed thee. See on *thy destroyers* (verse 17).

20. *children of thy bereavement.* The children who were lost to Zion when they were taken into captivity (Rashi, Kimchi).

give place. Cf. the use of the verb in Gen. xix. 9, *stand back.*

21. Zion, bereaved and solitary for so long, cannot believe that all the returning children are really her own.

an exile, and wandering to and fro. The exiled and wandering Israelites are personified in Zion (Kimchi).

where were they? Or, 'from where have they come?' (Kimchi).

22-1.3. Three short oracles on the restoration of exiled Israel with the aid of the highest personages of the Gentiles; a reassurance that God will champion their cause; and a reaffirmation of the covenant relation between Him and His people.

22f. The Gentiles, the common people as well as their kings and queens, in response to a Divine signal, will assist in the restoration of Israel and at the same time pay him the highest marks of homage.

Behold, I will lift up My hand
  to the nations,
And set up Mine ensign to the
  peoples,
And they shall bring thy sons in
  their bosom,
And thy daughters shall be
  carried upon their shoulders.
23. And kings shall be thy foster-
  fathers,
And their queens thy nursing
  mothers;
They shall bow down to thee
  with their face to the earth,
And lick the dust of thy feet;
And thou shalt know that I am
  the LORD,
For they shall not be ashamed
  that wait for Me.
24. Shall the prey be taken from
  the mighty,
Or the captives of the victorious
  be delivered?
25. But thus saith the LORD:
Even the captives of the mighty
  shall be taken away,
And the prey of the terrible shall
  be delivered;
And I will contend with him that
  contendeth with thee,

הִנֵּה אֶשָּׂא אֶל־גּוֹיִם יָדִי
וְאֶל־עַמִּים אָרִים נִסִּי
וְהֵבִיאוּ בָנַיִךְ בְּחֹצֶן
וּבְנֹתַיִךְ עַל־כָּתֵף תִּנָּשֶׂאנָה:
²³ וְהָיוּ מְלָכִים אֹמְנַיִךְ
וְשָׂרוֹתֵיהֶם מֵינִיקֹתַיִךְ
אַפַּיִם אֶרֶץ יִשְׁתַּחֲווּ־לָךְ
וַעֲפַר רַגְלַיִךְ יְלַחֵכוּ
וְיָדַעַתְּ כִּי־אֲנִי יְהֹוָה
אֲשֶׁר לֹא־יֵבֹשׁוּ קוָֹי:
²⁴ הֲיֻקַּח מִגִּבּוֹר מַלְקוֹחַ
וְאִם־שְׁבִי צַדִּיק יִמָּלֵט:
²⁵ כִּי־כֹה ׀ אָמַר יְהֹוָה
גַּם־שְׁבִי גִבּוֹר יֻקָּח
וּמַלְקוֹחַ עָרִיץ יִמָּלֵט
וְאֶת־יְרִיבֵךְ אָנֹכִי אָרִיב

v. 25. קמץ בז"ק

22. *lift up ... peoples.* As a signal for
them to perform the enumerated ser-
vices for the returning exiles (Rashi,
Metsudath David).

in their bosom ... shoulders. i.e. with great
honor (Metsudath David).

23. Kings and queens of the foreign
nations will look after the welfare of
God's people.

bow down ... earth. Will pay homage
(Abarbanel).

lick the dust of thy feet. They will display

abject self-humiliation in Oriental fashion (cf. Mic. vii. 17; Ps. lxxii. 9).

24-26. God will fight for the liberation of Israel against the all-powerful
nations who oppressed him.

24. The natural answer to the question
is obviously in the negative; but, as the
following verse announces, God can do
even that which is humanly impossible
(Kimchi).

mighty. Or, 'a hero.'

victorious. The Hebrew word is usually
rendered 'righteous' (see on xli. 2).

And I will save thy children.

26. And I will feed them that
oppress thee with their own
flesh;
And they shall be drunken with
their own blood, as with sweet
wine;
And all flesh shall know that
I the LORD am the Saviour,
And thy Redeemer, the Mighty
One of Jacob.

וְאֶת־בָּנַיִךְ אָנֹכִי אוֹשִׁיעַ׃

26 וְהַאֲכַלְתִּי אֶת־מוֹנַיִךְ אֶת־בְּשָׂרָם
וְכֶעָסִיס דָּמָם יִשְׁכָּרוּן
וְיָדְעוּ כָל־בָּשָׂר כִּי אֲנִי יְהֹוָה מוֹשִׁיעֵךְ
וְגֹאֲלֵךְ אֲבִיר יַעֲקֹב׃

50   CHAPTER L   נ

1. Thus saith the LORD:

Where is the bill of your mother's
divorcement,
Wherewith I have put her away?
Or which of My creditors is it
To whom I have sold you?
Behold, for your iniquities were
ye sold,
And for your transgressions was
your mother put away.

2. Wherefore, when I came, was
there no man?

1 כֹּה ׀ אָמַר יְהֹוָה
אֵי זֶה סֵפֶר כְּרִיתוּת אִמְּכֶם
אֲשֶׁר שִׁלַּחְתִּיהָ
אוֹ מִי מִנּוֹשַׁי
אֲשֶׁר־מָכַרְתִּי אֶתְכֶם לוֹ
הֵן בַּעֲוֹנֹתֵיכֶם נִמְכַּרְתֶּם
וּבְפִשְׁעֵיכֶם שֻׁלְּחָה אִמְּכֶם׃
2 מַדּוּעַ בָּאתִי וְאֵין אִישׁ

---

26. *feed . . . flesh.* They will be annihilated in their own mutually destructive
feuds (cf. Zech. xi. 9) (Kimchi).

CHAPTER L

1–3. Israel need not fear that his exile
had created a permanent break in his
covenant relation with God. Though he
was banished, no bill of divorcement
was ever written; and though long
oppressed by his enemies, no bill of sale
was ever made out. Israel, in expiation
for his sins, was only temporarily sold
and banished, and God will surely
redeem him when the appointed time
comes.

1. *where is . . . her away?* The answer

expected is nowhere; never was such a
bill written. There has been separation,
but not a divorce (Malbim).

My creditors . . . sold you? A father, driven
by poverty, had sometimes to sell his
children to his cruel creditors (cf. 2
Kings iv. 1; Neh. v. 5); but God has no
creditors. Israel, therefore, was never
sold (Malbim).

for your iniquities . . . put away. Now that
the term of punishment is over, they
may again return to their homeland
(Metsudath David).

2. The weaklings and despondent are
rebuked for their failure to respond to
the prophet's message of liberation.

When I called, was there none
to answer?
Is My hand shortened at all, that
it cannot redeem?
Or have I no power to deliver?
Behold, at My rebuke I dry up
the sea,
I make the rivers a wilderness;
Their fish become foul, because
there is no water,
And die for thirst.
3. I clothe the heavens with blackness,
And I make sackcloth their
covering.
4. The Lord GOD hath given me
The tongue of them that are
taught,
That I should know how to
sustain with words him that is
weary;
He wakeneth morning by morning,
He wakeneth mine ear
To hear as they that are taught.

קָרָאתִ֙י וְאֵ֣ין עוֹנֶ֔ה
הֲקָצ֤וֹר קָֽצְרָה֙ יָדִ֣י מִפְּד֔וּת
וְאִם־אֵֽין־בִּ֥י כֹ֖חַ לְהַצִּ֑יל
הֵ֣ן בְּגַעֲרָתִ֞י אַחֲרִ֣יב יָ֗ם
אָשִׂ֤ים נְהָרוֹת֙ מִדְבָּ֔ר
תִּבְאַ֤שׁ דְּגָתָם֙ מֵאֵ֣ין מַ֔יִם
וְתָמֹ֖ת בַּצָּמָֽא:
3 אַלְבִּ֥ישׁ שָׁמַ֖יִם קַדְר֑וּת
וְשַׂ֖ק אָשִׂ֥ים כְּסוּתָֽם:
4 אֲדֹנָ֤י יֱהֹוִה֙ נָ֣תַן לִ֔י
לְשׁ֖וֹן לִמּוּדִ֑ים
לָדַ֗עַת לָע֣וּת אֶת־יָעֵף֮ דָּבָ֒ר
יָעִ֣יר ׀ בַּבֹּ֣קֶר בַּבֹּ֗קֶר
יָעִ֥יר לִי֙ אֹ֔זֶן
לִשְׁמֹ֖עַ כַּלִּמּוּדִֽים:

---

no man. To respond to the message
(Rashi).

shortened. Incapable (cf. xxxvii. 27, lix. 1)
(Metsudath David).

I dry up the sea. As happened at the Red
Sea when Israel passed through it
(Exod. xiv. 29).

rivers a wilderness. Cf. Ps. cvii. 33.

fish become foul. Cf. Exod. vii. 21.

3. *blackness . . . sackcloth.* A reference to
eclipses, storms and clouds, God's
powerful manifestation against Israel's
enemies and oppressors, *blackness* and
sackcloth symbolizing depression and
gloom (Kimchi).

4–9. The servants' suffering and perseverance, and his trust in God's pro-

tection. The word 'servant' does not
occur in the passage, but the description
of his characteristics is strikingly similar
to those of the servant in xlii. 1–4, xlix.
1–6, lii. 13-liii. 12. The servant is said to
be Isaiah himself (Rashi, Ibn Ezra,
Kimchi).

4. *them that are taught.* Or, 'the
learned,' i.e. of cultivated and fluent
speech (Kimchi).

to sustain. Or, 'to instruct' (Targum, Ibn
Ganah). Others prefer the rendering 'to
speak a word in season' (Menahem,
Rashi, Ibn Ezra, Kimchi).

weaketh. Me (Ibn Ezra, Kimchi).

as they that are taught. Or, 'after the
manner of disciples.' The servant is
God's disciple (Metsudath David).

5. The Lord GOD hath opened
   mine ear,
   And I was not rebellious,
   Neither turned away backward.

6. I gave my back to the smiters,
   And my cheeks to them that
   plucked off the hair;
   I hid not my face from shame
   and spitting.

7. For the Lord GOD will help me;
   Therefore have I not been confounded;
   Therefore have I set my face like
   a flint,
   And I know that I shall not be
   ashamed.

8. He is near that justifieth me;
   Who will contend with me? let
   us stand up together;
   Who is mine adversary? let him
   come near to me.

5 אֲדֹנָי יְהוִה פָּתַח־לִי אֹזֶן
וְאָנֹכִי לֹא מָרִיתִי
אָחוֹר לֹא נְסוּגֹתִי:
6 גֵּוִי נָתַתִּי לְמַכִּים
וּלְחָיַי לְמֹרְטִים
פָּנַי לֹא הִסְתַּרְתִּי מִכְּלִמּוֹת וָרֹק:
7 וַאדֹנָי יְהוִה יַעֲזָר־לִי
עַל־כֵּן לֹא נִכְלָמְתִּי
עַל־כֵּן שַׂמְתִּי פָנַי כַּחַלָּמִישׁ
וָאֵדַע כִּי־לֹא אֵבוֹשׁ:
8 קָרוֹב מַצְדִּיקִי
מִי־יָרִיב אִתִּי נַעַמְדָה יָּחַד
מִי־בַעַל מִשְׁפָּטִי
יִגַּשׁ אֵלָי:

[handwritten annotations: "disgraced", "call for unity"]

---

6. *opened mine ear.* To impart His message (Rashi, Ibn Ezra).

was not rebellious. But implicitly obeyed (Rashi, Kimchi).

neither turned away backward. He boldly delivered God's message to the misguided people, though he incurred persecution and humiliation (Kimchi).

6. The servant readily acquiesces in the sufferings and disgrace inflicted upon him in the course of the performance of his mission.

plucked off the hair. Of the beard. Forcible removal of the beard was regarded as one of the worst forms of degradation (cf. vii. 20; 2 Sam. x. 4).

7. *confounded.* Better, 'disgraced.' Since God helped me by fulfilling the proph-

ecy I was not ashamed to deliver His message in public (Kimchi). Alternatively, Isaiah was not subjected to the derision and disgrace suffered by other prophets, e.g. Jeremiah, Amos, and Micah. Since he occupied a high position, the people did not molest him (Abarbanel).

like a flint. Expressive of unbreakable determination (Metsudath David).

not be ashamed. Not be subjected to shame (Metsudath David).

8. *that justifieth me.* viz. God Who will not allow His servant to suffer much longer (Rashi).

stand up together. To contend (Metsudath David).

let him come near to me. To justify his enmity (Metsudath David).

9. Behold, the Lord GOD will help
me;

Who is he that shall condemn
me?

Behold, they all shall wax old as
a garment,

The moth shall eat them up.

10. Who is among you that feareth
the LORD,

That obeyeth the voice of His
servant?

Though he walketh in darkness,

And hath no light,

Let him trust in the name of the
LORD,

And stay upon his God.

11. Behold, all ye that kindle a fire,

That gird yourselves with firebrands,

Begone in the flame of your fire,

And among the brands that ye
have kindled.

This shall ye have of My hand;

Ye shall lie down in sorrow.

9 הֵ֣ן אֲדֹנָ֤י יֱהֹוִה֙ יַֽעֲזָר־לִ֔י

מִי־ה֖וּא יַרְשִׁיעֵ֑נִי

הֵ֤ן כֻּלָּם֙ כַּבֶּ֣גֶד יִבְל֔וּ

עָ֖שׁ יֹאכְלֵֽם׃

10 מִ֤י בָכֶם֙ יְרֵ֣א יְהֹוָ֔ה

שֹׁמֵ֖עַ בְּק֣וֹל עַבְדּ֑וֹ

אֲשֶׁ֣ר ׀ הָלַ֣ךְ חֲשֵׁכִ֗ים

וְאֵ֥ין נֹ֨גַהּ֙ ל֔וֹ

יִבְטַח֙ בְּשֵׁ֣ם יְהֹוָ֔ה

וְיִשָּׁעֵ֖ן בֵּֽאלֹהָֽיו׃

11 הֵ֧ן כֻּלְּכֶ֛ם קֹ֥דְחֵי אֵ֖שׁ

מְאַזְּרֵ֣י זִיק֑וֹת

לְכ֣וּ ׀ בְּא֣וּר אֶשְׁכֶ֗ם

וּבְזִיקוֹת֙ בִּֽעַרְתֶּ֔ם

מִיָּדִי֙ הָיְתָה־זֹּ֣את לָכֶ֔ם

לְמַֽעֲצֵבָ֖ה תִּשְׁכָּבֽוּן׃

---

9. *condemn me.* Prove that I am wrong.

wax old. Or, 'be worn out.'

the moth. A symbol of destruction (cf.
Hos. v. 12; Ps. xxxix. 12).

10f. An addendum to the passage of
the servant, bringing assurance and
encouragement to the faithful and
threats and a warning to the godless.

10. *among you.* This is addressed to the
people generally (Abarbanel).

in darkness. In trouble and suffering
(Rashi).

11. *that kindle a fire . . . firebrands.* That
arouse God's wrath (Rashi, Kimchi).

begone in the flame of your fire. You ignited
fire and you will receive your retribution through fire; your iniquity will
destroy you (Kimchi).

this shall ye have. As retribution for the
mischievous designs (Rashi).

51

CHAPTER LI   נא

1. Hearken to Me, ye that follow
   after righteousness,
   Ye that seek the LORD;   [the few]
   Look unto the rock whence ye
   were hewn,   hammer or quarry
   And to the hole of the pit whence
   ye were digged.
2. Look unto Abraham your father,
   And unto Sarah that bore you;
   For when he was but one I called
   him,
   And I blessed him, and made
   him many.
3. For the LORD hath comforted
   Zion;
   He hath comforted all her waste
   places,
   And hath made her wilderness
   like Eden,
   And her desert like the garden
   of the LORD;   prophetic perfects

1 שִׁמְע֤וּ אֵלַי֙ רֹ֣דְפֵי צֶ֔דֶק
מְבַקְשֵׁ֖י יְהֹוָ֑ה
הַבִּ֙יטוּ֙ אֶל־צ֣וּר חֻצַּבְתֶּ֔ם
וְאֶל־מַקֶּ֥בֶת בּ֖וֹר נֻקַּרְתֶּֽם׃
2 הַבִּ֙יטוּ֙ אֶל־אַבְרָהָ֣ם אֲבִיכֶ֔ם
וְאֶל־שָׂרָ֖ה תְּחוֹלֶלְכֶ֑ם
כִּֽי־אֶחָ֣ד קְרָאתִ֔יו
וַאֲבָרְכֵ֖הוּ וְאַרְבֵּֽהוּ׃
3 כִּֽי־נִחַ֨ם יְהֹוָ֜ה צִיּ֗וֹן
נִחַם֙ כָּל־חָרְבֹתֶ֔יהָ
וַיָּ֤שֶׂם מִדְבָּרָהּ֙ כְּעֵ֔דֶן
וְעַרְבָתָ֖הּ כְּגַן־יְהֹוָ֑ה

CHAPTER LI

1-8. The prophet's address of consolation to the true believers, interrupted
by the speech of the servant (i. 4-9), is
now resumed (Ibn Ezra).

1-3. Though the faithful are few in
number, they need have no fear that
they are too insignificant to receive the
promised blessings. They have but to
look to Abraham and Sarah to realize
that a whole nation may arise from one
small family (Ibn Ezra).

1. *rock . . . pit.* The ancestors of the
nation are compared to a quarry and its
members to the stones hewn therefrom.
The Hebrew word for *hole* elsewhere
means 'hammer.' Indeed, Rashi and
Kimchi render, 'the hammer of the pit,'
etc.'

2. *Abraham . . . Sarah.* The names
define *rock* and *pit* in the preceding
verse.

he was but one . . . made him many. So will

the faithful few increase and live to see
the restoration and rehabilitation of
Zion. God's promise to Abraham (Gen.
xii. 2) was fulfilled; similarly the
promises made to them would be carried out (Rashi, Metsudath David).

and I blessed . . . made. This follows
Kimchi. Others render, 'and I will bless
him . . . make' in the future, meaning, 'I
promised to bless him and make him
great, and I fulfilled My promise.' This
applies likewise to the present situation
(Ibn Ezra).

3. *hath comforted . . . hath made.* These
are prophetic perfects (see on xliii. 1) or
perfects of certainty, signifying 'shall
surely comfort . . . shall surely make'
(Kimchi, Metsudath David).

her waste places. The prophet compares
Zion to Abraham and Sarah, who were
childless for many years. So will Zion be
bereft of her children for many years,
but will eventually become like Eden,
the garden of the Lord, cf. Gen. xiii. 10
(Abarbanel).

Joy and gladness shall be found
  therein,
Thanksgiving, and the voice of
  melody.
4. Attend unto Me, O My people,
  And give ear unto Me, O My
    nation;
  For instruction shall go forth
    from Me,
  And My right on a sudden for a
    light of the peoples.
5. My favour is near,
  My salvation is gone forth,
  And Mine arms shall judge the
    peoples;
  The isles shall wait for Me,
  And on Mine arm shall they
    trust.
6. Lift up your eyes to the heavens,
  And look upon the earth beneath;
  For the heavens shall vanish
    away like smoke,
  And the earth shall wax old like
    a garment,
  And they that dwell therein shall
    die in like manner;
  But My salvation shall be for
    ever,
  And My favour shall not be
    abolished.

שָׂשׂוֹן וְשִׂמְחָה יִמָּצֵא בָהּ
תּוֹדָה וְקוֹל זִמְרָה:
4 הַקְשִׁיבוּ אֵלַי עַמִּי
וּלְאוּמִּי אֵלַי הַאֲזִינוּ
כִּי תוֹרָה מֵאִתִּי תֵצֵא
וּמִשְׁפָּטִי לְאוֹר עַמִּים אַרְגִּיעַ:
5 קָרוֹב צִדְקִי
יָצָא יִשְׁעִי
וּזְרֹעַי עַמִּים יִשְׁפֹּטוּ
אֵלַי אִיִּים יְקַוּוּ
וְאֶל־זְרֹעִי יְיַחֵלוּן:
6 שְׂאוּ לַשָּׁמַיִם עֵינֵיכֶם
וְהַבִּיטוּ אֶל־הָאָרֶץ מִתַּחַת
כִּי־שָׁמַיִם כֶּעָשָׁן נִמְלָחוּ
וְהָאָרֶץ כַּבֶּגֶד תִּבְלֶה
וְיֹשְׁבֶיהָ כְּמוֹ־כֵן יְמוּתוּן
וִישׁוּעָתִי לְעוֹלָם תִּהְיֶה
וְצִדְקָתִי לֹא תֵחָת:

v. 3. עד כאן v. 4. דגש אחר שורק v. 6. קמץ בפשטא

joy . . . melody. In this, it will differ from
Eden, where Adam and Eve met tragedy
(Abarbanel).

4–6. Divine instruction, justice and
salvation will be a light to the world.
The nations will seek guidance from
God and the righteous be assured of
His everlasting salvation and favour.

4. *My nation.* Who is obligated to
believe My prophecy, know ye that My
'instruction shall go forth from Me,'
that My decree of the exile and the ultimate redemption therefrom will definitely be realized (Abarbanel).

right. Or, 'judgment.' As above, this
refers to the decree of the exile and the
redemption (Abarbanel).

on a sudden. Others translate, 'I will
cause to rest' (Rashi, Ibn Ezra).

5. *arm.* i.e. power; again in verse 9.

6. Even if nature were transitory,
God's salvation and favour are eternal
(Kimchi).

vanish away. Or, 'be dissolved' (Rashi).

7f. The eternal salvation and favour
promised should provide the faithful

7. Hearken unto Me, ye that know
   righteousness,
   The people in whose heart is
   My law;
   Fear ye not the taunt of men,
   Neither be ye dismayed at their
   revilings.

8. For the moth shall eat them up
   like a garment,
   And the worm shall eat them
   like wool;
   But My favour shall be for ever,
   And My salvation unto all
   generations.

9. Awake, awake, put on strength,
   O arm of the LORD;
   Awake, as in the days of old,
   The generations of ancient times.
   Art thou not it that hewed
   Rahab in pieces,
   That pierced the dragon?

10. Art thou not it that dried up the
    sea,
    The waters of the great deep;

7 שִׁמְעוּ אֵלַי יֹדְעֵי צֶדֶק
עַם תּוֹרָתִי בְלִבָּם
אַל־תִּירְאוּ חֶרְפַּת אֱנוֹשׁ
וּמִגִּדֻּפֹתָם אַל־תֵּחָתּוּ:
8 כִּי כַבֶּגֶד יֹאכְלֵם עָשׁ
וְכַצֶּמֶר יֹאכְלֵם סָס
וְצִדְקָתִי לְעוֹלָם תִּהְיֶה
וִישׁוּעָתִי לְדוֹר דּוֹרִים:
9 עוּרִי עוּרִי לִבְשִׁי־עֹז
זְרוֹעַ יְהֹוָה
עוּרִי כִּימֵי קֶדֶם
דּוֹרוֹת עוֹלָמִים
הֲלוֹא אַתְּ־הִיא
הַמַּחְצֶבֶת רַהַב מְחוֹלֶלֶת תַּנִּין:
10 הֲלוֹא אַתְּ־הִיא הַמַּחֲרֶבֶת יָם
מֵי תְּהוֹם רַבָּה

v. 9. מלרע

with moral courage and strength to
withstand the ephemeral taunts and
abuse of the ungodly.

7. *law.* Better, 'instruction' as in verse
4 (Abarbanel).

men. Hebrew *enosh,* denoting human
frailty: here the ungodly.

8. *moth.* See on 1. 9 where, however, a
different Hebrew noun is used.

My favour . . . salvation. For the faithful
(Kimchi).

9f. The prophet's prayer to God
(Rashi).

9. *art thou not it.* Addressed to the *arm
of the* LORD (Abarbanel).

Rahab. A poetical name for Egypt meaning 'the proud' (Rashi).

the dragon. viz. Pharaoh (Rashi).

10. *the sea.* The Red Sea through which
the children of Israel passed after their
departure from Egypt (Kimchi).

252

That made the depths of the sea
  a way
For the redeemed to pass over?

11. And the ransomed of the LORD
  shall return,
  And come with singing unto
  Zion,
  And everlasting joy shall be upon
  their heads;
  They shall obtain gladness and
  joy,
  And sorrow and sighing shall flee
  away.

12. I, even I, am He that comforteth
  you;
  Who art thou, that thou art
  afraid of man that shall die,
  And of the son of man that shall
  be made as grass;

13. And hast forgotten the LORD thy
  Maker,
  That stretched forth the heavens,
  And laid the foundations of the
  earth;
  And fearest continually all the
  day
  Because of the fury of the
  oppressor,
  As he maketh ready to destroy?

הַשָּׂמָה֙ מַעֲמַקֵּי־יָ֔ם
דֶּ֖רֶךְ לַעֲבֹ֥ר גְּאוּלִֽים׃
11 וּפְדוּיֵ֨י יְהֹוָ֜ה יְשׁוּב֗וּן
וּבָ֤אוּ צִיּוֹן֙ בְּרִנָּ֔ה
וְשִׂמְחַ֥ת עוֹלָ֖ם עַל־רֹאשָׁ֑ם
שָׂשׂ֤וֹן וְשִׂמְחָה֙ יַשִּׂיג֔וּן
נָ֖סוּ יָג֥וֹן וַאֲנָחָֽה׃
12 אָנֹכִ֧י אָנֹכִ֛י ה֖וּא מְנַחֶמְכֶ֑ם
מִי־אַ֤תְּ וַתִּֽירְאִי֙ מֵאֱנ֣וֹשׁ יָמ֔וּת
וּמִבֶּן־אָדָ֖ם חָצִ֥יר יִנָּתֵֽן׃
13 וַתִּשְׁכַּ֞ח יְהֹוָ֣ה עֹשֶׂ֗ךָ
נוֹטֶ֤ה שָׁמַ֙יִם֙
וְיֹסֵ֣ד אָ֔רֶץ
וַתְּפַחֵ֨ד תָּמִ֤יד כָּל־הַיּוֹם֙
מִפְּנֵי֙ חֲמַ֣ת הַמֵּצִ֔יק
כַּאֲשֶׁ֖ר כּוֹנֵ֣ן לְהַשְׁחִ֑ית

v. 12. הפטרת שופטים   v. 13. קמץ בסגולתא

---

11. The Divine reply to the prayer in
verses 9f. The verse is almost identical
with xxxv. 10.

the ransomed. The exiles returning to
Zion in Messianic times (Abarbanel).

12–16. The Comforter of Israel is the
Creator of the universe. Israel, therefore, n   have no fear of his puny
mortal oppressors. The passage may be
regarded as continuing the Divine
answer to the prayer in verses 9f (Metsudath David).

12. The people or the faithful remnant
at first addressed as individuals, *comforteth you,* then collectively as one group,
keneseth, that thou (fem.) *art afraid.* In the

next verse this is changed to the masculine, *hast* (masc.) *forgotten* (Kimchi).

who art thou, etc. The meaning is, 'thou
hast no need to fear' (Rashi).

man. Hebrew *enosh* (see on verse 7).

son of man. A mortal being (Metsudath
David).

made of grass. lit. 'given up (to destruction as) grass.'

13. *forgotten the* LORD. This refers to
Gog, who will attack Israel before the
Messianic era (Rabbenu Yeshayah).

as he maketh ready to destroy. The object to
be understood is Jerusalem. Israel fears
destruction at his hands when he makes

And where is the fury of the oppressor?

14. He that is bent down shall speedily be loosed;
And he shall not go down dying into the pit,
Neither shall his bread fail.

15. For I am the LORD thy God,
Who stirreth up the sea, that the waves thereof roar;
The LORD of hosts is His name.

16. And I have put My words in thy mouth,
And have covered thee in the shadow of My hand,
That I may plant the heavens,
And lay the foundations of the earth,
And say unto Zion: 'Thou art My people.'

וְאַיֵּה חֲמַת הַמֵּצִיק׃

14 מִהַר צֹעֶה לְהִפָּתֵחַ
וְלֹא־יָמוּת לַשַּׁחַת
וְלֹא יֶחְסַר לַחְמוֹ׃

15 וְאָנֹכִי יְהוָה אֱלֹהֶיךָ
רֹגַע הַיָּם וַיֶּהֱמוּ גַּלָּיו
יְהוָה צְבָאוֹת שְׁמוֹ׃

16 וָאָשִׂם דְּבָרַי בְּפִיךָ
וּבְצֵל יָדִי כִּסִּיתִיךָ
לִנְטֹעַ שָׁמַיִם
וְלִיסֹד אָרֶץ
וְלֵאמֹר לְצִיּוֹן עַמִּי אָתָּה׃

v. 16. קמץ בז״ק

ready his war machines to destroy Jerusalem (Isaiah of Trani).

where is the fury of the oppressor? The answer is that the fury is nowhere. In a short time God will wreak vengance upon them, and you will look for them and not find them (Isaiah of Trani).

14. *he that is bent down.* Better, 'bound' (Ibn Ezra), or 'wanderer' (Kimchi). This alludes to Israel in bondage.

shall speedily. [The Hebrew, lit. 'was speedily,' is the prophetic perfect.]

the pit. i.e. the grave (Kimchi).

15. *stirreth . . . roar.* Others render: 'rebukes' (Targum), 'splits' (Kimchi), 'stills' (Ibn Ezra). God has full control over Nature. He can stir the sea to make its waves roar, and so also He can restrain its fury and still it. The clause *Who stirreth . . . His name* is repeated in Jer. xxxi. 34.

16. *I have put . . . mouth.* God's message to the nations was given through Israel (cf. lix. 21) (Hirsch).

covered thee . . . hand. Figuratively of Divine protection (cf. xlix. 2) (Metsudath David).

plant the heavens . . . people. I will protect you throughout the long years of the Diaspora, until the time arrives for the ingathering of the exiles, when Israel will veritably become a new world (Kimchi).

plant the heavens. Figurative of Israel, compared to the stars of the heavens (Targum, Rashi).

lay the foundations of the earth. Figurative of Israel, compared to the dust of the earth (Targum).

My people. It will now be manifest that Zion is God's people (Metsudath David).

[handwritten: Wake yourselves]

17. Awake, awake,
    Stand up, O Jerusalem,
    That hast drunk at the hand of
        the LORD
    The cup of His fury;
    Thou hast drunken the beaker,
        even the cup of staggering,
    And drained it.

18. There is none to guide her
    Among all the sons whom she
        hath brought forth;
    Neither is there any that taketh
        her by the hand
    Of all the sons that she hath
        brought up.

19. These two things are befallen
        thee;
    Who shall bemoan thee?
    Desolation and destruction, and
        the famine and the sword;
    How shall I comfort thee?

20. Thy sons have fainted, they lie
        at the head of all the streets,
    As an antelope in a net;

17 הִתְעוֹרְרִי הִתְעוֹרְרִי
קוּמִי יְרוּשָׁלַםִ
אֲשֶׁר שָׁתִית
מִיַּד יְהוָה אֶת־כּוֹס חֲמָתוֹ
אֶת־קֻבַּעַת כּוֹס הַתַּרְעֵלָה
שָׁתִית מָצִית:

18 אֵין מְנַהֵל לָהּ
מִכָּל־בָּנִים יָלָדָה
וְאֵין מַחֲזִיק בְּיָדָהּ
מִכָּל־בָּנִים גִּדֵּלָה:

19 שְׁתַּיִם הֵנָּה קֹרְאֹתַיִךְ
מִי יָנוּד לָךְ
הַשֹּׁד וְהַשֶּׁבֶר *[handwritten: Shattering / destroy]*
וְהָרָעָב וְהַחֶרֶב מִי אֲנַחֲמֵךְ: *[handwritten: by whom?]*

20 בָּנַיִךְ עֻלְּפוּ שָׁכְבוּ *[handwritten: sleep]*
בְּרֹאשׁ כָּל־חוּצוֹת כְּתוֹא מִכְמָר *[handwritten: Markets]*

17-lii. 12. The end of the captivity and the glorious restoration of Zion.

17-20. A call to Jerusalem to awaken from the stupor of her affliction and degradation (Metsudath David).

17. *awake.* Or, 'arouse thee.'

the cup of His fury. A common metaphor of the prophets to describe Divine retribution (cf. Jer. xxv. 15ff.,; Ezek. xxiii. 32ff.).

drained it. Suffered the full measure of punishment (Ibn Ezra).

18. The nation has suffered loss of leadership and support (Kimchi).

19. *desolation and destruction.* Better, 'plunder and destruction.' The two lat-ter are identical with the two former: plunder being caused by the sword and destruction by famine. This twofold disaster befell Israel in his own land before he had been driven from it (Ibn Ezra, Kimchi).

how shall I comfort thee? The calamity being so overwhelming. For the Hebrew *mi* in the sense of *how,* cf. Amos vii. 2, 5 (after Ibn Kaspi). Others translate: 'by whom shall I comfort thee?' No other nation has suffered so bitterly that I could cite it as a fellow in distress (Ibn Ezra, Kimchi).

20. *at the head.* At the corners of the streets (cf. Lam. ii. 19, iv. 1).

as an antelope in a net. Exhausted and helpless. The comparison may go

They are full of the fury of the
LORD,
The rebuke of thy God.

21. Therefore hear now this, thou
afflicted,
And drunken, but not with wine;

22. Thus saith thy Lord the LORD,
And thy God that pleadeth the
cause of His people:
Behold, I have taken out of thy
hand
The cup of staggering;
The beaker, even the cup of My
fury,
Thou shalt no more drink it
again;

23. And I will put it into the hand of
them that afflict thee;
That have said to thy soul:
'Bow down, that we may go
over';
And thou hast laid thy back as
the ground,
And as the street, to them that
go over.

הַמְלֵאִים חֲמַת־יְהֹוָה
גַּעֲרַת אֱלֹהָיִךְ ׃
21 לָכֵן שִׁמְעִי־נָא זֹאת עֲנִיָּה
וּשְׁכֻרַת וְלֹא מִיָּיִן ׃
22 כֹּה־אָמַר אֲדֹנַיִךְ יְהֹוָה
וֵאלֹהַיִךְ יָרִיב עַמּוֹ
הִנֵּה לָקַחְתִּי
מִיָּדֵךְ אֶת־כּוֹס הַתַּרְעֵלָה
אֶת־קֻבַּעַת כּוֹס חֲמָתִי
לֹא־תוֹסִיפִי לִשְׁתּוֹתָהּ עוֹד ׃
23 וְשַׂמְתִּיהָ בְּיַד־מוֹגַיִךְ
אֲשֶׁר־אָמְרוּ לְנַפְשֵׁךְ
שְׁחִי וְנַעֲבֹרָה
וַתָּשִׂימִי כָאָרֶץ גֵּוֵךְ
וְכַחוּץ לַעֹבְרִים ׃

deeper: Zion's graceful children, reared
on the mountains of Judah, now
swooning with exhaustion at the feet of
the invaders, are like the mountain
gazelle, an elegantly formed species of
antelope, graceful and swift, lying
exhausted after its vain efforts to free
itself from the net of its hunters (See
Abarbanel).

full of the fury, etc. Their sad plight is due
to the *fury of the* LORD, etc. (Malbim).

21-23. Israel's suffering will pass over
to his oppressors.

21. *therefore.* Because of the long and
intense suffering (Metsudath David).

not with wine. But with misery and tribulation, or with *the fury of the* LORD (Ibn
Ezra).

23. *them that afflict thee.* (Metsudath
David). Or, 'thy tormentors' (Kimchi).

to thy soul. For the soul feels the pain of
the body (Kimchi).

that we may go over. [History records
instances of conquerors who literally
trod or even rode over the backs of
vanquished enemies.]

laid thy back as the ground. It has been
suggested that a distinction is here
drawn between Israel's *soul* (said to thy
soul) and *back.* The enemy aims to *go over*
Israel's *soul* but is permitted to pass only
over his *back.* Israel would never allow a
persecutor to master his *soul*; and that is
the secret of his survival (Alschich,
Malbim).

52   CHAPTER LII   נב

1. Awake, awake,
   Put on thy strength, O Zion;
   Put on thy beautiful garments,
   O Jerusalem, the holy city;
   For henceforth there shall no
       more come into thee
   The uncircumcised and the un-
       clean.
2. Shake thyself from the dust;
   Arise, and sit down, O Jeru-
       salem;
   Loose thyself from the bands of
       thy neck,
   O captive daughter of Zion.
3. For thus saith the LORD:
   Ye were sold for nought;
   And ye shall be redeemed
       without money.
4. For thus saith the Lord GOD:

1 עוּרִי עוּרִי
לִבְשִׁי עֻזֵּךְ צִיּוֹן
לִבְשִׁי ׀ בִּגְדֵי תִפְאַרְתֵּךְ
יְרוּשָׁלִַם עִיר הַקֹּדֶשׁ
כִּי לֹא יוֹסִיף
יָבֹא־בָךְ עוֹד עָרֵל וְטָמֵא:
2 הִתְנַעֲרִי מֵעָפָר
קוּמִי שְּׁבִי יְרוּשָׁלִָם
הִתְפַּתְּחוּ מוֹסְרֵי צַוָּארֵךְ
שְׁבִיָּה בַּת־צִיּוֹן:
3 כִּי־כֹה אָמַר יְהֹוָה
חִנָּם נִמְכַּרְתֶּם
וְלֹא בְכֶסֶף תִּגָּאֵלוּ:
4 כִּי כֹה אָמַר אֲדֹנָי יְהֹוִה

v. 1. התתפתחי ק׳   v. 2. מלרע

CHAPTER LII

1–6. Let Jerusalem break off the chains of her captivity and array herself in festal garments. No longer will God endure the desecration of His name through the enslavement of His people by rulers who fail to understand that it was He Who had for a time delivered Israel into their hands. They have no claim whatsoever upon Israel who will, therefore, be redeemed without money but at the will of God.

awake . . . strength. Repeated from li. 9. Zion is called upon to throw off the stupor which is the effect of drinking the cup of God's wrath (cf. li. 17).

1. *Zion* and *Jerusalem* are synonymous.

the holy city. See on xlviii. 2.

uncircumcised and the unclean. The heath-

en enemies who had hitherto infested the city. The uncircumcised are the kingdoms of Edom, and the unclean are the kingdom of Ishmael, who, in spite of their cleansing themselves, are unclean through their deeds (Kimchi).

2. *from the dust.* Of the ground on which Zion had been sitting as a mourner (see on xlvii. 1).

sit down. On thy throne; resume thy regal state (Targum).

bands. The chains of captivity (Metsudath David).

3. *for nought.* No price was paid to God for them by their captors (Kimchi).

redeemed without money. God Who delivered them to the captors will redeem them without having to pay compensation (Metsudath David).

My people went down aforetime
into Egypt to sojourn there;
And the Assyrian oppressed
them without cause.

5. Now therefore, what do I here,
saith the LORD,
Seeing that My people is taken
away for nought?
They that rule over them do
howl, saith the LORD,
And My name continually all the
day is blasphemed.

6. Therefore My people shall know
My name;
Therefore they shall know in
that day
That I, even He that spoke,
behold, here I am.

7. How beautiful upon the mountains
Are the feet of the messenger of
good tidings,
That announceth peace, the
harbinger of good tidings,
That announceth salvation;

מִצְרַיִם יָרַד־עַמִּי בָרִאשֹׁנָה לָגוּר שָׁם
וְאַשּׁוּר בְּאֶפֶס עֲשָׁקוֹ׃

5 וְעַתָּה מַה־לִּי־פֹה נְאֻם־יְהוָֹה
כִּי־לֻקַּח עַמִּי חִנָּם
מֹשְׁלָו יְהֵילִילוּ נְאֻם־יְהוָֹה
וְתָמִיד כָּל־הַיּוֹם שְׁמִי מִנֹּאָץ׃

6 לָכֵן יֵדַע עַמִּי שְׁמִי
לָכֵן בַּיּוֹם הַהוּא
כִּי־אֲנִי־הוּא הַמְדַבֵּר הִנֵּנִי׃

7 מַה־נָּאווּ עַל־הֶהָרִים
רַגְלֵי מְבַשֵּׂר
מַשְׁמִיעַ שָׁלוֹם
מְבַשֵּׂר טוֹב מַשְׁמִיעַ יְשׁוּעָה

v. 5. משליו ק׳

4. *aforetime.* Or, 'at first,' at the beginning of their history.

to sojourn there. Hence, their enslavement
was not completely unjustified (Rashi).

without cause. Without any legal or moral
right or claim (Rashi, Ibn Ezra).

5. *what do I here,* etc. In the third exile
God was, so to speak, in captivity
together with His people, and the
oppressor has now become so degrad-
ing and unendurable that both the
safety of Israel and the honour of his
God demand his immediate deliverance
from the exile (Kimchi).

taken away. Into captivity as slaves
(Abarbanel).

howl. Or, 'boast, exult' (Metsudath
Zion).

My name . . . blasphemed. The degradation and affliction of Israel are attributed by his enemies to the weakness
and helplessness of his God (Ibn Kaspi).

6. *know My name.* They will appreciate

its significance. The wonders of the
redemption which God will reveal to
His people will enable them to *know* the
power and the greatness that name
imports (Rashi).

that spoke. Promising deliverance
(Metsudath David).

here I am. To fulfill the promise made
(Metsudath David).

7-12. The leisurely return to Zion of
the exiles under the leadership of God,
heralded by messengers announcing
peace and salvation. They will be
received with exultation, and even the
waste places are invited to join in joyful
song because God's people is comforted, Jerusalem is redeemed and the
power and the salvation of the Lord are
made known to the uttermost ends of
the earth.

7. The triumphal procession of the
returning exiles is preceded by a messenger hastening over the mountains to
bring the good news to Zion.

That saith unto Zion:
'Thy God reigneth!'
8. Hark, thy watchmen! they lift up
    the voice,
    Together do they sing;
    For they shall see, eye to eye,
    The LORD returning to Zion.
9. Break forth into joy, sing to-
    gether,
    Ye waste places of Jerusalem;
    For the LORD hath comforted
    His people,
    He hath redeemed Jerusalem.
10. The LORD hath made bare His
     holy arm
     In the eyes of all the nations;
     And all the ends of the earth
     shall see
     The salvation of our God.
11. Depart ye, depart ye, go ye out
     from thence,
     Touch no unclean thing;
     Go ye out of the midst of her; be
     ye clean,

אֹמֵר לְצִיּוֹן
מָלַךְ אֱלֹהָיִךְ׃
8 קוֹל צֹפַיִךְ נָשְׂאוּ קוֹל
יַחְדָּו יְרַנֵּנוּ
כִּי עַיִן בְּעַיִן יִרְאוּ
בְּשׁוּב יְהוָה צִיּוֹן׃
9 פִּצְחוּ רַנְּנוּ יַחְדָּו
חָרְבוֹת יְרוּשָׁלָ͏ִם
כִּי־נִחַם יְהוָה עַמּוֹ
גָּאַל יְרוּשָׁלָ͏ִם׃
10 חָשַׂף יְהוָה אֶת־זְרוֹעַ קָדְשׁוֹ
לְעֵינֵי כָּל־הַגּוֹיִם
וְרָאוּ כָּל־אַפְסֵי־אָרֶץ
אֵת יְשׁוּעַת אֱלֹהֵינוּ׃
11 סוּרוּ סוּרוּ צְאוּ מִשָּׁם
טָמֵא אַל־תִּגָּעוּ
צְאוּ מִתּוֹכָהּ הִבָּרוּ

v. 10. קמץ בז״ק

God reigneth. Or, 'God hath (again) become King,' has manifested His kingdom to all nations (Metsudath David).

8. watchmen. Being posted on the towers and city walls, the watchmen are the first to see and report the approach of the procession (Rashi).

eye to eye. Clearly and distinctly, as when one looks straight into the eyes of another (again in Num. xiv. 14) (Ibn Ezra).

9. hath comforted . . . redeemed. A perfect of certainty; it is certain that God will comfort His people and redeem the holy city (Targum).

10. made bare His holy arm. A metaphor for readiness to enter into combat (Metsudath David).

the salvation. The deliverance of His people (Kimchi).

11. A call to the exiles.

depart. From Babylon (Rabbi Moshe Hakohen, quoted by Ibn Ezra).

touch no unclean thing . . . be ye clean. Because God is at their head and there must be no defilement in His Presence (cf. Deut. xxiii. 15).

vessels of the LORD. The vessels of the

Ye that bear the vessels of the
LORD.

12. For ye shall not go out in haste,
Neither shall ye go by flight;
For the LORD will go before you,
And the God of Israel will be
your rearward.

13. Behold, My servant shall
prosper,
He shall be exalted and lifted up,
and shall be very high.

14. According as many were appalled
at thee—
So marred was his visage unlike
that of a man,
And his form unlike that of the
sons of men—

נֹשְׂאֵי כְּלֵי יְהוָה׃

12 כִּי לֹא בְחִפָּזוֹן תֵּצֵאוּ
וּבִמְנוּסָה לֹא תֵלֵכוּן
כִּי־הֹלֵךְ לִפְנֵיכֶם יְהוָה
וּמְאַסִּפְכֶם אֱלֹהֵי יִשְׂרָאֵל׃

13 הִנֵּה יַשְׂכִּיל עַבְדִּי
יָרוּם וְנִשָּׂא וְגָבַהּ מְאֹד׃

14 כַּאֲשֶׁר שָׁמְמוּ עָלֶיךָ רַבִּים
כֵּן־מִשְׁחַת מֵאִישׁ מַרְאֵהוּ
וְתֹאֲרוֹ מִבְּנֵי אָדָם׃

v. 12. עד כאן

Sanctuary which were taken to Babylon when the Temple was destroyed and brought back (cf. Ezra i. 7ff.) by the returning exiles (Targum, Ibn Ezra).

12. The departure from Babylon, unlike that from Egypt which was in haste (cf. Exod. xii. 11, 39), will be leisurely. For God will be the Leader of the redeemed exiles in the vanguard and also their Protector from pursuers in the rear.

before you. As Guide (Targum).

rearward. To collect the stragglers (Rashi) and to provide protection from pursuing enemies (Abarbanel).

13-liii. 12. The servant's martyrdom and ultimate triumph. The servant is the ideal Israel or the faithful remnant. Cf. supra xli. 8f., xliv. 1f., xlv. 4. (Kimchi). That he is not an individual is the opinion of all Jewish and most modern non-Jewish commentators. The best proof is the fact that this passage is preceded by 'the Lord will go before you,' etc., which undoubtedly refers to the Israelites, and is followed by 'Sing, O barren,'

etc., which is likewise advised to the Israelites (Ibn Ezra).

13-15. Introduction and summary, contrasting the servant's past and present depths of humiliation with his future dignity and glory. The marvellous and unexpected transformation in his fortunes will change the amazement and horror of the nations into admiration and homage.

13. *prosper,* etc. The text presents an ascending climax: *prosper, exalted and lifted up, very high.*

14f. Both verses form one compound sentence. The first clause in verse 14, *according . . . thee,* is the protasis; the remaining part of the verse is a parenthesis, explaining why the *many were appalled*; and verse 15 begins the apodosis (Metsudath David).

14. *at thee.* The servant is addressed in the second person which is soon changed, by the interruption of the parenthesis, to the third (Kimchi).

so marred . . . man. His suffering had been so intense that their mark upon

15. So shall he startle many nations,
Kings shall shut their mouths
because of him;
For that which had not been
told them shall they see,
And that which they had not
heard shall they perceive.

טו בֵּן יַזֶּה גּוֹיִם רַבִּים
עָלָיו יִקְפְּצוּ מְלָכִים פִּיהֶם
כִּי אֲשֶׁר לֹא־סֻפַּר לָהֶם רָאוּ
וַאֲשֶׁר לֹא־שָׁמְעוּ הִתְבּוֹנָנוּ׃

---

53   CHAPTER LIII   נג

1. 'Who would have believed our
report?
And to whom hath the arm of
the Lord been revealed?
2. For he shot up right forth as a
sapling,
And as a root out of a dry
ground;
He had no form nor comeliness,
that we should look upon him,
Nor beauty that we should
delight in him.

א מִי הֶאֱמִין לִשְׁמֻעָתֵנוּ
וּזְרוֹעַ יְהוָה עַל־מִי נִגְלָתָה׃
ב וַיַּעַל כַּיּוֹנֵק לְפָנָיו
וְכַשֹּׁרֶשׁ מֵאֶרֶץ צִיָּה
לֹא־תֹאַר לוֹ וְלֹא הָדָר
וְנִרְאֵהוּ וְלֹא־מַרְאֶה וְנֶחְמְדֵהוּ׃

---

him made him lose the look of a human
being (Abarbanel).

15. *startle.* Cause to spring or rise suddenly in admiration and reverence.
Others render: 'scatter' (Targum):
'speak to' (Kimchi); 'shed blood' (Ibn
Ezra).

shut their mouths. In amazement at the
exaltation of the despised servant
(Metsudath David).

for that which had not been told them, etc.
Such a miraculous and sudden transformation had never before been heard
or seen (Rashi).

CHAPTER LIII

REINSTATEMENT OF THE
MARTYRED SERVANT

1-9. The Babylonians, or their representatives, having known the servant,
i.e. exiled Israel idealized, in his humiliation and martyrdom, and now seeing
his exaltation and new dignity, describe
their impressions and feelings (Ibn
Kaspi).

1. *our report.* The information received
by us concerning the servant's greatness; such news is incredible (Kimchi,
Metsudath David).

to whom ... revealed? To none, is the
answer. No one of the nations ever
merited the manifestation of God's
power as Israel has today (Rashi, Ibn
Ezra, Kimchi).

the arm. The Divine power which
became manifest at the time of the
redemption (Rashi).

2f. Reason for the unbelief expressed
in verse 1. The servant appeared so
despicable.

2. *shot up ... dry ground.* He was like a
stunned growth in arid soil (Ibn Ezra).

dry ground. Some see in the phrase an
allusion to the exile (Kimchi, Abarbanel).

look upon him. i.e. when we looked upon
him, we saw that he had no beauty
(Kimchi).

beauty. lit. 'appearance,' i.e. fair appearance (Kimchi).

3. He was despised, and forsaken
   of men,
   A man of pains, and acquainted
   with disease,
   And as one from whom men hide
   their face:
   He was despised, and we
   esteemed him not.
4. Surely our diseases he did bear,
   and our pains he carried;
   Whereas we did esteem him
   stricken,
   Smitten of God, and afflicted.
5. But he was wounded because of
   our transgressions,
   He was crushed because of our
   iniquities:
   The chastisement of our welfare
   was upon him,
   And with his stripes we were
   healed.
6. All we like sheep did go astray,
   We turned every one to his own
   way;
   And the LORD hath made to
   light on him
   The iniquity of us all.

3 נִבְזֶה וַחֲדַל אִישִׁים
אִישׁ מַכְאֹבוֹת וִידוּעַ חֹלִי
וּכְמַסְתֵּר פָּנִים מִמֶּנּוּ
נִבְזֶה וְלֹא חֲשַׁבְנֻהוּ:

4 אָכֵן חֳלָיֵנוּ הוּא נָשָׂא
וּמַכְאֹבֵינוּ סְבָלָם
וַאֲנַחְנוּ חֲשַׁבְנֻהוּ נָגוּעַ
מֻכֵּה אֱלֹהִים וּמְעֻנֶּה:

5 וְהוּא מְחֹלָל מִפְּשָׁעֵינוּ
מְדֻכָּא מֵעֲוֹנֹתֵינוּ
מוּסַר שְׁלוֹמֵנוּ עָלָיו
וּבַחֲבֻרָתוֹ נִרְפָּא־לָנוּ:

6 כֻּלָּנוּ כַּצֹּאן תָּעִינוּ
אִישׁ לְדַרְכּוֹ פָּנִינוּ
וַיהוָה הִפְגִּיעַ בּוֹ
אֵת עֲוֹן כֻּלָּנוּ:

---

3. *forsaken of men.* Treated like an outcast (Kimchi).

pains . . . disease. These are explained in the following verse.

hide their face. So as not to behold such a repellent sight (Kimchi).

esteemed him not. Or, 'held him of no account.'

4–6. Recognition that the servant's sufferings were not due to his secret sins. It is now frankly acknowledged that he was the victim who bore the dire penalties which the iniquities of others have incurred.

4. *our diseases.* The diseases that should have been inflicted upon us (Rashi, Kimchi).

did bear. He was called upon to endure (Rashi, Kimchi).

smitten of God. For his own sins (Rashi, Kimchi).

5. The servant suffered that it may be well with them.

the chastisement. For the transgressions committed and for which suffering was the expiation (Metsudath David).

of our welfare. That we may procure well-being, he having been punished for our guilt (Rashi, Kimchi).

6. The people wandered from the right path and indulged in ungodly desires.

like sheep. Without a shepherd. They forsook the leadership of God.

to his own way. Following his own false religion (Abarbanel).

7. He was oppressed, though he
humbled himself
And opened not his mouth;
As a lamb that is led to the
slaughter,
And as a sheep that before her
shearers is dumb;
Yea, he opened not his mouth.
8. By oppression and judgment he
was taken away,
And with his generation who did
reason?
For he was cut off out of the
land of the living,
For the transgression of my
people to whom the stroke
was due.
9. And they made his grave with
the wicked,
And with the rich his tomb;
Although he had done no
violence,
Neither was any deceit in his
mouth.'

7 נִגַּשׂ וְהוּא נַעֲנֶה
וְלֹא יִפְתַּח־פִּיו
כַּשֶּׂה לַטֶּבַח יוּבָל
וּכְרָחֵל לִפְנֵי גֹזְזֶיהָ נֶאֱלָמָה
וְלֹא יִפְתַּח פִּיו׃
8 מֵעֹצֶר וּמִמִּשְׁפָּט לֻקָּח
וְאֶת־דּוֹרוֹ מִי יְשׂוֹחֵחַ
כִּי נִגְזַר מֵאֶרֶץ חַיִּים
מִפֶּשַׁע עַמִּי נֶגַע לָמוֹ׃
9 וַיִּתֵּן אֶת־רְשָׁעִים קִבְרוֹ
וְאֶת־עָשִׁיר בְּמֹתָיו
עַל לֹא־חָמָס עָשָׂה
וְלֹא מִרְמָה בְּפִיו׃

v. 7. קמץ בז"ק   v. 8. קמץ בז"ק

7-9. The gentle spirit and meek
demeanor of the persecuted servant
under undeserved harsh treatment.

7. *he was oppressed ... himself.* Or,
'robbed, he was afflicted' (Kimchi).
Others render: 'taunted, he was afflicted' (Rashi).

opened not his mouth. In protest; he suffered in silence (Rashi).

8. *judgment.* i.e. from the place in
which he was judged (Metsudath
David).

and with his generation ... reason. Or, 'the
tribulations of his generation who can
relate?' Who can relate the numerous
tribulations they suffered throughout all
generations of his exile? (Metsudath
David).

he was cut off ... living. He was cut off
from his homeland by the Babylonians
(Ibn Kaspi).

the stroke was due. The suffering that
should have been inflicted upon the

wicked members of the community was
borne by the innocent servant (Rashi).

9. *and they made.* lit. 'and he gave'; the
subject being indefinite. Jewish exegetes
explain, 'he gave' to mean that he sub-
mitted himself to be buried wherever
the heathens would decree upon him
(Rashi).

his grave. The graves of the Jews in exile
(Ibn Ezra).

with the wicked. On account of his sufferings he was deemed to be a sinner, and,
therefore, classed with them. He was,
therefore, often put to death as a criminal (Kimchi).

the rich. The word, in the context, seems
to be synonymous with *wicked*; but such
a meaning of the word is rare. It may
perhaps refer to the wealthy who were
killed because of their wealth (Kimchi).

tomb. Or, 'mound,' lit. 'his high places.'
The punctuation of the Hebrew word is
unusual (Ibn Ezra).

10. Yet it pleased the LORD to crush
    him by disease;
    To see if his soul would offer
    itself in restitution,
    That he might see his seed,
    prolong his days,
    And that the purpose of the
    LORD might prosper by his
    hand:
11. Of the travail of his soul he shall
    see to the full, even My
    servant,
    Who by his knowledge did
    justify the Righteous One to
    the many,
    And their iniquities he did bear.
12. Therefore will I divide him a
    portion among the great,
    And he shall divide the spoil
    with the mighty;
    Because he bared his soul unto
    death,
    And was numbered with the
    transgressors;
    Yet he bore the sin of many,
    And made intercession for the
    transgressors.

10 וַיהֹוָה֙ חָפֵ֣ץ דַּכְּאוֹ֙ הֶֽחֱלִ֔י
אִם־תָּשִׂ֤ים אָשָׁם֙ נַפְשׁ֔וֹ
יִרְאֶ֥ה זֶ֖רַע יַאֲרִ֣יךְ יָמִ֑ים
וְחֵ֥פֶץ יְהֹוָ֖ה בְּיָד֥וֹ יִצְלָֽח׃
11 מֵעֲמַ֤ל נַפְשׁוֹ֙ יִרְאֶ֣ה יִשְׂבָּ֔ע
בְּדַעְתּ֗וֹ יַצְדִּ֥יק צַדִּ֛יק עַבְדִּ֖י לָֽרַבִּ֑ים
וַעֲוֺנֹתָ֖ם ה֥וּא יִסְבֹּֽל׃
12 לָכֵ֞ן אֲחַלֶּק־ל֣וֹ בָֽרַבִּ֗ים
וְאֶת־עֲצוּמִים֮ יְחַלֵּ֣ק שָׁלָל֒
תַּ֗חַת אֲשֶׁ֨ר הֶעֱרָ֤ה לַמָּ֙וֶת֙ נַפְשׁ֔וֹ
וְאֶת־פֹּשְׁעִ֖ים נִמְנָ֑ה
וְהוּא֙ חֵטְא־רַבִּ֣ים נָשָׂ֔א
וְלַפֹּשְׁעִ֖ים יַפְגִּֽיעַ׃

v. 11. קמץ בז״ק

10–12. The servant's patiently borne
suffering for other people's sins will cul-
minate in the spiritual uplift of many
and in his own physical or spiritual
rejuvenation. He will enjoy a glorious
future, offspring, long life, prosperity
and influence.

10. The purpose of the servant's
crushing misery.

by disease. lit. 'he made sick.'

to see. Implied from the context.

restitution. The Hebrew usually signifies
'a guilt-offering.'

see his seed. The Hebrew is 'see seed,' i.e.
have children and grandchildren.

prolong his days. Enjoy long life.

purpose of the LORD. Universal recognition of His sovereignty and commandments (Ibn Ezra).

11. *to the full.* lit. 'he shall be satisfied.'

he will be compensated for *the travail of
his soul* by an abundant fulfilment of his
wishes, both material and spiritual
(Kimchi).

knowledge. Of God.

did justify. More accurately, 'shall justify.' The servant will live to use his
knowledge of God to justify His ways to
man (Metsudath David).

12. *therefore.* For his unmerited suffering, for sacrificing himself on behalf of
others and for interceding in favour of
his tormentors (Rashi, Kimchi).

divide him a portion. Give him his due
reward (Metsudath David).

divide the spoil. Conquer his enemies
(Kimchi).

numbered. Howbeit erroneously (Ibn
Ezra, Metsudath David).

bore. In reality (Rashi).

54   CHAPTER LIV   נד

1. Sing, O barren, thou that didst
   not bear,
   Break forth into singing, and cry
   aloud, thou that didst not
   travail;
   For more are the children of the
   desolate
   Than the children of the married
   wife, saith the LORD.
2. Enlarge the place of thy tent,
   And let them stretch forth the
   curtains of thy habitations,
   spare not;
   Lengthen thy cords, and
   strengthen thy stakes.
3. For thou shalt spread abroad on
   the right hand and on the left;
   And thy seed shall possess the
   nations,
   And make the desolate cities to
   be inhabited.
4. Fear not, for thou shalt not be
   ashamed.

1 רָנִּי עֲקָרָה לֹא יָלָדָה
  פִּצְחִי רִנָּה וְצַהֲלִי לֹא־חָלָה
  כִּי־רַבִּים בְּנֵי־שׁוֹמֵמָה
  מִבְּנֵי בְעוּלָה אָמַר יְהוָה׃
2 הַרְחִיבִי ׀ מְקוֹם אָהֳלֵךְ
  וִירִיעוֹת מִשְׁכְּנוֹתַיִךְ יַטּוּ אַל־תַּחְשֹׂכִי
  הַאֲרִיכִי מֵיתָרַיִךְ וִיתֵדֹתַיִךְ חַזֵּקִי׃
3 כִּי־יָמִין וּשְׂמֹאול תִּפְרֹצִי
  וְזַרְעֵךְ גּוֹיִם יִירָשׁ
  וְעָרִים נְשַׁמּוֹת יוֹשִׁיבוּ׃
4 אַל־תִּירְאִי כִּי־לֹא תֵבוֹשִׁי

v. 1. הפטרת נח וגם הפטרת כי תצא   v. 3. מלא ו'   v. 3. קמץ בז"ק

CHAPTER LIV

VISION OF ZION RESTORED

ZION's suffering and humiliation will be
forgotten in her glorious future.

1-3. The return of the exiles to
mother Zion.

1. The prophet addresses the desolate
city.

barren. The depopulated Jerusalem
which is like a childless woman (Targum, Rashi).

more are the children of the desolate. The
exiled Judeans returning to the devastated city of Jerusalem (Metsudath
David).

married wife. The populated cities of the
heathens, which are compared to a
married woman, living with her husband and children (Kimchi).

2. *enlarge the place of thy tent.* To make
room for the increased population (cf.
xlix. 20ff.). Jerusalem is likened to a *tent,*
the *curtains* being the tent-hangings (Ibn
Ezra, Kimchi).

habitations. The other cities of the Holy
Land (Kimchi).

3. The verse supplies the reason why
the *tent* and *habitations* must be enlarged
and extended.

possess the nations. Or, 'take possession of
the nations,' the reference is to the
nations who occupied the Land of Israel
and to those around (Ibn Ezra, Kimchi).

4-6. Israel, returning to God like a
deserted wife to her husband, will forget
the shame of the past in the love and joy
of the reunion.

4. *fear not.* Lest the humiliating conditions of the exile mar the new relationship between God and His people
(Malbim).

265

Neither be thou confounded, for
  thou shalt not be put to shame;
For thou shalt forget the shame
  of thy youth,
And the reproach of thy widowhood shalt thou remember no
  more.
5. For thy Maker is thy husband,
  The LORD of hosts is His name;
  And the Holy One of Israel is
  thy Redeemer,
  The God of the whole earth shall
  He be called.
6. For the LORD hath called thee
  As a wife forsaken and grieved
  in spirit;
  And a wife of youth, can she be
  rejected?
  Saith thy God.
7. For a small moment have I
  forsaken thee;
  But with great compassion will
  I gather thee.
8. In a little wrath I hid My face
  from thee for a moment;

וְאַל־תִּכָּלְמִי כִּי־לֹא תַחְפִּירִי
כִּי בֹשֶׁת עֲלוּמַיִךְ תִּשְׁכָּחִי
וְחֶרְפַּת אַלְמְנוּתַיִךְ לֹא תִזְכְּרִי־עֽוֹד׃
5 כִּי בֹעֲלַיִךְ עֹשַׂיִךְ
יְהֹוָה צְבָאוֹת שְׁמוֹ
וְגֹאֲלֵךְ קְדוֹשׁ יִשְׂרָאֵל
אֱלֹהֵי כָל־הָאָרֶץ יִקָּרֵא׃
6 כִּי־כְאִשָּׁה עֲזוּבָה
וַעֲצוּבַת רוּחַ קְרָאָךְ יְהֹוָה
וְאֵשֶׁת נְעוּרִים
כִּי תִמָּאֵס אָמַר אֱלֹהָיִךְ׃
7 בְּרֶגַע קָטֹן עֲזַבְתִּיךְ
וּבְרַחֲמִים גְּדוֹלִים אֲקַבְּצֵךְ׃
8 בְּשֶׁצֶף קֶצֶף הִסְתַּרְתִּי פָנַי רֶגַע מִמֵּךְ

קמץ בז״ק v. 4.

---

the shame of thy youth. The backsliding
and chastisement of the earlier days, the
days of the First Temple (Malbim).

widowhood. The former lonely state of
the nation; Israel's years in exile when
he seemed to be cast off by God
(Malbim).

5. Israel need have no doubts of the
fulfilment of a promise made by the
Lord of hosts, the God of all the earth.

thy husband. Who will take thee back and
put an end to the separation (Kimchi).

6. Israel holds a permanent place in
God's love like a wife married in one's
youth who, despite temporary estrangement, continues to occupy a warm
corner in her husband's heart.

forsaken. For a time by her husband
(Abarbanel).

a wife of youth. Wooed and married in
youth with all the ardour of love characteristic of that age.

can she be rejected? Obviously she cannot.
An estrangement can only last for a
while until tempers cool (Hirsch).

7f. God's anger is momentary, His
love everlasting.

7. *a small moment.* Compared with the
long period of Israel's glory and happiness, the exile will seem but a brief
space of time (Kimchi).

gather thee. From the dispersion back to
Zion.

8. *little wrath.* Or, 'outbreak of wrath'
(Rashi). The Hebrew assonance, *shetseph
ketseph,* may bear either meaning.

9f. God's new covenant of peace and

But with everlasting kindness
will I have compassion on thee,
Saith the LORD thy Redeemer.

9. For this is as the waters of Noah
unto Me;
For as I have sworn that the
waters of Noah
Should no more go over the
earth,
So have I sworn that I would not
be wroth with thee,
Nor rebuke thee.

10. For the mountains may depart,
And the hills be removed;
But My kindness shall not
depart from thee,
Neither shall My covenant of
peace be removed,
Saith the LORD that hath com-
passion on thee.

11. O thou afflicted, tossed with
tempest,
And not comforted,
Behold, I will set thy stones in
fair colours,
And lay thy foundations with
sapphires.

12. And I will make thy pinnacles of
rubies,

וּבְחֶסֶד עוֹלָם רִחַמְתִּיךְ
אָמַר גֹּאֲלֵךְ יְהוָה׃
9 כִּי־מֵי נֹחַ זֹאת לִי
אֲשֶׁר נִשְׁבַּעְתִּי מֵעֲבֹר מֵי־נֹחַ
עוֹד עַל־הָאָרֶץ
כֵּן נִשְׁבַּעְתִּי
מִקְּצֹף עָלַיִךְ וּמִגְּעָר־בָּךְ׃
10 כִּי הֶהָרִים יָמוּשׁוּ
וְהַגְּבָעוֹת תְּמוּטֶנָה
וְחַסְדִּי מֵאִתֵּךְ לֹא־יָמוּשׁ
וּבְרִית שְׁלוֹמִי לֹא תָמוּט
אָמַר מְרַחֲמֵךְ יְהוָה׃
11 עֲנִיָּה סֹעֲרָה
לֹא נֻחָמָה
הִנֵּה אָנֹכִי מַרְבִּיץ בַּפּוּךְ אֲבָנַיִךְ
וִיסַדְתִּיךְ בַּסַּפִּירִים׃
12 וְשַׂמְתִּי כַּדְכֹד שִׁמְשֹׁתַיִךְ

v. 9. נ״א כימי   v. 10. עד כאן   v. 11. הפטרת ראה

---

mercy with Israel will be eternal, like
the covenant He made with mankind
after the flood in the days of Noah,
more permanent than the apparently
everlasting mountains and hills.

9. *for this*. viz. the exile and the
redemption. The sufferings of the exile
are compared to the flood and the glories of the redemption to the subsequent
covenant (Kimchi).

10. *for the mountains . . . but My kindness.*
Or, 'though the mountains . . . My
kindness.'

11f. The external splendour and
beauty of Zion in her restored state.

11. *thou afflicted*. Zion is addressed
(Metsudath David).

fair colours. lit. 'antimony,' used by
oriental women as a powder or ointment in painting the edges of their eye-
lids to enhance the brilliance of their
eyes (cf. 2 Kings ix. 30). Here it is a type
of stone, according to Kimchi, the car-
buncle (Shorashim).

12. *pinnacles* (*shimshothayich*). The
Hebrew noun denotes windows through
which the sun (*shemesh*) shines (Rashi,
Kimchi).

13f. The inner splendour of Zion:

267

And thy gates of carbuncles,
And all thy border of precious
   stones.

13. And all thy children shall be
taught of the LORD;
And great shall be the peace of
thy children.

14. In righteousness shalt thou be
established;
Be thou far from oppression, for
thou shalt not fear,
And from ruin, for it shall not
come near thee.

15. Behold, they may gather together, but not by Me;
Whosoever shall gather together
against thee shall fall because
of thee.

16. Behold, I have created the smith
That bloweth the fire of coals,
And bringeth forth a weapon for
his work;

וּשְׁעָרַיִךְ לְאַבְנֵי אֶקְדָּח
וְכָל־גְּבוּלֵךְ לְאַבְנֵי־חֵפֶץ׃

13 וְכָל־בָּנַיִךְ לִמּוּדֵי יְהֹוָה
וְרַב שְׁלוֹם בָּנָיִךְ׃

14 בִּצְדָקָה תִּכּוֹנָנִי
רַחֲקִי מֵעֹשֶׁק כִּי־לֹא תִירָאִי
וּמִמְּחִתָּה כִּי לֹא־תִקְרַב אֵלָיִךְ׃

15 הֵן גּוֹר יָגוּר אֶפֶס מֵאוֹתִי
מִי־גָר אִתָּךְ עָלַיִךְ יִפּוֹל׃

16 הִנֵּה אָנֹכִי בָּרָאתִי חָרָשׁ
נֹפֵחַ בְּאֵשׁ פֶּחָם
וּמוֹצִיא כְלִי לְמַעֲשֵׂהוּ

v. 16. הנה ק

learning, peace, righteousness and
security.

13. *taught of the* LORD. Or, 'disciples of
the LORD' (cf. 1.4). 'The disciples of the
sages,' it is stated in the Babylonian
Talmud (at the end of the tractate Bera-
choth), 'increase peace throughout the
world; as it is said, *And all thy children
shall be taught of the* LORD*; and great shall
be the peace of thy children.* Read not here
banayich (thy children) but *bonayich* (thy
builders).'

14. *in righteousness . . . established.* The
existence of a State, can rest on sure
foundations only if it is upheld by right
conduct (Ibn Ezra, Kimchi).

be thou far from oppression. From those
who oppressed thee (Rashi, Kimchi).

thou shalt not fear. i.e. thou shalt have no
cause to fear (Kimchi).

15. A difficult verse, the rendering of
which is rather free.

gather together. Against Israel (Kimchi).
Another possible rendering is: 'he shall
fear, who is not with Me' (Rashi).

not by Me. Without My consent (Kimchi).

whosoever, etc. Or, 'whosoever contends
with thee shall fall against thee' (Rashi).

16f. Neither violent action nor malicious speech will be effective against
Israel because his Protector is God, the
Creator of both the maker of the instrument of destruction and the man who
uses it; neither can act against His will.

16. *for his work.* (Kimchi). Or, 'for its
work,' the work for which the instrument is intended (Rashi).

the waster. The user of the destructive

And I have created the waster to destroy.

17. No weapon that is formed against thee shall prosper;
And every tongue that shall rise against thee in judgment thou shalt condemn.
This is the heritage of the servants of the LORD,
And their due reward from Me, saith the LORD.

וְאָנֹכִי בָּרָאתִי מַשְׁחִית לְחַבֵּל׃

17 כָּל־כְּלִי יוּצַר עָלַיִךְ לֹא יִצְלָח
וְכָל־לָשׁוֹן
תָּקוּם־אִתָּךְ לַמִּשְׁפָּט תַּרְשִׁיעִי
זֹאת נַחֲלַת עַבְדֵי יְהֹוָה
וְצִדְקָתָם מֵאִתִּי נְאֻם־יְהֹוָה׃

justice

---

55   CHAPTER LV   נה

1. Ho, every one that thirsteth, come ye for water,
And he that hath no money;
Come ye, buy, and eat;

spiritual feast!
Pt 8,3

go forth

1 הוֹי כָּל־צָמֵא לְכוּ לַמַּיִם
וַאֲשֶׁר אֵין־לוֹ כָּסֶף
לְכוּ שִׁבְרוּ וֶאֱכֹלוּ

v. 17. קָמֵץ בְּז״ק

shever —
G42-12

---

weapon. His use of it is subject to the control of God without Whose consent the waster cannot act (Kara).

17. Israel's future safety is, therefore, assured.

prosper. i.e. succeed in the purpose for which it is used (Kara).

rise ... judgment. To make malicious accusations (Metsudath David).

condemn. Frustrate in argument, prove it to be in the wrong (Metsudath David).

this. viz. the safe and happy future described in the prophecy (Metsudath David).

the servants of the LORD. All Israel will be servants of the LORD from the redemption onward (Kimchi).

due reward. The Hebrew noun, usually rendered 'righteousness,' stands here for 'the reward of righteousness.' Similarly, the Hebrew for 'sin' may also signify 'the punishment for sin' (According to Malbim).

CHAPTER LV

SUMMONS TO ENJOY THE NEW ERA

1-5. The prosperity and blessings of Jerusalem when restored.

1f. Rich and poor are invited to the spiritual feast, the metaphorical *water, wine* and *milk.*

1. *that thirsteth.* For the word of God (Abarbanel).

water. Figurative for the Torah (Rashi, Kimchi).

and he. Better, 'even he' (Metsudath David).

come ye. lit. 'go ye,' and so throughout the passage (Targum).

buy. This root, *shever,* is used only in the context of buying food and drink. Its usual meaning is 'buy corn' (cf. Gen. xlii. 2). The noun from the same root means 'grain, corn' (Badarschi).

Yea, come, buy wine and milk
Without money and without
price.

2. Wherefore do ye spend money
for that which is not bread?
And your gain for that which
satisfieth not?
Hearken diligently unto Me, and
eat ye that which is good,
And let your soul delight itself
in fatness.

3. Incline your ear, and come unto
Me;
Hear, and your soul shall live;
And I will make an everlasting
covenant with you,
Even the sure mercies of David.

4. Behold, I have given him for a
witness to the peoples,
A prince and commander to the
peoples.

5. Behold, thou shalt call a nation
that thou knowest not,

וּלְכוּ שִׁבְרוּ בְּלוֹא־כֶסֶף
וּבְלוֹא מְחִיר יַיִן וְחָלָב:
2 לָמָּה תִשְׁקְלוּ־כֶסֶף בְּלוֹא־לֶחֶם
וִיגִיעֲכֶם בְּלוֹא לְשָׂבְעָה
שִׁמְעוּ שָׁמוֹעַ אֵלַי וְאִכְלוּ־טוֹב
וְתִתְעַנַּג בַּדֶּשֶׁן נַפְשְׁכֶם:
3 הַטּוּ אָזְנְכֶם וּלְכוּ אֵלַי
שִׁמְעוּ וּתְחִי נַפְשְׁכֶם
וְאֶכְרְתָה לָכֶם בְּרִית עוֹלָם
חַסְדֵי דָוִד הַנֶּאֱמָנִים:
4 הֵן עֵד לְאוּמִּים נְתַתִּיו
נָגִיד וּמְצַוֵּה לְאֻמִּים:
5 הֵן גּוֹי לֹא־תֵדַע תִּקְרָא

v. 4. דגש אחר שורק

---

wine and milk. Learning, which is better
than wine and milk (Rashi).

2. Worldly pursuits involve the spend-
ing of money and labour without satis-
fying the soul that craves for the spiritual life.

spend money. lit. 'weigh silver.'

is not bread. Gives no satisfaction (Ibn
Ezra, Kimchi).

gain. The Hebrew noun means 'labour'
as well as gain, the proceeds of labour.
See the note on due reward in liv. 17 (Ibn
Ezra, Ps. cxxviii. 2).

hearken diligently . . . and eat. Or, 'if ye
but hearken diligently . . . ye shall eat.'

let your soul. Or, 'your soul shall.' The
Hebrew noun nephesh here signifies the
soul in the World to Come (Ibn Ezra,
Kimchi).

fatness. The most nourishing and wholesome food, figurative for ethical and
spiritual satisfaction (Kimchi).

3-5. The reward of a return to God
and His Torah will be a new and everlasting covenant, Israel's supremacy and
influence and the fulfilment of the
hopes centered in the Davidic dynasty.

3. incline your ear. [God is addressing
Israel.]

hear. Obey the Divine commandments
(Targum).

the sure mercies of David. Promised to him
in 2 Sam. vii. 8-16 (Metsudath David).

4. given him. David, meaning the
Messiah, a representative of his dynasty
(Ibn Ezra, Kimchi).

a witness. To warn the nations against
any misdeeds (Kimchi).

a prince. The Hebrew word nagid is used
of David in 2 Sam. vii. 8.

5. thou. [The address is to Israel].

call. i.e. exercise influence upon to follow the true faith (Malbim).

And a nation that knew not thee
    shall run unto thee;
Because of the LORD thy God,
And for the Holy One of Israel,
    for He hath glorified thee.
6. Seek ye the LORD while He may
    be found,
Call ye upon Him while He is
    near;
7. Let the wicked forsake his way,
And the man of iniquity his
    thoughts;
And let him return unto the
    LORD, and He will have com-
    passion upon him,
And to our God, for He will
    abundantly pardon.
8. For My thoughts are not your
    thoughts,
Neither are your ways My ways,
    saith the LORD.
9. For as the heavens are higher
    than the earth,
So are My ways higher than
    your ways,
And My thoughts than your
    thoughts.
10. For as the rain cometh down and
    the snow from heaven,
And returneth not thither,
Except it water the earth,
And make it bring forth and bud,

וְגוֹי לֹא־יְדָעוּךָ אֵלֶיךָ יָרוּצוּ
לְמַעַן יְהֹוָה אֱלֹהֶיךָ
וְלִקְדוֹשׁ יִשְׂרָאֵל כִּי פֵאֲרָךְ׃
6 דִּרְשׁוּ יְהֹוָה בְּהִמָּצְאוֹ
קְרָאֻהוּ בִּהְיוֹתוֹ קָרוֹב׃
7 יַעֲזֹב רָשָׁע דַּרְכּוֹ
וְאִישׁ אָוֶן מַחְשְׁבֹתָיו
וְיָשֹׁב אֶל־יְהֹוָה וִירַחֲמֵהוּ
וְאֶל־אֱלֹהֵינוּ כִּי־יַרְבֶּה לִסְלוֹחַ׃
8 כִּי לֹא מַחְשְׁבוֹתַי מַחְשְׁבוֹתֵיכֶם
וְלֹא דַרְכֵיכֶם דְּרָכָי נְאֻם יְהֹוָה׃
9 כִּי־גָבְהוּ שָׁמַיִם מֵאָרֶץ
כֵּן גָּבְהוּ דְרָכַי מִדַּרְכֵיכֶם
וּמַחְשְׁבֹתַי מִמַּחְשְׁבֹתֵיכֶם׃
10 כִּי כַּאֲשֶׁר יֵרֵד הַגֶּשֶׁם וְהַשֶּׁלֶג
מִן־הַשָּׁמַיִם
וְשָׁמָּה לֹא יָשׁוּב
כִּי אִם־הִרְוָה אֶת־הָאָרֶץ
וְהוֹלִידָהּ וְהִצְמִיחָהּ

a nation. The term is equivalent to 'many a nation' (Abarbanel).

6f. A call to repentance.

6. *while He may be found . . . while He is near.* When the decree has not yet been resolved upon. Repent while God still allows His presence to rest in the temple, before He exiles you to Babylon (Ibn Ezra).

7. *forsake his way . . . his thoughts.* Penitence to be effective must be complete, in thought as well as in deed (Ibn Ezra, Kimchi).

8f. The two verses stress the transcendence of God's thoughts and ways.

10f. The efficacy of God's word.

10. *except it water.* Or, 'without having watered.'

271

And give seed to the sower and
    bread to the eater;

11. So shall My word be that goeth
    forth out of My mouth:
It shall not return unto Me void,
Except it accomplish that which
    I please,
And make the thing whereto
    I sent it prosper.

12. For ye shall go out with joy,
And be led forth with peace;
The mountains and the hills
    shall break forth before you
    into singing,
And all the trees of the field
    shall clap their hands.

13. Instead of the thorn shall come
    up the cypress,
And instead of the brier shall
    come up the myrtle;
And it shall be to the Lord for a
    memorial,
For an everlasting sign that shall
    not be cut off.

וְנָתַן זֶרַע לַזֹּרֵעַ וְלֶחֶם לָאֹכֵל׃

11 כֵּן יִהְיֶה דְבָרִי אֲשֶׁר יֵצֵא מִפִּי
לֹא־יָשׁוּב אֵלַי רֵיקָם
כִּי אִם־עָשָׂה אֶת־אֲשֶׁר חָפַצְתִּי
וְהִצְלִיחַ אֲשֶׁר שְׁלַחְתִּיו׃

12 כִּי־בְשִׂמְחָה תֵצֵאוּ
וּבְשָׁלוֹם תּוּבָלוּן
הֶהָרִים וְהַגְּבָעוֹת
יִפְצְחוּ לִפְנֵיכֶם רִנָּה
וְכָל־עֲצֵי הַשָּׂדֶה יִמְחֲאוּ־כָף׃

13 תַּחַת הַנַּעֲצוּץ יַעֲלֶה בְרוֹשׁ
תַּחַת הַסִּרְפַּד יַעֲלֶה הֲדַס
וְהָיָה לַיהֹוָה לְשֵׁם
לְאוֹת עוֹלָם לֹא יִכָּרֵת׃

v. 13. ותחת ק׳   v. 13. פתח באתנח

12f. The peaceful and joyful return from exile which is the purpose of God's *word* spoken of in the previous verse.

12. *go out.* From the Babylonian exile (Ibn Ezra).

be led forth. To Zion (Metsudath David).

the mountains . . . hands. The people in their joyful mood will feel all Nature joining them in exultation (cf. Ps. xcviii. 8) (Kimchi). Others read in the words a description of the transformation that will take place in Nature (cf. verse 13). The bare mountains and desolate hills will be clothed with luxuriant vegeta-tion and all the trees of the field will produce rich fruits (Rashi).

13. The transformation of Nature, evident on the road from Babylon to Zion, will remain an everlasting memorial to the marvellous deeds God had wrought for His people (Kimchi).

and it. viz. the miraculous transforma-tion (Ibn Ezra, Kimchi).

a memorial. Of His power and greatness. The Rabbis regarded *the thorn* and *the brier* as representing the wicked, and *the cypress* and *the myrtle* as symbolizing the righteous. In the new Jerusalem the former will be replaced by the latter;

56   CHAPTER LVI   נ

(handwritten: 4/2t)

1. Thus saith the LORD:
   Keep ye justice, and do right-
   eousness;
   For My salvation is near to come,
   And My favour to be revealed.
2. Happy is the man that doeth this,
   And the son of man that holdeth
   fast by it:
   That keepeth the sabbath from
   profaning it,
   And keepeth his hand from doing
   any evil.
3. Neither let the alien,
   That hath joined himself to the
   LORD, speak, saying:
   'The LORD will surely separate
   me from His people';
   Neither let the eunuch say:
   'Behold, I am a dry tree.'

1 כֹּה אָמַר יְהֹוָה
שִׁמְרוּ מִשְׁפָּט וַעֲשׂוּ צְדָקָה
כִּי־קְרוֹבָה יְשׁוּעָתִי לָבוֹא
וְצִדְקָתִי לְהִגָּלוֹת׃

2 אַשְׁרֵי אֱנוֹשׁ יַעֲשֶׂה־זֹּאת
וּבֶן־אָדָם יַחֲזִיק בָּהּ
שֹׁמֵר שַׁבָּת מֵחַלְּלוֹ
וְשֹׁמֵר יָדוֹ מֵעֲשׂוֹת כָּל־רָע׃

3 וְאַל־יֹאמַר בֶּן־הַנֵּכָר
הַנִּלְוָה אֶל־יְהֹוָה לֵאמֹר
הַבְדֵּל יַבְדִּילַנִי יְהֹוָה מֵעַל עַמּוֹ
וְאַל־יֹאמַר הַסָּרִיס
הֵן אֲנִי עֵץ יָבֵשׁ׃

(handwritten notes:)
3rd Is - no exile, no new Exodus
Know Temple & cult
Why delay in redemption of people?
Social evil condemned
Pluralism of community - "Spurious Israel"

the ungodly will perish and the righteous flourish (Rashi).

CHAPTER LVI

1–8. The reward in store for all who
keep justice, righteousness and observance of the Sabbath, irrespective of
whether they are Israelites, eunuchs, or
proselytes.

1f. A call to justice, righteousness and
Sabbath observance.

1. *near to come ... revealed.* To those
who act justly and practise righteousness (Kimchi).

My favour. lit. 'My righteousness,' i.e.
vindication of the virtuous (Malbim).

2. *doeth this.* What follows, viz. hallow-

ing the Sabbath and refraining from
evil.

from profaning. So as not to profane. An
exhortation regarding the Sabbath is
found in lviii. 13.

3–8. An assurance to the proselyte and
the eunuch.

3. *joined himself to the* LORD. Became a
proselyte and observed the commandments enjoined upon Israel (Rashi).

separate me from His people. When He
bestows His blessings upon them
(Rashi).

a dry tree. Without children to perpet-
uate his name. Here it is asserted that he
will not be excluded from God's blessings.

273

4. For thus saith the Lord
Concerning the eunuchs that keep My sabbaths,
And choose the things that please Me,
And hold fast by My covenant:
5. Even unto them will I give in My house
And within My walls a monument and a memorial
Better than sons and daughters;
I will give them an everlasting memorial,
That shall not be cut off.
6. Also the aliens, that join themselves to the Lord, to minister unto Him,
And to love the name of the Lord,
To be His servants,
Every one that keepeth the sabbath from profaning it,
And holdeth fast by My covenant:
7. Even them will I bring to My holy mountain,
And make them joyful in My house of prayer;
Their burnt-offerings and their sacrifices
Shall be acceptable upon Mine altar;
For My house shall be called
A house of prayer for all peoples.

4 כִּי־כֹה ׀ אָמַ֣ר יְהֹוָ֗ה
לַסָּרִיסִים֙ אֲשֶׁ֤ר יִשְׁמְרוּ֙ אֶת־שַׁבְּתוֹתַ֔י
וּבָחֲר֖וּ בַּאֲשֶׁ֣ר חָפָ֑צְתִּי
וּמַחֲזִיקִ֖ים בִּבְרִיתִֽי׃
5 וְנָתַתִּ֨י לָהֶ֜ם
בְּבֵיתִ֤י וּבְחֽוֹמֹתַי֙ יָ֣ד וָשֵׁ֔ם
ט֖וֹב מִבָּנִ֣ים וּמִבָּנ֑וֹת
שֵׁ֤ם עוֹלָם֙ אֶתֶּן־ל֔וֹ
אֲשֶׁ֖ר לֹ֥א יִכָּרֵֽת׃
6 וּבְנֵ֣י הַנֵּכָ֗ר הַנִּלְוִ֤ים עַל־יְהֹוָה֙ לְשָׁ֣רְת֔וֹ
וּֽלְאַהֲבָה֙ אֶת־שֵׁ֣ם יְהֹוָ֔ה
לִהְי֥וֹת ל֖וֹ לַעֲבָדִ֑ים
כָּל־שֹׁמֵ֤ר שַׁבָּת֙ מֵֽחַלְּל֔וֹ
וּמַחֲזִיקִ֖ים בִּבְרִיתִֽי׃
7 וַהֲבִיאוֹתִ֞ים אֶל־הַ֣ר קָדְשִׁ֗י
וְשִׂמַּחְתִּים֙ בְּבֵ֣ית תְּפִלָּתִ֔י
עוֹלֹתֵיהֶ֧ם וְזִבְחֵיהֶ֛ם
לְרָצ֖וֹן עַל־מִזְבְּחִ֑י
כִּ֣י בֵיתִ֔י
בֵּית־תְּפִלָּ֥ה יִקָּרֵ֖א לְכָל־הָעַמִּֽים׃

4f. The religious eunuchs will enjoy everlasting fame which is superior to perpetuation through sons and daughters.

5. *a monument.* The Hebrew is literally 'hand,' and the noun occurs again in this sense in 2 Sam. xviii. 18 where it is related that Absalom's monument was erected by him because he said, *I have no son to keep my name in remembrance.* Kimchi renders: 'a place,' meaning a status. Abarbanel interprets it as a place in the hereafter.

7. *My holy mountain.* The Temple mount in Jerusalem (Kimchi).

My house. The Temple (Kimchi).

a house of prayer for all peoples. Fulfilling the hope expressed by king Solomon when he dedicated the Temple (cf. 1 Kings viii. 41ff.).

8. Saith the Lord GOD who
   gathereth the dispersed of
   Israel:
   Yet will I gather others to him,
   beside those of him that are
   gathered.
9. All ye beasts of the field, come to
   devour,
   Yea, all ye beasts in the forest.
10. His watchmen are all blind,
    Without knowledge;
    They are all dumb dogs,
    They cannot bark;
    Raving, lying down, loving to
    slumber.
11. Yea, the dogs are greedy,
    They know not when they have
    enough;
    And these are shepherds
    That cannot understand;

נְאֻם אֲדֹנָי יֱהֹוִה מְקַבֵּץ נִדְחֵי יִשְׂרָאֵל
עוֹד אֲקַבֵּץ עָלָיו לְנִקְבָּצָיו׃ 8

כֹּל חַיְתוֹ שָׂדָי 9
אֵתָיוּ לֶאֱכֹל כָּל־חַיְתוֹ בַּיָּעַר׃

צֹפָו עוְרִים כֻּלָּם 10
לֹא יָדָעוּ
כֻּלָּם כְּלָבִים אִלְּמִים
לֹא יוּכְלוּ לִנְבֹּחַ
הֹזִים שֹׁכְבִים אֹהֲבֵי לָנוּם׃

וְהַכְּלָבִים עַזֵּי־נֶפֶשׁ 11
לֹא יָדְעוּ שָׂבְעָה
וְהֵמָּה רֹעִים
לֹא יָדְעוּ הָבִין

handwritten: Neh 5:1-13
handwritten: ehet
handwritten: angry of soul
handwritten: slumbering (Tg's) חֹזִים viewing

v. 8. עד כאן   v. 10. צ׳ רבתי וצופיו ק׳   v. 10. קמץ בז״ק

8. *saith the* LORD. It should be noted
that this phrase, which usually follows
the statement to which it relates, here
precedes it.

gather others to him. An allusion to Gentiles who will offer themselves as proselytes (Rashi, Ibn Ezra).

9-12. A new section begins with denunciation of the greedy, sensual and
incompetent leaders.

9. In irony and bitterness of the heart
the prophet invites the wild beasts leisurely to devour the defenceless sheep,
because they were left unprotected by
their shepherds. A scathing satire
against the slothful leaders of the peoples. Similar imagery is used in Jer. xii.
9; Ezek. xxxiv. 8.

10. *his watchmen.* The people's spiritual
guides (Rashi).

blind. They cannot see the difference
between good and evil (Kimchi).

without knowledge. lit. 'they know not.'

dumb dogs. They do not speak the truth,
and are afraid to rebuke evil-doers
(Rashi).

they cannot bark. To give warning of
danger which menaces as do watch-
dogs (Rashi).

raving. The Hebrew *hozim,* which is to be
found only here, has a parallel in Arabic
describing the delirious talk of a sick
man. Jewish exegetes, however, almost
unanimously, accept Targum's rendering of 'slumbering' (Rashi, Ibn
Kimchi).

lying down. Through slothfulness they
are inactive when they should be alert
(Metsudath David).

11. *greedy.* lit. 'fierce of soul,' of big
appetite (Rashi).

and these. The leaders who are compared
to greedy dogs (Rashi).

They all turn to their own way,
Each one to his gain, one and all.

12. 'Come ye, I will fetch wine,
And we will fill ourselves with
strong drink;
And to-morrow shall be as this
day,
And much more abundant.'

כֻּלָּם לְדַרְכָּם פָּנוּ
אִישׁ לְבִצְעוֹ מִקָּצֵהוּ׃
אֵתָיוּ אֶקְחָה־יַיִן ¹²
וְנִסְבְּאָה שֵׁכָר
וְהָיָה כָזֶה יוֹם מָחָר
גָּדוֹל יֶתֶר מְאֹד׃

57   CHAPTER LVII   נז

1. The righteous perisheth,
And no man layeth it to heart,
And godly men are taken away,
None considering
That the righteous is taken away
from the evil to come.
2. He entereth into peace,
They rest in their beds,
Each one that walketh in his
uprightness.

¹ הַצַּדִּיק אָבָד
וְאֵין אִישׁ שָׂם עַל־לֵב
וְאַנְשֵׁי־חֶסֶד נֶאֱסָפִים
בְּאֵין מֵבִין
כִּי־מִפְּנֵי הָרָעָה נֶאֱסַף הַצַּדִּיק׃
² יָבוֹא שָׁלוֹם
יָנוּחוּ עַל־מִשְׁכְּבוֹתָם
הֹלֵךְ נְכֹחוֹ׃

v. 1. קמץ בז״ק

turn to their own way. Seek their own interests without caring for the welfare of the people (Rashi).

one and all. lit. 'from his end,' i.e. from end to end, without exception (Rashi).

12. A quotation from an invitation which one of the degenerate leaders might address to his fellows (Targum, Rashi).

CHAPTER LVII

THE theme of lvi. 9–12 is continued in this chapter.

1f. The righteous and godly are perishing under the misrule and apathy of the nation's leaders, but no one pays heed.

1. *godly men.* lit. 'men of kindness.'

from the evil to come. So that he may escape the approaching catastrophe (Rashi, Ibn Ezra).

2. *he.* The subject is *each one that walketh,* etc. (Rashi).

entereth into peace. In contrast with the troubled time in store for the wicked and the ungodly. The *peace* is that of death (cf. Job iii. 13) (Rashi, Ibn Ezra).

they rest in their beds. The *beds* are their graves (cf. Ezek. xxxii. 25) which have no terrors for them. Death is but a peaceful transformation for the upright man (Kimchi).

3. But draw near hither,
   Ye sons of the sorceress,
   The seed of the adulterer and the
   harlot.
4. Against whom do ye ~~sport~~ *entertain*
   yourselves?
   Against whom make ye a wide
   mouth,
   And draw out the tongue?
   Are ye not children of transgression,
   A seed of falsehood,
5. Ye that inflame yourselves among *high places*
   the terebinths,
   Under every leafy tree;
   That slay the children in the *Hinnom*
   valleys,
   Under the clefts of the rocks?
6. Among the smooth stones of the
   valley is thy portion;

וְאַתֶּם קִרְבוּ־הֵנָּה ³
בְּנֵי עֹנְנָה
זֶרַע מְנָאֵף וַתִּזְנֶה:
עַל־מִי תִּתְעַנָּגוּ ⁴
עַל־מִי תַּרְחִיבוּ פֶה
תַּאֲרִיכוּ לָשׁוֹן
הֲלוֹא־אַתֶּם יִלְדֵי־פֶשַׁע
זֶרַע שָׁקֶר:
הַנֵּחָמִים בָּאֵלִים ⁵
תַּחַת כָּל־עֵץ רַעֲנָן
שֹׁחֲטֵי הַיְלָדִים בַּנְּחָלִים
תַּחַת סְעִפֵי הַסְּלָעִים:
בְּחַלְּקֵי־נַחַל חֶלְקֵךְ ⁶

3–13. The transgressors and scoffers are addressed.

3. *but draw near.* Better, 'but as for you, draw near.' The emphasis is on 'you,' the mass of the people, after the demise of the righteous and godly spoken of in the previous passage (Rashi).

sons of . . . seed of. Both sons and parents are equally degenerate (Kimchi).

4. *do ye sport yourselves?* lit. 'enjoy yourselves.' The context shows that the enjoyment was malevolent, and that they would mock the prophets during their drinking bouts (Kimchi).

make a wide mouth . . . tongue. Scornful facial contortions (Kimchi).

are ye not, etc. Degenerates of your type should mock yourselves (Kimchi).

5–9. A description of the abominable rites practised.

5. *inflame yourselves.* With sexual lust, referring to the immorality which was part of idolatrous rites (cf. Hos. iv. 13f.) (Rashi).

slay the children. To Molech or some other false deity (cf. Jer. vii. 31, xxxii. 35) (Rashi, Ibn Ezra, Kimchi).

clefts of the rocks. These spots were selected for their revolting ritual. It was believed that the children slaughtered there would attain lofty heights in heaven (Malbim).

6. One of the rites in primitive heathendom, particularly among the Semites, was the worship in the wadis or watercourses of upright stones, water-worn and smoothed by the winter floods,

They, they are thy lot;
Even to them hast thou poured
    a drink-offering,
Thou hast offered a meal-
    offering.
Should I pacify Myself for these
    things?
7. Upon a high and lofty mountain
Hast thou set thy bed;
Thither also wentest thou up
To offer sacrifice.
8. And behind the doors and the
    posts
Hast thou set up thy symbol;
For thou hast uncovered, *from me* and art
    gone up ~~from Me,~~
Thou hast enlarged thy bed, *at the high places*
And chosen thee of them

cut (a covenant [handwritten]

הֵם הֵם גּוֹרָלֵךְ
גַּם־לָהֶם שָׁפַכְתְּ נֶסֶךְ
הֶעֱלִית מִנְחָה
הַעַל אֵלֶּה אֶנָּחֵם׃
7 עַל הַר־גָּבֹהַּ וְנִשָּׂא
שַׂמְתְּ מִשְׁכָּבֵךְ
גַּם־שָׁם עָלִית
לִזְבֹּחַ זָבַח׃
8 וְאַחַר הַדֶּלֶת וְהַמְּזוּזָה
שַׂמְתְּ זִכְרוֹנֵךְ
כִּי מֵאִתִּי גִּלִּית וַתַּעֲלִי
הִרְחַבְתְּ מִשְׁכָּבֵךְ
וַתִּכְרָת־לָךְ מֵהֶם

upon which was poured or smeared the blood or oil of sacrificial offerings to the deity the stones represented (Abarbanel).

thy portion. The Hebrew *chelkech* is an alliterative play on *chalkë, smooth stones* of (Kimchi).

they, they are thy lot. The worthless stones are contrasted with the greatness of God, the *lot* of loyal Israel (cf. Ps. xvi. 5, cxix. 57, cxlii. 6).

should I pacify . . . things? A rhetorical question. The answer expected is that no appeasement is possible. Such revolting worship demands not pacification but condign punishment (Rashi, Kimchi, Abarbanel).

7. The mountains, like the valleys in the preceding verse, were also places of worship to false deities (Abarbanel).

bed. An altar or site for pagan worship and sacrifice. The image of the *bed* is suggested by the close relationship between idolatry and immorality (Rashi).

8f. We meet here not only with difficulties of syntax, but also with obscure allusions.

8. *behind the doors . . . posts.* Of private houses or sanctuaries where household gods and patron deities were kept (Kimchi, Abarbanel).

symbol. An emblem or figure of a heathen deity (cf. Ezek, xvi. 17) (Kimchi).

for thou hast . . . bed. Better, 'far away from Me hast thou uncovered and ascended and enlarged thy bed,' increased occasions for lustful indulgence (Rashi).

chosen thee of them. Or, 'made thee a covenant with some of them' (Rashi, Ibn Ezra, Kimchi).

Whose bed thou lovedst,
Whose hand thou sawest.

9. And thou wentest to the king
   with ointment,
   And didst increase thy perfumes,
   And didst send thine ambas-
   sadors far off,
   Even down to the nether-world.

10. Thou wast wearied with the
    length of thy way;
    Yet saidst thou not: 'There is no
    hope';
    Thou didst find a renewal of thy
    strength,
    Therefore thou wast not affected.

11. And of whom hast thou been
    afraid and in fear,
    That thou wouldest fail?

אַהֲבְתְּ מִשְׁכָּבָם
יָד חָזִית:
9 וַתָּשֻׁרִי לַמֶּלֶךְ בַּשֶּׁמֶן
וַתַּרְבִּי רִקֻּחָיִךְ
וַתְּשַׁלְּחִי צִירַיִךְ עַד־מֵרָחֹק
וַתַּשְׁפִּילִי עַד־שְׁאוֹל:
10 בְּרֹב דַּרְכֵּךְ יָגַעַתְּ
לֹא אָמַרְתְּ נוֹאָשׁ
חַיַּת יָדֵךְ מָצָאת
עַל־כֵּן לֹא חָלִית:
11 וְאֶת־מִי דָּאַגְתְּ וַתִּירְאִי
כִּי תְכַזֵּבִי

v. 9. חסר ב

---

whose hand. 'With a beckoning finger' implied. All Jewish exegetes, however, render: 'whose place thou sawest' (Rashi, Ibn Ezra, Kimchi).

thou wentest. With gifts (Ibn Ezra, Kimchi).

to the king. Of Assyria, who ruled over the entire Middle East at that time (Ibn Ezra, Kimchi).

ointment. Or, 'oil' (so lit.).

didst send thine ambassadors. To the distant land of Assyria (Kimchi).

to the nether-world. You humbled yourself to such an extent that it was as though you humbled yourself to the nether-world (Kimchi).

10f. While they were wooing the foreign potentates, they never remembered

or thought of the true God Who alone gave them life and strength.

10. *length of thy way.* To the kings of the foreign lands (Kimchi).

there is no hope. All the efforts to secure aid from rulers are futile. I may as well stay where I am and rest (Kimchi).

a renewal of thy strength. lit. 'the life of thine hand,' restoration of vigour. The Israelite idolaters deluded themselves that their wooing of foreign potentates was helpful to them (Kimchi).

affect. lit. 'sick'; i.e. they do not abandon the practices (Metsudath David).

11. *of whom hast thou been afraid . . . fail?* The answer implied is: certainly not of Me. There was nothing to deter them from pursuing their evil course, since no fear of God stood in the way (Kimchi).

And as for Me, thou hast not
   remembered Me,
Nor laid it to thy heart.
Have not I held My peace even
   of long time?
Therefore thou fearest Me not.
12. I will declare thy righteousness;
   Thy works also—they shall not
   profit thee.
13. When thou criest, let them that
   thou hast gathered deliver
   thee;
   But the wind shall carry them all
   away,
   A breath shall bear them off;
   But he that taketh refuge in Me
   shall possess the land,
   And shall inherit My holy
   mountain.
14. And He will say:
   Cast ye up, cast ye up, clear the
   way,
   Take up the stumblingblock out
   of the way of My people.

וְאוֹתִי לֹא זָכַרְתְּ
לֹא־שַׂמְתְּ עַל־לִבֵּךְ
הֲלֹא אֲנִי מַחְשֶׁה וּמֵעֹלָם
וְאוֹתִי לֹא תִירָאִי:
12 אֲנִי אַגִּיד צִדְקָתֵךְ
וְאֶת־מַעֲשַׂיִךְ וְלֹא יוֹעִילוּךְ:
13 בְּזַעֲקֵךְ יַצִּילֻךְ קִבּוּצַיִךְ
וְאֶת־כֻּלָּם יִשָּׂא־רוּחַ יִקַּח הָבֶל
וְהַחוֹסֶה בִי יִנְחַל־אֶרֶץ
וְיִירַשׁ הַר־קָדְשִׁי:
14 וְאָמַר
סֹלּוּ־סֹלּוּ פַּנּוּ־דָרֶךְ
הָרִימוּ מִכְשׁוֹל מִדֶּרֶךְ עַמִּי:

v. 14. הפטרת יום כפור

---

and as for Me. The sense is, seeing that so
far as I am concerned.

have not I held My peace, etc. God did not
intervene to put an end to their evil
conduct by the affliction of punishment;
so they believed that there was no
reason to fear His retribution (Kimchi).

12f. God's apparent indifference to
their way of life is now ended and He is
proceeding to pronounce judgment.

12. *I will declare.* Better, 'I, even I, will
declare,' the subject being emphasized
in the text.

thy righteousness. Ironical for 'pretended
righteousness' (Kimchi, Abarbanel).

13. *them that thou hast gathered.* The varied collections of their idols (Rashi).

but that he taketh . . . mountain. This forms
a connecting link between the severities

and strictures of the previous passage
and the comforting assurance in the
following.

14–21. In elegant diction and flowing
periods, the penitent sufferers returning
to God are promised relief from their
oppressors and Divine comforts and
peace. The passage stands in remarkable contrast with the scathing denun-
ciations and heavy style of the preceding
(After Rashi).

14. The *way* in the verse is to be
understood as the spiritual approach to
God by the people who had hitherto
strayed from Him (Rashi).

clear the way. Remove the evil inclination
from your hearts which blocks the path
to redemption (Rashi).

the stumblingblock. i.e. sinful thoughts
which bar the way to justice and righteousness (Rashi).

15. For thus saith the High and
    Lofty One
    That inhabiteth eternity, whose
      name is Holy:
    I dwell in the high and holy
      place,
    With him also that is of a contrite
      and humble spirit,
    To revive the spirit of the
      humble,
    And to revive the heart of the
      contrite ones.

16. For I will not contend for ever,
    Neither will I be always wroth;
    For the spirit that enwrappeth
      itself is from Me,
    And the souls which I have
      made.

17. For the iniquity of his covetous-
      ness was I wroth and smote
      him,
    I hid Me and was wroth;
    And he went on frowardly in the
      way of his heart.

18. I have seen his ways, and will
      heal him;
    I will lead him also, and requite
      with comforts him and his
      mourners.

15 כִּי כֹה אָמַר רָם וְנִשָּׂא
שֹׁכֵן עַד וְקָדוֹשׁ שְׁמוֹ
מָרוֹם וְקָדוֹשׁ אֶשְׁכּוֹן
וְאֶת־דַּכָּא וּשְׁפַל־רוּחַ
לְהַחֲיוֹת רוּחַ שְׁפָלִים
וּלְהַחֲיוֹת לֵב נִדְכָּאִים׃

16 כִּי לֹא לְעוֹלָם אָרִיב
וְלֹא לָנֶצַח אֶקְצוֹף
כִּי־רוּחַ מִלְּפָנַי יַעֲטוֹף
וּנְשָׁמוֹת אֲנִי עָשִׂיתִי׃

17 בַּעֲוֹן בִּצְעוֹ
קָצַפְתִּי וְאַכֵּהוּ הַסְתֵּר וְאֶקְצֹף
וַיֵּלֶךְ שׁוֹבָב בְּדֶרֶךְ לִבּוֹ׃

18 דְּרָכָיו רָאִיתִי וְאֶרְפָּאֵהוּ
וְאַנְחֵהוּ וַאֲשַׁלֵּם נִחֻמִים לוֹ וְלַאֲבֵלָיו׃

15. God is high and lofty, far above all human eminence, and at the same time He is near to the contrite and humble. His exaltation and condescension are neither identical nor mutually exclusive, but two different manifestations of His inscrutable nature.

the high and holy place. i.e. heaven (Ibn Ezra).

16. The verse explains why God is near to the contrite in spirit. Divine anger lasts only for a time, until chastisement has produced the desired purification and humility of spirit. Long continuance of His wrath and judgment would have utterly destroyed the souls He had created (Rabbenu Yeshayah).

that enwrappeth itself is from Me. i.e. the spirit that enwrappeth itself in the body is from Me (Kimchi). Others render: 'would faint before Me' (Ibn Ezra).

17f. God's estrangement, anger and punishment are the fruits of the people's iniquity; but after the discipline come healing and comfort.

17. *covetousness.* Which led to the exploitation of the poor and weak (Kimchi).

I hid Me and was wroth. lit. 'hiding and being wroth,' i.e. repeatedly. As often as the people were guilty of covetousness God hid Himself and was wroth (Rashi).

and he went. Or, 'for he went' (Targum).

18. *seen his ways.* His sufferings and his penitence (Rashi).

lead him. Give him the support a convalescent needs (Rashi).

his mourners. Those who sympathized with him in his sorrow and distress (Rashi).

19. Peace, peace, to him that is far
off and to him that is near,
Saith the LORD that createth the
fruit of the lips;
And I will heal him.
20. But the wicked are like the
troubled sea;
For it cannot rest,
And its waters cast up mire and
dirt.
21. There is no peace,
Saith my God concerning the
wicked.

58   CHAPTER LVIII

1. Cry aloud, spare not,
Lift up thy voice like a horn,
And declare unto My people
their transgression,
And to the house of Jacob their
sins.

19 בּוֹרֵא נוֹב שְׂפָתָיִם
שָׁלוֹם ׀ שָׁלוֹם לָרָחוֹק וְלַקָּרוֹב
אָמַר יְהֹוָה וּרְפָאתִיו:
20 וְהָרְשָׁעִים כַּיָּם נִגְרָשׁ
כִּי הַשְׁקֵט לֹא יוּכָל
וַיִּגְרְשׁוּ מֵימָיו רֶפֶשׁ וָטִיט:
21 אֵין שָׁלוֹם
אָמַר אֱלֹהַי לָרְשָׁעִים:

נח

1 קְרָא בְגָרוֹן אַל־תַּחְשֹׂךְ
כַּשּׁוֹפָר הָרֵם קוֹלֶךָ
וְהַגֵּד לְעַמִּי פִּשְׁעָם
וּלְבֵית יַעֲקֹב חַטֹּאאתָם:

v. 19. ניב ק'   v. 20. קמץ בז״ק

---

19. *far off.* Those far from Jerusalem (Kimchi).

near. Those near Jerusalem. All will have peace after the war of Gog and Magog (Kimchi).

fruit of the lips. i.e. speech. In this context it denotes the new attitude of the nations toward Israel. Whereas heretofore they were always critical of Israel, now they will greet them with the expression of "Peace, peace" (Kimchi).

20f. In contrast with the abundant peace promised to the penitent, unrest like that of the troubled sea with its mire and dirt is the lot of the impenitent wicked.

20. *the wicked.* Who do not abandon their evil practices (Rashi).

like the troubled sea. Their life is full of unrest and unsatisfied lust, instead of the *peace* which God offers to the righteous (Malbim).

21. Repeated from xlviii. 22 with the substitution of *My God* for *the* LORD.

CHAPTER LVIII

THE futility of prayer and fasting without amendment, and the supreme importance of moral and religious conduct.

1f. God's call to the prophet.

1. *aloud.* lit. 'with the throat,' with a loud and clear voice (Abarbanel).

spare not. The throat or the voice but call constantly (Kimchi).

2. Yet they seek Me daily,
   And delight to know My ways;
   As a nation that did righteous-
   ness,
   And forsook not the ordinance of
   their God,
   They ask of Me righteous ordi-
   nances,
   They delight to draw near unto
   God.

3. 'Wherefore have we fasted, and
   Thou seest not?
   Wherefore have we afflicted our
   soul, and Thou takest no
   knowledge?'—
   Behold, in the day of your fast
   ye pursue your business,
   And exact all your labours.

4. Behold, ye fast for strife and
   contention,
   And to smite with the fist of
   wickedness;
   Ye fast not this day
   So as to make your voice to be
   heard on high.

2 וְאוֹתִי יוֹם ׀ יוֹם יִדְרֹשׁוּן
וְדַעַת דְּרָכַי יֶחְפָּצוּן
כְּגוֹי אֲשֶׁר־צְדָקָה עָשָׂה
וּמִשְׁפַּט אֱלֹהָיו לֹא עָזָב
יִשְׁאָלוּנִי מִשְׁפְּטֵי־צֶדֶק
קִרְבַת אֱלֹהִים יֶחְפָּצוּן:
3 לָמָּה צַּמְנוּ וְלֹא רָאִיתָ
עִנִּינוּ נַפְשֵׁנוּ וְלֹא תֵדָע
הֵן בְּיוֹם צֹמְכֶם תִּמְצְאוּ־חֵפֶץ
וְכָל־עַצְּבֵיכֶם תִּנְגֹּשׂוּ:
4 הֵן לְרִיב וּמַצָּה תָּצוּמוּ
וּלְהַכּוֹת בְּאֶגְרֹף רֶשַׁע
לֹא־תָצוּמוּ כַיּוֹם
לְהַשְׁמִיעַ בַּמָּרוֹם קוֹלְכֶם:

v. 2. הצ' בדגש ק בז"ק קמץ v. 3.

2. The people's worship is formal and insincere.

yet. Despite their sins and transgressions (Kimchi).

seek Me. lit. 'enquire of Me,' pretending a desire to know the ways of God (Targum).

delight. They wish to know the ways of Divine Providence (Abarbanel). Others explain: They constantly ask questions of law, as if they wished to observe them (Rashi).

righteous ordinances. Ordinances of the practice of righteousness (Malbim, Laniado).

to draw near unto God. They ask for instruction in the observance of pious practices in order to draw near unto God, whereas they do not observe the obligatory laws properly (Malbim).

3. wherefore . . . knowledge? This is the people's complaint when they saw no alleviation in their lot despite their fasting (Kimchi).

behold, in the dry, etc. The prophet's reply to the question which is continued in the following verses.

pursue your business . . . labours. The fast has no spiritual or religious significance. It is merely a means for securing material gain (Kimchi).

4. ye fast for strife. In the absence of a religious motive, the public gatherings on fastdays bring about quarrels and strife, since one meets his enemies, whom he would otherwise not meet (Metsudath David).

the fist of wickedness. These quarrels would often lead to violence (Metsudath David).

this day. Or, 'at present' (Ibn Ezra).

so as . . . on high. Fasts of that description are no aid to the ascent of a man's prayers to heaven (Rashi).

5. Is such the fast that I have
   chosen?
   The day for a man to afflict his
   soul?
   Is it to bow down his head as a
   bulrush,
   And to spread sackcloth and
   ashes under him?
   Wilt thou call this a fast,
   And an acceptable day to the
   LORD?
6. Is not this the fast that I have
   chosen?
   To loose the fetters of wickedness,
   To undo the bands of the yoke,
   And to let the oppressed go free,
   And that ye break every yoke?
7. Is it not to deal thy bread to the
   hungry,
   And that thou bring the poor
   that are cast out to thy house?
   When thou seest the naked, that
   thou cover him,
   And that thou hide not thyself
   from thine own flesh?
8. Then shall thy light break forth
   as the morning,

5 הֲכָזֶה יִהְיֶה צוֹם אֶבְחָרֵהוּ

יוֹם עַנּוֹת אָדָם נַפְשׁוֹ

הֲלָכֹף כְּאַגְמֹן רֹאשׁוֹ

וְשַׂק וָאֵפֶר יַצִּיעַ

הֲלָזֶה תִּקְרָא־צוֹם

וְיוֹם רָצוֹן לַיהוָה׃

6 הֲלוֹא זֶה צוֹם אֶבְחָרֵהוּ

פַּתֵּחַ חַרְצֻבּוֹת רֶשַׁע

הַתֵּר אֲגֻדּוֹת מוֹטָה

וְשַׁלַּח רְצוּצִים חָפְשִׁים

וְכָל־מוֹטָה תְּנַתֵּקוּ׃

7 הֲלוֹא פָרֹס לָרָעֵב לַחְמֶךָ

וַעֲנִיִּים מְרוּדִים תָּבִיא בָיִת

כִּי־תִרְאֶה עָרֹם וְכִסִּיתוֹ

וּמִבְּשָׂרְךָ לֹא תִתְעַלָּם׃

8 אָז יִבָּקַע כַּשַּׁחַר אוֹרֶךָ

5. *is such the fast . . . chosen?* Can a fast
with the motive of securing material
gains, leading to strife and blows, be
acceptable to God? (Kimchi).

to afflict his soul. With no spiritual sincerity behind it (Malbim).

to bow down . . . under him. As a mere
ceremonial formality (Kimchi, Malbim).

spread sackcloth and ashes. An outward
mark of contrition (Kimchi, Malbim,
Hirsch).

6f.   The right ways of observing a fast
are indicated. One of these is the abolition of unjust slavery and oppression;
the other is the practice of benevolent
deeds.

6.   *this.* Defined by what follows.

oppressed. lit. 'crushed,' referring to
Hebrew slaves who were overworked

and who were not freed after working
the prescribed six years of slavery.
Jeremiah, too, castigated the people for
this sin (Jer. xxxiv. 8–16) (Kimchi,
Abarbanel).

7.   *deal thy bread.* The force of Hebrew
is 'share thy food' (Malbim).

the poor that are cast out. Better, 'the wandering poor,' the homeless (Targum,
Kimchi).

own flesh. i.e. relatives in need of help
(Rashi, Ibn Ezra, Kimchi).

8.   *then.* If you perform these good
deeds, you will no longer find it necessary to proclaim fastdays and don sackcloth, but 'then shall thy light break
forth, etc.' (Kimchi).

thy light. The joy which dispels the
gloom of distress (Kimchi).

And thy healing shall spring
forth speedily;
And thy righteousness shall go
before thee,
The glory of the LORD shall be
thy rearward.
9. Then shalt thou call, and the
LORD will answer;
Thou shalt cry, and He will say:
'Here I am.'
If thou take away from the midst
of thee the yoke,
The putting forth of the finger,
and speaking wickedness;
10. And if thou draw out thy soul to
the hungry,
And satisfy the afflicted soul;
Then shall thy light rise in
darkness,
And thy gloom be as the noonday;
11. And the LORD will guide thee
continually,
And satisfy thy soul in drought,
And make strong thy bones;
And thou shalt be like a watered
garden,
And like a spring of water, whose
waters fail not.
12. And they that shall be of thee
shall build the old waste places,
Thou shalt raise up the foundations of many generations;

וְאָרֻכָתְךָ֖ מְהֵרָ֣ה תִצְמָ֑ח
וְהָלַ֤ךְ לְפָנֶ֙יךָ֙ צִדְקֶ֔ךָ
כְּב֥וֹד יְהוָ֖ה יַאַסְפֶֽךָ׃
9 אָ֤ז תִּקְרָא֙ וַיהוָ֣ה יַעֲנֶ֔ה
תְּשַׁוַּ֖ע וְיֹאמַ֣ר הִנֵּ֑נִי
אִם־תָּסִ֤יר מִתּֽוֹכְךָ֙ מוֹטָ֔ה
שְׁלַ֥ח אֶצְבַּ֖ע וְדַבֶּר־אָֽוֶן׃
10 וְתָפֵ֤ק לָֽרָעֵב֙ נַפְשֶׁ֔ךָ
וְנֶ֥פֶשׁ נַעֲנָ֖ה תַּשְׂבִּ֑יעַ
וְזָרַ֤ח בַּחֹ֙שֶׁךְ֙ אוֹרֶ֔ךָ
וַאֲפֵלָֽתְךָ֖ כַּֽצָּהֳרָֽיִם׃
11 וְנָחֲךָ֣ יְהוָה֮ תָּמִיד֒
וְהִשְׂבִּ֤יעַ בְּצַחְצָחוֹת֙ נַפְשֶׁ֔ךָ
וְעַצְמֹתֶ֖יךָ יַחֲלִ֑יץ
וְהָיִ֙יתָ֙ כְּגַ֣ן רָוֶ֔ה
וּכְמוֹצָ֣א מַ֔יִם אֲשֶׁ֥ר לֹֽא־יְכַזְּב֖וּ מֵימָֽיו׃
12 וּבָנ֤וּ מִמְּךָ֙ חָרְב֣וֹת עוֹלָ֔ם
מֽוֹסְדֵ֥י דֽוֹר־וָד֖וֹר תְּקוֹמֵ֑ם

healing. Or, 'recovery.'

go before thee. As a protection (Ibn
Ezra).

thy rearward. Cf. lii. 12.

9. *the yoke.* Cf. verse 6.

putting forth of the finger. A gesture of
scorn by the rich against the poor, the
powerful against the weak (cf. Prov. vi.
13) (After Targum).

10. *draw out thy soul.* Display sympathy
with (Metsudath David).

satisfy. With food (Kimchi).

the afflicted soul. Equals 'the famished
person' (Metsudath David).

11. *in drought.* Even during dry times
(Rashi, Kimchi).

make strong thy bones. Invigorate the body
(Metsudath David).

like a watered garden, etc. A metaphor for
prosperity and well-being (Kimchi).

12. *old waste places.* Or, 'ancient ruins'
(again in lxi. 4).

foundations of many generations. Foundations that lay waste for many years
(Kimchi).

And thou shalt be called The
repairer of the breach,
The restorer of paths to dwell in.

13. If thou turn away thy foot
because of the sabbath,
From pursuing thy business on
My holy day;
And call the sabbath a delight,
And the holy of the LORD
honourable;
And shalt honour it, not doing
thy wonted ways,
Nor pursuing thy business, nor
speaking thereof;

14. Then shalt thou delight thyself
in the LORD,
And I will make thee to ride
upon the high places of the
earth,
And I will feed thee with the
heritage of Jacob thy father;
For the mouth of the LORD hath
spoken it.

וְקֹרָ֣א לְךָ֮ גֹּדֵ֣ר פֶּ֒רֶץ֒
מְשֹׁבֵ֥ב נְתִיב֖וֹת לָשָֽׁבֶת׃

13 אִם־תָּשִׁ֤יב מִשַּׁבָּת֙ רַגְלֶ֔ךָ
עֲשׂ֥וֹת חֲפָצֶ֖ךָ בְּי֣וֹם קָדְשִׁ֑י
וְקָרָ֨אתָ לַשַּׁבָּ֜ת עֹ֗נֶג
לִקְד֤וֹשׁ יְהוָה֙ מְכֻבָּ֔ד
וְכִבַּדְתּוֹ֙ מֵעֲשׂ֣וֹת דְּרָכֶ֔יךָ
מִמְּצ֥וֹא חֶפְצְךָ֖ וְדַבֵּ֥ר דָּבָֽר׃

14 אָ֗ז תִּתְעַנַּג֙ עַל־יְהוָ֔ה
וְהִרְכַּבְתִּ֖יךָ עַל־במותי אָ֑רֶץ
וְהַאֲכַלְתִּ֗יךָ נַחֲלַת֙ יַעֲקֹ֣ב אָבִ֔יךָ
כִּ֛י פִּ֥י יְהוָ֖ה דִּבֵּֽר׃

v. 14. יתיר ר׳   v. 14. עד כאן

---

thou shalt be called. i.e. thy fame shall
spread (Kimchi).

paths to dwell in. Inhabited settlements
(Kimchi).

13f. The pleasures and delights to be
derived from the proper observance of
the Sabbath.

13. *turn away thy foot.* From going outside Sabbath limits (Kimchi).

call the sabbath a delight. Observe the holy
day in a spirit of joy and cheerfulness
(Kimchi).

the holy of the LORD. An epithet applied
to the Sabbath (Ibn Ezra, Kimchi).

doing thy wonted ways. Attending to the

usual secular affairs of a week-day
(Kimchi).

speaking thereof. The phrase may mean
'speaking idle words' (cf. Hos. x. 4)
instead of concentrating upon holy
matters (Kimchi) or 'making business
propositions' (cf. Gen. xxiv. 33, *told mine
errand*) (Rashi, Shab. 113b).

14. *shalt thou delight thyself* Or, 'shalt
thou have thy delight.'

ride upon ... earth. Thou wilt have
honor, power and influence (cf. Deut.
xxxii. 13) (Metsudath David).

and I will feed thee with. Or, 'and I will
cause thee to enjoy' (Hirsch).

the heritage of Jacob. The extensive territory promised to him (cf. Gen. xxviii.
14) (Rashi).

59   CHAPTER LIX   נט

1 הֵן לֹא־קָצְרָה יַד־יְהֹוָה מֵהוֹשִׁיעַ
וְלֹא־כָבְדָה אָזְנוֹ מִשְּׁמוֹעַ ׃
2 כִּי אִם־עֲוֹנֹתֵיכֶם הָיוּ מַבְדִּלִים
בֵּינֵכֶם לְבֵין אֱלֹהֵיכֶם
וְחַטֹּאותֵיכֶם הִסְתִּירוּ פָנִים
מִכֶּם מִשְּׁמוֹעַ ׃
3 כִּי כַפֵּיכֶם נְגֹאֲלוּ בַדָּם
וְאֶצְבְּעוֹתֵיכֶם בֶּעָוֺן
שִׂפְתוֹתֵיכֶם דִּבְּרוּ־שֶׁקֶר
לְשׁוֹנְכֶם עַוְלָה תֶהְגֶּה ׃
4 אֵין־קֹרֵא בְצֶדֶק
וְאֵין נִשְׁפָּט בֶּאֱמוּנָה
בָּטוֹחַ עַל־תֹּהוּ וְדַבֶּר־שָׁוְא
הָרוֹ עָמָל וְהוֹלֵיד אָוֶן ׃

v. 2. מלא ר

1. Behold, the LORD's hand is not
   shortened, that it cannot save,
   Neither His ear heavy, that it
   cannot hear;
2. But your iniquities have separated
   Between you and your God,
   And your sins have hid His face
   from you,
   That He will not hear.
3. For your hands are defiled with
   blood,
   And your fingers with iniquity;
   Your lips have spoken lies,
   Your tongue muttereth wickedness.
4. None sueth in righteousness,
   And none pleadeth in truth;
   They trust in vanity, and speak
   lies,
   They conceive mischief, and
   bring forth iniquity.

CHAPTER LIX

THE flagrant sins of the nation have
formed a barrrier between God and
them, and in consequence they were
plunged into the direst misery. When,
however, their plight was at its worst
and their position seemed hopeless,
God intervened and delivered them.

1–4. Not God's inability or indifference, but the sin of the people, is the
cause of Israel's sorrow and suffering
(Rashi, Kimchi).

1. *not shortened . . . save.* Or, 'not too
short to save'; similarly *heavy . . . hear*
may be rendered: 'too heavy to hear.'
The languages occurred in vi. 10, 1. 2.

2. *hid His face.* Alienated His Presence
(Ibn Ezra). The pronoun is not in the
text.

3. The general accusation in this verse
is specified in detail in what follows.

4. Perversion of justice, lying and mis-
chief-making are rife.

sueth. lit. 'calleth,' i.e. summons to a
lawsuit; *pleadeth* signifies 'defends himself against a charge' (Abarbanel).

they trust. The Hebrew form of this verb,
as of the following verbs in the verse, is
in the infinitive and might be rendered:
'trusting in vanity and speaking lies,
conceiving mischief and bringing forth
iniquity.'

5. They hatch basilisks' eggs,
   And weave the spider's web;
   He that eateth of their eggs dieth,
   And that which is crushed
   breaketh out into a viper.

6. Their webs shall not become
   garments,
   Neither shall men cover themselves with their works;
   Their works are works of
   iniquity,
   And the act of violence is in
   their hands.

7. Their feet run to evil,
   And they make haste to shed
   innocent blood;
   Their thoughts are thoughts of
   iniquity,
   Desolation and destruction are in
   their paths.

8. The way of peace they know not,
   And there is no right in their
   goings;
   They have made them crooked
   paths,
   Whosoever goeth therein doth
   not know peace.

5 בֵּיצֵי צִפְעוֹנִי בִּקֵּעוּ
וְקוּרֵי עַכָּבִישׁ יֶאֱרֹגוּ
הָאֹכֵל מִבֵּיצֵיהֶם יָמוּת
וְהַזּוּרֶה תִּבָּקַע אֶפְעֶה:
6 קוּרֵיהֶם לֹא־יִהְיוּ לְבֶגֶד
וְלֹא יִתְכַּסּוּ בְּמַעֲשֵׂיהֶם
מַעֲשֵׂיהֶם מַעֲשֵׂי־אָוֶן
וּפֹעַל חָמָס בְּכַפֵּיהֶם:
7 רַגְלֵיהֶם לָרַע יָרֻצוּ
וִימַהֲרוּ לִשְׁפֹּךְ דָּם נָקִי
מַחְשְׁבֹתֵיהֶם מַחְשְׁבוֹת אָוֶן
שֹׁד וָשֶׁבֶר בִּמְסִלּוֹתָם:
8 דֶּרֶךְ שָׁלוֹם לֹא יָדָעוּ
וְאֵין מִשְׁפָּט בְּמַעְגְּלוֹתָם
נְתִיבוֹתֵיהֶם עִקְּשׁוּ לָהֶם
כֹּל דֹּרֵךְ בָּהּ לֹא יָדַע שָׁלוֹם:

v. 8. קמץ בז״ק

5f. A series of striking similes on the people's machinations, deep-laid plots and deadly designs.

5. *hatch basilisks' eggs.* As the eggs produce basilisks so do their projects mature into fatal acts (Kimchi, Metsudath David).

weave the spider's web. Their deeds have no permanence (Ibn Ezra, Kimchi).

he that eateth . . . viper. Their plots are so deadly that whether one falls victim to them, or one attempts to counteract them, the effects are equally fatal (Metsudath David).

6. Even when their acts appear to be beneficent, they are in reality useless if not dangerous.

shall not become garments. Can never be made into garments. They are too frail and flimsy for the purpose (Ibn Ezra, Kimchi).

neither shall men . . . works. Because they are unsuitable as coverings. Wicked deeds ultimately benefit no one (Kimchi).

7f. They not only devise mischievous plans, but hasten to put them into operation.

7. The first half of the verse closely resembles Prov. 1. 16.

8. *goings.* Better, 'tracks' (Metsudath Zion).

they have made . . . paths. lit. 'their paths— they have made crooked for themselves.'

9. Therefore is justice far from us,
Neither doth righteousness over-
take us;
We look for light, but behold
darkness,
For brightness, but we walk in
gloom.

10. We grope for the wall like the
blind,
Yea, as they that have no eyes do
we grope;
We stumble at noonday as in the
twilight;
We are in dark places like the
dead.

11. We all growl like bears,
And mourn sore like doves;
We look for right, but there is
none;
For salvation, but it is far off
from us.

12. For our transgressions are multiplied before Thee,
And our sins testify against us;
For our transgressions are present to us,
And as for our iniquities, we
know them:

13. Transgressing and denying the
LORD,
And turning away from following
our God,

9 עַל־כֵּ֞ן רָחַ֤ק מִשְׁפָּט֙ מִמֶּ֔נּוּ
וְלֹ֥א תַשִּׂיגֵ֖נוּ צְדָקָ֑ה
נְקַוֶּ֤ה לָאוֹר֙ וְהִנֵּה־חֹ֔שֶׁךְ
לִנְגֹה֖וֹת בָּאֲפֵלֹ֥ות נְהַלֵּֽךְ׃

10 נְגַֽשְׁשָׁ֤ה כַֽעִוְרִים֙ קִ֔יר
וּכְאֵ֥ין עֵינַ֖יִם נְגַשֵּׁ֑שָׁה
כָּשַׁ֤לְנוּ בַֽצָּהֳרַ֨יִם֙ כַּנֶּ֔שֶׁף
בָּאַשְׁמַנִּ֖ים כַּמֵּתִֽים׃

11 נֶהֱמֶ֤ה כַדֻּבִּים֙ כֻּלָּ֔נוּ
וְכַיּוֹנִ֖ים הָגֹ֣ה נֶהְגֶּ֑ה
נְקַוֶּ֤ה לַמִּשְׁפָּט֙ וָאַ֔יִן
לִישׁוּעָ֖ה רָחֲקָ֥ה מִמֶּֽנּוּ׃

12 כִּֽי־רַבּ֤וּ פְשָׁעֵ֨ינוּ֙ נֶגְדֶּ֔ךָ
וְחַטֹּאותֵ֖ינוּ עָ֣נְתָה בָּ֑נוּ
כִּֽי־פְשָׁעֵ֣ינוּ אִתָּ֔נוּ
וַעֲוֺנֹתֵ֖ינוּ יְדַֽעֲנֽוּם׃

13 פָּשֹׁ֤עַ וְכַחֵשׁ֙ בַּֽיהֹוָ֔ה
וְנָס֖וֹג מֵאַחַ֣ר אֱלֹהֵ֑ינוּ

v. 12. מלא ר

9–11. The physical and moral darkness that enveloped the people deprived
them of the light, justice and salvation
for which they longed.

9. *therefore.* [Because of the prevalent
corruption and not for the reason stated
in verse 1.]

10. *for the wall.* Or, 'along the wall.'

we are in dark places like the dead. The
translation follows Menahem. Dunash,
however, contends that since the
Hebrew for *dark places* (ashmannim),
which occurs only here, seems to come
from a root meaning 'fatness' it may,
therefore, be translated 'lusty'; hence he

renders: 'among them that are lusty we
are as dead men' (Rashi).

11. *growl like bears.* In distress (Metsudath David).

mourn sore like doves. Cf. xxxviii. 14 where
the same verb is translated *moan.*

12–15a. The prophet voices a confession to God to the sins of the people.

12. *are present to us . . . we know them.*
We are conscious of them (Kimchi).

13. *transgressing and denying the* LORD.
Or, 'rebellion and denial of the LORD'
(Targum). All the verbs in the verse are
infinitives. The 'denial' consists in denying just claims against them, which is, in

Speaking oppression and per-
    verseness,
Conceiving and uttering from the
    heart words of falsehood.

14. And justice is turned away back-
    ward,
And righteousness standeth afar
    off;
For truth hath stumbled in the
    broad place,
And uprightness cannot enter.

15. And truth is lacking,
And he that departeth from evil
    maketh himself a prey.
And the LORD saw it, and it
    displeased Him
That there was no justice;

16. And He saw that there was no
    man,
And was astonished that there
    was no intercessor;
Therefore His own arm brought
    salvation unto Him;
And His righteousness, it sus-
    tained Him;

דַּבֶּר־עֹשֶׁק וְסָרָה
הֹרוֹ וְהֹגוֹ מִלֵּב דִּבְרֵי־שָׁקֶר׃

14 וְהֻסַּג אָחוֹר מִשְׁפָּט
וּצְדָקָה מֵרָחוֹק תַּעֲמֹד
כִּי־כָשְׁלָה בָרְחוֹב אֱמֶת
וּנְכֹחָה לֹא־תוּכַל לָבוֹא׃

15 וַתְּהִי הָאֱמֶת נֶעְדֶּרֶת
וְסָר מֵרָע מִשְׁתּוֹלֵל
וַיַּרְא יְהוָה וַיֵּרַע בְּעֵינָיו
כִּי־אֵין מִשְׁפָּט׃

16 וַיַּרְא כִּי־אֵין אִישׁ
וַיִּשְׁתּוֹמֵם כִּי־אֵין מַפְגִּיעַ
וַתּוֹשַׁע לוֹ זְרֹעוֹ
וְצִדְקָתוֹ הִיא סְמָכָתְהוּ׃

כצ״ל v. 16.

---

effect, a denial of God's knowledge of their deeds (Kimchi).

uttering. Or, 'drawing out,' 'executing' (Kimchi).

14. *and justice . . . afar off.* Or, 'and justice is forced back and righteousness stands afar' (Kimchi).

broad place. [The *rechob,* 'open space,' is the market-place close to the city gate where the people assembled, public orations were delivered and judges tried cases. It was also the children's playground and travellers sometimes spent the night there.]

15a. *maketh himself a prey.* The virtuous are penalized because they do not follow the bad example of the majority (Ibn Ezra). Other renderings are: 'withdraws himself' (Targum, Kimchi); 'is regarded as a fool' (Rashi). The Hebrew

root may bear any of the three meanings.

15b. The sentence forms a link between the description of the misery and hopeless moral and religious decay, and the announcement that God is about to put an end to the deplorable state of affairs by taking matters into His own hand.

it. The state of affairs described.

that there was no justice. The absence of justice is specially emphasized as outweighing all the other transgressions because it is fundamental (Kimchi).

16. *no man.* Worthy of the name to protest against the prevalent evil (cf. lxiii. 5) (Rashi).

intercessor. On behalf of the people to God (Kimchi). The verbs in the verse may be regarded as prophetic perfects.

17. And He put on righteousness as
a coat of mail,
And a helmet of salvation upon
His head,
And He put on garments of
vengeance for clothing,
And was clad with zeal as a cloak.

18. According to their deeds, accordingly He will repay,
Fury to His adversaries, recompense to His enemies;
To the islands He will repay
recompense.

19. So shall they fear the name of
the LORD from the west,
And His glory from the rising of
the sun; (east)
For distress will come in like a
flood,
Which the breath of the LORD
driveth.

20. And a redeemer will come to
Zion,
And unto them that turn from
transgression in Jacob,
Saith the LORD.

21. And as for Me, this is My
covenant with them, saith the LORD;
My spirit that is upon thee, and My
words which I have put in thy
mouth, shall not depart out of thy
mouth, nor out of the mouth of thy
seed, nor out of the mouth of thy
seed's seed, saith the LORD, from
henceforth and for ever.

17 וַיִּלְבַּשׁ צְדָקָה כַּשִּׁרְיָן
וְכוֹבַע יְשׁוּעָה בְּרֹאשׁוֹ
וַיִּלְבַּשׁ בִּגְדֵי נָקָם תִּלְבֹּשֶׁת
וַיַּעַט כַּמְעִיל קִנְאָה׃

18 כְּעַל גְּמֻלוֹת כְּעַל יְשַׁלֵּם
חֵמָה לְצָרָיו גְּמוּל לְאֹיְבָיו
לָאִיִּים גְּמוּל יְשַׁלֵּם׃

19 וְיִירְאוּ מִמַּעֲרָב אֶת־שֵׁם יְהֹוָה
וּמִמִּזְרַח־שֶׁמֶשׁ אֶת־כְּבוֹדוֹ
כִּי־יָבוֹא כַנָּהָר צָר
רוּחַ יְהֹוָה נֹסְסָה בוֹ׃

20 וּבָא לְצִיּוֹן גּוֹאֵל וּלְשָׁבֵי פֶשַׁע בְּיַעֲקֹב
נְאֻם יְהֹוָה׃

21 וַאֲנִי זֹאת בְּרִיתִי אוֹתָם אָמַר יְהֹוָה
רוּחִי אֲשֶׁר עָלֶיךָ וּדְבָרַי אֲשֶׁר־
שַׂמְתִּי בְּפִיךָ לֹא־יָמוּשׁוּ מִפִּיךָ וּמִפִּי
זַרְעֲךָ וּמִפִּי זֶרַע זַרְעֲךָ אָמַר יְהֹוָה
מֵעַתָּה וְעַד־עוֹלָם׃

v. 17. המ' רפה

17. God is represented as a warrior
whose coat of mail, helmet and other
equipment consist of righteousness, salvation, vengeance and zeal, attributes
for the chastisement of the wicked and
the deliverance of the godly.

18. their deeds. Better, 'their deserts.'

to the islands. Since Israel was scattered
all over the world, God will punish even
the dwellers of distant islands for the
harm they inflicted upon them (Kimchi).

19. The consequences of God's inter-

vention will be a world-wide recognition of His Sovereignty.

distress. For the guilty (Rashi).

20f. A promise of the final redemption
of Zion and of those who turn away
from transgression, and God's eternal
covenant with them.

20. with them. With the loyal Israel
(Abarbanel).

My words. The Torah, the revelation at
Sinai (R. Joseph Kimchi).

thy mouth, etc. All faithful Israelites are
personified in the prophet (Kimchi).

60   CHAPTER LX   ס

1. Arise, shine, for thy light is come,
   And the glory of the LORD is risen upon thee.
2. For, behold, darkness shall cover the earth,
   And gross darkness the peoples;
   But upon thee the LORD will arise,
   And His glory shall be seen upon thee.
3. And nations shall walk at thy light,
   And kings at the brightness of thy rising.
4. Lift up thine eyes round about, and see:
   They all are gathered together, and come to thee;
   Thy sons come from far,
   And thy daughters are borne on the side.

1 יְקוּמִי אוֹרִי כִּי־בָא אוֹרֵךְ
וּכְבוֹד יְהוָה עָלַיִךְ זָרָח׃
2 כִּי־הִנֵּה הַחֹשֶׁךְ יְכַסֶּה־אֶרֶץ
וַעֲרָפֶל לְאֻמִּים
וְעָלַיִךְ יִזְרַח יְהוָה
וּכְבוֹדוֹ עָלַיִךְ יֵרָאֶה׃
3 וְהָלְכוּ גוֹיִם לְאוֹרֵךְ
וּמְלָכִים לְנֹגַהּ זַרְחֵךְ׃
4 שְׂאִי סָבִיב עֵינַיִךְ וּרְאִי
כֻּלָּם נִקְבְּצוּ בָאוּ־לָךְ
בָּנַיִךְ מֵרָחוֹק יָבֹאוּ
וּבְנֹתַיִךְ עַל־צַד תֵּאָמַנָה׃

ע. 1. הפטרת כי תבא ע. 4. המ׳ בפתח

CHAPTER LX

THE main theme of chapters lx-lxii is the pre-eminence, wealth and glory of the new Jerusalem which is addressed as a lady in distress.

1–3. The surrounding landscape is shrouded in thick darkness, but Jerusalem is glittering in the rays of the rising sun.

1. *arise.* From the ground on which thou liest prostrate and dejected; or from thy misery and depression (Kimchi).

thy light. The time of salvation and deliverance (Kimchi).

2. *darkness.* Figurative of trial and tribulation (Kimchi).

3. *shall walk at thy light.* The nations will learn the ways of God, religion and morality, from His chosen people (Abarbanel).

4–9. The return of the exiles to Zion, carried on the shoulders or sides of the nations who had hitherto oppressed them, enriched by the precious gifts presented to them in compensation and as offerings to the Deliver of Israel.

4. *they all.* All the exiles (Kimchi).

borne on the side. lit. 'supported, or, nursed on a side.' [A child in Oriental countries is carried by his mother (or nurse) on her *side* or hip, being upheld by her arm resting on his back.] In xlix. 22 it is said that they will be carried in the *bosom* and upon the *shoulder* (Kimchi).

5. Then thou shalt see and be
    radiant,
And thy heart shall throb and be
    enlarged;
Because the abundance of the
    sea shall be turned unto thee,
The wealth of the nations shall
    come unto thee.
6. The caravan of camels shall
    cover thee,
And of the young camels of
    Midian and Ephah,
All coming from Sheba;
They shall bring gold and
    frankincense,
And shall proclaim the praises of
    the LORD.
7. All the flocks of Kedar shall be
    gathered together unto thee,
The rams of Nebaioth shall
    minister unto thee;
They shall come up with accept-
    ance on Mine altar,
And I will glorify My glorious
    house.
8. Who are these that fly as a cloud,
And as the doves to their cotes?

5 אָז תִּרְאִי וְנָהַרְתְּ
וּפָחַד וְרָחַב לְבָבֵךְ
כִּי־יֵהָפֵךְ עָלַיִךְ הֲמוֹן יָם
חֵיל גּוֹיִם יָבֹאוּ לָךְ:
6 שִׁפְעַת גְּמַלִּים תְּכַסֵּךְ
בִּכְרֵי מִדְיָן וְעֵיפָה
כֻּלָּם מִשְּׁבָא יָבֹאוּ
זָהָב וּלְבוֹנָה יִשָּׂאוּ
וּתְהִלֹּת יְהוָה יְבַשֵּׂרוּ:
7 כָּל־צֹאן קֵדָר יִקָּבְצוּ לָךְ
אֵילֵי נְבָיוֹת יְשָׁרְתוּנֶךְ
יַעֲלוּ עַל־רָצוֹן מִזְבְּחִי
וּבֵית תִּפְאַרְתִּי אֲפָאֵר:
8 מִי־אֵלֶּה כָּעָב תְּעוּפֶינָה
וְכַיּוֹנִים אֶל־אֲרֻבֹּתֵיהֶם:

---

5. *and be radiant*. Or, 'beam' with happiness (so again Ps. xxxiv. 6).

throb. The Hebrew verb, which is usually
rendered 'fear,' means here 'trembling
with joy,' 'happy excitement' (Kimchi).

be enlarged. Experiencing a sense of freedom and exultation (Kimchi).

the abundance of the sea. The rich sea-
borne merchandise or the products of
maritime countries (Ibn Kaspi).

6. *caravan*. lit. 'abundance,' or 'multitude' (Rashi, Kimchi).

shall cover thee. Long trains of caravans,
laden with precious treasures of the
lands enumerated, will be wending their
way along the roads to Jerusalem
(Metsudath David).

Ephah. One of the Midianite tribes (cf.
Gen. xxv. 4) resident in the territory east
of the Gulf of Akaba.

Shebna. Modern Yemen in South Arabia
(Abarbanel, 1 Kings x. 1).

7. *Kedar*. See on xxi. 16.

Nebaioth. Also a pastoral tribe (cf. Gen.
xxv. 13) identified by some authorities,
though disputed by others, with the
Nabateans of the classical writers (Targum 1 Chron. 1. 29; Josephus, Antiquities 1:12:4).

minister. Serve as sacrifices (Abarbanel)

glorify, etc. Or, 'beautify My beautiful
house,' referring to the rebuilt Temple
(Metsudath David).

8f. The prophet now turns from the
East, from where he saw the richly laden
caravans coming, to the West where he
sees the white sails of the Mediterranean
ships speeding towards the coast of the
Holy Land (Kimchi).

as the doves to their cotes. The speed of the
ships is compared with the swiftness of
doves when returning to their young in
the cote. They fly more swiftly when
they return with food to their young

9. Surely the isles shall wait for Me,
And the ships of Tarshish first,
To bring thy sons from far,
Their silver and their gold with
  them,
For the name of the LORD thy
  God,
And for the Holy One of Israel,
  because He hath glorified thee.

10. And aliens shall build up thy
  walls,
And their kings shall minister
  unto thee;
For in My wrath I smote thee,
But in My favour have I had
  compassion on thee.

11. Thy gates also shall be open
  continually,
Day and night, they shall not be
  shut;
That men may bring unto thee
  the wealth of the nations,
And their kings in procession.

9 כִּי־לִי ׀ אִיִּים יְקַוּוּ
וָאֳנִיּוֹת תַּרְשִׁישׁ בָּרִאשֹׁנָה
לְהָבִיא בָנַיִךְ מֵרָחוֹק
כַּסְפָּם וּזְהָבָם אִתָּם
לְשֵׁם יְהֹוָה אֱלֹהַיִךְ
וְלִקְדוֹשׁ יִשְׂרָאֵל כִּי פֵאֲרָךְ:

10 וּבָנוּ בְנֵי־נֵכָר חֹמֹתַיִךְ
וּמַלְכֵיהֶם יְשָׁרְתוּנֶךְ
כִּי בְקִצְפִּי הִכִּיתִיךְ
וּבִרְצוֹנִי רִחַמְתִּיךְ:

11 וּפִתְּחוּ שְׁעָרַיִךְ תָּמִיד
יוֹמָם וָלַיְלָה לֹא יִסָּגֵרוּ
לְהָבִיא אֵלַיִךְ חֵיל גּוֹיִם
וּמַלְכֵיהֶם נְהוּגִים:

than when they depart in search of it
(Kimchi).

9. *isles.* The reference is to their
inhabitants (Kimchi, Metsudath David).

shall wait. To receive their reward for
bringing the exiles back to Zion
(Kimchi).

Tarshish. See on ii. 16.

first. Shall be the first to bring back their
exiles (Kimchi).

to bring, etc. This explains why the
inhabitants of the isles or coastlands
shall wait, etc.

their silver and their gold. Belonging to the
returning exiles. They will no longer be
robbed of their valuable possessions,
and all loot will be restored to them by

the peoples who had despoiled them
(Kimchi).

glorified. Or, 'beautified' as in verse 7.

10-12. Foreign nations and their
kings will be Israel's servants. They will
rebuild Jerusalem's walls through
whose open gates will flow the wealth of
the nations.

10. *aliens shall build.* The destroyers of
Zion will now rebuild her (Abarbanel).

thy walls. The address is to Jerusalem
(Kimchi).

for in My wrath, etc. Cf. liv. 7f.

11. *in procession.* Or, 'led' by their
routine (Kimchi). They will flock to
Zion, which will be the world's source of
wealth and prosperity.

5/19

12. For that nation and kingdom that
    will not serve thee shall perish;
    Yea, those nations shall be
    utterly wasted.
13. The glory of Lebanon shall come
    unto thee,
    The cypress, the plane-tree, and
    the larch together;
    To beautify the place of My
    sanctuary,
    And I will make the place of
    My feet glorious.
14. And the sons of them that
    afflicted thee
    Shall come bending unto thee,
    And all they that despised thee
    shall bow down
    At the soles of thy feet;
    And they shall call thee The city
    of the LORD,
    The Zion of the Holy One of
    Israel.
15. Whereas thou hast been forsaken
    and hated,
    So that no man passed through
    thee,
    I will make thee an eternal ex-
    cellency,
    A joy of many generations.

כִּי־הַגּוֹי וְהַמַּמְלָכָה 12
אֲשֶׁר לֹא־יַעַבְדוּךְ יֹאבֵדוּ
וְהַגּוֹיִם חָרֹב יֶחֱרָבוּ׃
כְּבוֹד הַלְּבָנוֹן אֵלַיִךְ יָבוֹא 13
בְּרוֹשׁ תִּדְהָר וּתְאַשּׁוּר יַחְדָּו
לְפָאֵר מְקוֹם מִקְדָּשִׁי
וּמְקוֹם רַגְלַי אֲכַבֵּד׃
וְהָלְכוּ אֵלַיִךְ שְׁחוֹחַ בְּנֵי מְעַנַּיִךְ 14
וְהִשְׁתַּחֲווּ
עַל־כַּפּוֹת רַגְלַיִךְ כָּל־מְנַאֲצָיִךְ
וְקָרְאוּ לָךְ עִיר יְהוָה
צִיּוֹן קְדוֹשׁ יִשְׂרָאֵל׃
תַּחַת הֱיוֹתֵךְ 15
עֲזוּבָה וּשְׂנוּאָה וְאֵין עוֹבֵר
וְשַׂמְתִּיךְ לִגְאוֹן עוֹלָם
מְשׂוֹשׂ דּוֹר וָדוֹר׃

12. *will not serve thee.* Will not pay to
Israel the tribute spoken of in the
preceding verse (Abarbanel).

13. The tree that made the Lebanon
famous shall be brought to beautify the
Temple, by being used either as building materials for its structure or as
ornamental groves in its surrounding
courts.

the glory of Lebanon. The trees that gave
Lebanon its fame (Malbim).

the cypress, etc. See on xli. 19.

*place of My sanctuary . . . the place of My
feet.* i.e. the Temple (Kimchi).

make . . . glorious. Better, 'do honour to.'

14. Homage, respect and glory will be
paid to Israel instead of the former
affliction and contempt.

15f. The loneliness and hatred which
Zion had experienced will be transformed into eternal honour and joy,
prosperity and salvation.

15. *no man passed through thee.* Because
of thy ruined condition (Kimchi).

16. Thou shalt also suck the milk of
the nations,
And shalt suck the breast of
kings;
And thou shalt know that I the
LORD am thy Saviour,
And I, the Mighty One of Jacob,
thy Redeemer.

17. For brass I will bring gold,
And for iron I will bring silver,
And for wood brass,
And for stones iron;
I will also make thy officers
peace,
And righteousness thy magis-
trates.

18. Violence shall no more be heard
in thy land,
Desolation nor destruction with-
in thy borders;
But thou shalt call thy walls
Salvation,
And thy gates Praise.

19. The sun shall be no more thy
light by day,
Neither for brightness shall the
moon give light unto thee;
But the LORD shall be unto thee
an everlasting light,
And thy God thy glory.

16 וְיָנַקְתְּ חֲלֵב גּוֹיִם

וְשֹׁד מְלָכִים תִּינָקִי

וְיָדַעַתְּ כִּי־אֲנִי יְהֹוָה מוֹשִׁיעֵךְ

וְגֹאֲלֵךְ אֲבִיר יַעֲקֹב׃

17 תַּחַת הַנְּחֹשֶׁת אָבִיא זָהָב

וְתַחַת הַבַּרְזֶל אָבִיא כֶסֶף

וְתַחַת הָעֵצִים נְחֹשֶׁת

וְתַחַת הָאֲבָנִים בַּרְזֶל

וְשַׂמְתִּי פְקֻדָּתֵךְ שָׁלוֹם

וְנֹגְשַׂיִךְ צְדָקָה׃

18 לֹא־יִשָּׁמַע עוֹד חָמָס בְּאַרְצֵךְ

שֹׁד וָשֶׁבֶר בִּגְבוּלָיִךְ

וְקָרָאת יְשׁוּעָה חוֹמֹתַיִךְ

וּשְׁעָרַיִךְ תְּהִלָּה׃

19 לֹא־יִהְיֶה־לָּךְ

עוֹד הַשֶּׁמֶשׁ לְאוֹר יוֹמָם

וּלְנֹגַהּ הַיָּרֵחַ לֹא־יָאִיר לָךְ

וְהָיָה־לָךְ יְהֹוָה לְאוֹר עוֹלָם

וֵאלֹהַיִךְ לְתִפְאַרְתֵּךְ׃

16. *suck the milk.* Cf. xlix. 23.

that I the LORD *... Redeemer.* Repeated
from xlix. 26.

17f. The materials lost in the days of
sorrow shall be replaced by others of
greater value, while violence and desolation will give way to salvation and
praise.

17. *I will also make ... magistrates.* Or,
'I will make Peace thy government and
Righteousness thy magistrates.' The
sway of peace and righteousness will

replace the present rule of tyranny and
oppression (Kimchi).

18. *Salvation.* A protection against
attack and invasion (Kimchi).

19f. The glorious light of the LORD
will shine eternally upon Zion, eclipsing
the natural luminaries which will no
longer be needed. This may be understood literally or metaphorically.

19. *an everlasting light.* Both by day and
by night (Ibn Ezra).

20. Thy sun shall no more go down,
Neither shall thy moon withdraw itself;
For the LORD shall be thine everlasting light,
And the days of thy mourning shall be ended.

21. Thy people also shall be all righteous,
They shall inherit the land for ever;
The branch of My planting, the work of My hands,
Wherein I glory.

22. The smallest shall become a thousand,
And the least a mighty nation;
I the LORD will hasten it in its time.

לֹא־יָבוֹא עוֹד שִׁמְשֵׁךְ 20

וִירֵחֵךְ לֹא יֵאָסֵף

כִּי יְהֹוָה יִהְיֶה־לָּךְ לְאוֹר עוֹלָם

וְשָׁלְמוּ יְמֵי אֶבְלֵךְ:

וְעַמֵּךְ כֻּלָּם צַדִּיקִים 21

לְעוֹלָם יִירְשׁוּ אָרֶץ

נֵצֶר מַטָּעוֹ

מַעֲשֵׂה יָדַי לְהִתְפָּאֵר:

הַקָּטֹן יִהְיֶה לָאֶלֶף 22

וְהַצָּעִיר לְגוֹי עָצוּם

אֲנִי יְהֹוָה בְּעִתָּהּ אֲחִישֶׁנָּה:

v. 21. ‏מטעי ק׳‎ v. 22. ‏עד כאן‎

glory. Or, 'beauty.'

20. thy mourning shall be ended. This will be the final redemption, after which there will be no more exile (Malbim).

21f. The two verses describe the new, purified, righteous and numerous community that will possess the land, and in their saintly lives bear witness to the glory of God.

21. The Rabbis of the Mishnah deduced from this verse that 'all Israel have a share in the world to come,' all will enjoy immortality (San. 10:1).

inherit. i.e. possess.

for ever. Never again will they be driven into exile (Kimchi).

the branch of My planting. God has planted them in the land (Kimchi).

wherein I glory. lit. 'to be glorified.'

22. a thousand. Some render: 'a clan,' 'a tribe' (See on Jud. vi. 15).

hasten it. The fulfilment of the entire prophecy (Kimchi).

in its time. When the appointed hour of deliverance has struck. The Rabbis detected an apparent contradiction in the last clause: if an event is to happen *in its time,* how can God *hasten it?* They explain: if Israel is worthy, God will hasten its coming; if not, it will happen *in its* (destined) time (Rashi, Kimchi, from Talmud, Sanh. 98a).

Isa Speaking (handwritten)

61   CHAPTER LXI   סא

1. The spirit of the Lord GOD is
   upon me;
   Because the LORD hath anointed
   me
   To bring good tidings unto the
   humble;
   He hath sent me to bind up the
   broken-hearted,
   To proclaim liberty to the
   captives,
   And the opening of the eyes to
   them that are bound;
2. To proclaim the year of the
   LORD's good pleasure,
   And the day of vengeance of our
   God;
   To comfort all that mourn;
3. To appoint unto them that
   mourn in Zion,
   To give unto them a garland for
   ashes,

רוּחַ אֲדֹנָי יֱהֹוִה עָלָי 1
יַעַן מָשַׁח יְהֹוָה אֹתִי
לְבַשֵּׂר עֲנָוִים
שְׁלָחַנִי לַחֲבֹשׁ לְנִשְׁבְּרֵי־לֵב
לִקְרֹא לִשְׁבוּיִם דְּרוֹר
וְלַאֲסוּרִים פְּקַח־קוֹחַ:
לִקְרֹא שְׁנַת־רָצוֹן לַיהֹוָה 2
וְיוֹם נָקָם לֵאלֹהֵינוּ
לְנַחֵם כָּל־אֲבֵלִים:
לָשׂוּם | לַאֲבֵלֵי צִיּוֹן 3
לָתֵת לָהֶם פְּאֵר תַּחַת אֵפֶר

CHAPTER LXI

1–3. The prophet announces his mission as herald (Targum, Ibn Ezra,
Kimchi).

1. *anointed me.* This is to be understood metaphorically as 'appointed.' We
find a similar expression in 1 Kings xix.
16. Only kings and high priests were
actually anointed (Rashi, Kimchi).

the humble. A term often used to denote
the faithful minority in Israel who
remained staunch throughout the
national trials and did not yield to the
pressure of the nations among whom
they were scattered (Kimchi).

bind up. The wounds, i.e. to cure
(Abarbanel).

opening of the eyes. The unusual Hebrew
form, which should be read as one
word, *pekachkoach,* means 'complete or
wide opening of the eyes.' It signifies the
ability to see clearly as contrasted with
the gloom of a prison (After Targum).

2. *good pleasure.* Or, 'favour.'

vengeance. On the enemies of Israel
(Kimchi, Abarbanel).

all that mourn. For Zion, as explained in
the following verse (Ibn Ezra).

3. *to appoint.* The verb (lit. 'to put')
seems to have no object unless it is to be
regarded as an anticipation of the following to *give,* the objects being *garland
. . . oil,* etc. (Ibn Ezra, Metsudath David).

a garland for ashes. Mourners, like others
in distress, sprinkled ashes on their
heads (cf. 2 Sam. xiii. 19; Jer. vi. 26)
(Kimchi). The garland of honour and
joy will replace the symbols of mourning and misery. There is a notable play
on words in the Hebrew: *pëer* for *epher,*
the first two letters being transposed
(Ibn Kaspi).

The oil of joy for mourning,
The mantle of praise for the
  spirit of heaviness;
That they might be called
  terebinths of righteousness,
The planting of the LORD,
  wherein He might glory.
4. And they shall build the old
  wastes,
They shall raise up the former
  desolations,
And they shall renew the waste
  cities,
The desolations of many generations.
5. And strangers shall stand and
  feed your flocks,
And aliens shall be your plow-
  men and your vinedressers.
6. But ye shall be named the
  priests of the LORD,
Men shall call you the ministers
  of our God;
Ye shall eat the wealth of the
  nations,
And in their splendour shall ye
  revel.

שֶׁמֶן שָׂשׂוֹן תַּחַת אֵבֶל

מַעֲטֵה תְהִלָּה תַּחַת רוּחַ כֵּהָה

וְקֹרָא לָהֶם אֵילֵי הַצֶּדֶק

מַטַּע יְהֹוָה לְהִתְפָּאֵר׃

4 וּבָנוּ חָרְבוֹת עוֹלָם

שֹׁמְמוֹת רִאשֹׁנִים יְקוֹמֵמוּ

וְחִדְּשׁוּ עָרֵי חֹרֶב

שֹׁמְמוֹת דּוֹר וָדוֹר׃

5 וְעָמְדוּ זָרִים וְרָעוּ צֹאנְכֶם

וּבְנֵי נֵכָר אִכָּרֵיכֶם וְכֹרְמֵיכֶם׃

6 וְאַתֶּם כֹּהֲנֵי יְהֹוָה תִּקָּרֵאוּ

מְשָׁרְתֵי אֱלֹהֵינוּ יֵאָמֵר לָכֶם

חֵיל גּוֹיִם תֹּאכֵלוּ

וּבִכְבוֹדָם תִּתְיַמָּרוּ׃

---

oil of joy. The application of oil to the body to temper the effects of the heat was regarded as a great comfort (cf. Ps. xxiii. 5, xlv. 8), and so its use was discontinued in time of mourning (cf. 2 Sam. xiv. 2).

spirit of heaviness. Or, 'dimmed, failing, spirit' (cf. xlii. 3, *dimly burning wick*) (Kimchi).

terebinths. Being evergreen and fresh, they symbolize the righteous life (Metsudath David).

planting of the LORD . . . *glory.* Cf. lx. 21.

4-7. The ruins of the waste cities of the Holy Land shall be rebuilt, and strangers will tend the flocks and cultivate the soil; while Israel, free from worldly cares, will consecrate his life to the service of God and, as His priests,

will teach religion and morality to the nations of the world.

4. *and they.* The subject may be indefinite, or refer to the *mourners in Zion* (verse 3) (Kimchi).

the old wastes. As in lviii. 12.

5. *aliens.* Cf. lx. 10.

6. *the priests of the* LORD. Cf. Exod. xix. 6. As the priests subsisted upon what the Israelites allocated to them, so the priestly nation will be supported by the other peoples since it is dedicated to the Divine service (Ibn Ezra, Kimchi).

in their splendour . . . revel. (Targum). The splendour that was hitherto the lot of the nations will now pass over to Israel. The verb translated *revel* has also been variously explained as 'succeed to' (lit.

7. For your shame which was
double,
And for that they rejoiced:
'Confusion is their portion';
Therefore in their land they shall
possess double,
Everlasting joy shall be unto
them.

8. For I the LORD love justice,
I hate robbery with iniquity;
And I will give them their re-
compense in truth,
And I will make an everlasting
covenant with them.

9. And their seed shall be known
among the nations,
And their offspring among the
peoples;
All that see them shall acknow-
ledge them,
That they are the seed which the
LORD hath blessed.

10. I will greatly rejoice in the LORD,
My soul shall be joyful in my
God;
For He hath clothed me with the
garments of salvation,
He hath covered me with the
robe of victory,
As a bridegroom putteth on a
priestly diadem,

7 תַּחַת בָּשְׁתְּכֶם מִשְׁנֶה
וּכְלִמָּה יָרֹנּוּ חֶלְקָם
לָכֵן בְּאַרְצָם מִשְׁנֶה יִירָשׁוּ
שִׂמְחַת עוֹלָם תִּהְיֶה לָהֶם:
8 כִּי אֲנִי יְהוָה אֹהֵב מִשְׁפָּט
שֹׂנֵא גָזֵל בְּעוֹלָה
וְנָתַתִּי פְעֻלָּתָם בֶּאֱמֶת
וּבְרִית עוֹלָם אֶכְרוֹת לָהֶם:
9 וְנוֹדַע בַּגּוֹיִם זַרְעָם
וְצֶאֱצָאֵיהֶם בְּתוֹךְ הָעַמִּים
כָּל־רֹאֵיהֶם יַכִּירוּם
כִּי הֵם זֶרַע בֵּרַךְ יְהוָה:
10 שׂוֹשׂ אָשִׂישׂ בַּיהוָה
תָּגֵל נַפְשִׁי בֵּאלֹהַי
כִּי הִלְבִּישַׁנִי בִּגְדֵי־יֶשַׁע
מְעִיל צְדָקָה יְעָטָנִי
כֶּחָתָן יְכַהֵן פְּאֵר

v. 7. קמץ בז״ק v. 10. הפטרת נצבים

take in exchange) (Rashi) or 'boast
yourselves' (Kimchi).

7. The prosperity and joy of the future
will be commensurate with the sorrow
and affliction of the past and present.
The former shall indeed be double the
latter (Kimchi).

double. Twice as much as they suffered in
full measure (cf. xl. 2) (Kimchi).

they rejoiced. viz. the nations under
whom Israel suffered (Abarbanel).

8f. God will make an everlasting
covenant with the people and His blessings upon them will be manifest to all.

8. *with iniquity.* This rendering follows
Targum, who interprets *olah* with *awlah*.
We find a similar word in the liturgy of

the High Holy Days, viz. *we'olathah.*
Abarbanel renders: 'because of exaltation.' God hates robbery perpetrated by
one nation upon another because the
perpetrator is in a more exalted and
advantageous position than the victim.
The traditional rendering, following the
Talmud, is 'for burnt-offering.' So
Rashi, Ibn Ezra, and Kimchi.

10f. The prophet voices the feelings of
the redeemed people.

10. *victory.* The usual rendering of the
Hebrew is 'righteousness' (in the sense
of 'vindication' (Targum).

putteth on a priestly diadem. Better 'deck-
eth himself with elegant attire.' The verb
is connected with *kohen* and denotes
intensification of elegance, just as the

300

And as a bride adorneth herself
with her jewels.

11. For as the earth bringeth forth
her growth,
And as the garden causeth the
things that are sown in it to
spring forth;
So the Lord GOD will cause
victory and glory
To spring forth before all the
nations.

וְכַכַּלָּה תַּעְדֶּה כֵלֶיהָ:
11 כִּי כָאָרֶץ תּוֹצִיא צִמְחָהּ
וּכְגַנָּה זֵרוּעֶיהָ תַצְמִיחַ
כֵּן ׀ אֲדֹנָי יֱהֹוִה
יַצְמִיחַ צְדָקָה וּתְהִלָּה
נֶגֶד כָּל־הַגּוֹיִם:

62   CHAPTER LXII   סב

God speaks

1. For Zion's sake will I not hold
My peace,
And for Jerusalem's sake I will
not rest,
Until her triumph go forth as
brightness,
And her salvation as a torch that
burneth.

1 לְמַעַן צִיּוֹן לֹא אֶחֱשֶׁה
וּלְמַעַן יְרוּשָׁלַם לֹא אֶשְׁקוֹט
עַד־יֵצֵא כַנֹּגַהּ צִדְקָהּ
וִישׁוּעָתָהּ כְּלַפִּיד יִבְעָר:

priest is exalted over the rest of the populace. Targum renders: 'like a bridegroom and like a high priest who adorneth himself with his raiment (Kimchi).

11. The Divine promises to Israel are
as assured as the natural course of
Nature. The comparison between the
survival of Israel and the growth of seed
may be carried farther. The seed in the
earth, though apparently decayed,
sprouts into fresh life and multiplies
itself. So Israel in exile, though apparently deteriorated and lost in his miser-
ies, will in God's time emerge into a
new existence, increased both in
strength and numbers.

victory and glory. lit. 'righteousness and
praise.'

CHAPTER LXII

ZION'S SALVATION AND GLORY

1–5. God will not be silent until Zion's
cause is vindicated, her fame and glory
are universally acknowledged, she and
her children are reunited and God
rejoices over her as a bridegroom over
his bride (Targum, Ibn Ezra, Rashi,
Kimchi Abarbanel). Ibn Ezra mentions
that some hold the speaker to be the
captive Israel.

1. Zion ... Jerusalem. The terms are
synonymous (Kimchi).

a torch that burneth. As the burning torch
can be seen far and wide, so will Zion's
salvation be visible to all (Kimchi).

2. And the nations shall see thy
      triumph,
   And all kings thy glory;
   And thou shalt be called by a
      new name,
   Which the mouth of the LORD
      shall mark out.
3. Thou shalt also be a crown of
      beauty in the hand of the
      LORD,
   And a royal diadem in the open
      hand of thy God.
4. Thou shalt no more be termed
      Forsaken,
   Neither shall thy land any more
      be termed Desolate;
   But thou shalt be called, My
      delight is in her,
   And thy land, Espoused;
   For the LORD delighteth in thee,
   And thy land shall be espoused.
5. For as a young man espouseth
      a virgin,
   So shall thy sons espouse thee;
   And as the bridegroom re-
      joiceth over the bride,
   So shall thy God rejoice over
      thee.

2 וְרָאוּ גוֹיִם צִדְקֵ֔ךְ
וְכָל־מְלָכִים כְּבוֹדֵ֑ךְ
וְקֹ֤רָא לָךְ֙ שֵׁ֣ם חָדָ֔שׁ
אֲשֶׁ֛ר פִּ֥י יְהוָ֖ה יִקֳבֶֽנּוּ׃
3 וְהָיִ֛יתְ עֲטֶ֥רֶת תִּפְאֶ֖רֶת בְּיַד־יְהוָ֑ה
וּצְנִיף מְלוּכָ֖ה בְּכַף־אֱלֹהָֽיִךְ׃
4 לֹא־יֵאָמֵר֩ לָ֨ךְ ע֜וֹד עֲזוּבָ֗ה
וּלְאַרְצֵךְ֙ לֹא־יֵאָמֵ֥ר עוֹד֙ שְׁמָמָ֔ה
כִּ֣י לָ֗ךְ יִקָּרֵא֙ חֶפְצִי־בָ֔הּ
וּלְאַרְצֵ֖ךְ בְּעוּלָ֑ה
כִּֽי־חָפֵ֤ץ יְהוָה֙ בָּ֔ךְ
וְאַרְצֵ֖ךְ תִּבָּעֵֽל׃
5 כִּֽי־יִבְעַ֤ל בָּחוּר֙ בְּתוּלָ֔ה
יִבְעָל֖וּךְ בָּנָ֑יִךְ
וּמְשׂ֤וֹשׂ חָתָן֙ עַל־כַּלָּ֔ה
יָשִׂ֥ישׂ עָלַ֖יִךְ אֱלֹהָֽיִךְ׃

v. 3. וּצְנִיף ק׳

2. *new name.* The name, according to
one opinion, is not disclosed (Ibn
Kaspi); according to another view, it is
given in verse 4 (Kimchi, Abarbanel).
The change of name indicates the alter-
ation in condition and status (Abarbanel).

3. *in the hand . . . open hand.* More cor-
rectly, 'in the closed hand.' This denotes
God's support and protection of Israel,
as one who holds an article tightly in his
hand, lest it fall (Kimchi, Shorashim).

4. *Forsaken.* Hebrew *Azubah,* a proper
noun actually found in 1 Kings xxii. 42.

My delight is in her. Hebrew *Chephtsibah,*

also a proper noun occurring in 2 Kings
xxi. 1.

Espoused. lit. 'married' (for the thought,
cf. liv. 1ff.).

5. *as a young man espouseth a virgin.*
Unlike the union between an old man
and a virgin or a young man and a
formerly married woman, that of a
young man and a virgin is well matched.
Likewise, the reunion of Israel and the
Holy Land will restore the splendour
which no other occupying nation was
able to achieve (Kimchi).

thy sons espouse thee. Metaphorically for
the restoration of the monarchy (Ibn

angelo?

6. I have set watchmen
   Upon thy walls, O Jerusalem,
   They shall never hold their
      peace
   Day nor night:
   'Ye that are the LORD's re-
      membrancers,
   Take ye no rest,

7. And give Him no rest,
   Till He establish,
   And till He make Jerusalem
   A praise in the earth.'

8. The LORD hath sworn by His
      right hand,
   And by the arm of His strength:
   Surely I will no more give thy
      corn
   To be food for thine enemies;
   And strangers shall not drink
      thy wine,
   For which thou hast laboured;

עַל־חוֹמֹתַיִךְ יְרוּשָׁלַם 6
הִפְקַדְתִּי שֹׁמְרִים
כָּל־הַיּוֹם וְכָל־הַלַּיְלָה
תָּמִיד לֹא יֶחֱשׁוּ
הַמַּזְכִּרִים אֶת־יְהֹוָה
אַל־דֳּמִי לָכֶם:
וְאַל־תִּתְּנוּ דֳמִי לוֹ 7
עַד־יְכוֹנֵן
וְעַד־יָשִׂים אֶת־יְרוּשָׁלַם
תְּהִלָּה בָּאָרֶץ:
נִשְׁבַּע יְהֹוָה בִּימִינוֹ 8
וּבִזְרוֹעַ עֻזּוֹ
אִם־אֶתֵּן אֶת־דְּגָנֵךְ
עוֹד מַאֲכָל לְאֹיְבַיִךְ
וְאִם־יִשְׁתּוּ בְנֵי־נֵכָר תִּירוֹשֵׁךְ
אֲשֶׁר יָגַעַתְּ בּוֹ:

Ezra). Or, the resettlement of the land by Israel (Targum, Kimchi).

6-9. God has set watchmen on the walls of Jerusalem to remind Him constantly of His promises to the city; for He has sworn that never again shall it be plundered by enemies or strangers, but it will enjoy the fruits of its labour in security and peace.

6. *I have set.* God is the Speaker (Ibn Ezra).

watchman. Invisible angelic beings (Rashi, Kimchi from Talmud Men. 87a). According to others, the *watchmen* or guardians are the 'mourners in Zion' or 'the company of prophets' who, by their prayers for the welfare of Jerusalem, remind God of His promises (Kimchi, Abarbanel).

never hold their peace. But would unceasingly intercede on behalf of the city until their prayers had been answered (Kimchi).

ye that are . . . rest. This clause, with its continuation in verse 7, is an address by the prophet to *the* LORD's *remembrancers,* to be identified with the *watchmen* mentioned earlier in the verse (Metsudath David).

remembrancers. Officials with the duty to keep records and bring them to the notice of the authorities when the occasion demanded it (cf. 2 Kings xviii. 18 where the noun is translated *recorder*) (Abarbanel).

8. *right hand.* Symbolizing power to be employed in the deliverance of Israel from his captors (Kimchi).

9. But they that have garnered it
     shall eat it,
   And praise the LORD,
   And they that have gathered it
     shall drink it
   In the courts of My sanctuary.

10. Go through, go through the
     gates,
   Clear ye the way of the people;
   Cast up, cast up the highway,
   Gather out the stones;
   Lift up an ensign over the
     peoples.

11. Behold, the LORD hath pro-
     claimed
   Unto the end of the earth:
   Say ye to the daughter of Zion:
   'Behold, thy salvation cometh;
   Behold, His reward is with Him,
   And His recompense before
     Him.'

12. And they shall call them The
     holy people,

9 כִּי מְאַסְפָיו יֹאכְלֻהוּ
וְהִלְלוּ אֶת־יְהֹוָה
וּמְקַבְּצָיו יִשְׁתֻּהוּ
בְּחַצְרוֹת קָדְשִׁי׃

10 עִבְרוּ עִבְרוּ בַּשְּׁעָרִים
פַּנּוּ דֶּרֶךְ הָעָם
סֹלּוּ סֹלּוּ הַמְסִלָּה
סַקְּלוּ מֵאֶבֶן
הָרִימוּ נֵס עַל־הָעַמִּים׃

11 הִנֵּה יְהֹוָה
הִשְׁמִיעַ אֶל־קְצֵה הָאָרֶץ
אִמְרוּ לְבַת־צִיּוֹן
הִנֵּה יִשְׁעֵךְ בָּא
הִנֵּה שְׂכָרוֹ אִתּוֹ
וּפְעֻלָּתוֹ לְפָנָיו׃

12 וְקָרְאוּ לָהֶם עַם־הַקֹּדֶשׁ

actually 'a people of holiness

---

9. *garnered . . . gathered*. The subject is the inhabitants of Zion restored (Abarbanel).

shall eat it. viz. *thy corn* mentioned in the preceding verse, and *drink it* refers to *thy wine* (Targum, Rashi, Ibn Ezra).

courts of My sanctuary. Or, 'My holy courts.' The allusion is to the bringing of the tithes to the Holy City where they were eaten with rejoicing (cf. Deut. xii. 17f.) (Kimchi).

10-12. The officers of the nations will call for preparation to be made for welcoming the homecoming exiles.

10. *go through the gates*. Of the cities, to make the following proclamation (Ibn Ezra).

cast up the highway. For the homeward journey of the exiles (cf. lvii. 14) (Metsudath David).

gather out the stones. From the highway, so that the exiles meet with no obstacles on the road (Metsudath David).

lift up an ensign. To signal the nations to bring their captives and their gift to the Holy Land (Metsudath David, Malbim).

11. The language of the verse is reminiscent of xl. 10, xlviii. 20.

12. *and they*. The nations (Metsudath David).

shall call them. viz. the inhabitants of Zion (Abarbanel, Metsudath David).

The redeemed of the LORD;
And thou shalt be called Sought
    out,
A city not forsaken.

נְּאוּלֵי יְהֹוֶה
וְלָךְ יִקָּרֵא דְרוּשָׁה
עִיר לֹא נֶעֱזָבָה:

Drushah

---

63   CHAPTER LXIII   סג

1. 'Who is this that cometh from
    Edom,
   With crimsoned garments from
    Bozrah?
   This that is glorious in his
    apparel,
   Stately in the greatness of his
    strength?'—

34.58
Edom

¹ מִי־זֶה ׀ בָּא מֵאֱדֹום
חֲמוּץ בְּגָדִים מִבָּצְרָה
זֶה הָדוּר בִּלְבוּשֹׁו
צֹעֶה בְּרֹב כֹּחֹו

---

and thou. Zion (Abarbanel, Metsudath
David).

Sought out. The city whose wellbeing
God Himself seeks (Metsudath David).
Cf. the saying of Israel's adversaries
which God promises to reverse, *She is
Zion, there is none that careth for her* (Jer.
xxx. 17) (Kimchi).

a city not forsaken. Repeating the promise
of verse 4.

CHAPTER LXIII

1-6. Execution of Divine vengeance
upon Edom. The passage forms an
independent oracle on the final triumph
of God over Israel's enemies which is
the preliminary to the redemption. The
prophet presents a symbolic vision of a
warrior coming from Edom, with
bloodstained clothing, indicative of the
massacre of Edom, which he has
exhausted. The hero is attired in
beautiful apparel, shouting at the top of
his voice, 'I that speak in victory, mighty
to save. I speak in justice, and I have

come to save My people. I alone have
come. This vengeance has not been
accomplished by man, but by Me
alone.' The Hero is none other than the
God of Israel (Abarbanel).

1. *who is this,* etc. The startled
prophet's question on seeing the
approach of the majestic blood-stained
figure (Abarbanel).

Edom. A general term for all the lands
of tyranny and oppression the inhabitants of which are descended from Esau.
One of its large cities was known as
Bozrah (Kimchi).

crimsoned. i.e. blood-stained (Rashi,
Metsudath Zion).

Bozrah. See on xxxiv. 6. The Hebrew
root of the noun is suggestive of *mivtsar,*
'fortress,' alluding to a large, fortified
city (Metsudath David).

glorious. Symbolic of 'garments of vengeance' (Kimchi). Others explain that
the hero's garments *were* glorious
before they became crimsoned with
blood (Metsudath David).

'I that speak in victory, mighty
to save.'—

2. 'Wherefore is Thine apparel red,
And Thy garments like his that
treadeth in the winevat?'—

3. 'I have trodden the winepress
alone,
And of the peoples there was no
man with Me;
Yea, I trod them in Mine anger,
And trampled them in My fury;
And their lifeblood is dashed
against My garments,
And I have stained all My
raiment.

4. For the day of vengeance that
was in My heart,
And My year of redemption are
come.

5. And I looked, and there was
none to help,
And I beheld in astonishment,
and there was none to uphold;

אֲנִי מְדַבֵּר בִּצְדָקָה
רַב לְהוֹשִׁיעַ׃

2 מַדּוּעַ אָדֹם לִלְבוּשֶׁךָ
וּבְגָדֶיךָ כְּדֹרֵךְ בְּגַת׃

3 פּוּרָה ׀ דָּרַכְתִּי לְבַדִּי
וּמֵעַמִּים אֵין־אִישׁ אִתִּי
וְאֶדְרְכֵם בְּאַפִּי
וְאֶרְמְסֵם בַּחֲמָתִי
וְיֵז נִצְחָם עַל־בְּגָדַי
וְכָל־מַלְבּוּשַׁי אֶגְאָלְתִּי׃

4 כִּי יוֹם נָקָם בְּלִבִּי
וּשְׁנַת גְּאוּלַי בָּאָה׃

5 וְאַבִּיט וְאֵין עֹזֵר
וְאֶשְׁתּוֹמֵם וְאֵין סוֹמֵךְ

פתח בס״פ v. 2.

I that speak . . . save. The answer of the
Divine warrior. None of the Divine
names, but only two of God's attributes,
are mentioned. He has been to Edom
for a specific purpose: to punish the
oppressors and save His people (Abarbanel).

2. The blood-stains on the garments
not having been explained, the prophet
seeks further enlightenment.

wherefore is . . . red. lit. 'wherefore is
there red on Thine apparel?' The
Hebrew for *red,* it should be noted, is of
the same root as Edom.

treadeth. Grapes were trodden under
foot, and the juice splashed the treader's garment (Metsudath Zion).

winevat. Or, 'wine-press' a figure for
slaughter and carnage (Kimchi, Ibn
Ezra).

3–6. The Divine answer.

3. *there was no man with Me.* To assist or
to withstand (Metsudath David).

stained. lit. 'defiled.'

4. *the day of vengeance.* On the enemies
of God and Israel, spoken of in lix. 2
(Ibn Ezra).

My year of redemption. Of Israel [This is
probably *the year of the* LORD's *good pleasure* mentioned, like *the day of vengeance,*
in lxi. 2. God's vengeance is only for a
while—a day; but *His good pleasure* is
everlasting— a *year* without end.] The
Talmud, however, takes this to mean
that the Messianic era will last for 365
years, corresponding to the number of
days in the solar year (San. 99a).

5. *none to help . . . none to uphold.* The
Divine Champion. There were no
nations to join My revenge against
Edom. They were all guilty of the same
crime (Kimchi).

Therefore Mine own arm brought salvation unto Me, And My fury, it upheld Me.

6. And I trod down the peoples in Mine anger, And made them drunk with My fury, And I poured out their lifeblood on the earth.'

7. I will make mention of the mercies of the LORD, And the praises of the LORD, According to all that the LORD hath bestowed on us; And the great goodness toward the house of Israel, Which He hath bestowed on them according to His compassions, And according to the multitude of His mercies.

8. For He said: 'Surely, they are My people, Children that will not deal falsely'; So He was their Saviour.

9. In all their affliction He was afflicted, And the angel of His presence saved them; In His love and in His pity He redeemed them; And He bore them, and carried them all the days of old.

וַתּ֤וֹשַׁע לִי֙ זְרֹעִ֔י
וַחֲמָתִ֖י הִ֥יא סְמָכָֽתְנִי׃
6 וְאָב֤וּס עַמִּים֙ בְּאַפִּ֔י
וַאֲשַׁכְּרֵ֖ם בַּחֲמָתִ֑י
וְאוֹרִ֥יד לָאָ֖רֶץ נִצְחָֽם׃
7 חַֽסְדֵ֨י יְהֹוָ֤ה ׀ אַזְכִּיר֙
תְּהִלֹּ֣ת יְהֹוָ֔ה
כְּעַ֕ל כֹּ֖ל אֲשֶׁר־גְּמָלָ֣נוּ יְהֹוָ֑ה
וְרַב־טוּב֙ לְבֵ֣ית יִשְׂרָאֵ֔ל
אֲשֶׁר־גְּמָלָ֖ם כְּרַחֲמָ֑יו
וּכְרֹ֖ב חֲסָדָֽיו׃
8 וַיֹּ֙אמֶר֙ אַךְ־עַמִּ֣י הֵ֔מָּה
בָּנִ֖ים לֹ֣א יְשַׁקֵּ֑רוּ
וַיְהִ֥י לָהֶ֖ם לְמוֹשִֽׁיעַ׃
9 בְּכָל־צָרָתָ֣ם ׀ לֹ֣א צָ֗ר
וּמַלְאַ֤ךְ פָּנָיו֙ הֽוֹשִׁיעָ֔ם
בְּאַהֲבָת֥וֹ וּבְחֶמְלָת֖וֹ ה֣וּא גְאָלָ֑ם
וַֽיְנַטְּלֵ֥ם וַֽיְנַשְּׂאֵ֖ם כָּל־יְמֵ֥י עוֹלָֽם׃

v. 9. ק' לֹ֑ו   v. 9. עד כאן

---

6. *made them drunk.* Several Hebrew MSS. and the Targum read *beth* for *kaph*, 'broke them in pieces.'

7–lxiv. 11. A prayer, confession and thanksgiving.

7–9. Gratitude to God for His past kindness and mercy to Israel.

7. *make mention.* Or, 'remind' Israel to praise and thank God for all the kindness He bestowed upon them (Rashi, Kimchi).

8. *so He was their Saviour.* Or, 'and so He became their Saviour.'

9. *in all their affliction He was afflicted.* God Himself, so to speak, participates in the sufferings of His people. This is the reading of the *kerë*; the sense of the *kethib* is: 'in all their adversity He was no adversary' (Kimchi).

the angel of His presence. The angel who ministers before (Ibn Ezra). This is the angel Mettatron (Laniado).

bore them. [Or, 'took them up,' as a parent raises a child and carries him.]

10–14. Israel's rebellion turned God from friend into foe; and when he was

307

10. But they rebelled, and grieved
    His holy spirit;
    Therefore He was turned to be
    their enemy,
    Himself fought against them.
11. Then His people remembered
    the days of old, the days of
    Moses:
    'Where is He that brought them
    up out of the sea
    With the shepherds of His flock?
    Where is He that put His holy
    spirit
    In the midst of them?
12. That caused His glorious arm to
    go
    At the right hand of Moses?
    That divided the water before
    them,
    To make Himself an everlasting
    name?

10 וְהֵמָּה מָרוּ וְעִצְּבוּ אֶת־רוּחַ קָדְשׁוֹ
וַיֵּהָפֵךְ לָהֶם
לְאוֹיֵב הוּא נִלְחַם־בָּם׃
11 וַיִּזְכֹּר יְמֵי־עוֹלָם מֹשֶׁה עַמּוֹ
אַיֵּה | הַמַּעֲלֵם מִיָּם
אֵת רֹעֵי צֹאנוֹ
אַיֵּה הַשָּׂם בְּקִרְבּוֹ
אֶת־רוּחַ קָדְשׁוֹ׃
12 מוֹלִיךְ לִימִין מֹשֶׁה
זְרוֹעַ תִּפְאַרְתּוֹ
בּוֹקֵעַ מַיִם מִפְּנֵיהֶם
לַעֲשׂוֹת לוֹ שֵׁם עוֹלָם׃

v. 11. נ״א רעי

plunged into abject misery, he could
but recall in anguish the wonders of
old, longing for a return of the preceding days of glory.

10. *but they.* The Hebrew is emphatic:
they of all people upon whom God had
bestowed such favour (Malbim).

to be their enemy. lit. 'to them as an
enemy.'

11. *the days of Moses.* The words *the
days,* which are a repetition from the
preceding verse, are implied. But the
rendering of A.J. obscures the fact that
in the text *His people* is attached to *Moses.*
R.V. has 'then He remembered the days
of old, Moses (and) his people, (saying),
Where,' etc. An ingenious interpretation was suggested by Ibn Ezra. He
understands *Mosheh* in its etymological
sense: 'then He remembered the

drawer-forth of His people,' the man
who had withdrawn the people of God
from the Red Sea. Then follow, and
with obvious intention, the words indicating God's co-operation with Moses.

where is He, etc. Down to the end of
verse 14 is the agonized question of the
suffering peoples (Kimchi).

the sea. i.e. the Red Sea (Ibn Ezra).

shepherds. The Hebrew is singular, but
the allusion is to Moses and Aaron
(Kimchi). Some Hebrew MSS. read the
plural.

12. *His glorious arm.* The overwhelming
might of God (Rashi).

to go at the right hand of Moses? To be ever
at his service (Rashi).

divided the water. Of the Red Sea
(Targum).

13. That led them through the deep,
    As a horse in the wilderness,
    without stumbling?
14. As the cattle that go down into
    the valley,
    The spirit of the LORD caused
    them to rest;
    So didst Thou lead Thy people,
    To make Thyself a glorious
    name.'
15. Look down from heaven, and see,
    Even from Thy holy and glorious
    habitation;
    Where is Thy zeal and Thy
    mighty acts,
    The yearning of Thy heart and
    Thy compassions,
    Now restrained toward me?
16. For Thou art our Father;
    For Abraham knoweth us not,
    And Israel doth not acknowledge
    us;

13 מוֹלִיכָם בַּתְּהֹמֹות
כַּסּוּס בַּמִּדְבָּר לֹא יִכָּשֵׁלוּ:
14 כַּבְּהֵמָה בַּבִּקְעָה תֵרֵד
רוּחַ יְהֹוָה תְּנִיחֶנּוּ
כֵּן נִהַגְתָּ עַמְּךָ
לַעֲשֹׂות לְךָ שֵׁם תִּפְאָרֶת:
15 הַבֵּט מִשָּׁמַיִם וּרְאֵה
מִזְּבֻל קָדְשְׁךָ וְתִפְאַרְתֶּךָ
אַיֵּה קִנְאָתְךָ וּגְבוּרֹתֶיךָ
הֲמֹון מֵעֶיךָ
וְרַחֲמֶיךָ אֵלַי הִתְאַפָּקוּ:
16 כִּי־אַתָּה אָבִינוּ
כִּי אַבְרָהָם לֹא יְדָעָנוּ
וְיִשְׂרָאֵל לֹא יַכִּירָנוּ

13. *the deep.* More lit. 'the depths.' Cf.
for the thought of the verse, Ps. cvi. 9.

as a horse in the wilderness. With firm and
sure steps like those of the horse in a
pasture-land (Rashi).

14. *as the cattle . . . valley.* This may be a
continuation of the preceding verse,
repeating the idea of firmness and
security in a new image (Rashi). Others
join it to *the spirit of the* LORD, etc., and
instead of *caused them to rest,* the translation is: 'led him (the nation)' i.e. led
him to Mount Sinai to receive the Torah
(Laniado).

so. In the manner described in verses
11–14.

15f. An appeal for mercy to God as
Father and Redeemer, recalling His
compassionate dealings with Israel in
the past.

15. *Thy zeal,* etc. Revealed by God to
Israel in bygone generations (Rashi).

16. *for Thou art our Father.* Who should
help His children (Rashi, Kimchi).

Abraham knoweth us not. In the Egyptian
bondage (Rashi).

Israel. Jacob, the third of the patriarchs
(Kimchi).

doth not acknowledge us. In the wander-
ings in the wilderness (Rashi).

Thou, O Lord, art our Father,
Our Redeemer from everlasting
is Thy name.

17. O Lord, why dost Thou make
us to err from Thy ways,
And hardenest our heart from
Thy fear?
Return for Thy servants' sake,
The tribes of Thine inheritance.

18. Thy holy people they have well
nigh driven out,
Our adversaries have trodden
down Thy sanctuary.

19. We are become as they over
whom Thou never borest rule,
As they that were not called by
Thy name.
Oh that Thou wouldest rend the
heavens, that Thou wouldest
come down,
That the mountains might quake
at Thy presence,

אַתָּה יְהֹוָה אָבִינוּ

גֹּאֲלֵנוּ מֵעוֹלָם שְׁמֶךָ׃

17 לָמָּה תַתְעֵנוּ יְהֹוָה מִדְּרָכֶיךָ

תַּקְשִׁיחַ לִבֵּנוּ מִיִּרְאָתֶךָ

שׁוּב לְמַעַן עֲבָדֶיךָ

שִׁבְטֵי נַחֲלָתֶךָ׃

18 לַמִּצְעָר יָרְשׁוּ עַם־קָדְשֶׁךָ

צָרֵינוּ בּוֹסְסוּ מִקְדָּשֶׁךָ׃

19 הָיִינוּ מֵעוֹלָם לֹא־מָשַׁלְתָּ בָּם

לֹא־נִקְרָא שִׁמְךָ עֲלֵיהֶם

לוּא־קָרַעְתָּ שָׁמַיִם יָרַדְתָּ

מִפָּנֶיךָ הָרִים נָזֹלּוּ׃

63.2

Thou . . . art our Father, our Redeemer.
Always, alike in the slavery of Egypt, the
troubles of the wilderness and the afflictions of the exile (Rashi).

17–19. The sufferings of Israel inflicted by God are themselves a hindrance
to his return to the paths of justice and
righteousness, and God is implored to
be reconciled to His people if not for
their sake, then for the sake of their
ancestors.

17. *make us to err.* Through the afflictions of the exile many Jews have lost
faith in the redemption (Kimchi).

from Thy fear. From reverence and worship of Thee (Metsudath David).

return. To Israel (Metsudath David).

for Thy servants' sake. For the merits of
the patriarchs (Ibn Ezra, Kimchi).

the tribes. The sons of Jacob (Kimchi).

18. *Thy holy people . . . out.* Better, 'For
a short time did Thy holy people inherit
(the land)' (Ibn Ezra, Kimchi, Abarbanel).

19. *are become.* In consequence of
God's estrangement (Rashi).

as they over whom, etc. It would appear
that the election of Israel as God's
people had finally ceased (Metsudath
David).

really, the End of 63, 19 ↓

64 CHAPTER LXIV סד

1. As when fire kindleth the brush-
   wood,
   And the fire causeth the waters
   to boil;
   To make Thy name known to
   Thine adversaries,
   That the nations might tremble
   at Thy presence,

2. When Thou didst tremendous
   things
   Which we looked not for—
   Oh that Thou wouldest come
   down, that the mountains
   might quake at Thy presence!—

3. And whereof from of old men
   have not heard, nor perceived
   by the ear,
   Neither hath the eye seen a God
   beside Thee,
   Who worketh for him that waiteth
   for Him.

4. Thou didst take away him that
   joyfully worked righteousness,
   Those that remembered Thee in
   Thy ways—
   Behold, Thou wast wroth, and
   we sinned—
   Upon them have we stayed of
   old, that we might be saved.

1 כִּקְדֹחַ אֵשׁ הֲמָסִים

מַיִם תִּבְעֶה־אֵשׁ

לְהוֹדִיעַ שִׁמְךָ לְצָרֶיךָ

מִפָּנֶיךָ גּוֹיִם יִרְגָּזוּ׃

2 בַּעֲשׂוֹתְךָ נוֹרָאוֹת

לֹא נְקַוֶּה

יָרַדְתָּ מִפָּנֶיךָ הָרִים נָזֹלּוּ׃

63, 19 repeat

3 וּמֵעוֹלָם לֹא־שָׁמְעוּ לֹא הֶאֱזִינוּ

עַיִן לֹא־רָאָתָה אֱלֹהִים זוּלָתְךָ

יַעֲשֶׂה לִמְחַכֵּה־לוֹ׃

4 פָּגַעְתָּ אֶת־שָׂשׂ וְעֹשֵׂה צֶדֶק

בִּדְרָכֶיךָ יִזְכְּרוּךָ

הֵן־אַתָּה קָצַפְתָּ וַנֶּחֱטָא

בָּהֶם עוֹלָם וְנִוָּשֵׁעַ׃

v. 3. קמץ ברביע

CHAPTER LXIV

1–3. This passage continues the wish
or prayer of the last part of the preceding verse, from *Oh that thou wouldest rend
the heavens . . . presence* which is counted
as lxiv. 1 in the English version.

1. This verse is to be connected with
what precedes.

2. *Oh that Thou wouldest,* etc. A verbal
repetition of the last four Hebrew words
of the preceding chapter, forming a
parenthesis. Others render: 'Thou
camest down; the mountains quaked at
Thy presence' (Rashi, Ibn Ezra).

3. *and whereof.* Referring to *tremendous
things* in verse 2 (Rashi).

4–6. A humble confession of sins and
weaknesses, preceded by the plea that
the death of the righteous men, whom
God had prematurely taken away
because of the people's iniquities, was
the cause of the nation's degeneration
and moral and religious helplessness.

4. *Thou didst take away.* Ibn Ezra and
Kimchi quote exegetes who render:
'Thou acceptest the prayer of,' but the
usual connotation of the verb is hostile
(Rashi, Kimchi, Ibn Ezra).

and we sinned. Or, 'because we sinned'
(Kimchi).

upon them have we stayed. The words *have
we stayed* are implied (Metsudath David).

5. And we are all become as one
that is unclean,
And all our righteousnesses are
as a polluted garment;
And we all do fade as a leaf,
And our iniquities, like the wind,
take us away.

6. And there is none that calleth
upon Thy name,
That stirreth up himself to take
hold of Thee;
For Thou hast hid Thy face
from us,
And hast consumed us by means
of our iniquities.

7. But now, O Lord, Thou art our
Father;
We are the clay, and Thou our
potter,
And we all are the work of Thy
hand.

8. Be not wroth very sore, O Lord,
Neither remember iniquity for
ever;
Behold, look, we beseech Thee,
we are all Thy people.

9. Thy holy cities are become a
wilderness,
Zion is become a wilderness,
Jerusalem a desolation.

10. Our holy and our beautiful
house,
Where our fathers praised Thee,

וַנְּהִי כַטָּמֵא כֻּלָּנוּ 5
וּכְבֶגֶד עִדִּים כָּל־צִדְקֹתֵינוּ
וַנָּבֶל כֶּעָלֶה כֻּלָּנוּ
וַעֲוֺנֵנוּ כָּרוּחַ יִשָּׂאֻנוּ׃
וְאֵין־קוֹרֵא בְשִׁמְךָ 6
מִתְעוֹרֵר לְהַחֲזִיק בָּךְ
כִּי־הִסְתַּרְתָּ פָנֶיךָ מִמֶּנּוּ
וַתְּמוּגֵנוּ בְּיַד־עֲוֺנֵינוּ׃
וְעַתָּה יְהֹוָה אָבִינוּ אָתָּה 7
אֲנַחְנוּ הַחֹמֶר וְאַתָּה יֹצְרֵנוּ
וּמַעֲשֵׂה יָדְךָ כֻּלָּנוּ׃
אַל־תִּקְצֹף יְהֹוָה עַד־מְאֹד 8
וְאַל־לָעַד תִּזְכֹּר עָוֺן
הֵן הַבֶּט־נָא עַמְּךָ כֻלָּנוּ׃
עָרֵי קָדְשְׁךָ הָיוּ מִדְבָּר 9
צִיּוֹן מִדְבָּר הָיָתָה
יְרוּשָׁלַ͏ִם שְׁמָמָה׃
בֵּית קָדְשֵׁנוּ וְתִפְאַרְתֵּנוּ 10
אֲשֶׁר הִלְלוּךָ אֲבֹתֵינוּ

---

5. *unclean.* The Hebrew denotes ritual
uncleanness, like that of the menstruant
or the leper (Malbim).

polluted garment. lit. 'garment of re-
moval'; hence filthy, polluted (Rashi).
Others render: 'garment of rags'
(Kimchi).

6. *there is none . . . name.* Since the righteous were taken away (Kimchi).

consumed. lit. 'melted.'

7-11. Supplication to the Father and
Creator of the nation. Let Him not be
wroth for ever, for the sufferings of His
people are beyond further endurance.
All that was precious is lost, burned,
destroyed. Can He calmly look on and
refuse His help?

7. *we are the clay,* etc. Cf. Jer. xviii. 6.

10. *house.* The First and Second Temples (Kimchi).

312

Is burned with fire;
And all our pleasant things are
laid waste.
11. Wilt Thou refrain Thyself for
these things, O LORD?
Wilt Thou hold Thy peace, and
afflict us very sore?

הָיָה לִשְׂרֵפַת אֵשׁ
וְכָל־מַחֲמַדֵּינוּ הָיָה לְחָרְבָּה:
11 הַעַל־אֵלֶּה תִתְאַפַּק יְהֹוָה
תֶּחֱשֶׁה וּתְעַנֵּנוּ עַד־מְאֹד:

from compassion

God's reply.

65   CHAPTER LXV   סה

1. I gave access to them that asked
   not for Me,
   I was at hand to them that
   sought Me not;
   I said: 'Behold Me, behold Me',
   Unto a nation that was not called
   by My name.

2. I have spread out My hands all
   the day
   Unto a rebellious people,

1 נִדְרַשְׁתִּי לְלוֹא שָׁאָלוּ
נִמְצֵאתִי לְלֹא בִקְשֻׁנִי
אָמַרְתִּי הִנֵּנִי הִנֵּנִי
אֶל־גּוֹי לֹא־קֹרָא בִשְׁמִי:
2 פֵּרַשְׂתִּי יָדַי
כָּל־הַיּוֹם אֶל־עַם סוֹרֵר

Here I am!   *or didn't call*   *should be gal*

v. 1. קמץ בז״ק

is burned with fire. lit. 'has become a burning of fire.'

pleasant things. 'Desirable places' (Targum Kimchi), referring to the Holy of Holies (Abarbanel).

11. *refrain Thyself.* From compassion and aid (Kimchi).

for these things. The humiliation of Israel, the Holy Land, and the Temple site (Abarbanel).

CHAPTER LXV

THE Divine answer to the prayers and pleas in the preceding chapter. A distinction is drawn between the loyal servants of God and the provoking rebels.

1–7. The reasons for Israel's tribulation and sorrow.

1. God's ready accessibility was spurned.

I gave access to them. lit. 'I allowed Myself to be inquired of by them.'

I was at hand. lit. 'I was found,' 'I let Myself be found.'

behold Me. Or, 'behold I am ready' to attend to you, to receive you (Rashi).

that was not called. The meaning is, that refused to be called (Rashi).

2. *spread out My hands.* An attitude of welcome (Rashi, Kimchi).

That walk in a way that is not
good,
After their own thoughts;

3. A people that provoke Me
To My face continually,
That sacrifice in gardens,
And burn incense upon bricks;

4. That sit among the graves,
And lodge in the vaults;
That eat swine's flesh,
And broth of abominable things
is in their vessels;

5. That say: 'Stand by thyself,
Come not near to me, for I am
holier than thou';
These are a smoke in My nose,
A fire that burneth all the day.

הַהֹלְכִים הַדֶּרֶךְ לֹא־טוֹב
אַחַר מַחְשְׁבֹתֵיהֶם:
³ הָעָם הַמַּכְעִיסִים אֹתִי
עַל־פָּנַי תָּמִיד
זֹבְחִים בַּגַּנּוֹת
וּמְקַטְּרִים עַל־הַלְּבֵנִים:
⁴ הַיֹּשְׁבִים בַּקְּבָרִים
וּבַנְּצוּרִים יָלִינוּ
הָאֹכְלִים בְּשַׂר הַחֲזִיר
וּפְרַק פִּגֻּלִים כְּלֵיהֶם:
⁵ הָאֹמְרִים קְרַב אֵלֶיךָ
אַל־תִּגַּשׁ־בִּי כִּי קְדַשְׁתִּיךָ
אֵלֶּה עָשָׁן בְּאַפִּי
אֵשׁ יֹקֶדֶת כָּל־הַיּוֹם:

v. 4. וּמְרַק ק׳

---

their own thoughts. [Which are evil.]

3–5. The abominable cults and superstitions followed by the Israelites are detailed.

3. *sacrifice ... burn incense.* To false gods (Targum, Ibn Ezra, Rashi, Kimchi).

in gardens. Cf. i. 29, xvii. 10, lxvi. 17.

upon bricks. The allusion is uncertain, but it may be to the heathenish practice of burning incense on the bricks when they are placed in a kiln (Kimchi).

4. *sit among the graves ... vaults.* Forms of ancestor-worship and invocation of the spirits of the dead (Rashi, Ibn Ezra).

swine's flesh. Which is forbidden food.

broth. The translation of the *kerë* as well

as the *kethib.* the fat adhering to the vessels was evidence of their consumption of swine's flesh (Kimchi).

abominable things. Referred to in lxvi. 17

is in their vessels. The preposition is implied, but the Hebrew may be rendered 'are their dishes.'

5. *that say.* To those who do not partake of their diet of abominable things (Ibn Ezra).

stand by thyself. lit. 'draw near unto thee,' i.e. keep away (Kimchi).

these. The practices described (Rashi).

a smoke in My nose. A source of provocation (cf. Deut. xxxii. 22; Jer. xvii. 4 (Metsudath David).

6. Behold, it is written before Me;
   I will not keep silence, except
   I have requited,
   Yea, I will requite into their
   bosom,

7. Your own iniquities, and the
   iniquities of your fathers together,
   Saith the LORD,
   That have offered upon the
   mountains,
   And blasphemed Me upon the
   hills;
   Therefore will I first measure
   their wage into their bosom.

8. Thus saith the LORD:
   As, when wine is found in the
   cluster,
   One saith: 'Destroy it not,
   For a blessing is in it';
   So will I do for My servants'
   sakes,
   That I may not destroy all.

9. And I will bring forth a seed out
   of Jacob,
   And out of Judah an inheritor of
   My mountains;
   And Mine elect shall inherit it,
   And My servants shall dwell
   there.

6 הִנֵּה כְתוּבָה לְפָנָי
לֹא אֶחֱשֶׁה כִּי אִם־שִׁלַּמְתִּי
וְשִׁלַּמְתִּי אֶל־חֵיקָם:
7 עֲוֹנֹתֵיכֶם וַעֲוֹנֹת אֲבוֹתֵיכֶם יַחְדָּו
אָמַר יְהֹוָה
אֲשֶׁר קִטְּרוּ עַל־הֶהָרִים
וְעַל־הַגְּבָעוֹת חֵרְפוּנִי
וּמַדֹּתִי פְעֻלָּתָם רִאשֹׁנָה עַל־חֵיקָם:
8 כֹּה ׀ אָמַר יְהֹוָה
כַּאֲשֶׁר יִמָּצֵא הַתִּירוֹשׁ בָּאֶשְׁכּוֹל
וְאָמַר אַל־תַּשְׁחִיתֵהוּ
כִּי בְרָכָה בּוֹ
כֵּן אֶעֱשֶׂה לְמַעַן עֲבָדַי
לְבִלְתִּי הַשְׁחִית הַכֹּל:
9 וְהוֹצֵאתִי מִיַּעֲקֹב זֶרַע
וּמִיהוּדָה יוֹרֵשׁ הָרָי
וִירֵשׁוּהָ בְחִירַי
וַעֲבָדַי יִשְׁכְּנוּ־שָׁמָּה:

v. 7. אל ק׳

---

6. *it is written*. The tale of their vile
practices is duly recorded in the heavenly annals never to be forgotten (Kimchi,
Ibn Ezra).

7. *your own ... together*. This is the
object of the predicate *requite* in the
previous verse (Rashi).

the mountains ... the hills. The shrines of
the false gods (Kimchi, Metsudath
David).

8-12. Despite the debased practices of
many, the nation will be preserved for
the sake of those who remained loyal to

their God. The degenerate, however,
who persist in their idolatrous ritual will
be delivered to slaughter.

8. As the cluster of grapes is preserved
on account of the little wine in it, so will
the nation be spared from annihilation
for the sake of the faithful servants of
God therein.

destroy it not ... in it. Although the skins
and the pits are of no use, spare the
cluster because of the wine that can be
extracted from it (Kimchi).

9. *shall inherit it*. The mountain region
in which Jerusalem is located (Kimchi).

10. And Sharon shall be a fold of
flocks,
   And the valley of Achor a place
for herds to lie down in,
   For My people that have sought
Me.

11. But ye that forsake the LORD,
   That forget My holy mountain,
   That prepare a table for Fortune,
   And that offer mingled wine in
full measure unto Destiny,

12. I will destine you to the sword,
   And ye shall all bow down to the
slaughter;
   Because when I called, ye did
not answer,
   When I spoke, ye did not hear;
   But ye did that which was evil in
Mine eyes,
   And chose that wherein I de-
lighted not.

13. Therefore thus saith the Lord
GOD:
   Behold, My servants shall eat,
   But ye shall be hungry;

וְהָיָה הַשָּׁרוֹן לִנְוֵה־צֹאן 10
וְעֵמֶק עָכוֹר לְרֵבֶץ בָּקָר
לְעַמִּי אֲשֶׁר דְּרָשׁוּנִי:
וְאַתֶּם עֹזְבֵי יְהוָה 11
הַשְּׁכֵחִים אֶת־הַר קָדְשִׁי
הָעֹרְכִים לַגַּד שֻׁלְחָן
וְהַמְמַלְאִים לַמְנִי מִמְסָךְ:
וּמָנִיתִי אֶתְכֶם לַחֶרֶב 12
וְכֻלְּכֶם לַטֶּבַח תִּכְרָעוּ
יַעַן קָרָאתִי וְלֹא עֲנִיתֶם
דִּבַּרְתִּי וְלֹא שְׁמַעְתֶּם
וַתַּעֲשׂוּ הָרַע בְּעֵינַי
וּבַאֲשֶׁר לֹא־חָפַצְתִּי בְּחַרְתֶּם:
לָכֵן כֹּה־אָמַר | אֲדֹנָי יְהוִה 13
הִנֵּה עֲבָדַי | יֹאכֵלוּ
וְאַתֶּם תִּרְעָבוּ

v. 12. קמץ בז"ק   v. 13. קמץ בז"ק

10. *Sharon.* The fertile plain between
the mountains and the Mediterranean,
stretching from Jaffa to the vicinity of
mount Carmel (cf. xxxv. 2).

the valley of Achor. The locality is uncertain. It is presumed to lie on the eastern
side of the mountain region in the Jordan valley not far from Jericho (referred
to in Josh. vii. 24, xv. 7; Hos. ii. 17) (See
Ibn Ezra, Kimchi).

that have sought Me. Contrasted with *them
that sought Me not* in verse i (Kimchi).

11. *forget My holy mountain.* That it is
the only place for sacrifices (Metsudath
David).

Fortune . . . Destiny. Hebrew *Gad* (cf.
Gen. xxx. 11) and *Meni* (identified by
Kimchi as the planet Jupiter and
another unnamed heavenly body),
names of deities whose worship consisted in spreading for them a table with
meats and drinks.

12. *I will destine.* The Hebrew *manithi* is
a play upon *Meni* in the preceding verse
(Ibn Ezra, Kimchi).

13-16. A contrast is drawn between
the fate of the loyal servants of God and
that of the faithless.

13. *My servants.* The devoted followers
of God (Rashi).

Behold, My servants shall drink,
But ye shall be thirsty;
Behold, My servants shall rejoice,
But ye shall be ashamed;

14. Behold, My servants shall sing
For joy of heart,
But ye shall cry for sorrow of
heart,
And shall wail for vexation of
spirit.

15. And ye shall leave your name for
a curse unto Mine elect:
'So may the Lord GOD slay
thee';
But He shall call His servants by
another name;

16. So that he who blesseth himself
in the earth
Shall bless himself by the God of
truth;
And he that sweareth in the earth
Shall swear by the God of truth;
Because the former troubles are
forgotten,
And because they are hid from
Mine eyes.

17. For, behold, I create new
heavens

הִנֵּה עֲבָדַי יִשְׁתּוּ

וְאַתֶּם תִּצְמָאוּ

הִנֵּה עֲבָדַי יִשְׂמָחוּ

וְאַתֶּם תֵּבֹשׁוּ׃

14 הִנֵּה עֲבָדַי יָרֹנּוּ

מִטּוּב לֵב

וְאַתֶּם תִּצְעֲקוּ מִכְּאֵב לֵב

וּמִשֵּׁבֶר רוּחַ תְּיֵלִילוּ׃

15 וְהִנַּחְתֶּם שִׁמְכֶם לִשְׁבוּעָה לִבְחִירַי

וֶהֱמִיתְךָ אֲדֹנָי יֱהֹוִה

וְלַעֲבָדָיו יִקְרָא שֵׁם אַחֵר׃

16 אֲשֶׁר הַמִּתְבָּרֵךְ בָּאָרֶץ

יִתְבָּרֵךְ בֵּאלֹהֵי אָמֵן

וְהַנִּשְׁבָּע בָּאָרֶץ

יִשָּׁבַע בֵּאלֹהֵי אָמֵן

כִּי נִשְׁכְּחוּ הַצָּרוֹת הָרִאשֹׁנוֹת

וְכִי נִסְתְּרוּ מֵעֵינָי׃

17 כִּי־הִנְנִי בוֹרֵא שָׁמַיִם חֲדָשִׁים

v. 13. קמץ בטרחא

---

14. *joy.* lit. 'goodness.'

sorrow. Or, 'pain.'

vexation. lit. 'breaking.'

15. *so may ... thee.* This is the form
which the curse will take.

another name. An appellation of fame
and glory (Ibn Ezra, Kimchi).

16. God, having fulfilled His promises
and His threats, will establish Himself
as the God of truth and thus gain the
confidence of all.

bless himself ... truth. He will use the

expression, 'May the God of truth bless
me' (Kimchi).

the former troubles are forgotten. So happy
will the lot of the faithful servants be
that the troubles of the past will vanish
from memory (Metsudath David).

hid from Mine eyes. Even God, so to
speak, will see them no more (Metsudath David).

17–25. The glories and marvels of a
new era in which all existing conditions
will undergo complete transformation.

17. *new heavens ... earth.* Metaphorical

And a new earth;
And the former things shall not
   be remembered,
Nor come into mind.

18. But be ye glad and rejoice for
   ever
   In that which I create;
   For, behold, I create Jerusalem a
    rejoicing,
   And her people a joy.

19. And I will rejoice in Jerusalem,
   And joy in My people;
   And the voice of weeping shall
    be no more heard in her,
   Nor the voice of crying.

20. There shall be no more thence an
   infant of days, nor an old man,
   That hath not filled his days;
   For the youngest shall die a
    hundred years old,
   And the sinner being a hundred
    years old shall be accursed.

21. And they shall build houses, and
   inhabit them;
   And they shall plant vineyards,
    and eat the fruit of them.

וְאֶרֶץ חֲדָשָׁה
וְלֹא תִזָּכַרְנָה הָרִאשֹׁנוֹת
וְלֹא תַעֲלֶינָה עַל־לֵב:

18 כִּי־אִם־שִׂישׂוּ וְגִילוּ עֲדֵי־עַד
אֲשֶׁר אֲנִי בוֹרֵא
כִּי הִנְנִי בוֹרֵא אֶת־יְרוּשָׁלַם
גִּילָה וְעַמָּהּ מָשׂוֹשׂ:

19 וְגַלְתִּי בִירוּשָׁלַם
וְשַׂשְׂתִּי בְעַמִּי
וְלֹא־יִשָּׁמַע בָּהּ עוֹד
קוֹל בְּכִי וְקוֹל זְעָקָה:

20 לֹא־יִהְיֶה מִשָּׁם עוֹד עוּל יָמִים וְזָקֵן
אֲשֶׁר לֹא־יְמַלֵּא אֶת־יָמָיו
כִּי הַנַּעַר בֶּן־מֵאָה שָׁנָה יָמוּת
וְהַחוֹטֶא בֶּן־מֵאָה שָׁנָה יְקֻלָּל:

21 וּבָנוּ בָתִּים וְיָשָׁבוּ
וְנָטְעוּ כְרָמִים וְאָכְלוּ פִּרְיָם:

for a new world order (Metsudath
David).

former things. The conditions prevailing
before the advent of the new era
(Malbim).

18. *rejoicing.* [An object and source of
joy to the people.]

joy. [To themselves and to the world.]

19. God, too, will rejoice in Jerusalem
and Israel.

20. In the new era, both young and
old will live to a hundred years, and
every one will attain the full allotted
span of life.

the sinner . . . accursed. He will live no
longer than the shortest period of life,
which will be a hundred years (Kimchi).
Others, taking the Hebrew for *sinner* in
its primary sense of 'missing,' render:
'and he that falls short of a hundred
years shall be deemed accursed' (Metsudath David).

21–23. Their longevity will enable
each of them to enjoy the fruit of his
labour.

21. The underlying thought is that the
land will be spared invasions which rob
the inhabitants of the fruits of their toil.

22. *as the days of a tree.* Which make up
many years (Ibn Ezra).

22. They shall not build, and another
    inhabit,
    They shall not plant, and another
    eat;
    For as the days of a tree shall be
    the days of My people,
    And Mine elect shall long enjoy
    the work of their hands.
23. They shall not labour in vain,
    Nor bring forth for terror;
    For they are the seed blessed of
    the LORD,
    And their offspring with them.
24. And it shall come to pass that,
    before they call, I will answer,
    And while they are yet speaking,
    I will hear.
25. The wolf and the lamb shall feed
    together,
    And the lion shall eat straw like
    the ox;
    And dust shall be the serpent's
    food.
    They shall not hurt nor destroy
    In all My holy mountain,
    Saith the LORD.

22 לֹא יִבְנוּ וְאַחֵר יֵשֵׁב
לֹא יִטְּעוּ וְאַחֵר יֹאכֵל
כִּי־כִימֵי הָעֵץ יְמֵי עַמִּי
וּמַעֲשֵׂה יְדֵיהֶם יְבַלּוּ בְחִירָי׃
23 לֹא יִיגְעוּ לָרִיק
וְלֹא יֵלְדוּ לַבֶּהָלָה
כִּי זֶרַע בְּרוּכֵי יְהֹוָה הֵמָּה
וְצֶאֱצָאֵיהֶם אִתָּם׃
24 וְהָיָה טֶרֶם יִקְרָאוּ וַאֲנִי אֶעֱנֶה
עוֹד הֵם מְדַבְּרִים וַאֲנִי אֶשְׁמָע׃
25 זְאֵב וְטָלֶה יִרְעוּ כְאֶחָד
וְאַרְיֵה כַּבָּקָר יֹאכַל־תֶּבֶן
וְנָחָשׁ עָפָר לַחְמוֹ
לֹא־יָרֵעוּ וְלֹא־יַשְׁחִיתוּ
בְּכָל־הַר קָדְשִׁי אָמַר יְהֹוָה׃

66 CHAPTER LXVI סו

1. Thus saith the LORD:
   The heaven is My throne,

1 כֹּה אָמַר יְהֹוָה
הַשָּׁמַיִם כִּסְאִי

v. 1. הפטרת שבת וראש חדש בטרחא | v. 24. קמץ

shall long enjoy. lit. 'shall wear out.'

23. *bring forth.* Children (Kimchi).

terror. Sudden or premature death (Kimchi).

their offspring with them. i.e. shall be with them all their lives. Several generations will live together simultaneously (Kimchi).

24f. All human desires will be Divinely fulfilled even before they have been expressed, and there will be peace and contentment even in the animal world.

25. The same words or ideas occur in xi. 6–9. *And dust shall be the serpent's food* recalls Gen. iii. 14.

CHAPTER LXVI

GOD's overwhelming greatness and profound condescension. Dire retribution will be the lot of the apostates, while eternal peace and happiness will be the reward of the faithful.

wedding marriages [handwritten]

And the earth is My footstool;
Where is the house that ye may
  build unto Me?
And where is the place that may
  be My resting-place?

2. For all these things hath My
  hand made,
And so all these things came to
  be,
Saith the LORD;
But on this man will I look,
Even on him that is poor and of
  a contrite spirit,
And trembleth at My word.

sacrifice [handwritten]

3. He that killeth an ox is as if he
  slew a man;
He that sacrificeth a lamb, as if
  he broke a dog's neck;
He that offereth a meal-offering,
  as if he offered swine's blood;
He that maketh a memorial-
  offering of frankincense, as if
  he blessed an idol;
According as they have chosen
  their own ways,

bad guys [handwritten]

וְהָאָרֶץ הֲדֹם רַגְלָי
אֵי־זֶה בַיִת אֲשֶׁר תִּבְנוּ־לִי
וְאֵי־זֶה מָקוֹם מְנוּחָתִי ׃
וְאֶת־כָּל־אֵלֶּה יָדִי עָשָׂתָה 2
וַיִּהְיוּ כָל־אֵלֶּה
נְאֻם־יְהֹוָה
וְאֶל־זֶה אַבִּיט
אֶל־עָנִי וּנְכֵה־רוּחַ
וְחָרֵד עַל־דְּבָרִי ׃
שׁוֹחֵט הַשּׁוֹר מַכֵּה־אִישׁ 3
זוֹבֵחַ הַשֶּׂה עֹרֵף כֶּלֶב
מַעֲלֵה מִנְחָה דַּם־חֲזִיר
מַזְכִּיר לְבֹנָה מְבָרֵךְ אָוֶן
גַּם־הֵמָּה בָּחֲרוּ בְּדַרְכֵיהֶם

v. 2. קָמֵץ בז״ק v. 2. למדנחאי אֵל v. 3. כצ״ל

1f. No man-made Temple can contain God in His infinity and majesty. The Heavens are but His throne and the earth only His footstool. Yet He is near to man and ready to listen to the voice of the humble, contrite and truly pious.

1. *where is the house,* etc. Nowhere, since God is infinite. The function of the Temple was not to provide a dwelling-place for God, but to serve as a religious centre for the people and as a symbol of the covenant between them and Him (Ibn Kaspi).

2. *these things.* Pointing to all visible creation (Rashi).

will I look. Take note of, listen to his supplications (Ibn Ezra).

trembleth at My word. Displaying devotion and eagerness to fulfil God's commandments (Metsudath Zion).

3f. The mechanical, unspiritual offering of sacrifices by men steeped in idolatry and addicted to its abominable rites is as contemptible in the eyes of God as the actual performance of these horrible practices and will receive retribution, measure for measure.

3. *he that killeth . . . man.* The former act is as hateful as the latter. i.e. if a wicked man kills an ox for an offering, since his sacrifice is unacceptable, it is equated with slaying a man (Ibn Ezra, Kimchi). Abarbanel explains that one would slay an ox in order to steal it and slay its owner in order to rob him of it.

broke a dog's neck. He kills the dog that watches the flock, in order to steal a lamb to slaughter it (Abarbanel).

according as they . . . abominations. The two clauses from the protasis to the following verse (Kimchi).

And their soul delighteth in their abominations;

4. Even so I will choose their mockings,
And will bring their fears upon them;
Because when I called, none did answer;
When I spoke, they did not hear,
But they did that which was evil in Mine eyes,
And chose that in which I delighted not.

5. Hear the word of the LORD,
Ye that tremble at His word:
Your brethren that hate you, that cast you out for My name's sake, have said:
'Let the LORD be glorified,
That we may gaze upon your joy',
But they shall be ashamed.

6. Hark! an uproar from the city,
Hark! it cometh from the temple,
Hark! the LORD rendereth recompense to His enemies.

וּבְשִׁקּוּצֵיהֶם נַפְשָׁם חָפֵצָה׃

4 גַּם־אֲנִי אֶבְחַר בְּתַעֲלֻלֵיהֶם
וּמְגוּרֹתָם אָבִיא לָהֶם
יַעַן קָרָאתִי וְאֵין עוֹנֶה
דִּבַּרְתִּי וְלֹא שָׁמֵעוּ
וַיַּעֲשׂוּ הָרַע בְּעֵינַי
וּבַאֲשֶׁר לֹא־חָפַצְתִּי בָּחָרוּ׃

5 שִׁמְעוּ דְּבַר־יְהֹוָה
הַחֲרֵדִים אֶל־דְּבָרוֹ
אָמְרוּ אֲחֵיכֶם שֹׂנְאֵיכֶם מְנַדֵּיכֶם
לְמַעַן שְׁמִי
יִכְבַּד יְהֹוָה
וְנִרְאֶה בְשִׂמְחַתְכֶם
וְהֵם יֵבֹשׁוּ׃

6 קוֹל שָׁאוֹן מֵעִיר
קוֹל מֵהֵיכָל
קוֹל יְהֹוָה מְשַׁלֵּם גְּמוּל לְאֹיְבָיו׃

(handwritten margin note: 'you obey for our sakes')

---

4. *their mockings,* i.e. I will choose to mock them (Rashi, Ibn Ezra, Kimchi).

their fears. The calamities they feared and sought to avert by their idolatrous cult (Rashi).

because when I called. Cf. lxv. 12, where the same passage occurs with the change of the third person to the second.

5. *ye that tremble.* The faithful and devoted mentioned in verse 2 (Rashi).

your brethren. Your sinful fellow-countrymen (Rashi)i.

cast you out . . . sake. Excluded you from their company because of your loyalty to Me. The Hebrew verb for *cast out* means in late Hebrew 'to excommunicate.'

let the LORD . . . *joy.* The sarcastic taunt of the enemies (Abarbanel).

but they shall be ashamed. The prophet's assurance to their faithful relating to their adversaries (Rashi, Kimchi, Abarbanel).

6. Vivid description of the impending retribution.

hark. lit. 'a voice.'

His enemies. The enemies of His faithful adherents mentioned in verse 5 (Isaiah of Trani).

7. Before she travailed, she brought
forth;
Before her pain came,
She was delivered of a man-
child.

8. Who hath heard such a thing?
Who hath seen such things?
Is a land born in one day?
Is a nation brought forth at
once?
For as soon as Zion travailed,
She brought forth her children.

9. Shall I bring to the birth, and
not cause to bring forth?
Saith the LORD;
Shall I that cause to bring forth
shut the womb?
Saith thy God.

10. Rejoice ye with Jerusalem,
And be glad with her, all ye that
love her;
Rejoice for joy with her,
All ye that mourn for her;

7 בְּטֶרֶם תָּחִיל יָלָדָה
בְּטֶרֶם יָבוֹא חֵבֶל לָהּ
וְהִמְלִיטָה זָכָר׃
8 מִי־שָׁמַע כָּזֹאת
מִי רָאָה כָּאֵלֶּה
הֲיוּחַל אֶרֶץ בְּיוֹם אֶחָד
אִם־יִוָּלֵד גּוֹי פַּעַם אֶחָת
כִּי־חָלָה גַם־יָלְדָה צִיּוֹן אֶת־בָּנֶיהָ׃
9 הַאֲנִי אַשְׁבִּיר
וְלֹא אוֹלִיד יֹאמַר יְהֹוָה
אִם־אֲנִי הַמּוֹלִיד
וְעָצַרְתִּי אָמַר אֱלֹהָיִךְ׃
10 שִׂמְחוּ אֶת־יְרוּשָׁלַםִ
וְגִילוּ בָהּ כָּל־אֹהֲבֶיהָ
שִׂישׂוּ אִתָּהּ מָשׂוֹשׂ
כָּל־הַמִּתְאַבְּלִים עָלֶיהָ׃

‏כצ״ל v. 8.

7–9. The sudden and speedy repopu-
lation of Zion is depicted to hearten the
loyal worshippers of God.

7. *before she travailed . . . forth.* Figurative of the speedy increase of the population by the return of the Godfearing
exiles (cf. xlix. 20f.). *She* refers to Zion
(Kimchi).

a man-child. The birth of a male was the
occasion of greater joy than that of a
female (Metsudath David).

8. *such a thing.* Such a rapid transformation from desolation to a teeming
population (Metsudath David).

a land. i.e. the people of a land (Isaiah of
Trani).

for as soon . . . brought forth. lit. 'for Zion
hath both travailed and brought forth.'

9. The speedy restoration which is
begun will be completed. God will not
leave His work unfinished.

10f. A summons to the mourners and
friends of Zion to rejoice in the city's
restored splendor.

10. *mourn for her.* A reference to the
fasts observed to commemorate the
destruction of Jerusalem (cf. Zech. vii.
3).

11. That ye may suck, and be satisfied
With the breast of her con-
solations;
That ye may drink deeply with
delight
Of the abundance of her glory.
12. For thus saith the LORD:
Behold, I will extend peace to
her like a river,
And the wealth of the nations
like an overflowing stream,
And ye shall suck thereof;
Ye shall be borne upon the side,
And shall be dandled upon the
knees.
13. As one whom his mother comforteth,
So will I comfort you;
And ye shall be comforted in
Jerusalem.
14. And when ye see this, your heart
shall rejoice,
And your bones shall flourish like
young grass;
And the hand of the LORD shall
be known toward His servants,
And He will have indignation
against His enemies.

11 לְמַ֤עַן תִּֽינְקוּ֙ וּשְׂבַעְתֶּ֔ם
מִשֹּׁ֖ד תַּנְחֻמֶ֑יהָ
לְמַ֥עַן תָּמֹ֖צּוּ
וְהִתְעַנַּגְתֶּ֖ם מִזִּ֥יז כְּבוֹדָֽהּ׃
12 כִּֽי־כֹ֣ה ׀ אָמַ֣ר יְהֹוָ֗ה
הִנְנִ֣י נֹטֶֽה־אֵ֠לֶיהָ כְּנָהָ֨ר שָׁל֜וֹם
וּכְנַ֧חַל שׁוֹטֵ֛ף כְּב֥וֹד גּוֹיִ֖ם וִינַקְתֶּ֑ם
עַל־צַד֙ תִּנָּשֵׂ֔אוּ
וְעַל־בִּרְכַּ֖יִם תְּשָׁעֳשָֽׁעוּ׃
13 כְּאִ֕ישׁ אֲשֶׁ֥ר אִמּ֖וֹ תְּנַחֲמֶ֑נּוּ
כֵּ֤ן אָֽנֹכִי֙ אֲנַ֣חֶמְכֶ֔ם
וּבִירֽוּשָׁלַ֖͏ִם תְּנֻחָֽמוּ׃
14 וּרְאִיתֶם֙ וְשָׂ֣שׂ לִבְּכֶ֔ם
וְעַצְמֽוֹתֵיכֶ֖ם כַּדֶּ֣שֶׁא תִפְרַ֑חְנָה
וְנוֹדְעָ֤ה יַד־יְהֹוָה֙ אֶת־עֲבָדָ֔יו
וְזָעַ֖ם אֶת־אֹיְבָֽיו׃

11. *that ye may drink deeply with delight.*
Or, 'that ye may drain out and delight
yourselves.'

abundance. Some render the noun
'desire' (Targum), some 'splendour'
(Kimchi).

12–14. Peace, wealth, honour and joy
promised to Zion and her returned
children.

12. *like a river.* i.e. in abundance
(Metsudath David).

wealth of the nations. Cf. lxi. 6.

borne upon the side. Of the nations that
had hitherto oppressed them (cf. xlix.

22, lx. 4). The figure of nursing is maintained (Kimchi).

13. *as one . . . comforteth.* A grown man,
hurt or weary, coming back to his
mother and finding in her the comfort
he needs (Hirsch).

14. *your bones.* Designating the body as
a whole (cf. Ps. li. 10) (Targum).

like young grass. Which is fresh and full of
sap (Kimchi).

hand of the LORD. His protecting power
(Targum, Kimchi).

His servants. His faithful followers (Targum).

15. For, behold, the LORD will come
in fire,
And His chariots shall be like the
whirlwind;
To render His anger with fury,
And His rebuke with flames of
fire.
16. For by fire will the LORD contend,
And by His sword with all flesh;
And the slain of the LORD shall
be many.
17. They that sanctify themselves
and purify themselves
To go unto the gardens,
Behind one in the midst,
Eating swine's flesh, and the
detestable thing, and the
mouse,
Shall be consumed together,
saith the LORD.
18. For I [know] their works and
their thoughts; [the time] cometh,
that I will gather all nations and
tongues; and they shall come, and

15 כִּי־הִנֵּה יְהֹוָה בָּאֵשׁ יָבוֹא
וְכַסּוּפָה מַרְכְּבֹתָיו
לְהָשִׁיב בְּחֵמָה אַפּוֹ
וְגַעֲרָתוֹ בְּלַהֲבֵי־אֵשׁ׃
16 כִּי בָאֵשׁ יְהֹוָה נִשְׁפָּט
וּבְחַרְבּוֹ אֶת־כָּל־בָּשָׂר
וְרַבּוּ חַלְלֵי יְהֹוָה׃
17 הַמִּתְקַדְּשִׁים וְהַמִּטַּהֲרִים
אֶל־הַגַּנּוֹת
אַחַר אַחַד בַּתָּוֶךְ
אֹכְלֵי בְּשַׂר הַחֲזִיר וְהַשֶּׁקֶץ וְהָעַכְבָּר
יַחְדָּו יָסֻפוּ נְאֻם־יְהֹוָה׃
18 וְאָנֹכִי מַעֲשֵׂיהֶם וּמַחְשְׁבֹתֵיהֶם בָּאָה
לְקַבֵּץ אֶת־כָּל־הַגּוֹיִם וְהַלְּשֹׁנוֹת

ק' אחת .v. 17

15f. God's judgment and vengeance
upon His enemies.

15. *to render.* lit. 'to bring back.' God's
anger against the wicked will be
brought again upon them, now raised
to its height of fury (Kimchi).

16. *by fire.* Of Gehenna in which the
adversaries of God are purged (Rashi).

contend. Or, 'enter into judgment.'

17. Description of the detestable rites
of idolatry resumed from verse 3.

to go unto the gardens. The first two words
are implied. The gardens were favourite
spots for the practice of the heathenish
rites (cf. lxv. 3).

behind one. The *kethib* reads the word as
masculine, the *kerë* as feminine. The
former may denote the leader of the
procession, the latter a goddess, pos-

sibly the *asherah* (Ibn Ezra). Maimonides
explains as 'behind one tree in the
midst,' which he understands as indulgence in forbidden lust (*Guide,* III, 33).

eating swine's flesh . . . mouse. The eating
of the flesh of that which is forbidden to
observing Israelites (cf. Lev. xi) formed
part of the sacrificial meals in the mystic
ceremonial of the heretical community
(Isaiah of Trani).

18-22. God's glory and power will be
manifest over all the nations of the
world who, as a tribute to His Sovereignty, will bring, with many marks of
respect and honour, all the Israelites
who lived among them in exile.

18. A difficult text which is made intelligible by the insertion in square brack-
ets of the apparently implied words
know after *for I,* and *the time* before *cometh*
(Metsudath David).

shall see My glory. 19. And I will work a sign among them, and I will send such as escape of them unto the nations, to Tarshish, Pul and Lud, that draw the bow, to Tubal and Javan, to the isles afar off, that have not heard My fame, neither have seen My glory; and they shall declare My glory among the nations. 20. And they shall bring all your brethren out of all the nations for an offering unto the LORD, upon horses, and in chariots, and in litters, and upon mules, and upon swift beasts, to My holy mountain Jerusalem, saith the LORD, as the children of Israel bring their offering in a clean vessel into the house of the LORD. 21. And of them also will I take for the priests and for the Levites, saith the LORD. 22. For as the new heavens and the new earth, which I will make, shall

וּבָאוּ וְרָאוּ אֶת־כְּבוֹדִי: וְשַׂמְתִּי 19
בָהֶם אוֹת וְשִׁלַּחְתִּי מֵהֶם | פְּלֵיטִים
אֶל־הַגּוֹיִם תַּרְשִׁישׁ פּוּל וְלוּד מֹשְׁכֵי
קֶשֶׁת תֻּבַל וְיָוָן הָאִיִּים הָרְחֹקִים
אֲשֶׁר לֹא־שָׁמְעוּ אֶת־שִׁמְעִי וְלֹא־
רָאוּ אֶת־כְּבוֹדִי וְהִגִּידוּ אֶת־כְּבוֹדִי
בַּגּוֹיִם: וְהֵבִיאוּ אֶת־כָּל־אֲחֵיכֶם | 20
מִכָּל־הַגּוֹיִם | מִנְחָה | לַיהֹוָה
בַּסּוּסִים וּבָרֶכֶב וּבַצַּבִּים וּבַפְּרָדִים
וּבַכִּרְכָּרוֹת עַל הַר קָדְשִׁי יְרוּשָׁלַ͏ִם
אָמַר יְהֹוָה כַּאֲשֶׁר יָבִיאוּ בְנֵי יִשְׂרָאֵל
אֶת־הַמִּנְחָה בִּכְלִי טָהוֹר בֵּית יְהֹוָה:
וְגַם־מֵהֶם אֶקַּח לַכֹּהֲנִים לַלְוִיִּם אָמַר 21
יְהֹוָה: כִּי כַאֲשֶׁר הַשָּׁמַיִם הַחֲדָשִׁים 22
וְהָאָרֶץ הַחֲדָשָׁה אֲשֶׁר אֲנִי עֹשֶׂה

19. *a sign.* A miracle, a striking act of judgment (Kimchi, Kara).

among them. The gathered nations (Metsudath David).

I will send. To proclaim the praise of God's power and greatness (Isaiah of Trani).

such as escape. The survivors of the war of Gog and Magog and the plague following in its wake, as related by the prophet Zechariah (xiv. 12) (Kimchi, Rashi).

Tarshish. See on ii. 16.

Pul and Lud. Presumed to be North African peoples or districts. Some believe them to be the Lydians of Asia Minor (See Abarbanel, Gen. x. 13; Biberfeld).

Tubal. A race that lived on the east of Cappadocia (Gen. x. 2) (Targum Jonathan, Gen. x. 3).

Javan. The Ionians, Greece (Gen. x. 2).

20. *and they.* The nations, hearing the marvellous deeds of God (Kimchi).

swift beasts. Or, 'dromedaries' (Ibn Ezra).

21.*and of them.* The reference is ambiguous; it may relate to the nations conveying the Israelites, or the Israelites who are conveyed, or both. Rashi and Kimchi accept the third. Those priests and Levites whose lineage has been forgotten, even those who have mingled with the nations, will be returned to their status. Some explain that they will be taken as asistants for the priests and the Levites, i.e. to hew wood and draw water for the temple service (R. Joseph Kimchi).

22. Israel's eternal existence and fame.

new heavens . . . earth. Spoken of in lxv. 17.

remain before Me, saith the LORD,
so shall your seed and your name
remain.

23. And it shall come to pass,
That from one new moon to
another,
And from one sabbath to an-
other,
Shall all flesh come to worship
before Me,
Saith the LORD.

24. And they shall go forth, and look
Upon the carcasses of the men
that have rebelled against Me;
For their worm shall not die,
Neither shall their fire be
quenched;
And they shall be an abhorring
unto all flesh.

And it shall come to pass,
That from one new moon to another,
And from one sabbath to another,
Shall all flesh come to worship before
Me,
Saith the LORD.

עֹמְדִים לְפָנַי נְאֻם־יְהֹוָה כֵּן יַעֲמֹד
זַרְעֲכֶם וְשִׁמְכֶם׃

23 וְהָיָה
מִדֵּי־חֹדֶשׁ בְּחָדְשׁוֹ
וּמִדֵּי שַׁבָּת בְּשַׁבַּתּוֹ
יָבוֹא כָל־בָּשָׂר
לְהִשְׁתַּחֲוֹת לְפָנַי אָמַר יְהֹוָה׃

24 וְיָצְאוּ וְרָאוּ
בְּפִגְרֵי הָאֲנָשִׁים הַפֹּשְׁעִים בִּי
כִּי תוֹלַעְתָּם לֹא תָמוּת
וְאִשָּׁם לֹא תִכְבֶּה
וְהָיוּ דֵרָאוֹן לְכָל־בָּשָׂר׃

והיה
מדי־חדש בחדשו
ומדי שבת בשבתו
יבוא כל־בשר
להשתחות לפני אמר יהוה׃

v. 23. סבירין יבראו

חֲזַק

23f. God's universal Sovereignty will
be recognized by all men, and they
will regularly, month by month and week by
week, come to worship in His holy
Temple; but the dead bodies of the
rebels and apostates will lie condemned
to everlasting disgrace and horror.

23. *from one new moon ... sabbath to
another.* lit. 'as often as there is a new
moon on its new moon, etc.,' i.e. on
every new moon and Sabbath, regularly
(Metsudath David).

all flesh. All mankind (Metsudath David).

before Me. In the Temple of Jerusalem
(Metsudath David).

24. *and they.* The worshippers (Kimchi).

shall go forth. To the heap of carcasses

(perhaps in the valley of Hinnom) outside the holy city (Kimchi).

their worm. The worms devouring the
dead bodies of the rebels (Rashi).

their fire. The fire of Gehenna which will
purge their souls (Rashi).

abhorring. The word occurs again only in
Dan. xii. 2 in a similar connection.
Jewish custom and tradition revolt
against ending upon an unhappy or
inauspicious note. Hebrew Bibles and
MSS., therefore, repeat the preceding
verse with its noble and universal
aspiration. The same practice is followed in the public and private reading
of this chapter which is the *haphtarah*
(prophetical lesson) of the Sabbath that
coincides with the new moon. Similar
repetitions are found at the end of
Malachi, Lamentations and Ecclesiastes
for the same reason.

326

Authorities consulted or quoted

Terms and Abbreviations

AUTHORITIES CONSULTED OR QUOTED

Abarbanel, Isaac (1437–1509), Bible Commentator.
Aboth—*Pirke Aboth, Sayings of the Fathers*: Mishnaic tractate.
Alschich, Moses (sixteenth century) *Maroth Hazovoth*.
Aruch-Lexicon of Talmud, Midrash, Targum, by Nathan of Rome (10th century).
Azulai, Abraham (seventeenth century) *Baalei Brith Avram*.
Ben Sira, Alfa-betha d'
Biberfeld, Philip (Contemporary Jewish Historian) *Universal Jewish History*.
Chotam Tochnit—Hebrew Synonyms, by Abraham Bedarschi (13th century).
Dunash (10th century Grammarian) *Teshuboth Dunash*.
Eisenstein, J.D. (Jewish Encyclopedist) *Otsar Yisrael, Otsar Midrashim*.
Elijah of Wilna (1720–1797), (Annotator of the Bible and Talmud).
Herodotus (Greek Historian, 5th century B.C.E.).
Hirsch, Mendel (19th century Educator) *The Haphtoroth*.
Ibn Ezra, Abraham (1092–1167, Bible Commentator.
Ibn Ganah, Jona (11th century, Grammarian and Lexicographer) *Shorashim*.
Ibn Kaspi, Joseph (1279–1340, Bible Commentator) *Adne Keseph*.
Isaiah of Trani (13th century Bible Commentator).
Josephus Flavius (Jewish Historian, 1st century C.E.).
Kara, Joseph (1060–1130, Bible Commentator).
Kimchi, David (1160–1235, Bible Commentator).
Kimchi, Joseph (12th century Bible Commentator and Grammarian).
Kohut, Alexander (19th century Jewish Scholar) *Aruch Completum*.
Laniado, Samuel (sixteenth century Bible Commentator) *K'li Paz*.
Levita, Elija (16th century Lexicographer) *Lexicon Chaldaicum*.
Maimonides, Moses (1135–1204, Jewish Philosopher) *Guide to the Perplexed*.
Malbim, Meyer Leibush (1809–1879, famed Bible Commentator).
Marcus, Aaron (19th century scholar and archeologist) *Kadmonioth*.
Mechilta—Ancient Rabbinical Commentary on Exodus.
Megillah—Talmudic tractate.
Menahem (10th century Grammarian) *Machbereth Menahem*.
Metsudath David ('Tower of David'), Hebrew Commentary on Books of the Bible by David Altschul (17th century).
Midrash—Rabbinic Homilies on the Pentateuch, etc.
Mishnah—Codification on Jewish law (c. 200 C.E.).
Otzar Midrashim
Ralbag
Rashi (Rabbi Solomon ben Isaac, 1040–1105, Bible Commentator).
Saadya (882–942, Bible Exegete and Philosopher).
Sanhedrin—Talmudic tractate.
Seder Olam—Early Jewish chronicle.
Septuagint—Greek Translation of the Bible, begun in the 3rd century B.C.E.
Ta'anith—Talmudic tractate.
Talmud—Corpus of Jewish Law and Thought (compiled at the end of the 5th century C.E.).
Tanchuma—Midrashic Commentary on the Pentateuch (original version 4th century C.E.).
Targum—Aramaic Translation of the Bible (1st and 2nd centuries C.E.).
Yalkut Shimoni—Midrashic compilation (13th century).

TERMS AND ABBREVIATIONS

A.J.   American-Jewish Translation of the Scriptures
A.V.   Authorized Version
B.C.E.   Before Common Era
Cant.   Song of Songs
C.E.   Common Era
Chron.   Chronicles
Dan.   Daniel
Deut.   Deuteronomy
Ecclus.   Apocryphal Book of Ecclesiasticus
Exod.   Exodus
Ezek.   Ezekiel
Gen.   Genesis
Hab.   Habakkuk
Hos.   Hosea
Jer.   Jeremiah
Josh.   Joshua
Judg.   Judges
Kerë   The Hebrew as it is read according to the Masoretes
Kethib   The Hebrew as it is written according to tradition
Lam.   Lamentations
Lev.   Leviticus
LXX   Septuagint
Mic.   Micah
Neh.   Nehemiah
Num.   Numbers
Ps.   Psalms
R.V.   Revised Version
Sam.   Samuel
Zech.   Zechariah
Zeph.   Zephaniah